The Psychology of Humor: An Integrative Approach

The Psychology of Humor: An Integrative Approach

ROD A. MARTIN

Department of Psychology
University of Western Ontario
London, Ontario, Canada N6A 5C2

ELSEVIER

AMSTERDAM • BOSTON • HEIDELBERG • LONDON
NEW YORK • OXFORD • PARIS • SAN DIEGO
SAN FRANCISCO • SINGAPORE • SYDNEY • TOKYO

Elsevier Academic Press
30 Corporate Drive, Suite 400, Burlington, MA 01803, USA
525 B Street, Suite 1900, San Diego, California 92101-4495, USA
84 Theobald's Road, London WC1X 8RR, UK

This book is printed on acid-free paper. ∞

Library of Congress Cataloging-in-Publication Data
APPLICATION SUBMITTED

British Library Cataloguing in Publication Data
A catalogue record for this book is available from the British Library

ISBN 13: 978-0-12-372564-6
ISBN 10: 0-12-372564-X

For all information on all Elsevier Academic Press publications
visit our Web site at www.books.elsevier.com

PRINTED IN the United States of America
09 10   9 8 7 6 5 4 3

To Myra, who keeps me laughing

CONTENTS

CHAPTER 1

Introduction to the Psychology of Humor   1

CHAPTER 2

Theories and Early Research I: Psychoanalytic and Superiority Theories   31

CHAPTER 3

Theories and Early Research II: Arousal, Incongruity, and Reversal Theories   57

CHAPTER 4

The Cognitive Psychology of Humor   83

CHAPTER 5

The Social Psychology of Humor   113

CHAPTER 8

The Developmental Psychology of Humor   229

CHAPTER 9

Humor and Mental Health   269

FOREWORD

Understanding the nature of humor is a problem for psychology. Humor, comedy, and laughter are important and engaging aspects of behavior. Consequently, they have received attention from many perspectives and approaches. The amount and diversity of relevant information should have made this book impossible to write. The material for a work on humor is widely scattered, both in space and time. Even if the focus is on psychology, all the other areas touching humor need to be examined. Not only empirical research, but rational and literary thought must be included. Rod Martin has not only brought this material together but turned it into an easy read. To borrow a simile from James Agee, it must have been like "putting socks on an octopus."

The Psychology of Humor: An Integrative Approach can stand at the head of a line of books that have presented a picture of this universal trait. Any philosopher who wrote on human nature discussed laughter and, at least by implication, humor. Bergson and Freud at the beginning of the last century focused on laughter and wit to present testable, if not tested, hypotheses. Psychologists in the middle of the century included humor as part of their assessments of personality. Chapman and Foot, and Goldstein and McGhee (as well as McGhee and Goldstein) gave humor scholars a platform in the 1970s and 1980s. Separate chapters in these various books permitted presentation of data and ideas, but little interaction or direct communication. Even now, with a yearly conference and a quarterly journal, disagreement is more typical than exchange and cooperation. Here, then, with a single voice Martin surveys and integrates a disparate field. After 100 years, we have some answers to the questions the theories have raised. It is possible to evaluate incongruity/surprise, aggression/superiority, tension/release, and so on. Their points of overlap and agreement as well as their conflicts can be examined and a decision advanced as to what predictions are most accurate.

As the past century has evolved, humor has broadened and increased in scope. Newspapers, magazines, radio, television, and the Internet supply more accessible—and to a degree less critical—outlets for humor. One might complain that increased quantity has led to decreased quality. On the other hand, quantity also leads to more variability, so the best is better yet! Humor has become a more significant reflection of society and humanity as a whole. In these pages, the current state of our knowledge is assessed. The direction of future inquiry and understanding can be seen.

Life, it has been said, would be meaningless without art. Perhaps it would be too meaningful without humor. Here, then, is a thorough description and evaluation of the good, the bad, and the playful behavior that is a common and significant part of life.

Peter Derks
Professor Emeritus
College of William and Mary

PREFACE

Humor is a ubiquitous human activity that occurs in all types of social interaction. Most of us laugh at something funny many times during the course of a typical day. Although it is a form of play, humor serves a number of "serious" social, cognitive, and emotional functions. Fascinating questions about humor and laughter touch on every area of psychology. Surprisingly, however, despite its obvious importance in human behavior, humor and related topics like laughter, irony, and mirth are hardly ever mentioned in psychology texts and other scholarly books. Although there is a sizable and continually expanding research literature on this subject, most psychologists seem to have little systematic knowledge of it.

The main purpose of this book, then, is to provide an integrative review of theory and research findings in all areas of the psychology of humor, with one chapter devoted to each branch of the discipline (cognitive, social, biologic, personality, developmental, clinical, etc.). The book is designed in part to be used as a textbook for senior undergraduate- or graduate-level courses in the psychology of humor. Although such courses are not currently part of the curriculum in most psychology departments, it is my hope that the availability of this book will encourage instructors to consider offering one. This course, like the book, would typically be organized around the different areas of psychology, with a week or two spent on each chapter. In my experience, this is always a very popular course, and it serves as an excellent vehicle for demonstrating to students how a very intriguing, enjoyable, and personally relevant aspect of behavior can be approached from the perspective of each branch of psychology, providing a comprehensive and compelling understanding of the topic.

In addition to its purpose as a course textbook, I have also attempted to make this book useful as a research handbook for students as well as more seasoned academics who might be interested in conducting their own research in this topic area. In each chapter, therefore, I point out interesting questions that remain to be answered, novel hypotheses arising from recent developments in various areas of psychology, and promising research methods for addressing these questions. Researchers will no doubt see other ways that concepts from their own field of investigation could be applied to an understanding of humor. I also include an extensive bibliography for those who wish to examine the primary sources more closely. It is my hope that this book will trigger many interesting new ideas and stimulate readers to branch into this research area.

In addition to students and academic psychologists, I hope this book will be beneficial to scholars from other disciplines who are interested in learning about how humor has been investigated by psychologists. At various points in the book, I touch on some of the contributions of several other disciplines, such as anthropology, biology, computer science, linguistics, and sociology, which augment the research of psychologists. Finally, this book is also intended for practitioners in health care (e.g., physicians, nurses, occupational and physical therapists), counseling, social work, education, and business, who may be interested in potential applications of humor in their respective fields. I therefore do not assume that readers necessarily have a strong background in psychology. For those who may be less familiar with the discipline, I try to provide enough information to make the theories, methods, and findings reasonably accessible. Thus, I am attempting to reach a fairly broad audience with this book. I ask the reader's indulgence if I seem to be "spreading myself too thin."

ACKNOWLEDGMENTS

This book could not have been written without the help of many people. My interest in the academic study of humor was first kindled by my graduate research adviser at the University of Waterloo, Herb Lefcourt, whose intellectual curiosity and enthusiasm for scholarship have provided an inspiration and role model for me throughout my career. Over the years, I have honed my thinking about humor in many hours of lively discussion with several colleagues, including Nick Kuiper at the University of Western Ontario, with whom I have collaborated on a number of projects, and my good friends and fellow members of the International Society for Humor Studies, Peter Derks, Willi Ruch, and Sven Svebak. I am also grateful to a number of other research collaborators, including Eric Bressler, Jay Brinker, Lorne Campbell, Guohai Chen, Kathy Dance, David Dozois, Paul Frewen, Shahe Kazarian, Paavo Kerkkänen, Joan Olinger, Tony Vernon, and Lynne Zarbatany. I have also learned a great deal from my students, whose inquisitiveness and fresh insights have provided me with ongoing inspiration. Those who have worked with me on the topic of humor include James Dobbin, Patricia Doris, Gwen Dutrizac, Jeanette Gray, Tim Hillson, Melissa Johari, Jennie Ward, Kelly Weir, and Jeremy Yip.

I also wish to thank the following individuals who read drafts of various sections of this book and provided me with helpful feedback and suggestions: Albert Katz, Martin Kavaliers, Nick Kuiper, Paul Lewis, Jim Olson, and Willi Ruch. I am especially indebted to Peter Derks, who read and responded to every chapter, and whose unfailing encouragement and enthusiasm for this project helped keep me going. Needless to say, however, I take full responsibility for all errors and omissions. I am also grateful for the support and encouragement of my good friends, Ed Beharry, Ray Cardey, George Vanderschaaf, and John Zinkann. I am blessed by a warm and caring family, and am buoyed by the love of my daughters Rachelle (and her husband Andrew and their children Caroline and Christina) and Julia (and her husband Ben), and my son Ben. Finally, and most importantly, I cannot fully express my gratitude to my wife, Myra, whose enduring love and cheerful sense of humor have sustained me, and to whom I dedicate this book.

Introduction to the Psychology of Humor

We all know what it is like to experience humor. Someone tells a joke, relates an amusing personal anecdote, makes a witty comment or an inadvertent slip of the tongue, and we are suddenly struck by how funny it is. Depending on how amusing we perceive the stimulus to be, it might cause us to smile, to chuckle, or to burst out in peals of convulsive laughter. Our response is accompanied by pleasant feelings of emotional well-being and mirth. Most of us have this sort of experience many times during the course of a typical day.

Because humor is so familiar and is such an enjoyable and playful activity, many people might think they already understand it and do not need research in psychology to explain it. However, the empirical study of humor holds many interesting surprises. Although it is essentially a type of mental play involving a lighthearted, nonserious attitude toward ideas and events, humor serves a number of "serious" social, emotional, and cognitive functions, making it a fascinating and rewarding topic of scientific investigation.

The topic of humor raises a host of intriguing questions of relevance to all areas of psychology. What are the mental processes involved in "getting a joke" or perceiving something to be funny? How is humor processed in the brain, and what effect does it have on our bodies? What is laughter and why do we laugh in response to humorous things? Why is humor so enjoyable? What role does humor play in our interactions with other people? What is a sense of humor and how does it develop in children? Is a good sense of humor beneficial for mental and physical health?

1

As is evident from these and other related questions, humor touches on all branches of academic psychology (R. A. Martin, 2000). Researchers in the area of cognitive psychology may be interested in the mental processes involved in the perception, comprehension, appreciation, and creation of humor. The interpersonal functions of humor in dyadic interactions and group dynamics are of relevance to social psychology. Developmental psychologists may focus on the way humor and laughter develop from infancy into childhood and throughout the lifespan. Personality researchers might examine individual differences in sense of humor and their relation to other traits and behaviors. Biological psychology can shed light on the physiological bases of laughter and the brain regions underlying the comprehension and appreciation of humor. The role of humor in mental and physical health, as well as its potential applications in psychotherapy, education, and the workplace, are of interest to applied branches of psychology such as clinical, health, educational, and industrial-organizational psychology. Thus, researchers from every branch of the discipline have potentially interesting contributions to make to the study of humor. Indeed, a complete understanding of the psychology of humor requires an integration of findings from all these areas.

Despite the obvious importance of humor in many different areas of human experience and its relevance to all branches of psychology, mainstream psychology has paid surprisingly little attention to this subject up to now. Humor research typically receives scant mention, if any at all, in undergraduate psychology texts or scholarly books. Nonetheless, there has been a steady accumulation of research on the topic over the years, producing a sizable body of knowledge. The overall aim of this book is therefore to introduce students and academics in psychology, as well as scholars and professional practitioners from other fields, to the existing research literature, and to point out interesting avenues for further study in this fascinating topic area.

In this chapter, I will begin by summarizing evidence of the universality and evolutionary origins of humor and laughter in humans. I will then explore the question of what humor is, discussing four essential elements of the humor process and the relevance of each to an integrative psychology of humor. This will be followed by a survey of the many different forms of humor that we encounter during our daily lives, and an examination of the psychological functions of humor and laughter. Next, I will summarize the history of the concept of humor, examining the way popular conceptions and assumptions about humor and laughter have changed dramatically over the centuries. Finally, I will discuss the psychological approach to humor and then present an overview of the rest of this book.

THE UNIVERSALITY OF HUMOR AND LAUGHTER

Humor and laughter are a universal aspect of human experience, occurring in all cultures and virtually all individuals throughout the world (Apte, 1985; Lefcourt, 2001). Laughter is a distinctive, stereotyped pattern of vocalization that is easily recognized and quite unmistakable (Provine and Yong, 1991). Although different cultures have their own norms concerning the suitable subject matter of humor and the types of situations in which laughter is considered appropriate, the sounds of laughter are indistinguishable from one culture to another. Developmentally, laughter is one of the first social vocalizations (after crying) emitted by human infants (McGhee, 1979). Infants begin to laugh in response to the actions of other people at about four months of age, and cases of gelastic (i.e., laughter-producing) epilepsy in newborns indicate that the brain mechanisms for laughter are already present at birth (Sher and Brown, 1976). The innateness of laughter is further demonstrated by the fact that even children born deaf and blind have been reported to laugh appropriately without ever having perceived the laughter of others (Provine, 2000). Indeed, there is evidence of specialized brain circuits for humor and laughter in humans, which researchers are beginning to identify by means of neural imaging studies. Thus, being able to enjoy humor and express it through laughter seems to be an essential part of what it means to be human.

Interestingly, though, humans are not the only animal that laughs. Primatologists have studied in some detail a form of laughter emitted by young chimpanzees, which was first described by Charles Darwin (1872). Similar types of laughter have also been observed in other apes, including bonobos, orangutans, and gorillas (Preuschoft and van Hooff, 1997; van Hooff and Preuschoft, 2003). Ape laughter is described as a staccato, throaty, panting vocalization that accompanies the *relaxed open-mouth* or "play face," and is emitted during playful rough-and-tumble social activities such as wrestling, tickling, and chasing games (see Figure 1). Although it sounds somewhat different from human laughter, it is quite recognizable as such, occurring in similar social contexts as laughter in human infants and young children. Indeed, there is good reason to believe that human and chimpanzee laughter have the same evolutionary origins and many of the same functions.

In addition to laughter, there is evidence that apes may even have the capacity for a rudimentary sense of humor. Chimpanzees and gorillas that have been taught to communicate by means of sign language have been observed to use language in playful ways that are very reminiscent of humor, such as punning, humorous insults, and incongruous word use (Gamble, 2001). Interestingly, these humorous uses of linguistic signs are sometimes also accompanied by laughter and the play face, indicating a close link between humor, play, and laughter even in apes.

All of these lines of evidence suggest that humor and laughter in humans are a product of natural selection (Gervais and Wilson, 2005). Laughter appears to have originated in social play and to be derived from primate play signals. It is viewed by evolutionary researchers as part of the nonverbal "gesture-call" system, which has a long evolutionary history, predating the development of language (Burling, 1993). With the evolution of greater intellectual and linguistic abilities, humans have adapted the laughter-generating play activities of their primate ancestors to the mental play with words and ideas that we now call humor (Caron, 2002). Thus, although they usually do not chase and tickle one another in rough-and-tumble play, human adults, by means of humor, continue to engage in frequent social play. These evolutionary

FIGURE 1   The chimpanzee play face. The characteristic "play face" (open mouth, upper teeth covered, lower teeth exposed) accompanies panting laughter. © Getty Images/PhotoDisc

origins of humor and laughter suggest that they likely have important social-emotional functions that have contributed to our survival as a species.

Although humor has a biological basis rooted in our genes, it is also evident that cultural norms and learning play an important role in determining how it is used in social interactions, and what topics are considered appropriate for it. In addition, although all forms of humor seem to originate in a basic play structure, the complexity of human language and imagination enables us to create humor in a seemingly endless variety of forms. As human language, culture, and technology have evolved, we have developed new methods and styles of communicating it, from spontaneous interpersonal joking and banter to oral storytelling traditions, comedic drama and humorous literature, comedy films, radio and television shows, and jokes and cartoons disseminated over the Internet.

Besides being a form of playful fun and entertainment, humor has taken on a wide range of social functions over the course of human biological and cultural evolution. Many of these interpersonal functions are contradictory and paradoxical. Humor can be a method of enhancing social cohesion within an in-group, but it can also be a way of excluding individuals from an out-group. It can be a means of reducing but also reinforcing status differences among people, expressing agreement and sociability but also disagreement and aggression, facilitating cooperation as well as resistance, and strengthening solidarity and connectedness or undermining power and status. Thus, while originating in social play, humor has evolved in humans as a universal mode of communication and social influence with a variety of functions.

WHAT IS HUMOR?

The Oxford English Dictionary defines humor as "that quality of action, speech, or writing which excites amusement; oddity, jocularity, facetiousness, comicality, fun." It goes on to say that humor is also "the faculty of perceiving what is ludicrous or amusing, or of expressing it in speech, writing, or other composition; jocose imagination or treatment of a subject" (Simpson and Weiner, 1989, p. 486). It is evident from these definitions that humor is a broad term that refers to anything that people say or do that is perceived as funny and tends to make others laugh, as well as the mental processes that go into both creating and perceiving such an amusing stimulus, and also the affective response involved in the enjoyment of it.

From a psychological perspective, the humor process can be divided into four essential components: (1) a social context, (2) a cognitive-perceptual process, (3) an emotional response, and (4) the vocal-behavioral expression of laughter.

The Social Context of Humor

Humor is fundamentally a social phenomenon. We laugh and joke much more frequently when we are with other people than when we are by ourselves (R. A. Martin and Kuiper, 1999; Provine and Fischer, 1989). People do occasionally laugh when they are alone, such as while watching a comedy show on television, reading a humorous book, or remembering a funny personal experience. However, these instances of laughter can usually be seen as "pseudo-social" in nature, because one is still responding to the characters in the television program or the author of the book, or reliving in memory an event that involved other people.

Humor can (and frequently does) occur in virtually any social situation. It can occur between spouses who have lived together for fifty years or between strangers waiting at a bus stop. It can take place in the conversation of a group of close friends casually sitting around a table in a coffee shop, or in the interactions of a group of business people participating in formal negotiations. It can be used by public speakers, such as politicians or religious leaders, addressing large audiences either in person or via the media.

The social context of humor is one of play. Indeed, humor is essentially a way for people to interact in a playful manner. As I have already noted, research on laughter in chimpanzees and other apes indicates that laughter originates in social play (van

Hooff and Preuschoft, 2003). In humans, our ability to create humor to amuse one another and evoke laughter appears to have evolved as a means of providing us with extended opportunities for play. Play seems to serve important social, emotional, and cognitive functions (Bateson, 2005). Indeed, all mammals engage in play as juveniles, but, unlike most other animals, humans continue to play throughout their lives, most notably through humor.

When they engage in play, people take a nonserious attitude toward the things they are saying or doing, and they carry out these activities for their own sake—for the fun of it—rather than having a more important goal in mind. Psychologist Michael Apter (1991) has referred to the playful state of mind associated with humor as the *paratelic* mode, which he distinguishes from the more serious, goal-directed *telic* mode (from Greek *telos* = goal). According to Apter, we switch back and forth between these serious and playful states of mind many times during the course of a typical day. The humorous, playful mode of functioning can occur for brief moments or for extended periods of time. In a business meeting, for example, someone may make a humorous quip that causes the group to laugh and enter the playful paratelic frame of mind for a brief moment, before resuming their more serious telic mode of discourse. In more casual settings, when people are feeling relaxed and uninhibited, they may engage in playful and humorous storytelling and joke swapping for several hours at a time.

Cognitive-Perceptual Processes in Humor

Besides occurring in a social context, humor is characterized by particular sorts of cognitions. To produce humor, an individual needs to mentally process information coming from the environment or from memory, playing with ideas, words, or actions in a creative way, and thereby generating a witty verbal utterance or a comical nonverbal action that is perceived by others to be funny. In the reception of humor, we take in information (something someone says or does, or something we read) through our eyes and ears, process the meaning of this information, and appraise it as nonserious, playful, and humorous.

What are the characteristics of a stimulus that cause us to perceive it to be funny? As we will see in the next two chapters, this question has been a topic of much scholarly debate and research for centuries (see also Roeckelein, 2002). Most investigators would agree, however, that humor involves an idea, image, text, or event that is in some sense incongruous, odd, unusual, unexpected, surprising, or out of the ordinary. In addition, there needs to be some aspect that causes us to appraise the stimulus as nonserious or unimportant, putting us into a playful frame of mind at least momentarily. Thus, the essence of humor seems to be incongruity, unexpectedness, and playfulness, which evolutionary theorists Matthew Gervais and David Wilson (2005) referred to as "nonserious social incongruity." This constellation of cognitive elements appears to characterize all forms of humor, including jokes, teasing, and witty banter, unintentional types of humor such as amusing slips of the tongue or the proverbial person slipping on the banana peel, the laughter-eliciting peek-a-boo games and rough-and-tumble play of children, and even the humor of chimpanzees and gorillas (Wyer and Collins, 1992).

Arthur Koestler (1964) coined the term *bisociation* to refer to the mental process involved in perceiving humorous incongruity. According to Koestler, bisociation occurs when a situation, event, or idea is simultaneously perceived from the perspective of two self-consistent but normally unrelated and even incompatible frames of reference. Thus, a single event "is made to vibrate simultaneously on two different wavelengths, as it were" (p. 35). A simple example is a pun, in which two different meanings of a word or phrase are brought together simultaneously (e.g., Two cannibals are eating a clown. One says to the other, "Does this taste funny to you?"). According to Koestler, this same process underlies all types of humor.

Michael Apter (1982) used the concept of *synergy* to describe this cognitive process, in which two contradictory images or conceptions of the same object are held in one's mind at the same time. In the playful paratelic state, according to Apter, synergies are enjoyable and emotionally arousing, producing the pleasurable sensation of having one's thoughts oscillate back and forth between two incompatible interpretations of a concept. Thus, in humor, we playfully manipulate ideas and activities so that they are simultaneously perceived in opposite ways, such as real and not real, important and trivial, threatening and safe. As we will see in later chapters, a great deal of theoretical discussion and research in the psychology of humor has focused on exploring in greater detail the cognitive processes underlying the perception and appreciation of humor.

Emotional Aspects of Humor

Our response to humor is not just an intellectual one. The perception of humor invariably also evokes a pleasant emotional response, at least to some degree. Psychological studies have shown that exposure to humorous stimuli produces an increase in positive affect and mood (Szabo, 2003). The emotional nature of humor is also clearly demonstrated by recent brain imaging research showing that exposure to humorous cartoons activates the well-known reward network in the limbic system of the brain (Mobbs et al., 2003). The funnier a particular cartoon is rated by a participant, the more strongly these parts of the brain are activated. From other research, we know that these same brain circuits underlie pleasurable emotional states associated with a variety of enjoyable activities including eating, listening to enjoyable music, sexual activity, and even ingestion of mood-altering drugs. This explains why humor is so enjoyable and why people go to such lengths to experience it as often as they can: whenever we laugh at something funny, we are experiencing an emotional high that is rooted in the biochemistry of our brains.

It can therefore be argued that humor is essentially an emotion that is elicited by the particular types of cognitive processes discussed in the previous section. Just as other emotions like joy, jealousy, or fear occur in response to specific types of appraisals of the social and physical environment (Lazarus, 1991), so humor comprises an emotional response that is elicited by a particular set of appraisals, namely the perception that an event or situation is incongruously funny or amusing. The pleasant emotion associated with humor, which is familiar to all of us, is a unique feeling of well-being that is described by such terms as *amusement, mirth, hilarity, cheerfulness,* and *merriment*. It is closely related to joy, and contains an element of exultation and a feeling of invincibility, a sense of expansion of the self that the seventeenth-century English philosopher Thomas Hobbes referred to as "sudden glory."

Surprisingly, although it is a feeling that is familiar to everyone, scholars have not yet settled on an agreed-upon technical term to denote this particular emotion. Researchers have specific terms to denote emotions like joy, love, fear, anxiety, depression, and so forth, but there is no common name for the emotion elicited by humor. This is because it is so closely aligned with laughter that, until recently, theorists and researchers have tended to focus on the more obvious behavior of laughter instead of the emotion that underlies it. Some researchers have used the expressions "humor appreciation" (e.g., Weisfeld, 1993) or "amusement" (e.g., Shiota et al., 2004) to denote this emotion, but these terms seem to be too cognitive and do not fully capture its emotional nature. Psychologist Willibald Ruch (1993) has proposed the word *exhilaration* (related to *hilarity*, from Latin *hilaris* = cheerful) as a technical term for this emotion. While exhilaration, in its common English meaning, contains a sense of excitement in addition to cheerfulness, Ruch suggested that this use of the term would de-emphasize the excitement component, underscoring instead the emotional quality of cheerfulness, amusement, and funniness. However, this term does not seem to have caught on with researchers, who likely have difficulty shedding the connotation of excitement.

To denote this emotion, we need a term that is clearly emotion-related and is associated with humor and laughter but without being synonymous with either one, and which can have a range of intensities. In my view, the word *mirth* works very well for this purpose. *The Oxford English Dictionary* defines mirth as "pleasurable feeling, . . . joy, happiness; gaiety of mind, as manifested in jest and laughter; merriment, hilarity" (Simpson and Weiner, 1989, p. 841). This seems to be exactly the required meaning. Some researchers have used the word *mirth* to refer to smiling and laughter, which are facial and vocal expressions of the emotion rather than the emotion itself, and therefore should be kept distinct. In this book, then, I will refer to this emotion as mirth.

Mirth, then, is the distinctive emotion that is elicited by the perception of humor. Like other emotions (e.g., joy, love, sadness, fear), mirth can occur with varying degrees of intensity, ranging from mild feelings of amusement to very high levels of hilarity (Ruch, 1993). Also like other emotions, mirth has physiological as well as experiential components. Along with the distinctive subjective feelings of pleasure, amusement, and cheerfulness, this emotion is accompanied by a range of biochemical changes in the brain, autonomic nervous system, and endocrine system, involving a variety of molecules, including neurotransmitters, hormones, opioids, and neuropeptides (Panksepp, 1993). This neurochemical cocktail has further effects on many parts of the body, including the cardiovascular, muskuloskeletal, digestive, and immune systems (W. F. Fry, 1994). The biological concomitants of the emotion of mirth form the basis of claims that have been made in recent years about potential health benefits of humor and laughter. However, the exact nature of the physiological changes accompanying mirth is not yet well understood, and further research is needed before we can say with confidence whether these effects have significant health benefits (R. A. Martin, 2001, 2002).

The essentially emotional nature of humor is something that many scholars have failed to recognize until quite recently. In the past, most theorists and researchers have viewed it as primarily a cognitive process rather than an emotional one. A great deal of philosophical debate and research effort has been expended on attempts to identify the precise cognitive-perceptual elements that are necessary and sufficient for humor to occur, with little recognition of the fact that what these cognitive appraisals elicit is an emotion. This would be like researchers who study depression or anxiety spending all their time debating about the specific types of events and cognitive appraisals that elicit these mood states without ever noticing their emotional nature. Although much has been learned about the cognitive aspects of humor (and there is still more work to do in this area), theory and research directed at the emotional component of humor has only recently begun. Recent research efforts bridging social and biological psychology hold particular promise for further exciting breakthroughs in this area.

Laughter as an Expression of the Emotion of Mirth

Like other emotions, the mirthful pleasure accompanying humor also has an expressive component, namely laughter and smiling. At low levels of intensity, this emotion is expressed by a faint smile, which turns into a broader grin and then audible chuckling and laughter as the emotional intensity increases. At very high intensities, it is expressed by loud guffaws, often accompanied by a reddening of the face as well as bodily movements such as throwing back the head, rocking the body, slapping one's thighs, and so on. Thus, laughter is essentially a way of expressing or communicating to others the fact that one is experiencing the emotion of mirth, just as frowning, scowling, yelling, and clenching one's fists communicate the emotion of anger. Laughter is therefore fundamentally a social behavior: if there were no other people to communicate to, we would not need laughter. This is no doubt why it is so loud, why it comprises such a distinctive and easily recognized set of sounds, and why it rarely occurs in social isolation.

As we have already seen, the laughter of chimpanzees and other apes is typically accompanied by a characteristic facial expression called the relaxed open-mouth display, or play face, which is also seen in other primates and is shown during play. Many theorists have suggested that the main function of laughter, in humans as well as apes, is to signal to others that one is engaging in play, rather than being serious (e.g., van Hooff, 1972). When chimpanzees are playfully fighting and chasing each other, it is important for them to be able to let each other know that they are just having fun and not seriously intending to harm one another. In humans also, laughter can be a signal of friendliness and playful intentions, indicating that one is in a nonserious frame of mind. The laughter accompanying friendly teasing, for example, signals that a seemingly insulting message is not to be taken seriously.

More recently, researchers have suggested that the purpose of laughter is not just to communicate that one is in a playful state, but to actually induce this state in others as well (Owren and Bachorowski, 2003; Russell, Bachorowski, and Fernandez-Dols, 2003). According to this view, the peculiar sounds of laughter have a direct effect on the listener, inducing positive emotional arousal that mirrors the emotional state of the laugher, perhaps by activating certain specialized brain circuits (Gervais and Wilson, 2005; Provine, 2000). In this way, laughter may serve an important biosocial function of coupling together the positive emotions of members of a group and thereby coordinating their activities. This would explain why laughter is so contagious; when we hear someone laughing, it is almost impossible not to feel mirthful and begin laughing too. Yet another potential social function of laughter is to motivate others to behave in particular ways (Shiota et al., 2004). For example, laughter can be a method of positively reinforcing others for desirable behavior ("laughing with"), as well as a potent form of punishment directed at undesirable behaviors ("laughing at").

In summary, the psychological process of humor involves a social context, a cognitive appraisal process comprising the perception of playful incongruity, the emotional response of mirth, and the vocal-behavioral expression of laughter. Neurological studies indicate that these different components of the humor process involve different but interconnected regions of the brain (Wild et al., 2003). The word *humor* is often used in a narrow sense to refer specifically to the cognitive-perceptual component, the mental processes that go into creating or perceiving something funny or amusing. I will also occasionally use it in this narrow sense, since there does not seem to be another word to denote this cognitive process. It is important to bear in mind, though, that in a broader sense, humor refers to all four components, and all of them need to be addressed in an integrative psychology of humor.

THE MANY FORMS OF HUMOR

We have seen that humor is essentially an emotional response of mirth in a social context that is elicited by a perception of playful incongruity and is expressed through smiling and laughter. Although these basic elements are common to all instances of humor, the range of social situations and events that can elicit the humor response is remarkably diverse. During the course of a typical day, we encounter many different forms of humor communicated by different means and for different purposes. Some of this humor comes to us via the mass media. Radio hosts frequently crack jokes and make witty comments; television provides us with a constant diet of humor in the form of sitcoms, blooper shows, stand-up comedy, political satire, and humorous advertisements; and we encounter it also in newspaper comic strips and cartoons, comedy movies, and humorous books. Humor is also often used in speeches, sermons, and lectures by politicians, religious leaders, motivational speakers, and teachers.

However, most of the humor and laughter that we experience in our daily lives arises spontaneously in the course of our normal relations with other people (R. A. Martin and Kuiper, 1999). This sort of interpersonal humor occurs in nearly every type of informal and formal interaction, including conversations between lovers, close friends, fellow students, coworkers, business associates, store clerks and customers, doctors and patients, teachers and students, and even complete strangers standing in line at a bank.

Individuals vary in the degree to which they produce humor in their daily interactions with others. Most of us enjoy the positive emotion of mirth so much that we highly value those individuals who are especially good at making us laugh. These are the people that we often describe as having a "good sense of humor," and they tend to be particularly sought out as friends and romantic partners. Some people develop such a talent at eliciting mirth in others and making them laugh that they become professional humor producers, entering the ranks of humorous authors, cartoonists, stand-up comedians, comedy writers, and actors. The billions of dollars spent on various forms of comedy each year further attest to the high value placed on the emotional pleasure associated with humor.

The humor that occurs in our everyday social interactions can be divided into three broad categories: (1) jokes, which are prepackaged humorous anecdotes that people memorize and pass on to one another; (2) spontaneous conversational humor, which is created intentionally by individuals during the course of a social interaction, and can be either verbal or nonverbal; and (3) accidental or unintentional humor.

Jokes

During the course of normal conversations, some people like to amuse others by telling jokes, which are short, amusing stories ending in a punch line. These are sometimes also referred to as "canned jokes" to distinguish them from the sorts of informal jesting and witty quips to which the words *joke* and *joking* can also refer. Here is an example of a joke of this sort (from Long and Graesser, 1988, p. 49):

> A man goes to a psychiatrist who gives him a battery of tests. Then he announces his findings. "I'm sorry to have to tell you that you are hopelessly insane." "Hell," says the client, indignantly, "I want a second opinion." "Okay," says the doctor, "You're ugly too."

The joke consists of a setup and a punch line. The setup, which includes all but the last sentence, creates in the listener a particular set of expectations about how the situation should be interpreted. The punch line suddenly shifts the meaning in an unexpected and playful way, thus creating the perception of nonserious incongruity that is necessary for humor to occur. In this particular joke, the punch line plays on the meaning of the phrase "second opinion," shifting the frame of reference from that of a serious, professional doctor-patient relationship to a nonsensical one in which one person is insulting another. The story is clearly playful and nonserious, conveying that the whole thing is meant to be taken as fun. Note, however, that there is also an aggressive element in this joke ("You're ugly too"). As we will see, there is much debate about the degree to which aggression is an essential aspect of all jokes (and perhaps even all humor).

In everyday conversation, joke-telling is usually prefaced by verbal or nonverbal cues (e.g., "Did you hear the one about . . .") or conforms to certain stock formats (e.g., "A man went into a bar . . .") that indicate to the audience that the story is meant to be humorous and that the listeners are expected to laugh (Cashion, Cody, and Erickson, 1986). Although joke-tellers typically try to draw links between the jokes they tell and the ongoing topic of conversation, a joke is a context-free and self-contained unit of humor that carries within itself all the information needed for it to be understood and enjoyed. It can therefore be told in many different conversational contexts (Long and Graesser, 1988). Riddles are another form of prepackaged humor closely related to jokes, which often involve a play on words and are particularly enjoyed by young children (e.g., Why did the cookie cry? Because his mother was a wafer so long).

Spontaneous Conversational Humor

Canned jokes represent only a small proportion of the humor that we experience in our everyday social interactions. In a daily diary study in which we had adults keep a record of every time they laughed over the course of three days, my colleague Nicholas Kuiper and I found that only about 11 percent of daily laughter occurred in response to jokes. Another 17 percent was elicited by the media, and fully 72 percent arose spontaneously during social interactions, either in response to funny comments that people made or to amusing anecdotes they told about things that had happened to them (R. A. Martin and Kuiper, 1999). This sort of spontaneous conversational humor is more context-dependent than joke-telling, and is therefore often not as funny when recounted afterwards ("You had to be there"). In such conversational humor, nonverbal cues indicating a humorous intent, such as a twinkle in the eye or a particular tone of voice, are often more ambiguous than in joke-telling, so that the listener is often not entirely sure if the speaker is jesting or being serious.

Spontaneous conversational humor takes many different forms, and many different words exist to describe them (e.g., *jest, witticism, quip, wisecrack, gag*). Neal Norrick (2003), a linguist who has conducted research on humor occurring in everyday conversation, suggested that, besides the telling of canned jokes, conversational humor may be classified into (1) *anecdotes* (relating an amusing story about oneself or someone else); (2) *wordplay* (creating puns, witty responses, or wisecracks that play on the meaning of words); and (3) *irony* (a statement in which the literal meaning is different from the intended meaning).

A more extensive classification system of spontaneous conversational humor (which they referred to as *wit*), was developed by psychologists Debra Long and Arthur Graesser (1988). To obtain a broad sample of the types of humor occurring in naturalistic conversations, these authors recorded a number of episodes of television talk shows (e.g., *The Tonight Show*) and then analyzed the different types of humor that arose in the interactions between the hosts and their guests. Audience laughter was used as an indicator of humor. Based on their analyses, these authors identified the following 11 categories, which were distinguished from one another on the basis of their intentions or uses of humor:

1. *Irony*—the speaker expresses a statement in which the literal meaning is opposite to the intended meaning (e.g., saying "What a beautiful day!" when the weather is cold and stormy).

2. *Satire*—aggressive humor that pokes fun at social institutions or social policy.

3. *Sarcasm*—aggressive humor that targets an individual rather than an institution (e.g., At a fashionable dinner, a dignified lady rebuked Winston Churchill: "Sir, you are drunk." "Yes," replied Churchill, "and you are ugly. But tomorrow I shall be sober and you shall still be ugly").

4. *Overstatement and understatement*—changing the meaning of something another person has said by repeating it with a different emphasis (e.g., A guest asks host Johnny Carson, who had been married several times: "Have you ever been married?" A second guest says, "Has he *ever* been married!").

5. *Self-deprecation*—humorous remarks targeting oneself as the object of humor. This may be done to demonstrate modesty, to put the listener at ease, or to ingratiate oneself with the listener.

6. *Teasing*—humorous remarks directed at the listener's personal appearance or foibles. Unlike sarcasm, the intention is not to seriously insult or offend.

7. *Replies to rhetorical questions*—because rhetorical questions are not asked with the expectation of a reply, giving an answer to one violates a conversational expectation and surprises the person who posed the question. This can therefore be perceived as funny, and the intention is usually to simply entertain a conversational partner.

8. *Clever replies to serious statements*—clever, incongruous, or nonsensical replies to a statement or question that was meant to be serious. The statement is deliberately misconstrued so that the speaker replies to a meaning other than the intended one.

9. *Double entendres*—a statement or word is deliberately misperceived or misconstrued so as to evoke a dual meaning, which is often sexual in nature.

10. *Transformations of frozen expressions*—transforming well-known sayings, clichés, or adages into novel statements (e.g., complaint of a bald man: "Hair today, gone tomorrow").

11. *Puns*—humorous use of a word that evokes a second meaning, usually based on a homophone (i.e., a word with a different meaning that sounds the same).

Although these categories are not mutually exclusive and there may be other forms of spontaneous wit that occur in natural conversation but are not observed in television talk shows (Wyer and Collins, 1992), this list does provide a useful starting point for thinking about the many different ways humor may be expressed. Neal Norrick (1984) also discussed what he called *stock conversational witticisms*, which are humorous sayings or expressions that are routinely and recurrently used in conversation (e.g., "faster than greased lightning," or "bring that up again and we'll vote on it" in response to someone belching). Besides these verbal forms of humor, people also often intentionally create humor in social interactions by nonverbal means, such as funny or exaggerated facial expressions, odd ways of walking, bodily gestures, or mannerisms.

Unintentional Humor

In addition to the things people say and do during social interactions with the intention of amusing others, much mirth and laughter also arise from utterances or actions that are not meant to be funny (Wyer and Collins, 1992). English literature professors Alleen Nilsen and Don Nilsen (2000) referred to these as *accidental humor*, which they divided into physical and linguistic forms. Accidental physical humor includes minor mishaps and pratfalls such as the person slipping on a banana peel or spilling a drink on one's shirt. These sorts of events are funny when they occur in a surprising and incongruous manner and when the person experiencing them is not seriously hurt or badly embarrassed. This type of humor also forms the basis of slap-stick and screwball comedy.

Accidental linguistic humor arises from misspellings, mispronunciations, errors in logic, and the kinds of speaker confusions called *Freudian slips*, *malapropisms*, and *spoonerisms*. This type of unintentional humor occurs, for example, in newspaper headlines in which an ambiguity creates a humorous alternative meaning (e.g., "Prostitutes appeal to pope"; "Dr. Ruth talks about sex with newspaper editors"; "Red tape holds up bridge"). Spoonerisms are a speech error in which the initial sounds of two or more words are transposed, creating an unintended and humorous new meaning. They were named after a nineteenth-century British clergyman named William Spooner who frequently made such mistakes in his sermons and speeches (e.g., he is said to have proposed a toast to Queen Victoria, saying "Three cheers for our queer old dean").

In sum, humor is a ubiquitous type of social interaction that takes many different forms. The conversational types of humor, including joke-telling, spontaneous wit, and unintentional humor, are of particular interest to psychologists. However, until quite recently, most of the psychological research on humor has focused largely on jokes and cartoons (which are essentially visual jokes), and has generally ignored the other types. This is in large part because of the self-contained and context-free nature of jokes and cartoons, which makes them very easy to transport into a laboratory setting. Over the years, a great many studies have been conducted in which participants (usually sitting by themselves in a laboratory) were presented with various types of jokes and cartoons under a variety of experimental conditions and were asked to rate them for funniness. Thus, in humor research, jokes and cartoons have long served as the equivalent of T-mazes or nonsense syllables in other fields, providing experimenters with an independent variable that can help control the input in investigations of this rather nebulous concept.

However, humor in these sorts of studies is removed from its natural social context, and, although these methods have enabled researchers to make many interesting discoveries, they are not as useful for studying the forms and functions of humor as it normally occurs in social interaction. In contrast to studying participants' responses to jokes in a laboratory, it is more difficult to investigate the spontaneous forms of humor that arise in everyday conversations and depend on the social context. For this type of research, investigators may need to go out of the laboratory and study humor as it occurs spontaneously in naturalistic settings, or at least have dyads or groups of people interact with one another in the laboratory.

Besides being the focus of most research, jokes have also served as the prototype of humor in many past theories, which have tended to focus particularly on the cognitive processes underlying the comprehension of these types of humor. Because joke comprehension may be somewhat different from the cognitive processes involved in other forms of humor, these theories were often inadequate for explaining all types of humor. More recently, researchers are beginning to develop theories that account for other sorts of humor occurring in social interaction besides jokes (e.g., Wyer and Collins, 1992). These theories often incorporate the emotional and social aspects of humor as well as the cognitive elements.

PSYCHOLOGICAL FUNCTIONS OF HUMOR

Although it is essentially a form of social play enabling us to have fun and derive emotional pleasure from nonserious incongruities, humor serves a number of important and "serious" psychological functions, which have likely contributed to our survival as a species. Some of the benefits of humor derive from the positive emotion associated with it, and many of these were likely already present in the laughter-evoking rough-and-tumble play activities ("proto-humor") of our early hominid ancestors even before the evolution of language. Other functions seem to have been added on over the course of human evolution through a process known as *co-optation* (Gervais and Wilson, 2005). As humans developed greater cognitive and linguistic abilities, complex patterns of group interaction, and the ability to infer the intentions and mental states of others, humor and laughter, while originating in rough-and-tumble social play, came to be used for additional purposes relating to social communication and influence, tension relief, and coping with adversity.

The psychological functions of humor can be classified into three broad categories: (1) cognitive and social benefits of the positive emotion of mirth, (2) uses of humor for social communication and influence, and (3) tension relief and coping.

Cognitive and Social Functions of the Positive Emotion of Mirth

Human emotions have important adaptive functions. Emotions such as fear and anger, for example, cause individuals to focus their attention on threats in the environment, mobilize their energies, and motivate them to take action to deal with these threats (Levenson, 1994). However, the functions of positive emotions like mirth and joy are less immediately obvious, since they do not seem to evoke specific action patterns. In the past, psychologists tended to focus primarily on negative emotions like depression, fear, and hostility, and did not give much attention to positive emotions like mirth, joy, happiness, and love. More recently, however, psychologists have begun to investigate positive emotions, and this research is beginning to shed light on their functions.

Alice Isen (2003) summarized a body of experimental research indicating that when people are experiencing positive emotions (including comedy-induced mirth), as compared to neutral or negative emotions, they show improvements in a variety of cognitive abilities and social behaviors. For example, they demonstrate greater cognitive flexibility, enabling them to engage in more creative problem solving; more efficient organization and integration of memory; more effective thinking, planning, and judgment; and higher levels of social responsibility and prosocial behaviors such as helpfulness and generosity (see also Lyubomirsky, King, and Diener, 2005). An experiment by Barbara Fredrickson and Robert Levenson (1998) also demonstrated that the induction of positive emotions, including mirth, helps to reduce physiological arousal caused by negative emotions.

Based on these sorts of findings, Barbara Fredrickson (1998, 2001) has proposed a "broaden-and-build" model of the psychological functions of positive emotions such as mirth. Unlike negative emotions, which tend to narrow one's focus of attention and motivate one to engage in specific actions, she suggested that positive emotions serve to *broaden* the scope of the individual's focus of attention, allowing for more creative problem-solving and an increased range of behavioral response options, and they also *build* physical, intellectual, and social resources that are available to the individual for dealing with life's challenges. She argued that positive emotions such as mirth are evolved adaptations that contribute to both mental and physical health. Recent research by Fredrickson and her colleagues on mirth and other positive emotions has provided further support for these hypotheses (e.g., Fredrickson and Branigan, 2005; Fredrickson et al., 2000).

Michelle Shiota and her colleagues (2004) have also proposed that positive emotions may play an important role in the regulation of interpersonal relationships. These authors pointed out that humans are social animals that require close relationships in order to survive. They suggested that positive emotions play a role in accomplishing three fundamental tasks required for relationships: (1) identifying potential relationship partners, (2) developing, negotiating, and maintaining key relationships, and (3) collective agency (i.e., working together with others to achieve goals that could not be accomplished alone). They suggested that the humor-related positive emotion of mirth is effective for accomplishing all three of these tasks in various types of relationships, including romantic partnerships, friendships, and group relations. For example, the mirth associated with mutual laughter can be a way of identifying members of an in-group, selecting and attracting partners, rewarding cooperative efforts, and enhancing interpersonal bonding and group cohesion.

One way in which humor likely provides important psychological benefits, then, is by inducing a positive emotional state that is typically shared among two or more individuals. The enjoyable subjective feelings accompanying this emotional state provide a strong incentive to seek out opportunities for humor and laughter, which in turn fulfill a number of important cognitive and social functions. Many of these emotion-related benefits were likely already present in the proto-humor of our early hominid ancestors, providing an evolutionary survival advantage.

Social Communication and Influence

As we have seen, humorous interactions between people take a wide variety of forms. When people engage in these sorts of humorous exchanges in their everyday lives, they often have some (perhaps unconscious) purpose or social goal beyond merely providing amusement and entertainment. Even when telling a joke or saying funny things to make others laugh, people also often have the underlying goal of impressing others with their wittiness and gaining attention, prestige, or approval. Sociologist Michael Mulkay (1988) suggested that humor may be viewed as a mode of interpersonal communication that is frequently used to convey implicit messages in an indirect manner and to influence other people in various ways. Because it involves playing with incongruities and contradictory ideas and conveys multiple meanings at once, humor is a particularly useful form of communication in situations in which a more serious and direct mode runs the risk of being too confrontational, potentially embarrassing, or otherwise risky.

For example, if two friends attempt to discuss a difference of opinion in a serious way, they may become embroiled in endless arguments and counterarguments, with an accompanying escalation in feelings of frustration and annoyance. However, by using humor to joke about each other's perspective, they can communicate a sense of acceptance and appreciation of one another while still maintaining and acknowledging their different points of view (Kane, Suls, and Tedeschi, 1977). Similarly, if a conflict between two people escalates to the point where it threatens their relationship, a joking comment from one of them can be a way of de-escalating the conflict while enabling both of them to save face. Thus, humor can be a means of smoothing over conflicts and tensions between people.

On the other hand, humor is also often used to convey critical or disparaging messages that might not be well received if communicated in a more serious manner. In friendly teasing, for example, a message of mild disapproval or censure is communicated using humor (Keltner et al., 2001). This allows the speaker to retract the message if it is not well received by saying "I was only joking." Indeed, since everyone recognizes the ambiguous nature of humor, such a disclaimer is usually not even necessary. Thus, humor is often a way for individuals to "save face" for themselves and others, using it to soften the impact of a message or to "test the water" to see how others will respond.

Some of the social functions of humor can also be quite aggressive, coercive, and manipulative. Although it is a form of play, humor is not necessarily prosocial and benevolent, and indeed a good deal of humor involves laughing at the behavior and characteristics of individuals who are perceived to be different in some way and therefore incongruous. Over the course of human evolution (much of which involved living in small groups of hunter-gatherers), humor and laughter seem to have been co-opted for the purpose of enhancing group identity by enforcing social norms within the group and excluding members of out-groups, and this function of humor is still very evident today (Alexander, 1986).

Whereas the "face-saving" communicative uses of humor often involve only two people, these more aggressive and even hostile uses typically involve three individuals or groups: the speaker who communicates the humorous message, the listener(s) who laugh at it, and the target(s) who are the "butt" of the humor. The target, who may or may not be physically present, may be a particular individual or a nonspecific member of a disparaged group, such as a particular gender, ethnic, or religious group. The humor may be a spontaneous humorous comment or a canned ethnic or sexist joke. This type of humor enables members of an in-group to enhance their feelings of group identity and cohesiveness while excluding and emphasizing their differences from members of an out-group. These aggressive types of humor are often perceived by participants to be extremely funny and they evoke genuine feelings of mirth and laughter, even though they occur at the expense of others.

The pleasurable emotion of mirth accompanying humor and laughter can therefore be gained at other people's expense, either by passively deriving amusement from their misfortunes (as described by the interesting German word *schadenfreude*), or by actively seeking to humiliate, embarrass, or ridicule them in some way and thereby enhancing one's own status relative to theirs. Thus, humor can involve "laughing at" as well as "laughing with." As we will see, many traditional theories suggest that aggression is actually an essential element of all humor and laughter. Although most theorists today would not take such an extreme view, few would disagree that humor can be used in aggressive and even hostile ways.

Since being the target of others' laughter is painful and something most people seek to avoid, aggressive forms of humor can also be used as a method of coercing people into conforming to desired behaviors. Within social groups, humor is often used to enforce group norms, either by making fun of the discrepant actions and traits of people who are outside the group or by teasing members within the group when they engage in deviant behavior. Thus, in aggressive types of joking, teasing, ridicule, or sarcasm, humor can be used to exclude individuals from a group, reinforce power and status differences, suppress behavior that does not conform to group norms, and have a coercive influence on others.

In summary, the social play of humor can be used to communicate a variety of messages and to achieve any number of social goals that individuals may have at any particular time, some of which may be congenial and prosocial while others may be more aggressive or coercive. Humor, then, is inherently neither friendly nor aggressive: it is a means of deriving emotional pleasure that can be used for both amiable and antagonistic purposes. This is the paradox of humor. If one's goal is to strengthen relationships, smooth over conflicts, and build cohesiveness, humor can be useful for those purposes. On the other hand, if one's goal is to ostracize, humiliate, or manipulate someone, or to build up one's own status at the expense of others, humor can be useful for those purposes as well. Either way, it can evoke genuine feelings of mirth.

Tension Relief and Coping with Adversity

Another function of humor that has often been noted is its role in coping with life stress and adversity (Lefcourt, 2001; Lefcourt and Martin, 1986). Over the course of evolution, humans appear to have co-opted the nonserious play of humor as a means of cognitively managing many of the events and situations that threaten their well-being, by making light of them and turning them into something to be laughed at (Dixon, 1980). Because it inherently involves incongruity and multiple interpretations, humor provides a way for the individual to shift perspective on a stressful situation, reappraising it from a new and less threatening point of view. As a consequence of this humorous reappraisal, the situation becomes less stressful and more manageable (Kuiper, Martin, and Olinger, 1993; R. A. Martin et al., 1993).

The positive emotion of mirth accompanying humor replaces the feeling of anxiety, depression, or anger that would otherwise occur, enabling the person to think more broadly and flexibly and to engage in creative problem solving (Fredrickson, 2001). In addition, this positive emotion may have a physiological benefit of speeding recovery from the cardiovascular effects of any negative stress-related emotions that may have been evoked (Fredrickson and Levenson, 1998). Thus, humor may be viewed as an important emotion regulation mechanism, which can contribute to mental health (Gross and Muñoz, 1995).

Studies of survivors of extreme adversity such as the brutal conditions of concentration camps indicate that humor, in the form of joking about the oppressors as well as the hardships endured, is often an important means of engendering positive emotions; maintaining group cohesion and morale; preserving a sense of mastery, hope, and self-respect; and thereby enabling individuals to survive in seemingly hopeless circumstances (C. V. Ford and Spaulding, 1973; Frankl, 1984; Henman, 2001). Less extreme examples of the liberating potential of humor as a means of triumphing over adversity and refusing to be defeated by the slings and arrows of life can be found in the daily lives of many people. Humor and laughter provide a means for cancer patients to make light of their illness and maintain a spirit of optimism, and jokes about death are a way for people to distance themselves emotionally from thoughts of their own mortality. Thus, by laughing at the fundamental incongruities of life and diminishing threats by turning them into objects of nonserious play, humor is a way of refusing to be overcome by the people and situations, both large and small, that threaten our well-being.

The aggressive aspects of humor discussed earlier also play a role in this coping function. Many of the threats to well-being that humans experience come from other people. By making fun of the stupidity, incompetence, laziness, or other failings of the people who frustrate, irritate, and annoy them and thwart their progress toward their goals, individuals are able to minimize the feelings of distress that these others might cause, and derive some pleasure at their expense. This use of aggressive humor in coping can be directed toward particular individuals who create difficulties or at nonspecific representatives of broader social groups or power structures that are perceived as irritants. While providing a means of enhancing personal feelings of well-being in the short run, however, such aggressive uses of humor for coping can also alienate others and have an adverse effect on valued relationships in the longer term (R. A. Martin et al., 2003).

Like all forms of humor, the use of humor for coping with adversity usually takes place in a social context. People typically do not begin laughing and cracking jokes about their problems when they are all alone. Instead, coping humor commonly takes the form of joking and laughing with other people, either in the midst of an adverse situation or shortly afterwards. For example, when the events of a particularly stressful day are discussed among a group of close friends later in the evening, difficulties that earlier seemed distressing and overwhelming can be perceived as humorously incongruous and become the basis of a great deal of hilarity and boisterous laughter. The greater the emotional arousal and tension engendered by the stressful events, the greater the pleasure and the louder the laughter when joking about them afterwards.

This tension-releasing function of humor has been noted by many theorists over the years, and some have even suggested that tension relief is a defining characteristic of all humor. Although this view is perhaps overstated, it does reflect one of the important functions of humor and laughter. Thus, it appears that over the course of human evolution, the cognitive play of humor has been adapted as a means of dealing with difficulties and hardships, contributing to the resilience and coping potentials that have enabled humans to survive and thrive.

A BRIEF HISTORY OF HUMOR

Today the word *humor* is an umbrella term with a generally positive, socially desirable connotation, which refers to anything people say or do that is perceived to be funny and evokes mirth and laughter in others. Interestingly, this broad meaning of humor has developed only quite recently. Indeed, the word has a very interesting and complex history, starting out with an entirely different meaning and gradually accumulating new connotations over the centuries. Cultural historian Daniel Wickberg (1998) has provided a detailed and fascinating analysis of the history of this concept, from which I have drawn much of what follows (see also Ruch, 1998a).

Etymology of Humor

Humor began as a Latin word (*humorem*) meaning fluid or liquid. It still retains this meaning in physiology in reference to bodily fluids, such as the aqueous and vitreous humors of the eye. The Greek physician Hippocrates (fourth century B.C.), who is considered to be the father of medicine, believed that good health depends on the proper balance of four fluids, or "humors," of the body, namely blood, phlegm, black bile, and yellow bile. Later, the Greek physician Galen (second century A.D.), who lived in Rome, introduced the idea that these four fluids possessed particular psychological qualities, so that an excess of any one of them in an individual created a certain kind of temperament or character. A predominance of blood caused one to have a sanguine or cheerful temperament, too much black bile produced a melancholic or depressive personality, and so on.

Besides being seen as the basis of relatively enduring character traits, fluctuations in these body fluids began also to be viewed as the cause of more temporary mood states. These meanings of humor as an enduring character trait or a temporary mood are still present today when we speak of someone being a "good-humored person" or "in a bad humor." Thus, having originally referred to a physical substance, humor gradually developed psychological connotations relating to both enduring temperament and temporary mood. Until the sixteenth century, however, it still did not have any connotation of funniness or association with laughter.

In the English language, the word *humor* (which had been borrowed from the French *humeur*) continued to evolve. In the sixteenth century, the idea of humor as an unbalanced temperament or personality trait led to its use to refer to any behavior that deviates from social norms. Thus, a "humor" came to mean an odd, eccentric, or peculiar person (cf. Ben Jonson's *Every Man Out of His Humour*, 1598, cited by Wickberg, 1998). Because such people were often viewed as ridiculous, or objects of laughter and ridicule, it was a small step from there to the association of humor with funniness and laughter, and its entry into the field of comedy (Ruch, 1998a).

Eventually, the odd or peculiar person who was the object of laughter became known as a "humorist," whereas a "man of humor" was someone who took pleasure in imitating the peculiarities of a humorist (e.g., Corbyn Morris in *An Essay Toward Fixing the True Standard of Wit, Humour, Raillery, Satire, and Ridicule*, 1744, cited by Wickberg, 1998). Thus, humor came to be seen as a talent involving the ability to make others laugh. It was not until the mid- to late nineteenth century, however, that the term *humorist* took on the modern meaning of someone who creates a product called "humor" in order to amuse others (Wickberg, 1998). Mark Twain is viewed by many scholars as one of the first humorists in this modern sense.

Changing Views of Laughter

At the same time that the meaning of the word *humor* was evolving in the English language, popular conceptions of laughter and the laughable were also changing (Wickberg, 1998). Prior to the eighteenth century, laughter was viewed by most authors almost entirely in negative terms. No distinction was made between "laughing with" and "laughing at," since all laughter was thought to arise from making fun of someone. Most references to laughter in the Bible, for example, are linked with scorn, derision, mockery, or contempt (Koestler, 1964). The philosophical conception of laughter as essentially a form of aggression can be traced to Aristotle, who believed that it was always a response to ugliness or deformity in another person, although he thought it would not occur if the object of laughter aroused other strong emotions such as pity or anger. Following in the long tradition of Aristotle, the seventeenth-century English philosopher Thomas Hobbes saw laughter as being based on a feeling of superiority, or "sudden glory," resulting from some perception of inferiority in another person.

During the eighteenth century, the word *ridicule* (from Latin *ridiculum* = joke and *ridiculus* = laughable) was used in much the same way that we use the word *humor* today, that is, as a generic term for anything that causes laughter and mirth. However, it had a much more negative and aggressive connotation than humor has today. Whereas laughter was a passive response, ridicule was seen as active and aggressive, a form of attack. Throughout Europe during this time, ridicule became a popular debating technique for outwitting and humiliating one's adversaries by making them laughable to others. It also grew into a socially accepted conversational art form for entertaining others in social gatherings. The person who was adept at generating clever remarks to skewer others and thereby provoke laughter was seen as a particularly desirable dinner guest. Other words that were commonly used during this time along with ridicule were *raillery* and *banter*. While both of these terms referred to aggressive forms of witty repartee used in conversation, banter was seen as a coarser, more impolite, and low-class type of ridicule, whereas raillery was more refined and socially pleasing.

With the growing view of ridicule as a socially acceptable verbal art form and a desirable part of amiable conversation, the idea of laughter as an expression of contempt and scorn gradually gave way to a view of it as a response to cleverness and gamesmanship. The sense of superiority inherent in laughter was now downplayed and seen as secondary, and the intellectual aspects were elevated over the emotional. Laughter was now associated with a game of wits, a way of showing off one's cleverness by creating intellectual surprise in novel relationships between ideas, rather than an expression of contempt, scorn, superiority, and aggression. By the early nineteenth century, Hobbes's superiority theory was being replaced by theories that viewed incongruity as the essence of laughter. This theory was epitomized in the statement by William Hazlitt, an English writer of the early nineteenth century, that "the essence of the laughable is the incongruous" (quoted by Wickberg, 1998, p. 56).

This shift away from an essentially aggressive view of laughter was motivated also by a new sensibility among middle-class British society in the eighteenth century that emphasized the importance of benevolence, kindness, civility, and sympathy in people of refinement. As reflected, for example, in the writings of Adam Smith (e.g., *Theory of Moral Sentiments*, 1759, cited by Wickberg, 1998), a new set of humanitarian values elevated emotional discernment above cold rational logic. In keeping with this general outlook, social reformers began to argue in favor of a more humanitarian form of laughter based on sympathy rather than aggression. This led to the need for a new word to describe this benevolent basis of laughter, and *humor* was co-opted to serve this purpose. In contrast, the word *wit* (from Old English *witan* = to know) began to be used to refer to the more aggressive types of laughter-evoking behaviors that had previously been described by the generic term *ridicule*. Thus, by the early nineteenth century, the umbrella term *ridicule* had been replaced by the two contrasting words *wit* and *humor*.

Wit versus Humor

Both wit and humor were seen as being based on incongruity and were methods of provoking laughter, but they were thought to do so in radically different ways. The distinction between these two concepts was first made in theories of dramatic comedy, where wit was associated with comedy based on intellect, while humor involved comedy based on character (Wickberg, 1998). Over time, wit took on the meaning of the old word *ridicule*, referring to aggressive cleverness and wordplay, whereas humor emphasized sympathy and benevolence, and was seen as a more positive and desirable basis for laughter. Wit was intellectual, sarcastic, and related to antipathy, whereas humor was emotional, congenial, and related to "fellow-feeling."

The two words also had different social class connotations. Wit was associated with the aristocracy and elitism, whereas humor was a more bourgeois, middle-class concept, associated with universality and democracy. Wit was also considered to be more artificial and something that could be acquired through learning and practice, whereas humor was viewed as more natural and an inborn talent in the individual. Thus, it was generally recognized that laughter could be either aggressive or benevolent, and the modern distinction between "laughing at" and "laughing with" was captured by wit and humor, respectively.

Not surprisingly, humor came to be seen as more socially desirable than wit, and was described by many writers in glowing terms. For example, one nineteenth-century author described humor as "the combination of the laughable with an element of love, tenderness, sympathy, warm-heartedness, or affection" (quoted by Wickberg, 1998, p. 65). The association between humor and democratic values (as opposed to the elitism and snobbery of wit) made humor a very popular concept in the egalitarian culture of the United States, particularly after the Civil War. In his writings on the subject, Sigmund Freud, like most of his contemporaries, also made the distinction between humor as benevolent and psychologically healthy and wit as aggressive and of questionable psychological value (Freud, 1960 [1905]).

Over the course of the twentieth century, however, the distinction between wit and humor gradually disappeared, and *humor* came to predominate as the umbrella term for all things laughable. Humor no longer represented just one (benign) way of eliciting laughter, but it now referred to all sources of laughter, including more aggressive forms that would previously have been described as wit. At the same time, though, the positive and socially desirable connotation of humor was retained, and all laughter therefore came to be seen as essentially benevolent and sympathetic. All the positive characteristics that had previously been ascribed to humor, as a subspecies of the laughable that was distinguished from wit, were now seen as applicable to all laughter-eliciting phenomena, including the more aggressive forms once identified with wit. Although laughter itself had once been viewed as essentially aggressive, by the early twentieth century, many theorists began to suggest that it almost always contains an element of sympathy. Even those who still subscribed to the superiority theory began to view the aggressive aspects of laughter as tempered in some way by sympathy or playfulness rather than being truly aggressive and malevolent (cf. Gruner, 1997).

Thus, from the seventeenth to the twentieth century, popular conceptions of laughter underwent a remarkable transformation, shifting from the aggressive antipathy of superiority theory, to the neutrality of incongruity theory, to the view that laughter could sometimes be sympathetic, to the notion that sympathy is a necessary condition for laughter (Wickberg, 1998). These changing views were also reflected in the prevailing social norms. As recently as the 1860s, it was considered impolite to laugh in public in the United States. Even in the early twentieth century, some spheres of social activity (e.g., religion, education, and politics) were considered inappropriate for humor and laughter. Today, of course, humor and laughter are not only considered acceptable, but are actively encouraged in virtually all social settings.

Evolution of the Concept of Sense of Humor

Along with changes in the meaning of humor and attitudes toward laughter, the concept of "sense of humor" has also evolved over the past two centuries (Wickberg, 1998). In the eighteenth and early nineteenth centuries, British philosophers developed the notion of various aesthetic and moral "senses," which were seen as refined sensitivities or abilities to discern or judge the quality of certain things. Thus, they spoke of a sense of beauty, a sense of honor, a sense of decency, moral sense, and common sense. The "sense of the ridiculous" was an early expression to describe sensitivity to laughable things. By the mid-nineteenth century, however, this had been replaced by the "sense of humor."

Although it began as a purely descriptive term, the sense of humor quickly became a highly valued virtue, taking on the positive connotations that were associated with humor (as opposed to wit) during that time. By the 1870s, the sense of humor acquired the very desirable meaning that it has today, referring to a cardinal virtue. To say that someone had a sense of humor was to say something very positive about his or her character. Indeed, a sense of humor came to be one of the most important characteristics a person could have. On the other hand, to say that someone lacked a sense of humor was seen as one of the worst things that could be said about him or her. No one wanted to admit that they did not have a sense of humor.

Over the course of the twentieth century, the concept of sense of humor continued to be very desirable, but also became increasingly vague and undefined. While it always retained some notion of the ability to make others laugh or the enjoyment of amusement and laughter, it took on the added meaning of a more general set of desirable personality characteristics. What it meant to have a sense of humor came to be defined in large part by what it meant *not* to have one. Saying that someone lacked a sense of humor came to mean that he or she was excessively serious, fanatical, or egotistical, an inflexible, temperamental extremist. The lack of a sense of humor was viewed as a defining characteristic of some forms of mental illness (particularly schizophrenia), denoting instability and paranoia (Wickberg, 1998).

By the 1930s, a sense of humor was seen by many psychologists as an essential ingredient of mental health. For example, Gordon Allport (1961) associated a sense of humor with self-awareness, insight, and tolerance, and viewed it as a characteristic of the mature or healthy personality. It is important to note, however, that he distinguished between this mature type of humor, which he saw as quite rare, and the less healthy "sense of the comic," or laughter at absurdities, puns, and the degradation of others, which he saw as much more common. In sum, having a sense of humor became synonymous with being stable and well-adjusted, being able to adapt to stress, being temperate, affable, not prone to anger, and easygoing.

During the twentieth century, the sense of humor also took on sociopolitical connotations and was used for propaganda purposes. In the United States, it came to be seen as a distinctly American virtue, having to do with tolerance and democracy, in contrast to those living in dictatorships, such as the Germans under Nazism or the Russians during the Communist era, who were thought to be devoid of humor. After the tragic events of September 11, 2001, many American commentators expressed the opinion that Al Qaeda terrorists, and perhaps even all Moslems, lacked a sense of humor (despite the fact that videotapes of Osama bin Laden clearly showed him laughing and joking with his comrades).

Whereas too much humor in the nineteenth century was considered a liability in someone wishing to run for office, by the mid-twentieth century a sense of humor became a necessary characteristic in a politician, especially someone aspiring to be president. A popular way for both liberals and conservatives to disparage one another was to claim that they lacked a sense of humor. There has also long been a sexist aspect to the concept, which was viewed as an essentially masculine characteristic. Until quite recently, it was commonly assumed by many writers that women generally lacked a sense of humor (Wickberg, 1998).

The positive qualities associated with the vague concept of sense of humor as a personality trait in turn fed back into popular connotations of humor and laughter more generally. By the end of the twentieth century, humor and laughter were not only seen as essentially benevolent, but as important factors in mental and physical health. This view gained greater prominence following the publication of a book by Norman Cousins (1979), a well-known magazine editor, describing how he supposedly cured himself of a painful and debilitating disease by means of hearty laughter (along with massive doses of vitamin C). This book appeared at a time of growing disenchantment with traditional Western approaches to medicine, and fed into the rising popularity of alternative or complementary medicines.

The idea that humor and laughter are beneficial for one's health, bolstered also by psychoneuroimmunology research suggesting links between emotions and immunity, led to the growth of a popular "humor and health movement" among many health care providers, including nurses, physicians, occupational therapists, social workers, and others. Hospital clowns and comedy rooms became familiar sights in many hospitals, as humor and laughter came to be viewed as a method of speeding recovery in patients suffering from chronic pain, cancer, and other ailments. These developments in health care also contributed to increased interest in applications of humor in other domains including business, education, and psychotherapy. Although this humor movement has always been seen as somewhat on the fringes rather than the mainstream, it has attracted considerable attention to potential benefits of humor and laughter in the popular media as well as professional journals.

A very positive view of humor and laughter continues to predominate in our culture today. Although there is some recognition that humor can occasionally be aggressive or inappropriate, this is perceived as an aberration; "normal" humor is sympathetic and benevolent. Aggression-based theories of humor are generally out of favor with contemporary humor scholars, having been replaced by more benign cognition-based incongruity theories. Thus, over the past century, humor has taken on a broad positive connotation. No longer does it merely involve the perception of incongruity, funniness, mirth, and laughter, but it is also very beneficial, desirable, and health-enhancing (for an interesting analysis of humor in contemporary American society, see Lewis, 2006).

This brief overview of the changes in social attitudes and conceptions of humor and laughter over the past few centuries helps us to put our current assumptions and biases into a broader historical perspective. Although humor and laughter are universal in humans and are likely a product of natural selection, the way people use and express them in a given time and place is strongly influenced by cultural norms, beliefs, attitudes, and values. Most people today view humor as essentially positive, benevolent, and desirable, and it is strongly encouraged in most areas of life. It is easy to assume that these attitudes and behavior patterns are universal and have always been present in all cultures. Not so long ago, however, laughter in our own culture was seen as essentially aggressive, malevolent, and undesirable, and too much laughter was frowned upon. The existence of such divergent views over the course of a relatively brief period of history suggests that there is likely an element of truth to both extremes. It is important to recognize that humor can be used in ways that are aggressive as well as sympathetic, and can involve "laughing at" as well as "laughing with."

If we wish to take a scientific approach to the study of humor, we need to be conscious of the assumptions and biases that we ourselves have absorbed from our culture and that may color our own thinking. As much as possible, we must try to approach the subject in an objective manner, using empirical research methods to evaluate popular beliefs instead of merely assuming them to be true. In our theories and research, we also need to be careful to distinguish between those aspects that are universal in the human species and those that are specific to particular cultures at particular times.

HUMOR AND PSYCHOLOGY

Psychology is often defined as the scientific study of behavior. The concept of behavior in this definition is a very broad one, embracing all kinds of overt actions, speech, and social interactions, as well as less easily observed processes such as thoughts, feelings, attitudes, and the biological mechanisms underlying all of these in the brain and nervous system. With such a diverse subject matter, psychology is a very broad discipline, and is divided into a number of subfields focusing on particular aspects of behavior, including cognitive, social, biologic, developmental, clinical, and so on. As I have already noted, humor touches on all of these areas. Psychologists view themselves as scientists, taking an empirical and predominantly quantitative research approach to test theories and hypotheses about behavior. Psychological research methods include controlled laboratory experiments in which one variable is manipulated to observe its effect on other variables, as well as correlational approaches in which variables are operationally defined and quantified and their association across individuals is assessed.

As Jon Roeckelein (2002) has noted, one of the curiosities of the psychology of humor is that, although it comprises quite a sizable research literature, it has gone largely unnoticed in mainstream psychology up to now. In a search of *PsycINFO*, a database of psychology publications, using the keywords *humor*, *humour*, *laughter*, *irony*, and other closely related terms, I found references to just over 3400 peer-reviewed journal articles published as of early 2006. Despite the extensiveness of this research literature, however, it is rarely mentioned in undergraduate textbooks or psychology reference works. Roeckelein (2002) examined 136 introductory psychology texts published between 1885 and 1996, and found only three—all published before 1930— that made any reference to humor or related topics. Although humor is occasionally mentioned in more advanced undergraduate texts devoted to particular branches of psychology (e.g., social, developmental), the treatment is usually only brief and superficial. Roeckelein also observed that this topic receives only rare and cursory mention in scholarly reference works such as the *Annual Review of Psychology*. The most recent two-volume edition of *The Handbook of Social Psychology* (Gilbert, Fiske, and Lindzey, 1998), a major reference work for social psychologists spanning more than 2000 pages, contains only a single brief mention, although early editions contained a whole chapter on humor, laughter, and play (Berlyne, 1969; Flugel, 1954).

Two main reasons have been suggested for this general neglect of humor in mainstream psychology until now. First, given its essentially nonserious nature and association with fun and mirth, some researchers may have seen it as too frivolous and unimportant a subject for serious academic study. However, as Berlyne (1969) pointed out more than 35 years ago, the apparent frivolity of humor is a good reason why it should receive more, rather than less, research attention than other psychological behaviors whose adaptive functions are easier to understand. The fact that all human societies expend a great deal of time and energy engaging in humor and laughter, while the purpose of this activity is not immediately obvious, makes this a puzzle worthy of careful and systematic study.

Several decades of research effort since Berlyne's time, approaching the subject from a number of psychological perspectives, are beginning to give us some intriguing answers to this puzzle. For example, recent evolutionary models suggest that humor and laughter may have played an important role in the formation and maintenance of social groups in our evolutionary history, and therefore have inter-esting implications for our understanding of human verbal and nonverbal communi-cation and social organization (Gervais and Wilson, 2005; Panksepp, 2000). Thus, the view of humor as too frivolous for serious study is becoming increasingly difficult to defend.

Fortunately, the idea that psychologists should concentrate only on "serious" topics like psychopathology and human deficits seems to be waning in recent years, as demonstrated by such developments as the "positive psychology" movement, with its emphasis on the study of human strengths and positive emotions (Aspinwall and Staudinger, 2003; Seligman and Csikszentmihalyi, 2000). One would hope that psy-chology has moved beyond the situation of 30 years ago when Walter O'Connell (1976) lamented that "anyone embarking upon research into the origins and devel-opment of humor will, more often than not, be seen as a deviant and a freak, one who does not take psychology seriously enough" (p. 316).

A second possible reason for the general neglect of humor, suggested by Dixon (1980), is the sheer elusiveness of the phenomena under investigation. The diversity of stimuli and situations that evoke mirth, the lack of a precise definition of the concept, the multiplicity of theories that have been proposed to account for it, and the difficulties one encounters in trying to capture and study it in controlled experi-ments in the laboratory may have caused researchers to shy away from it as a subject of investigation.

Once again, however, the complexity and elusiveness of the topic is all the more reason for researchers to apply their efforts, skills, and ingenuity to an understanding of it. Furthermore, as I will try to demonstrate in this book, the cumulative efforts of many researchers over the past few decades have brought increasing focus to the field, generating several fairly circumscribed theories with testable hypotheses and devel-oping practical and reliable research methods for investigating them. Thus, although it certainly continues to pose interesting challenges for researchers to tackle, humor no longer seems to be such an intractable topic of study.

In addition to psychology, humor is also a topic of study in a number of other disciplines, including anthropology, biology, computer science, linguistics, literary and cultural studies, neuroscience, philosophy, religious studies, and sociology. There are even scholarly works on the mathematics of humor (Casadonte, 2003; Paulos, 1980). The International Society for Humor Studies (ISHS) is a multidisciplinary organiza-tion of humor scholars that holds annual conferences and publishes a scholarly journal entitled *Humor: International Journal of Humor Research* (for more information, see the ISHS website, available at www.hnu.edu/ishs). At various points in this book, I will touch on some of the contributions of these other disciplines that have augmented the research of psychologists.

In addition, humor is a topic of interest to many professional practitioners in health care (e.g., physicians, nurses, occupational and physical therapists), counseling, social work, education, and business. The Association for Applied and Therapeutic Humor (AATH) is a professional society of individuals from many of these profes-sions who are interested in applications of humor in their respective fields (available at www.aath.org). Besides addressing psychologists, an additional purpose of this book is therefore to introduce interested individuals from these other academic disciplines and professions to the methods, theories, and empirical findings of psychological research on humor.

CONCLUSION

In summary, humor is a universal human activity that most people experience many times over the course of a typical day and in all sorts of social contexts. There is a good deal of evidence suggesting that humor and laughter have an evolutionary origin and therefore confer adaptive benefits. At the same time, there are obviously important cultural influences on the way humor is used and the situations that are considered appropriate for laughter. From a psychological perspective, humor is essentially a positive emotion called mirth, which is typically elicited in social contexts by a cognitive appraisal process involving the perception of playful, nonserious incongruity, and which is expressed by the facial and vocal behavior of laughter. In social interactions, humor takes on many different forms, including canned jokes, spontaneous witticisms, and unintentionally funny utterances and actions.

Psychological functions of humor include the cognitive and social benefits of the positive emotion of mirth, and its uses as a mode of social communication and influence, and as a way of relieving tension, regulating emotions, and coping with stress. Popular conceptions of laughter have changed dramatically over the past two or three centuries, from being viewed as essentially aggressive and somewhat socially inappropriate to being seen as positive, psychologically and physically healthy, and socially desirable. The meaning of the word *humor* has also evolved from a narrow focus on benign and sympathetic sources of mirth distinguished from more aggressive types of wit, to its use as a broad umbrella term to refer to all sources of laughter. Although humor has important psychological functions and touches on all branches of psychology, and there is a sizable and growing research literature on the topic, mainstream psychology has paid relatively little attention to it until now.

In the next two chapters, I will give an overview of early research in the psychology of humor that was conducted prior to the early 1980s. My review of this research will be organized around five major theoretical approaches that have their roots in earlier philosophical conceptualizations of humor and laughter and have been particularly influential in psychological research over the years. This discussion of theories and early research will provide a background for the remaining chapters, which will focus particularly on research conducted during the past two decades.

In Chapters 4 to 8, I will explore relevant theories, research approaches, and empirical findings in the study of humor from the perspective of each of the basic research domains of psychology, with individual chapters devoted to cognitive, social, biological, personality, and developmental psychology. Chapters 9 and 10 will focus on research examining the implications of humor for mental and physical health, corresponding to the fields of clinical and health psychology, respectively. Finally, in

Chapter 11, I will examine theories and research pertaining to potential applications of humor in several applied areas, including psychotherapy and counseling, education, and industrial-organizational psychology. By the end of the book, I hope it will be evident that the study of humor has relevance to every area of the discipline.

It has often been noted that the academic study of humor is not in itself very funny, and that nothing kills a joke like analyzing it. As McComas (1923) observed, "he who approaches laughter upon science bent will find it no laughing matter" (p. 45). Journalists reporting on the annual conferences of ISHS often take delight in pointing out the apparent irony of scholars presenting very weighty and unfunny research papers on the subject of humor. There is no reason, though, why a scholarly work on humor needs to be funny any more than studies of human sexuality should be titillating or depression research should be gloomy. In my experience, humor scholars, while taking their research seriously, tend to be just as funny as anyone else, or perhaps even more so, in their everyday lives.

In keeping with a long-standing tradition of scholarly books on humor, I therefore warn the reader at the outset that you are not likely to find this book particularly funny. However, I do hope you will find it interesting and informative, and that it will pique your curiosity and eagerness to engage in further study of this intriguing topic.

CHAPTER 2

Theories and Early Research I: Psychoanalytic and Superiority Theories

What are the mental processes involved in "getting a joke" or perceiving something to be funny? What are the elements that need to be present (i.e., necessary and sufficient conditions) for humor and laughter to occur? Why is humor so enjoyable, and what motivates us to engage in it? These sorts of questions have perplexed thinkers for centuries, and numerous theories of humor have been proposed by philosophers, psychologists, linguists, and other theorists (for more detailed discussion, see Keith-Spiegel, 1972; Roeckelein, 2002). Greig (1923) listed 88 different theories, although he acknowledged that many of them differed from one another in only minor ways. In this chapter and the next, I will focus on five general theoretical approaches that have been most influential in psychological humor research, namely, psychoanalytic, superiority/disparagement, arousal, incongruity, and reversal theory. The first two will be reviewed in the present chapter, and the remaining three in the next one.

Theories are a way of organizing information and seeking to explain phenomena in a parsimonious way. Theories are not judged so much on the basis of whether they are right or wrong, but on the basis of their usefulness in accounting for phenomena and generating testable hypotheses. Thus, good theories have "heuristic" value in suggesting directions for research. A good theory is one that is clearly defined and well specified. A theory should define the conditions that are both necessary and sufficient for a given phenomenon to occur. A good theory is also potentially falsifiable. In other words, it makes predictions which, if proven untrue, require a rejection, or at least a modification, of the theory.

Unfortunately, most of the general theories of humor that have been proposed do not meet all these stringent criteria. They often use rather vaguely defined concepts, are unable to specify all the necessary and sufficient conditions for humor, and are not falsifiable, since a way can typically be found to account for any discrepant research findings. Nonetheless, different humor theories are useful for suggesting particular avenues for research. In many ways, the different theories are like the six blind men and the elephant, each of whom felt a different part of the animal and came away with a different conclusion about what an elephant is like (Berger, 1995). Thus, each theory accounts for some aspects or types of humor, but fails to give a complete picture. To gain a broad understanding of humor, we need to combine insights from all the different theories.

My review of theoretical issues in these two chapters is also an opportunity to provide an overview of the early psychological humor research that was generated by each theory. In these two chapters I will focus particularly on research conducted prior to the early 1980s, to set the stage for the discussion of more recent investigations in subsequent chapters. As we will see, interest in the various theoretical approaches has shifted over time, with different theories being particularly popular at different times. This changing popularity of various humor theories parallels the rise and fall of broader theoretical approaches, research methodologies, and research topics that have gone in and out of fashion throughout the history of psychology as a whole.

Thus, the psychoanalytic approach to humor predominated in the research of the 1940s and 1950s and had largely disappeared by the 1980s, reflecting the rise and fall of psychoanalytic theory during that time in psychology as a whole. In the 1960s and 1970s, interest among social psychologists in the roles of physiological arousal and cognitive appraisal processes in emotion was reflected in the revival of arousal-based theories of humor. The popularity of research on aggression around the same time also contributed to a renewed interest in superiority theories, which view humor as a form of aggression. With the rise of cognitive approaches to psychology in the 1970s (when computers had become widely accessible and began to be viewed as a model of human information processing), cognitively oriented incongruity theories of humor also began to be popular.

Today, with the cognitive approach dominating all areas of psychology and related disciplines, cognitive theories of humor tend to predominate. However, as we will see throughout this book, many of the themes from each of the traditional theories continue to influence research today. As in other areas of contemporary psychology, in humor research we are seeing a movement away from "grand theories" that attempt to explain all aspects of humor toward smaller "mini-theories" that focus on more circumscribed aspects (e.g., teasing, irony). Researchers today also tend to draw on a variety of theoretical influences to develop their models and hypotheses, rather than remaining committed to a single traditional theoretical approach.

PSYCHOANALYTIC THEORY

Sigmund Freud's psychoanalytic view of humor was by far the most influential theory in psychological humor research during the first half of the twentieth century, a period when Freudian theory was quite prominent in psychology as a whole. Freud's general theory of psychology posited that each of us embodies a seething cauldron of conflicting motives and desires (Freud, 1935). Childish, immature, and largely unconscious sexual and aggressive (libidinal) drives, residing in the id, seek instant gratification and expression on the basis of the pleasure principle. The superego, which incorporates the demands and dictates of society as embodied in the internalized parents, strongly opposes the impulses of the id. The ego, functioning on the reality principle, attempts to find some adaptive compromise among the demands of the id, the superego, and the real world, employing a variety of more or less adaptive defense mechanisms to protect itself from the otherwise overwhelming anxiety that arises from these conflicting forces. Early in his writing career, Freud turned his attention to the role of humor in this psychological drama. Freud's theoretical writings on humor are contained in two publications: the book *Jokes and Their Relation to the Unconscious* (Freud, 1960 [1905]), and a short paper simply entitled "Humour" (Freud, 1928).

Overview of the Theory

From the writer and popular philosopher Herbert Spencer (1860), Freud borrowed the idea that the purpose of laughter is to release excess nervous energy. In this view, when energy that has built up in the nervous system is no longer needed, it must be released in some way, and laughter is one way for this to occur. According to Freud, there are three different types or categories of laughter-related phenomena: (1) wit or jokes, (2) humor, and (3) the comic. Each of these involves a different mechanism by which psychic energy is saved or economized and is consequently dissipated in the form of laughter. *Jokes* (or wit) make use of a number of clever cognitive "jokework" techniques, such as displacement, condensation, unification, and indirect representation, that serve as a kind of distraction to the superego, allowing unconscious aggressive and sexual impulses arising from the id (which would normally be repressed) to be briefly expressed and enjoyed. The inhibitory energy that would normally be required to repress these libidinal impulses becomes briefly redundant as a result of the joke, and it is this energy that is released in the form of laughter. Freud referred to the release of libidinal (sexual or aggressive) drive as the *tendentious* element of jokes, while the cognitive techniques involved in the jokework were called the *nontendentious* elements. Thus, according to Freud, the reason we enjoy jokes so much is that they enable us to experience for a moment the illicit pleasure derived from releasing some of our primitive sexual and aggressive impulses. We do not feel guilty about this, because our superego (conscience) is temporarily distracted by the clever cognitive trick included in the joke, and we are often not even consciously aware of the degree to which the joke contains such aggressive and sexual themes.

These ideas can be illustrated with the following joke (from McGhee, 1979, p. 9):

> One bachelor asked another, "How did you like your stay at the nudist camp?"
> "Well," he answered, "It was okay after a while. The first three days were the hardest."

The jokework here involves the cognitive effort required to detect the double meaning of the last word in the joke, which can refer either to the difficulty of the experience or to the man getting an erection. The initial interpretation of the word implies a negative connotation, but the second one reveals that the experience was actually sexually arousing and enjoyable. According to Freudian theory, this clever play on words diverts our attention from the fact that the joke has allowed us to vicariously enjoy the erotic pleasure of this sexually inexperienced man ("bachelor") who finds himself surrounded by naked women. The psychic energy that our conscience would normally employ to suppress such illicit pleasure becomes momentarily redundant, and it is therefore diverted to fuel the activity of laughter.

As another example, consider the following joke (also taken from McGhee, 1979, p. 9):

> Mr. Brown: "This is disgusting. I just found out that the janitor has made love to every woman in the building except one."
> His wife: "Oh, it must be that stuck-up Mrs. Johnson on the third floor."

Here the jokework involves the mental process of pursuing the inference of the wife's seemingly off-hand comment to its logical conclusion: she herself has had a sexual liaison with the janitor. Although the tendentious element in this joke again appears initially to be a sexual one, a closer examination reveals that the pleasure for the listener actually derives more from aggression than sex. We take aggressive delight in laughing at the cuckolding of the hapless husband, as well as the stupidity of the wife, who reveals her unfaithfulness to her husband in such a naïve manner, and will likely soon suffer the consequences of his jealous anger. Again, the cleverness of the logical processes involved in interpreting the joke enables us to distract our attention from the fact that we are deriving pleasure from other people's pain and stupidity, an activity that would normally cause us to feel somewhat guilty.

In summary, for a joke to be effective, there are two important requirements: it must involve a clever use of jokework, and it must allow for the expression of some repressed sexual or aggressive impulse. Either of these elements alone may be pleasurable, but neither is likely to be viewed as truly funny.

Although Freud believed that most jokes involve this release of sexual or aggressive drives, he tentatively suggested that there may be some non-aggressive and non-sexual ("non-tendentious" or "innocent") jokes in which the enjoyment is derived only from clever cognitive processes (jokework) that enable us momentarily to regress to less logical and rational (i.e., more childish) modes of thinking. However, some authors such as Grotjahn (1966) and Gruner (1978) have pointed out that Freud was unable to provide any examples of such innocent jokes (a fact that Freud himself acknowledged). These theorists argued that this is because no such jokes actually exist: all jokes are tendentious.

Freud's second category of laughter-related phenomena, which was the only one that he referred to as *humor*, occurs in stressful or aversive situations in which persons would normally experience negative emotions such as fear, sadness, or anger, but the perception of amusing or incongruous elements in the situation provides them with an altered perspective on it and enables them to avoid experiencing this negative affect. The pleasure of humor (in this restricted meaning of the word) arises from the release of energy that would have been associated with this painful emotion but has now become redundant. For example, the individual who is able to "see the funny side of things" despite having recently suffered a serious financial loss would be demonstrating this kind of humor. This type of humor is especially seen in the ability to laugh at one's own foibles, weaknesses, and social blunders. Thus, humor referred specifically to the tension-release function of mirth and laughter, and its use in coping with stress, as discussed in the previous chapter.

It is important to note that Freud, like most of his contemporaries, drew a sharp distinction between humor and wit. Humor referred to a benign and sympathetic amusement at the ironical aspects of the misfortunes of life, whereas wit (which he identified primarily with canned jokes) was more aggressive and less clearly psychologically healthy. As we saw in the previous chapter, since Freud's time the word *humor* has evolved into a broad umbrella term that encompasses all types of laughter-evoking phenomena, including aggressive teasing, sexual jokes, and slapstick comedy, as well as irony. This difference in terminology can be very confusing, and it has led many researchers and theorists to confuse Freud's theory of wit or jokes with his theory of humor. I will have more to say about this when I discuss the relation between humor and mental health in Chapter 9.

According to Freud, humor (in this old-fashioned narrow sense) is one of a number of different types of defense mechanisms that enable us to face difficult situations without becoming overwhelmed by unpleasant emotion. Indeed, according to Freud, humor is the "highest of the defense mechanisms," since it enables the individual to avoid unpleasant emotions while still maintaining a realistic view of the situation. To Freud (1928), humor is very beneficial:

> Like wit and the comic, humor has in it a liberating element. But it has also something fine and elevating, which is lacking in the other two ways of deriving pleasure from intellectual activity. Obviously, what is fine about it is the triumph of narcissism, the ego's victorious assertion of its own invulnerability. It refuses to be hurt by the arrows of reality or to be compelled to suffer. It insists that it is impervious to wounds dealt by the outside world, in fact, that these are merely occasions for affording it pleasure.

Whereas jokes and the comic are commonly enjoyed by nearly everyone, Freud (1928, p. 220) described humor as "a rare and precious gift" which is possessed only by a few lucky people. Interestingly, Freud (1928, p. 220) saw humor as the action of the parental superego attempting to comfort and reassure the anxious ego, asserting

"Look here! This is all this seemingly dangerous world amounts to. Child's play—the very thing to jest about!" This is a much more positive view of the superego than the harsh, punitive taskmaster that is typically portrayed in Freudian theory. As we will see in Chapter 9, Freud's conception of humor (in this narrow sense) is closely related to contemporary views of humor as a way of coping with stress and regulating emotions.

Whereas wit and humor are verbal, Freud's third category, the *comic*, refers to nonverbal sources of mirth, such as slapstick comedy, circus clowns, and the pompous person slipping on the banana peel. In such situations, according to Freud, the observer mobilizes a certain amount of mental or ideational energy in anticipation of what is expected to happen. When the expected does not occur, this mental energy becomes redundant and is released in laughter. Freud suggested that the comic involves delighted laughter at childish behavior in oneself or others, which he described as "the regained lost laughter of childhood" (Freud, 1960 [1905], p. 224). Comical situations may also contain some tendentious elements, allowing for the pleasurable release of libidinal energy. The person slipping on the banana peel is a good example. The fact that he is pompous and ostentatious makes the scene all the more amusing because it permits the expression of some aggressive impulses. It would not be nearly as funny if the mishap occurred to a small child or to a person for whom we felt some sympathy. Thus, like wit, the comic often contains at least a tinge of aggression.

Empirical Investigations

A variety of hypotheses were derived from Freudian theory (particularly the theory of jokes or wit), and these were investigated in a large number of early psychological studies. Kline (1977) listed several hypotheses having to do with individual differences. For example, based on Freudian theory, individuals finding aggressive or sexual jokes funniest would be expected to be those whose aggression or sexuality is normally repressed. Psychopaths should not find jokes amusing, since they have no need to lift their repression in this way. Witty people should tend to have powerful unconscious aggressive drives and to be more neurotic than the normal population. Moreover, highly repressed people should prefer jokes with more complex jokework rather than "simple" jokes.

In the 1950s, psychologist Jacob Levine and his colleagues published a number of studies investigating these sorts of hypotheses. Levine and Redlich (1955) presented an anxiety-reduction theory of humor, in which they reconceptualized Freud's ideas about the release of psychic energy in terms of relief from anxiety. They suggested that jokes that are perceived by an individual as being particularly funny touch on anxiety-arousing themes, such as aggression and sexuality, which are normally repressed or suppressed. Thus, a joke initially evokes feelings of anxiety due to its libidinal themes, and these feelings are then suddenly reduced by the punch line. The pleasure of a joke derives from this sudden reduction in anxiety, and the greater this reduction, the greater the pleasure and mirth. If the anxiety produced by the joke is too great, however, the punch line will be inadequate for reducing it, and the response will be one of aversion, disgust, shame, or even horror. On the other hand, if the individual experiences no arousal of anxiety with a particular joke, the response will be one of indifference.

To investigate these hypotheses, Redlich, Levine, and Sohler (1951) developed the Mirth Response Test as a method of assessing the types of humor that individuals prefer and thereby drawing inferences about their basic needs and conflicts. This test consisted of a series of 36 cartoons that were judged to tap a wide range of aggressive and sexual themes. Research participants were presented with each cartoon individually, and their spontaneous verbal and nonverbal responses were noted. Jokes that elicited mirth and enjoyment were assumed to contain themes relating to the individual's underlying needs and conflicts, whereas those that were viewed with indifference presumably contained themes that were irrelevant to the individual. Negative responses to jokes, particularly those associated with a failure to "get" the joke, were seen as indicative of powerful and threatening unresolved needs or conflicts in the individual.

In one typical study, Levine and Abelson (1959) used the Mirth Response Test to compare hospitalized psychiatric patients with schizophrenia, patients with anxiety disorders, and normal controls. The cartoons were first rated by a number of psychiatrists for the degree to which they evoked potentially disturbing themes such as overt aggression and sexuality. Among the psychiatric patients (who presumably had a greater number of unresolved conflicts and repressed impulses), mirth responses to the cartoons were strongly negatively related to these clinician ratings of disturbingness, the least disturbing cartoons being viewed as most humorous and enjoyable. In contrast, the nonpatient controls showed a curvilinear relationship between their mirth responses and the disturbingness of the cartoons, preferring those that were moderately disturbing and disliking those that were either very low or very high on this dimension. These results were taken to be supportive of psychoanalytic theory.

Another early humor test based on Freudian theory was the Wit and Humor Appreciation Test (WHAT) developed by Walter O'Connell (1960). This test was composed of 30 jokes, 10 of which were judged by a panel of clinical psychologists to represent hostile wit, 10 nonsense wit, and 10 humor (in the narrow Freudian sense). Research participants were instructed to rate the degree to which they liked or disliked each joke. In several studies with this test, O'Connell attempted to show that better adjusted, less hostile individuals are more likely to enjoy humor and nonsense wit than hostile wit. However, the findings were only partially supportive of these hypotheses (O'Connell, 1969, 1976).

One theoretical difficulty with this test seems to be that, since Freud identified jokes with wit, which he conceptualized quite differently from humor, it was inconsistent with his theory to attempt to assess humor using jokes. Furthermore, as we will see in later chapters, the degree to which people use humor in healthy versus unhealthy ways in their daily lives has been found to be generally unrelated to their enjoyment of different types of jokes or cartoons. Consequently, joke appreciation tests do not seem to be very useful for assessing these mental health–related dimensions of humor; self-report measures developed for this purpose appear to have greater validity (e.g., R. A. Martin et al., 2003).

A number of early studies examined Freud's hypothesis that the enjoyment of hostile jokes is related to repressed aggressive drives. Contrary to psychoanalytic theory, however, most of this research found that aggressive humor is enjoyed most by individuals who express hostility and aggression openly rather than by those who suppress or repress it. For example, Byrne (1956) presented a series of cartoons depicting hostile or nonhostile themes to male psychiatric patients who had been rated by hospital staff as either overtly hostile, covertly hostile (passive-aggressive), or nonhostile (compliant). Overtly and covertly hostile patients, as compared to nonhostile ones, rated the hostile cartoons as funnier. Thus, individuals who exhibited hostile behavior in their interactions with others were more likely to enjoy cartoons that reflected hostile themes. Byrne argued that these results contradicted Freudian theory and were more consistent with behavioral learning theory. According to learning theory, aggressive behavior is learned through positive reinforcement, and aggressive individuals would therefore be expected to find aggressive humor to be reinforcing and enjoyable. Similar findings were obtained by Ullmann and Lim (1962). Taking a somewhat different approach, Epstein and Smith (1956) also found no correlation between the degree to which subjects repress hostility and their enjoyment of cartoons containing hostile or aggressive themes.

Other investigators examined the Freudian hypothesis that individuals who repress their sexual drives should be more likely to enjoy sexual humor. As with the research on aggressive humor, the results tended to contradict psychoanalytic theory, indicating instead that subjects who are *less* sexually inhibited are more likely to enjoy sexual jokes and cartoons. For example, Ruch and Hehl (1988) found that sexual jokes and cartoons were rated as significantly funnier by both male and female participants who had more positive attitudes toward sexuality, greater sexual experience and enjoyment, higher sexual libido and excitement, and lower prudishness (cf. also Prerost, 1983, 1984). Interestingly, more sexually active individuals were found to enjoy all types of humor, regardless of content, more than did less sexually active individuals. Thus, contrary to Freudian theory, the expression and enjoyment of sexual activities, rather than the repression of sexuality, seems to be associated with enjoyment of humor generally and sexual content humor in particular.

A study by Holmes (1969) bears on the hypothesis that psychopaths will show less enjoyment of humor because they are less prone to inhibit unacceptable impulses. Contrary to psychoanalytic predictions, this study found that men with greater psychopathic tendencies, as shown by higher scores on the psychopathic deviate (PD) scale of the Minnesota Multiphasic Personality Inventory (MMPI), were quicker at understanding cartoons than were less psychopathic men, and enjoyed sexual and hostile cartoons more than nonsense cartoons. Thus, once again, the expression rather than the inhibition of impulses seems to be related to the enjoyment of humor, and particularly humor containing sexual and aggressive themes.

However, Rosenwald (1964) criticized the rationale of these studies, arguing that overt expression of an impulse such as aggression does not necessarily mean that there are no inhibitions against that impulse. He suggested that enjoyment of a joke does not simply reflect unconscious conflicts or anxiety associated with the theme of the joke, but rather the degree to which the individual is able to relax inhibitions or defenses. If a person rigidifies inhibitions in response to a joke, he or she will not find it amusing, but if the person is able momentarily to release inhibitory energies, the joke will be found to be funny. In support of these hypotheses, Rosenwald found that male high school students with flexible inhibitions against aggression—as measured by the Thematic Apperception Test (TAT)—enjoyed hostile humor more than did either those with overly constricted inhibitions or those with impulsivity and a lack of inhibitions. These findings were taken to be supportive of Freudian theory. Overall, though, most of the correlational studies provided little support for the hypothesis that the enjoyment of aggressive and sexual humor is associated with repression of the corresponding drives.

Other researchers took an experimental approach to test various hypotheses derived from psychoanalytic theory. Singer, Gollob, and Levine (1967) hypothesized that, when people's inhibitions regarding the expression of aggression are increased, this will result in a decreased ability to enjoy aggressive humor, but will not affect their enjoyment of nonaggressive humor. To mobilize research participants' aggression-related inhibitions, they had a group of subjects study drawings by Goya depicting extreme brutality and sadism, while control subjects viewed benign Goya works. All participants then rated the funniness of 12 cartoons, four of which were considered to be nonsense cartoons, four portraying mild interpersonal aggression, and four depicting high interpersonal aggression. As predicted, the participants who had viewed the disturbing art (and in whom inhibitions against aggression had presumably been mobilized) rated the highly aggressive cartoons as significantly less funny in comparison to the control subjects, whereas there were no differences between the two groups in their enjoyment of the nonsense and mildly aggressive cartoons. These results appeared to provide support for the Freudian view that increased mobilization of inhibitions concerning aggression will result in decreased enjoyment of aggressive humor.

As we saw, Freud suggested that the jokework involved in successful aggressive jokes distracts the listeners so that they are not fully aware of the aggressive content at which they are laughing. Based on this view, Gollob and Levine (1967) hypothesized that if people focus their attention on the fact that humor expresses aggressive impulses, their inhibitions will be mobilized and they will then be relatively unable to enjoy the humor. They had a group of female subjects make ratings of the funniness of a number of cartoons before and after focusing their attention on the cartoon content by asking them to explain why the cartoons were funny. As predicted, highly aggressive cartoons were given significantly lower ratings on the post-test than were low-aggressive or nonsense cartoons, presumably because the act of explaining the cartoons drew attention to their aggressiveness and thereby circumvented the distracting effects of the clever jokework. These results were viewed as supportive of Freudian theory.

If jokes provide an outlet for sexual and aggressive drives, as suggested by psychoanalytic theory, then they should be particularly enjoyed when drives associated with the relevant themes have previously been activated. Additionally, these jokes should have a cathartic effect, reducing the levels of previously aroused drives. A number of experiments were conducted to test these hypotheses. For example, Dworkin and Efran (1967) aroused feelings of anger (i.e., aggression) in male undergraduate participants by having an experimenter treat them in a very rude and critical manner. The participants were then asked to listen to recordings of either hostile or nonhostile humor or a nonhumorous tape, and to rate these stimuli for funniness. A separate control group of subjects rated the humor without having been angered by the experimenter. Mood adjective checklists were completed before and after the humor rating task.

As predicted, participants who had been angered rated the hostile humor as significantly funnier than did those who had not been angered, whereas no difference was found between the two groups in their ratings of the nonhostile humor. In addition, exposure to both types of humor led to a significant reduction in self-reported feelings of hostility and anxiety in the angered subjects, whereas no change in mood was observed in the angered subjects who listened to the nonhumorous recordings. Thus, activation of angry feelings led to greater appreciation for hostile (but not nonhostile) humor, while both hostile and nonhostile humor led to a reduction in angry feelings. The latter finding was only partially supportive of Freudian theory, since this theory would predict a greater reduction in anger with the hostile than with the nonhostile humor. Subsequent attempts to replicate these findings, however, were mixed. Some studies similarly found increased enjoyment of hostile humor in research participants following exposure to a hostility-arousing situation (e.g., Prerost and Brewer, 1977; Strickland, 1959), but these findings were not replicated in others (e.g., Landy and Mettee, 1969; Singer, 1968).

Other experiments examined the effects of humor on aggressive *behavior* (rather than just reported feelings and humor ratings) following exposure to a hostility-arousing situation. Aggressive behavior was assessed in a variety of ways, including the severity of electric shocks that subjects administered to someone who had previously insulted them (under the guise of research on the effects of electric shocks on learning). Unfortunately, these experiments also yielded inconsistent results. In support of Freudian theory, some showed that previously angered subjects were less likely to behave aggressively toward the insulting person following exposure to hostile as opposed to nonhostile humor (e.g., Baron, 1978a; Leak, 1974). Others, however, found a reduction in aggression following the nonhostile instead of the hostile humor (e.g., Baron and Ball, 1974). Yet other experiments showed the opposite pattern of effects, with an *increase* in aggressive behavior occurring after exposure to hostile humor (e.g., Baron, 1978b; Berkowitz, 1970; Mueller and Donnerstein, 1983). Thus, evidence for cathartic effects of hostile humor on aggressive behavior is inconclusive to say the least.

Other researchers examined the effects of sexual arousal on the enjoyment of sexual humor. For example, Strickland (1959) had male research participants rate the funniness of a number of cartoons containing sexual, hostile, or neutral ("nonsense") themes after they had either been insulted and criticized by the experimenter (hostile group), or shown a series of photographs of nude females (sexual group). A control group of participants rated the cartoons immediately after being brought into the experimental situation. The results indicated that, as predicted, participants who had been in the hostility-arousing situation gave significantly higher funniness ratings for the hostile cartoons than for the sexual or nonsense cartoons, whereas those who had been in the sexually-arousing situation gave significantly higher funniness ratings for the sexual cartoons than for the other two types of cartoons.

However, in a study with a very similar design, Byrne (1961) did not replicate these findings. Instead, he found that hostile cartoons were rated as most funny by participants in all three conditions. In another experiment, Lamb (1968) found that participants exposed to sexually arousing photographs showed greater appreciation for all types of cartoons (hostile and neutral as well as sexual), in comparison with those who were not sexually aroused. Thus, as with the aggression research, studies of the cathartic effects of sexual humor on sexual arousal produced contradictory and inconclusive results.

Whereas the preceding research investigated hypotheses derived from Freudian theory by focusing on participants' *appreciation* or enjoyment of humorous stimuli, a study conducted by Ofra Nevo and Baruch Nevo (1983) looked at humor *production*. Male high school students were presented with a series of drawings depicting one person behaving in a frustrating way toward another, and were asked to generate verbal responses that might be given by the recipient of the frustrating behavior. Half of the participants were instructed to try to make their responses as humorous as possible, while no mention of humor was made in the instructions to the other half. Experimenter ratings of the responses revealed that the humorous responses, compared to the nonhumorous ones, contained significantly more aggression and sexual themes, as predicted by psychoanalytic theory. The relatively high frequency of sexual content was especially striking in view of the fact that the pictures did not contain obvious sexual themes. In addition, the authors noted that many of the jokework techniques described by Freud were observed in the humorous responses, including displacement, play on words, absurdity and fantasy, and representation by the opposite. The authors concluded that the "subjects applied Freud as if they had read him!" (p. 192). Similar findings were also reported in a more recent study by Avner Ziv and Orit Gadish (1990) in which male and female participants were asked to generate either humorous or nonhumorous stories in response to TAT pictures. Once again, the humorous stories, compared to the nonhumorous ones, contained significantly more aggressive and sexual elements.

Evaluation

As this brief review of the early research shows, the large number of studies conducted to test hypotheses derived from the psychoanalytic theory of jokes produced limited and inconsistent supportive evidence. Although there was some evidence that people find aggressive jokes less funny when their attention is drawn to the aggressive nature of the humor, little consistent support was found for the hypotheses that individuals who habitually repress sexual or aggressive drives show greater enjoyment for jokes containing such themes; that arousal of sexual and aggressive drives leads to increased enjoyment of drive-related jokes; or that exposure to aggressive or sexual jokes has a cathartic effect, decreasing drive arousal. On the other hand, some support for Freudian theory was found in research showing increased aggressive and sexual themes in participants' responses when they are instructed to generate humor. Apart from the inconsistency of the research evidence, the "hydraulic model" of psychic energy on which Freudian theory is built, viewing laughter as a way of "burning off" excess tension, is not consistent with our modern understanding of the nervous system. Consequently, the psychoanalytic theory of humor (like Freudian theory in general) has been largely abandoned by empirical researchers since the 1980s, although some further theoretical work has appeared in the psychoanalytic literature (e.g., Sanville, 1999).

It is important to note, however, that most of this early research focused only on Freud's theory of jokes (or wit) and not his theory of humor (in the old-fashioned sense). Part of the reason for this was methodological, since almost all the research made use of jokes and cartoons (which are also essentially a type of joke) as stimuli. Since Freud's theory of humor does not apply to jokes, these sorts of stimuli could not be used to test hypotheses about humor. As we will see in Chapter 9, more recent research evidence for the role of humor in mental health and coping with stress, although generally not explicitly inspired by Freudian theory, may be viewed as support for some of Freud's ideas about humor (narrowly defined) as an adaptive defense mechanism.

It is also worth noting that the concept of defense mechanisms is one psychoanalytic idea that continues to be widely accepted by contemporary psychologists who might not consider themselves to be psychoanalytically oriented. The idea of humor as a mature or healthy defense mechanism (but without the outdated Freudian notions of energy release through laughter) continues to have credibility (Vaillant, 2000). Indeed, the current version of the Diagnostic and Statistical Manual (DSM-IV; American Psychiatric Association, 1994), which is used by psychiatrists and clinical psychologists to diagnose psychological disorders, contains a section on defense mechanisms that includes humor as an adaptive or mature defense.

A limitation of Freud's theory is that it does not consider the interpersonal context and social functions of humor, focusing instead on dynamics taking place within the individual. Thus, jokes were seen by Freud as serving a primarily intrapsychic function, enabling the individual to express and enjoy libidinal drives that are normally repressed by one's own conscience. As we will see in later chapters, humor scholars have recently begun to focus more on the social aspects of humor, noting that jokes and other types of humor are essentially a form of communication between people. Sociologist Michael Mulkay (1988) suggested that the function of jokes may have more to do with the social expression of topics that are considered taboo by the culture than with the intrapsychic release of drives. He noted that topics like sex and aggression have great personal relevance to most people, but are considered inappropriate for discussion in normal discourse. Humor enables people to communicate sexual information, attitudes, and emotions in a form that is more socially acceptable because it implies that the speaker is "only joking" and is therefore not to be taken seriously. Because the meaning of a humorous communication is inherently ambiguous, people can get away with saying things in a humorous way that they could not express using a more serious mode of communication.

Similarly, Eliot Oring (1994) suggested that, in addition to sex and aggression, humor is often used to communicate a variety of topics with which the culture has some discomfort. For example, he suggested that contemporary American culture is uncomfortable with the expression of sentimental feelings like affection, tenderness, admiration, and sympathy, and humor is therefore often used to convey these sorts of feelings in an indirect way. Examples of this use of humor include "roasts," in which friends and coworkers humorously belittle the personality, behaviors, and achievements of an honored guest, and humorous greeting cards, in which insulting messages are used to indirectly express feelings of affection (e.g., "I wish I had a nickel for every time I've thought of you . . . I'd buy some gum"). Although the overt message appears to be negative, the humorous manner in which it is delivered makes it apparent that the opposite, more affectionate meaning is actually the intended one. Thus, by focusing on the inherently interpersonal nature of humor, some contemporary theorists and researchers have reconceptualized Freud's original ideas about intrapsychic functions of humor and applied them to an understanding of its social functions.

Although psychoanalytic theory may not provide a completely satisfactory account of humor (in the broad, modern sense), it did draw attention to certain aspects that need to be explained in any comprehensive theory. In particular, we note the predominance of aggressive and sexual themes in most (if not all) jokes, the feelings of emotional pleasure and enjoyment (i.e., mirth) that are engendered by humor, and the strong motivation to engage in it. As we will see in later chapters, these aspects of humor continue to be of great interest to theorists and researchers today.

SUPERIORITY/DISPARAGEMENT THEORIES

As we have seen, Freud viewed aggression as an important aspect of jokes, which he identified with the old concept of wit. Indeed, there is abundant evidence that much humor (broadly defined) is based on aggression and hostility. The aggressive basis of laughter is evident in ancient writings. Koestler (1964) noted that, of 29 references to laughter in the Old Testament, most are linked with scorn, derision, mockery, or contempt, and only two are "born out of a joyful and merry heart" (p. 53). The aggression in humor can be blatant or subtle. Herbert Lefcourt (2001) gives some examples of the more extremely sadistic or heartless forms of humor. For example, Nazi soldiers during World War II, particularly the Gestapo, were known to laugh mirthfully at the panicky behavior of Jews attempting to flee from them. Anthropologist Colin Turnbull (1972) described how members of a nomadic mountain tribe in Africa, during a time of starvation and misery, would laugh uproariously at the suffering of individuals that would normally be expected to arouse sympathy. In one instance, a group of people laughed loudly at the spectacle of an elderly blind woman writhing weakly at the bottom of a canyon after losing her footing on a steep trail and falling over a cliff.

The aggressive side of humor is also evident in the merciless teasing that children often inflict on one another. I remember well a regrettable incident from my own childhood when an overweight girl in the fourth grade fell to the floor after her chair broke. The ensuing raucous laughter and teasing from the rest of the class continued for several days afterwards. As every child knows, being laughed at can be extremely painful and humiliating. At a milder level, a great many of the jokes that are so popular in our culture quite obviously involve the disparagement of others, including members of either sex (but most often women), various national or ethnic groups, or people of low intelligence. Sociologist Christie Davies (1990a) described how people of every country and region make jokes about members of a particular nationality or subculture who are considered to be similar yet different enough from the cultural mainstream to be objects of ridicule.

Overview of the Theories

As we saw in Chapter 1, a long-standing theoretical approach views aggression of some sort as the essential characteristic of all humor. In this view, humor is actually a form of aggression. Theories of this kind have been referred to as superiority, disparagement, aggression, or degradation theories. This is the oldest approach to humor, dating at least as far back as the philosophers Plato and Aristotle. Plato (428–348 B.C.) stated that laughter originates in malice. According to him, we laugh at what is ridiculous in other people, feeling delight instead of pain when we see even our friends in misfortune (Plato in *Philebus*, reprinted in Morreall, 1987). Similarly, Aristotle (348–322 B.C.) saw comedy as an imitation of people who are worse than the average and viewed it as a "species of the ugly" (in *Poetics*, reprinted in Morreall, 1987, p. 14). According to Aristotle, "people who carry humor to excess are considered vulgar buffoons. They try to be funny at all costs, and their aim is more to raise a laugh than to speak with propriety and to avoid giving pain to the butt of their jokes" (in *Nicomachean Ethics*, reprinted in Morreall, 1987, p. 15). He evidently did not care much for it.

The writings of the seventeenth-century British philosopher Thomas Hobbes (1588–1679) further reinforced the general acceptance of the superiority view for several centuries. According to Hobbes, "the passion of laughter is nothing else but sudden glory arising from some sudden conception of some eminency in ourselves, by comparison with the infirmity of others, or with our own formerly . . . It is no wonder therefore that men take heinously to be laughed at or derided, that is, triumphed over." (in *Human Nature*, reprinted in Morreall, 1987, p. 20). Thus, humor is thought to result from a sense of superiority derived from the disparagement of another person or of one's own past blunders or foolishness. Elements of the superiority view continue to be seen in some theories of humor proposed over the past century (e.g., Bergson, 1911; Leacock, 1935; Ludovici, 1933; Rapp, 1951).

The most outspoken contemporary advocate of this approach is Charles Gruner, a professor of speech communication at the University of Georgia (Gruner, 1978, 1997). Gruner views humor as "playful aggression." It is not "real" aggression, in the sense that it does not involve physically attacking and injuring people; rather, it is more like the play fighting of children and young animals. Thus, Gruner emphasizes the idea that humor is a form of play. In particular, the type of play he has in mind is a game, competition, or contest, where there are winners and losers. Gruner suggests that the enjoyment of humor is akin to the jubilant, triumphant feelings one has after suddenly winning a very close game after a long and difficult struggle. "Successful humor," stated Gruner, "like enjoying success in sports and games (including the games of life), must include *winning* ("getting what we want"), and *sudden* perception of that winning" (Gruner, 1997, p. 9, emphasis in original).

Gruner based his theory on an evolutionary view in which the propensity for competitiveness and aggressiveness is the main characteristic that enabled humans to survive and flourish. Following Rapp's (1951) phylogenetic (i.e., evolutionary) theory, Gruner (1978) suggested that laughter originated in the "roar of triumph" following a hard-fought battle (typically occurring between males). During the course of a physical struggle with another person, much emotional and physical energy is built up, as adrenaline is pumped into the bloodstream. When the fight ends suddenly, the winner must dispel this excess tension, and he does so through laughter: he "bares his teeth, pumps his shoulders, and chops up his breath into grunts and moans, with appropriate grimaces" (p. 43). Thus, laughter serves the physiological function of rapidly restoring homeostasis, as well as the psychological function of signaling victory over the enemy. (The loser, meanwhile, expels his excess energy by weeping.)

According to Gruner, "the many generations of men who responded to their sudden victories in violent encounters with roars of triumph, over hundreds of thousands of years, wore a groove, a riverbed, into the collective human unconscious" (p. 52), and this continues to be the basis of laughter to the present day. This early precursor of laughter evolved into our modern-day humor. With the evolution of language in the context of communal living, people were able to begin poking fun at others with words, rather than relying only on physical aggression. Soon people could use language to ridicule anyone who appeared inferior, such as those with a physical or mental defect. Today, this form of humor is evident in slapstick comedy and practical jokes, laughter at others' clumsiness and verbal mistakes, laughter at "dumb blond" jokes, and any jokes that make fun of individuals from other ethnic groups.

Those who disagree with this aggression theory of humor might point to simple riddles and puns as forms of humor to which it does not seem to apply. These kinds of humor merely involve a play on words and seem to be completely devoid of aggression and hostility. However, according to Gruner, riddles and puns have their origins in ancient "duels of wits" in which people attempted to display their intellectual superiority over others by means of their facility with words. Still today, creating puns is a way of "beating" others in conversation. This is why people respond to puns with groans, which are seen as an admission of defeat. The person who constantly interrupts the flow of conversation with puns is often perceived by others as disruptive, frustrating, and distracting, and puns are seen as a way of controlling social interactions. The competitive nature of punning is particularly evident in "punning duels," in which two people attempt to outdo one another with exchanges of witty wordplay. Gruner (1997, p. 136) gave the following example:

> Bob: The cops arrested a streaker yesterday.
> Rob: Could they pin anything on him?
> Bob: Naw. The guy claimed he was hauled in on a bum wrap.
> Rob: You'd think the case was supported by the bare facts.
> Bob: We can probably hear more about the case tonight on the TV nudecast.
> Rob: Tomorrow's nudespaper might have more details.

Puns in everyday conversation may be a way of "defeating" the listener, but canned jokes in which the punch line is based on a pun are seen as a way of enabling the listener to share feelings of mastery and superiority along with the joke-teller. The ability to "get the joke" gives the listener a feeling of superiority and victory, presumably over hypothetical others who might not be able to understand it, perhaps due to their lower intelligence. Thus, according to Gruner, all jokes, no matter how seemingly innocent, contain a contest, a winner, and a loser.

Gruner (1997) analyzed a large number of examples of different types of jokes, demonstrating how each of them may be viewed as an expression of playful aggression. "To understand a piece of humorous material," stated Gruner (1978, p. 14), "it is necessary only to find out who is ridiculed, how, and why." Thus, he finds aggression in jokes about death, destruction, or disaster; "sick" jokes (such as "dead baby" jokes and those that followed the *Challenger* space shuttle disaster); slapstick comedy and children's television cartoons; practical jokes; ethnic and sexist jokes; and so on. Whereas Freud saw sexuality as a possible joke mechanism that can operate without any aggression, Gruner argued forcefully that all sexual, sexist, and scatological ("toilet") humor is based on aggression. According to Gruner (1997, p. 109), "'dirty' jokes differ from 'clean' jokes only in subject matter and language, not in form or technique; both 'types' of jokes follow the formula of a contest, resulting in both a winner and a loser." Gruner claimed that he has never encountered a joke or other laughter-provoking event that cannot be explained by application of his theory, and at the end of his 1997 book he challenged the reader to try to find one.

What about all the "innocent" or "nonsense" jokes and cartoons that were used in much of the psychoanalytically inspired research, reviewed earlier, comparing the effects of hostile versus nonhostile humor? Although he acknowledged that the aggression in humor can sometimes be quite muted and subtle, Gruner (1997) argued forcefully that even the most seemingly innocuous jokes contain some element of aggression. Here his analyses sometimes seem a little forced. For example, he discussed a published cartoon in which "two tipplers coming home from a wild night on the town are gaily staggering up and down walls, as well as back and forth across the sidewalk and street" (p. 162). Although this cartoon seems to be playing in a purely innocent way with incongruity and absurdity, Gruner interpreted it as ridiculing drunkenness: drunks are so oblivious to reality that they don't realize that defying gravity is impossible and don't stop to think about the dangers involved. In another example, a cartoon shows a plumber plugging the hole in a water pipe with his finger, as water pours out his ear. Again, this seems to be merely an innocent and whimsical exercise in absurdity, but Gruner suggested that the cartoon causes the viewer to laugh at the damage being done to the plumber's brain cells by the water going through his head. Although many of Gruner's analyses seem quite convincing about the aggressive basis of humor, some examples such as these seem rather contrived.

What about self-deprecatory humor? How can laughing at oneself be explained in terms of superiority theory? Like Hobbes, Gruner responds that we can laugh at our own past stupidities and failings, feeling superiority over the person we once were in the past. Furthermore, even in the present, one part of ourselves can laugh at another part. For example, when I am feeling lazy, I can laugh at the part of me that is overly ambitious, and when I am in an ambitious mood I can laugh at my lazy self. We all have multiple roles, mood states, and conflicting personality characteristics, and a sense of humor is what keeps these many varied aspects of ourselves in balance. People with no sense of humor are people who are rigid and unidimensional, unable to see anything funny about themselves or their beliefs. Thus, the disparagement at the root of humor can be directed at oneself in a healthy manner.

Implications of Superiority/Disparagement Theories

As we saw in Chapter 1, the extremely positive view of humor held by most people today has made the superiority theory very unpopular because of the negative way it seems to portray humor. Although they might acknowledge that some humor is occasionally aggressive, hostile, and even cruel, most people today wish to believe that most humor (perhaps particularly their own!) is free of aggression, nonhostile, sympathetic, friendly, and healthy. Psychotherapists, educators, and business consultants who promote humor for its presumed beneficial qualities (which I will discuss in Chapter 11) often draw a distinction between "laughing at" and "laughing with." They may espouse "political correctness" views, regarding ethnic, racist, and sexist humor, like smoking in restaurants, as offensive and inappropriate in polite society. Instead, they seek to promote the use of more affirming and caring types of humor. However, Gruner argues that such people are simply deluding themselves, denying the reality of the true source of pleasure underlying their enjoyment of humor. If we try to eliminate aggression from humor, according to Gruner, we will eliminate humor altogether.

At the same time, Gruner denies that this view of humor actually paints a negative picture of human nature. He emphasizes that the aggression involved in humor is just play, a game that should not be taken seriously and is not intended to inflict actual harm. Individuals who tell ethnic jokes do not necessarily believe the stereotypes conveyed in their jokes. Gruner (1997) stated that "a stereotype is merely a very handy kind of shorthand to provide the essential framework for understanding the content of a joke" (p. 99). Of course, some people who are truly hostile, racist, sexist, or anti-Semitic might use such jokes as a way of expressing their hostility. But such people will likely express their attitudes in more direct and openly hostile ways as well. This does not mean that all people who enjoy such jokes are racist or sexist. A similar view is expressed by sociologist Christie Davies, who has argued, for example, that jokes making fun of "Jewish American princesses" (JAPs) are not really based on anti-Semitism, but are actually affirming of the qualities of Jewish culture (C. Davies, 1990b). Although Davies rejected the superiority/aggression theory of humor because it seems to confuse the playful aggression of humor with "real-world" aggression (C. Davies, 1990a, p. 326), Gruner argued that these objections reveal a misunderstanding of his theory.

The more positive perspective on superiority/disparagement theories espoused by Gruner (as opposed to the negative views held by more traditional superiority theorists) has also allowed some authors to emphasize the value of humor for self-esteem, feelings of competence, and personal well-being generally. Rather than focusing on the hostile, sarcastic, and derisive aspects of humor, these views emphasize the positive feelings of well-being and efficacy, and the sense of liberation and freedom from threat experienced when one is able to poke fun at other people or situations that would normally be viewed as threatening or constrictive. As Holland (1982, p. 45) pointed out, "we can state the disproportion the other way around, calling the purpose of laughter not so much a glorifying of the self as a minimizing of the distresses menacing the self." Similarly, Kallen (1968, p. 59) wrote, "I laugh at that which has endangered or degraded or has fought to suppress, enslave, or destroy what I cherish and has failed. My laughter signalizes its failure and my own liberation."

Similar views have been expressed by authors taking an existential approach to humor, who emphasize that it provides one with a sense of liberation or freedom from the constraints of life. For example, Knox (1951, p. 543) defined humor as "playful chaos in a serious world," and stated that "humor is a species of liberation, and it is the liberation that comes to us as we experience the singular delight of beholding chaos that is playful and make-believe in a world that is serious and coercive" (p. 541). Similarly, Mindess (1971) noted that our social roles require us to suppress and deny many of our impulses and desires and to conform to our surroundings and the expectations placed on us by others. Although these constraints and routines are necessary for survival in our group-based existence, they also lead to feelings of self-alienation and loss of spontaneity and authenticity. Humor, according to Mindess, is a means of coping with this paradox, enabling one to gain a sense of freedom, mastery, and self-respect while continuing to live within the social constraints of human life. In humor we can temporarily break all the rules, playing with reality in a way that denies the normal physical and social constraints and ignores the usual consequences of behavior (see also Svebak, 1974b, for a similar view).

This coping aspect of aggressive humor is also evident in the "gallows humor" described by Obrdlik (1942) as a form of joking used by people in oppressive regimes, such as Nazi-occupied nations during World War II. The term *gallows humor* comes from Freud's (1960 [1905]) description of condemned prisoners making lighthearted jokes on their way to the gallows (e.g., the prisoner who, when offered a last cigarette before his execution, says, "No thanks, I'm trying to quit"). It has come to be used to refer to aggressive forms of humor with a grotesque or macabre character ("black humor") used as a means of maintaining one's sanity in seemingly hopeless or extremely harrowing situations. By poking fun at the ineptness and stupidity of oppressors, gallows humor can be a subversive activity that allows one to gain a sense of freedom from their power, a refusal to be completely subjugated by them, despite their apparent domination. Such forms of humor were also very popular in the former Soviet Union and Eastern European countries during the Communist era (Raskin, 1985).

Along with Freud's concept of humor (in the narrow sense) as a defense mechanism, the superiority approach provides a basis for contemporary views of humor as a way of coping with stress in daily life (which I will discuss in Chapter 9). As a defense mechanism (à la Freud), humor enables us to protect ourselves from painful emotions associated with adverse circumstances. As a way of asserting our superiority (à la Gruner), humor is a way of refusing to be overcome by the people and situations, large and small, which threaten our well-being. It must be recognized, though, that while such aggressive uses of humor in coping may make us feel better, when directed at spouses, close friends, and family members, they can have a negative effect on the relationship.

Humor also enables us to avoid becoming too emotionally involved in the distress and problems of others. McDougall (1903, 1922) viewed humor as a sort of "emotional anesthesia," that enables us to avoid feeling too much sympathy for others, which might otherwise overwhelm us. He believed that humor and laughter evolved in humans as an antidote to sympathy, a protective reaction that shields us from the depressive influence of other people. Thus, when we make a joke about our own problems or those of another person, we are separating ourselves, at least momentarily, from the emotional pain involved.

Empirical Investigations

As we saw in the earlier section on psychoanalytic theory, a great deal of research has been devoted to the study of aggression and hostility in humor. Although much of this research was inspired by Freudian theory, it can also be viewed as relevant to superiority/disparagement theories, since both approaches share the idea of aggression as a motive in humor. The theory that all humor is based on aggression leads to the prediction that there will be a positive correlation between the amount of hostility present in a joke and its perceived funniness. Gruner (1997) stated that "usually, everything else being equal, the more hostile the humor, the funnier" (p. 110). Some research has provided support for this hypothesis. McCauley and associates (1983) conducted a series of six studies in which they had separate groups of participants rate the aggressiveness and the funniness of different sets of cartoons taken from magazines. In each of these studies, significant positive correlations were found between the median humor and aggressiveness ratings across the sets of cartoons ($r = .49$ to .90), indicating that the more aggressive a cartoon, the funnier it was perceived to be.

These results were found with children and adults, individuals of high and low socioeconomic status, and native- and foreign-born participants. Singer, Gollob, and Levine (1967) and Epstein and Smith (1956) also found evidence that hostile cartoons are enjoyed more than nonhostile cartoons.

However, some other research suggests that a moderate amount of hostility or aggression in humor is funnier than either too little or too much. Zillmann and Bryant (1974) found that humorous "squelches" given in response to an aggressor were perceived as most funny when they involved a moderate and equitable amount of retaliation rather than an over- or under-retaliation. Similarly, Zillmann, Bryant, and Cantor (1974) found that, when research participants were shown political cartoons in which mild, moderate, or extreme levels of disparagement were depicted against presidential candidates, the cartoons showing mild attacks on a rejected candidate were rated as most funny. Bryant (1977) also found that a moderate amount of hostility expressed in put-down humor was rated funnier than either mild or intense hostility, even when the equitableness of the "squelch" was controlled. Although they suggest a curvilinear (inverted-U) rather than a linear relationship between hostility and funniness, these findings could perhaps still be taken as supportive of Gruner's theory of humor as "playful aggression," since more extreme forms of aggression might no longer be perceived as playful and would therefore no longer be expected to be funny.

There is also some evidence that the funniness of disparagement humor arises more from the perceived pain experienced by the victim than from the hostility displayed by the protagonist. In three separate studies, Deckers and Carr (1986) obtained ratings of funniness, the amount of hostility/aggression displayed by the protagonist, and the amount of pain experienced by the victim in a wide variety of cartoons. Although the hostility and pain ratings were highly correlated, funniness ratings were significantly correlated with pain ratings but not with hostility ratings. Funniness ratings increased as pain ratings increased up to a point, and then leveled off as pain increased further. Thus, moderate pain experienced by the victim or target of a joke is perceived as funnier than no pain, but extreme pain is no more (or less) funny than moderate pain. Thus, consistent with superiority/disparagement theory, the enjoyment of humor seems to arise from seeing someone suffer (in an unreal, playful context). A similar correlation between funniness and pain ratings was found by Wicker et al. (1981).

Although this research seems to support the aggression view of humor, Willibald Ruch has questioned this theory on the basis of his extensive investigations involving factor analyses of jokes and cartoons (e.g., Ruch and Hehl, 1998). In a series of studies (which will be described in more detail in Chapter 7), Ruch and his colleagues factor analyzed subjects' positive and negative responses to a wide range of humor stimuli with participants from different age groups, socioeconomic backgrounds, and nationalities. These researchers consistently found three stable factors, two of which related to structural aspects of the humor (labeled incongruity-resolution and nonsense) and only one content factor (sexual themes). Although they included a number of jokes and cartoons containing hostile and aggressive themes in their studies, these did not form a separate factor, but instead loaded on one or the other of the two structural factors, suggesting that hostility is not a very salient dimension in people's responses to humor. In defense of his theory, Gruner might perhaps argue that, since all humor is by definition based on aggression, it is not surprising that there is not a separate factor for aggression. However, these factor analytic findings do raise questions about the importance of aggression and hostility in humor. Incidentally, these findings also cast some doubt on the validity of the numerous past studies (discussed earlier) that have investigated participants' responses to jokes and cartoons that were categorized by the researchers themselves into hostile and nonhostile types.

Another prediction of superiority/disparagement theory would seem to be that people with more hostile and aggressive personality traits will enjoy all kinds of humor (not just hostile humor) more than do less aggressive people. However, several studies have found no significant correlations between a variety of trait measures of aggressiveness and appreciation for various types of humor (Ruch and Hehl, 1998). Other studies, as we have already seen, have found that aggressive people are more likely to enjoy more hostile forms of humor (Donn Byrne, 1956; Ullmann and Lim, 1962). Thus, while aggressiveness as a personality trait may be related to enjoyment of aggressive forms of humor, it does not appear to be related to enjoyment of humor in general, contrary to the predictions of superiority theory.

In addition to these studies that bear on the relationship between funniness and aggressiveness in humor, a considerable amount of social psychological research has been conducted on disparagement or "put-down" humor, as a particular category of humor. Indeed, superiority/disparagement theories enjoyed a period of considerable popularity among social psychologists during the 1960s and 1970s. This was particularly evident in the research programs of Dolf Zillmann and his colleagues at Indiana University (Zillmann and Cantor, 1976) and Lawrence La Fave and his colleagues at the University of Windsor, Canada (La Fave, 1972). Much of this research focused on the way the funniness of disparagement humor is determined by the social relationships among the protagonists, the victims, and the audience. In general, these researchers hypothesized that people will find humor in the misfortunes of those toward whom they have some antipathy. In one of the earliest experiments on humor, Wolff et al. (1934) presented a series of anti-Jewish jokes to both Jewish and non-Jewish participants. Not surprisingly, they found that the Jewish participants, as compared to the non-Jews, displayed less appreciation for these jokes. In addition, men showed more appreciation for jokes ridiculing women than women did, while women exceeded men in their appreciation of jokes ridiculing men.

However, mere membership in a particular racial or religious group may not be sufficient for predicting a person's response to jokes about that group. Middleton (1959) found that, although Black participants exceeded Whites in their appreciation of jokes disparaging Whites, Blacks and Whites did not differ in their appreciation of anti-Black jokes. He speculated that this was due to the fact that the Blacks in his sample, who were predominantly middle-class, may not have identified themselves with the stereotyped lower-class Blacks portrayed in the jokes. Similarly, Cantor (1976) found that both female and male college students showed greater appreciation for disparagement humor in which a male had the last laugh at a female's expense, as compared to jokes in which a female disparaged a male. Furthermore, subjects of both sexes preferred disparaging jokes in which women (rather than men) were the victims of both men and women. These findings suggest a possible identification of women with male aggressors in this era before women's liberation had made an impact on the culture.

In view of these sorts of findings, Zillmann and Cantor (1976) emphasized the importance of assessing individuals' attitudes toward a target group, rather than relying merely on their group membership. They proposed a "dispositional model of humor," in which they posited that individuals' disposition toward other people or objects varies along a continuum from extreme positive affect through indifference to extreme negative affect. They hypothesized that "humor appreciation varies inversely with the favorableness of the disposition toward the agent or entity being disparaged, and varies directly with the favorableness of the disposition toward the agent or entity disparaging it" (p. 100). According to these authors, an individual's disposition toward the target of a joke is not necessarily a permanent trait, but may be a temporary attitude evoked by the situation, including features of the joke itself. Importantly, though, they emphasized that humor always involves disparagement in some form: "something malicious and potentially harmful must happen, or at least, the inferiority of someone or something must be implied, before a humor response can occur" (p. 101).

Zillmann and Cantor (1972) found evidence in support of this theory in a study in which a group of college students and a group of middle-aged business and professional people were presented jokes involving people in superior-subordinate relationships (father-son, employer-employee, etc.). As predicted, students gave higher ratings of funniness to the jokes in which the subordinate disparaged the superior than to those in which the superior disparaged the subordinate, whereas the ratings of professionals revealed the opposite pattern (see also Zillmann and Bryant, 1980).

Similar research by Lawrence La Fave and his colleagues (reviewed by La Fave, Haddad, and Maesen, 1976) employed the concept of the "identification class," which is either a positive or negative attitude-belief system regarding a given class or category of persons. These authors also emphasized the importance of self-esteem in humor appreciation. Jokes that enhance a positively valued identification class or disparage a negatively valued identification class were assumed to increase the individual's self-esteem and lead to greater mirth and enjoyment. La Fave, Haddad, and Maesen (1976) reviewed a series of five studies that provided general support for their theory. Each of these studies examined humor appreciation responses of research participants holding opposing views on different social issues, such as religious beliefs, women's liberation, and Canadian-American relations. The subjects were asked to rate the funniness of jokes in which individuals identified with one or the other of these opposing views were either the protagonist or the target of disparagement. As predicted, participants rated the jokes as funnier when the protagonist was a member of a positively valued identification class and the target was a member of a negatively valued identification class.

Although the dispositional theory of humor suggests that humor results from the demeaning or humiliation of someone that we dislike, Zillmann and Bryant (1980) pointed out that there are normally strong social proscriptions against displaying amusement and pleasure at the misfortunes of others, even those we dislike. Drawing from Freud's idea that nontendentious elements of a joke (the jokework) serve as a distraction from the tendentious (aggressive or sexual) elements, these authors suggested a "misattribution theory" of disparagement humor. According to this theory, we can permit ourselves to laugh and display amusement at the debasement or discomfiture of someone for whom we feel antipathy if there are incongruous or peculiar aspects of the situation to which we can (mis)attribute our amusement. "If, for example, we witness our neighbor backing his brand-new car into his mailbox, and a negative disposition predisposes us to enjoy this and makes us burst out in laughter, we can always tell ourselves that we laughed because of the peculiar way in which the mailbox was deformed, the peculiar expression on the neighbor's face, the peculiar squeaking noise of the impact, or a dozen other peculiar things" (Zillmann and Bryant, 1980, p. 150).

Zillmann and Bryant tested this theory in an experiment in which participants were first either treated rudely or in a normal manner by a female experimenter to establish either a negative or neutral affective disposition toward her. The subjects then witnessed her in one of three conditions: (1) a mishap condition with humorous cues, in which the experimenter accidentally spilled a hot cup of tea on herself when a jack-in-the-box suddenly popped out of a box; (2) a mishap condition without humorous cues, in which she spilled hot tea on herself but the jack-in-the-box remained closed; or (3) a no-mishap condition with humorous cues, in which the jack-in-the-box popped up but she did not spill her tea. The dependent variable was the amount of mirth (smiling and laughter) displayed by the subjects following this event.

The results were consistent with the predictions from misattribution theory. The subjects who had a negative disposition toward the experimenter, and who witnessed the mishap along with the humor cues, smiled and laughed much more than did the subjects in all the other conditions. Thus, the presence of innocuous humor cues seems to have a disinhibiting effect that intensifies mirth in response to seeing resented others suffer misfortunes. A similar process presumably occurs in aggressive jokes in which one can misattribute one's amusement to humorous elements such as incongruity and clever wordplay while enjoying the disparagement of someone toward whom one has a negative disposition. These findings are consistent with Freud's ideas about the jokework fooling the superego and thereby allowing libidinal pleasure to be enjoyed, but the misattribution account provides a more cognitive explanation in place of Freud's generally outmoded psychoanalytic concepts.

Evaluation

There seems to be little doubt that aggressive elements play a role in many jokes and other forms of humor. There is considerable evidence that the playfully aggressive elements in jokes and the perception of pain in others (within a nonserious, playful context) contribute to the funniness of the humor. There is also evidence that humorous cues in the situation have a disinhibiting effect, enabling one to misattribute one's mirth in response to the misfortunes experienced by disliked others. The research on disparagement humor by Zillmann and La Fave and their colleagues explored in some detail the parameters influencing the degree to which people are amused by humorous put-downs. However, there is little evidence supporting the view held by superiority/disparagement theorists that *all* humor involves some form of aggression and that hostile people enjoy all types of humor more than do nonhostile people.

There are also several problems with Gruner's (1978, 1997) version of superiority/disparagement theory. First, the evolutionary theory that he presents is essentially an outmoded Lamarkian view. The idea that laughter and humor have survived in humans because they were frequently used by our ancestors does not explain their adaptive value, that is, the ways in which humor and laughter provide an advantage to individuals in the struggle to survive and produce offspring. This is not an insurmountable problem, however, as compatible theories could be devised that would be more consistent with contemporary evolutionary thinking. For example, Alexander (1986) proposed an evolutionary theory of humor that is essentially a superiority/disparagement view, making use of concepts such as ostracism and indirect reciprocity to account for the survival value of humor and laughter (evolutionary theories of humor will be discussed in more detail in Chapter 6). Another problem with Gruner's theory is that, like Freud, he proposes an outdated tension-release model of laughter. However, this is not essential to his theory.

Apart from these theoretical problems, comparative animal research does not support Gruner's view that laughter evolved in the context of aggression. Ethological studies of the silent bared-teeth display and the relaxed open-mouth (play face) display in apes, which are viewed as primate homologues of human smiling and laughter, respectively, reveal that these facial displays occur exclusively in the context of friendly social and play activities, and not in the context of aggression (van Hooff, 1972). I will discuss this research in more detail in Chapter 6.

A major problem with Gruner's theory is that it is essentially unfalsifiable and therefore cannot be tested empirically. Gruner claims that his theory could be falsified by finding just one example of humor that cannot be shown to be based on aggression. However, since Gruner sets himself up as the judge of whether or not a given example of humor fits his theory, it seems highly unlikely that a joke will be found that does not pass the test. No matter how dubious the evidence may appear to everyone else, Gruner always seems to be able to satisfy himself that he can identify the aggression in even the most seemingly innocuous examples of humor. Even if a joke involves nothing more than a clever play on words, Gruner can argue that this conveys the feelings of superiority of the person who came up with the cleverness.

Indeed, one suspects that Gruner could find aggression not just in all humor, but in all human activity. It appears that, to Gruner, humans are fundamentally aggressive, in his broad sense of the word. Thus, he has defined aggression so broadly that his theory seems to account for all human activity and therefore fails to explain the uniqueness of humor. Furthermore, by lumping all humor into the single category of aggression, Gruner ignores the many other ways in which different types of humor might be distinguished from one another, which might be of theoretical and practical importance.

Consistent with favorable views of humor in contemporary culture as a whole, the extreme view that all humor involves aggression has generally fallen into disfavor among humor researchers. Superiority theories have largely been replaced by cognitive incongruity theories, which will be discussed in the next chapter. In addition, recent decades have seen a resurgence of views of humor and laughter as a source of psychological and physical health, and a growing interest in applications of humor in psychotherapy, health care, education, and the workplace. The view of humor as a form of aggression (albeit playful aggression), having its roots in derision and disparagement, seems to many to be incompatible with benign views of humor as a pathway to health. However, as I have pointed out, the superiority view can actually provide a theoretical basis for conceptualizing humor as a way of coping with stress and adversity. If humor is a way of playfully asserting a sense of victory over the people and situations that threaten us, mastery over our oppressors, and liberation from life's constraints, then it is not difficult to see how it can be an important way of maintaining our self-esteem and mental sanity in the face of adversity. Thus, the superiority theory may actually be more compatible with views of humor as coping than is often recognized.

In summary, although an extreme view of humor as aggression is generally rejected today, most researchers agree that humor can often be used to express aggression. Recent research on teasing (discussed in Chapters 5 and 8) exemplifies the continuing interest in aggressive aspects of humor (Keltner, Young, Heerey, Oemig, and Monarch, 1998; Kowalski, Howerton, and McKenzie, 2001). This research also highlights the paradox that humor can be both aggressive and prosocial at the same time, a theme that is central to the superiority theory.

CONCLUSION

In this chapter, I have begun my discussion of the major humor theories and my review of the early empirical research by focusing on psychoanalytic and superiority/disparagement theories, two broad theoretical approaches that were very influential in previous decades. Both of these approaches generated a good deal of interesting research, contributing substantially to our knowledge of the psychology of humor. Although they are not as prominent today, these two approaches call attention to a number of questions about humor that continue to be the focus of much research and theoretical work: why so much humor seems to be based on sexuality and/or aggression; why humor gives us so much pleasure and why we are so motivated to engage in it; the role of humor in coping with stress; and the functions of humor in interpersonal interactions. We will return to these themes repeatedly throughout this book. In the next chapter, I will explore conceptual and early empirical contributions from three other broad theoretical approaches that have strongly influenced humor research, namely arousal, incongruity, and reversal theories.

CHAPTER 3

Theories and Early Research II: Arousal, Incongruity, and Reversal Theories

In the previous chapter we examined psychoanalytic and superiority theories of humor. Both emphasize emotional aspects of humor, seeking to account for its pleasurable nature by focusing on ways it allows us to express strong emotions (i.e., sexuality and aggression) in a playful way. Although these theories are not very popular today, they introduced themes that continue to be of theoretical and empirical importance.

In this chapter, I will discuss three additional theoretical approaches: (1) arousal theories, which focus on the role of psychological and physiological arousal in humor; (2) incongruity theories, which emphasize the cognitive aspects; and (3) reversal theory, which views humor as a form of mental play. Although there are many overlapping ideas in these different approaches, each emphasizes particular aspects that are seen as central to humor. By combining insights and findings from all of these approaches, along with those we discussed in the last chapter, we gain a more comprehensive understanding of the multifaceted phenomenon of humor.

AROUSAL THEORIES

Overview of the Theories

As we saw in the previous chapter, both Freudian and superiority theories (at least the version advanced by Gruner, 1997) hypothesized that the function of laughter is to dissipate excess physiological energy. This energy-release theory of laughter can be traced to the ideas of nineteenth-century writer Herbert Spencer (1860). Spencer was strongly influenced by the then-popular "hydraulic" theory of nervous energy (modeled after the steam engine) in which energy is thought to build up in our bodies and must be released through muscular movement. According to Spencer, the respiratory and muscular action of laughter is a specialized way for the body to release excess nervous energy, much like a safety valve on a steam engine. Needless to say, this view is inconsistent with our current understanding of the nervous system.

Other theorists, both before and after Spencer, have conceptualized humor more generally as a way of relieving built-up psychological tension or strain. For example, Immanuel Kant (1724–1804) stated that "laughter is an affection arising from the sudden transformation of a strained expectation into nothing" (in *Critique of Judgment*, reprinted in Morreall, 1987, p. 47). Writing early in the twentieth century, Gregory (1924) viewed relief as the common factor in all forms of humor. According to Gregory, the relief that leads to laughter can arise from many sources, including the successful outcome of a struggle or the sudden perception of the weakness of an opponent (as in Gruner's theory), or when one builds up tension in anticipation of a difficult task and it turns out to be much less demanding than expected. It can also be relief from pain or fear, or from socially imposed constraints on behavior or language.

Tension-relief theories focus on the role of psychological and physiological arousal in the humor process. A more modern arousal-related theory of humor was that of Daniel Berlyne at the University of Toronto (Berlyne, 1960, 1969, 1972). Berlyne was interested in psychological aspects of aesthetic experiences in general, including the appreciation of art and the enjoyment of play, as well as humor. He focused particularly on various stimulus properties, which he referred to as *collative variables*, that make a stimulus such as a work of art, music, or literature aesthetically pleasing. These included such properties as novelty, level of surprise, complexity, change, ambiguity, incongruity, and redundancy. They were called collative variables because they require the individual to perceive various elements of a stimulus together in order to compare and contrast them. According to Berlyne, jokes and humorous events also contain collative variables, such as surprise, incongruity, ambiguity, and so on. Berlyne (1960) reviewed psychophysiological research showing that collative variables strongly attract our attention, because we find them interesting and unusual, and they are associated with increases in arousal in the brain and autonomic nervous system.

In his theory of humor, Berlyne (1972) rejected Spencer's outdated notion that laughter derives from a release of pent-up energy. Instead, he based his theory on the well-known concept of an inverted-U relationship between physiological arousal and subjective pleasure (Hebb, 1955). According to this view, the greatest pleasure is associated with a moderate amount of arousal, whereas too little or too much arousal is unpleasant. Berlyne postulated two arousal-related mechanisms in humor, which he called the arousal boost and arousal jag mechanisms. The *arousal boost mechanism* operates during the telling of a joke or perception of a humorous situation, when arousal is elevated by means of the collative variables in the stimulus. This increase in arousal up to an optimal level is experienced as pleasurable.

The *arousal jag mechanism* takes over when arousal has been elevated beyond the optimal level and has therefore begun to be aversive. The joke punch line is a sudden resolution of the arousing properties of the joke, causing the arousal level to be reduced very quickly to a pleasurable level once again. This sudden reduction of arousal from an aversive to a pleasurable level adds to the enjoyment of the joke. The subjective pleasure associated with both the arousal boost and the arousal jag is expressed by laughter. Thus, rather than viewing laughter as a method of releasing excess arousal, Berlyne saw it as an expression of the pleasure resulting from changes in arousal to an optimal level (not too high and not too low). Although similar processes occur in the appreciation of art and in play, Berlyne suggested that humor is distinguished from these other types of aesthetic experience by the brief time scale on which the arousal changes occur, the cues precluding seriousness that accompany it, and the extreme bizarreness of the collative variables involved.

Empirical Investigations

Arousal theories of humor received a considerable amount of research attention during the 1960s and 1970s, a period when there was great interest in the role of arousal in emotions generally. The focus of much of this research was therefore on the emotional component of humor, which I refer to as *mirth*. In a well-known experiment, Schachter and Wheeler (1962) manipulated the degree of sympathetic nervous system activation in research participants by injecting them with either epinephrine (which increases arousal of the sympathetic nervous system), chlorpromazine (which decreases sympathetic arousal), or a placebo saline solution. The participants were then exposed to a slapstick comedy film. Those who had been injected with epinephrine showed greater amusement (smiling and laughter) in response to the film and rated it as funnier, as compared to those in the placebo group, who in turn showed greater amusement and higher funniness ratings than did those in the chlorpromazine group. Thus, higher levels of autonomic arousal, even when produced by a drug, resulted in greater expressions of mirth and perceptions of amusement in response to a humorous stimulus.

These results were interpreted as providing support for the view that emotions involve a combination of autonomic arousal (which determines the intensity of the emotion) and cognitive appraisal (which determines its quality or valence). Thus, the amount of mirth elicited by a joke or humorous experience seems to be a function of both the cognitive appraisal or evaluation of the amusing qualities of the humor stimulus and the physiological arousal present at the time. Interestingly, although this physiological arousal may be activated by elements of the joke itself, it may also arise from factors separate from the joke, such as the ingestion of an arousing drug. Subsequent research (Gavanski, 1986) has shown that smiling and laughter (the facial and vocal expressions of the emotion of mirth) are more strongly associated with the emotional enjoyment of humor (humor appreciation), whereas funniness ratings are related more to the cognitive evaluation component (humor comprehension).

In addition to research on the effects of arousal on the positive emotional response to humor, a number of studies were conducted to investigate Berlyne's hypotheses that humorous stimuli themselves produce changes in autonomic arousal and that the perceived funniness of the stimuli is related to this arousal level in a curvilinear manner (i.e., inverted-U relationship). Levi (1965) showed female office clerks a series of four different films (emotionally neutral, fear-arousing, anger-arousing, and comedy) on different days. After each film, he collected urine samples from the participants and analyzed them for levels of epinephrine and norepinephrine, hormones that are associated with activation of the sympathetic nervous system. The results showed that, whereas the emotionally neutral film resulted in decreases in these hormones, the other three films all produced significant increases. Thus, the amusement associated with comedy produces similar arousal of the sympathetic-adrenomedullary system (the well-known fight or flight response) as do feelings of fear and anger. More recent research has also shown comedy-related increases in levels of cortisol, a hormone that is normally associated with the stress response (Hubert, Moeller, and de Jong-Meyer, 1993).

Other researchers monitored various psychophysiological variables associated with arousal of the sympathetic nervous system while participants were exposed to comedy. Averill (1969) found increased skin conductance (a measure of emotion-related sweating) and heart rate in participants watching a comedy film, indicating sympathetic arousal. Langevin and Day (1972) examined the relationship between psychophysiological changes in participants and the rated funniness of humor across a series of cartoons. The results showed that cartoons that were rated as funnier were associated with greater increases in heart rate and skin conductance. Contrary to Berlyne's theory, there was no evidence of an inverted-U relationship between arousal and funniness; instead, the relationship was found to be linear.

Godkewitsch (1976) further evaluated Berlyne's theory of arousal boost and arousal jag mechanisms by assessing physiological responses in research participants during the presentation of both the joke body and the punch line of a series of jokes, as well as having the participants afterwards rate their subjective arousal level and the funniness of the jokes. The results revealed that jokes that were rated as funnier were associated with greater increases in skin conductance during both the joke body and the punch line, greater increases in heart rate during the punch line, and greater subjective arousal ratings subsequently. These results supported Berlyne's notion of an "arousal boost" mechanism in humor, but did not support the "arousal jag" concept. Instead of lowering arousal to a supposedly optimal level, the punch lines were found to increase arousal even further than that found with the joke bodies.

The results of Godkewitsch's study, combined with the findings of several other investigations examining heart rate, skin conductance, blood pressure, muscle tension, and other psychophysiological variables (e.g., Chapman, 1973a, 1976; Goldstein, Harman, McGhee, and Karasik, 1975; J. M. Jones and Harris, 1971), provide consistent evidence that exposure to humor produces increased sympathetic nervous system activation, with almost no evidence for the inverted-*U* relationship predicted by optimal arousal theories like Berlyne's. The relationship between humor enjoyment and autonomic arousal appears to be linear; the more arousal, the more enjoyment and the funnier the humor is perceived to be (McGhee, 1983b). These findings are consistent with the view of humor as essentially an emotional response (i.e., mirth) which, like other emotions, is associated with increased physiological arousal.

Based on evidence that the degree of humor appreciation is largely determined by the level of emotional arousal, Cantor, Bryant, and Zillmann (1974) conducted a "transfer of excitation" experiment to test the hypothesis that residual arousal associated with either strong positive or strong negative emotions could increase the enjoyment of subsequent humor. In a 2 × 2 design, participants were randomly assigned to either a positive or negative hedonic tone condition and to either a high or low arousal condition. In the low arousal positive condition, they read mildly interesting articles from a newspaper; in the high arousal positive condition, they read a graphically descriptive erotic passage from a novel. In the low arousal negative condition, they read a mildly disturbing newspaper article; in the high arousal negative condition, they read a graphic description of a lynch mob's brutal torture and mutilation of a young boy. In a supposedly different experiment, the participants were subsequently asked to rate the funniness of a series of jokes and cartoons that did not contain obvious sexual or hostile themes.

As predicted, participants who had been exposed to either of the high arousal emotion conditions (positive or negative) rated the humor stimuli as much funnier than did those in the two low arousal conditions. These results indicate that increased emotional arousal, regardless of whether it is produced by a positive or a negative emotion, can contribute to greater enjoyment of humor. These findings also provide a more plausible explanation of the tension-relief function of humor than the old "steam-engine" model. The arousal associated with negative emotions like fear, anxiety, or anger that are evoked by an unpleasant or stressful event can later be transferred to the positive feelings of mirth accompanying any humor that may occur, intensifying the pleasurable feelings to a degree that is proportional to the amount of negative emotion, and this heightened feeling of pleasure is then expressed through intense laughter.

Shurcliff (1968) conducted an interesting experiment to test the hypothesis that humor represents a sudden relief from strong emotion, using anxiety as the emotion. To manipulate their levels of anxiety, participants were informed that they would be required to perform various tasks with a white rat that they were to remove from a cage. They were randomly assigned to different conditions involving tasks evoking varying degrees of anxiety, ranging from merely holding the rat to giving it an injection with a large syringe. When the subjects reached into the cage and removed the rat, they discovered that it was just a rubber toy. They were then asked to rate their anxiety and the funniness of the experience.

As predicted by relief theory, the reported level of anxiety of the participants prior to the discovery of the toy rat was found to be positively correlated with the funniness ratings: those who thought they would need to give the rat an injection with an imposing-looking needle found the surprising outcome funnier than did those who merely thought they would need to hold it. However, the idea of relief from anxiety (i.e., anxiety-reduction) was not directly tested in the study. These findings seem to be better explained in terms of the "transfer of excitation" concept, whereby the mirthful emotion associated with the perception of funniness was enhanced by the residual arousal resulting from the anticipatory anxiety, rather than by a sudden reduction in that arousal.

Evaluation

Research based on arousal theories of humor has contributed important information to our understanding of the humor process. Berlyne's theory, and the research it inspired, supports the view that humor represents a complex, physiologically-based interaction between cognition and emotion. Humor is clearly an emotional phenomenon as well as a cognitive one. With regard to the cognitive aspects, Berlyne's ideas about collative properties in humor have not received much further research attention. With regard to his ideas about the emotional aspects, though, there is consistent support for the idea that humor is associated with increased autonomic arousal and that increases in arousal, regardless of their source, can increase the subsequent emotional enjoyment of humor. However, there is little evidence for an inverted-U relationship between arousal level and enjoyment; instead, the relationship appears to be linear. Rather than reducing emotional arousal levels, humor itself is an emotional response that is accompanied by increases in arousal, and is expressed by the vocal and facial behavior of laughter.

The emotional component of humor has gained increasing attention among researchers in recent years. As one example, Willibald Ruch (1997) has investigated the positive emotion associated with humor, using Ekman and Friesen's (1978) Facial Action Coding system. Research on biological aspects of humor, mirth, and laughter has also continued to the present time. The early psychophysiological investigations of arousal led to further studies of physiological processes associated with humor and mirth in the autonomic nervous system, the endocrine and immune systems, and the brain. Today, this line of research continues in studies of brain processes in humor using sophisticated methodologies such as functional magnetic resonance imaging (fMRI). This research will be discussed in more detail in Chapter 6.

INCONGRUITY THEORIES

Overview of the Theories

We have seen that most of the different theories have something to say about the cognitive-perceptual aspects of humor. For example, Freud's ideas about *jokework* and Berlyne's *collative variables* both referred to cognitive components. Incongruity theories of humor focus even more specifically on cognition and give less attention to the social and emotional aspects of humor. These theories suggest that the perception of incongruity is the crucial determinant of whether or not something is humorous: things that are funny are incongruous, surprising, peculiar, unusual, or different from what we normally expect. As we saw in Chapter 1, the idea that incongruity is the basis of humor has been proposed by many philosophers and theorists over the past 250 years.

The eighteenth-century writer Beattie stated that "laughter arises from the view of two or more inconsistent, unsuitable, or incongruous parts or circumstances, considered as united in one complex object or assemblage, or as acquiring a sort of mutual relation from the peculiar manner in which the mind takes notice of them" (quoted in Ritchie, 2004, p. 48). Similarly, the German philosopher Arthur Schopenhauer (1788–1860) stated that "the cause of laughter in every case is simply the sudden perception of the incongruity between a concept and the real objects which have been thought through it in some relation, and laughter itself is just the expression of this incongruity" (in *The World as Will and Idea*, reprinted in Morreall, 1987, p. 52). Thus, humor occurs when there is a mismatch or clash between our sensory perceptions of something and our abstract knowledge or concepts about that thing. Summarizing the cognitive elements involved in humor, psychologist Hans Eysenck (1942, p. 307) stated that "laughter results from the sudden, insightful integration of contradictory or incongruous ideas, attitudes, or sentiments which are experienced objectively."

The incongruity approach to humor was further elaborated by Arthur Koestler (1964), who developed the concept of *bisociation* to explain the mental processes involved in humor, as well as in artistic creativity and scientific discovery. According to Koestler, bisociation occurs when a situation, event, or idea is simultaneously perceived from the perspective of two self-consistent but normally incompatible or disparate frames of reference. Thus, a single event "is made to vibrate simultaneously on two different wavelengths, as it were" (p. 35). A simple example is a pun, in which two different meanings of a word or phrase are brought together simultaneously (e.g., "Why do people become bakers? Because they knead the dough").

The following joke (from Suls, 1972, p. 90) may be used to illustrate these ideas:

> O'Riley was on trial for armed robbery. The jury came out and announced, "Not guilty."
> "Wonderful," said O'Riley, "does that mean I can keep the money?"

The punch line of this joke is incongruous, or inconsistent with the setup, since the man is implicitly admitting his guilt after just having been found not guilty. This surprising ending triggers two incompatible thoughts: he is guilty and not guilty at the same time. Thus, in the humorous mode of thinking, contrary to the rational logic of normal, serious thought, a thing can be both X and not-X at the same time (Mulkay, 1988). Indeed, it is this simultaneous activation of two contradictory perceptions that is the essence of humor. It is worth noting incidentally that a proponent of superiority theory, such as Gruner (1997), would say that we are laughing at the stupidity of the crook who inadvertently admits his guilt after just being found innocent (the name O'Riley indicates that it is also an ethnic joke playing on the stereotype of the Irish as slow-witted). Although Koestler (1964) agreed that bisociation must be accompanied by some aggression in order for it to be funny, later incongruity theorists have generally focused only on the cognitive aspects of humor and have downplayed or even denied the importance of aggressive elements.

Although some form of incongruity is generally viewed as a necessary condition for humor, most theorists would acknowledge that incongruity by itself is not sufficient, since not all incongruity is funny (being hit by a car while walking on the sidewalk is incongruous but not funny). Different theories have different ways of explaining this "something extra." For example, some theories have suggested that the incongruity must occur suddenly (Suls, 1983), or must take place in a playful and nonthreatening context (Rothbart, 1976). One idea that was popularized by several cognitive theorists in the 1970s was that, for incongruity to be funny, it must also be resolved or "make sense" in some way. According to these "incongruity-resolution" theories, resolution of incongruity in a joke is what makes it possible for us to "get the joke." Thomas Shultz (1972), at McGill University, developed an incongruity-resolution theory in which he suggested that the punch line of a joke creates an incongruity by introducing information that is not compatible with our initial understanding of the joke setup. This then prompts the listener to go back and search for an ambiguity in the setup that can be interpreted in a different way and that allows for the punch line to make sense. The ambiguity that provides this resolution of the incongruity can take a number of different forms, including phonological, lexical, surface structure, deep structure, and nonlinguistic forms of ambiguity.

These ideas may be illustrated by the following joke (from Ritchie, 2004, p. 62):

> A lady went into a clothing store and asked "May I try on that dress in the window?" "Well," replied the sales clerk doubtfully, "don't you think it would be better to use the dressing room?"

Here the punch line is initially incongruous because it seems incompatible with the first part of the joke. To understand the joke, we search through the setup for an ambiguity and discover that "in the window" is ambiguous. On first hearing the setup, we interpret this phrase as referring to the current location of the dress, but after the punch line we realize that there is also an alternate meaning, i.e., the place where the shopper wishes to try on the dress. When we recognize that the clerk understood it in this second meaning, we are able to resolve the incongruity and thereby "get" the joke.

Similar to Shultz, Jerry Suls (1972, 1983), then at the State University of New York at Albany, proposed a two-stage model of humor comprehension that is frequently cited by humor researchers. This theory also views humor comprehension as a sort of problem-solving task (see Figure 2). According to the model, a joke setup causes the listener to make a prediction about the likely outcome. When the punch line does not conform to the prediction, the listener is surprised and looks for a cognitive rule that will make the punch line follow from the material in the joke setup. When this cognitive rule is found, the incongruity is removed, the joke is perceived as funny, and laughter ensues. If a cognitive rule is not found, however, the incongruity remains, and the joke leads only to puzzlement instead of humor. Thus, in this

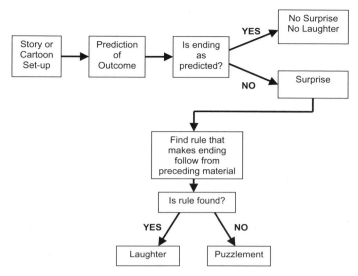

FIGURE 2 Suls' Incongruity Resolution Model. Comprehension of humor is viewed as a process of problem solving. (Adapted from Suls, 1972).

view, humor arises from the removal or resolution of an incongruity, rather than from the ongoing presence of an incongruity.

The two-stage model may be illustrated with the following joke (from Raskin, 1985, p. 106):

> An English bishop received the following note from the vicar of a village in his diocese: "Milord, I regret to inform you of my wife's death. Can you possibly send me a substitute for the weekend?"

In the joke setup we learn that a vicar (local priest) has sent a note to the bishop following the death of the vicar's wife. This leads us to predict a possible outcome, perhaps having to do with the vicar seeking the sympathy of the bishop in some way. In the punch line, the vicar's request for a substitute seems surprising (incongruous), as he seems to be asking the bishop to send him a replacement for his dead wife for the coming weekend. The puzzlement created by this unexpected ending causes the listener to go back over the joke setup and search for a "cognitive rule" that will make the surprising ending fit with the setup. When it is realized that the vicar is actually asking for another clergyman to officiate at the church service in his place while the vicar is mourning the death of his wife, the joke makes sense (the incongruity is resolved), and we find it amusing. Thus, in this model, joke comprehension and appreciation is essentially a sort of cognitive problem-solving task.

Note, once again, that Freud would likely see an important sexual aspect to this joke. Our initial interpretation of the punch line implies that the vicar, seeking another woman so soon after his wife died (and apparently just for the weekend), is particularly interested in sex. However, incongruity theorists tend to ignore the "tendentious" (sexual and aggressive) elements of humor that are emphasized in psychoanalytic and superiority/disparagement theories. Indeed, several cognitively oriented theorists have sought to subsume these latter theories within incongruity theory. For example, Suls (1977) argued that the aspects of jokes that are usually thought to be aggressive and disparaging are not really aggressive, but instead are a way of providing the information needed for the incongruity to be resolved. To illustrate, he used the following joke (p. 42):

> Question: If your son flunks out of school and is illiterate and anti-social, what can he grow up to be?
> Answer: An Italian policeman.

From the perspective of disparagement and superiority theories, this joke is amusing to people who dislike Italians because it disparages people of that nationality, and more specifically Italian policemen. Analyzing the joke from the perspective of incongruity-resolution theory, however, Suls argued that the aggressive element merely provides a way of resolving the incongruity. There is an incongruity between the joke setup and the punch line, since being uneducated, illiterate, and antisocial does not seem to be consistent with being a policeman. This incongruity is resolved, however, when we recognize the existence of a stereotype that Italians are stupid.

Although Suls suggested that we may actually need to believe this stereotype in order to "get" the joke, other authors have argued that simply recognizing that such a stereotype exists, without actually agreeing with it, is all that is needed to enjoy a joke (e.g., Attardo and Raskin, 1991). According to these authors, seemingly aggressive (e.g., ethnic, sexist) forms of humor are not really aggressive at all: they simply make use of common stereotypes to play with ideas in an amusing way. Goldstein, Suls, and Anthony (1972) referred to this view as the *salience hypothesis,* since the purpose of aggressive and sexual elements in jokes is to make salient the information needed to resolve the incongruity. In this way, cognitive theorists were able to completely sanitize humor, removing any residue of the aggression and other tendentious elements that were once seen as being essential to it.

Although incongruity-resolution theorists saw resolution as essential for humor to occur in response to a joke, they recognized that the incongruity is never completely resolved. As Forabosco (1992) pointed out, the resolution is really just a "pseudo-resolution," which makes sense only within the fantasy world of the joke. If a joke truly made sense, and the incongruity was completely resolved, it would simply be a nonhumorous puzzle instead of a joke. Similarly, McGhee (1972) wrote about the "fantasy assimilation" that occurs in jokes as being quite different from the "reality assimilation" of more serious cognitive processing. Pien and Rothbart (1977) also noted that the resolution of a joke often introduces new incongruities that can add to its enjoyment.

Empirical Investigations

The incongruity-resolution theory of humor was investigated in a series of studies by Thomas Shultz and his colleagues at McGill University. Shultz (1974b) presented undergraduate students a series of jokes and asked them to identify the order in which they noticed various elements within each. The results supported the predictions of Shultz's incongruity-resolution theory: subjects reported that they did not notice the hidden meaning of an ambiguous element in the joke setup until the incongruity of the punch line caused them to search for a resolution. A second study using visual cartoons instead of verbal jokes also showed that participants tended to notice incongruous elements before noticing details that resolved the incongruity.

Shultz and his colleagues also examined the role of incongruity and resolution by creating incongruity-removed and resolution-removed versions of jokes and cartoons. If incongruity and resolution are essential to humor, then removal of either of them should decrease humor appreciation. For example, one of the original jokes was the following:

> Mother: "Doctor, come at once! Our baby swallowed a fountain pen!"
> Doctor: "I'll be right over. What are you doing in the meantime?"
> Mother: "Using a pencil."

In this joke, the incongruous reply of the mother in the punch line is resolved by recognizing the ambiguity in the doctor's question, which could mean either "What are you doing in the meantime to treat the baby?" or "What are you using as a substitute for a fountain pen?" In the incongruity-removed version of the joke, Shultz changed the punch line to: "We don't know what to do." In this version, there is no incongruity between the joke setup and the punch line and therefore no puzzle to solve. In the resolution-removed version, Shultz had the parents saying that the baby had swallowed a rubber band instead of a fountain pen. Now the punch line ("Using a pencil") is still incongruous and puzzling, but there is no resolution, since there is no logical connection between the baby swallowing a rubber band and the parents using a pencil.

Shultz and Horibe (1974) presented these different versions of a number of jokes to children in grades 1, 3, 5, and 7. The children were asked to rate the funniness of the jokes, and the experimenters also observed the degree to which they smiled and laughed. As predicted, the results showed that, by grade 3, the children found the original versions of the jokes funnier than the resolution-removed versions, which in turn were found to be funnier than the incongruity-removed versions. Thus, incongruity without resolution is funnier than no incongruity, but resolution of the incongruity is even funnier. Similar results were found using original, incongruity-removed, and resolution-removed versions of cartoons (Shultz, 1972) and riddles (Shultz, 1974a).

Interestingly, in the study by Shultz and Horibe (1974), children in grade 1 showed no difference between the original and resolution-removed jokes, but both were funnier than the versions without incongruity. The authors suggested that, at an early stage of development (prior to the development of concrete operational thought) incongruity alone is sufficient to elicit a humor response, whereas both incongruity and resolution are required at a later stage. However, Pien and Rothbart (1976) found that younger children also appreciate joke resolutions if the humor is easy to understand.

Problems with this methodology were noted, however, by some researchers, who pointed out that it is difficult to hold some of the elements of a joke constant while varying others (Nerhardt, 1977; Pien and Rothbart, 1977). For example, removing the resolution from jokes and cartoons may also eliminate some of the incongruity. If participants then prefer the original jokes over those with resolution removed, it is difficult to know whether this is due to the differences in resolution or incongruity. Frank Wicker and colleagues (1981) at the University of Texas at Austin attempted to get around these problems by taking a different approach. They had research participants rate a number of jokes on a funniness scale and also on 13 other scales assessing dimensions suggested by various theories of humor, including incongruity-resolution, superiority, psychoanalytic, and arousal theories. These ratings included: surprise, nonsense, resolution, difficulty, emotional involvement, superiority, sympathy, pain, freedom, and anxiety. Participants' ratings on each of the scales were averaged for each joke, and a factor analysis was conducted on these averaged ratings.

This analysis revealed three factors relating to: (1) cognitive incongruity-resolution elements (surprise, resolution, originality), (2) superiority, and (3) emotional elements (anxiety, pain, importance, emotional involvement). The funniness ratings loaded primarily on the cognitive factor, a finding that was interpreted as indicating that funniness is primarily determined by information-processing mechanisms relating to incongruity and resolution. The emotionality factor also correlated with funniness, but this association was mediated by incongruity and resolution ratings, suggesting that the effects of emotional elements on humor appreciation (such as those described by superiority and psychoanalytic theories) may depend in part on the cleverness of the cognitive elements described by incongruity-resolution theories. This finding was taken as support for the salience hypothesis advocated by proponents of incongruity-resolution theories.

However, not all cognitive theorists were convinced by the evidence for incongruity-resolution theories. For example, Swedish psychologist Göran Nerhardt, at the University of Stockholm, argued that incongruity alone is sufficient for humor, and that resolution of the incongruity is not necessary. Nerhardt (1970) was dissatisfied with the use of jokes and cartoons as stimuli in experiments on cognitive processes in humor. Since jokes incorporate many unmeasured and uncontrolled linguistic elements and emotional themes, he argued, it is difficult to know which dimensions are responsible for research participants' funniness ratings. Also, when subjects are asked to rate the funniness of jokes, their own assumptions and implicit theories of humor may influence their responses. To avoid these problems, Nerhardt developed a rather clever methodology, called the *weight judgment paradigm*, as a way of experimentally manipulating incongruity, which he defined as divergence from expectation.

In this paradigm, participants, who were led to believe that they were involved in a psychophysical study, were asked to compare a series of identical-looking weights with a standard reference weight. A number of very similar weights (averaging 500 +/– 50 g) were evaluated first, and then one that was much lighter or heavier than the standard (50 g or 3000 g) was presented (see Deckers, 1993, for a detailed description of the methodology). Interestingly, when participants lifted this greatly discrepant weight, they frequently smiled, chuckled, or even laughed aloud, and Nerhardt (1970, 1976) found that the more discrepant this weight was from the mean of the other comparisons, the more the subjects displayed such expressions of mirth. Thus, the size of the incongruity (the discrepancy in weight) was directly related to the amount of smiling and laughter evoked. Furthermore, several studies using this paradigm showed sizable correlations between the intensity of these mirth responses and participants' ratings of the funniness of the experience (Deckers, 1993; Deckers, Jenkins, and Gladfelter, 1977; Deckers, Pell, and Lundahl, 1990), indicating that the smiling and laughter was a reflection of humorous amusement and not just embarrassment or nervousness. The weight judgment paradigm, then, is a way of operationally defining incongruity without using inherently humorous stimuli such as jokes and cartoons, and it seems to reliably produce an emotional mirth response that is expressed by smiling and laughter.

Lambert Deckers and his colleagues at Ball State University used this procedure in a number of experiments, in which they varied different parameters to examine their effects on the mirth response. For example, Deckers and Kizer (1975) found that a minimum number of initial comparisons was needed in order to build up an expectation about the weight before a discrepancy would evoke expressions of mirth. In addition, studies that manipulated the degree of discrepancy between the final and earlier weights showed a negatively accelerated relationship with the amount of smiling and laughter evoked: greater discrepancies evoked a greater amount of these responses up to a point, after which additional increases in the weight discrepancy did not produce more mirth (Deckers and Edington, 1979; Deckers and Salais, 1983; Gerber and Routh, 1975).

Studies comparing the effects of unexpectedly heavy versus light weights indicated that weights that were heavier than expected evoked more humor than did those that were lighter than expected (Deckers and Kizer, 1974; Gerber and Routh, 1975). When subjects were asked to make judgments about either the height or the weight of a series of stimuli and then presented with stimuli that were incongruous in either height or weight, mirth reactions were greater when the critical comparison was discrepant in the particular dimension that the subject had been judging (Deckers, Edington, and VanCleave, 1981).

Nerhardt (1976) and Deckers (1993) argued that the weight judgment findings demonstrate that incongruity without resolution is capable of eliciting humor, contradicting incongruity-resolution theories which suggest that incongruity must be resolved for it to be funny. At the same time, they recognized that there are other necessary conditions in addition to incongruity for a humor response to be evoked. Interestingly, Nerhardt (1976) was initially unsuccessful in his early experiments with the weight judgment paradigm, which he carried out in the guise of a consumer survey in a railroad station. There he found that train passengers who were asked to judge weights of a series of suitcases did not respond with expressions of mirth to unexpectedly heavy or light ones. This was apparently because they were inclined to take the experiment too seriously, were perhaps in a hurry to get somewhere, and were not easily put into the playful frame of mind that also seems to be necessary for a humor response to occur (cf. Apter, 1982). When the experimental paradigm was moved into a laboratory, using undergraduate participants who were more familiar with psychological research, and an effort was made to put the subjects at ease, smiling and laughter began to be elicited by the discrepant weight. Thus, although resolution of incongruity may not be necessary for humor, it does appear that there are other requirements besides incongruity, having to do with the emotional climate or mental set of the perceiver. In sum, incongruity seems to be a necessary but not a sufficient condition for humor.

Several studies have also investigated the salience hypothesis proposed by incongruity-resolution theorists. As we saw in the previous chapter in our discussion of psychoanalytic theory, earlier research showed that participants are more likely to enjoy aggressive humor after they have been made angry and to enjoy sexual humor after they have been sexually aroused (e.g., Strickland, 1959). These findings were interpreted by psychoanalytic theorists as demonstrating support for drive theory. In contrast, incongruity-resolution theorists Goldstein, Suls, and Anthony (1972) suggested that these experimental manipulations simply increased the salience of sexual and aggressive themes, thereby creating a cognitive set that made the corresponding jokes easier to understand.

To test this idea, Goldstein and colleagues (1972) conducted an experiment in which they presented participants with photographs depicting either scenes of violence or automobiles. After rating the photographs for aesthetic value, the subjects were asked to rate the funniness of a number of cartoons that were either aggressive or contained automobiles as a major element. As predicted by the salience hypothesis, those who had been exposed to aggressive photographs rated aggressive humor as funnier, whereas those who had been exposed to photographs of automobiles preferred the cartoons about automobiles.

In a second study, the researchers showed that exposure to music-related jokes increases subsequent enjoyment of other jokes about music, whereas exposure to jokes about medical topics increases subsequent enjoyment of medical jokes. Since pictures of automobiles and jokes about music and medicine are not likely to arouse specific drives, the results appear to support the hypothesis that it is the salience of the content, rather than arousal of a drive, that accounts for the increased appreciation of the humor. The authors concluded that "the most parsimonious explanation of the data would rule out motivation as an explanatory concept, since the salience hypothesis can account for the appreciation of nonsense as well as aggressive and sexual humor" (p. 169).

A subsequent study by Kuhlman (1985), however, provided less support for the salience hypothesis. Kuhlman manipulated salience in a less obvious way by having participants rate the funniness of a series of jokes either in a normal college classroom, or just before they were to take an examination, or in the middle of an exam. One-third of the jokes contained social taboo themes (sex, profanity, violence), one third contained themes relating to academic examinations (salient jokes), and one third involved neutral themes. An effort was made to equate the jokes for characteristics that might affect funniness, such as difficulty, the incongruity techniques used, length, and so on. The salience hypothesis would predict that the exam-related jokes should be enjoyed more just before or during an exam than during a normal class.

However, the results showed that the jokes containing taboo themes were preferred over the other two types in all three experimental conditions. Rather than supporting the salience hypothesis, these results appear to support motivational-emotional views such as psychoanalytic and superiority/disparagement theories. An additional finding was that all three types of jokes were enjoyed more by the subjects who were in the middle of an exam than by those in the other two conditions. This result, consistent with arousal theories of humor, suggests that humor appreciation is elevated by increased levels of state anxiety. A study by Derks and Arora (1993) also found little support for the salience hypothesis. In summary, the existing evidence for the salience hypothesis is inconsistent. This is a topic that merits further investigation.

According to incongruity theories, the funniness of a joke depends on the unexpectedness or surprisingness of the punch line. Thus, the funniest jokes should be those having the most unpredictable or surprising endings (e.g., Shultz, 1976; Suls, 1972). However, this hypothesis has not been supported by research, which has tended to show instead that more predictable joke endings are actually funnier than less predictable ones. For example, Kenny (1955) had a group of participants rate a number of jokes on the degree to which the punch line corresponded to what they expected it would be, and another group of participants were asked to rate the same jokes for funniness. Mean ratings on these two scales were computed for each joke, and the correlation between them was analyzed. Contrary to the predictions of incongruity-resolution theory, a significant positive correlation was found: the jokes with the most predictable punch lines were rated as most funny.

A difficulty with Kenny's study was that the ratings of predictability were made retrospectively by the participants after they had already heard the punch lines, and it may therefore have been difficult for them to judge accurately the degree to which they had been expecting those particular punch lines. To correct this problem, Pollio and Mers (1974) had participants listen to a number of tape recordings of comedy routines by Bill Cosby and Phyllis Diller. The recordings were stopped immediately before the punch lines of the jokes were delivered, and the subjects were instructed to write out what they thought the punch lines would be. The researchers subsequently rated the degree to which these predicted punch lines conformed to the actual punch lines delivered by the comedians. These similarity ratings were found to be positively correlated with the funniness ratings, smiling, and laughter of a different set of subjects in response to the same recordings: jokes that were most predictable were most funny. Like the findings of Kenny (1955), these results appear to contradict incongruity theory. People seem to find a joke funnier when they "see the punch line coming" than when it is completely unexpected. Pollio and Mers concluded that "laughter is a partial exclamation of achievement rather than an expression of surprise over incongruity" (p. 232).

Evaluation

Incongruity theories have made an important contribution to our understanding of humor. When they were introduced in the late 1960s and early 1970s, they drew researchers' attention to cognitive-perceptual aspects of humor, which had been seen as only having secondary importance in other approaches such as psychoanalytic, superiority/disparagement, and arousal theories. Incongruity theories stimulated a great deal of research and further theoretical development that have continued to the present day (more recent cognitive theory and research will be discussed in the next chapter). In 1967, when topics such as aggression, sexual drive, and arousal were the main focus of attention in research on humor, Zigler, Levine, and Gould noted a tendency for researchers to "underestimate the importance of cognitive factors in determining the degree of laughter" (p. 332). However, the situation has since then been reversed, as cognitive approaches to humor became the prevailing view, and emotional aspects became much less frequently studied. This growing focus on cognition in humor paralleled the trend toward an information-processing orientation in psychology generally, as well as related disciplines such as linguistics. More recently, however, there has been some renewed interest in emotional aspects. In particular, the emotional nature of humor has been highlighted by recent brain-imaging studies (Berns, 2004). The contemporary movement known as "positive psychology" has also generated new interest in the study of positive emotions in general and the emotion of mirth in particular (e.g., Aspinwall and Staudinger, 2003; Fredrickson, 2001).

The research evidence to date generally supports the idea that incongruity of some sort is an essential element of humor. Some variation of Koestler's (1964) idea that humor involves the activation of two normally incompatible frames of reference continues to form the basis of most humor theories today. However, it is important to note that the concept of incongruity is still rather vague and not well defined (Ritchie, 2004). Moreover, the different variants of incongruity and incongruity-resolution theories present somewhat different conceptualizations of the function of incongruity. For example, in both Shultz's and Suls' theories, incongruity is no longer present at the point where a joke is perceived to be funny, since it has been "resolved" by then. This is quite different from Koestler's original view, in which the "bisociation" (i.e., the ongoing incongruity) is what creates the humorous effect, rather than its removal. Ritchie (2004) has also noted that, although the theories of Shultz and Suls are generally viewed as essentially interchangeable, there are some subtle but important differences between them. He suggested that these different theories may apply to different subclasses of jokes rather than to all jokes, much less all humor. As we will see in the next chapter, theorists and researchers continue to make refinements to the ideas and research methodologies of the earlier incongruity theorists.

Although some sort of incongruity (however defined) seems to be necessary for all types of humor, there is less evidence for the idea that resolution is also essential. Theorists subscribing to the incongruity-resolution view typically based their theories on the joke as the prototype of humor, and tested their hypotheses with research using jokes and cartoons. In contrast, much of the evidence for humorous incongruity without resolution comes from non-joke–related humor, such as the weight judgment paradigm. The processes involved in jokes may not be the same as those in other forms of humor, such as spontaneous conversational humor (e.g., witticisms, puns, slips of the tongue, spoonerisms) and nonverbal humor (e.g., slapstick comedy). It may be that incongruity-resolution theories apply particularly to a certain class of jokes and cartoons, whereas resolution may be less important in other jokes and other forms of humor. In Chapter 7, I will discuss research by Willibald Ruch (e.g., Ruch and Hehl, 1998) indicating that jokes and cartoons can be divided into two general categories on the basis of whether or not they involve the resolution of incongruity.

As Long and Graesser (1988) noted, jokes and cartoons, which are context-independent, can be enjoyed in almost any situation, since they contain within themselves all the information needed for their understanding. Other forms of humor are more context-sensitive, requiring information arising from the situation to create the humor. This is why the latter types of humor often lose their funniness when described out of context ("You had to be there"). This portability of jokes and cartoons is also the reason why they have been most commonly used in humor research, while more spontaneous forms of humor that arise in the course of social interactions, which are more difficult to create in a laboratory, are less frequently studied. However, the study of jokes and cartoons may provide only limited information about other more spontaneous types of humor. Since jokes and cartoons also play only a minor role in the humor that most people experience in their daily lives (Mannell and McMahon, 1982; R. A. Martin and Kuiper, 1999; Provine, 2000), it is important for researchers to study the cognitive processes involved in other forms of humor besides jokes. Fortunately, as we will see in the next chapter, theorists and researchers in recent years have begun to pay more attention to cognitive processes involved in non-joke–related humor.

Another weakness of incongruity-resolution theories is that they try to explain the cognitive processes involved in joke comprehension without taking the social context of joke-telling into account. The suggestion that listeners are surprised or puzzled by an unexpected punch line assumes that they are seeking to understand humor as they would serious forms of communication, where contradictory information is puzzling and unsettling. However, as more recent theorists have noted (e.g., Norrick, 2003; Wyer and Collins, 1992), when jokes are told in normal social situations, they are usually prefaced by cues alerting the listeners to the fact that they are about to hear a joke ("Did you hear the one about . . ."). Even in the research context, when jokes are used as stimuli, subjects are told that they will be presented with jokes, or they are alerted to this fact by instructions to rate their funniness. Since listeners usually know that they are hearing a joke, they are likely more actively involved in anticipating the outcome and are not as surprised by the punch line as incongruity-resolution theories suggested. Rather than being surprising or unexpected, incongruity is actually expected in humor, and, indeed, a *lack* of incongruity would be surprising. When people know that they are hearing a joke, then, they likely anticipate and search for an incongruity, and their ability to predict the incongruity may even enhance the funniness of the joke. This would explain why Pollio and Mers (1974) found that the funniest jokes were those in which the subjects were best able to predict the punch lines. Thus, while the perception of some sort of incongruity seems to play a central role in humor, the incongruity may not need to be unanticipated to be enjoyed. This would also account for the fact that jokes and humorous incidents can often continue to be amusing even after repeated retelling (Eysenck, 1942).

Although incongruity theories and other cognitive approaches make important contributions to the study of humor, it is important also to note that they do not adequately account for all aspects of humor. In particular, these approaches do not explain the emotional and social aspects of humor that are the focus of other theories. As we have seen, many cognitive theorists attempt to subordinate these "tendentious" elements to the cognitive mechanisms, denying their importance in humor. While reading these theorists' analyses of various jokes, one is often struck by the degree to which they completely ignore the seemingly obvious sexual, aggressive, and other emotion-arousing aspects. As we have seen, though, there is considerable evidence that sexual and aggressive elements can contribute to the enjoyment of humor independently of the cognitive mechanisms. Many jokes are difficult to explain on the basis of cognitive processes alone. Consider the following joke (from Gruner, 1978, p. 35), for example:

> A woman sideswiped a car driven by a man. The woman climbed out and apologized for the accident. The man demurred: "That's O.K. lady, it was all my fault. I could see it was a woman driving your car from half a mile away, and I had lots of time to drive off into a field and avoid all this."

Incongruity-resolution theories would suggest that the main source of the humor here is the incongruity of a person taking the blame for an accident that he did not cause and saying he should have avoided it by driving into a field. This incongruity is resolved by accessing the stereotype that women are inherently such terrible drivers that they cannot do anything about it and therefore should not be held responsible. What appears to be aggression is merely what enables one to "get" the joke; it wouldn't be resolved otherwise. However, this sort of explanation seems to ignore the emotional nature of humor and turn it into a purely intellectual exercise. What is the source of pleasure in this joke? Is it merely the intellectual enjoyment of playing with a puzzling incongruity and then discovering its resolution, or is it the emotional pleasure of taking a playfully aggressive jab at women drivers? It is likely a combination of both. Cognitive processes involving incongruity and resolution are what make the joke funny, while aggressive elements enhance the feelings of enjoyment. Without the cognitive elements peculiar to humor, aggression is not funny, but without the aggression (or some other emotional element), incongruity is not very enjoyable. Again, it is important to remember that any aggression in humor is only playful and not necessarily "serious" (Gruner, 1997).

The importance of noncognitive factors in humor was also emphasized by Arthur Koestler (1964), whose concept of bisociation is often seen as the basis of contemporary incongruity theories. He spoke of the "aggressive-defensive or self-asserting tendency" in humor (p. 52), and suggested that, to be humorous, bisociation must be accompanied by at least a tinge of aggression. It is likely an exaggeration to say that all humor involves aggression, but it does seem accurate to say that it involves an emotional experience that can be intensified by a range of emotion-arousing topics. Other emotion-arousing topics besides aggression seem to work as well, including sex and just plain exuberant fun. As Suls (1983) rather tentatively acknowledged, incongruity-based cognitive theories appear to be theories of humor *comprehension* but not humor *appreciation*. They describe the elements needed to understand and "get" the joke, but they do not explain the emotional aspects that make the humorous experience so enjoyable.

REVERSAL THEORY

Overview of the Theory

As noted in Chapter 1, humor is a playful, nonserious activity. Chimpanzees laugh in the context of rough-and-tumble play and tickling, suggesting that laughter in our common ancestry with chimpanzees was likely also associated with play. Laughter in children also occurs most frequently in the context of play, and humor can be seen as a way for adults to continue to engage in playful activities, using words and ideas as playthings. However, surprisingly few of the early theorists recognized the essentially playful nature of humor. One exception was Max Eastman (1936), who stated that "humor is play . . . Therefore no definition of humor, no theory of wit, no explanation of comic laughter, will ever stand up, which is not based upon the distinction between *playful* and *serious*" (p. 15). He pointed out that, from reading the serious-sounding descriptions of humor written by many of the past theorists, one would not know that humor is a playful, lighthearted activity. More recently, Berlyne (1969) noted the close connection between humor and play, and Gruner (1997) emphasized the playful nature of humorous aggression. William Fry (1963) also viewed humor as essentially a form of play.

The idea of humor as play is made explicit in the theory of humor proposed by the Anglo-American psychologist Michael Apter (1982; Apter and Smith, 1977), which is derived from a broader theory of motivation and personality called reversal theory (Apter, 2001). Although not as well known as the other theories I have discussed, Apter's theory of humor is quite comprehensive, incorporating many of the strengths of other theories, and can account for many of the research findings. I include it here because I view it as a promising framework for an integrative theory of humor.

What is play? According to Apter (1991), it is "a state of mind, a way of seeing and being, a special mental 'set' towards the world and one's actions in it" (p. 31). To experience humor, we need to be in this playful state of mind. He suggested that play is characterized by a "protective frame," which is a "psychological safety zone" that we create to isolate ourselves from the serious concerns of the real world. In play, stated Apter (p. 14):

> we seem to create a small and manageable private world which we may, of course share with others; and this world is one in which, temporarily at least, nothing outside has any significance, and into which the outside world of real problems cannot properly impinge. If the "real world" does enter in some way, it is transformed and sterilized in the process so that it is no longer truly itself, and can do no harm.

Apter refers to this playful frame of mind as the *paratelic* state, to distinguish it from the *telic* (goal-directed) state that underlies more serious activities. He suggests that we reverse back and forth between these two states of mind at different times throughout a typical day (hence the name *reversal theory*).

In the serious, telic state, one is concerned primarily with attaining important goals, while the means to achieve the goals are secondary. In contrast, in the playful, paratelic state, one's goals are of secondary importance, and the ongoing activities are enjoyed for their own sake. The telic state is future-oriented, whereas the paratelic state is present-oriented. With regard to the relation between arousal and emotion, Apter rejected traditional optimal arousal theories such as Berlyne's (discussed earlier). Instead, he suggested that arousal is experienced differently depending on whether one is in the telic or the paratelic state. In the telic state, high arousal is unpleasant (anxiety) and low arousal is preferred (relaxation), whereas in the paratelic state, low arousal is unpleasant (boredom) and high arousal is enjoyable (excitement).

Apter (1992) described the many ways in which people seek to increase their level of arousal in the paratelic state by means of exciting activities such as riding on roller coasters, hang gliding, and taking other kinds of risks. Even normally negative emotions can be experienced as exciting and enjoyable when one is in the paratelic state, as demonstrated by the popularity of horror movies. As a paratelic activity, humor also involves the enjoyment of arousal. According to Apter (1982), emotionally arousing elements that may be present in humor, such as sexual and aggressive themes, are a means of enhancing these pleasurable feelings of arousal and thus making the humor seem funnier. Similarly, humor involving topics that would normally arouse feelings of horror, revulsion, or disgust (such as humorous parodies of horror movies, "sick" jokes, etc.) may be enjoyed because of the way these normally negative emotions add to the pleasurable arousal when one is in a playful frame of mind. Thus, this theory accounts for the "tendentious" aspects of humor in terms of their arousal-boosting effects. It is also consistent with the research findings discussed earlier indicating that greater levels of physiological arousal are associated with greater enjoyment of humor, and that residual arousal from exposure to either positive or negative emotional material increases subsequent enjoyment of humor.

Reversal theory also addresses the cognitive aspects of humor that are the focus of incongruity theories. Apter (1982) used the concept of "synergy" to describe a cognitive process in which two contradictory ideas or concepts about the same object are held in one's mind at the same time. This is very similar to Koestler's (1964) concept of bisociation, discussed earlier. Like Koestler, Apter believes that this process occurs in artistic creativity and aesthetic enjoyment, as well as in humor. In the playful, paratelic state, according to Apter, synergies are found to be enjoyable and, like the collative properties in Berlyne's theory, they are thought to increase arousal. Apter disagrees with incongruity-resolution theories, suggesting instead that humor involves the simultaneous recognition of incongruous or contradictory viewpoints, rather than the removal (resolution) of an incongruity. He argues that the punch line of a joke functions to create an incongruous synergy rather than resolving it.

Although humor and art both involve these kinds of cognitive synergies or incongruities, Apter suggests that the difference between the two is that in humor one of the simultaneously held viewpoints involves a diminishment or devaluation of the object being considered, whereas in art the object is elevated. Thus, the incongruity occurring in humor makes us see a person, object, action, or situation as less important, dignified, serious, valuable, worthy of respect, etc., than what at first appeared. Without diminishment, an incongruity or synergy is not funny. Although not mentioned in most incongruity theories, this diminishment idea was proposed in the nineteenth century by Herbert Spencer, who stated that "laughter naturally results only when consciousness is unawares transferred from great things to small—only when there is what we may call a *descending* incongruity" (from *The Physiology of Laughter*, reprinted in Morreall, 1987, p. 108, emphasis in original). Thus, Apter accounts for the aggressive elements frequently occurring in humor (which are the focus of superiority/disparagement theories) by suggesting that disparagement in humor is one way of creating diminishment. However, Apter disagrees with the view of superiority theorists that humor always involves aggression or disparagement, since diminishment does not need to be aggressive: it can simply be a perception of something as more mundane or trivial than it first appeared.

In sum, Apter's theory proposes that humor involves the perception of a cognitive synergy (i.e., two concurrent but contradictory interpretations of the same object), in which the second interpretation of an object involves a diminishment relative to the first, which is experienced in a playful, or paratelic, state of mind. The individual is either already in this playful frame before encountering the humorous event, or the event itself causes him or her to switch into the paratelic state. Environmental cues, such as the laughter of other people or their amusing facial expressions may help to induce the paratelic frame of mind. Arousal associated with emotional elements in the joke or situation (and also induced by laughter itself) contributes to the experience of enjoyment of the humor. Such arousal-increasing elements include surprise, sex, violence, taboo topics, and disgust. Humor is also enhanced by multiple synergies occurring simultaneously or within a short period of time, especially if they are interconnected and play off each other to produce further comic effects (A. S. Coulson, 2001).

Psychologists Robert Wyer and James Collins (1992; see also Wyer, 2004), at the University of Illinois, have developed a "comprehension-elaboration theory" of humor that reformulates and extends Apter's synergy concept in terms of social cognition using schema theory (which will be discussed in more detail in the next chapter). They extended Apter's theory by examining the way people comprehend humor within a social context and exploring information-processing factors such as comprehension difficulty and cognitive elaboration. They suggested that humor is enhanced when it requires a moderate degree of mental effort to understand it, rather than being too easy or too difficult to understand, and when there is greater opportunity to elaborate the cognitive synergies involved. Wyer and Collins (1992, p. 667) used the following joke to illustrate the ideas of reversal theory:

> A young Catholic priest is walking through town when he is accosted by a prostitute. "How about a quickie for twenty dollars?" she asks.
> The priest, puzzled, shakes her off and continues on his way, only to be stopped by another prostitute. "Twenty dollars for a quickie," she offers. Again, he breaks free and goes up the street.
> Later, as he is nearing his home in the country, he meets a nun. "Pardon me, sister," he asks, "but what's a quickie?"
> "Twenty dollars," she says, "The same as it is in town."

The synergy in this joke involves the sudden shift in interpretation brought about by the punch line. The joke setup leads us to believe that the priest's question, "What's a quickie?" should be interpreted as "What does 'a quickie' mean?' However, the nun's reply introduces a different interpretation, namely, "How much does a quickie cost?" There is also a second shift in interpretation from our perception of the woman as being a nun to being a prostitute. In each of these contradictory perceptions, both interpretations are held simultaneously. The diminishment criterion is satisfied by the fact that the nun, who is first seen as a chaste and holy woman, turns out to be a prostitute on the side. Although not mentioned by Wyer and Collins, this joke also includes a sexual theme that may add to its enjoyment. The contemplation of a usually chaste nun as a sexually loose woman may be somewhat titillating. Any associated increases in arousal would enhance the feelings of amusement.

Like Apter (1982), Wyer and Collins (1992) emphasized the importance of taking the social context of humor into account, pointing out that humor is primarily a form of social communication. For example, they explained the findings of research using the weight judgment paradigm (discussed earlier) in terms of cognitive reinterpretation and diminishment in a social context. They suggested that participants in these experiments, on picking up a weight that is much heavier or lighter than the previous ones, begin to infer that they are being tricked and that the experiment is not a serious study of weight judgment after all. In other words, the participants reinterpret the entire social situation of the experiment, and not just the weights, perceiving it to be less important than they had originally viewed it to be, and this reinterpretation elicits amusement. Wyer and Collins went on to discuss in some detail the ways in which their elaboration of reversal theory can be used to explain all types of humor, including conversational witticisms (irony, satire, teasing, puns), unintentional humor (slips of the tongue, clumsy actions), and slapstick comedy, in addition to a wide variety of joke types. A detailed explanation of their theory and its applications is outside the scope of the present discussion. I will return to some of these ideas in the next chapter.

EMPIRICAL INVESTIGATIONS

Many of the research findings discussed earlier can be viewed as supportive of the reversal theory account of humor. As already noted, research indicating a positive linear correlation between physiological arousal and enjoyment of humor (rather than a curvilinear relationship) is more consistent with reversal theory than with optimal arousal theories (e.g., Godkewitsch, 1976). The theory is also supported by "transfer of excitation" research showing that residual arousal from both positive and negative emotions can subsequently enhance the enjoyment of humor (Cantor et al., 1974). The study by Shurcliff (1968), in which subjects who expected to remove a rat from a cage found a rubber toy instead, is also consistent with reversal theory. The discovery of the rubber toy leads to a reinterpretation of the situation that entails a diminishment of its seriousness and importance as a scientific experiment, inducing a shift to the paratelic mode, and the amount of anxiety-related arousal generated previously influences the degree to which the humor is enjoyed. Nerhardt's (1976) initial difficulties in eliciting mirth with the weight judgment paradigm in the context of a railroad station also point to the importance of the mental set of the participant for humor to occur. Reversal theory would suggest that these subjects, engaged in the goal-oriented activity of traveling from one place to another, were in the telic state, and were unable to switch into the paratelic state that is necessary for humor.

A study by Mio and Graesser (1991), although designed to test disparagement theory using metaphors, can also be viewed as a test of the diminishment hypothesis in reversal theory. In this study, undergraduate students were asked to rate the funniness of a number of metaphor pairs. One metaphor in each pair disparaged the topic of the sentence, whereas the other one uplifted the topic. Consistent with the diminishment hypothesis, the disparaging metaphors were perceived to be more humorous than their uplifting counterparts.

In one of my own studies, I found a significant negative correlation between the Telic Dominance Scale and several measures of sense of humor, indicating that people who are more likely to be in the paratelic state at any given time also tend to laugh and smile more frequently, to notice humorous aspects of the environment, to enjoy humor, and to use humor in coping with stress (R. A. Martin, 1984). Similar results were also found by Ruch (1994). Svebak and Apter (1987) also found that the presentation of humorous material was likely to induce the paratelic state even in individuals who normally tend to remain in the telic state. These findings support the view that humor is associated with the playful paratelic state.

Wyer and Collins (1992) also described two studies that were designed to test some of the hypotheses of reversal theory. In one of these, participants read stories that could be interpreted in two different ways, one of which was less likely to be identified spontaneously than the other. In each case, the less obvious interpretation was more mundane, and therefore involved a diminishment of importance. One story, for example, appeared to be about two people planning a murder, but it could also be interpreted as a discussion of the difficulties encountered in opening a pickle jar. Another story appeared to be the comments of a man making love to a woman, but could also be interpreted as washing a dog. In different versions of the story, cues were inserted to make the subordinate theme more or less obvious. The participants were instructed either to read the stories for understanding (as they would read a magazine article) or to read them with the goal of evaluating their humor, and all subjects were later asked to rate their funniness.

As predicted by reversal theory, the participants were more likely to rate the stories as amusing when statements activating the subordinate theme were included, and this difference was more pronounced in the story comprehension condition than in the humor evaluation condition. The latter finding, which seems counterintuitive, is explained by reversal theory on the basis of the motivational state of the subjects. Those who were instructed to read the stories with a goal in mind were more likely to be in the serious, goal-oriented telic state, even though this goal involved making a humor judgment. They would therefore be less likely to respond to humor than would those who read the stories without a specific goal, an activity that is more compatible with the playful, paratelic state. Incidentally, these findings raise questions about much of the humor appreciation research conducted over several decades, in which subjects have been instructed to evaluate the funniness of various stimuli, where a serious telic state of mind may have interfered with the enjoyment of the humor. This may explain in part why funniness ratings have usually been quite low in such research.

In a second experiment, Wyer and Collins (1992) presented participants with variants of the "quickie" joke about the priest and nun. In the different versions, they selectively removed one or the other of the alternative interpretations of the priest's question and of the nun's identity. In addition, in some versions, the second interpretation of the nun as a prostitute replaced the first (as in incongruity-resolution theory), whereas in other versions the two contradictory interpretations (nun and prostitute) continued to apply simultaneously. Differences in participants' funniness ratings of the different joke versions supported the prediction that the effects on funniness of the two shifts in meaning to more mundane interpretations were independent and additive. However, no support was found for the prediction that the simultaneous retention of the two interpretations would be funnier than the replacement of one interpretation by the other. Further research with a wider range of humor stimuli is needed to provide more definitive tests of this reversal theory hypothesis.

Evaluation

The account of humor provided by reversal theory integrates many of the ideas from the other theories that I have discussed. Like psychoanalytic and superiority theories, it provides an explanation for aggressive, sexual, and other emotional elements in humor. These components are seen as functioning to increase arousal, which is experienced as enjoyable and exciting when one is in the playful frame of mind associated with humor. As well, this theory explains the enjoyment of humor and people's strong motivation for engaging in it in terms of the enjoyment of play. The theory appears to be more consistent with research findings on the role of arousal in humor appreciation than are optimal arousal theories such as Berlyne's. With further developments of the theory proposed by Wyer and Collins (1992) and by Wyer (2004), it also provides a framework for understanding cognitive processes in many different forms of everyday humor and not just jokes. Unlike most of the other theories that we have discussed, this theory also focuses more explicitly on the social context in which humor occurs. Thus, it opens the door to examinations of humor as a form of interpersonal communication from the perspective of social psychology (which I will explore in Chapter 5).

The reversal theory of humor also provides an account of the role of humor in coping with stress (Svebak and Martin, 1997). The capacity of humorous synergies to induce the paratelic state may make it possible for stressful situations to be experienced as challenges to be approached in a playful way rather than as serious threats (R. A. Martin, Kuiper, Olinger, and Dobbin, 1987). In addition, the diminishment aspect of humorous synergies means that humor may be used to reframe anxiety-arousing events or problems as less threatening than they first appear (Kuiper et al., 1993). Although reversal theory is not as widely known among humor researchers, it offers a number of hypotheses that are deserving of further investigation.

More generally, the view of humor as play reminds us that humor is a nonserious, playful activity that differs from more serious modes of thinking. Many of the theories of humor seem to forget this fact, describing the cognitive processes involved in humor comprehension as though they had to do with serious information processing. A play view of humor suggests that jokes may be viewed as a way of playing with cognitive structures and mechanisms, which have evolved in humans for the normally "serious" purpose of making sense and surviving in the world, but in humor are temporarily being manipulated "for fun." Both the teller and the listener of a joke are collaborating in a playful activity, in which multiple interpretations of events are activated and elaborated in an enjoyable way by introducing an incongruous element into the narrative. In more spontaneous forms of humor, people may play with language and ideas or use humor to playfully tease one another. However, although humor is playful and nonserious, this does not mean that it does not have serious functions. For example, humorous teasing may be a way of expressing disapproval or criticism to another person in a way that would be difficult to do using a serious mode of discourse. If the criticism is not well received, one can always say that one was "just joking." These sorts of interpersonal functions of humor will be examined in more detail in Chapter 5.

CONCLUSION

Each of the theories that we have examined in these two chapters contributes a useful perspective, highlighting certain aspects of humor. By combining elements from all of the theories, we obtain a more complete understanding of this multi-faceted phenomenon. Psychoanalytic theory calls our attention to the predominance of aggressive and sexual themes in many jokes, the feelings of emotional pleasure and enjoyment that are engendered by humor, and the strong motivation that most people therefore experience for engaging in it. It also suggests that some of the elements contributing to our enjoyment of humor may be outside our conscious awareness. Superiority/disparagement theories emphasize the social and emotional aspects of humor and call attention to its paradoxical nature, combining both prosocial and aggressive elements. This approach also provides a theoretical basis for views of humor as a way of asserting a sense of victory over the people and situations that threaten us, mastery over the circumstances of life that can otherwise oppress us, and liberation from life's constraints.

Arousal theories underscore the view that humor represents a complex mind-body interaction of cognition and emotion that is rooted in the biological substrates of our brain and nervous system. Incongruity theories shed light on the cognitive-perceptual processes involved in humor, the way it causes us to view people, situations, and events from the perspective of two or more incongruous and seemingly incompatible perspectives at the same time. Finally, the reversal theory perspective combines many of the elements of the other theories, emphasizing that humor is a form of play in which incongruities are enjoyed for their own sake in the context of our interactions with other people. It also highlights the diverse ways we experience humor, including jokes, nonverbal humor, conversational witticisms, and the humorous outlook on the adversities of life that forms the basis of humor as a coping mechanism.

Our review of the early psychological research on humor provides an introduction to the empirical methods that have been used by researchers to answer age-old philosophical questions about humor. Based on the findings of these early studies, as well as theoretical and methodological developments in other areas of psychology, the theories and research methods used by humor researchers have evolved over the years. Some of the ideas and methodologies of these early studies now seem outdated, and many of the answers they provided are still only tentative, but some patterns have emerged. These studies set the stage for subsequent research, guiding the ongoing questions and pointing to potentially useful topics of investigation. In the following chapters, I will discuss more recent developments in the sorts of questions, methods, and findings of humor research in each of the branches of psychology.

CHAPTER 4

The Cognitive Psychology of Humor

We saw in Chapter 1 that humor is a form of play, comprising a social context, a cognitive process, and an emotional response that is expressed through laughter. In this chapter, we focus on the cognitive process, the mental events leading to the perception of incongruity that is the basis of humor. What are the mental processes involved in "getting a joke" or perceiving a situation or event to be funny? In addition, we will examine ways that humor in turn affects other cognitive processes, particularly memory and creative thinking. Are we likely to remember humorous information better than serious information? Does experiencing humor cause people to think more creatively?

These sorts of questions fall into the domain of cognitive psychology, which has been defined as "the study of human mental processes and their role in thinking, feeling, and behaving" (Kellogg, 1995, p. 4). Cognitive psychologists use experimental methods to study how the mind works. Although they recognize that the brain does not function exactly like an electronic computer, they often find it useful to employ a computer analogy in conceptualizing mental processes. Thus, they take an information processing approach to understand how information is taken in through our sensory organs, encoded, stored and retrieved from memory, and used in the comprehension and production of language, problem solving, creativity, decision making, and reasoning. In short, cognitive psychology is concerned with mental representations of meaning and the mental processes that operate on those representations.

For the most part, cognitive psychologists have not taken much interest in the study of humor. Indeed, an examination of the subject indexes of cognitive psychology textbooks reveals almost no references to humor, laughter, or related topics. This is because most cognitive psychologists tend to be interested in more basic mental processes such as attention, perception, memory, and so on. However, one subarea within this field where there is some interest in humor is psycholinguistics. As the name suggests, this is the study of cognitive processes involved in language comprehension and production. Since much humor is based on language, psycholinguistics is a natural domain for the cognitive study of humor. In particular, some researchers within this field who study nonliteral language (e.g., metaphor) have been interested in humorous types of nonliteral language such as irony (e.g., Colston, Giora, and Katz, 2000; Giora, Fein, and Schwartz, 1998) and sarcasm (e.g., Gibbs, 1986; A. N. Katz, Blasko, and Kazmerski, 2004).

Cognitive psychology is part of a broader interdisciplinary enterprise known as cognitive science, which also includes some branches of neuroscience, computer science (artificial intelligence), and linguistics. All of these disciplines have also made important contributions to the study of humor, applying their particular research methods and theoretical approaches. It would be difficult to review the psychology of humor without also touching on the contributions of these other disciplines. In this chapter, I will therefore also briefly review some of the contributions to a cognitive understanding of humor from the disciplines of linguistics and computer science, and I will explore the contributions of neuroscience in Chapter 6.

We saw in Chapter 3 that cognitive theories of humor have been proposed by a number of philosophers since the eighteenth century (e.g., Schopenhauer). During the 1970s, several psychological theories were developed that attempted to provide more rigorous and testable formulations of these ideas (e.g., Rothbart, 1976; Shultz, 1976; Suls, 1972), and these stimulated a number of psychological investigations with many interesting findings (e.g., Deckers and Salais, 1983; Shultz, 1974b; Wicker et al., 1981). However, these theories were still rather vague and not clearly specified. Over the past two decades, there has been a flurry of renewed theoretical activity coming particularly from scholars in linguistics (e.g., Attardo, 1994; Raskin, 1985), but also in psycholinguistics (e.g., Giora, 1991) and computer science (e.g., Ritchie, 2004). These formulations, based on theoretical, empirical, and methodological advances in other areas of their respective disciplines, have generated new hypotheses about cognitive aspects of humor that have only begun to be investigated by psychologists (e.g., Vaid, Hull, Heredia, Gerkens, and Martinez, 2003). These advances will hopefully stimulate further interest among psychologists in the study of cognitive processes in humor.

In this chapter, I will first review ways in which cognitive theorists have made use of concepts from schema theory to understand how we mentally process humorous incongruities. Then I will briefly look at some of the schema-based theories proposed in recent years by linguists. I will then discuss some of the research methods that have been developed by cognitive psychologists to study schemas and related cognitive processes, and will describe some applications of these methods to the study of how we understand humorous information, such as jokes and ironic statements. After this overview of research on cognitive mechanisms and processes in humor comprehension, I will discuss research that has looked at the effects of humor on other aspects of cognition, particularly memory and creativity. Next, I will discuss the contributions of artificial intelligence researchers in the field of computer science. Finally, I will comment on the implications of a view of humor as a form of cognitive play.

HUMOR, INCONGRUITY, AND SCHEMAS

As we saw in the last chapter, cognitively oriented theorists and researchers generally view some type of incongruity as being a defining characteristic of humor. Arthur Koestler's (1964) concept of *bisociation* is an early formulation of incongruity, in which a situation, person, event, or idea is simultaneously perceived from the perspective of two self-consistent but normally incompatible or disparate frames of reference. Apter's (1982) concept of *cognitive synergy* has a similar meaning: two incompatible or even contradictory interpretations of the same object or event are active in the mind at the same time. Typically, humor begins with one interpretation of the situation, and then a second contradictory interpretation is suddenly activated.

Theorists have debated about whether incongruity alone is sufficient for humor (Nerhardt, 1977), or whether incongruity must also be resolved in some way for it to be funny (Shultz, 1972; Suls, 1972). As we saw in Chapter 3, research evidence suggests that incongruity-resolution theories may apply to certain types of jokes, but do not appear to account for all forms of humor (e.g., Nerhardt, 1977). Some theorists have also suggested that the incongruity must occur suddenly (Suls, 1983), must take place in an emotionally pleasant, safe, and nonthreatening context (Rothbart, 1976), must involve an extreme or bizarre discrepancy (Berlyne, 1972), or must be perceived in a playful, nonserious frame of mind (Apter, 1982). Wyer and Collins (1992), following Apter (1982), suggested that, for an incongruity to be funny, the second interpretation that is activated must involve diminishment, that is, the situation or event must be viewed as less important, valuable, or admirable than the view provided by the initial interpretation.

Schemas, Frames, and Scripts

How might these concepts of incongruity be understood from the perspective of cognitive science? Cognitive psychologists have conducted a great deal of research on the way knowledge is represented and organized in our minds. These studies suggest that information is organized in knowledge structures called *schemas* (Bartlett, 1932; Mandler, 1979; Rumelhart and Ortony, 1977). The concept of a schema was originally based on the data structures used in programming languages such as Pascal and Lisp that were commonly employed in artificial intelligence research (Ritchie, 2004). A schema is a dynamic mental representation that enables us to build mental models of the world. Mandler (1979) stated that a schema "is formed on the basis of past experience with objects, scenes, or events and consists of a set of (usually unconscious) expectations about what things look like and/or the order in which they occur" (p. 263).

Schemas describe the general characteristics of an object or event and contain variables or slots that can assume different values in particular instances. For example, a schema for birds would include variables such as the types of wings, feet, beaks, tails, and bodies, which may be instantiated in a number of ways in individual birds. Many different kinds of birds all fit the general schema, with different values for the different variables. The variables often contain default values that represent the prototypical characteristic of the object or event. When we catch a glimpse of a bird or hear about a bird in a story, the schema for birds is activated, and, unless we are given information to the contrary, we expect this particular bird to conform to the default values. The acceptable values of variables in a given schema have certain limits. If we see a drawing of a bird with wings that look like airplane propellers, this would not fit the expected values of the bird schema, and would therefore be an incongruity, something that "does not compute" with respect to our mental model of birds.

Frames (Minsky, 1977) and scripts (Abelson, 1981; Schank and Abelson, 1977) are particular types of schemas that relate to knowledge about the physical environment and routine activities, respectively. For example, Schank and Abelson (1977) described the restaurant script, which organizes information about the normal sequence of events involved in going to a restaurant (sitting at a table, ordering from a menu, being served, eating, paying the bill, leaving the restaurant, etc.). When we hear a narrative about someone going to a restaurant, this script is activated and it leads us to expect certain activities that are normally associated with the script. This also makes it possible for the narrator to leave out many details that we automatically fill in as defaults.

The script also tells us what details of the narrative are appropriate and relevant, and how to evaluate people's actions. As Wyer (2004, p. 199) noted, if we heard that a man went to a restaurant and proceeded to take off his clothes and start playing a guitar, this does not fit with the expected values in our restaurant script, and would be perceived as incongruous. This would stimulate us to reassess the situation and perhaps modify the script or seek another script that might account for the information. For example, we might surmise that the restaurant was in a nudist colony and the man was an entertainer rather than a patron of the restaurant.

Applications of Schema Theory to Humor

These concepts of schemas, frames, and scripts can be used to explain the nature of incongruity in humor, and a number of psychological and linguistic theories of humor, based on these ideas, have been proposed (e.g., Norrick, 1986; Raskin, 1985; Wyer and Collins, 1992). In general, these theories suggest that, while we are hearing the setup of a joke, a schema (or script) is activated to enable us to make sense of the incoming information. However, information in the joke punch line does not fit with the schema, causing us to search for another schema that will make better sense. This second schema typically gives an altogether different (and even contradictory) interpretation of the situation, rather than just a slightly modified perspective. The second script does not completely replace the first one, however, and so the two are activated simultaneously. This simultaneous activation of two incompatible scripts is the essence of humorous incongruity and is experienced as enjoyable and amusing. Different schema-based theories provide somewhat different accounts of these processes, and some also attempt to account for non-joke–related humor, such as conversational witticisms and unintentional humor, as well as jokes.

As an example of a schema-based psychological theory relating to social cognition, Robert Wyer and James Collins (1992) proposed a comprehension-elaboration theory of humor elicitation (see also Wyer, 2004, for further discussion of the model in the context of a broader theory of social cognition). They suggested that humor involves the simultaneous activation of two different schemas to understand the same situation or event. In addition, humor is elicited only if the second schema to be activated produces an interpretation that is diminished in value or importance relative to that of the initial schema. Thus, humor always involves reinterpreting an action or situation as being less admirable and more trivial (i.e., less serious) than it first seemed.

In addition, Wyer and Collins proposed that the elicited humor is greatest when an intermediate amount of time and effort is required to identify and apply the concepts necessary to activate the alternative schema. If it is too difficult or too easy to find the second schema, less humor will be elicited. The amount of humor elicited also depends on the amount of cognitive elaboration that is generated concerning the event and its implications. Cognitive elaboration has to do with the degree to which the activated schemas play back and forth on each other, eliciting further concepts and mental imagery. The more cognitive elaboration is elicited by the humorous event, the more it will be enjoyed and perceived to be funny. Wyer and Collins also discussed the social context in which humor occurs, noting that expectations, norms, motives, and information-processing goals relating to speaker and listener roles need to be considered in explaining humor elicitation. They showed how the theory can be applied to account for humor not only in jokes and funny narratives, but also in witticisms, ironic comments, and fortuitous events that occur spontaneously in social situations.

Thus, the schema-based cognitive theory proposed by Wyer and Collins is a very comprehensive one that is intended to account for all types of humor and not just jokes. It offers numerous interesting hypotheses for future research. While many of their hypotheses are consistent with previous research findings, others still need to be tested empirically. In particular, there has been very little research so far addressing the hypotheses about non-joke–related humor elicited spontaneously in social situations.

One of their hypotheses that has not been supported is the idea that the funniest jokes are the ones that take an intermediate amount of time to process, whereas jokes that are too easy or too difficult to understand are less amusing. This would suggest a curvilinear (inverted-U) relationship between difficulty of comprehension and funniness. Contrary to this view, Peter Derks and his colleagues at the College of William and Mary found a strong negative linear correlation between participants' ratings of the difficulty of comprehension of a series of jokes and their rated funniness, with no curvilinear component (Derks, Staley, and Haselton, 1998). Thus, the easier a joke was to understand, the funnier it was rated to be.

Similarly, two more recent studies reported by William Cunningham and Peter Derks (2005) showed that the more quickly participants were able to identify paragraphs as being jokes, the funnier they found them to be. These authors suggested that humor comprehension should be viewed as an automatic, expert skill that involves implicit and sophisticated knowledge of language and multiple meanings. Consequently, the more automatically accessible a humorous message is (due to its personal relevance and the expertise of the listener), the more amusing and enjoyable it is. Although these findings suggest that some modifications of Wyer and Collins' theory are needed, they are not a serious threat to the theory as a whole.

In Chapter 3 I described research on incongruity using the weight judgment paradigm, in which humor is elicited when research participants lift weights that are greatly discrepant from those in a series of preceding trials. Lambert Deckers and Robert Buttram (1990) reconceptualized the weight judgment paradigm in terms of schema theory, suggesting that the initial weight judgments cause a schema to be built up, and the final weight is perceived as an incongruity with respect to this schema. They also drew parallels between the mental processes involved in the weight judgment task and the processing of jokes. They suggested that two kinds of incongruity may generate humor: incongruity between an expected value and the perceived value of a variable within a single schema (as in the weight judgment paradigm), and incongruity between two different schemas (as occurs in most jokes). In either case, they argued, it is incongruity that produces humor, and not resolution of incongruity.

Wyer and Collins (1992), however, conceptualized the incongruity occurring in the weight judgment paradigm somewhat differently. Taking a broader social cognition perspective, rather than focusing only on the discrepancy between the expected weight and the observed weight, these authors discussed the paradigm in terms of the schemas presumably involved in the participants' perceptions of the experimental situation as a whole. Initially, subjects view the experiment as a serious, scientific enterprise, but when they encounter the extremely light or heavy weight, they begin to suspect that the experimenter may be playing a trick on them. After having them compare a number of barely discernible differences in weights, why is the experimenter suddenly asking them to test a weight that is so obviously much heavier or lighter? A new schema concerning the situation is evoked ("Could this be a joke?"), and this schema is enough to trigger a smile or chuckle. In Apter's (1982) terms, this may also cause them to momentarily shift from a serious, scientific mode into a playful (paratelic) mode. Thus, Wyer and Collins' approach takes into account the broader social context of all humor, instead of focusing narrowly on the immediate joke or stimulus as have most past researchers and theorists. These competing hypotheses about the incongruities occurring in the weight judgment paradigm could be tested in further research, perhaps using some of the schema-based methodologies that I will describe shortly.

LINGUISTIC APPROACHES TO HUMOR

In recent years, a considerable amount of work has been done by linguists in the development of formal theories of humor (for a review, see Attardo, 1994). Not surprisingly, linguists who are interested in humor focus on types of humor that are communicated through language, rather than nonverbal forms like practical jokes or slapstick comedy. Linguistics comprises a number of subfields, including phonology (the study of speech sounds), syntax (grammatical rules that specify the acceptable form of sentences), semantics (language meaning), and pragmatics (rules for appropriate social use and interpretation of language in context). The areas that are most relevant to humor research are semantics and pragmatics.

Linguists working in the field of semantics are interested in many of the issues that I have been discussing concerning the way humorous narratives ("texts") are processed, understood, and interpreted as funny (e.g., Norrick, 1986; Raskin, 1985). In the area of pragmatics, linguists are interested in the way humor is communicated in everyday conversation and the functions of humorous communications, such as joke-telling, teasing, and irony, in interpersonal interactions (e.g., Graham, Papa, and Brooks, 1992; Norrick, 2003). I will touch briefly on pragmatics later in this chapter, and will examine it in more detail in Chapter 5 in relation to the social psychology of humor. In this section I will focus particularly on a linguistic theory from the field of semantics.

The script-based semantic theory developed by linguists Victor Raskin, at Purdue University, and Salvatore Attardo, at Youngstown State University (Attardo and Raskin, 1991; Raskin, 1985), is the most well-developed linguistic theory of humor and the one that is best known to psychologists. This theory attempts to model the comprehension of verbal humor, with a particular focus on jokes. The theory incorporates ideas about scripts (discussed above) and was also influenced by Noam Chomsky's (1957, 1971) concepts of transformational generative grammars for relating the deep structure, or underlying meaning, of a text to its surface structure (the actual words that are used). Raskin's (1985) original Semantic Script Theory of Humor (SSTH) is meant to provide a formal model of humor competence (i.e., how can a text be recognized as humorous?).

The goal of this theory, then, is to provide a model of a hypothetical information-processing system that is capable of making sense of a humorous text, but not necessarily the way humans actually do it. In theory, the model could eventually be turned into a computer program for processing humor. Thus, in the linguistics approach, the concern is not so much whether the theory describes actual human information processing, and therefore linguists typically do not conduct experiments to test their theories on human subjects. Instead, they use logical reasoning to see whether the theory is internally coherent and whether it accounts for a wide range of text examples (i.e., jokes). The ideal test would be to implement it in a computer program and demonstrate that it is capable of distinguishing between humorous and nonhumorous scripts.

Raskin's theory conceives of scripts as graphs with lexical nodes and semantic links between nodes. Scripts are assumed to be nested within scripts and, in theory, all the scripts of the language make up a single continuous graph, forming a multidimensional semantic network that contains all the information a speaker has about his or her culture. Words in a sentence are thought to evoke the script or scripts with which they are associated. The theory also assumes a set of combinatorial rules for combining all the possible meanings of the scripts that are evoked by a text, discarding those that do not yield a coherent reading, and coming up with an overall, coherent meaning of the text.

Based on these concepts, Raskin (1985, p. 99) stated the main hypothesis of his theory as follows:

> A text can be characterized as a single-joke-carrying text if both of the [following] conditions . . . are satisfied: (i) The text is compatible, fully or in part, with two different scripts; and (ii) the two scripts with which the text is compatible are opposite in a special sense . . .

Thus, when an individual is attempting to understand a joke, a mental script is activated to make sense of the events that are described in the joke setup. However, the punch line of the joke introduces elements that are not compatible with that original script, triggering a switch from one script to another. The punch line makes the listener backtrack and realize that a different interpretation (i.e., an alternative script) was possible from the beginning. In order for the text to be viewed as humorous, this second, overlapping script must be opposite to the first. There are three general ways in which the scripts may be in opposition to one another: actual versus nonactual, normal versus abnormal, or possible versus impossible. At a more concrete level, script oppositions may be manifested in terms of such pairs as good versus bad, life versus death, obscene versus nonobscene, money versus no money, high stature versus low stature, clean versus dirty, intelligent versus unintelligent, and so on.

Raskin used the following joke to illustrate how the model works:

> "Is the doctor at home?" the patient asked in his bronchial whisper. "No," the doctor's young and pretty wife whispered in reply. "Come right in."

According to Raskin's theory, the first part of this joke evokes a standard "doctor" script (which is presumably stored in the listener's semantic network) in which a patient presents himself at a doctor's residence to be treated for an illness that causes him to have a hoarse voice, and is told that the doctor is not there. However, the doctor's wife's invitation for the patient to enter the house anyway does not fit with the "doctor" script, so the listener must backtrack and reevaluate the text. The information that the doctor's wife is young and pretty and that she is inviting the patient into her house when her husband is away activates a different (i.e., "lover") script. Both the "doctor" script and the "lover" script are compatible with the text, and these two scripts are opposed to one another on the sex versus no-sex basis. Consequently, the joke fulfills the requirements of the theory and is evaluated as humorous. Note that Raskin's theory is more consistent with Koestler's and Apter's ideas of "bisociation" and "cognitive synergy" than with Shultz's and Suls' incongruity-resolution theories because, in Raskin's theory, both scripts are activated at the same time, rather than one replacing the other.

Attardo and Raskin (1991) further extended and revised Raskin's original SSTH into a broader linguistic theory, which they called the General Theory of Verbal Humor (GTVH), which addresses other areas of linguistics such as pragmatics and discourse analysis, in addition to semantics. This revised theory is a model of joke representation, which posits a hierarchical arrangement of six Knowledge Resources (KRs), or hypothetical databases, that are thought to be involved in the cognitive representation and analysis of humorous texts. The six KRs, in order from most abstract to most concrete, are: Script Oppositions (SO), Logical Mechanisms (LM), Situations (SI), Targets (TA), Narrative Strategies (NS), and Language (LA). Raskin's original SSTH theory corresponds to the SO component, and is thus just one subset of this broader theory. LM refers to the "joke techniques" or "pseudo-logic" used to activate the alternate script in a joke. These include such mechanisms as figure-ground reversal, juxtaposition, analogy, parallelism, and faulty reasoning. SI refers to the people, objects, activities, and so on, involved in the particular joke. TA (which are not necessarily present in all jokes) refers to the "butt" or victim of the joke. NS refers to the "genre" or format of the joke (e.g., riddle or expository text). Finally, LA is the actual wording of the joke.

Attardo (1997) discussed the relationship between the GTVH and traditional incongruity-resolution theories of humor. He argued for a "three-stage" (setup-incongruity-resolution) rather than a "two-stage" (incongruity-resolution) model of joke comprehension. Attardo suggested that incongruity has to do with the SO component, resolution corresponds to the LM component, and setup refers to the overlap between the two scripts. Note, however, that this formulation is different from traditional incongruity-resolution theories, since it views the resolution as coming before the incongruity, that is, the logical mechanism (which Attardo identifies with resolution) activates the alternative script, which, along with the initial script, creates the incongruity. Thus, the GTVH (like the SSTH that it subsumes) assumes that humor arises from the concurrent activation of two incompatible scripts, and is therefore similar to the views of Koestler (1964), Apter (1982), and Wyer (2004) and different from the incongruity-resolution models of Shultz (1976) and Suls (1972), which posit that humor is elicited only after the incongruity has been eliminated (i.e., resolved).

Attardo, Hempelmann, and Di Maio (2002) developed further the concept of logical mechanisms, and proposed formulations of the model using graph theory and set theory. Attardo (1998) extended the GTVH to allow for the analysis of humorous texts that are longer than jokes. To do this, he introduced a variety of additional concepts such as jab and punch lines, macro- and micro-narratives, levels of narratives, strands of lines, stacks of strands, and intertextual jokes. (An explanation of these concepts is beyond the scope of the present discussion.) Attardo also demonstrated how this more complex model could be applied by using it to analyze a segment of a television sitcom. Thus, an attempt has been made to extend the theory so that it can account for spontaneous conversational humor in addition to canned jokes.

Although this brief overview certainly does not do justice to linguistic theories of humor, it should give readers from psychology some sense of the kinds of theories that have been developed by linguists, which could potentially be used as a source of testable hypotheses for psychological research. For example, psychologist Willibald Ruch teamed up with Attardo and Raskin (Ruch, Attardo, and Raskin, 1993) to conduct an empirical study designed to test some aspects of the GTVH. In particular, they evaluated the hypothesis that subjects' perceptions of similarities between pairs of jokes will decrease in a linear fashion as the jokes differ from each other at successively higher levels of the KR hierarchy. Research participants were presented with pairs of jokes differing from one another at various levels of the hierarchy. For example, two jokes might be identical in every way except that they involved different script oppositions, or different logical mechanisms. The participants were instructed to rate how similar the jokes were in each pair. In general, the results conformed to predictions, with greater similarities being found between jokes that differed at lower levels of the hierarchy. However, there were some inconsistencies in the exact ordering of the KRs, particularly in the case of LM, suggesting that some modification of this aspect of the theory may be required.

Another empirical investigation making use of the GTVH was reported by Italian psychologist Giovannantonio Forabosco (1994), who conducted two experiments examining the effects of seriality on joke appreciation. In particular, he was interested in determining whether, when presented with a series of jokes, people find particular jokes to be less funny if they are similar to ones that they have already seen. Using the GTVH framework, the degree of similarity between jokes was manipulated by varying the number of knowledge resources that they shared. As predicted, the more similar a group of jokes were, the more they exhibited a seriality effect, such that those presented later in the series were rated as being less funny than those presented earlier. These investigations provide examples of how psychological research methods might be used to test linguistic theories of humor, as well as how linguistic theories might be used to inform psychological research.

PSYCHOLOGICAL APPROACHES TO THE STUDY OF SCHEMAS IN HUMOR

Semantic Distance

Cognitive psychologists have developed a number of experimental techniques for investigating hypotheses derived from schema theories. An early approach made use of the idea of semantic distances between words or concepts based on semantic differential ratings. This methodology was pioneered by Charles Osgood and his colleagues as a means of exploring the way meaning is represented in the mind (Osgood, Suci, and Tannenbaum, 1957; Snider and Osgood, 1969). It involved having a large number of research participants rate particular words or concepts on a series of rating scales, each scale representing a dimension between a pair of adjectives with opposite meanings (e.g., hot-cold, fast-slow, likable-unlikable). These ratings were then factor analyzed to identify a smaller number of basic dimensions (factors) that capture most of the variance in the ratings.

Using ratings of a large number of concepts and many different samples of participants, Osgood and his colleagues repeatedly found three basic orthogonal factors, which he labeled Activity (active-passive), Evaluative (good-bad), and Potency (strong-weak). These three factors appear to be basic dimensions by which people mentally organize meanings that they attach to a wide range of concepts. The factors can be conceptualized as dimensions of a hypothetical three-dimensional cognitive "space" in which people store words and concepts in their minds. The factor loadings of a particular word or concept can be used to identify where the concept is stored in this space. Concepts that are similar in meaning are stored closely together in this hypothetical semantic space, since they have similar loadings on the three factors, whereas those that are quite different in meaning have different loadings and are stored at more distant locations. Thus, semantic distances between pairs of words or concepts can be quantified by means of the difference in their loadings on the semantic differential factors. This technique provided cognitive researchers a method for investigating the way knowledge or meanings of concepts are organized in people's minds.

This method was applied to the study of humor by Michael Godkewitsch (1974), at the University of Toronto, using the semantic distances between pairs of words as a method of quantifying incongruity. Participants were presented with a number of adjective-noun pairs and asked to rate them for funniness and wittiness. The degree of smiling and laughter of participants was also observed. The semantic distance between the words in each pair was computed on the basis of their loadings on the semantic differential factors. As predicted by incongruity theory, adjective-noun pairs that were more discrepant from one another in semantic space were judged to be funnier and evoked more smiles. For example, the adjective-noun pair "happy child," in which both words load similarly on the semantic differential factors, was not seen as very funny. In contrast, "wise egg," with an intermediate distance, was funnier, and "hot poet," with a high semantic distance, was even funnier. Although, admittedly, the humor evoked by these word pairs was not very great, it was systematically related to the semantic distance between the two words in each pair, providing support for incongruity theories of humor.

Tim Hillson and I also employed a semantic distance procedure to model the concept of resolution as well as incongruity in such simple verbal stimuli (Hillson and Martin, 1994). We hypothesized that word pairs that are quite distant on some dimensions of semantic space (incongruity) but are also quite close on other dimensions (resolution of incongruity) might be funnier than those that are either distant or close on all dimensions. We employed a methodology, called the domain-interaction approach, which had previously been used in the study of metaphors by other researchers (e.g., Trick and Katz, 1986). As humor stimuli, we used simple metaphor-like statements combining two concepts in the form "A is the B of A's domain" (e.g., "George Bush is the buzzard of world leaders"). The domains used were actors, world leaders, birds, makes of cars, foods, and magazines, and within each domain we used four nouns (e.g., Sylvester Stallone and Woody Allen were two of the actors).

Semantic differential ratings provided by a group of subjects on these nouns and domain names were factor analyzed, yielding four factors. We identified two of the factors as domain-distinguishing (i.e., different nouns within a given domain were found to have very similar loadings on these two factors, while nouns from different domains had more distant loadings). The other two factors were identified as domain-insensitive (i.e., different nouns within the same domain could have quite different loadings on these two factors). On the basis of these factor loadings, two types of semantic distance between the nouns were computed: a within-domain distance (using the domain-insensitive factor loadings), and a between-domain distance (using the domain-distinguishing factor loadings). We considered between-domain distance to be a way of operationally defining incongruity (greater distance = greater incongruity), and within-domain distance to be a way of operationalizing resolution (less distance = greater resolution).

We then created metaphor-like sentences using pairs of nouns from different domains and asked a second group of participants to rate them for funniness. As predicted (and consistent with the findings of Godkewitsch, 1974), the between-domain distance (incongruity) of the noun pairs in each sentence showed a significant positive correlation with the funniness ratings of the jokes. That is, noun pairs with greater between-domain distance were rated as more funny. Also as predicted, within-domain distance (resolution) showed no simple correlation with funniness, but did produce a significant interaction with between-domain distance in predicting funniness ratings. In particular, sentences that were rated as most funny were those that showed both high between-domain distance (incongruity) and low within-domain distance (resolution). To illustrate, a sentence that received a relatively high mean humor rating was "Woody Allen is the quiche of actors." The between-domain semantic distance between Woody Allen and quiche was large (actors are quite different from foods on some dimensions), but the within-domain distance was small (Woody Allen and quiche are quite similar in some ways within their respective domains). Thus, there is incongruity but also some sort of resolution to the incongruity (i.e., the incongruity "makes sense" in some way).

The semantic distance approach did seem to capture some relevant dimensions of humor, as it was able to systematically predict funniness ratings of simple verbal material. It could still be a useful method for exploring various additional parameters that may be relevant to some types of humor. However, this technique has several limitations. It provides only a static picture of the organization of semantic meaning, and is therefore not useful for examining the processes whereby cognitive structures (schemas) are activated over time in processing humorous information. It also assumes that cognitive organization is the same in all people, and, because mean ratings are averaged across large numbers of participants, it is not amenable to studying individual differences in humor comprehension. In addition, it allows only for the study of simple "pseudo-jokes" made up of word pairs, rather than more complex real jokes and other natural forms of humorous material.

Semantic Priming Techniques

More recently, cognitive psychologists have developed a number of more sophisticated experimental techniques for studying schema activation in real time with more naturalistic stimuli. An example of such techniques is the use of lexical decision tasks to determine whether or not a particular schema has been activated (primed) as a result of exposure to some previous information. In these tasks, research participants are presented with a string of letters on a computer screen and are asked to indicate as quickly as possible whether the letter string is a real word or a nonword (i.e., a random string of letters) by pressing one of two keys associated with each of these options. The reaction time for making this response is measured in milliseconds.

Studies have shown that, on those trials in which the target letters form a word, if the word on the screen is semantically related to a schema that has been previously activated (or "primed"), participants will respond faster than if it is not related to an activated schema, presumably because the information is more readily accessible in their minds. For example, if participants have been thinking about cats (and therefore the cat schema has been activated) they will respond more quickly to the word *whiskers* (which is semantically related to the cat schema) than they would if they had been thinking about automobiles and an automobile schema was therefore primed. Consequently, this methodology can be used by researchers to determine whether or not a particular schema has been activated in an individual at a given point in time. For example, this sort of lexical decision task has been used by psycholinguists to determine the way various scripts become activated while people are reading narrative texts (e.g., Sharkey and Mitchell, 1985).

Recently, psychologists have begun to make use of techniques such as the Lexical Decision Semantic Priming Task in the study of humor comprehension. For example, Jyotsna Vaid and her colleagues (2003) at Texas A&M University used this technique to study schema activation during the reading of jokes. Based on incongruity theory, they hypothesized that an initial schema (S1) is activated during the joke setup, and a second, surprising or incongruous, schema (S2) is activated later in the joke. For example, in the joke about the patient and the doctor's wife discussed previously, S1 would be the "doctor" script and S2 would be the "lover" script. These researchers were interested in determining whether S2 becomes activated relatively early while reading the setup or whether it is not activated until the punch line. They also wished to determine whether S2 replaces S1, so that only S2 remains active by the end of the joke (the selective attention view), or whether both S1 and S2 remain activated concurrently right up to the end of the joke (the concurrent activation view). This question is relevant to the competing predictions made by incongruity-resolution theories, such as those of Suls (1972) and Shultz (1976), versus concurrent activation theories such as those of Attardo and Raskin (1991) and Wyer and Collins (1992).

Vaid and her colleagues presented participants with a series of jokes printed on a computer screen. Each joke was divided into three segments, with the setup being divided into two parts to form the first two segments, and the punch line forming the third segment. After each segment, the subjects were presented with a lexical decision probe involving words that were semantically related to either the initial schema (S1) or the second (incongruous) schema (S2) (the schemas had been identified in pretesting of the jokes with a different group of subjects). If, after a particular joke segment, reaction times for making a particular word-nonword discrimination were significantly shorter than those found in a baseline test, this would indicate that the schema associated with the particular word was activated by that point in processing the joke.

The results revealed that the initial schemas (S1) were activated during the presentation of the first two segments of the jokes (i.e., throughout the setup), whereas the incongruous second schemas (S2) became activated during the second segment (i.e., the second half of the setup). Unexpectedly, however, *neither* of the schemas was found to be activated at the final time point (immediately after the punch line). These results were difficult to explain. On the one hand, they seemed to show some support for the concurrent activation view, since S2 was not more strongly activated than S1 by the end of the joke. On the other hand, though, the lack of activation of either schema by that point was inconsistent with either hypothesis. This finding needs to be replicated in further research before firm conclusions can be drawn. Interestingly, the finding that S2 was primed well before the punch line suggests that numerous potential schemas may be activated even before the incongruity is encountered. This finding seems to provide additional evidence, consistent with the findings of Kenny (1955) and Pollio and Mers (1974), discussed in Chapter 3, that the recipients of a joke have already anticipated the "true" meaning of the joke well before they hear the punch line, rather than it being unexpected (as suggested by incongruity-resolution theories).

In a second experiment, Vaid and her colleagues (2003) used the same methodology to examine the activation of the two schemas more than four seconds after a joke was presented, giving the participants ample time to process the joke meaning. Here, the results showed priming for the second schema (S2) but not for the initial schema (S1). These findings were interpreted as supporting the selective attention view, since only the second joke meaning appears to be primed after the joke is fully processed. Because they did not include lexical decision probes at times closer to the ending of the joke, however, these results are not conclusive. Further research is needed to replicate these studies and to investigate the priming of schemas at multiple time points during and after the presentation of jokes.

Other methods that have been developed for psycholinguistic research on schema activation could also be adapted to address research questions relating to humor. An example is the Cross-Modal Lexical Priming Task, which was used by Stewart and

Heredia (2002) to study schema activation during metaphor comprehension. In this technique, auditory information (e.g., a joke or funny narrative) is presented to research participants via headphones, and probe words related to various schemas are presented visually on a computer screen at precise moments during the auditory presentation. The participants are instructed to read these probe words aloud as quickly as possible, and the reaction times for reading the words are recorded. Since words that are semantically related to currently activated schemas are spoken more quickly than those unrelated to activated schemas, this is another way of testing whether or not particular schemas have been primed.

Another method is the Word Fragment Completion Test (e.g., Giora and Fein, 1999) in which participants are instructed to complete a fragmented (partially spelled out) word with the first word they can think of. Words that are semantically more closely related to currently primed schemas can be completed more quickly. Thus, these methods can be used to determine whether particular schemas have been activated at particular points during the processing of jokes and other humorous texts.

As this brief overview shows, these sorts of techniques hold a great deal of promise for cognitive research on humor, enabling researchers to test specific hypotheses about the time course of schema activation during the processing of humorous texts. More studies are needed to replicate the initial findings of Vaid et al. (2003), to clarify the patterns that have been observed, and to broaden the scope of inquiry. These authors listed a number of unanswered research questions, including the precise timing and duration of activation of the schemas, the role of individual differences in joke processing, the effects of manipulating subjects' expectations about whether or not they will be encountering humorous materials, the degree to which meaning activation in joke processing is subject to strategic versus automatic control, and the processes involved in different types of humorous texts besides jokes, such as humor occurring spontaneously in conversation (e.g., irony, witticisms). Besides greatly enriching our understanding of the cognitive processes involved in humor, the results of these sorts of investigations should help to address long-standing debates among theorists, such as the debate about incongruity versus incongruity-resolution as the basis of humor.

COGNITIVE PROCESSES IN CONVERSATIONAL HUMOR: IRONY AND SARCASM

Much of the past theoretical and empirical work on cognitive aspects of humor has focused particularly on jokes. For example, Attardo and Raskin's GTVH was designed primarily to explain joke comprehension. However, as noted in Chapter 1, most of the humor that we encounter in everyday life is not in the form of "canned" jokes (R. A. Martin and Kuiper, 1999; Provine, 2000). Much everyday humor arises from spontaneous intentional and unintentional verbal and nonverbal behaviors of people interacting with one another, such as witty retorts, wordplay, banter, teasing, irony, sarcasm, slips of the tongue, practical jokes, and pratfalls (Long and Graesser, 1988; Norrick, 1993, 2003).

Since jokes are context-free and self-contained, and can be told in many conversational contexts, they are relatively easy to analyze and they lend themselves well to experimental research. Conversational humor, however, depends more on the constantly changing social context and therefore poses greater challenges for theorists and researchers. Nonetheless, some theoretical and empirical work has been done in this area in recent years by cognitive psychologists (particularly psycholinguists) and linguists (primarily those working in the areas of pragmatics and discourse analysis). For example, Wyer and Collins (Wyer, 2004, 1992) showed how their comprehension-elaboration theory of humor elicitation can be used to account for many types of witticisms as well as unintentional humor and even nonverbal humor. Norrick (1986) also applied his schema conflict theory to a variety of conversational witticisms in addition to jokes, including witty retorts, quips, and one-liners. Lippman and Dunn (2000) also conducted a series of experiments on appreciation and memory for puns.

One type of conversational humor that has received particular theoretical and empirical attention in recent years is irony. Irony is a figure of speech that communicates the opposite of what is said. For example, someone who says "What a beautiful day!" during a bleak and miserable day is actually communicating "What an awful day." Although irony is not always funny, it can be a source of humor. Irony is also closely related to sarcasm, which depends for its effect on "bitter, caustic, and other ironic language that is usually directed against an individual" (Gibbs, 1986, p. 3). For example, if someone says "You're a fine friend" to someone who has been unkind, this is an ironic statement that is also sarcastic.

Psycholinguist Rachel Giora and her colleagues at Tel Aviv University have proposed a graded salience theory of humor that is based on pragmatics and focuses primarily on irony. Giora (1985, 1995) suggested that there are implicit rules that people follow while engaging in conversation ("discourse"): (1) all messages should be relevant to the topic of conversation (the relevance requirement); (2) successive messages should be gradually more informative, and not less informative, than preceding ones (the graded informativeness requirement); and (3) any deviation from the first two rules should be "marked" with an explicit semantic connector such as "by the way" or "after all." When we are attempting to understand the meaning of something another person says during a conversation, we are initially guided by the "graded salience principle," which dictates that salient meanings (i.e., the more conventional, common, familiar, or prototypical meanings) are always activated first. If the salient meaning does not match the context (doesn't make sense), then less salient meanings are activated. Subsequently, there is a contextual integration phase, in which any meanings that have been activated are either retained, or suppressed as irrelevant or disruptive, or permitted to fade.

An ironic statement in a conversation, according to Giora (1995, 1998), conforms to the relevance requirement, since it introduces information about the current topic of conversation, but it violates the graded informativeness requirement, since it introduces an improbable message whose salient meaning is either too informative or not informative enough. To understand the ironic statement, the listener first activates its salient (literal) meaning, but, since this does not make sense in the context, must then activate an "unmarked" interpretation (the "implicature"), and both of these meanings remain activated in order for them to be compared. The incongruity between the two activated meanings causes the irony to be humorous. In addition to explaining irony, Giora (1991) also applied her graded salience theory to the understanding of jokes. Although this theory is similar in many ways to Raskin's (1985) script-based theory, Giora's theory takes the social context of humor into account, and is therefore more applicable to non-joke–related humor. Indeed, Norrick (2003) has applied Giora's theory to various types of conversational witticisms, including puns and amusing anecdotes.

Some implications of Giora's theory are that comprehension of ironic statements should take longer than nonironic statements (since it involves activating two meanings), and that both meanings should remain activated after the "true" meaning of the ironic statement has been understood. These predictions are in contrast to some other theories (e.g., H. H. Clark and Gerrig, 1984; Gibbs, 1994; Sperber, 1984) that suggest that, given enough contextual information, irony (and other nonliteral language) is processed in the same way as literal language (known as the Processing Equivalence Hypothesis). According to these views, irony should take no longer to understand than literal language, and only the ironic meaning will be activated.

Although some research findings seem to provide support for the Processing Equivalence Hypothesis (e.g. Gibbs, 1986), Giora (1995) reinterpreted these findings in light of her own theory. In addition, Giora and her colleagues have conducted several experiments that provide evidence in support of her graded salience theory and against the Processing Equivalence Hypothesis. For example, Giora, Fein, and Schwartz (1998) showed that reading a statement in an ironically biased context (i.e., at the end of a story in which the statement is clearly meant to be taken ironically) takes longer than reading the same utterance in a literally biased context (where the preceding story supports a literal interpretation), indicating that more processing is taking place in the case of irony comprehension. In another experiment, using the Lexical Decision Semantic Priming Technique described earlier, they showed that both the ironic and literal meanings of sentences were activated when they were presented in an ironically biased context, but only the literal meanings were activated in a literally biased context. Giora and Fein (1999) also found similar results using the Word Fragment Completion Procedure to test meaning activation.

More recent research suggests that the conflict between the Processing Equivalence and Graded Salience Hypotheses may be resolved by taking the social context into account. Albert Katz, a cognitive psychologist at the University of Western Ontario, and his colleagues summarized a body of research investigating the way individuals process sarcastic statements when they have been provided with information about the interpersonal context, such as the degree of relatedness and shared knowledge of the participants in a conversation, or the gender and occupation of the speaker (A. N. Katz et al., 2004). Taken together, these studies showed that the speed with which people recognize statements as sarcasm depends on their prior information about the context.

For example, some studies found that, when subjects are told that a statement was made by a male, they take no longer to read sarcastic statements than literal statements (supporting the Processing Equivalence Hypothesis), whereas when the statement is made by a female, sarcastic sentences take longer to read than literal ones (supporting the Graded Salience Hypothesis). These findings suggest that, since males are generally perceived as being more likely to use sarcasm than are females, the sarcastic meaning of an utterance by a male is more readily available during the comprehension process. In contrast, when a woman makes a sarcastic comment, the literal meaning tends to be activated initially, before the sarcastic meaning is accessed, resulting in lengthier processing. Similar differences in processing time were found when participants were given information about the occupation of the speaker. Sarcastic statements were processed very quickly when the speaker was described as being either a comedian or a factory worker, but they required longer processing time when the speaker was said to be a priest or teacher (occupations that are stereotypically viewed as less likely to use sarcasm).

Katz and his colleagues (2004) proposed a constraint-satisfaction model to account for these sorts of findings. According to this theory, different sources of information about the social context (i.e., constraints) provide probabilistic support for different possible interpretations of an utterance (e.g., whether it is literal or sarcastic). These constraints operate in parallel while a sentence is being processed. If the constraints all point in the same direction, competition between alternative interpretations is resolved rapidly, whereas settling on an interpretation takes longer if support for different alternatives is nearly equal. Thus, the social context in which ironic or sarcastic statements are made plays an important role in determining how efficiently they are interpreted. If all indicators point toward a humorous interpretation right from the start, the incongruity of humor can be interpreted very quickly.

Other recent psycholinguistic investigations of the comprehension of nonliteral humorous language have provided further evidence of the importance of taking the interpersonal context into account. For example, Penny Pexman and Meghan Zvaigzne (2004), at the University of Calgary, examined the effect of the closeness of a relationship on participants' comprehension of ironic insults and compliments. Ironic insults are positive statements that are intended to be taken as criticisms (e.g., saying "You're a fine friend" when someone has done something unkind), whereas ironic compliments are negative statements that are intended to be taken positively (e.g., saying "Too bad you can't play baseball" when someone has just scored a home run). Participants were presented with vignettes describing either a close friend or a casual acquaintance making a positive or a negative statement in a positive or a negative social context, and were asked to rate these statements on a number of dimensions.

As expected, when the positivity of the statement was incongruent with the positivity of the context (e.g., a positive statement in a negative context), the statements were perceived by the participants to be ironic, regardless of whether the statement took place between close friends or casual acquaintances. However, the closeness of the relationship affected the perceived funniness of these ironic statements: irony occurring between close friends, as compared to casual acquaintances, was rated as more humorous, especially if it was an ironic compliment. Irony between close friends (as compared to acquaintances) was also more likely to be perceived as friendly teasing and less likely to be viewed as having either a positive or negative impact on their relationship. Interestingly, ironic compliments were rated as being less polite than literal compliments, whereas ironic insults were rated as being more polite than literal insults. The authors concluded from their overall findings that humor in the form of irony plays a role in building and maintaining close relationships. In addition, the presence of solidarity and closeness in a relationship acts as a cue for interpreting the intention of the ironic speaker, facilitating the second-order inferences that are needed to understand such nonliteral remarks. Thus, social factors as well as linguistic factors are important for understanding irony.

Overall, then, in recent years there has been some debate among psycholinguists concerning the cognitive processes involved in the comprehension of irony and sarcasm, and this has stimulated a considerable amount of interesting research (see Creusere, 1999, for a review). Moreover, as cognitive psychologists have moved beyond the study of jokes to these more conversational forms of humor, their research has increasingly taken the interpersonal context into account, examining the effects of social as well as linguistic factors on cognitive processing of humor. Similar research efforts will hopefully be applied to investigate other types of conversational humor besides irony and sarcasm. The techniques for assessing schema activation that I have discussed are potentially useful tools for further creative research in this area.

EFFECTS OF HUMOR ON COGNITION

Thus far, I have examined cognitive processes that are involved in humor comprehension. I now turn to a discussion of the possible effects of humor on other aspects of cognition, focusing particularly on creativity and memory.

Creativity

Many theorists and researchers have noted a close relationship between humor and creativity. Koestler (1964) considered humor, along with scientific discovery and artistic creation, to be forms of creativity, all of which involved the process of bisociation (discussed earlier). Just as elements like incongruity, surprise, and novelty are seen by theorists as necessary elements of humor, these are also seen by creativity theorists as defining characteristics of creativity (e.g., Besemer and Treffinger, 1981; Mednick, 1962). Thus, both humor and creativity involve a switch of perspective, a new way of looking at things. Indeed, many creativity researchers consider humor to be essentially a type of creativity. Consequently, some measures of creative ability or creative personality that they have developed include assessments of humor among their items (e.g., G. A. Davis and Subkoviak, 1975; Torrance, 1966).

Several studies have also investigated the creativity involved in subjects' humor-ous productions (e.g., Derks, 1987; Derks and Hervas, 1988). Murdock and Ganim (1993) reviewed the theoretical literature on humor and creativity, and concluded that humor can be considered a subset of creativity, recommending that they be studied within similar conceptual frameworks. However, O'Quin and Derks (1997) disagreed with this view. On the basis of the existing research evidence, they concluded that, although there are close theoretical links between the two, creativity and humor should be considered two separate but partially overlapping domains.

A large number of studies have examined the relation between trait measures of sense of humor and measures of creative abilities and traits, indicating a moderate relationship between the two (see O'Quin and Derks, 1997, for a review). Thus, indi-viduals with a greater sense of humor also tend to be more creative in other areas. However, this correlational research does not provide evidence of a causal influence. Indeed, O'Quin and Derks (1997) pointed out that the two may be related due to the common influence of a third variable, such as intelligence. Here I am interested par-ticularly in the potential effects of humor on creativity. Does exposure to humor cause people to be more creative in their thinking? There are at least two possible mecha-nisms by which humor may be expected to affect creativity. First, the flexible thought processes and activation of multiple schemas involved in the processing of incon-gruities in humor may facilitate the flexible and divergent thinking required for cre-ativity (Belanger, Kirkpatrick, and Derks, 1998). Second, the positive emotion (i.e., mirth) associated with humor may reduce tension and anxiety, resulting in less rigid-ity of thinking and an enhanced ability to relate and integrate divergent material (Isen, Daubman, and Nowicki, 1987).

A number of experiments have provided considerable evidence that exposure to humor produces an increase in people's creative potential. Israeli psychologist Avner Ziv (1976) compared scores of tenth grade students on two tests of verbal creativity after they had either listened to a recording of a popular comedian or engaged in a nonhumorous activity. Compared to the controls, those in the humor condition obtained significantly higher scores on measures of fluency, flexibility, and original-ity, as well as total creativity.

In the 1980s, psychologist Alice Isen, at the University of Maryland, and her col-leagues conducted a series of studies demonstrating facilitative effects of positive emotion on creativity (Isen et al., 1987; Isen, Johnson, Mertz, and Robinson, 1985). Creativity was assessed by a variety of methods, including the Remote Associates Test, unusual word associations, and problem-solving tasks requiring creative ingenuity. Although Isen and her colleagues conceptualized their findings in terms of positive affect in general rather than humor in particular, in most of these studies they used exposure to comedy films as one method of inducing positive emotion. The studies generally showed that exposure to comedy resulted in more creative responses as com-pared to emotionally neutral or negative control conditions. Since these findings also occurred with nonhumorous methods of inducing positive emotions, it appears that the creativity-enhancing effects of humor are likely due to effects of mirth (i.e., the emotional component of humor) on cognition rather than to a more cognitive mechanism such as the idea that activation of multiple schemas in humor produces increased cognitive flexibility. Other research has shown that positive emotional states (including humor-related mirth) affect a variety of cognitive processes including memory, judgment, willingness to take risks, cognitive organization, and decision making (Isen, 1993, 2003; Isen and Daubman, 1984).

In summary, there is evidence that exposure to humor can enhance creative thinking, and that this effect is likely mediated by the positive emotion (i.e., mirth) associated with humor. These findings may have practical implications for applications of humor for enhancing creative thinking and problem solving in such fields as education and business (which will be discussed in Chapter 11).

Memory

Does humor enhance memory? More specifically, is humorous material remembered better than nonhumorous material? Educators and advertisers have long believed in the beneficial effects on memory of humorous lectures and advertisements. There are several reasons why humor might be expected to enhance memory (Schmidt, 1994). First, the positive emotion associated with humor may have positive effects on memory in a manner similar to the demonstrated effects of nonhumorous emotional arousal. Second, humor may enhance attention to stimuli due to the novelty and surprise involved in humorous incongruity. Third, humorous material may be rehearsed more than nonhumorous material, resulting in increased retention. Finally, humor may affect retrieval strategies, biasing subjects to retrieve humorous material before nonhumorous material.

Several early studies investigated memory-enhancing effects of humor in the contexts of education (e.g., Kaplan and Pascoe, 1977; Kintsch and Bates, 1977) and advertising (e.g., C. P. Duncan, Nelson, and Frontzak, 1984; Gelb and Zinkhan, 1986) with mixed results. However, most of these did not provide adequate control over possible confounding factors such as the emotional content of the materials to be remembered. More recently, Steven Schmidt, a psychologist at Middle Tennessee State University, has conducted a series of well-designed experiments that demonstrated enhanced memory effects of humor, and explored a number of competing hypotheses regarding the mechanisms involved (Schmidt, 1994, 2002; Schmidt and Williams, 2001).

In a series of six experiments, Schmidt (1994) examined the effects of humor on sentence memory by presenting participants with lists of humorous and nonhumorous sentences. To control for possible nonhumor-related differences between the sentences, humorous and nonhumorous versions of the same sentences were used. Pretesting of the sentences revealed that they did not differ on ratings of bizarreness, difficulty, meaningfulness, or familiarity, but did differ greatly on rated funniness. The studies revealed that humorous sentences were recalled better than nonhumorous sentences when they were presented in lists containing both types of sentences. In fact, enhanced recall of the humorous sentences was found at the expense of the nonhumorous sentences in the same list. In other words, when both humorous and nonhumorous sentences were presented in the same list, participants performed better in recalling the humorous sentences but worse in recalling the nonhumorous sentences, relative to their performance when either type of sentence was presented alone. However, when the two types of sentences were presented in separate homogeneous lists, there was no difference in recall for the two types. These effects were found with free and cued recall, in incidental and intentional learning, and on a variety of measures of sentence access. As to the possible mechanisms involved, Schmidt concluded that the findings were inconsistent with simple arousal, surprise, and retrieval explanations, but consistent with the hypothesis that humorous material receives both increased attention and rehearsal as compared to nonhumorous material.

Schmidt and Williams (2001) examined further the effects of humor on memory, using cartoons instead of humorous sentences. Participants were better able to recall the gist of original cartoons than nonhumorous or "weird" (but not funny) versions of the same cartoons. However, these memory differences were not found for detailed cartoon information such as the actual wording of the captions. Schmidt (2002) replicated the findings with cartoon stimuli and also took heart rate measures of participants to examine the role of physiological arousal in the memory effect of humor. The heart rate results did not show evidence for an enhanced orienting response to the humorous materials (contrary to the prediction of Deckers and Hricik, 1984), but a greater secondary heart-rate deceleration to the humorous cartoons suggested that different encoding processes occurred with the humorous as compared to the nonhumorous stimuli. Overall, these findings suggest that humor serves as a sort of mnemonic technique or memory aid, causing greater elaboration of information and therefore enhancing its transfer and storage in long-term memory.

If humor aids memory, why is it often so difficult to remember a joke? Schmidt and Williams (2001) commented that their findings help to explain this phenomenon, since humor enhances memory for the gist of the material, but not for details such as the exact wording. The funniness of a joke may help us to remember what it was generally about, but may not help us to remember the exact wording of the punch line. More effortful repetition and elaboration seems to be needed to memorize a joke if one wishes to be able to recall it later. The authors also suggest that past research showing mnemonic benefits of bizarre imagery (the "bizarreness effect") may have been due to humorousness rather than bizarreness, since the weird cartoons without humor in their study did not have an effect on memory.

Peter Derks and his colleagues, at the College of William and Mary, used experimental procedures similar to those of Schmidt (1994) to examine potential memory effects of "tendentious" (i.e., sexual and aggressive) humor compared to nontendentious humor (Derks, Gardner, and Agarwal, 1998). They partially replicated Schmidt's findings of memory-enhancing effects of humorous material, and also found a strong effect for tendentiousness, indicating that emotionally arousing elements such as sex and aggression further enhance these memory effects. Lippman and Dunn (2000) also found some evidence for memory-enhancing effects of humor using puns.

In summary, these studies provide quite convincing evidence that humorous information is recalled better than nonhumorous information when both are presented in the same context. If only humorous material is presented, there is no apparent benefit for memory. However, the recall of humorous material appears to be at the expense of memory for nonhumorous information presented at the same time. These findings have potential implications for education and advertising. For example, humor may enhance memory for the humorous material but diminish memory for other information contained in a lecture or advertisement. Humor therefore should be integrated with the course content or product. In addition, constant use of humor will have little effect on retention. Instead, humor should be used to illustrate important concepts and not background or peripheral material.

COMPUTATIONAL APPROACHES TO HUMOR

Is it possible to program a computer to generate and/or understand humor? Although researchers in the field of artificial intelligence (AI) have, for the most part, ignored humor, it can be argued that any attempt to develop a truly intelligent computer system will ultimately need to address the problem of humor. Graeme Ritchie, a linguist and AI researcher at the University of Edinburgh, along with his students and colleagues, is currently the most active scholar in the field of computational humor (Binsted and Ritchie, 1997, 2001; Ritchie, 2001, 2004). Ritchie (2001) suggested that AI investigations of humor can not only help to clarify our theories of humor, but can also lead to important discoveries about human intelligence, language, problem solving, and information processing more generally.

Moreover, as artificial intelligence systems, such as robots, become increasingly sophisticated in the future, it may be important for them to be able to generate and understand humor in order to communicate more effectively and in a more congenial way with the humans with whom they interact. On a more philosophical note, we can consider whether truly intelligent robots might even *require* a sense of humor in order to cope with the incongruous and inconsistent perspectives that confront any intelligent being functioning autonomously in the real world and interacting with other intelligent beings. The idea that humor is more than just a luxury is suggested by theories that it evolved in humans as a mode of interpersonal communication for dealing with conflicting perspectives (Mulkay, 1988), or as a cognitive coping mechanism that is necessary for survival (Dixon, 1980). These questions are similar to questions about whether artificially intelligent systems functioning in the real world would require some analog of emotion (Trappl, Petta, and Payr, 2002).

Ritchie (2001, 2004) has advocated an "experimental AI" approach, in which computer programming is used as a means of testing cognitive (and particularly linguistic) theories of humor. In order for a theory to be implemented in a computer program, it needs to be formal, precise, detailed, and rigorous, conforming to the principles of generative linguistics and AI. Thus, AI investigations provide a way of sniffing out fuzzy thinking and faulty logic that might not otherwise be apparent in theoretical formulations. Unfortunately, according to Ritchie, most of the existing theories of humor are too vague and imprecise to be of much use to AI. For example,

Ritchie (1999) criticized the traditional incongruity-resolution theories (which I discussed in Chapter 3), pointing out that the ideas of incongruity and resolution have not been defined clearly enough and that different theories use these concepts in different ways. In particular, although they are often seen as being equivalent, Shultz's (1976) theory (which Ritchie refers to as the "surprise disambiguation model") is, on close analysis, actually quite different from Suls' (1972) theory (the "two-stage model"). The two theories have different implications and apply to different classes of jokes (see also Ritchie, in press). Ritchie (2004) has also criticized Raskin and Attardo's General Theory of Verbal Humor (discussed earlier), as being too vague in its present form for computer implementation.

One reason for the vagueness and imprecision of many theories, according to Ritchie, is that they attempt to explain too many different types of humor. Ritchie strongly rejects the quest for a "grand theory of humor" at the present time, arguing instead that we need to identify specific subclasses that can be thoroughly characterized and implemented on a computer. Only after we have done this with a large number of types can we build up a comprehensive theory that accounts for all kinds of humor. Accordingly, Ritchie has narrowed his focus to verbal jokes, and even more narrowly to certain types of jokes that share particular verbal mechanisms (e.g., punning riddles).

Although one could theoretically attempt to develop a program that is able to process verbal texts that are fed into it and determine whether or not they are funny, Ritchie suggests that the more practical place to begin is with programs that apply a given theory to generate humorous texts. Human judges can then determine whether the output of the program is indeed humorous. By observing the behavior of the program (i.e., the types of jokes it produces), one can obtain useful insights into the weaknesses of the theory underlying it. This can then lead to further refinements of the theory and corresponding "tweaking" of the program. Thus, the goal of this sort of programming enterprise is not so much the program itself but the refinement of the theoretical ideas underlying it.

Kim Binsted and Graeme Ritchie (1997) have taken this approach in developing a computer program called Joke Analysis and Production Engine (JAPE) that generates a specific class of jokes known as punning riddles. These are question-answer jokes that are based on a pun (e.g., What's the difference between a hairy dog and a painter? One sheds his coat, the other coats his shed.). Binsted and Ritchie began by developing a formal model of the punning mechanisms underlying these types of riddles, identifying a set of symbolic rules about the meaning combinations and textual forms involved. These rules were then built into a program that also has access to a large natural language lexicon (dictionary) of the kind used in AI research generally. This lexicon contains a large number of words, along with information about their phonetic pronunciation, lexical usage, and syntactic meaning. It is important to note that this lexicon does not contain any information that could be conceived as inherently "funny." Nonetheless, by searching through the lexicon for suitable word pairs that meet the criteria described by the rules, and applying various basic templates of riddle structure, the program is able to generate a virtually limitless number of novel riddles.

The following are some examples of the funnier riddles that were generated by JAPE (from Ritchie, 2004):

> What do you call a ferocious nude? A grizzly bare.
> What do you get when you cross breakfast food with a murderer? A cereal killer.
> What's the difference between leaves and a car? One you brush and rake, the other you rush and brake.
> What's the difference between a horse and a wagon? One bolts and jumps, the other jolts and bumps.

Binsted, Pain, and Ritchie (1997) conducted a study to evaluate the output of JAPE, using a sample of 8- to 11-year-old children as judges. They presented these subjects with a random selection of JAPE-produced riddles, human-produced riddles (taken from published joke books), nonsense nonjokes, and sensible nonjokes. The children were asked to determine whether each text was a joke and, if so, how funny it was and whether they had heard it before. The results showed that the JAPE-produced riddles were identified as jokes just as reliably as the human-produced ones, and both were easily distinguished from the non-jokes. Although the JAPE-produced jokes were rated as less funny, on average, than the human-produced jokes, a number of the JAPE riddles were rated as being just as funny as those produced by humans. Further analysis of the less funny riddles produced by JAPE may lead to future refinements of the program and, at the same time, a more precise linguistic theory of this type of humor.

In addition to the JAPE program, Binsted and Ritchie (2001) analyzed the structure and formal regularities of another class of joke, which they referred to as "story puns," and offered some suggestions about a possible computational model for their production. Ritchie (2004) also described a number of other computer programs that have been developed by other researchers using a variety of approaches. As one example, Bruce Katz (1993) took a connectionist approach in developing a neural network model of incongruity in humor that attempted also to incorporate concepts of arousal, sexual and aggressive themes, and hedonic tone (i.e., mirth).

Although computational models such as JAPE appear to be quite promising, Ritchie (2001, 2004) acknowledges that they are still at a very early stage of development. The implementation rules underlying this program are not tied to any real hypotheses about humor in general, and it is not clear how to generalize from this model to other forms of humor. In addition, a complete computational model of humor will ultimately require the development of truly intelligent systems with a vast foundation of encyclopedic knowledge coupled with sophisticated reasoning abilities. Nonetheless, Ritchie contends that steps can be taken toward this ultimate goal by breaking the problem into smaller chunks, identifying specific classes of humor, and developing rigorous formal descriptions that can be implemented using existing technology. "The overall message," states Ritchie (2001, p. 132), "is that endeavoring to develop computational models of humor is a worthwhile enterprise both for artificial intelligence and for those interested in humor, but we are starting from a very meager foundation, and the challenges are significant."

Ritchie has argued that attempts to implement cognitive theories of humor in computer programs are beneficial to psychologists as well as linguists by providing a way of testing theories and alerting theorists to weaknesses in their models. To be psychologically relevant, however, it is important that the computer simulations carry out the tasks in the same way that humans are assumed to do. For example, although computer chess programs are capable of outplaying most of the best human players, they operate very differently than human chess players, and are therefore not a very good test of cognitive theories of human chess playing. Similarly, it is not entirely clear that programs like JAPE generate humor in the same way that humans do.

Ritchie's recommendation for more narrowly focused theories applied to discrete types of humor may also be a useful suggestion for psychological humor research, although this arguably depends on the goals of the individual researcher. If the goal is to identify general characteristics of humor that distinguish it from other human activities, then broader, more general theories may be appropriate. On the other hand, if the goal is to describe in detail how people cognitively process particular types of humor, then greater progress will likely be made with research aimed at testing specific hypotheses derived from narrowly focused theories. However, for the purposes of understanding psychological aspects of humor, it may not be as necessary to make such fine-grained distinctions (e.g., distinguishing between several different classes of puns), and psychologists may find it useful to partition the humor domain ("carve nature at its joints") in different ways than do AI researchers. In any case, for the psychologist, advances in AI research on humor may be viewed as a rich source of potential hypotheses for further experimental research. Ritchie (1999) listed a number of research questions that would be amenable to psychological investigations as well as studies in AI.

HUMOR AS COGNITIVE PLAY

Most of the cognitive theories that have been developed to date attempt to explain the processes involved in the comprehension of humor, but they do not address the question of what makes humor so enjoyable. They may explain how we come to understand a joke and recognize that something is funny, but they do not explain why we are so motivated to seek out and participate in many forms of humor during our daily lives. Indeed, as Max Eastman (1936) noted many years ago, humor theorists often discuss humor as though it were a very serious business, and you would not know from reading their writings that they are dealing with something that is inherently pleasurable.

As I noted in previous chapters, humor involves emotional and social as well as cognitive aspects. The relation between cognition and emotion is a thorny topic in cognitive psychology generally, and most cognitive psychologists view it as outside the scope of their research activities. Ultimately, though, it would seem that a complete understanding of human cognition in general will require an understanding of the role of emotion. Indeed, there is some evidence that seemingly purely rational processes, such as decision making, are impossible without some emotional input (Damasio, 1994).

The view of humor as cognitive play may provide a framework for thinking about the interaction of cognitive, emotional, and social elements. When we engage in humor, we are playing with language and ideas (schemas, scripts) in much the same way that children (and adults) play with physical objects, exploring new and unusual ways of using them, and delighting in these novel applications. For a child, an ordinary stick can be an airplane, a person, or a rifle, evoking multiple schemas concurrently. The incongruity of humor that we have been discussing can be seen as a manifestation of this play with ideas, where words and concepts are used in ways that are surprising, unusual, and incongruous, activating schemas with which they are not normally associated. As discussed in the previous chapter, Michael Apter (1982) referred to the playful elaborations of multiple cognitive schemas as "synergy," and noted that there is something inherently enjoyable about this activity when we are in a playful, nonserious state of mind.

This view of humor as cognitive play also sheds light on the mechanisms of jokes that we have been discussing. The simultaneous activation of multiple schemas to try to make sense of a joke enables both the joke teller and the listener to engage in playful cognitive synergies. As Forabosco (1992) has pointed out, the "resolutions" involved in jokes are really "pseudo-resolutions," since they do not actually make sense in a literal way. Thus, they are a way of playing creatively with the cognitive mechanisms that we normally use in more "serious" contexts for seeking meaning in the world.

Evolutionary theories of emotions suggest that they evolved because they motivate us to behave in certain ways that have proven beneficial for survival and reproduction, avoiding certain situations and approaching others (Plutchik, 1991). As I noted in Chapter 1 (and will discuss more fully in Chapter 6), research on primates and other animals indicates that the playful cognitive activity involved in humor likely evolved from mammalian rough-and-tumble social play. The associated positive emotion of mirth is what motivates individuals to engage in this activity. Panksepp (1998) has proposed a "ludic" (playful) emotion system in the brain that underlies presumably adaptive playful activities (including humor) and their associated positive emotions. The fact that the cognitive play of humor elicits the positive emotion of mirth suggests that this sort of flexible, exploratory cognitive behavior has an adaptive function, perhaps because of its benefits for flexible thinking, creativity, and problem solving (Fagen, 1981) or as a means of facilitating social interaction and bonding (Panksepp and Burgdorf, 2003). Also, as we have seen, the research of Isen and her colleagues indicates that positive emotional states, in themselves, promote creative thinking and problem solving as well as fostering social responsibility and prosocial behaviors such as helpfulness and generosity (Isen, 2003). I will return to these evolutionary issues in Chapter 6.

CONCLUSION

What have we learned about cognitive processes in humor? The idea that some sort of incongruity is the basis of all humor seems to be generally supported. However, it is far from clear exactly how incongruity should be defined or conceptualized, and whether it is a single mechanism that applies to all forms of humor or whether we need to invoke different types of incongruity for different types of humor. Contemporary theories based on schema and script concepts have contributed a great deal to our understanding, although further work is needed to make them more precise and rigorous. These theories suggest that "resolution" of incongruity in jokes may be best conceived as a mechanism for activating several schemas simultaneously, rather than a way of replacing one schema with another (as suggested by earlier incongruity-resolution theories). Cognitive psychologists have developed a number of techniques for investigating the activation of particular schemas "on line" during the processing of information. Future research using these methodologies will be beneficial for conducting empirical tests of the hypotheses derived from schema-based theories.

Much of the past theoretical and empirical work focused on jokes as a prototype of humor. However, jokes are a relatively insignificant source of humor in most people's daily lives, and the cognitive mechanisms involved in them may be somewhat different from those in other forms of humor. It is risky for theorists to attempt to develop general theories of humor based only on analyses of jokes. Fortunately, there is growing interest among cognitive psychologists and linguists in other types of humor apart from jokes, such as conversational witticisms, irony, puns, and sarcasm. Here, as well, a positive trend is the increased interest in the pragmatics as well as the semantics of humor.

Research examining how people actually use humor in everyday conversations and interactions (including, but not limited to, telling jokes) will likely lead to better understanding of cognitive as well as social aspects of humor. How a joke is cognitively processed in the context of everyday social interactions (including the social context of a psychology laboratory) may be quite different from the idealized processes invoked in semantic theories that do not take pragmatics into account. Indeed, as we have seen, recent research indicates that information about the social context plays an important role in the comprehension of conversational types of humor such as irony and sarcasm. Future cognitive research should also go beyond the linguistic types of humor and begin to address nonverbal forms, such as slapstick comedy and accidental humor.

Another limitation of cognitive research on humor is that it has focused almost exclusively on humor comprehension rather than humor creation. This reflects the more general state of affairs in psycholinguistics and linguistics, where research on language comprehension far outstrips work on language production. Although there have been some isolated attempts by psychologists to address the cognitive processes involved in the creation of humor (Shultz and Scott, 1974), this is a topic that awaits further investigation.

There is considerable evidence that exposure to humor affects other cognitive processes, particularly memory and creativity. Enhanced memory for humorous material seems to be due to selective attention to and greater elaboration of humorous elements at the expense of less humorous information. The effects of humor on creativity appear to be due to emotional rather than purely cognitive mechanisms. The emotional component of humor has not received much attention from cognitively oriented psychologists and linguists. The view of humor as cognitive play may provide a framework for integrating the pleasurable emotional aspect with the cognitive mechanisms of humor.

As in cognitive science generally, the interdisciplinary nature of the cognitive study of humor is apparent, with important contributions coming from linguistics and computer science as well as psychology. Indeed, many important theoretical advances in recent decades have originated in linguistics rather than psychology. However, there is also a small but active nucleus of psycholinguists who have continued to make valuable theoretical and empirical contributions, particularly in the study of irony and sarcasm.

At the present time, the field is ripe for further psychological research on cognitive aspects of humor. As noted throughout this chapter, there are a great many research questions and hypotheses coming from a variety of theories that could be readily investigated empirically using the experimental methodologies available to psychologists. Further research on cognitive aspects of humor may not only provide a better understanding of the ubiquitous phenomena of humor, but may also shed light on other more basic questions of interest to psychologists, such as the interface between cognition and emotion, comprehension of ambiguous meaning, and cognitive aspects of nonverbal as well as verbal interpersonal communication. Research questions relating to cognitive aspects of humor could form the basis of a good many Masters and PhD theses for years to come.

CHAPTER 5

The Social Psychology of Humor

As I have noted previously, humor is fundamentally a social phenomenon. We laugh and joke much more frequently when we are with other people than when we are alone (R. A. Martin and Kuiper, 1999; Provine and Fischer, 1989). Those rare occasions when we do laugh by ourselves typically involve "pseudo-social" situations, such as reading a book, watching a television program, or recalling an amusing experience with other people. The interpersonal aspects of humor are of particular interest to social psychology, which has been defined as "the scientific study of how individuals' thoughts, feelings, and behaviors are influenced by other people" (Breckler, Olson, and Wiggins, 2006, p. 5). As we will see in this chapter, humor is one of the methods that people use to influence each other in a complex variety of ways. Social psychologists study such topics as social perception, interpersonal attraction, communication, attitudes, prejudice, persuasion, close relationships, group processes, and so on. It is easy to see that humor can play an important role in all of these areas.

Social psychology is closely related to several other academic disciplines, including sociology, anthropology, and linguistics, each of which has made important contributions to our understanding of social aspects of humor. In this chapter, I will therefore discuss some of the contributions of these other disciplines along with those of psychology. I will begin by discussing humor as a method of interpersonal communication and influence, followed by an overview of its many social functions, and an exploration of how these relate to humorous forms of teasing. I will then examine social aspects of laughter, the vocal and facial expression of the humor-related emotion of mirth. In the remainder of the chapter, I will review research findings on the role of humor in several of the major topic areas of social psychology, including social perception and interpersonal attraction, persuasion, attitudes and prejudice, intimate relationships, and gender.

HUMOR AS SOCIAL INTERACTION

Many of the traditional theories and much of the early research on the psychology of humor neglected the interpersonal aspects, focusing instead on cognitive and emotional processes taking place within the individual. Most of the early studies examined participants' reactions to jokes and cartoons in the laboratory, which does not provide much information about how humor is normally expressed in everyday social interactions. In recent years, however, researchers in psychology, as well as other disciplines, have been giving more attention to social aspects of humor, examining in particular its functions in interpersonal communication and influence. This change in perspective has been accompanied by a shift in focus away from canned jokes as the prototype of humor to other forms that occur spontaneously in the course of ordinary conversation, such as teasing, irony, and witty banter.

I have been suggesting in this book that humor is best viewed as a form of play that comprises cognitive (nonserious incongruity), emotional (mirth), and expressive (laughter) components. All of these elements of humor have a social dimension. The nonserious incongruities that elicit humor typically have to do with funny things that people say or do. Jokes are almost always about people, not animals or inanimate objects. The emotion of mirth is also typically shared with other people (see Figure 3). As Michelle Shiota and her colleagues (2004) have suggested, the shared experience of mirth serves important social functions in establishing and maintaining close relationships, enhancing feelings of attraction and commitment, and coordinating mutually beneficial activities. Laughter is also inherently social, communicating one's mirthful emotional state to others as well as inducing this emotion in one's listeners (Owren and Bachorowski, 2003; Russell et al., 2003). Thus, while humor is a form of play that we enjoy for its own sake, it also serves important social functions that likely contributed to our evolutionary survival. As I suggested in Chapter 1, some of the social functions of humor may be co-optations in which, with the emergence of higher linguistic and cognitive abilities and more complex social organization, play-related mirthful activities were adapted in human evolution for a wide variety of purposes having to do with interpersonal communication and influence (Gervais and Wilson, 2005).

Sociologist Michael Mulkay (1988) suggested that people interact with one another using two basic modes of communication: serious and humorous (referred to by Victor Raskin, 1985, as the "bona-fide" and "non-bona-fide" modes, respectively). According to Mulkay, both of these are ordinary, everyday methods of discourse, but they operate according to fundamentally different principles. In the serious mode, we

FIGURE 3 Most humor occurs spontaneously in the context of ordinary social interactions. © Monica Lau/Getty Images/PhotoDisc

attempt to be logically consistent and coherent, we seek to avoid ambiguity and contradiction, and we assume that there is a unitary external reality that is shared by everyone. However, this mode of communication is often inadequate, since different individuals and groups often have quite different perceptions of reality and disagree about their interpretations of events. When people attempt to communicate, these multiple realities frequently collide, producing contradiction, incongruity, and incoherence, which the serious mode of discourse is unable to handle easily.

According to Mulkay, the social play activity of humor was co-opted over the course of human evolution as a way for people to deal with this multiplicity and inherent contradiction in their communications with one another. Making use of Arthur Koestler's (1964) concept of *bisociation* (discussed in Chapters 1, 3, and 4), Mulkay views humor as a way of incorporating, embracing, and even celebrating the contradictions, incongruities, and ambiguities inherent in interpersonal relationships. By simultaneously expressing opposite meanings, the humorous mode provides a shared conceptual framework that embraces contradictions, rather than avoiding them, and thereby enables people to negotiate otherwise difficult interpersonal transactions.

For example, humorous joking and playful teasing can be a way for spouses or other partners in a close relationship to communicate about a topic on which they strongly disagree, instead of using the more serious mode and getting into endless arguments that cannot resolve the issue and only lead to an escalation of anger and bitterness, destabilizing the relationship. The humorous mode allows them to express their strongly opposing views and acknowledge their conflict while, at the very same time, communicating an opposite message about their continuing commitment to the relationship. Thus, their humor is a way of playing with, and laughing about, the incongruity inherent in the contradictory feelings and attitudes that they simultane-ously hold toward one another. The positive feelings of mirth generated by this per-ception of playful incongruity, and the laughter that they share, help to maintain cohesion and positive feelings about the relationship, despite their differing views. This is just one example of the many ways humor enables people, in many different kinds of relationships, to communicate information about their beliefs, attitudes, motives, feelings, and needs, which may not be as amenable to the serious mode of discourse. Not only does this mode of communication convey information, but it also induces mirth and laughter, further influencing the attitudes and feelings of others.

As noted in Chapter 1, humor is a ubiquitous form of interaction that occurs in all types of social contexts and takes many different forms. These include canned jokes, amusing personal anecdotes, spontaneous witty comments, ironic observations, puns, teasing, sarcasm, double entendres, and so on. Humor can also be evoked uninten-tionally, such as when people laugh in response to someone misusing a word or behav-ing in a clumsy manner (e.g., tripping, or spilling a drink). All of these forms of humor can serve important interpersonal functions.

INTERPERSONAL FUNCTIONS OF HUMOR

Anthropologists studying preliterate societies have noted the widespread existence of "joking relationships" (Radcliffe-Brown, 1952) in which individuals who are related in particular ways are expected to interact with humor, including joking, teasing, banter, ridicule, and practical jokes (see Apte, 1985, for a review of this research). For example, joking relationships occur in various cultures between individuals who are potential sexual partners, between a man and his brothers-in-law, between grandpar-ents and grandchildren, or between members of different clans. Although the form and pattern of joking relationships vary across cultures, they all seem to serve an important function of regulating social interactions and maintaining social harmony and stability. A number of ethnographic studies suggest that similar kinds of joking relationships commonly exist in industrialized societies as well, as in the sorts of joking and teasing relationships that develop in work settings and in friendship groups to establish group identity and exclude outsiders (Apte, 1985).

Humor serves a variety of functions, not only in these sorts of joking relation-ships, but in all types of interpersonal interactions (Kane et al., 1977; Long and Graesser, 1988; Martineau, 1972; Norrick, 1993). Most of these have to do with the fact that it is inherently ambiguous and even contradictory, and can therefore be inter-preted in several different ways at the same time. When someone says something in a humorous way, he or she can always take it back by saying "I was only joking." Indeed, since everyone recognizes the ambiguous nature of humor, it is often not even necessary to make such a disclaimer. In this way, humor enables individuals to "save face" for themselves and others. The concept of "face" comes from Erving Goffman's (1967) analyses of social interactions. Goffman defined *face* as "an image of self delin-eated in terms of approved social attributes" (p. 5). He noted that people are strongly motivated to avoid communications that are potentially face-threatening, putting themselves or others in an awkward or embarrassing situation. Because of its ambiguity and potential for retraction, humor, like politeness, can be a useful tactic for protecting the face of oneself and others, thus playing an important role in facilitating social interaction (Keltner et al., 1998; Zajdman, 1995).

It is important to note that when we speak of humor being "used" for particular purposes, this does not mean that individuals are always consciously aware of these functions or are using it in a volitional, strategic manner. Since it is usually spontaneous and unplanned, individuals typically perceive their experiences of humor to be nothing more than playful fun. Nonetheless, in many instances, humor may be serving various purposes of which the individuals involved are not fully aware. Indeed, the ability to deny any serious intentions, even to oneself, is part of what makes humor so effective in many types of social interaction.

These uses of humor in communication can have any number of different purposes. In a ground-breaking early paper on this topic, social psychologists Thomas Kane, Jerry Suls, and James Tedeschi (1977) observed that humor "can help the source to claim or disclaim responsibility for his actions, can reveal courage or relieve embarrassment, may invoke normative commitments or release the individual from commitments" (p. 13). In the following sections, I will discuss several of the interpersonal functions of humor that have been identified. These are not mutually exclusive, since any given instance of humor may serve more than one function at the same time.

Self-Disclosure, Social Probing, and Norm Violation

Kane and colleagues (1977) noted that we are continually exploring our social environments in order to determine the values, attitudes, knowledge, emotional states, motives, and intentions of others. This sort of information is necessary for achieving our goals in interactions with others, whether these are to increase intimacy, obtain desired favors and rewards, or exert influence over others. Because of the potential "face threat" involved, the unspoken rules of social propriety often make it difficult or uncomfortable to ask direct questions about these sorts of issues. There is a risk that our motives will be misconstrued, that we will be resented for our intrusiveness, or that we or others will be embarrassed in some way. Humor can often be a more acceptable and indirect way of gaining such information. By making a humorous remark about certain attitudes, feelings, or opinions, we can reveal something about ourselves in a way that allows us to deny it if it is not well received. Moreover, by observing whether or not others respond with laughter or reciprocate with similar humorous comments, we can ascertain whether they share similar views.

The communication of attitudes and motives relating to sex is often particularly fraught with risks of misunderstanding and rejection, and humor is often used to deal with these problems. This is likely why there are so many words with alternate sexual meanings, allowing people to use humorous double entendre and innuendo to discuss sexual matters in a safe way (Long and Graesser, 1988). In an observational study of conversations among customers and staff in an all-night diner in upstate New York, sociologist Alf Walle (1976) described the way humor was used by men and women to express interest in a possible sexual liaison. If they were to use serious modes of communication in this context, participants would run the risk of causing offense to the other person and being personally humiliated by rejection. However, by telling sexual jokes and making humorous comments containing sexual innuendo, they were able to probe the other person's level of interest in a way that enabled them to save face if their interest was not reciprocated.

This role of humor as self-disclosure and social probing in sexual communication was also illustrated in an early experiment by social psychologists Jay Davis and Amerigo Farina (1970). Male college students were asked by either an attractive or an unattractive female experimenter to rate the funniness of either aggressive or sexual cartoons. The ratings were either given orally to the experimenter or on paper-and-pencil scales. The results indicated that the highest funniness ratings were given by the male participants when they were rating sexual cartoons orally to the attractive female. The researchers suggested that these responses to humor provided a socially acceptable method for the participants to let the experimenter know that they were sexually interested in her.

Besides sexual topics, humor can be used to self-disclose and probe beliefs and attitudes regarding a wide variety of issues, such as political and religious views and attitudes toward people of different ethnicities, nationalities, occupations, or gender. By making a racist or sexist comment in a humorous manner, an individual can probe the degree to which such attitudes are tolerated or shared by others. Humor can also be used to probe people's emotional reactions to situations. For example, during times of stress or danger (e.g., in a high-pressure work situation or prior to a battle during wartime) where showing distress or fear might be construed as weakness, gallows humor may be used to probe the degree to which others are experiencing negative emotions (Kane et al., 1977). Thus, humor can be a useful tool for social comparison, a process whereby we seek information about others in order to evaluate our own feelings and performance (Morse and Gergen, 1970).

Humor can also be used to push the boundaries of social propriety, attack "sacred cows," and rebel against social norms. For example, by using obscenities or other types of shocking language in a humorous manner, one is able to violate social norms in a way that reduces the likelihood that others will take offense, since everyone knows that humor is not to be taken seriously. Thus, one is more likely to get away with breaking various taboos, expressing prejudiced attitudes, or engaging in boorish behavior if these are done in a humorous rather than a serious manner. When carried into the public domain, iconoclastic forms of humor such as satire and comedy can be used to challenge widely held assumptions, expose social ills, and bring about social change (Ziv, 1984).

Decommitment

People often use humor to save face when they experience some sort of failure, when they are about to be unmasked in some way, or when they have been caught in a lie or are found to have engaged in inappropriate behavior (Kane et al., 1977). By using humor to indicate that the proposed or past action was intended as a joke and was therefore not meant to be taken seriously, one can save face by "decommitting" oneself from the action. For example, if Person A threatens Person B in some way and this provokes a counter-threat from Person B, Person A can back down by turning the original threat into a joke. Alternatively, if Person B does not comply with the original threat and it comes time for Person A to back up the threat ("put up or shut up"), he or she can use humor instead of carrying out the threat, thus avoiding an escalation of conflict in the relationship while still maintaining his or her reputation for credibility. By laughing in response to the humor, Person B in turn indicates a tacit agreement to treat the original threat as nonserious. Similarly, two friends who have allowed a disagreement to escalate into an argument can, by interjecting a humorous remark, relieve the tension and avoid the loss of face that would occur if either one was forced to back down (Long and Graesser, 1988).

Over the course of a year in a small community in Newfoundland, Craig Palmer (1993) conducted an observational study of males playing floor hockey, a rough sport involving quite a lot of verbal and physical aggression. He found that, while engaging in overtly aggressive actions, middle-aged players (who were more concerned with establishing and maintaining friendships with each other) were more likely to display humor (smiling, laughter, and humorous comments) as compared to adolescents and young adults, who were more concerned with competition. In addition, humor was more likely to accompany aggressive behaviors between players with marked differences in skill level, as compared to those of equal skill. This is presumably because confrontations between individuals with discrepancies in skill present more potential for one person being hurt or embarrassed. Thus, the use of humor with what would otherwise be interpreted as aggressive or provocative actions appeared to be a form of decommitment, a way for participants to communicate that the action was not to be taken seriously, and to reassure each other of the friendly nature of their relationship.

Social Norms and Control

Besides being used to test and even violate social norms, Long and Graesser (1988) pointed out that humor can be used to enforce social norms and indirectly exert control over others' behavior. By using irony, teasing, sarcasm, or satire to make fun of certain attitudes, behaviors, or personality traits, members of a group can communicate implicit expectations and rules concerning the kinds of behavior that are considered acceptable within the group. These types of humor can take the form of ridiculing members of an out-group, or they can be directed at deviant behaviors of individuals within an in-group (Martineau, 1972). Either way, this humor can have a coercive function, intimidating group members into conforming to the implied norms out of fear of embarrassment.

Similarly, humor can also be used as an "unmasking tactic" (Kane et al., 1977). By poking fun at another person, one is communicating a refusal to accept the identity projected by that person, exposing or belittling his or her motives. Since the message is communicated in a humorous way, and is therefore subject to multiple interpretations simultaneously, it is difficult for the target to retaliate or to hold the source accountable for embarrassing him or her. Thus, a humorous communication reduces the risk of hostility and rancor that might be generated using a more serious mode of communication in confrontation. I will discuss teasing in greater detail later in the chapter.

Dews, Kaplan, and Winner (1995) conducted several experiments to investigate the effects of using irony, as compared to direct statements, to deliver both criticisms and compliments. An example of an ironic criticism is saying "Great game" to a person who has played poorly, whereas an ironic compliment would be "You sure sucked in that game" after someone has played particularly well. Not surprisingly, the studies showed that ironic statements are perceived as more humorous than direct statements. More importantly, irony also seemed to mute the message conveyed by literal language: ironic criticism was perceived as less aggressive and insulting than direct criticism, whereas ironic compliments were perceived as less positive than direct compliments. Thus, irony can have a social control function, enabling people to express both criticism and praise indirectly and ambiguously, avoiding loss of face for speakers and listeners in the process.

Status and Hierarchy Maintenance

The role of humor in controlling behavior and enforcing social norms also implies that it can be used by individuals to reinforce their own status in a group hierarchy. For example, you are more likely to crack jokes and amuse others in a group in which you are the leader or have a position of dominance than in a group in which you have lower status and less power than others. In a frequently cited early study, sociologist Rose Laub Coser (1960) observed the use of humor during staff meetings in a psychiatric hospital. She found that humor in this context served to reinforce the hierarchical structure of the relationships among staff members. Higher-status senior staff (psychiatrists) were much more likely to use humor than were junior staff (psychiatric residents or nurses), and they frequently directed their humor at junior staff in a way that conveyed a critical or corrective message. In turn, the junior staff members refrained from directing humor at senior staff, but instead tended to use it either in a self-deprecating manner or as a way of making fun of outsiders. Coser concluded that humor helps to "overcome the contradictions and ambiguities inherent in the complex social structure, and thereby to contribute to its maintenance" (p. 95). These findings were replicated more recently in another study of humor among staff members in a psychiatric unit (Sayre, 2001).

Dawn Robinson and Lynn Smith-Lovin (2001) used a statistical technique called event history regression to analyze the use of humor during conversations in 29 six-person task groups that were instructed to work together on a problem. The data supported a model of humor as a status-related activity. Individuals who more frequently interrupted others in conversation (a behavior that indicates higher status) were also more likely to engage in humor and make others laugh, even after controlling for the frequency of overall participation in group discussion. Conversely, those who were more frequently interrupted by others (reflecting their lower status) were less likely to produce humor. There was also evidence that the use of humor early on in the group discussion was a means for participants to establish status in the group hierarchy. In mixed-sex groups, males (who tended to be more dominant in a variety of ways) were more likely to express humor than were females, and were more likely to elicit laughter from others. The status differences in traditional male and female gender roles may explain the findings of many studies (which I will discuss later in the chapter) showing that men tend to produce humor more than women, whereas women tend to laugh more in response to men's humor.

The use of humor to maintain a position of dominance is also evident in an ethnographic study by James Spradley and Brenda Mann (1975) of interactions between bartenders and waitresses in an American bar. Much of the humor that occurred in these interactions took the form of ridicule, sexual insults, and lewd comments, and was directed by the male bartenders toward the female waitresses. The authors discussed this humor in terms of joking relationships, seeing it as a way of relieving tensions resulting from structurally created conflict in the relationships. However, Mulkay (1988) pointed out that, rather than relieving tension for the women, the humor tended to increase their frustration, and was primarily a strategy adopted by the men to sustain their domination over the women. The women were not permitted to take offense at the bartenders' ribald and denigrating remarks, whereas the men could object when a "girl" went "too far" with her humorous comments. These types of humor, which today would likely be viewed as workplace harassment, have long been used to reinforce the subordinate position of women and members of disadvantaged minority groups. Because the denigration occurs in a humorous rather than a serious mode, it is difficult for the targets to complain, since the sources can claim that they were "only joking." Indeed, the sources may even convince themselves that it is "all in fun," and that the targets really have no reason to take offense.

Ingratiation

Whereas humor may be used by higher-status individuals to maintain dominance over others, it can also be used by lower-status persons as an *ingratiation tactic* to gain attention, approval, and favors from others (Kane et al., 1977). Ingratiation refers to behaviors such as other-enhancement, opinion conformity, self-deprecation, and feigned interpersonal similarity, which are used to garner favors from a higher-status person. When done in a serious communication mode, ingratiation runs the risk of having one's insincerity unmasked, especially when there is considerable advantage to be gained and when the target's status is very high. However, if ingratiation is done in a humorous way, such as using a "backhanded compliment," there is less likelihood that the source will be exposed as insincere (Long and Graesser, 1988, p. 54). For example, to avoid sounding ingratiating, one might say to a basketball star, "You would make a great basketball player if you could only learn to dribble the ball," rather than "You are an amazing player."

Laughing at another person's jokes can also be a form of ingratiation. The higher the status of a public speaker, the more likely are his or her jokes and funny anecdotes to evoke laughter in the audience (Kane et al., 1977). In addition, ingratiation may involve efforts to amuse others at one's own expense, engaging in silly or inappropriate behavior to get a laugh from others, making excessively self-disparaging witty comments, or laughing along with others when one is the target of their teasing or ridicule. As we will see in Chapter 9, individuals who frequently engage in this sort of "self-defeating humor", although they may be very funny and witty, tend to have low self-esteem and high neuroticism and have difficulties maintaining satisfactory personal relationships (R. A. Martin et al., 2003).

Group Identity and Cohesion

Although humor can be used to reinforce status differences between people, it can also be a way of enhancing cohesion and a sense of group identity. Gary Alan Fine (1977) used the term *idioculture* to describe the system of knowledge, beliefs, and customs by which a small group of people defines itself and enables its members to share a sense of belonging and cohesion. He suggested that humor, in the form of friendly teasing, funny nicknames, shared "in-jokes," and slang terms, can contribute to the idioculture of a group, providing a way for members to construct a shared reality and sense of meaning. This function of humor also occurs in close dyads, such as married couples, for whom private humor can create a shared identity and thus strengthen their feelings of cohesion.

In task-oriented groups such as those found in work settings, interactions among members have two important functions: (1) to accomplish group goals and (2) to maintain smooth relations (Robinson and Smith-Lovin, 2001). Humor may help group members to maintain smooth relations by serving as a stress reliever when the pressures of task accomplishment begin to build. In a field study of humor among employees in a small, family-owned business, Karen Vinton (1989) observed that humor tended to create bonds among the employees and thereby facilitated the accomplishment of work tasks.

Jenepher Terrion and Blake Ashforth (2002) examined the role of "putdown humor" in an observational study of a six-week executive development course for senior police officers at the Canadian Police College in Ottawa. They concluded that, rather than having a disruptive effect, putdown humor "played a prominent role in melding this temporary group into a more or less cohesive unit" (p. 80). They observed a progression in the targets of humor over the six weeks, from putdowns of oneself to putdowns of shared identities, external groups, and, finally, other group members. The use of putdown humor appeared to be influenced by a set of implicit social rules regarding the appropriate targets, methods, and responses, which served to maintain self-esteem and a positive group climate.

For example, putdowns of group members targeted relatively inconsequential characteristics, and were only directed toward those individuals who did not take offense but demonstrated an ability to laugh along in a good-natured way. Interestingly, when group members were later interviewed about particular humorous exchanges that had taken place within the group, they often had differing interpretations about the meaning of the event, but assumed that their own interpretations were shared by everyone else. Thus, the multiplicity and ambiguity of meaning in humor seemed to enable group members to interact as if they shared common perceptions, thereby fostering a sense of community despite their actual differences in perspective. The authors of this study observed that humor seemed to serve the function of a collective social ritual that was governed by implicit norms and enhanced the sense of group solidarity.

Discourse Management

During the course of a conversation, participants need to attend not only to the content of what is being said, but they also need to monitor and manage the flow of the conversation (Ervin-Tripp, 1993). Conversations are mutual activities that require the cooperation of all participants to make the discussion intelligible and satisfactory. This involves such discourse activities as turn-taking, exchanging control, setting the tone or style of the conversation, introducing topics, shifting topics, checking for meaning, eye gaze, repetition, paraphrasing, and terminating the conversation. Humor may be used for many of these purposes.

In research using the method of conversational analysis, Neal Norrick (1993) studied these functions in some detail, observing the way humor can be used to shift the conversation away from a threatening topic, to change the tone of the conversation from one that is serious to one that is more lighthearted, and so on. As one example, making a pun based on multiple meanings of a word that has been used in a conversation can be a way for one person to humorously call attention to the ambiguity in something another person has said. Humor can also be used to initiate conversations in situations in which there is little shared knowledge between the participants (e.g., strangers). For example, a witty comment about the weather might generate further conversation, whereas a more serious comment that simply states the obvious might seem trite (Long and Graesser, 1988).

Discourse management functions of humor were studied by social psychologist John La Gaipa (1977) at the University of Windsor in Canada, who videotaped 22 small groups of male friends engaging in spontaneous conversations in a college pub. Sequential analyses revealed that when one group member made a humorous comment, this typically resulted in a significant increase in the conversational tempo, or rate of participation of all the group members, immediately afterwards. The type and target of the humor affected the tempo in various ways. For example, when the humor involved friendly putdowns, it led to a greater increase in tempo if it was directed at a group member (i.e., friendly teasing of someone within the group) than if it was in reference to someone outside the group. However, this pattern was reversed when the humor was more hostile or aggressive. When directed at a person within the group, this type of sarcastic humor led to a reduction in the rate of conversation, whereas nasty humorous remarks about someone outside the group led to an increased tempo. These different types of humor also produced different amounts of laughter, but the effects of humor on the flow of conversation remained even after controlling for the amount of laughter generated.

Depending on whether or not participants share the same goals in a conversation, the use of humor in discourse management can be disruptive to conversation as well as facilitative. For example, individuals who frequently make puns in response to ambiguous words of others can be quite disruptive to the flow of the conversation, diverting the focus away from the current topic and toward their own cleverness. Similarly, joke-telling can be a way of taking control of a conversation for a relatively extended period of time, putting on a performance to which listeners are expected to respond with approving laughter (Norrick, 2003). If other participants in the conversation desire a more serious mode of discussion or a more equitable give-and-take, these uses of humor may be viewed as intrusive and even aggressive.

Social Play

Besides these "serious" functions of humor in social interactions, humor can also be enjoyed purely for its own sake as a pleasurable form of social play. This type of humor most frequently occurs in groups of friends or close acquaintances of equal status in informal settings. As previously noted, Michael Apter (1982) viewed humor as a playful paratelic activity that is enjoyed for its own sake, as opposed to the serious, goal-oriented, arousal-avoidant telic mode of functioning in which we find ourselves during much of our daily lives.

In engaging in humor as social play, participants typically abandon, at least temporarily, any serious conversational goals. Playing off one another, they amuse themselves with the multiple meanings of words and ideas, relating funny anecdotes about incongruous events and experiences, and often using exaggeration, gestures, and facial expressions to maximize the humorous effect. Participants often experience high levels of mirth, and laughter can be loud and unconstrained during these times. While such humor is enjoyed for its own sake, it nonetheless often serves additional interpersonal functions of enhancing group cohesiveness, laughing at outsiders, and strengthening social bonds.

TEASING

Teasing is a particular form of humor that serves many of the interpersonal functions just discussed. Like other types of humor, teasing is paradoxical, combining both prosocial and aggressive functions. As Keltner and his colleagues (1998) noted, "teasing criticizes yet compliments, attacks yet makes people closer, humiliates yet expresses affection" (p. 1231). According to Shapiro, Baumeister, and Kessler (1991), teasing comprises three components: aggression, humor, and ambiguity. In recent years, a considerable amount of research attention has been devoted to teasing by social psychologists as well as sociologists, anthropologists, and linguists (for reviews, see Keltner et al., 2001; Kowalski et al., 2001).

Social psychologist Dacher Keltner and his colleagues (2001) proposed a "face threat" analysis of teasing, conceptualizing it in terms of Goffman's (1967) ideas about the importance of saving face in social interactions, particularly those interactions that involve confrontation or communication of information that is potentially embarrassing to the speaker or listener. They defined teasing as "an intentional provocation accompanied by playful off-record markers that together comment on something relevant to the target" (p. 234). In this definition, "provocation" refers to the fact that teasing is a verbal or nonverbal act that is intended to have some effect and to elicit a reaction from the target. Off-record markers are the verbal and nonverbal cues (such as smiling, exaggeration, or certain vocal inflections) that accompany a tease and indicate that it is to be taken in jest, making it a humorous as well as an ambiguous communication that is delivered indirectly rather than directly (P. Brown and Levinson, 1987). The humorous and ambiguous nature of teasing enables the source to say things that would be face-threatening and potentially unacceptable if communicated in a serious mode, since the source can always say "I was just joking" if the communication is not well received by the target.

Teasing can be used for a number of different purposes, ranging from prosocial and friendly to hostile and malicious. The aggressiveness of the tease depends on the degree of identity confrontation and the amount of ambiguity and humor that are present (Kowalski et al., 2001). In playful, friendly teasing, close friends might say things to one another that, if taken literally, would appear to be rather demeaning or critical. The playful manner of the tease, however, communicates that the message is not intended to be taken literally and, indeed, the opposite meaning is intended: the source actually means to compliment the target in an ironic way. This playful aggression is similar to play fighting among children and young animals. Rather than being aggressive, the unspoken subtext in such friendly teasing is an affirmation of the strength of the relationship between the two individuals, calling attention to the fact that they are close enough that they can say negative things and not take offense. The laughter of both the source and the target signals that the tease is not taken seriously by either, and this can help to increase further the feelings of closeness (Terrion and Ashforth, 2002).

This sort of friendly teasing is also seen in "roasts," in which friends and coworkers take turns humorously belittling a guest of honor, as well as in humorous greeting cards that indirectly convey feelings of affection and sentimentality in the guise of an overtly insulting message (Oring, 1994). Since teasing is seen as inappropriate between people who do not know each other well, this sort of friendly teasing can also be a way for individuals to signal a desire to move an acquaintanceship to a more intimate level of friendship. Although these forms of teasing are essentially nonaggressive, however, there is always a potential for them to backfire if the recipient misperceives the humorous intention or for some reason takes the message seriously. Also, even the most friendly teasing tends to elicit less positive feelings in the target than in the source of the teasing (Keltner et al., 1998).

Practical jokes are another form of humor closely related to this sort of friendly teasing. Whereas teasing involves saying things that would normally be viewed as somewhat insulting, practical jokes involve playing tricks on another person that would normally be viewed as rather unkind. Like teasing, practical jokes can be a way of indirectly demonstrating (or testing) the strength of a relationship, showing that partners feel good enough about each other that they can put up with these playful inconveniences. If the target takes offense, the source can say "it was all in fun," and back away gracefully. On the other hand, if the target responds with laughter, this affirmation of goodwill and tolerance generates feelings of greater closeness between them. Since the source of a practical joke tends to enjoy it more and finds it funnier than the target does, the target typically feels a need to respond in kind, in order to "even the score." Consequently, practical joking can become a kind of tit-for-tat game, in which each person tries to think up ever more outrageous tricks to play on the other. As long as the participants continue to enjoy it, this game adds pleasure to the friendship. However, there is always a risk that practical joking might escalate to the point where it is no longer enjoyable to one of the partners, potentially destabilizing the relationship.

A somewhat more aggressive form of teasing, which often takes place between close friends, romantic partners, or parents and children, involves its use as a mild form of censure, communicating disapproval of some aspect of the target's habits, behaviors, or preferences (Keltner et al., 1998). For example, if a person perceives a friend to be overly demanding or rigid, he or she might use teasing as a way of drawing attention to the excessiveness of this behavior. This use of humor allows both the source and the target to save face, diminishing the risk of defensiveness on the part of the target and increasing the likelihood of compliance. Thus, this form of teasing involves the use of humor as a form of social influence. Studies have shown that recipients of this sort of teasing usually respond in a serious way to the underlying message, explaining or justifying the targeted behavior, rather than laughing along with the source (Keltner et al., 1998).

In even more aggressive forms of teasing, the confrontation becomes more direct, and the humor and ambiguity of the message are reduced. In its most aggressive forms, teasing can take the form of bullying (Whitney and Smith, 1993) and even violent behavior (Arriaga, 2002). Even at these more aggressive levels, though, the humorous nature of teasing allows the source to disclaim the aggressive intent, claiming that the communication was intended as a joke, and thereby making it difficult for the target to take offense. These aggressive forms of teasing can therefore be very coercive and manipulative.

Keltner and his associates at the University of California at Berkeley conducted two experiments to investigate hypotheses derived from their face-threat analysis of teasing (Keltner et al., 1998). In one study, they asked high- and low-status members of a college fraternity to generate teasing comments about one another and rate their feelings afterwards. As predicted, low-status members teased in more prosocial ways, while high-status members were more aggressive. Overall, most teasing concerned negative rather than positive characteristics, consistent with the idea that teasing is generally used to point out flaws and norm violations in the target. However, when positive characteristics did appear as the topic of teasing, this was more likely to occur when low-status sources teased high-status targets, rather than the other way around. Not surprisingly, individuals with higher scores on a measure of the personality trait of agreeableness tended to use less aggressive forms of teasing. The aggressive nature of teasing was also seen in the fact that targets reported and displayed more negative emotions than did the sources. Furthermore, low-status members showed more embarrassment, pain, and fear in their facial expressions, whereas high-status members showed more hostility, both when teasing and when being teased.

In the second study, a similar methodology was used with heterosexual dating couples who were asked to generate teases about each other. Individuals who were less satisfied with their relationship teased their partners in more aggressive ways. As in the previous study, teasing was more frequently about negative than positive characteristics of the target, and targets of teasing displayed more negative emotions than did sources. More prosocial teasing produced more positive emotional responses in both targets and sources. Although men and women did not differ in the aggressiveness of their teasing, women experienced more negative and less positive feelings in response to being teased by their male partners. Overall, these studies provided support for the view of teasing as a way of expressing censure and dominance in a face-saving way.

How does aggressive teasing affect observers who are not themselves the target of the teasing? Leslie Janes and James Olson (2000), social psychologists at the University of Western Ontario, conducted two experiments in which they examined the inhibiting effects of observing another person being ridiculed in a humorous way (i.e., teased), which they referred to as "jeer pressure." In both experiments, they had university students watch videotapes depicting a male actor either ridiculing another person, or directing the same humorous disparaging remarks at himself, or using nondisparaging humor. In both studies, those who had viewed the other-disparaging videotape, as compared to those in the other two groups, subsequently exhibited greater inhibition in their performance on several tasks. In particular, they showed greater conformity with the views of others in a rating task and, on a ring-toss task, they revealed greater fear of failure as demonstrated by less willingness to take risks. In addition, they responded more quickly to rejection-related words on a lexical decision task, indicating activation of a rejection schema.

Janes and Olson interpreted their findings as demonstrating that seeing someone else being ridiculed or aggressively teased makes people perceive themselves to be at increased risk of rejection themselves, and consequently they avoid behaving in ways that might make them stand out and become a potential target of teasing too. The strength of these effects is quite remarkable, considering the fact that the subjects were merely watching a videotape and therefore the likelihood of being targets of teasing themselves was minimal. Overall, this study indicates that aggressive teasing can have a detrimental effect not only on the targets of negative teasing but also on those who observe another person being teased.

SOCIAL ASPECTS OF LAUGHTER

As noted in Chapter 1, laughter is an expressive behavior signaling the presence of the emotion of mirth. The reason it is so loud and comprises unique sounds and facial expressions is because it is a method of communication, designed to capture the attention of others, to convey important emotional information, and to activate similar emotions in others. Thus, laughter is inherently social. Research indicates that people are 30 times more likely to laugh when they are with others than when they are alone (Provine and Fischer, 1989). Laughter originated long before the development of language as a method of communication. Thus, it seems to be "a unique and ancient mode of prelinguistic auditory communication that is now performed in parallel with modern speech and language" (Provine, 1992, p. 1).

What is the interpersonal function of laughter? As noted in Chapter 1, it appears to have evolved in humans from the rapid, breathy panting vocalization seen in chimpanzees and other apes during rough-and-tumble social play, which is accompanied by the relaxed open-mouth display or "play face" (Preuschoft and van Hooff, 1997; van Hooff and Preuschoft, 2003). A number of theorists have therefore suggested that laughter is a communication signal designed to indicate to others that one is experiencing the playful emotional state of mirth. In this view, the meaning of laughter is to convey the message "This is play" (e.g., van Hooff, 1972).

More recently, however, some researchers have proposed an affect-induction view, arguing that laughter not only conveys cognitive information to others but it also serves the function of inducing and accentuating positive emotions in others, in order to influence their behavior and promote a more favorable attitude toward the one who is laughing (e.g., Bachorowski and Owren, 2003; Owren and Bachorowski, 2003; Russell et al., 2003). These authors have suggested that the peculiar sounds of laughter have a direct effect on the listener, inducing positive emotional arousal that mirrors the emotional state of the laugher, perhaps by activating certain brain circuits in the listener (Provine, 1996). Gervais and Wilson (2005) suggested that these brain circuits may be akin to the mirror neurons, or mirror-matching systems, that have been the subject of a good deal of recent research in social neuroscience and are thought to form an important neural basis for human social relationships by enabling individuals to experience and appreciate the actions and emotions of others (Rizzolatti and Craighero, 2004). In Chapter 6, I will discuss some recent brain-imaging studies that investigated the regions of the brain that are activated when we hear others laughing.

The view of laughter as a means of inducing mirth in others helps to explain why it is so contagious. When we hear other people laughing heartily, it is difficult not to begin laughing also. Presumably, it is the emotion of mirth that is "caught" in such instances of laughter contagion. Hearing others laugh induces this positive emotion, which in turn causes us to laugh. Numerous experiments have shown that participants who are exposed to humorous stimuli (e.g., jokes, cartoons, or comedy films) in the presence of a laughing person or while listening to recorded laughter, in comparison to those in no-laughter control conditions, are more likely to laugh themselves and tend to rate the stimuli as being more funny (G. E. Brown, D. Brown, and Ramos, 1981; Donoghue, McCarrey, and Clement, 1983; Fuller and Sheehy-Skeffington, 1974; G. N. Martin and Gray, 1996; Porterfield et al., 1988). These findings account for the widespread use of recorded laughter sound tracks accompanying television comedy programs, which presumably enhance audience enjoyment and perceptions of funniness. Other experiments have shown that the larger the audience, the more likely they will be to laugh at a comedy performance, as long as they are not overly crowded into a small space (Prerost, 1977).

A study by Robert Provine (1992), using a "laughter box," showed that the sound of laughter alone, without any other humorous stimuli being present, is enough to trigger laughter in most listeners. However, repeated exposure to the same laughter recording quickly becomes aversive and no longer elicits laughter after a few repetitions. In a similar vein, Jo-Anne Bachorowski and her colleagues found that laughter containing variable acoustic properties is rated as more enjoyable by listeners than laughter that is more repetitious (Bachorowski, Smoski, and Owren, 2001).

Early research on social aspects of laughter consisting primarily of laboratory studies examined the effects of listening to rather artificial recorded laughter on people's enjoyment of jokes, cartoons, and comedy films. More recently, however, investigators have gone out of the laboratory and begun to study spontaneous laughter occurring in the context of more naturalistic social interactions. In a study reported by Robert Provine (1993), at the University of Maryland, small groups of people interacting in public places were surreptitiously observed, and each time someone laughed, the dialogue immediately preceding the laughter was written down. In a sample of 1200 such episodes, laughter was found to occur almost exclusively at the end of completed sentences rather than in the middle, suggesting that "laughter punctuates speech" (see Nwokah, Hsu, Davies, and Fogel, 1999, however, for evidence of laughter co-occurring with speech in mother-infant interactions). Provine also found that people were significantly more likely to laugh after something they themselves said than after something said by another person, and that women tended to laugh more frequently than men.

Interestingly, Provine noted that in these naturalistic conversations most of the laughter did not occur in response to joke-telling or other obvious structured attempts at humor. Instead, it frequently followed seemingly mundane statements and questions (e.g., "It was nice meeting you too," or "What is that supposed to mean?"). Provine therefore argued that much of our everyday laughter actually has little to do with humor *per se*, but instead is a social signal of friendliness and positive emotion generally. It is not clear from this research, however, whether the subjects were actually perceiving these utterances as being funny (i.e., containing some sort of nonserious incongruities) and therefore experiencing genuine mirth, or whether their laughter was simply a friendly social signal as Provine argued (Gervais and Wilson,

2005). Since Provine only recorded the last sentence spoken before each episode of laughter, we do not have enough information to know whether the larger conversational context may have made these statements funny, just as we would not perceive the humor if we simply heard a series of joke punch lines without the setups. This is a question that merits further investigation.

In another study of laughter in social interaction, Julia Vettin and Dietmar Todt (2004), at the Free University of Berlin, tape-recorded 48 hours of conversations among dyads of friends and strangers in naturalistic settings. They found an average of 5.8 bouts of laughter occurring in each 10-minute period of conversation, with a range of 0 to 15 bouts. A laughter bout was defined as the series of "ha-ha-ha" sounds emitted during a single exhalation. These rates appear to be much higher than the frequencies that have been reported in self-report daily diary studies of laughter (Mannell and McMahon, 1982; R. A. Martin and Kuiper, 1999). This suggests that, when completing such records, people tend to underestimate how frequently they laugh and may not even notice some of the times when they are laughing. Interestingly, this study found that, on average, participants laughed just as frequently with strangers as they did with close friends.

As in Provine's (1993) investigations, individuals in Vettin and Todt's study laughed more frequently following their own utterances than following an utterance of their conversational partner. Also similar to Provine's findings, speakers generally did not laugh in the middle of a sentence. However, unlike Provine, this study found that listeners often laughed while their conversational partners were still speaking. Acoustical analyses of the laughter revealed a great deal of variability, both within and between individuals (cf. Bachorowski et al., 2001). In addition, it was found that some of the acoustical parameters of laughter varied systematically according to the context and whether the laughter was produced by the speaker or the listener. These findings further highlight the conversational nature of laughter, indicating that it is a nonverbal method of communication.

To study listeners' affective responses to different types of laughter, Jo-Anne Bachorowski and Michael Owren (2001), at Vanderbilt University, conducted five experiments in which they asked male and female participants to complete a number of ratings after listening to recordings of different types of laughs produced by men and women. These included voiced, harmonically rich songlike laughs, and unvoiced gruntlike, snortlike, and cacklelike laughs. In each of the studies, the voiced songlike laughs elicited more positive evaluations than did any of the unvoiced laughs. This occurred regardless of whether listeners rated their own emotional responses, the likely responses of others, or perceived attributes of the laughers (e.g., friendliness, sexiness, or listener's interest in meeting the laugher). Based on these findings, the authors suggested that the acoustic variability in laughter is important for its affect-induction function, eliciting a range of different emotional responses in listeners.

A subsequent study by Moria Smoski and Jo-Anne Bachorowski (2003) also examined the role of laughter in social interaction. They proposed that "antiphonal" laughter (i.e., laughter that occurs during or immediately after a social partner's laugh) is part of an affect-induction process that promotes affiliative, cooperative behavior between social partners. They hypothesized that antiphonal laughter should therefore increase in frequency as friendships develop between people. To test this hypothesis, they audiotaped same-sex and mixed-sex friend and stranger dyads while they played brief games designed to facilitate laugh production. As predicted, significantly more antiphonal laughter (controlling for overall laughter rates) occurred in friend dyads than in stranger dyads. In addition, in mixed-sex dyads, females were more likely to laugh antiphonally than were males, suggesting that females may be particularly attuned to positive affective expressions by males.

Taken together, these studies provide considerable support for the view that laughter is a form of social communication that is used to express positive emotions and also to elicit positive emotional responses in others. As such, it seems to have an important social facilitation and bonding function, promoting and helping to synchronize and coordinate social interactions by coupling the emotions of group members (Gervais and Wilson, 2005; Provine, 1992).

HUMOR, SOCIAL PERCEPTION, AND INTERPERSONAL ATTRACTION

How do we gather information and form impressions of other people? What factors cause us to be attracted to some people and to dislike others? How do these processes of social perception and attraction influence our decisions in selecting a mate or forming a close friendship with someone? These types of questions have long been of particular interest to social psychologists. In the following sections, I will explore some of the ways humor may play an important role in all these processes.

Social Perception

When we meet other people for the first time, we tend to quickly form impressions and make judgments about their personality characteristics such as their friendliness, trustworthiness, motives, and so on (E. E. Jones, 1990). Indeed, the ability to form relatively accurate impressions of others rapidly and efficiently may have been important for survival in our evolutionary history. One source of information that contributes to our initial impressions of others is the way they express humor. As we have seen, humor is a form of interpersonal communication, and a good sense of humor is therefore an important social skill that we typically admire in others.

Although a sense of humor is generally viewed as a positive characteristic in other people, the way another person's humor influences our impressions may depend in part on our previous expectations about that person. In an early study of the role of humor in person perception, undergraduate participants were asked to evaluate a professor after watching a videotaped lecture (Mettee, Hrelec, and Wilkens, 1971). Before the lecture, the participants were given a summary of the professor's personality characteristics; half of the subjects were told that he was an aloof, humorless person, and half were told that he was somewhat "clownish" and given to being indiscreet in his use of humor. The participants all watched videotapes of the same professor giving the same lecture, except that for some subjects he told a joke at one point in the lecture, whereas for others he did not. Analyses of the participants' ratings indicated that, in the joke condition, those who had been led to expect an aloof and humorless lecturer found the joke funnier and rated the lecturer as more competent, as compared to those who were told that he was "clownish" and given to silly humor. However, regardless of whether they had been told he was aloof or clownish, subjects rated the lecturer as more likable when he told a joke than when he did not.

Our perceptions of other people may also be influenced by the type of humor they use, the responses of others to their humor, and the social context in which they express it. Peter Derks and Jack Berkowitz (1989) randomly assigned almost 800 male and female undergraduates to various conditions in which they read alternate versions of a story in which a male (or female) tells a cute (or dirty) joke to a group of friends (or strangers) at a party (or at work), and everyone (or no one) laughs. The participants were then asked to rate their impressions of the joke-teller on a number of dimensions. The joke-teller who told a "dirty," as compared to a "cute" joke, was rated as significantly less sincere, less friendly, less intelligent, more thoughtless, and more obnoxious. Dirty jokes were viewed particularly negatively if they were told to strangers rather than friends, and by males rather than by females. Thus, telling "dirty" jokes does not appear to be a very good way of making a positive first impression on others.

Regardless of which type of joke was told, if the audience laughed at it, the joke-teller was perceived as more attractive, but also as less sincere, than if the audience did not laugh. Males found joke-tellers to be particularly attractive if they made people laugh at work, whereas females rated most attractive those who made people laugh at a party. Overall, those who told jokes at work were rated as more friendly than were those who told jokes at a party. This latter finding may be explained by attribution theory (H. H. Kelley, 1972), which suggests that we attribute the causes of behavior to internal personality traits when it occurs in situations where it is not normally expected, and to external causes when it occurs in situations where the behavior is more expected. Since people typically tell jokes at parties more frequently than at work, telling a joke at work is more likely to elicit attributions that the behavior is due to internal traits such as friendliness.

A later study by Derks and his colleagues replicated and extended these findings (Derks, Kalland, and Etgen, 1995). One finding in the later study was that the failure of an audience to laugh at a joke led to perceptions of the joke-teller as being more aggressive and less affiliative as compared to situations where the audience laughed at the joke. Overall, then, the effect of humor on impression formation depends on a variety of factors, including the type of humor, the social context, and the degree to which other people find the person amusing.

Interpersonal Attraction

In general, we tend to be attracted to people who display a sense of humor. In the cost-benefit analyses underlying interpersonal attraction (K. S. Cook and Rice,

2003), a sense of humor in another person increases the perceived benefits of a relationship (the pleasant feelings associated with laughter) and decreases the perceived costs (there is less likelihood that the person will become easily offended or burden us with negative emotional reactions). An experiment by Barbara Fraley and Arthur Aron (2004) examined the degree to which a shared humorous experience during a first encounter between strangers leads to greater feelings of closeness. In this study, same-sex stranger pairs participated together in a series of tasks that were designed either to generate a great deal of humor or to be enjoyable but not humorous. After completing these tasks, they were each asked to rate their perceptions of their partner and their feelings on a number of scales, including how close they felt to the other person.

The participants in the humorous task condition laughed much more frequently and rated the activity as being significantly more humorous than did those in the non-humorous condition, indicating that the manipulation of humor was successful. At the same time, the two conditions were rated as being equally enjoyable. As predicted, the participants in the humorous condition reported feeling much closer and more attracted to each other afterwards, as compared to those in the nonhumorous condition. Further analyses revealed that this effect was due to differences in the perceived funniness and not merely the enjoyableness of the conditions.

The authors also tested several hypotheses concerning possible mediators and moderators of the observed effects of shared humor. They found that the effect of humor on perceived closeness was mediated in part by perceptions of "self-expansion" (feeling that one has gained a new perspective on things and a greater sense of awareness as a result of the interaction), as well as by distraction from the initial discomfort associated with interacting with a stranger, but not by perceptions of self-disclosure or greater acceptance by the partner. Furthermore, the effect of humor on closeness was stronger for participants with a greater sense of humor and for those with a more anxious attachment style. In summary, sharing humor in an initial encounter between strangers appears to enhance feelings of closeness and mutual attraction by expanding each person's sense of self and by reducing their feelings of discomfort and anxiety, particularly among people who generally have a good sense of humor as well as those who usually tend to feel anxious about their close relationships.

While we tend to be attracted to people with whom we have a humorous interaction in our first encounter, we may be particularly attracted to those who laugh at our jokes, since this indicates that they share our sense of humor. In an experiment by Arnie Cann and his colleagues, participants were instructed to tell a joke to a same-sex stranger who was actually a confederate of the experimenter (Cann, Calhoun, and Banks, 1997). For half of the subjects, the stranger laughed at the joke, and for the other half he or she did not. Half of the participants were also given information indicating that the stranger held attitudes and beliefs about social issues that were very similar to their own, whereas the other half were led to believe that the stranger held dissimilar views. The participants subsequently rated their perceptions of the stranger and their feelings of attraction to him or her.

As predicted, the results indicated that both greater similarity in attitudes and the stranger's laughter in response to the joke led to more positive perceptions and greater attraction to the stranger. Interestingly, the effect of laughter on the part of the stranger was even powerful enough to overcome the well-established negative effect of attitude dissimilarity on attraction. A stranger with dissimilar social attitudes who laughed in response to the participant's joke was perceived more positively than was a stranger with similar attitudes who did not laugh. The authors suggested that laughter from the stranger indicates that this person has a sense of humor, and, moreover, that he or she shares the subject's style of humor, both of which contribute to positive attraction. These humor perceptions seem to be even more important than the well-established effect on attraction of sharing similar attitudes and beliefs. Viewed in another way, these findings suggest that laughing at the funny things another person says is a way not only of expressing feelings of attraction but also of enhancing one's own attractiveness to the other person (Grammer, 1990).

Humor as a Desirable Trait in Friendship and Mate Selection

As noted in Chapter 1, over the past century a sense of humor has become a highly prized personality characteristic, but it is also rather vaguely defined in most people's minds. In much the same way as physical attractiveness is highly valued and is perceived to be associated with many desirable traits (Eagly, Ashmore, Makhijani, and Longo, 1991), we tend to hold positive stereotypes about individuals whom we perceive to have a sense of humor. Studies have shown that people tend to assume that individuals with a strong sense of humor are also characterized by a number of other desirable traits, such as being friendly, extraverted, considerate, pleasant, interesting, imaginative, intelligent, perceptive, and emotionally stable (Cann and Calhoun, 2001). Due to this positive stereotype, we often use other people's sense of humor as a guide in choosing our friends and romantic partners. Sprecher and Regan (2002) surveyed 700 men and women about their preferences for a number of attributes in either a casual sex partner, dating partner, marriage partner, same-sex friend, or opposite-sex friend. Across all these relationship types, a good sense of humor was one of the most highly rated characteristics, along with warmth and openness. Similar findings have been obtained in a number of other studies (Goodwin, 1990; Goodwin and Tang, 1991; Kenrick, Sadalla, Groth, and Trost, 1990).

Analyses of the kinds of characteristics sought in potential romantic partners in personal ads placed in newspapers and singles magazines have found that women particularly look for a sense of humor in male partners, whereas men, although they still place a high value on a sense of humor in a woman, rate physical attractiveness as somewhat more important (Provine, 2000; J. E. Smith, Waldorf, and Trembath, 1990). A similar pattern of sex differences has been found in some survey studies (e.g., Daniel, O'Brien, McCabe, and Quinter, 1985). A meta-analysis of the research on mate selection preferences concluded that there is a significant but relatively small tendency for women to place greater weight than men on the importance of a sense of humor in a potential partner (Feingold, 1992).

An experiment by Duane Lundy and his colleagues examined the effects of self-deprecating humor and physical attractiveness on observers' desire for future interaction in various types of heterosexual relationships (Lundy, Tan, and Cunningham, 1998). Male and female college students were shown a photograph and a transcript of an interview with a person of the opposite sex (the target person). The participants were randomly assigned to conditions in which the photograph depicted either an attractive or unattractive person, and the transcript either did or did not contain a self-deprecating humorous comment supposedly made by the target. The participants were asked to rate the target in terms of mate qualities by indicating the degree to which they would be interested in several types of relationships with him or her, including dating, sexual intercourse, long-term relationship, marriage, and marriage with children.

As in previous research, men rated the more physically attractive female target as a more desirable partner for almost all types of relationships. Men's ratings of desirability were not affected by the presence or absence of humor in the transcript. In contrast, for women, physical attractiveness of the male target did not directly influence their ratings of desirability. Instead, for female participants, there was an interaction between the physical attractiveness of the target and whether or not he expressed humor. In particular, humor increased the perceived desirability if the target was physically attractive, but it had no effect if he was unattractive. This pattern held for ratings of desirability for both short- and long-term relationships. These results suggest that self-deprecating humor may increase romantic attraction of women toward men, but only when other variables (such as physical attractiveness) are favorable. Further analyses of the rating data indicated that women viewed the humorous, physically attractive male as being more caring than the nonhumorous, physically attractive male.

Contrary to previous research evidence that humor is perceived as an indicator of intelligence (Cann and Calhoun, 2001), both male and female participants tended to view the humorous target as being slightly *less* intelligent than the nonhumorous one. However, the results of this study may have been influenced by the self-deprecating nature of the humor displayed by the target and not to humor in general. In particular, the humor in this experiment may not have been sufficient or of the right type to evoke perceptions that the target had a "sense of humor," along with all the positive qualities that are associated with this stereotype. Additional research is needed to determine whether these findings can be replicated using different degrees or types of humor. Some other research suggests that, for women, having a good sense of humor (as well as being emotionally stable) can make up for being relatively less physically attractive in determining the degree to which they are seen by males as attractive romantic partners (Feingold, 1981). I will review some additional research along these lines in my discussion of evolutionary theories of humor in Chapter 6.

Overall, the research on humor, social perception, and attraction indicates that we tend to have positive attitudes toward people who demonstrate a sense of humor. People with a sense of humor are generally assumed also to have a number of other positive characteristics, and this trait is highly desirable in the selection of a friend or romantic partner. As we saw earlier, research indicates that the sound of laughter in others induces positive feelings in the listener (Bachorowski and Owren, 2001). The positive emotion elicited by shared laughter with someone who has a sense of humor may serve to reinforce mutual feelings of attraction, strengthening positive attitudes, instilling a sense of trust and loyalty, and promoting the development of close relationships (Smoski and Bachorowski, 2003).

HUMOR AND PERSUASION

Is a humorous message more persuasive than a serious one? The widespread use of humor in television and radio advertisements suggests that advertisers view humor as a useful tool in persuading people to buy their products. Also, politicians frequently sprinkle humor in their campaign speeches, presumably because they believe this will help in persuading people to vote for them. Surprisingly, however, there is little research evidence that humorous messages are more persuasive, overall, than are non-humorous ones. A review of the relevant research (Weinberger and Gulas, 1992) found five studies on humor in advertising that indicated a positive effect on persuasion, eight studies that indicated only mixed or no effect, and one that even found humorous advertisements to be *less* persuasive than serious ones.

In research on humor and persuasion outside of advertising (e.g., persuasive speeches or essays), none of the studies demonstrated an overall superiority of humorous over nonhumorous messages, seven studies found neutral or mixed results, and one study found a negative effect of humor on persuasiveness (Weinberger and Gulas, 1992). Thus, simply making a message humorous does not necessarily make it more persuasive. This conclusion is perhaps less surprising than it may initially seem: if humorous messages were always more persuasive, advertisers and politicians would likely have figured that out by now, and we would see nothing but humorous advertisements on television and politicians constantly cracking jokes throughout their campaign speeches!

The wide variation in research findings suggests that the role of humor in persuasion is more complex, with certain types of humor contributing to persuasiveness in some circumstances but not in others. For example, one study found that humorous advertisements were more effective than nonhumorous ones with viewers who already had a positive attitude toward the product, whereas humor was less effective with those who had pre-existing negative brand attitudes (Chattopadhyay and Basu, 1990). Another study found that the addition of humor to a low-intensity, soft-sell advertising approach increased the level of persuasion, whereas the addition of humor to a hard-sell approach actually decreased persuasiveness (Markiewicz, 1974). Weinberger and Gulas (1992) suggested that the effectiveness of humor in advertising depends on the objectives one seeks to achieve, the target audience, the product being advertised, and the type of humor used.

The complex role of humor in persuasion may be better understood if we consider the factors that have been found to be relevant to persuasion in general. Contemporary research suggests that the persuasiveness of a message depends not only on the message itself but also on characteristics of the audience, such as attention, distraction, involvement, motivation, self-esteem, and intelligence. According to the Elaboration Likelihood Model developed by Richard Petty and John Cacioppo (1986), persuasion can be achieved by means of two potential routes: a central processing route and a peripheral processing route. The *central route*, which involves active elaboration of the message by the listener, occurs when the listener finds the message personally relevant and has pre-existing ideas and beliefs about the issue. In this route, listeners will become convinced of an argument if they find it logically compelling. In contrast, the *peripheral route* involves less well-thought-out responses based on "heuristic" cues such as moods and emotions, familiar phrases, or the attributes of the message source (e.g., level of expertise, likeability, or perceived lack of self-interested motives). This route occurs when the listener is less highly invested or motivated, is not able to understand the message, or does not like to deal with complex information, and it generally leads to less stable changes in attitudes and behavior.

Research suggests that the effects of humor on persuasion may have more to do with the peripheral than the central processing route. In particular, humor seems to be more effective in influencing emotional variables, such as liking and positive mood, than cognitive ones, such as comprehension of the message (Calvin P. Duncan and Nelson, 1985). There is little evidence that humor increases the perceived credibility of the source of a message, or that it improves comprehension of the message (Weinberger and Gulas, 1992). However, there is considerable evidence that humor has emotional effects on the audience, tending to put them into a more positive mood (C. C. Moran, 1996). Studies also indicate that humor enhances the listener's liking of the source and the product being advertised (Weinberger and Gulas, 1992). Humor also has an attention-grabbing effect, causing people to attend to the humorous aspects of the message (Madden and Weinberger, 1982), and distracting them from weaknesses in the logical argument (J. A. Jones, 2005). Taken together, these findings suggest that humor has more of an emotional than a cognitive effect, and that it may play a greater role in the peripheral processing route than in the central processing route to persuasion.

Jim Lyttle (2001) suggested that humor may influence the peripheral processing route in several ways. First, by creating a positive mood in the audience, it might make them less likely to disagree with a persuasive message. Second, by increasing liking for the source, humor might implicitly convey a sense of shared values and thereby make the source appear more credible. Third, by distracting the attention of the audience, humor might prevent them from constructing counter-arguments against the message. Finally, self-disparaging or self-effacing humor might convey the impression that the source has less personal investment in the outcome and this might increase audience perceptions of trustworthiness of the source.

An experiment by Diane Mackie and Leila Worth (1989) examined the role of humor-induced positive mood on the persuasiveness of a message. Participants were either put in a good mood by having them watch a humorous videotape (a comedy segment from *Saturday Night Live*) or they were put in a neutral mood by having them watch a documentary film about wine. They were then exposed to a persuasive message about gun control (advocating a position contrary to their original views) that contained either strong or weak arguments, and that was delivered by either an expert or a nonexpert source. The participants' subsequent ratings of their attitudes toward gun control revealed that those who had been exposed to the humorous videotape were equally likely to change their attitudes following the weak and strong arguments, but were more strongly influenced by the expert source than by the nonexpert source. This pattern of results indicates that they were engaging in peripheral rather than central processing of the information, relying on heuristic cues instead of the strength of the argument to make a decision. In contrast, those who had watched the nonhumorous videotape were more strongly influenced by the strong than the weak arguments, whereas they were equally persuaded by the expert and nonexpert sources. Thus, they were engaging in central processing, focusing on the strength of the arguments rather than heuristic cues such as the credibility of the source.

Similar findings were obtained in another experiment in which positive moods were induced in participants by having them win a small prize in a lottery, indicating that the pattern of the humor-related persuasion effects was due to the induction of positive emotion rather than the more cognitive aspects of humor. Thus, humor may influence the persuasiveness of a message by inducing positive moods in listeners, causing them to attend to peripheral, heuristic cues rather than to the strength of the argument via central processing (see also Wegener, Petty, and Smith, 1995, regarding the complicated relationship between positive moods and information processing). These findings may also explain the broad appeal of some politicians who sprinkle their speeches with humor, inducing voters to respond to peripheral cues instead of engaging in more critical thinking about their policies.

Because it involves the peripheral processing route, humor may be particularly effective as a method of persuasion with people who are motivated to avoid thinking too much about an issue. This hypothesis was tested in two studies that examined the effects of a humorous persuasive message concerning potentially threatening topics, specifically the use of sunscreen to prevent skin cancer and the use of condoms to prevent sexually transmitted diseases (Conway and Dube, 2002). The authors hypothesized that a humorous message would be more effective than a nonhumorous message for high-masculinity individuals, but not for low-masculinity people. Masculinity (a characteristic that can apply to both men and women) consists of an assertive, instrumental orientation characterized by being independent, forceful, and dominant. Previous research has shown that high-masculinity people are particularly averse to feelings of distress, and they therefore avoid thinking about threatening topics by engaging in distraction, denial, or a focus on the positive.

To test these hypotheses, male and female participants who were either high or low in masculinity were presented with either a humorous or a nonhumorous message, both of which contained an equal amount of information about the topic. The participants were then asked to indicate how likely they would be to engage in the preventive behaviors in the future (sunscreen use in the first study and condom use in the second). As predicted, high-masculinity participants (both male and female) were more strongly persuaded by the humorous message than by the nonhumorous message, whereas low-masculinity subjects were equally persuaded by both messages. The authors suggested that the humorous appeals were more effective for high-masculinity subjects in promoting preventive behaviors because the humor matched the avoidant manner in which these individuals typically respond to a threatening topic, allowing them to engage in peripheral (heuristic) rather than central (elaborative) processing of the persuasive message.

The research discussed so far focused on the effectiveness of humor in persuasive messages such as advertisements. An experiment by Karen O'Quin and Joel Aronoff (1981) examined whether humor is effective in an interpersonal bargaining situation. The participants in this study were instructed to act as buyers of a painting, negotiating a sale price with another person who played the part of the seller (and who was actually a confederate of the experimenter). At one point during the negotiation, the confederate made either a nonhumorous or a humorous offer to the subject ("Well, my final offer is $100, and I'll throw in my pet frog"). The results showed that the participants who received the humorous offer during the course of negotiations agreed to pay a higher final price for the painting, on average, than did those who received the nonhumorous offer. Thus, the use of humor by the seller appears to provide an advantage in sales negotiations. Interestingly, further analyses indicated that this effect was not simply due to the humor causing the participants to like the seller more. Instead, the authors proposed an explanation based on the face-saving effects of humor discussed earlier. In particular, they suggested that humor may convey the message that the seller does not take the situation very seriously, thereby allowing the buyer to save face when agreeing to pay a higher price. This hypothesis should be examined further in future research.

In summary, there does not appear to be a simple relationship between humor and persuasion. The role of humor in persuasion depends on the kind of processing involved (peripheral or central), and characteristics of the audience, the topic, and the source of the message.

HUMOR, ATTITUDES, AND PREJUDICE

Many jokes make use of a stereotype about a particular group of people to enable the listener to resolve an incongruity and "get" the joke. Consider the following old English riddle (from Raskin, 1985, p. 189):

> How do you make a Scotsman mute and deaf?
> By asking him to contribute to a charity.

To resolve the puzzle of why someone would suddenly become mute and deaf when asked to contribute money to a charity, one needs to be aware of the English stereotype of Scottish people as being excessively stingy. The presence of such stereotypes in many jokes raises the question of whether jokes making fun of women, people of disadvantaged ethnic or racial groups, homosexuals, and so on, reinforce negative stereotypes and contribute to prejudice and discrimination. As noted in Chapter 3, theorists holding to the salience hypothesis have argued that people do not need to agree with such stereotypes in order to enjoy these types of disparaging jokes, and that they are therefore not inherently aggressive or offensive (Attardo and Raskin, 1991; Goldstein et al., 1972).

We saw earlier in this chapter that humor is often used to communicate contradictory and ambiguous messages. When people make disparaging statements about others in a humorous way, they can leave open the question of whether they "really mean it" or are "just joking," and whether or not the target of the humorous disparagement has reason to take offense. This ambiguity in the meaning of humor is played out in the "political correctness" debate, which has generated a great deal of controversy in recent years. When historically disadvantaged groups, such as minorities and women, began to decry the use of disparaging humor in the workplace and in public discourse generally, others reacted against what they perceived to be an unwarranted restriction of their right to free speech, suggesting that such humor was all in fun and should not be taken so seriously (Saper, 1995).

Much like the general public, humor scholars have also been divided over this issue, as demonstrated by an extended debate that was conducted via email among 19 humor researchers and was subsequently published in *Humor: International Journal of Humor Research* (Lewis, 1997). Some scholars, such as Paul Lewis, argued that degrading forms of sexist and racist humor can serve to legitimize and perpetuate negative stereotypes and contribute to a culture of prejudice. Others, like Arthur Asa Berger, countered that humor is inherently iconoclastic, is valuable for rebelling against norms, rules, and restrictions of all kinds, and should not be restricted. Still others, such as John Morreall, suggested that the offensiveness of a joke depends not so much on its content but the manner and context in which it is told. Such differences of opinion among humor scholars are also seen in two sociological studies analyzing jokes making fun of "Jewish American princesses" (JAPs), which arrived at radically different conclusions. Gary Spencer (1989) concluded that these jokes are essentially anti-Semitic and contribute to prejudice and negative stereotypes of Jews, whereas Christie Davies (1990b) argued that they are not based on anti-Semitism at all, but actually affirm the positive qualities of Jewish culture.

We saw in Chapter 2 that Freud (1960 [1905]) viewed jokes as a socially acceptable means of expressing aggressive and hostile impulses. In addition, Zillmann and Cantor's (1976) dispositional theory of humor suggested that people enjoy jokes that disparage a particular group of people when they have negative attitudes toward that group and/or positive attitudes toward the source of the disparagement. A number of studies have found evidence to support this theory (Cantor, 1976; La Fave, Haddad, and Marshall, 1974; Wicker, Barron, and Willis, 1980). More recently, a study by

Brigitte Bill and Peter Naus (1992) showed that people who perceive incidents involving sexist attitudes and behaviors to be more humorous also tend to view them as less sexist and more socially acceptable. Several other studies have revealed that individuals who rate sexist and female-disparaging humor as more funny and enjoyable are also more likely to endorse sexist attitudes and rape-related beliefs and have less liberal, pro-feminist attitudes (Greenwood and Isbell, 2002; Henkin and Fish, 1986; Moore, Griffiths, and Payne, 1987; Ryan and Kanjorski, 1998).

Caroline Thomas and Victoria Esses (2004), at the University of Western Ontario, found that men with higher scores on a measure of hostile sexism, as compared to those with lower scores, rated female-disparaging (but not male-disparaging) jokes as funnier and less offensive, and were more likely to indicate that they would repeat these sexist jokes to others. Further analyses revealed that these differences were not merely due to stereotypical attitudes or prejudice toward women, but to hostile attitudes. Thus, there is considerable evidence that disparagement humor, such as that found in sexist and racist jokes, is enjoyed partly because it enables people to express negative sentiments and attitudes toward the target groups in a manner that is perceived to be socially acceptable.

In addition to research indicating that enjoyment of disparagement humor reveals negative attitudes toward the target of the humor, researchers have recently begun to examine the question of whether exposure to these types of humor can actually have an influence on listeners' attitudes and stereotypes. James Olson and colleagues (1999), at the University of Western Ontario, conducted three experiments testing whether exposure to disparaging humor would produce more extreme or more accessible stereotypes and attitudes concerning the disparaged group. Participants in the experimental conditions were exposed to disparaging humor about men (in two studies) or lawyers (in the third study), while those in the control groups were exposed to nondisparaging humor, nonhumorous disparaging information, or nothing at all. Dependent measures included ratings of the target group on stereotypic attributes, attitudes toward the target group, and latencies of stereotypic and attitudinal judgments about the target group (to assess activation of prejudice schemas).

Across the three experiments, a total of 83 analyses yielded only one significant difference in the predicted direction. In sum, exposure to disparaging humor had no demonstrable effects on stereotype or attitude extremity or accessibility. Thus, simply hearing someone tell jokes that disparage a particular target group does not seem to cause the listener to have more negative attitudes toward that group. A limitation of these studies, however, is that the disparaged groups in these studies (men and lawyers) are relatively advantaged in the culture; different results might have been found if the jokes had targeted more disadvantaged groups. The authors had chosen these targets rather than jokes disparaging women or racial minorities because of ethical concerns. However, given their null results, it seems important for future research to replicate these findings using disparagement humor targeting truly disadvantaged groups. If the same results are found, this would provide more conclusive evidence that this type of humor does not influence the attitudes of the listeners.

Although these studies found little evidence that listening to disparagement humor creates more negative stereotypes and attitudes in the audience, other studies by the same research group have shown that *telling* such jokes can affect joke-tellers' stereotypes about the target group. Hobden and Olson (1994) had participants tell disparaging jokes that played upon the stereotype that lawyers are greedy. Participants' attitudes toward lawyers were then measured. The results indicated that freely reciting the disparaging humor about lawyers caused participants to indicate more negative attitudes toward lawyers afterwards.

In another experiment, Maio, Olson, and Bush (1997) manipulated whether participants recited jokes that disparaged Newfoundlanders, who are a relatively disadvantaged group in Canada, or nondisparaging jokes. In a supposedly unrelated study, the participants were then asked to complete a measure of their stereotypes and attitudes toward Newfoundlanders. The results indicated that those who recited disparaging humor subsequently reported more negative stereotypes (e.g., perceptions of Newfoundlanders as having low intelligence) than did those who recited nondisparaging humor. However, the participants' evaluative attitudes toward Newfoundlanders (e.g., ratings of good/bad, likable/unlikable) were not affected by the manipulation.

Taken together, the results of these experiments provide some evidence that telling disparaging jokes (as opposed to merely listening to them) can reinforce, and perhaps even exacerbate, negative stereotypes about the target group. It is not clear, however, whether these results were due to the participants' attitudes or stereotypes becoming more negative as a result of reciting the jokes, or whether the jokes simply made pre-existing beliefs more salient and therefore more accessible from memory. Another possible explanation is that the instructions to tell such jokes may have caused participants to perceive that it was more acceptable to express their pre-existing negative attitudes or stereotypes in this situation, whereas those in the control groups suppressed any such attitudes in their responses. Future research is needed to explore these alternative explanations of the results.

Even if exposure to disparaging humor does not make the listeners' attitudes more negative (as suggested by the study of J. M. Olson et al., 1999), it may make prejudiced attitudes seem more socially acceptable and thereby increase tolerance for discrimination, particularly in people who already have negative attitudes toward the target group. Thomas Ford (2000) conducted three experiments to investigate these hypotheses. In the first experiment, participants were exposed either to sexist jokes, neutral jokes, or nonhumorous sexist communications, and were then asked to rate the acceptability of a sexist event (a vignette describing a situation in which a young woman was treated in a patronizing manner at work by her male supervisor). The results showed that, after exposure to sexist jokes, those participants (both male and female) who had previously been identified in a questionnaire as being high in hostile sexism showed greater tolerance for the sexist event, in comparison to those exposed to neutral jokes or nonhumorous sexist communications. This effect was not found among participants who were low in hostile sexism. Thus, exposure to sexist attitudes communicated in a humorous (but not a serious) manner seems to cause people with pre-existing sexist attitudes to become more tolerant of sex discrimination.

These findings were replicated in two further experiments, which also showed that these effects of sexist humor on participants high in hostile sexism were nullified when sexist jokes were interpreted in a serious, critical manner, as a result of either explicit instructions or contextual cues such as information about the group membership of the joke-teller. These findings suggest that it is the activation of a noncritical mindset (which is presumably a natural by-product of humorous communication) that makes it possible for sexist humor to increase tolerance of sex discrimination. This would explain why nonhumorous, serious sexist communications did not have the same effect. A follow-up experiment indicated that exposure to sexist humor causes people who are high in hostile sexism to perceive the social norm as being more tolerant of sexism, and they therefore feel less guilty about behaving in a sexist manner themselves (T. E. Ford, Wentzel, and Lorion, 2001).

In summary, the existing research indicates that simply being exposed to sexist or other forms of disparaging humor is not likely to change people's attitudes, stereotypes, or prejudices (which tend to be quite stable schemas). However, telling these kinds of jokes may create more negative stereotypes in the joke-teller, and hearing them can cause negative stereotypes to become more salient in the listener. In addition, the sexist or racist attitudes underlying disparaging jokes may be interpreted less critically than when these attitudes are expressed in a serious manner, and this can create a social climate in which individuals who already have these sorts of attitudes perceive sexual or racial discrimination to be more socially acceptable, causing them to be more tolerant of such behavior (T. E. Ford and Ferguson, 2004). This does not mean that everyone who enjoys disparagement humor necessarily has sexist, racist, or homophobic attitudes (Attardo and Raskin, 1991); however, the research indicates that there is a strong tendency for the two to go together. Furthermore, although simply telling such jokes is not likely to change other people's feelings about the targets of the jokes, for those who do have such attitudes this kind of humor can implicitly communicate a level of social tolerance for prejudice that may help to perpetuate discrimination and social inequities.

HUMOR AND INTIMATE RELATIONSHIPS

We saw earlier that a sense of humor is viewed by most people as a very desirable characteristic in a friend or romantic partner. Most of us assume that a person with a greater sense of humor will be someone with whom we can have a more satisfying relationship compared to someone with less humor. The humorous person is seen as likely to be enjoyable to be with, cheering us up when we are under stress, and refraining from becoming ill-humored and burdening us unduly when he or she is having problems. Are these stereotypes accurate, however? Is there evidence that humor actually contributes to better relationships and greater relationship satisfaction?

A common view is that couples who share similar preferences in humor styles will be more satisfied with their relationship. A study of undergraduate dating couples found evidence in support of this hypothesis (Murstein and Brust, 1985), but a more recent investigation of married couples did not (Priest and Thein, 2003). Although spouses in the latter study generally tended to have similar styles of humor, greater similarity was not related to greater marital satisfaction. Thus, the current evidence is unclear as to whether a tendency to share similar humor preferences is correlated with relationship satisfaction.

On the other hand, there is consistent evidence from studies of dating and married couples that relationship satisfaction is correlated with positive appraisals of a partner's sense of humor. That is, the more people are satisfied with their relationship, the more they report that their partner has a good sense of humor, regardless of whether they like the same types of jokes (Rust and Goldstein, 1989; Ziv and Gadish, 1989). Research also indicates that people who are happily married often attribute their marital satisfaction in part to the humor they share with their spouse (Ziv, 1988a). When men and women who had been married for over 50 years were asked about the reasons for the stability and longevity of their marriages, "laughing together frequently" was close to the top of the list (Lauer, Lauer, and Kerr, 1990). However, it is important to note that such correlational findings do not demonstrate that humor has a causal effect on marital satisfaction. They may simply indicate that people who are happy with their marriage (for whatever reason) tend to appreciate many things about their spouses, including their sense of humor.

For several decades, psychologist John Gottman and his colleagues have been studying marital satisfaction and factors predicting marital longevity over time (Gottman, 1994). Their main research method involves videotaping married couples engaging in discussions about problem areas in their marriage, such as differences of opinion about dealing with finances or disciplining the children. Although these discussions take place in a research laboratory, they often become quite emotionally intense. Indeed, the couples apparently behave in these laboratory discussions in much the same way they normally interact when discussing problems in their daily lives. The videotapes are then analyzed to determine the degree to which various verbal and nonverbal expressions of emotion, conflict-resolution styles, and so on, are predictive of marital satisfaction and stability in the couples, both concurrently and prospectively over a period of years (Gottman, 1993).

One variable that these researchers have examined is the degree to which partners use benign (nonsarcastic) humor during these discussions. Overall, the studies indicate that individuals who are more satisfied with their marriage, as compared to those who are unhappily married, show higher levels of humor and laughter and more reciprocated laughter during the problem discussions (Carstensen, Gottman, and Levenson, 1995; Gottman, 1994). Thus, greater use of humor while discussing problems is indicative of greater marital harmony. In these concurrent analyses, however, the direction of causality is still not clear: humor use in problem discussions may be a result, rather than a cause, of current marital satisfaction.

A more convincing test of the causal role of humor is provided by longitudinal research that examines whether greater expression of humor at one point in time predicts long-term marital stability several years later, after controlling for the level of marital satisfaction at time one. In this type of research, though, the findings have been less clear-cut. Gottman and his colleagues have consistently found that more frequent expression of positive emotions (such as joy and affection) during the problem discussions, as compared to negative emotions (such as anger and contempt), is strongly related to long-term marital stability. However, the specific contribution of humor to this prediction has been inconsistent (Gottman, 1994). For example, Gottman and Levenson (1999) were able to predict with 93 percent accuracy the likelihood of marital stability versus divorce over a four-year period on the basis of the amount of affection, anger, disgust, and sadness displayed by spouses during 15-minute discussions in the laboratory. However, the amount of humor observed in the discussions did not significantly differentiate between those who remained together and those who were divorced or separated four years later.

Other studies using this methodology suggest that the effects of humor on marital stability may depend on several additional factors, and may differ for men and women. For example, a study of newly married couples by Cohan and Bradbury (1997), using Gottman's methodology, found that when humor expression by *husbands* during a problem discussion was associated with high levels of major stressful events in the couple's life, the couples were more likely to be separated or divorced 18 months later. The authors suggested that husbands' use of humor during times of stress may be a way for them to temporarily deflect problems and avoid the anxiety associated with talking about them, but without actively confronting and resolving the problems. Hence, humor expressed by the husband in the context of major life stress might be associated with less distress in the short term but not with longer-term marital stability.

On the other hand, another study of newlywed couples by Gottman and his colleagues found that more humor expression by *wives* during a problem discussion was predictive of greater marital stability over six years, but only when the wives' humor led to a reduction in the husbands' heart rate during the conversation (Gottman, Coan, Carrere, and Swanson, 1998). Since men have generally been found to become more emotionally aroused and agitated than their wives during discussions of marital problems, this finding suggests that humor may be beneficial to marriage when it is used by wives in ways that are emotionally calming to their partners. Thus, while husbands' use of humor during times of stress can sometimes be a way of avoiding dealing with problems, wives' use of humor can be a way of helping to calm their spouse emotionally while encouraging him to continue dealing with the problems. In turn, these two different uses of humor by husbands and wives can have different effects on the long-term stability of the marriage.

The evidence discussed so far indicates that the amount of humor communicated by spouses to each other relates to their current level of marital satisfaction, but is not always predictive of the long-term stability of their marriage. Some recent research on younger dating couples suggests that a sense of humor may even be *detrimental* to relationship longevity, at least in this early stage of heterosexual relationships. As part of her doctoral research, one of my students, Patricia Doris (2004), investigated humor in university students who were in dating relationships. She found that, for both males and females, those who had higher scores on a measure of affiliative humor were significantly *more* likely to experience a breakup in their dating relationship within five months, especially if the other partner expressed some dissatisfaction with the relationship at time one. Similarly, Keltner and colleagues (1998) found that dating partners who engaged in more prosocial, friendly teasing when instructed to tease one another, as compared to those who used more aggressive teasing, were *more* likely to break up within several months.

A possible explanation of these surprising findings is that, because people with a good sense of humor are seen by others as being especially attractive, they are more likely to be able to find another relationship quite easily if things go badly in their current one. Consequently, they may be quicker to leave a dating relationship rather than staying in it and attempting to resolve any problems that may arise. Thus, ironically, a characteristic that makes individuals appear to others to be more desirable as a dating partner may actually tend to cause their relationships to be less stable over time. In a similar vein, a study of "fatal attractions" in dating relationships found that, while a sense of humor may be a characteristic that initially makes a person attractive as a potential dating partner, this same characteristic can later become an irritant that causes dissatisfaction in the partner, leading to a breakup of the relationship (Felmlee, 1995). This was exemplified by one female participant who reported that she "was attracted to her partner because he was 'funny and fun,' but later disliked his 'constant silliness' and the fact that he 'never seemed to take the relationship seriously'" (Felmlee, 1995, p. 303). Further research is needed to determine whether these counterintuitive findings of greater relationship *instability* in dating partners with a higher sense of humor are also found in more committed relationships such as marriage.

In summary, research on humor in relationships indicates that, although a sense of humor is perceived to be a very desirable characteristic in a romantic partner, it does not necessarily increase the likelihood that the relationship will be more satisfying and stable over time. The concept of sense of humor has become associated in popular views with a number of positive connotations and assumptions that are not necessarily accurate. As we have seen, humor can be used for a range of social purposes, some of which can contribute to cohesiveness and enjoyment, whereas others are more aggressive and manipulative. The degree to which humor is beneficial to a relationship therefore depends on the ways it is used in interactions between partners.

In recent years, researchers in this area have increasingly emphasized the importance of distinguishing between potentially beneficial and detrimental uses of humor in investigating its role in relationships, rather than viewing it as a unitary and purely positive construct. For example, the Relational Humor Inventory (de Koning and Weiss, 2002), a recently developed measure for studying humor in relationships, contains separate scales for positive, negative, and instrumental uses of humor by each partner (see also R. A. Martin et al., 2003). In Chapter 9, I will discuss research using these sorts of measures to examine positive and negative effects of humor in dating relationships and marriage, as well as in nonromantic friendships.

HUMOR AND GENDER

A number of studies were conducted over the past four decades to investigate gender differences in various aspects of humor. Many additional studies, although not specifically focusing on gender, reported comparisons of the responses of male and female participants. Consequently, there is a large amount of data on gender differences in humor (see Lampert and Ervin-Tripp, 1998, for a review of this literature). Much of the early theory and research, prior to the emergence of the women's movement, suggested that, "when it comes to humor, men are more likely to joke, tease, and kid, whereas women are more likely to act as an appreciative audience than to produce humor of their own" (Lampert and Ervin-Tripp, 1998, p. 235). Studies of humor appreciation generally also indicated that men were more likely than women to enjoy humor containing aggressive and sexual themes, whereas women were more likely to enjoy "nonsense" (i.e., nontendentious) humor (Groch, 1974; Terry and Ertel, 1974; W. Wilson, 1975). In addition, there was some evidence that both men and women tended to enjoy jokes making fun of women more than jokes targeting men (Cantor, 1976; Losco and Epstein, 1975).

More recently, researchers have challenged many of the conclusions drawn from these earlier studies, pointing out a number of biases inherent in their research methods (e.g., Crawford, 1989). Almost all of the early research examined sex differences in appreciation of jokes and cartoons, rather than the spontaneous creation of humor in naturalistic social contexts. For both men and women, jokes and cartoons are a relatively minor source of humor in everyday life, compared to spontaneous, socially situated humor (Graeven and Morris, 1975; R. A. Martin and Kuiper, 1999; Provine, 1993). Moreover, joke-telling tends to be relatively more characteristic of male humor, whereas women are more likely to relate humorous personal anecdotes (Crawford and Gressley, 1991). Consequently, studies testing the enjoyment of jokes likely do not provide a representative view of women's (or even men's) humor more generally.

In addition, sexual and aggressive jokes are frequently disparaging of women, and it is therefore not surprising if women enjoy them less than men do (Chapman and Gadfield, 1976; Love and Deckers, 1989). Indeed, when researchers have used non-sexist sexual jokes as stimuli (i.e., jokes about sex that do not disparage either women or men), they generally have not found gender differences in enjoyment ratings (Chapman and Gadfield, 1976; Hemmasi, Graf, and Russ, 1994; Henkin and Fish, 1986; Prerost, 1983; D. W. Wilson and Molleston, 1981). These studies indicate that women enjoy sexual humor just as much as men do when it is not demeaning toward women. Furthermore, whereas women's lower enjoyment ratings of sexual and hostile jokes were interpreted by researchers as evidence of greater sexual inhibition or conventionality, little thought was given to the possibility that women may also use uninhibited and unconventional humor, but for social functions other than the release of hostility or sexual tension. In sum, much of the past research examining gender differences in humor has been characterized by gender biases in the choice of topics examined, the types of stimuli presented to participants, the operationalization of variables, and the interpretation of findings (Crawford, 1989).

Some researchers have attempted to remedy these biases in laboratory studies of gender differences in humor appreciation by varying the gender of the source and target of disparagement humor or by including examples of feminist humor (Brodzinsky, Barnet, and Aiello, 1981; Gallivan, 1992; Stillion and White, 1987). However, since the focus in these studies continues to be on the appreciation of humor stimuli selected by the experimenter, they still do not examine the ways men and women actually create and use humor in their daily interactions with others. Recently, researchers in this area, as in other social psychological research on humor, have begun to shift their attention away from the appreciation of jokes to the use of humor in everyday discourse. Using methods such as questionnaires, daily diaries, and conversational analysis, these studies have attempted to examine gender differences in humor more naturalistically.

For example, Mary Crawford and Diane Gressley (1991) administered a 68-item questionnaire to men and women, asking them about their typical appreciation and creation of humor involving a broad range of topics, styles, and types of humor. Overall, men and women showed more similarities than differences in their responses. No gender differences were found, for example, for creativity in humor production, tendency to laugh at oneself, enjoyment of cartoons and comic strips in newspapers and magazines, and enjoyment of sexual humor. However, men reported greater enjoyment and creation of hostile humor, a greater tendency to tell canned jokes, and greater enjoyment of slapstick comedy. On the other hand, women reported greater use of anecdotal humor, such as recounting funny stories about things that happen to themselves or others.

My colleague Nicholas Kuiper and I conducted a naturalistic study of laughter in which we asked men and women to complete daily logs recording all the experiences that caused them to laugh over a three-day period (R. A. Martin and Kuiper, 1999). The sources of humor were grouped into four categories: media, spontaneous social situations, canned jokes, and recall of humorous past events. Men and women did not differ in their overall frequency of reported laughter (averaging 17.5 reported laughs per day). However, women were significantly more likely than men to report laughing in response to humor arising spontaneously in social situations. No significant gender differences were found on the other three categories.

Jennifer Hay (2000) analyzed the interpersonal functions of humor occurring in 18 tape-recorded conversations among small groups of adult friends, including all-female, all-male, and mixed-sex groups. The conversations took place in homes of group members, and, although the participants were aware of being recorded, they were not aware that humor was to be the focus of the study. A number of different humor functions were identified in the conversations, and these were classified into three broad categories: (1) power-based (e.g., aggressive teasing), (2) solidarity-based (e.g., sharing humorous memories, friendly teasing), and (3) psychological (e.g., using humor to cope with problems). The data analyses indicated that women were much more likely than men to use humor to create or maintain group solidarity, both in same-sex and mixed-sex groups. This function of humor was over eight times more frequent for women than for men. In particular, women's greater solidarity-based humor involved humorous disclosure of personal information, which presumably enabled the conversational partners to get to know the speaker better and communicated a sense of trust.

Both friendly and aggressive forms of teasing were more likely to occur in all-female and in all-male than in mixed-sex groups, and teasing was only slightly more frequent in groups of men as compared to groups of women. Thus, women were nearly as likely to tease their female friends as men were to tease their male friends. The use of humor for coping was also more common in single-sex than in mixed-sex groups. However, a difference was found in the way men and women tend to use humor to cope. Men were more likely to engage in "contextual" coping (using humor to cope with an immediate problem arising in the context of the conversation), whereas women were more likely to engage in "noncontextual" coping (using humor in talking about life problems outside the conversational context). Other studies of gender differences in humor in naturalistic discourse were reported by Lampert and Ervin-Tripp (1998) and by Robinson and Smith-Lovin (2001).

As these examples of recent research demonstrate, the general shift in humor studies away from a focus on appreciation of jokes in the laboratory to an exploration of the interpersonal functions of spontaneous humor in naturalistic contexts has produced changes in researchers' ideas about the relation between humor and gender. Further research is needed to replicate the findings of these and other similar studies and to examine their generalizability to other populations. However, the data collected thus far indicate that, although women and men do not differ in their overall tendency to create and enjoy humor, and there are many similarities in their uses of humor, they also tend to use humor for somewhat different social purposes.

These gender differences in humorous discourse may be understood in terms of the way gender is expressed in social interactions more generally (Crawford, 1992; 2003). According to Deborah Tannen (1986; 1990), men and women have somewhat different conversational goals: for women, the primary goal of friendly conversation is intimacy, whereas for men the goal is positive self-presentation. These different goals are also reflected in the ways men and women use humor. Women more often use humor to enhance group solidarity and intimacy through self-disclosure and mild self-deprecation, whereas men more often use humor for the purpose of impressing others, appearing funny, and creating a positive personal identity. Thus, humor is a mode of communication that, along with more serious communication, is used to achieve gender-relevant social goals.

CONCLUSION

In this chapter we have seen that humor may be viewed as a mode of communication that occurs in a wide range of everyday social contexts. Although it is playful and nonserious, and is often seen as frivolous and unimportant, humor can be used for a number of "serious" functions, extending into every aspect of social behavior. As sociologist Linda Francis (1994) pointed out, "there is more to explain about humor than just why it is funny. People have reasons for using humor, goals they wish to accomplish with it" (p. 157).

According to recent theory, many of the interpersonal functions of humor derive from its inherently ambiguous nature due to the multiple concurrent meanings that it conveys. Because of this ambiguity, humor is a useful vehicle for communicating certain messages and dealing with situations that would be more difficult to handle using a more serious, unambiguous mode of communication. Importantly, a message communicated in a humorous manner can be retracted more easily than if it were expressed in the serious mode, allowing both the speaker and the listener to save face if the message is not well received. These insights concerning the ambiguity and face-saving potential of humor have been applied by theorists and researchers to account for a wide variety of social uses of humor, including self-disclosure and social probing, decommitment and conflict de-escalation, enforcing social norms and exerting social control, establishing and maintaining status, enhancing group cohesion and identity, discourse management, and social play.

The multiple interpersonal functions of humor suggest that it may be viewed as a type of social skill or interpersonal competence. Employed in an adept manner, humor can be a very useful tool for achieving one's interpersonal goals. This does not mean, however, that humor is always used in prosocial ways. If an individual's goals in a particular situation are to establish meaningful relationships, enhance intimacy, and resolve conflicts, the sensitive use of humor may be an effective vehicle for furthering these aims. However, if the goal is to gain an advantage, manipulate, dominate, or belittle others, humor can be a useful skill for those purposes as well.

Because of its inherent ambiguity, humor can be employed for a variety of contradictory purposes. It can be used to bring people closer together or to exclude them, to violate social norms or to enforce them, to dominate over and manipulate people, or to ingratiate oneself with others. Humor can also be used to reinforce stereotypes or to shatter prejudices, to resolve conflicts in relationships or to avoid dealing with problems, to convey feelings of affection and tolerance, or to denigrate and express hostility. Most people likely use humor for many of these different purposes at different times and in different contexts. For example, when you are at work, you might use humor to reinforce your status, whereas when you are relaxing with a group of friends, you might use it to enhance group cohesion.

Besides being an interesting topic of study in its own right within social psychology, humor also has important implications for our understanding of a number of other topic areas that have long been of interest to social psychologists, including person perception and attraction, persuasion, attitudes and prejudice, intimate relationships, and gender differences. By studying the role of humor in each of these areas, we gain new insights that would not be apparent if we focused only on the serious mode of communication.

The role of humor often turns out to be more complex than one might initially expect. For example, although a sense of humor is generally viewed as a desirable characteristic in a friend or romantic partner, research indicates that it can contribute in both positive and negative ways to relationship satisfaction and stability, depending on how it is used in the relationship. Similarly, in the area of persuasion, a humorous message may contribute to greater persuasiveness with certain topics and audiences, but it can reduce persuasiveness with others.

The existing research suggests that the role of humor in many areas of social psychology may be at least as important, if not more so, than some other factors that have typically received greater research attention. For example, there is some evidence (Cann et al., 1997; Feingold, 1981) that humor may have a stronger influence on interpersonal attraction than do attitude similarity and physical attractiveness, both of which have been the focus of considerably more research. The importance of humor in the areas of prejudice and stereotypes, gender differences, and intimate relationships may also be more substantial than has generally been recognized in the existing research on these topics. Clearly, to gain a full understanding of most aspects of social behavior, researchers need to give attention to the complex contributions of humor.

In view of the ubiquity of humor in social interaction, its obviously important social functions, and its relevance to most of the topics of interest to social psychology, one might expect that humor would be a fairly prominent topic in social psychology as a whole. Surprisingly, however, the study of humor tends to be a relatively minor topic that is largely ignored by the mainstream. Most of the leading social psychology textbooks contain no mention of humor or its cognates. The most recent edition of *The Handbook of Social Psychology* (Gilbert et al., 1998), a two-volume "bible" for the field that spans more than 2000 pages, contains only a single brief mention of humor. By and large, social psychologists seem to focus almost exclusively on serious modes of communication in social interactions, while ignoring the important functions of the humorous mode.

Recent insights about the interpersonal uses of humor that I have discussed in this chapter could provide a basis for interesting new theoretical models and hypotheses for future research. As these ideas become more widely known, they will hopefully stimulate greater interest among social psychologists in the topic of humor. Because humor is such a broad topic, the greatest empirical advances will likely be achieved by developing more narrowly focused theoretical models concerning specific humor components or processes. A good example of the types of relatively focused and heuristically useful theoretical models that are needed in this area is the face threat analysis of teasing developed by Keltner and colleagues (2001). Numerous research questions and hypotheses derived from this model remain to be addressed in future research (see Keltner et al., 1998, for further research ideas).

As we will see throughout this book, recognition of the essentially social nature of humor also has important implications for other domains of psychology. In Chapter

4, we saw that recent research on cognitive processes involved in the comprehension of irony and sarcasm has increasingly taken into account the influence of interpersonal aspects of these forms of humor. The interpersonal view of humor has also influenced recent approaches to the study of individual differences in sense of humor, which we will explore in Chapter 7. In Chapter 8, we will examine social aspects of the development of humor and laughter in infancy and childhood. A social perspective may also be very useful for increasing our understanding of mental health aspects of humor and its role in coping with life stress, as we will see in Chapter 9. In sum, while the existing research on the social psychology of humor has provided a number of interesting insights into the interpersonal functions of humor, this continues to be a potentially very fertile field for future investigation, with important implications for all areas of psychology.

CHAPTER 6

The Psychobiology of Humor and Laughter

Like all psychological phenomena, humor is based on a large number of complex biological processes taking place in the brain and nervous system. To experience humor, an individual must first perceive playful incongruity in a stimulus event. This perceptual process draws on systems located in many regions of the cerebral cortex involved in visual and auditory perception, language comprehension, social cognition, logical reasoning, and so forth. When humor is perceived, these cognitive processes stimulate emotional systems associated with positive feelings of mirth and amusement, involving areas in the prefrontal cortex and limbic system. These emotion systems also release a cocktail of biochemical molecules, producing further changes in the brain and throughout the body via the autonomic nervous system and endocrine system. In addition, the activation of mirthful emotion typically triggers the expressive responses of smiling and laughter, which involve the brainstem and its connections to the forebrain, as well as nerves leading to muscles in the face, larynx, and respiratory system.

The investigation of these sorts of biological processes in humor lies within the domain of biological psychology (also known as psychobiology or physiological psychology), the branch of the discipline that studies the relation between behavior and the body, particularly the brain. Biological psychology is part of a broader field of study known as neuroscience, which also includes disciplines such as neurophysiology, neuroanatomy, and brain biochemistry. Although the study of humor and laughter has not been a major focus in biological psychology, there has been a small

153

but steady output of research on this topic over the years. The recent publication of several functional magnetic resonance imaging (fMRI) studies (e.g., Azim et al., 2005) as well as articles on topics such as the evolution of humor and laughter (e.g., Gervais and Wilson, 2005) suggest that interest in this topic is increasing (see also Vaid, 2002).

As we will see, biological research on humor and laughter highlights the importance of emotional components of humor in addition to the cognitive aspects, pointing to humor as an interesting topic for investigating the interplay between emotion and cognition more generally. As such, the psychobiological study of humor may be viewed as a subject within the newly developing field of affective neuroscience (Panksepp, 1998). Our discussion of biological aspects of humor also provides an opportunity to focus more closely on many interesting questions concerning the nature and functions of laughter.

In this chapter, I will begin by discussing laughter as an emotional display that expresses the positive emotion of mirth, followed by an overview of research on the acoustics, respiration, phonation, and facial expressions of laughter, as well as the autonomic and visceral concomitants of mirth. The subsequent discussion of laughter in nonhuman animals will underscore the close connection between humor, laughter, and play. I will then explore several other laughter-related topics, including pathological laughter conditions, laughter and the brain, and tickling as a stimulus for laughter. Next, I will turn to investigations of the brain areas involved in the cognitive and emotional processing of humor, including studies of humor in patients with localized brain damage as well as studies of normal subjects using EEG and fMRI. Finally, I will discuss theories about the evolutionary origins and adaptive functions of humor and laughter.

THE NATURE OF LAUGHTER

As many authors have noted, boisterous laughter comprises a very strange set of behaviors. A hypothetical alien from outer space would certainly be struck by the oddity of this behavior, noting the loud, barking noises that are emitted, the repetitive contractions of the diaphragm and associated changes in respiration, the open mouth and grimaces caused by contractions of facial muscles, the flushing of the skin, increased heart rate and general physiological arousal, production of tears in the eyes, loss of strength in the extremities, and flailing body movements (cf. Askenasy, 1987; Keith-Spiegel, 1972). Such hearty laughter seems to take over the whole organism in an uncontrollable and compulsive way, conveying almost overwhelming feelings of enjoyment and amusement. It is also very contagious and difficult to fake (van Hooff and Preuschoft, 2003). What a peculiar way for people to respond to the perception of humor!

Koestler (1964) characterized laughter as a physiological reflex, and suggested that it is the only domain in which a highly complex mental stimulus (i.e., humor) produces such a stereotyped reflexive response. However, as van Hooff and Preuschoft

(2003) have pointed out, the term *reflex* is a misnomer because, unlike reflexes, laughter is highly dependent on motivational and emotional states and social context. Instead, laughter seems to be best characterized as a "fixed action pattern," a ritualized and largely stereotyped behavior pattern that serves as a communication signal.

Laughter and Emotion

As Charles Darwin (1872) noted in *The Expression of the Emotions in Man and Animals*, laughter is essentially an emotional expression, a way of communicating to others that one is feeling a particular emotion. Thus, laughter is one of many largely hardwired behavior patterns used by humans to communicate a wide range of positive and negative emotions, including various facial expressions (e.g., scowling, frowning), vocal sounds (e.g., gasping, screaming), bodily actions (e.g., trembling, shaking the fist), changes in speech patterns (e.g., shouting, whining), and so on. In the case of laughter, the particular emotion that is communicated is a pleasurable feeling closely related to joy. As noted in Chapter 1, researchers have not yet settled on an agreed-upon technical name for this emotion, with different scholars referring to it as "amusement," "humor appreciation," or "exhilaration." I prefer the term *mirth*, which captures its emotional nature as well as its association with humor and laughter.

The emotion of mirth is therefore primary, with laughter (along with smiling) being an emotional display. The more intense the emotion, the stronger the expressive display. At low levels of intensity, mirth is expressed by a faint smile, which turns into a broader smile and then audible chuckling and laughter as the emotional intensity increases. At very high intensity, it is expressed by loud guffaws, often accompanied by a reddening of the face as well as bodily movements such as throwing back the head, rocking the body, slapping one's thighs, and so on. Although, as we will see, there is evidence that smiling and laughter may have different evolutionary origins, they are very closely related in humans, with smiling and laughter occurring along a continuum of emotional intensity. The same facial muscles are involved in laughter and smiling, with stronger contractions of longer duration occurring in laughter than in smiling (Ruch, 1993). The close connection between smiling and laughter is also evident in the fact that laughter typically begins as a smile and, after the laughter ends, gradually fades smoothly back into a smile once again (Pollio, Mers, and Lucchesi, 1972).

Like all emotions, mirth has behavioral, physiological, and experiential components. In addition to the vocalizations, facial expressions, and bodily actions that characterize the expressive behavior of laughter, mirth involves a range of physiological changes that take place in the brain, autonomic nervous system, and endocrine system, along with subjective feelings of pleasure, amusement, and cheerfulness. I will discuss each of these components in the following sections. As we will see, the emotion of mirth that is expressed by laughter also appears to be closely related to play. Much of the laughter of early childhood may be seen as an expression of the exuberant delight associated with physical play activities such as running, chasing, and rough-and-tumble play-fighting, as well as incongruous playful actions such as peek-a-boo games.

Since social play is an important activity in juveniles of all mammal species, the evolutionary origins of mirth and laughter in play may well extend to our earliest mammalian ancestors some 60 million years ago. As children's cognitive and linguistic abilities develop, they begin to laugh not only at physical play, but also in response to the sorts of playful manipulation of incongruous ideas, words, and concepts that we call "humor." Thus, humor may be viewed as a cognitive-linguistic form of play that elicits the emotion of mirth which, in turn, is typically expressed through laughter.

Humor may not be the only stimulus that elicits the emotion of mirth and the laughter that expresses it. This emotion may also be elicited by several other stimuli, including nitrous oxide (N_2O, or "laughing gas") and possibly tickling (Niethammer, 1983; Ruch, 1993). At any particular time, an individual's threshold for experiencing mirth can be raised or lowered by a variety of factors, such as the social context (e.g., feelings of safety, the presence of other people who are laughing), one's current mood (cheerfulness versus depression; Deckers, 1998; Ruch, 1997), health status, level of fatigue, ingestion of alcohol or psychoactive drugs (Lowe et al., 1997; J. B. Weaver et al., 1985), and more enduring personality traits such as one's overall sense of humor (Ruch, 1993).

Acoustics of Laughter

The characteristic that most strikingly distinguishes laughter from other human activities is the loud and distinctive sounds that are emitted. As we will see, the function of these laughter sounds appears to be both to communicate to others one's joyful and playful emotional state, and to induce this same emotional state in the listeners (Gervais and Wilson, 2005). In recent years, researchers have begun to study the acoustics (sound properties) of laughter, employing methods commonly used by ethologists to investigate animal vocalizations such as bird songs. In this research, recordings of human laughter are digitized and then analyzed using computer-based spectrographic procedures to examine their audio waveforms, frequency patterns, and other acoustical characteristics. The unit of analysis in these studies is usually the series of "ha-ha-ha" sounds that are made during a single exhalation. Researchers refer to such a laugh episode as a *laughter bout*, and the individual "ha" syllables are referred to as *calls* (Bachorowski et al., 2001), *notes* (Provine and Yong, 1991), or *pulses* (Ruch and Ekman, 2001).

Psychologists Robert Provine and Yvonne Yong (1991), at the University of Maryland, analyzed the acoustical properties of 51 laughter bouts produced by male and female university students and staff members. To obtain recordings of laughter, they approached people in public places with a tape recorder and asked them to "simulate hearty laughter." Most people found it very difficult to laugh on command, and their first attempts were typically strained and artificial, presumably because they were not actually experiencing the emotion of mirth that laughter normally expresses. However, the funniness of the activity itself, along with the clowning and kidding of the experimenters, typically caused the subjects to begin feeling amused and they started laughing spontaneously and naturally. It was these natural and spontaneous bouts of laughter that were subsequently analyzed.

These analyses revealed that, on average, each laugh bout consisted of four individual notes or calls, although there was considerable variability in this number, ranging from one to as many as 16 in some laughter samples, but typically no more than eight. Each laugh note within a bout was found to begin with a protracted voiceless aspirant (i.e., a hissing *h* sound not produced by vibration of the vocal cords). This was followed by a forcefully voiced vowellike sound with an average duration of about 75 milliseconds. Another voiceless aspirant then followed, with an average duration of about 135 milliseconds, followed by the next voiced vowel sound. Thus, each complete "ha" note was about 210 milliseconds in duration, resulting in about five notes typically being emitted per second. Not surprisingly, the fundamental frequency (corresponding to the perceived pitch) of male laughter (averaging 276 Hertz) was lower than that of females (502 Hertz), reflecting the lower pitch of men's voices. Each laugh note showed a clear harmonic structure, with numerous secondary frequencies occurring as multiples of the fundamental frequency, producing a richly harmonious quality.

Based on their analyses, Provine and Yong emphasized the stereotypical nature of laughter, observing that there was very little variability across people in such characteristics as the overall duration of individual notes. Regardless of the number of notes in a given bout of laughter, the duration of each note (onset-to-onset inter-note interval, or INI) seemed to remain fairly constant, at about 210 milliseconds. However, the voiced segment ("vowel sound") of each note became slightly shorter from the beginning to the end of a laugh bout, while the intervening unvoiced (*h* sound) segments became correspondingly longer, thus maintaining the same overall duration for each note. They also observed that the amplitude (loudness) of each voiced note segment decreased from the beginning to the end of a bout. Interestingly, when played backwards, a laugh bout sounds quite normal, except for the fact that it becomes progressively louder instead of quieter. This is quite different from human speech, which does not sound at all normal when played backwards.

Because Provine and Yong's (1991) analyses were conducted on a relatively small sample of laughs obtained from people who were asked to produce laughter on demand, they may not have been representative of the full range of laughter that occurs naturally in social settings. Consequently, they may have concluded that laughter is more stereotyped and unvarying than it actually is. More recently, Jo-Anne Bachorowski and her colleagues (2001), at Vanderbilt University, conducted more extensive acoustical analyses of laughter using recordings of 1024 laughter bouts from 97 male and female university students. To obtain a wide range of naturalistic laughter samples, recordings were made while the participants were watching humorous videotapes in a comfortable laboratory setting, either alone or in same-sex or mixed-sex dyads.

In contrast to the stereotypy of laughter emphasized by Provine and Yong, these researchers found evidence of a great deal of variability and complexity in the acoustic properties of laughter. Several different types of individual laugh calls (notes) were identified, including voiced "songlike," unvoiced "gruntlike," and unvoiced "snort-like" calls, in addition to "glottal pulses," and "glottal whistles." Several of these different types of calls were often observed within a single bout of laughter, and there was little consistency within individual participants in the types of calls that they produced from one laugh bout to another. However, some general sex differences were observed. Females produced significantly more bouts containing voiced, songlike calls, whereas males produced more unvoiced, gruntlike laughs. Men and women did not differ, though, in the frequency of unvoiced snortlike laughs. Although there were no sex differences in the overall number of laugh bouts produced in response to the humorous videotapes, men's bouts tended to be slightly longer than women's, with more calls per bout.

On average, laugh bouts were comprised of 3.4 calls per bout, with a total duration of 870 milliseconds, but there was a great deal of variability in these numbers. Laugh bouts typically began with a fairly long call (280 milliseconds duration) followed by a series of shorter calls (lasting 130 milliseconds each). Like Provine and Yong, these researchers found that the unvoiced *h*-sound segments between calls tended to be shorter at the beginning of a bout and then became progressively longer toward the end. Analyses of fundamental frequencies of calls also indicated a considerable amount of variability, both between and within individuals. Indeed, the fundamental frequencies were often found to change over the course of an individual call, either rising or falling in pitch. Compared to shorter bouts, longer bouts of laughter tended to have higher mean fundamental frequencies and greater shifts in frequency within calls.

Analyses of the vowel sounds in voiced calls revealed that these are not nearly as distinct or clearly articulated as the vowels of speech, but tend to be a central, unarticulated *schwa* (like the *a* sound in "about"). Contrary to the observations of Provine and Yong (1991), "ho-ho" and "he-he" laughs were extremely rare, while "ha-ha" was much more common. Nonetheless, there was some evidence that individuals tend to have distinct laughs based on slight variations in the vowel sounds and other vocal characteristics that they produce while laughing. Bachorowski and her colleagues concluded that laughter is much less stereotyped than claimed by Provine and Yong (1991), but instead should be conceptualized as a "repertoire of sounds." Arguing that laughter has an important social communication function (discussed in Chapter 5), they suggested that these different sounds of laughter are combined in various ways to communicate subtle differences in emotional meanings to other people.

In a series of experiments, Silke Kipper and Dietmar Todt (2001, 2003a, 2003b), at the Free University of Berlin, took a somewhat different approach to studying the acoustics of laughter. Using computer equipment, they systematically modified various acoustical parameters of natural laughter bouts, such as the duration of laugh notes, the fundamental frequencies, and amplitude (loudness). They then had participants listen to these altered laugh bouts and asked them to rate the degree to which these laughs sounded like normal laughter, as well as rating their emotional responses to them. Among a number of interesting findings, these researchers found that laughter can diverge to a considerable degree on various acoustical parameters and still be perceived as normal laughter. Moreover, laugh bouts that showed substantial variability across calls were considered more natural and elicited more positive emotional responses as compared to more stereotyped bouts containing little variability. These findings cast further doubt on the view of laughter as a highly stereotyped vocalization. Additional findings from these studies supported the view of laughter as a method of communicating positive emotions and eliciting similar emotional responses in others. For example, the more natural-sounding a laugh bout was rated to be, the more it elicited a positive emotional response (for additional acoustical research on laughter, see Mowrer, 1994; Mowrer, LaPointe, and Case, 1987; Nwokah et al., 1999; Vettin and Todt, 2004).

Laughter Respiration and Phonation

To produce the distinctive sounds of laughter, we make use of a number of muscles that control our breathing, larynx, and vocal apparatus (for a detailed description see Ruch and Ekman, 2001). The normal human breathing cycle consists of inspiration, inspiration pause, expiration, and expiration pause. Regardless of where the person happens to be in this cycle, laughter typically begins with an initial forced exhalation (Lloyd, 1938), which brings the lung volume down to around functional residual capacity (i.e., the volume that remains after a normal expiration). This is followed by a sustained sequence of repeated, rapid, and shallow expirations, which, when accompanied by phonation, produce the "ha-ha-ha" of laughter. By the end of this expiratory laugh bout, the lungs reach residual volume (i.e., the air volume remaining in the lungs after maximal expiration). Thus, laughter typically occurs at a low lung volume, forcing out more air from the lungs than occurs during normal breathing. Following a laughter bout, a quick inhalation occurs, filling the lungs once again to normal capacity. Another laughter bout may then follow. Due to this unusual amount of expiration, laughter produces a greatly increased breathing amplitude, up to 2.5 times greater than that which occurs during normal breathing.

The predominantly expiratory respiration pattern during laughter is produced by saccadic contractions of muscles that are normally passive during expiration, including the diaphragm, abdominal (*rectus abdominus*), and rib cage (*triangularis sterni*) muscles (Ruch and Ekman, 2001). Along with the action of these respiratory muscles, respiration during laughter is also regulated by the larynx, which serves as a valve separating the trachea from the upper aerodigestive tract. In the larynx, the glottis (comprising the vocal folds) initially closes to prevent the air from being exhaled too quickly, causing a buildup of subglottal air pressure. The glottis, aided by the arytenoid cartilages, then begins to open and close rhythmically, permitting short bursts of pressurized air to escape. Each time the glottis closes to a narrow slit, the vocal cords begin to vibrate, producing the "ha" sounds. Because the glottis continues to move and change shape while these vibrations are occurring, the fundamental frequency (pitch) of the sound produced rises and falls during each individual call, as well as changing from one call to the next, rather than maintaining a constant frequency. Each time the glottis opens more widely, it stops vibrating, and the escaping air produces the unvoiced *h* sound between each voiced call.

These sound vibrations are carried through the vocal tract, whose shape amplifies or dampens various frequency characteristics of the sounds, and finally the air escapes through the mouth or nose. The amount of tension on the vocal cords; position of the larynx, tongue, and jaw; shape of the mouth and lips; and even the degree of contraction of various facial muscles (all of which can be influenced by the person's current emotional state) further influence the sound quality of the laughter. As found in research on the acoustics of laughter (Bachorowski et al., 2001), there is also a great deal of variability, both within and between individuals, in the patterns of respiration and phonation during laughter (W. F. Fry and Rader, 1977; Svebak, 1975, 1977). Thus, people seem to have distinctive "laugh signatures," making their laughs as recognizable as their voices. However, individuals also demonstrate a great deal of variability in their laughter acoustics depending in part on their current emotional state, resulting in characteristic fearful, embarrassed, aggressive, and other emotionally tinged laughs in addition to pure enjoyment laughs.

Facial Expressions of Laughter and Smiling

Besides the loud and distinctive "ha-ha-ha" sounds, laughter is characterized by a distinctive facial display, which closely resembles smiling. This emotional facial display is another way laughter serves as a communication signal. Paul Ekman and his colleagues, at the University of California at San Francisco, have conducted extensive research on facial expressions of emotion, including smiling and laughter (Ekman, Davidson, and Friesen, 1990; Ekman and Friesen, 1978; Frank and Ekman, 1993). Although they have identified 18 different types of smiles, Ekman and his colleagues have found only one that is reliably associated with genuine enjoyment or amusement. They have named this smile the *Duchenne display*, after the French anatomist who first identified it in 1862. Other types of smiles are associated with feigned amusement ("forced" or "faked" smiles) or the presence of negative emotions such as embarrassment or anxiety mixed with the enjoyment.

The Duchenne display involves symmetrical, synchronous, and smooth contractions of both the *zygomatic major* and the *obicularis oculi* muscles of the face (see Figure 4). The zygomatic major is the muscle in the cheeks that pulls the lip corners upwards and backwards, while the obicularis oculi is the muscle that surrounds each eye socket and causes wrinkling of the skin at the outer sides of the eyes ("crow's feet"). Although most types of smiles involve contractions of the zygomatic major, only genuine enjoyment smiles also involve the obicularis oculi, which is less subject to voluntary control. Smiles that involve other facial muscles besides these two generally indicate the presence of other (often negative) emotions besides pure enjoyment. For example, contractions of muscles in the forehead during smiling tend to be associated with negative emotions (S. L. Brown and Schwartz, 1980).

FIGURE 4 The Duchenne display expresses genuine mirth. Note the "crow's feet" at outsides of eyes due to contraction of *obicularis oculi* muscles. © Barbara Penoyar/Getty Images/PhotoDisc

The Duchenne display occurs in laughter as well as smiling, although laughter often includes some additional muscles, such as those involved in opening the mouth and lowering the jaw (Ruch and Ekman, 2001). Thus, the presence or absence of the Duchenne display can be used by researchers (as well as any careful observer in social interactions) to determine whether a person's smiling or laughter is expressing genuine, spontaneous enjoyment or if it betrays other emotions or is being used to feign amusement. In particular, the presence of "crow's feet" wrinkles along the outsides of the eyes is an indicator of genuine amusement.

Ekman and Friesen (1978) have developed the Facial Action Coding System (FACS) for use by trained observers to code the various facial action units controlled by different muscles of the face in the expression of different emotions. Although this system requires some training and practice, it is very useful for researchers who are interested in studying laughter, as it provides them a way of distinguishing between Duchenne and non-Duchenne laughter. There is a considerable amount of research evidence that laughter with and without the Duchenne display has very different psychological meanings.

Differences between Duchenne and nonDuchenne laughter were demonstrated in a study by Dacher Keltner and George Bonanno (1997) at the University of California at Berkeley. They videotaped interviews of adults whose spouses had died six months previously, and used the FACS to code the laughter produced by these participants during the interviews. Greater frequencies of Duchenne laughter were found to be significantly correlated with more positive emotions such as happiness and joy, and less negative emotions such as anger, distress, and guilt. The amount of Duchenne laughter was also positively associated with better social adjustment, recollections of a more satisfactory relationship with the deceased spouse, and better current relationships with others. In contrast, non-Duchenne laughter was not related to any of these variables.

The videotapes, with the sound turned off, were later shown to college students who were asked to rate them on a number of dimensions. More frequent Duchenne laughter in the bereaved participants was significantly correlated with higher self-ratings of positive emotions in the observers themselves and with the observers' judgments that the participant was healthier, better adjusted, less frustrated, and more amusing. Thus, subtle differences in facial expressions during laughter, signaling the presence or absence of the Duchenne display, communicate quite different emotional states, and these expressions in turn influence the emotional responses of observers. These findings further highlight the role of laughter as a form of emotional communication.

AUTONOMIC AND VISCERAL CONCOMITANTS OF MIRTH

Like other emotions, the emotion of mirth that is expressed by laughter also produces changes in many parts of the body via the autonomic nervous system and the endocrine (hormone) system (Cacioppo et al., 2000). Since the 1960s, many researchers have investigated mirth-related changes in heart rate, skin conductance, blood pressure, skin temperature, muscle tension, and so on. In these studies, participants are attached via electrodes and sensors to polygraph machines, and various psychophysiological variables are assessed while they are exposed to humorous stimuli such as comedy videotapes. Control conditions involving nonhumorous, emotionally neutral stimuli, or stimuli that elicit other emotions (e.g., fear, sadness, anger), are also included for comparison. Although there have been some inconsistent findings (e.g., Harrison et al., 2000; Hubert and de Jong-Meyer, 1991), the results of these investigations generally indicate that mirth is associated with increased activity of the sympathetic nervous system, the branch of the autonomic nervous system associated with the well-known fight-or-flight response (see McGhee, 1983b, for a review of early research).

Lennart Levi (1965) found significant increases in adrenaline and noradrenaline output (measured in urine samples) while subjects watched a comedy film as compared to watching an emotionally neutral nature film, and these humor-related increases were comparable to those found with fear- and anger-evoking films. Other experiments have found mirth-related increases in heart rate, skin conductance, and other variables associated with sympathetic arousal (Averill, 1969; P. S. Foster, Webster, and Williamson, 2002; Godkewitsch, 1976; Goldstein et al., 1975; Hubert and de Jong-Meyer, 1990; J. M. Jones and Harris, 1971; Langevin and Day, 1972; Marci, Moran, and Orr, 2004). These effects indicate activation of the sympathetic-adrenal-medullary (SAM) system, the well-known fight-or-flight response of sympathetic nervous system arousal under the control of the hypothalamus, which is also involved in stress-related emotional responses such as fear and anger. In several of these experiments, the participants were asked to rate the funniness of the humor stimuli, and significant positive correlations were found between these funniness ratings and the amount of increase in physiological arousal. Thus, higher levels of amusement (which presumably indicate stronger feelings of mirth) were systematically related to greater increases in sympathetic nervous system activation.

In addition to SAM activation, there is some evidence that extended periods of mirth are associated with activation of the hypothalamic-pituitary-adrenocortical (HPA) system, the classic stress response that causes the adrenal cortex to release cortisol into the bloodstream. Although exposure to a fairly brief (nine minutes duration) humorous animated cartoon did not produce an increase in salivary cortisol levels (Hubert and de Jong-Meyer, 1990), a longer (90 minutes duration) and arguably more humorous film (a Monty Python movie) did produce significant increases in cortisol compared to an emotionally neutral nature film (Hubert et al., 1993). In the latter study, 50 percent of participants showed HPA activation, as indicated by significantly increased cortisol levels relative to baseline, starting about one hour after the beginning of the comedy film and continuing for one hour after the film ended. The amount of increase in cortisol over baseline was also found to be positively correlated with participants' ratings of the funniness of the film, indicating that the more amusing the film was perceived to be (and therefore the more mirth experienced), the more cortisol was released.

It is worth noting that these increases in physiological arousal are likely best viewed as a function of the emotion of mirth rather than being a consequence of laughter *per se*. Significant increases in heart rate and skin conductance have also been found when a mirthful emotional state was induced by having research participants vividly remember or imagine a humorous experience, without actually laughing (P. S. Foster et al., 2002). In addition, the observed correlations between funniness ratings and changes in physiological variables support the view that the degree of arousal is related to subjective feelings of amusement rather than to the amount of laughter. Thus, rather than laughter causing physiological arousal, it seems more accurate to view both laughter and peripheral autonomic arousal as being relatively independent (although correlated) consequences of the emotional state of mirth.

Overall, these research findings indicate that mirth is associated with a pattern of increased arousal similar to the fight-or-flight response, which prepares the body for vigorous activity. However, there is also some evidence for the common notion that mirth causes a loss of muscle tone. With vigorous laughter, people often feel a weakness in their limbs and occasionally even fall to the floor, and the expression "weak with laughter" is common to many languages (Overeem, Lammers, and Van Dijk, 1999). An early study found a decrease in muscle tone in the forearm of subjects while they were laughing (Paskind, 1932). More recently, Sebastiaan Overeem and his colleagues (1999) examined the effects of mirth on the *H*-reflex, which is assessed by electrically stimulating a nerve in the leg and using electromyography (EMG) to measure the resultant activation of an adjacent muscle. The strength (amplitude) of this reflex is governed by descending pathways from the brain. A severe reduction in amplitude is indicative of motor inhibition or muscle weakness, such as that seen in cases of cataplexy, in which afflicted individuals suddenly collapse due to a general loss of muscle tone.

In their study, Overeem and colleagues found that the *H*-reflex decreased by almost 90 percent while individuals were laughing in response to humorous slides. A subsequent study demonstrated that this effect is due to the emotion of mirth underlying laughter, rather than the respiratory or motoric effects of laughter itself (Overeem et al., 2004). Thus, there appears to be truth to the idea that laughter causes muscle weakness, although it seems more accurate to say that this weakness is caused by the mirthful emotion underlying laughter. This phenomenon is the basis of theories suggesting that laughter is a "disabling mechanism" whose function is to prevent individuals from acting in counterproductive ways (Chafe, 1987), as well as suggestions that humor and laughter might be used in psychotherapy as a relaxation induction technique (Prerost and Ruma, 1987).

It may seem puzzling that the positive emotion of mirth is accompanied by the same general pattern of physiological arousal as are stress-related negative emotions like fear and anger. If mirth is a positive emotion that is presumably beneficial to health, why does it have the same physiological effects as stress-related emotions that are known to be injurious to health? One possible explanation for these findings has to do with the hypothesis that the positive emotion associated with laughter originated in rough-and-tumble play. Just as many systems of the body are rapidly mobilized for the exertion of either fighting or fleeing during times of threat, many of these same systems may also be activated for the exuberant, exciting, and prosocial chasing, fleeing, jumping, and wrestling of mammalian play. It should also be noted that stress-related illnesses tend to result from chronic activation and inadequate recovery from sympathetic arousal (Mayne, 2001). The more phasic short-term arousal associated with mirth is therefore less likely to have such adverse consequences.

Moreover, it is still unclear whether the physiological arousal associated with mirth is identical to the arousal accompanying negative stress-related emotions, or whether it is different in some respects. There is some evidence that mirth and other positive emotions may be distinguished from negative emotions on the basis of the overall pattern of physiological changes associated with them (Christie and Friedman, 2004; Harrison et al., 2000). For example, positive emotions, compared to negative emotions, seem to involve a smaller increase in blood pressure and less autonomic activation overall (Cacioppo et al., 2000). However, the research to date is inconclusive, and there continues to be some controversy concerning the "emotional specificity" of autonomic nervous system activity.

Some researchers (e.g., Gray, 1994; LeDoux, 1994) have also pointed out that peripheral changes in the autonomic nervous system and endocrine system may be the wrong place to look for physiological differences among different emotions, since these systems have to do with functions that may be common to many different emotions, such as energy requirements, metabolism, and tissue repair. Instead, they have argued that more important differences are likely to be found in the brain systems that underlie different emotions. Thus, although the somatovisceral changes accompanying mirth may be quite similar to those associated with negative emotions like anger and fear, there are likely to be important differences in the brain systems underlying these emotions, including the biochemical molecules (e.g., neuropeptides, neurotransmitters, opioids) that are produced (Panksepp, 1993, 1994). These in turn may have different implications for health, such as different effects on components of the immune system (Kennedy, Glaser, and Kiecolt-Glaser, 1990). This is an important topic for future investigation. Potential effects of humor and laughter on physical health will be discussed in greater detail in Chapter 10.

LAUGHTER IN NONHUMAN ANIMALS

Although some writers have suggested that humans are the only animal that laughs (e.g., Stearns, 1972), there is good reason to believe that homologous behaviors also exist in other animals, particularly our closest ape relatives. Charles Darwin (1872), who viewed laughter as an expression of the positive emotions of joy and happiness, described a form of laughter that is emitted by young chimpanzees when they are being tickled. This observation has been supported by more recent primate research, which suggests that laughter in humans is homologous with (i.e., has the same evolutionary origin as) the *relaxed open-mouth display* or "play face" seen in monkeys and apes (Preuschoft and van Hooff, 1997; van Hooff, 1972; van Hooff and Preuschoft, 2003).

The Play Face

Van Hooff and Preuschoft (2003, p. 267) described this facial expression as follows:

> The mouth is opened wide and the mouth corners may be slightly retracted. In most (but not all!) primate species the lips are not retracted but still cover the teeth. In many species this facial posture is often accompanied by a rhythmic staccato shallow breathing (play chuckles) and by vehement but supple body movements. The posture and movements, both of the face and of the body as a whole, lack the tension, rigidity, and brusqueness that is characteristic of expressions of aggression, threat, and fear.

The play face, as the name suggests, occurs while the animals are involved in social play. Play is a common activity among juveniles, not only in primates but in all mammal species and even some birds. In play, many activities that are normally important for survival, such as hunting, fighting, mating, fleeing, and simple locomotion (jumping, sliding, pirouetting), are performed "just for fun," with a great deal of exuberance and energy. Young primates spend many hours in playful mock fighting, chasing, attacking, wrestling, and tickling one another, perhaps as a way of program-ming various cortical functions and developing the social skills needed to perform such behaviors in more "serious" contexts later in life (Gervais and Wilson, 2005; Panksepp, 1998). Since many of these behaviors would normally be construed by other individuals as aggressive and could lead to serious retaliation and physical harm, animals need a way of clearly signaling to others that these activities are not serious, but are merely intended "for fun." In primates, this communicative signal is the play face, along with the breathy, panting laughter-like grunts that accompany it in some species.

It is interesting to note that, by means of the play face, animals demonstrate an ability to distinguish between reality and pretense, seriousness and play, which, as we have seen in Chapters 1 and 5, are arguably the essence of humor. Thus, one can make the case that a rudimentary form of humor—in addition to laughter—is evident even in nonhuman animals. Interestingly, chimpanzees and gorillas that have been taught to communicate by means of sign language have been observed to use language in playful ways, such as punning, humorous insults, and incongruous word use, indicat-ing a rudimentary sense of humor (see Gamble, 2001, for a review). Moreover, this humorous use of sign language in apes is typically accompanied by the play face, providing further evidence for the close connection between linguistic humor and play.

With our more highly developed cognitive and linguistic capacities, we humans are able to extend these playful behaviors into the realm of concepts and ideas, cre-ating nonserious, playful alternative realities that we share with one another through language. Thus, humor in humans appears to have originated in social play, an ancient mammalian emotion-behavior complex. Interestingly, comparable play faces occur in many other mammals besides primates. For example, the canidae (dogs, wolves, and foxes) and ursinae (bears) have a gape-mouthed play face in which the upper teeth remain covered, which is accompanied by boisterous, frolicsome body movements and rapid panting that is very reminiscent of the play panting of primates (van Hooff and Preuschoft, 2003). Thus, the evolutionary origins of the relaxed open-mouth play face, which in humans seems to have evolved into laughter, appear to go back many millions of years.

Laughter and Smiling in Apes

The "laughter" that was observed by Darwin in chimpanzees is a staccato, gut-tural, throaty panting sound associated with rapid and shallow breathing, which typ-ically accompanies the relaxed open-mouth play face display. A similar pattern is seen in many other primates, including gorillas, orangutans, and macaques, although the vocalization is less pronounced in some species (van Hooff and Preuschoft, 2003). A major difference between the laughter of humans and chimpanzees is that, in chim-panzee laughter, the breathing involves a rapid alternation between shallow inhala-tions and exhalations, with single sounds being produced during each inhalation and exhalation. In contrast, as we have seen, human laughter involves a series of multiple "ha-ha-ha" sounds occurring during a single exhalation, with no vocalization during the intervening inhalations. Consequently, chimpanzee laughter sounds very different from that of humans (Provine, 2000). Thus, although the two forms of laughter appear to have the same evolutionary origins, they have diverged considerably in the 6 million or so years since our common ancestor with chimpanzees (Gervais and Wilson, 2005; Owren and Bachorowski, 2001).

Chimp laughter and the play face are readily elicited during playful interactions between human caretakers and juvenile chimpanzees in zoos. As with human infants, tickling and peek-a-boo games containing an element of surprise, occurring in a relaxed and trusting social atmosphere, are particularly effective elicitors of laughter in chimps. Among conspecifics (i.e., members of the same species), play faces and the voiced breathing laughter occur during boisterous rough-and-tumble play-wrestling and play-chasing. The individuals alternate between chasing and being chased, coordinating their activities by means of these play signals (van Hooff and Preuschoft, 2003). It is easy to see parallels in the boisterous laughter of human children during rough-and-tumble play, and only a short step to the more intellectually-based play with words and ideas in the laughter-evoking humor of human adults.

Although the play face and laughter in primates often occur in the context of play fighting and "quasi-aggression" (Butovskaya and Kozintsev, 1996), comparative research does not support the view that laughter originated in aggressive displays used to intimidate and ridicule adversaries and signal one's superiority over them (cf. Gruner, 1997). Instead, the research tends to support Darwin's view of laughter as an original expression of happiness, joy, and high spirits associated with play (van Hooff and Preuschoft, 2003). Drawing on his studies of the neural bases of play in laboratory rats, Panksepp (1998) provided considerable evidence that play and aggression are mediated by different brain systems (see also D. P. Fry, 2005).

At the same time, though, researchers recognize that laughter, like play, tends to be competitive and can be used in aggressive ways. Indeed, Panksepp (1998) describes rough-and-tumble play in all mammal species as "joyful social exchange with a strong competitive edge" (p. 284). During bouts of play, animals frequently pin each other down, and one individual often emerges as the more dominant. However, for the playful interactions to continue, this individual must also allow the less dominant one to "win" quite frequently. In much the same way, teasing and other forms of verbal play in humans appear to be ways of competing in a friendly way, and those who tease others are required also to playfully accept the teasing directed at them by others.

Interestingly, smiling likely has a somewhat different evolutionary origin than laughter (van Hooff and Preuschoft, 2003). While laughter appears to be related to the relaxed open-mouth display, smiling in humans seems to be homologous to another facial pattern, the *silent bared-teeth display*, which is seen in primates as well as many other species of mammals. In this display, the animal retracts its mouth corners and lifts its lips, baring its teeth, while keeping its mouth more or less closed. When shown by a lower-status individual, this display is a signal of fearful submission and appeasement; in a higher-status individual, it signals friendly reassurance and lack of hostile intent. Thus, rather than simply being a more subdued, low-intensity form of laughter, smiling seems to have originated in a different signal altogether. Functional differences between smiling and laughter are still apparent to some degree in humans, with smiling occurring more often than laughter in nonhumorous contexts such as friendly greeting, signaling of appeasement, and embarrassment.

Nonetheless, smiling and laughter, though apparently originating in different displays, seem to have moved quite closely together in humans, to the point where they often represent different degrees of intensity of the same emotional state. Thus, a smile may be an expression of mild amusement in response to a joke, whereas a laugh communicates much greater enjoyment (Ruch, 1993). This is reflected in many languages, in which the word for smile is a diminutive of the word for laughter (e.g., French *sourire* and *rire*). I will return to the discussion of possible evolutionary origins of smiling and laughter in a later section.

"Laughter" in Rats?

Thus far, we have considered evidence that the origins of human laughter go back at least as far as the evolutionary ancestors that we share with our closest living relative, the chimpanzee, and, in the form of the play face, even to the common ancestors of all primates. Recently, biological psychologist Jaak Panksepp and his colleagues at Bowling Green State University have provided intriguing evidence that a form of laughter may even exist in rats (Panksepp, 2000; Panksepp and Burgdorf, 2000, 2003). They have found that laboratory rats produce a high-frequency (approximately 50 kHz), ultrasonic chirping sound during social rough-and-tumble play and also when being tickled by human handlers. Although humans are unable to hear these sounds without the aid of specialized sound equipment, they are within the auditory range in which rats communicate.

Rats seem to be most ticklish on the nape of the neck, although they also apparently enjoy a "full body" tickle. When they have previously been tickled by a human hand, they will eagerly approach that hand rather than one that has merely petted them, chirping all the while. Like laughter among humans, this rat "laughter" appears to be contagious, and young rats generally prefer to spend time with older animals that produce more of this chirping sound as compared to those that do not. This chirping "laughter" is also readily conditioned using both classical and operant methods, and animals will run mazes and press levers for an opportunity to be tickled and "laugh." Rat "laughter" can easily be amplified or reduced by selective genetic breeding, indicating that it reflects a heritable emotional trait. As we will see in later chapters, a comparable genetically based trait in humans may underlie our concept of "sense of humor" (Ruch and Carrell, 1998).

Panksepp and Burgdorf (2003) have suggested that this chirping "laughter" arises from organized "ludic" (from Greek *ludos* = play) brain circuits that form the "emotional operating system" for the positive emotion of joy (or what I call mirth), which is activated during social play, and which may be common to all mammals. They postulated that play-related joy has an important social facilitation and bonding function in mammals, promoting cooperative forms of social engagement and helping to organize social dynamics. They suggested that rough-and-tumble play in rats, accompanied by chirping "laughter," may provide a useful animal model for researchers to investigate the brain structures mediating positive emotions relating to play and laughter, in much the same way that other animal models have been used to elucidate the brain mechanisms of negative emotions such as fear and anger (Panksepp, 1998).

Research using this model has already begun to shed light on the neural bases of positive playful emotion. For example, this research suggests an important role of endorphins and other opioids, the morphine-like substances created in certain brain sites. Low doses of morphine increase play in rats, whereas the opiate antagonist naloxone (which inhibits the effect of opioids) decreases play (Panksepp, 1998). These findings suggest that opioid systems may also be involved in mirthful humor and laughter in humans. Human laughter is very different from ultrasonic chirping in rats, and many researchers believe it is too much of a stretch to view the two as having any real evolutionary connection (Gervais and Wilson, 2005). Nonetheless, they may both relate to homologous brain structures found in all mammals which have an important social-emotional function and an ancient evolutionary origin relating to social play. Thus, these animal studies suggest that the feelings of hilarity and mirth that we experience in humor originated in the exhilaration and joy of rough-and-tumble social play that is a prominent activity of all mammals.

PATHOLOGICAL LAUGHTER

Brain disorders involving pathological laughter are well known in the neurological literature, and numerous cases have been reported since the late 1800s (Duchowny, 1983; Forabosco, 1998; Poeck, 1985). The study of pathological laughter, in connection with knowledge of the underlying brain abnormalities, is one way that neuroscientists have been able to make inferences about the brain sites that may be involved in normal laughter. Although pathological laughter closely resembles natural laughter, it is considered abnormal because of the presence of unusual motor patterns, or a lack of accompanying pleasant and mirthful emotional experience, or because it occurs in an inappropriate social context in the absence of humorous stimuli.

Duchowny (1983) distinguished three major categories of pathological laughter, each of which has different clinical manifestations and anatomical substrates: (1) excessive laughter, (2) forced laughter, and (3) gelastic epilepsy. *Excessive laughter* conditions involve emotional lability, heightened feelings of mirth and euphoria, an inability to inhibit laughter, and a lack of insight into the abnormality of the laughter. These conditions most commonly occur in adulthood and tend to be associated with disorders such as schizophrenia, mania, and dementia. These disorders appear to affect parts of the brain involved in emotion production and regulation, including structures in the limbic system and parts of the frontal lobes.

In *forced laughter* conditions, the second broad category of pathological laughter, patients experience involuntary outbursts of explosive, self-sustained laughter, often accompanied by autonomic disturbances of heart rate, vasomotor control, and sphincter tone. Although they may appear to others to be feeling genuinely amused, these patients usually do not subjectively experience the positive emotion of mirth that normally accompanies laughter, but instead often experience it as unpleasant, embarrassing, and something to be endured. Many patients with this condition also exhibit pathological crying, with fits of laughter merging into crying or vice versa. It is occasionally even difficult to tell whether they are laughing or crying. This indicates that some of the brain centers controlling laughter and crying are located very close together (likely in the part of the brainstem called the pons), suggesting a close link between the positive emotions of social play and the distressing emotions associated with social separation (Panksepp, 1998).

Conditions involving forced laughter typically begin in adulthood and can result from a variety of disorders, including degenerative brain conditions such as Parkinson's disease, multiple sclerosis (MS), and amyotrophic lateral sclerosis (ALS), as well as tumors and lesions in various parts of the brain due to cerebrovascular accidents (strokes) and brain injury. In the condition called *fou rire prodromique*, uncontrolled laughter lasting up to a half hour or even longer signals the onset of a stroke in the brainstem. In some tragic cases, people have literally laughed themselves to death. Pathological "forced laughter" conditions have been associated with lesions in many areas of the brain, ranging from the frontal and temporal lobes of the cortex and the pyramidal tracts to the ventral mesencephalon, the cerebellum, and the pons (Wild et al., 2003; Zeilig et al., 1996). In most of these cases, the effect of the lesions seems to be chronic disinhibition of laughter-generating circuitry (i.e., an inability to inhibit or modulate laughter normally), rather than an excitatory effect.

The third general category of pathological laughter, *gelastic epilepsy* (from Greek *gelos* = laughter) involves relatively rare epileptic conditions in which the seizures predominantly take the form of bouts of laughter. These seizures are often accompanied by motor convulsions, eye movement abnormalities, and autonomic disturbances. During the seizures, patients typically (but not always) lose consciousness and are therefore unaware of the laugh attack. In cases in which the patients remain conscious during the seizure, some report a pleasant feeling of mirth, but others experience the laughter as inappropriate and even unpleasant. The laughter typically lasts less than a minute, but can be more prolonged when associated with complex partial seizures (Arroyo et al., 1993). Gelastic epilepsy usually begins in childhood, and cases have even been reported in newborn infants, demonstrating that the neural circuits for laughter are fully developed at birth (Sher and Brown, 1976).

Brain-imaging studies have identified several brain regions that are associated with gelastic seizures, most importantly the hypothalamus, temporal lobes, and medial frontal lobe (Arroyo et al., 1993). The most common type of gelastic epilepsy, which has also been studied most extensively, is associated with hypothalamic hamartomas, which consist of nonmalignant abnormal tissue growth in the hypothalamus. Research has shown that hypothalamic and pituitary hormones are released during these seizures, and it appears that the abnormal hypothalamic electrical activity has excitatory effects, spreading to areas in the neighboring limbic system and also to the brainstem to produce the psychophysiological manifestations of laughter (Wild et al., 2003). These findings suggest that the hypothalamus likely has an important role in normal laughter as well. As noted earlier, the hypothalamus is well-known as a control center for the autonomic arousal associated with the fight-flight response, as well as regulating a range of motivational states including hunger and sexual arousal (as psychology professors frequently explain to their students, the hypothalamus is responsible for the four "*f*'s": feeding, fighting, fleeing, and sexual intercourse).

LAUGHTER AND THE BRAIN

Studies of patients with brain lesions demonstrate that there are two separate pathways in the brain that can lead to the production of smiling and laughter, one voluntary and unemotional, and the other involuntary and emotional. Some patients who have suffered a stroke or other brain injury, causing them to be unable to voluntarily move their facial muscles (volitional facial paresis), are nonetheless able to smile and laugh normally when they find something funny (i.e., when they experience the emotion of mirth). On the other hand, some patients with lesions of subcortical nuclei in regions such as the basal ganglia (as in Parkinson's disease) are unable to show spontaneous, emotional facial expressions when they are subjectively feeling amused, but are able to smile voluntarily on command (Wild et al., 2003).

The voluntary facial movements likely originate in the motor strip on the cerebral cortex and arrive quite directly at the face via the corticospinal tracts of the pyramidal motor system, whereas the involuntary, emotional movements arise from subcortical nuclei and arrive at the face via the extrapyramidal system, involving many emotion-related regions in the basal ganglia, limbic system, and brainstem (Frank and Ekman, 1993). There is also evidence that voluntary control of laughter is mediated by ventral areas of the mesencephalon and pons, whereas emotional control involves dorsal areas of these same structures (Wild et al., 2003). These findings help to explain the differences in facial expressions associated with genuine (Duchenne) and feigned (non-Duchenne) smiling and laughter, discussed earlier.

Further evidence for separate neural substrates of emotional and voluntary smiling and laughter was provided by a recent study that made use of positron emission tomography (PET), a brain-imaging technique (Iwase et al., 2002). The brains of healthy participants were scanned while they were smiling, either spontaneously in response to humorous videotapes or voluntarily while watching nonhumorous videotapes. The results showed different patterns of regional cerebral blood flow (rCBF) during the two different types of facial expression. In particular, emotional smiling led to greater activation of areas of the cortex involved in the processing and integration of visual information (bilateral occipital and occipitotemporal cortices and left anterior temporal cortex), as well as cortical areas that are closely related to the limbic system and are involved in emotional reward (ventromedial orbitofrontal cortex and medial prefrontal cortex). In contrast, nonemotional voluntary facial movements mimicking smiling led to greater activation of areas of the frontal cortex involved in voluntary facial movement (facial area of the left primary motor strip and bilateral supplementary motor area).

In addition to evidence that different brain circuits are involved in voluntary and emotional forms of smiling and laughter, there is also evidence from cases involving electrical brain stimulation that the cognitive aspects of humor can be dissociated from the emotional and motoric components. When patients are undergoing brain surgery for treatment of epileptic seizures, surgeons commonly electrically stimulate various areas of the exposed surface of the brain, in order to localize areas that should and should not be removed. The patients remain conscious during this procedure. These electrical probes occasionally trigger laughter in the patients, with or without accompanying feelings of mirth.

As one example, Fried and colleagues (1998) described a 16-year-old female patient who consistently began to laugh whenever her brain was stimulated in a small region of the supplementary motor area located on the left frontal lobe of the cortex. The laughter was accompanied by subjective feelings of merriment and mirth in the patient. Interestingly, each time she laughed due to electrical stimulation, the patient attributed her laughter to various stimuli in her environment. For example, she would say that she had laughed because of the funny appearance of a picture of a horse that she happened to be looking at, or because the people in the room seemed to be behaving in an amusing way. It is important to note that this patient's epilepsy never involved gelastic seizures.

Although the exact brain mechanisms are not fully understood, this remarkable case provides evidence of the way cognitive components of humor can be dissociated from the emotional and motor components of mirth and laughter. In our normal experience, higher-level cognitive processes involved in the perception of humorous incongruity cause stimulation of the limbic and brainstem regions involved in the experience of mirth and production of laughter, but when those same mirthful feelings and laughter behaviors are triggered artificially with an electrical probe, the brain generates cognitive-perceptual incongruities to try to account for these emotional experiences.

Based on evidence from cases of pathological laughter, electrical brain stimulation, and animal studies, neuroscientists are beginning to piece together the circuits of the brain that are involved in the positive emotion of mirth and the production of laughter, although many of the details are still unknown (Arroyo et al., 1993; MacLean, 1987; Parvizi et al., 2001; Wild et al., 2003). As with other emotional systems (Panksepp, 1998), the structures and systems underlying laughter and mirth are distributed throughout the brain, including regions in the neocortex, basal ganglia, diencephalon, limbic system, and brainstem.

Parvizi and colleagues (2001) distinguished between emotion induction and emotion effector sites involved in mirth and laughter. Normal emotional laughter is initiated by perceptions of humorous incongruity or the recall of humorous memories, involving association areas of the cerebral cortex. These activate various *emotion induction* sites located in the telencephalon (cerebral cortex and limbic system), which are involved in "turning on" the emotion of mirth, and likely include areas of the ventromedial prefrontal cortex, basal temporal cortex, anterior cingulate cortex, amygdala, and ventral striatum (part of the basal ganglia). I will discuss these brain bases of cognitive and emotional aspects of humor in more detail in a later section describing neuroimaging studies.

When activated, the induction sites work on *emotion effector* (expression) sites, including the motor and premotor areas of the cerebral cortex (initiating facial and bodily movements), the hypothalamus (subserving autonomic responses such as increased heart rate and flushing), thalamus, periaqueductal gray matter, reticular formation, cranial nerve nuclei (controlling facial, laryngeal, and respiratory actions), and parts of the brainstem, all of which are involved in smiling and laughter as the expression of mirth. Most authors agree that there is likely a final common pathway for laughter located in the brainstem (possibly in the dorsal area of the pons) that coordinates the respiratory, laryngeal, and facial components of laughter (Wild et al., 2003). Laughter is triggered at this site by input from the various effector sites, and signals are sent out from here to the cranial nerves to activate the relevant muscles of the body.

In addition to excitatory input triggering laughter, inhibitory signals arriving in the brainstem from various higher centers in the brain serve to inhibit inappropriate laughter. Most researchers believe that the "forced laughter" type of pathological laughter described earlier is due to damage involving the corticobulbar tract, a motor pathway originating in the frontal cortex and terminating in cranial motor nuclei in the pons and medulla, which results in a failure of these laughter-inhibition mechanisms (Mendez, Nakawatase, and Brown, 1999). Parvizi and colleagues (2001) have also hypothesized a possible role of the cerebellum in modulating the intensity and duration of laughter. According to this view, the cerebellum receives information concerning the current social-emotional context from the cortex and telencephalic structures and feeds this information back to various effector sites.

In this way, laughter may be inhibited or amplified, depending on its appropriateness to the social and emotional situation (e.g., whether one is at a party or a funeral). However, when a stroke or other disease causes lesions to specific regions of the cerebellum or to the relevant structures and pathways leading into or out of it, this modulation does not take place, resulting in pathological laughter occurring in socially and emotionally inappropriate contexts (Parvizi et al., 2001). In sum, although further research is needed to clarify the exact brain sites and pathways involved, it is clear that laughter is a complex activity involving cognition, emotion, and motoric behavior, and requiring the coordinated activation of a wide range of brain regions, including parts of the cerebral cortex, the limbic system, and the brainstem.

TICKLING AS A STIMULUS FOR LAUGHTER

Why do we laugh in response to being tickled? Why is it impossible to tickle oneself? As we have seen, many juvenile animals tickle each other during play, and tickling frequently stimulates laughter in human children and adults, as well as chimpanzees and other primates, and possibly even rats (Panksepp and Burgdorf, 2000). Provine (2004) suggested that the pleasurable, reciprocal give-and-take of tickling may be viewed as a prototype of mammalian social play. The laughter associated with tickling appears to be accompanied by a pleasurable feeling of mirth similar to the emotion accompanying laughter when it is elicited by humor. However, tickling can also be quite aversive, and it was reportedly even used as a form of torture in medieval times. The social context is also important: tickling only produces laughter in a safe and trusting environment (Harris, 1999).

Tickling and its curious relationship to humor and laughter raise a number of intriguing questions that have been pondered by philosophers since the time of Socrates and Aristotle. Although the first survey study of tickling and laughter was conducted more than 100 years ago (Hall and Allin, 1897), more systematic empirical investigations of tickling have only begun quite recently.

Jaak Panksepp (2000) has argued that the merriment and laughter associated with tickling involve the same emotional brain regions as humor-elicited laughter. Hence, he suggested that the study of brain processes involved in tickling-related "laughter" in rats can tell us a good deal about the neural bases of humor and laughter in humans. This view is similar to the one proposed much earlier by Charles Darwin (1872), who suggested that tickling is essentially a humorous experience, eliciting laughter via the same emotional mechanisms as those involved in humor. In other words, both humor and tickling elicit the emotion of mirth, which in turn is expressed through laughter. Since a similar idea was proposed at about the same time by a German physiologist named Hecker, this view has come to be known as the Darwin-Hecker Hypothesis.

The current research evidence regarding this hypothesis is somewhat mixed, however. Alan Fridlund and Jennifer Loftis (1990), at the University of California in Santa Barbara, found some support for the hypothesis in a questionnaire study that showed that the more individuals reported being very ticklish, the more they also reported that they tend to laugh, giggle, and smile in response to jokes and other forms of humor. Similarly, Christine Harris and Nicholas Christenfeld (1997), at the University of California in San Diego, found a positive correlation between the degree to which participants were actually observed to laugh and smile while they were being tickled in the laboratory, and how much they laughed in response to a comedy film. Both these studies indicate that people who are more ticklish also tend to laugh more in response to humor, suggesting a close relationship between tickling and humor as elicitors of laughter, and thus providing support for the Darwin-Hecker Hypothesis.

However, a second part of the study by Harris and Christenfeld failed to support the prediction that tickling and humor would have a "warm-up effect" on each other. Participants were no more likely to laugh in response to being tickled after having seen a comedy film than after watching a nonhumorous control film. Similarly, participants laughed the same amount in response to a comedy film regardless of whether or not they had previously been tickled. These results appear to cast doubt on the idea that tickling and laughter both elicit the same positive emotion of mirth. If this were the case, then when this emotion is elicited by means of tickling, it should subsequently lead to greater laughter in response to humor, and vice versa. The authors concluded that, although there seem to be relatively stable individual differences in people's threshold for laughter regardless of whether it occurs in response to tickling or to humor, the two types of laughter do not share a common emotional basis.

A more recent experiment by Christine Harris and Nancy Alvarado (2005) casts further doubt on the Darwin-Hecker Hypothesis. They used the FACS to analyze the facial expressions of participants who were laughing and smiling while being tickled, and compared them with facial expressions of the same individuals while listening to a comedy audiotape and while experiencing the pain of having their hand immersed in ice-cold water. Both tickling and comedy were associated with Duchenne smiles and laughter, whereas these expressions did not occur during pain. However, tickling was also associated with a greater proportion of non-Duchenne smiles along with a number of facial movements indicating negative emotions and distress, which were not seen in the comedy condition but were evident in the pain condition. The participants also reported lower levels of amusement and higher levels of unpleasant feelings, anxiety, and embarrassment in the tickling condition compared to the comedy condition. Furthermore, Duchenne smiles were correlated with self-reported unpleasant feelings as well as positive feelings in the tickling condition, but only with positive feelings in the comedy condition. Overall, these results suggested that the laughter elicited by tickling is not as purely pleasant and enjoyable as that elicited by humor.

The results of the latter two studies cast doubt on the Darwin-Hecker Hypothesis that humor and tickling both produce the same emotion of mirth, which is expressed through laughter. The authors suggested that, whereas humor-elicited laughter is mediated by a pleasant emotional state, laughter in response to tickling is a more reflexlike, nonemotional response. If these conclusions are correct, then they cast doubt on views that posit a close connection among tickling, mirth, and humor, including Panksepp's (2000) suggestion that tickling-elicited "laughter" in rats can be used as an animal model to study mirth. This issue requires further investigation, perhaps using brain-imaging techniques to compare the brain areas activated by tickling and humor.

Why are we unable to tickle ourselves? Since the same cutaneous stimulation is experienced very differently depending on whether it is produced by the self or by another person, there must be some mechanism whereby the brain distinguishes between these two sources of stimulation, canceling the ticklish effect when it is self-produced. As Provine (2004) noted, in the absence of such a mechanism, people might be constantly tickling themselves accidentally! One study used fMRI to examine differences in brain activity when participants tickled themselves on the hand compared to when the tickling was done by an experimenter (Blakemore, Wolpert, and Frith, 1998). The results showed lower activity in the cerebellum when the tickling was self-produced rather than externally produced, suggesting that the differentiation may take place in this structure of the hindbrain. As we saw earlier, the cerebellum has also been implicated in the modulation of laughter based on information about the social context (Parvizi et al., 2001).

Although we cannot tickle ourselves, there is some evidence that it may be possible to be tickled by a nonhuman machine. Harris and Christenfeld (1999) led blindfolded participants to believe that they would be tickled either by a "tickle machine" or by a human hand, although in both conditions they were actually tickled in the same way by a research assistant. The results showed that the subjects laughed just as much when they believed they were being tickled by a machine as when they thought they were being tickled by a person. Thus, laughter elicited by tickling does not seem to be dependent on the belief that it is being done by a human being.

Although this research has begun to address the interesting phenomena of tickling and laughter, there are still many questions that await further investigation. In particular, further study of the brain areas involved in tickling versus humor should help to answer the question of whether tickling elicits the same pleasurable emotion as that produced by humor (as suggested by Panksepp, 2000), or whether it is emotionally quite distinct from humor (as suggested by Harris, 1999). Further investigations may also provide some clues to the evolutionary functions of ticklish laughter. Did ticklishness evolve (as some theorists have suggested) as a means of motivating individuals to develop combat skills to protect certain vulnerable areas of the body from attack (Gregory, 1924; Harris, 1999)? Or is it a way of facilitating social bonding in the context of joyful play, as others have proposed (Panksepp, 2000; Provine, 2004)?

THE NEURAL BASIS OF COGNITIVE PROCESSES IN HUMOR

So far in this chapter, I have been focusing particularly on laughter and the emotion of mirth that it expresses. In this section I will turn to research on the neural underpinnings of the cognitive component of humor. If we think of the cognitive processes involved in humor (discussed in Chapter 4) as the "software" or "mental programs," here I am discussing the "hardware," the brain structures and circuits in which these programs "run." Our understanding of the brain bases of humor comes from several lines of research, including neuropsychological studies of deficits in humor comprehension observed in patients with brain damage, EEG studies of brain-wave activity during humor processing in normal individuals, and, more recently, neuroimaging studies using fMRI to identify the brain regions that are activated when people are exposed to humorous stimuli.

Humor and Brain Injury

Clinical observations of patients with right hemisphere damage (RHD) resulting from strokes or other injury to the brain have long suggested that the right hemisphere likely plays an important role in the processing of humor. Although these patients typically have normal linguistic abilities, they often (but not always) display marked changes in their personality, engaging in socially inappropriate behavior, making humorous but often crude or offensive comments, and laughing inappropriately (Brownell and Gardner, 1988). They are also often impaired in understanding the discourse and behavior of others, failing to understand jokes told by other people, and missing the main point of a story. Although they understand the details of a story, they seem to be unable to piece them together into a coherent interpretation. In addition, they often have difficulty extracting inferences and nuances from communication, misunderstanding sarcasm and indirect requests.

In contrast, patients with unilateral left hemisphere damage (LHD) typically do not show the same personality changes and inappropriate social behavior. Although they are often aphasic (i.e., they have marked language impairment due to the fact that language functions are located in the left hemisphere in right-handed people), they typically display a normal level of social awareness and understanding. In addition, to the extent allowed by their linguistic impairments, they are usually able to extract the main point of a story or conversation, to draw inferences, and to combine elements of a story into a coherent whole. These clinical observations suggest that RHD patients may have particular difficulty in understanding and appreciating at least some forms of humor.

Amy Bihrle and her colleagues at the Boston University School of Medicine conducted a study in which they compared RHD and LHD patients in their ability to comprehend humor (Bihrle, Brownell, and Powelson, 1986). Due to the language impairments common in LHD patients, it was important to use nonverbal humor stimuli to ensure that any differences between the groups were not simply due to differences in language abilities. Accordingly, the humor stimuli used in the experiment were a series of captionless comic strips, each containing four picture panels forming a narrative, with the final picture introducing a humorous ending much like the punch line of a verbal joke. The participants were presented with the first three panels of each comic strip and were instructed to select which of two alternative pictures would make the funniest ending. In each case, one of the alternatives was the original, humorous "punch line" picture, whereas the other (less humorous) alternative varied in the degree to which it contained incongruity (surprising elements) and resolution (coherence with the preceding narrative). By examining the types of alternatives that were chosen incorrectly by the participants, the researchers could identify particular components of humor comprehension with which they had difficulties.

Overall, RHD patients performed significantly more poorly than did LHD patients in selecting the correct joke ending, suggesting a particularly important role of the right hemisphere in humor comprehension. More specifically, RHD patients were found to be much more likely than LHD patients to select incorrect endings that contained an incongruous non sequitur but that did not show coherence with the earlier part of the narrative. In other words, these incorrect endings contained incongruity without resolution. For example, instead of the correct, funny ending, they would often select a slapstick ending (e.g., a picture of someone slipping on a banana peel) that did not have any relevance to the story. Thus, they seemed to be aware that humor involves some sort of incongruity (and often some element of aggression), and were able to recognize the presence of incongruity, but they had difficulty identifying which incongruous endings made most sense in relation to the rest of the story.

This lack of relevance or coherence may account for the clinical observation that RHD patients often engage in silly, socially inappropriate forms of humor (i.e., humor that is not relevant to the social situation). On the other hand, when LHD patients made errors, they were more likely than RHD patients to choose incorrect endings that did not contain any incongruity, but simply provided an ordinary, unsurprising completion to the story. Thus, they had some difficulty in recognizing incongruity.

In a second part of their study, which examined only the RHD patients, Bihrle and her colleagues (1986) employed a similar methodology using verbal jokes instead of visual cartoons as humor stimuli, to determine whether a similar pattern of deficits would be found with verbal humor. The results closely replicated the findings with the nonverbal humor, with RHD patients frequently selecting incorrect joke punch lines that contained incongruity (often of a slapstick nature) but no coherence or resolution. Similar findings were also obtained in other studies by Brownell et al. (1983) and by Wapner et al. (1981). Overall, these results suggested that the left hemisphere of the brain plays a role in perceiving incongruity, whereas the right hemisphere is important for making coherent sense of (i.e., resolving) the incongruity within the social context (Bihrle, Brownell, and Gardner, 1988; Gillikin and Derks, 1991; McGhee, 1983b).

More recent research suggests that part of the difficulty of RHD patients in comprehending humor may have to do with deficits in "theory of mind," which is the ability to attribute beliefs and intentions to other people in order to explain or predict their behavior (Brownell and Stringfellow, 2000). Francesca Happé, Hiram Brownell, and Ellen Winner (1999) tested humor comprehension in groups of RHD and LHD patients and non-brain–damaged control participants using nonverbal cartoons that either did or did not require a sophisticated theory of mind in order to understand and appreciate the humor fully. In the theory of mind cartoons, the humor depended on what a character mistakenly thought or did not know. For example, in one cartoon a man is playing a guitar and singing on a balcony of a high-rise apartment building, while two women, one on the balcony above him and the other on the balcony below, are listening with rapt attention, each apparently thinking that he is serenading her. To understand the joke, one must be able to recognize differences in the knowledge of each of the characters.

Participants were presented with pairs of cartoons, each pair comprising an original humorous cartoon and a modified version in which the key humorous element was replaced, and were asked to choose which of the two was funnier. The results indicated that RHD patients, as compared with both the LHD patients and normal control subjects, showed significantly more errors in identifying the humorous cartoons involving theory of mind, but did not differ in their ability to identify the cartoons that did not require theory of mind. In contrast, LHD patients did not differ from non-brain–damaged controls on either type of cartoon.

Brownell and Stringfellow (2000) suggested that deficits in theory of mind, which have also been found in RHD patients in other research, may account for the pattern of humor comprehension deficits that were found in these patients in previous research. In particular, they speculated that the resolution of humor (i.e., the ability to "make sense" of incongruity), which has been found to be the aspect of humor in which RHD patients have particular difficulty, often depends on a theory of mind. Impairments in theory of mind, which is very important for appropriate social and emotional functioning, may also help to account for the socially inappropriate forms of humor often observed in these patients. Further research is needed to explore these hypotheses more fully (see also Lyons and Fitzgerald, 2004, for a discussion of humor in autism and Asperger syndrome, which are thought to involve deficits in theory of mind).

Although previous research indicated an important role of the right hemisphere in humor comprehension, a study by Prathiba Shammi and Donald Stuss (1999), at the University of Toronto, indicated that it is the right frontal lobe in particular that seems to be most important. They tested patients with single focal brain damage restricted to the frontal (right, left, or bilateral) or nonfrontal (right or left) brain regions as well as age-matched normal controls. The participants were given several humor tests to assess various aspects of humor comprehension and appreciation, including both verbal and nonverbal forms of humor. In general, similar deficits in humor comprehension that were previously found in RHD patients were found in this study, but only for patients with right frontal lobe damage. In addition, the patients with right frontal lesions reacted with less emotional responsiveness (smiling and laughter) to all the humorous materials as compared to those with lesions in other brain areas.

The authors noted that the frontal lobes, and particularly the right frontal lobe, appear to be especially involved in the integration of cognition and emotion, due to their connections to the limbic system as well as many other cortical regions. In addition to the integration of cognition and emotion, the frontal lobes have been shown to play a crucial role in a number of cognitive functions that are likely important for humor comprehension, including narrative discourse, abstract and nonliteral interpretation, working memory, problem solving, and indirect forms of communication such as irony, affective intonation, and sarcasm.

EEG Studies

In addition to studying deficits in humor comprehension in patients with brain damage, researchers have investigated the brain areas involved in humor in healthy subjects using EEG techniques, in which the electrical activity of the brain is measured by means of electrodes attached to the scalp. To determine whether the left or right hemisphere is more active in humor, Sven Svebak (1982), then at the University of Bergen in Norway, measured the amount of discordant alpha wave activity occurring at sites on the right and left occipital lobes of subjects while they watched a comedy film. Those who laughed while watching the film (and therefore presumably found it highly amusing) showed less discordant right-left alpha activity than did those who did not laugh, suggesting coordinated activity of both hemispheres during mirth.

To test whether this finding was simply due to respiratory effects of laughter (perhaps causing differences in blood oxygen levels), a second study included conditions in which subjects were instructed to hyperventilate and hypoventilate, as well as humorous and nonhumorous film conditions. The results replicated the first study and also demonstrated that the greater concordance in alpha activity across the hemispheres associated with laughter was not simply caused by laughter-related changes in respiration. Overall, then, these studies suggested that both hemispheres of the brain work together in a coordinated manner during humor and mirth rather than one hemisphere being more active than the other.

In another EEG study of humor, Peter Derks and colleagues, at the National Aeronautics and Space Administration, examined event-related potentials (ERPs) associated with joke comprehension and appreciation (Derks et al., 1997). ERPs are spikes in positively or negatively polarized brain wave activity occurring at very brief intervals after an event, and have been found to indicate different types of information processing. Using 21 EEG electrodes at various locations on the scalp, brain wave activity was monitored while participants were presented with a series of verbal jokes on a computer screen. Electromyographic (EMG) recordings were also taken on the zygomatic muscle of the face to detect the presence or absence of smiling and laughter, indicating whether or not each joke was found amusing by the subject.

The results showed that all of the jokes, regardless of whether or not smiling or laughter occurred, produced an increase in positive polarization of brain waves with peak amplitude about 300 milliseconds (P300) following presentation of the punch line. In addition, for the jokes that were associated with zygomatic muscle activity, this was followed by a negative polarization with peak amplitude at about 400 milliseconds (N400). In contrast, this N400 wave did not occur after jokes that did not elicit zygomatic activity, and were therefore presumably not found to be amusing.

Previous research has shown that P300 waves indicate the cognitive activity of categorization, whereas N400 waves occur when categorization is disrupted due to an incongruous or unexpected element, resulting in an extension of the categorization process. In terms of the schema concepts discussed in Chapter 4, P300 following a joke can be viewed as indicating the activation of a schema to make sense of the information in the joke, whereas N400 indicates the disruption of this process and the search for an alternative schema due to the detection of an incongruity ("frame-shifting"). The fact that the N400 wave only occurred with jokes that were found to be amusing suggests that these were the jokes that triggered the activation of an alternate schema (corresponding to the "resolution" stage in two-stage theories of humor). As noted in Chapter 4, the simultaneous activation of two or more incompatible schemas seems to be the hallmark of humor. Thus, this study provided EEG evidence that corresponds quite well to the schema-based cognitive research discussed previously. In addition, consistent with the findings of Svebak (1982), this study found similar levels of activity in both hemispheres of the brain, suggesting that both hemispheres are involved in humor processing.

A more recent EEG study by Seana Coulson and Marta Kutas (2001), at the University of California at San Diego, found the N400 wave following the presentation of humorous sentences but not nonhumorous sentences, replicating the finding of Derks and colleagues (although the results were somewhat less consistent). Although this study also found evidence of a positively polarized wave, this occurred at 500 to 700 milliseconds, considerably later than that observed in the study by Derks and colleagues. In addition, subjects who showed a high level of joke comprehension revealed simultaneous positive and negative waves in different brain regions during this time period.

These authors interpreted the positive polarities as reflecting the surprise component of joke processing and the negative polarities as indicating the frame-shifting needed to reestablish coherence. They argued that the fact that these occurred during the same time period indicates that the surprise and coherence components of humor comprehension occur simultaneously in different brain regions, rather than following the temporally sequential pattern suggested by two-stage incongruity-resolution models of humor (e.g., Suls, 1972). In summary, although there were some differences between these two studies, both seem to provide evidence of positive and negative polarity ERPs corresponding to incongruity and resolution components of humor comprehension.

Brain-Imaging Studies

Recent advances in neuroimaging techniques such as fMRI have enabled researchers to study the brain regions involved in a wide range of psychological processes in normal individuals. fMRI uses high-powered, rapidly oscillating magnetic fields to scan the brain and detect small changes in blood oxygenation levels (which are indicative of changes in neuronal activity) in specific regions of the brain. Several recent studies have employed this method to investigate humor. These investigations have begun to map out the areas in the cortex involved in the cognitive comprehension of humor as well as subcortical areas in the limbic system underlying the emotional response of mirth.

In a study conducted at University College London, MRI was used to scan the brains of participants while they listened to riddles containing either phonological jokes (simple puns based on word sounds) or semantic jokes (containing more complex incongruities based on semantic meaning), as well as a set of nonhumorous control riddles (Goel and Dolan, 2001). After each item, the subjects were instructed to indicate, by pressing a key, whether or not they found it amusing, and after the scan they reviewed the jokes and rated them for funniness. Analyses of the brain areas that were differentially activated by the two different types of jokes indicated that somewhat different networks were involved. In particular, the semantic jokes induced greater activation in regions of both the left and right temporal lobes that are involved in semantic processing of language. In contrast, the phonological jokes induced greater activation in areas of the left frontal lobe that have been implicated in the processing of speech sounds, which have particular relevance in puns. Thus, different brain areas appear to be involved in the cognitive processing of different types of humor.

Besides these cognitive processes, this study also examined emotional components of humor by identifying brain areas that were differentially activated in response to jokes that were rated as funny, as compared to those rated as unfunny. Funniness ratings presumably reflect the degree to which each stimulus elicited mirth in the participants. These analyses revealed that, regardless of joke type, funnier jokes were associated with significantly greater activation of the medial ventral prefrontal cortex, an area at the front of the brain with connections to the limbic system that plays an important role in integrating cognitive and emotional processes. This was one of the areas that was also found to be activated during emotional, as opposed to voluntary, laughter in the study by Iwase and colleagues (2002) discussed previously.

Another fMRI study, conducted at Stanford University, found further evidence for the involvement of emotion-related brain centers in humor, particularly the well-known mesolimbic reward centers (Mobbs et al., 2003). While being scanned in an MRI machine, participants viewed, in random order, 42 humorous cartoons and 42 nonhumorous control cartoons in which the humorous elements had been removed. The data were analyzed to identify the brain regions that were differentially activated in response to humorous versus nonhumorous cartoons. Several of the regions that showed greater activation to humorous cartoons were in the left hemisphere of the cerebral cortex, presumably involving cognitive processing of humorous information. These included: (1) an area at the junction of the left temporal and occipital lobes (which was suggested by the authors to be important in the perception of incongruous or surprising elements of humor); (2) an area of the left frontal lobe including Broca's area (which is involved in semantic processing and integrating language and long-term memory, and may therefore be important for the perception of coherence or resolution of incongruity); and (3) the supplementary motor area of the left frontal lobe (presumably reflecting motor aspects of expressive smiling and laughter). The latter area is the one found by Fried and colleagues (1998) to produce mirthful laughter when electrically stimulated during surgery.

In addition to these cortical areas, this study found that humorous as compared to nonhumorous cartoons also produced significantly greater activation in several subcortical regions, including the anterior thalamus, ventral striatum, nucleus accumbens, ventral tegmental area, hypothalamus, and amygdala (Figure 5). These regions form the core of the so-called mesolimbic reward network, a well-researched system that employs dopamine as the major neurotransmitter, and which is implicated in a variety of pleasurable, emotionally rewarding activities, including ingestion of mood-altering drugs like heroin and alcohol, eating, sexual activity, listening to enjoyable music, looking at photographs of attractive faces, and playing video games (for a review, see Schultz, 2002). Thus, at a neurological level, the positive emotion elicited by humor appears to be closely related to the pleasurable feelings associated with these other activities. Of particular interest was the finding of a significant positive correlation between the funniness ratings of individual cartoons and the degree of activation of the nucleus accumbens, which has consistently been shown to be important in psy-

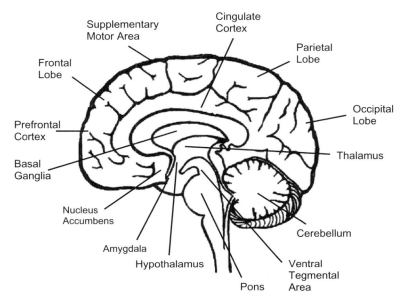

FIGURE 5   Brain regions involved in cognitive and emotional components of humor and laughter.

chologically and pharmacologically driven rewards, suggesting that this structure is particularly important in the pleasurable emotion associated with humor.

These patterns of cortical and subcortical regions activated by humorous versus nonhumorous cartoons were replicated in three subsequent investigations, two by the same team of researchers at Stanford University (Azim et al., 2005; Mobbs et al., 2005), and one by researchers at the California Institute of Technology (K. K. Watson, Matthews, and Allman, in press). One of these studies also examined sex differences in brain responses to humor (Azim et al., 2005). Although women and men showed similar overall patterns of brain activity, women revealed greater activation in the left prefrontal cortex and in the mesolimbic regions including the nucleus accumbens, suggesting that they enjoyed the cartoons more. Another of these studies examined correlations between personality traits and brain activation in response to humor (Mobbs et al., 2005). Participants with lower scores on a measure of neuroticism were found to have higher levels of activation in the mesolimbic reward circuitry, including the nucleus accumbens, suggesting that humor induces a stronger pleasure response in more emotionally stable individuals. There was also greater humor-related brain activation in extraverted as compared to introverted participants, indicating a greater responsiveness to humor in these individuals as well. These findings suggest a biological basis to correlations that have been found between these personality traits and various measures of sense of humor, which I will discuss in greater detail in Chapter 7.

Taken together, these brain-imaging studies provide intriguing evidence concerning the regions of the cerebral cortex that are involved in the cognitive processing of various types of humor, as well as the cortical and subcortical (limbic) regions mediating the pleasurable emotion of mirth that is induced by the perception of humor. Although the studies of humor in patients with brain lesions seem to suggest a particularly important role of the right hemisphere, the brain-imaging research (like the EEG studies) indicates that humor involves coordinated activities of many regions in both hemispheres. As noted earlier, the brain lesion findings implicating right hemisphere involvement in humor may reflect a particular role of that hemisphere in social comprehension skills, such as theory of mind, which are important for understanding humor within its social context. The brain-imaging studies suggest that the left hemisphere is also very much involved in processing other aspects of humor.

In addition to research investigating brain regions involved in the comprehension and enjoyment of jokes, some fMRI studies have looked at the brain areas that are activated by the sound of laughter. As we saw in the Chapter 5, Provine (2000) suggested that the contagiousness of laughter might be due to a hypothetical center in the brain that responds selectively to the distinct sounds of laughter, inducing feelings of mirth and causing the listener to laugh in turn. Gervais and Wilson (2005) suggested that this laughter-response center may consist of specialized mirror neurons, a type of neuron that is active not only when the individual is performing a particular behavior but also when observing someone else perform the same behavior (Rizzolatti and Craighero, 2004). Research has shown that certain mirror neurons also respond to the perception of emotions in others, inducing an empathic response in the observer.

An fMRI study by Kerstin Sander and Henning Scheich (2001) found that listening both to laughter and to crying elicited strong activation in the amygdala, part of the limbic system which, as we have seen, is an important center of emotion processing that is activated by humor. A more recent fMRI investigation compared the brain areas that were active when participants listened either to laughter, speech, or nonvocal sounds (M. Meyer et al., 2005). While both speech and laughter produced activation in auditory processing regions of the temporal lobes, the activation was stronger in the right hemisphere with laughter and in the left hemisphere with speech. Thus, the right hemisphere may be more strongly involved in responses to laughter if not to humor. This study also found that hearing laughter activated a section of the motor area in the right frontal lobe that has previously been implicated in the vocal expression of laughter, providing further evidence for a close link between laughter reception and expression mechanisms. Further research is needed to determine whether any of these areas can be identified as the laughter-mirroring center hypothesized by Provine (2000) and by Gervais and Wilson (2005).

Although only a small number of fMRI investigations of humor and laughter have been conducted as yet, they are beginning to provide intriguing information about how the brain responds to humor. It is important to note, though, that the confined space of an MRI machine does not permit researchers to study events in the brain associated with the creation and perception of spontaneous forms of humor occurring in naturalistic social interactions, and this research is therefore limited to the comprehension and enjoyment of jokes and cartoons and responses to recorded laughter. There are also some discrepancies in findings across these studies, likely due to differences in the types of humor stimuli and experimental paradigms that were used. Despite the limitations of the methodology, there is still much more to learn with this approach, and this will likely continue to be an exciting area of research in coming years.

EVOLUTIONARY THEORIES OF HUMOR AND LAUGHTER

Several lines of evidence indicate that humor, mirth, and laughter are likely a product of natural selection (Gervais and Wilson, 2005; Weisfeld, 1993). Humor and laughter are universal in the human species, and laughter as an expression of mirth emerges early in life. Infants begin to laugh in response to social stimuli by around four months of age, and cases of gelastic epilepsy in newborns indicate that the mechanisms for laughter are present at birth (Sher and Brown, 1976). Additional evidence that laughter is an innate behavior pattern, rather than being learned through imitation, comes from the fact that children who are born blind and deaf laugh normally (Goodenough, 1932). As we have seen, the evidence from studies of pathological laughter, brain lesion studies, and brain-imaging research all suggest that there are specific neural circuits for humor, mirth, and laughter. Moreover, the evidence of laughter and play-related positive emotion in other animals further attests to their evolutionary origins.

The animal research discussed earlier indicates that humor and laughter in humans likely originated in social play. Thus, the adaptive functions of humor are likely closely linked to the functions of play more generally. Many theorists have suggested that the evolutionary benefits of play have to do with facilitating the development of various adaptive skills (Bateson, 2005; Panksepp, 1998). For example, some have suggested that play helps individuals learn competitive and noncompetitive social skills, such as behaviors that facilitate social bonding and cooperation or those that promote social rank, leadership, and communication. Others have suggested nonsocial functions of play, such as increasing physical fitness, cognitive abilities, and creativity (P. K. Smith, 1982). Panksepp (1998) summarized research showing that adult rats that have been deprived of play during the juvenile period, as compared to those that have abundant play experience, are less effective in competitive encounters, are less valued as social partners by others, are more fearful in social situations, and have decrements in certain problem-solving abilities.

With the evolution of an enlarged cerebral cortex and increased capacity for language, abstract thinking, self-awareness, theory of mind, and so on, humans have extended the functions of play, mirth, and laughter by developing the ability to play with ideas, words, and alternative realities by means of the ludic mental activity of humor (Caron, 2002). Glenn Weisfeld (1993) proposed an evolutionary theory of the adaptive functions of humor that emphasizes its continuity with play. Just as physical play in animals seems to provide them the opportunity to practice competitive and noncompetitive social and physical survival skills in a nonthreatening context, humor, in this theory, is a means for humans to playfully practice important skills relating to social cognition and interpersonal behavior. Through humorous anecdotes, teasing, joking, and wordplay, humans are able to safely probe sensitive social issues concerning such topics as sexuality, aggression, and social status; engage in playful competition; explore incongruous counterexamples, and so on. Thus, the adaptive functions of humor as playful cognitive activity in a social context appear to be an extension of the original functions of mammalian physical play into the realm of cognition.

Besides these benefits of the cognitive aspects of humor, part of its adaptive function may have to do with the positive emotion associated with it. According to Barbara Fredrickson's (2001) Broaden-and-Build Theory, the adaptive functions of positive emotions in general, including the humor-related emotion of mirth, is to *broaden* the scope of the individual's focus of attention, allowing for more creative problem solving and an increased range of behavioral response options, and to *build* physical, intellectual, and social resources that are available to the individual for dealing with life's challenges. Evidence in support of this theory has been provided by recent research conducted by Fredrickson and her colleagues on mirth and other positive emotions (e.g., Fredrickson and Branigan, 2005; Fredrickson et al., 2000). These ideas are also consistent with the suggestion made by Michelle Shiota and her colleagues (2004) that positive emotions, including humor-related mirth, play an important role in the regulation of interpersonal relationships.

Although human laughter appears to have originated in play, it has evidently undergone considerable evolutionary change since we diverged from our nearest living relative, the chimpanzee, some 6 million years ago. As noted earlier, human laughter sounds quite different from that of chimpanzees and other primates, and is based on a different respiratory pattern. Thus, there appears to have been some adaptive pressure on the formal characteristics of laughter in the evolutionary history of our species. Matthew Gervais and David Wilson (2005) refer to these modifications as a process of ritualization, whereby "a signal changes in structure so that it is more prominent and unmistakable, and thus more readily perceptible" (p. 415).

When did this distinctively human form of laughter evolve? Robert Provine (2000) argued that the divergence from apelike to humanlike laughter did not begin until after the development of bipedalism in our hominid ancestors (presumably the *australopithecines*) some 4 million years ago, since walking on two legs freed the thorax from the mechanical constraints of quadrupedal locomotion and allowed for the greater control over respiration that is needed for human laughter (as well as language). In turn, Gervais and Wilson (2005) suggested that the human form of laughter was likely fully developed before the evolution of language (which is thought to have begun with *Homo habilis* around 2 million years ago), since brain studies indicate that laughter originates in subcortical, limbic, and brainstem areas shared with other primates, and not in the more recently evolved neocortical areas in which language is based. If this reasoning is correct, laughter must have taken its contemporary human form sometime between 2 and 4 million years ago.

Why did laughter in humans become ritualized in this way? Gervais and Wilson (2005) proposed a theory drawing on contemporary views of laughter as an emotion-induction mechanism. In particular, they suggested that the changes that occurred in laughter were ones that made it increasingly effective at inducing the play-related positive emotion of mirth in other members of a group, and thereby recruiting them to engage in social play. In turn, social play and the positive emotion associated with it presumably provided the various adaptive benefits discussed earlier. Individuals who were more adept at becoming playful during times of safety and eliciting a playful state in others through laughter would have benefited from increased fitness within the group. In addition, groups composed of members who more frequently engaged in laughter would have a competitive advantage over other groups. (For an alternative, "selfish gene" theory of the evolution of laughter, see Owren and Bachorowski, 2001.)

Besides the play-related functions of humor, mirth, and laughter, over the course of human evolution humor seems to have been adapted for a number of additional functions by means of co-optation. A number of such additional functions have been proposed by various theorists (see Vaid, 1999, for a review of evolutionary theories of humor). For example, as we saw in Chapter 5, Mulkay (1988) suggested that humor was co-opted as a mode of interpersonal communication. Along the same line, Richard Alexander (1986) proposed an evolutionary theory of humor that emphasizes its aggressive as well as its bonding aspects. Using the concepts of ostracism and indirect reciprocity, he suggested that humor evolved as a way of favorably manipulating one's status in a social group to improve one's access to resources for reproductive success. Jokes and other disparaging forms of humor that make fun of members of an out-group are a means of lowering their status and ostracizing them, while more affiliative forms of humor are a method of enhancing the status and fostering the cohesiveness of members of the in-group.

Geoffrey Miller (1997, 2000) has proposed a theory that focuses on the creativity of humor rather than its aggressiveness, suggesting that sexual selection played a major role in its evolution. According to this view, a witty sense of humor, like linguistic skills and creativity, is an indicator of superior intellectual aptitude, a genetically based trait that enhances one's ability to compete successfully for resources. Thus, humor is a "fitness indicator," a signal for "good genes," increasing the individual's perceived desirability as a potential mate. This theory accounts for the well-replicated finding (discussed in Chapter 5) that a sense of humor is seen by people in all cultures as one of the most desirable characteristics in a prospective mate, and particularly in women's choice of a male partner (Feingold, 1992). The preferred selection of partners with a sense of humor would ensure that, over time, genes involved in the formation of brain systems underlying humor creation and appreciation would proliferate in the population.

Some recent studies have investigated hypotheses derived from Miller's sexual selection theory. Eric Bressler and Sigal Balshine (2006) presented male and female undergraduates photographs of two individuals (both either male or female) along with statements that were supposedly written by them. The statements from one of each pair always contained humor, and the other did not. The participants were then asked to rate these individuals on a number of perceived personality traits and to select the one that was most desirable as a relationship partner. The results revealed that female subjects preferred the humorous over the nonhumorous male as a potential partner, whereas no such preference appeared when males were rating females or when participants of either gender were rating individuals of the same sex. These results were interpreted as providing support for Miller's theory that a sense of humor evolved as a means of attracting potential sexual partners, and particularly for males to attract females.

Although research has shown that both men and women consider a sense of humor to be a desirable characteristic in a prospective mate (Daniel et al., 1985; Feingold, 1992), sexual selection theory would suggest that the two sexes may have somewhat different ideas about what a desirable sense of humor is. Women may think of a man with a good sense of humor as someone who makes them laugh, whereas men may think of a woman with a sense of humor as someone who laughs at their jokes. A recent study by Bressler and colleagues provided some support for this hypothesis (Bressler, Martin, and Balshine, 2006). When presented with descriptions of two individuals of the opposite sex and asked to choose which one was more attractive as a potential romantic partner, women were more likely to choose the one who produced humor and made them laugh over the one who appreciated their humor, whereas men were more likely to choose the humor appreciator over the humor producer.

A number of other evolutionary theories have been proposed, each suggesting somewhat different adaptive functions for humor. For example, humor and laughter have been viewed as a "disabling mechanism" that prevents us from doing things that would be counterproductive (Chafe, 1987), or as a form of "vocal grooming" which, like physical grooming in primates, facilitates social bonding (Dunbar, 1996). Another theory views laughter as a "false alarm," signaling to others that a stimulus or event is unimportant and nonserious (Ramachandran, 1998). Although many of these theories seem quite plausible, there is little research evidence to support most of them. Like evolutionary psychology in general, evolutionary theories of humor need to provide testable hypotheses making them potentially falsifiable so that they can be more than merely "just so" stories (Gould, 2002). In the end, we may never have definitive answers concerning the origins and adaptive functions of humor. Nonetheless, these sorts of evolutionary theories are useful if they generate interesting new hypotheses, stimulating new lines of research, and providing a better understanding of the phenomena.

CONCLUSION

The psychobiological study of humor, mirth, and laughter contributes interesting new perspectives and insights, complementing the findings from other areas of psychology. The biological approach to humor calls our attention particularly to the emotional aspects of this phenomenon. The cognitive-perceptual component of humor draws on many cortical brain circuits involved in information processing. When humorous incongruity is perceived, a distinctive emotional state is elicited, which I have referred to as mirth. Comparative studies of nonhuman animals suggest that this emotion originates in play, a social activity that apparently serves important adaptive functions. Recent brain studies, using animal models as well as neuroimaging in humans, are just beginning to unravel the "emotional operating system" of mirth, the specialized brain structures and circuits that underlie this emotion. These studies have already implicated the well-known dopaminergic mesolimbic reward centers, as well as the role of opiates and various neuropeptides. Further research in this area, part of the growing field of affective neuroscience, will likely yield many interesting discoveries, not only about the brain circuits, but also the brain biochemistry of humor-related mirth and the potential interactions of these biochemicals with other systems of the body, including the endocrine and immune systems.

The emotion of mirth typically also triggers the expressive behavior of laughter, which communicates to others the presence of this emotional state in the individual. Laughter is characterized by a distinctive pattern of vocalizations, respiration, and facial expression. Although we often view laughter as the "cause" of changes in autonomic arousal and brain biochemistry, it seems more appropriate to view all of these as effects of the emotion of mirth. Laughter is essentially a social behavior, a fixed action pattern that serves an interpersonal communication function. It has a contagious effect, as the sound of laughter elicits feelings of mirth in others, causing them to laugh as well.

The biological approach also draws attention to the evolutionary basis of humor. A type of play-related laughter occurs in our closest ape relative, the chimpanzee, as well as other primates, and it has even been suggested that homologues of laughter may be seen in the play activities of rats, suggesting that the origins of mirth and laughter may extend to our earliest mammalian ancestors. The play face and related vocalizations in nonhuman animals signal a distinction between reality and pretense, seriousness and fun, indicating a rudimentary conception of humor. With the exponential growth in the human cortex, and the associated increase in cognitive abilities including language, abstract reasoning, self-awareness, and theory of mind, humans have taken social play to a new level. By playing with language and ideas in the verbal equivalent of competitive rough-and-tumble play, an activity that we call "humor," we activate the same emotional brain circuits, autonomic arousal patterns, and behavioral displays that are involved in actual physical play. Although play is largely a juvenile activity in most animals, and rough-and-tumble play typically ends with childhood in humans as well, play in the form of humor continues to be an important activity throughout adulthood in humans, serving important social functions. By testing hypotheses derived from various evolutionary theories of humor, research in the field of evolutionary psychology may help to elucidate its adaptive functions, as well as take research on humor into interesting new avenues. In sum, while research in the field of psychobiology has made considerable progress in furthering our understanding of the origins, nature, and biological bases of humor, mirth, and laughter, this promises to be an exciting area of further research in the future.

CHAPTER 7

Personality Approaches to the Sense of Humor

How would you describe one of your friends to another person? In addition to physical characteristics such as height and hair color, you would likely mention various personality traits, describing his or her level of friendliness, intelligence, competitiveness, or generosity. Chances are that you would also mention his or her sense of humor, saying something like "She often makes me laugh," or "He always sees the funny side of things." Thus, sense of humor may be viewed as a personality trait (or, more accurately, a set of loosely related traits), referring to consistent tendencies to perceive, enjoy, or create humor in one's daily life.

Personality has to do with "an individual's habitual way of thinking, feeling, perceiving, and reacting to the world" (Magnavita, 2002, p. 16). Personality traits are hypothetical constructs that describe the ways people differ from one another and that enable us to make predictions about how they will behave in various situations. Although people's behavior is partly influenced by situational factors (you are more likely to tell jokes at a party than at a funeral, for instance), individuals also display some degree of consistency across situations (some people are more likely than others to tell jokes in any particular situation).

A personality trait may be viewed as a dimension along which all people can be placed, with some falling at the very high or low ends of the scale and others somewhere between the extremes. Personality psychologists seek to identify the various traits that account for behavioral, cognitive, and affective differences among people, to create reliable and valid measures for quantifying these traits, to explore the relationships among different traits and their ability to predict particular behaviors and affects, and to investigate the biological, social, and psychological factors that account for such individual differences.

Among the many traits that they have investigated, sense of humor has long been a topic of interest to personality psychologists. Several of the most influential early personality researchers and theorists, including such disparate thinkers as Hans Eysenck (1942), Raymond Cattell (Cattell and Luborsky, 1947), Gordon Allport (1961), and Sigmund Freud (1960 [1905]), investigated humor and found a place for it in their theoretical systems (for a review, see R. A. Martin, 1998). In the past few decades, the study of sense of humor as a personality trait has continued to be one of the most active areas of research in the psychology of humor. Researchers have developed a number of tests for measuring different aspects or components of this construct, and numerous studies have been conducted to investigate how these humor-related traits correlate with other personality dimensions and predict relevant behavior.

A particular interest in much of the recent research has been the role of sense of humor in mental health and coping with stress. I will discuss the mental health implications of sense of humor in Chapter 9. In this chapter, I will focus on the conceptualization and measurement of individual differences in humor and their association with other personality dimensions. I will begin by exploring what we mean by sense of humor, noting that this concept seems to comprise several different dimensions. I will then discuss various approaches that researchers have taken in defining and measuring this concept and will review research examining relationships between these different humor measures and other personality traits. These approaches include: humor appreciation measures, which assess the degree to which individuals enjoy different types of humor; self-report measures of various components of sense of humor; measures of people's ability to produce humor; and a *q*-sort technique for assessing humor styles. I will then discuss factor analytic research examining interrelationships among these different measurement approaches. Finally, I will review some research investigating the personality traits of professional comedians.

WHAT IS SENSE OF HUMOR?

As we saw in Chapter 1, the concept of sense of humor developed in the nineteenth century. In its original meaning, it had an aesthetic connotation, referring to a faculty or capacity for the perception or appreciation of humor, something like a sense of beauty in art or an ear for music. At that time, the word *humor* also had a narrower meaning than it has today, referring to a sympathetic form of amusement that was linked to pathos, and was distinguished from wit, which was seen as more aggressive and less socially desirable (Ruch, 1998a; Wickberg, 1998). The sense of humor, as a character trait relating to this positive form of amusement, therefore also took on a very socially desirable connotation, and came to be viewed as one of the most positive traits a person could have. Over the years, however, the meaning of *humor* has broadened to cover all types of mirthful phenomena, and *sense of humor* has also been extended to include a much wider range of humor-related traits, while retaining its very positive connotation. Thus, a sense of humor has become a very desirable but also a very poorly defined personality characteristic.

Most people think of themselves as having a good sense of humor. As the American essayist Frank Moore Colby wittily observed, "Men will confess to treason, murder, arson, false teeth, or a wig. How many of them will own up to a lack of humor?" (quoted in Andrews, 1993, p. 431). Gordon Allport (1961) found that, when asked to assess their own sense of humor, 94 percent of research participants rated it as either average or above average, with only 6 percent acknowledging a below-average sense of humor (statistically, of course, 50 percent of the population are below average). Herbert Lefcourt and I (1986) replicated this finding 25 years later in a study of university students.

People generally associate a sense of humor with many desirable characteristics beyond merely the tendency to create or enjoy humor. When research participants were asked to rate the personality traits of a hypothetical person with a "well above average sense of humor," as well as someone with a "below average sense of humor," the high-humor person was rated as being significantly more friendly, pleasant, cooperative, interesting, imaginative, creative, clever, admirable, intelligent, and perceptive, and significantly less complaining, cold, mean, and passive (Cann and Calhoun, 2001). At the same time, though, the high-humor person was also rated as being more impulsive, boastful, and restless, and less mature, indicating that the sense of humor concept does contain some less desirable characteristics as well. On the major personality dimensions of the well-known Five Factor Model (FFM) of personality (McCrae and John, 1992), this same study found that people with an above average sense of humor are perceived to be more emotionally stable, extraverted, open to experience, and agreeable, but less conscientious than their low-humor counterparts.

While everyone wants to believe they have a good sense of humor, which is thought to be associated with many desirable qualities and characteristics, no one seems to know exactly what a sense of humor *is*. Indeed, Cann and Calhoun (2001) questioned whether this popular but nebulous concept has any consistent, specific referents at all, or whether it is simply a relatively nonspecific configuration of socially desirable characteristics. As Louise Omwake (1939, p. 95) stated over 65 years ago, the sense of humor "is so all-inclusive and highly prized that to say of another: 'He has a grand sense of humor' is almost synonymous with: 'He is intelligent, he's a good sport, and I like him immensely.'" If sense of humor is to be a scientifically useful trait concept that can be measured reliably and validly in personality research, it obviously needs to be defined more carefully and precisely.

As I have noted in earlier chapters, humor is a complex phenomenon that touches on many aspects of our daily lives. It is a type of mental play comprising social, cognitive, emotional, and expressive components. It also takes many forms, including canned jokes, spontaneous conversational witticisms, irony, puns, double entendres, amusing anecdotes, and unintentionally funny speech and actions. In addition, it serves a wide variety of psychological functions, including the cognitive and social benefits of the positive emotion of mirth; its many uses in interpersonal communication and influence, which can be both prosocial and aggressive; and its use as a tension-relief and coping mechanism. People can be producers of humor, amusing others and making them laugh, and they can also respond to the humor created by others. As a personality trait or individual difference variable, the concept of sense of humor can relate to any of these different components, forms, and functions of humor. Indeed, researchers investigating this trait have taken many different approaches, each focusing on somewhat different aspects of this complex phenomenon. Not surprisingly, when sense of humor is conceptualized in these different ways, it tends to be associated with different dimensions of human behavior, cognition, and personality.

When we say that someone has a sense of humor, then, we may mean many different things. Personality psychologist Hans Eysenck (1972) pointed out three different possible meanings. First, saying someone has a sense of humor may mean that he or she laughs at the same things that we do (*qualitative* meaning). Second, we may mean that the person laughs a great deal and is easily amused (*quantitative* meaning). Third, we may mean that the person is the "life and soul of the party," telling funny stories and amusing other people (*productive* meaning). Eysenck went on to argue that these three different "senses of humor" are not necessarily highly correlated with each other.

Franz-Josef Hehl and Willibald Ruch (1985) expanded on Eysenck's list, noting that individual differences in sense of humor may relate to variation in: (1) the *ability to comprehend* jokes and other humorous stimuli (i.e., to "get" the joke); (2) the way in which individuals *express* humor and mirth, both quantitatively and qualitatively; (3) their *ability to create* humorous comments or perceptions; (4) their *appreciation* of various types of jokes, cartoons, and other humorous materials; (5) the degree to which they actively *seek out* sources that make them laugh, such as comedy movies and television programs; (6) their *memory* for jokes or funny events in their own lives; and (7) their tendency to use humor as a *coping mechanism*. Elisha Babad (1974) also distinguished between humor *production* (the ability to create humor) and *reproduction* (the tendency to retell jokes that one has heard from others) and showed that the two are uncorrelated. Yet another meaning commonly associated with sense of humor is the idea of *not taking oneself too seriously* and the ability to laugh at one's own foibles and weaknesses.

Sense of humor may therefore be variously conceptualized as a *habitual behavior pattern* (tendency to laugh frequently, to tell jokes and amuse others with spontaneous witticisms, to laugh at other people's humor productions), an *ability* (to create humor, to amuse others, to "get the joke," to remember jokes), a *temperament trait* (habitual cheerfulness, playfulness), an *aesthetic response* (enjoyment of particular types of humorous material), an *attitude* (positive attitude toward humor and humorous people), a *world view* (bemused, nonserious outlook on life), or a *coping strategy* or *defense mechanism* (tendency to maintain a humorous perspective in the face of adversity).

These different ways of conceptualizing sense of humor also lend themselves to different measurement approaches in personality research. For example, humor appreciation tests employing funniness ratings of jokes and cartoons may be used to measure sense of humor when it is defined as an aesthetic response. If sense of humor is conceived as a habitual behavior pattern, however, it may be better to measure it with self-report scales in which respondents rate the degree to which various statements describe their typical humor-related behaviors, thoughts, feelings, and attitudes. Alternatively, ratings obtained from peers or trained observers may be used to quantify typical humor behaviors. On the other hand, the measurement of sense of humor as a cognitive ability requires the use of maximal performance tests similar to measures of intelligence or creativity, such as tasks in which participants' humor productions are judged for funniness and originality. As we will see, each of these different conceptualizations and measurement approaches has been employed by different researchers.

In summary, sense of humor does not seem to be a unitary trait. Instead, it is best conceived as a group of traits and abilities having to do with different components, forms, and functions of humor. Some of these may be closely related to each other, while others are likely to be quite distinct (R. A. Martin, 2003). For example, whereas people with a good ability to create humor likely also tend to enjoy making other people laugh, they do not necessarily also tend to use humor in coping with stress in their daily lives. Researchers who wish to investigate hypotheses concerning sense of humor need to be careful to identify which meaning of the construct is theoretically most relevant to their research questions, and select the measurement approach that is most appropriate.

INDIVIDUAL DIFFERENCES IN HUMOR APPRECIATION

Does the type of humor that a person finds most amusing tell us something about his or her personality? This idea, which has been popular for centuries, is reflected in the observation of the German poet Johann Wolfgang von Goethe that "men show their character in nothing more clearly than by what they think laughable" (quoted by Ruch and Hehl, 1998, p. 109). Based on this idea, some clinicians have proposed that asking psychotherapy patients to tell their favorite jokes might be a useful type of projective test that could be analyzed to diagnose their problems and identify their unresolved needs and conflicts (e.g., Strother, Barnett, and Apostolakos, 1954; Zwerling, 1955).

This view is also the basis of a number of humor appreciation tests that have been developed by personality researchers over the past 50 years to indirectly assess various personality traits (e.g., Cattell and Tollefson, 1966). Indeed, most of the research on individual differences in sense of humor prior to the 1980s was based on this humor appreciation approach, and it continues to have some popularity today. In this approach, research participants are presented with a series of jokes, cartoons, and other humorous materials, and are asked to rate them on such dimensions as funniness, enjoyment, and aversiveness. The humor stimuli are clustered into various categories, either on a theoretical basis or by means of factor analysis, and separate scores are computed by summing participants' ratings within each category. In this approach, then, sense of humor is defined in terms of the degree to which the individual enjoys particular types or categories of humor.

Theoretically-Based Content Approaches

In many of the early humor appreciation tests, the humor stimuli (primarily jokes and cartoons) were categorized by the experimenters or other experts on the basis of their content themes. These content categories were typically derived from particular theories of humor, and the measures were then used in research to test these theories. For example, to test Freud's theory that repressed sexual and aggressive drives are released through humor, jokes, and cartoons were typically classified into sexual, aggressive, and nonsense (also referred to as innocent or nontendentious) categories. As noted in Chapter 2, most of the research on psychoanalytic humor theory used this approach. For example, the Mirth Response Test, developed by Jacob Levine and his colleagues (1951), consisted of 36 cartoons that were judged to tap various sex- and aggression-related themes. Subjects' positive and negative responses to the cartoons were thought to reveal their unconscious needs and unresolved conflicts relating to these themes.

Research using the theoretically derived content-based humor appreciation approach provided some evidence that people's level of enjoyment of various types of jokes and cartoons is related to certain personality traits. For example, one early study found that participants who preferred jokes containing sexual and aggressive themes over more intellectually-based humor had more aggressive themes in their Thematic Apperception Test (TAT) stories, lower scores on a measure of intellectual values, less psychological complexity, and higher scores on a measure of extraversion (Grziwok and Scodel, 1956). Some other studies also found positive correlations between extraversion and liking of sexual humor (e.g., G. D. Wilson and Patterson, 1969).

In addition, participants with more conservative attitudes tended to prefer "safe" types of humor (e.g., puns), whereas those endorsing more liberal views expressed greater appreciation of overtly "libidinal" (e.g., sick and sexual) types of humor (G. D. Wilson and Patterson, 1969). In general, more highly anxious individuals, as compared to their less anxious counterparts, were found to enjoy humorous materials less, although studies differed as to whether this effect occurred with all types of humor (Hammes and Wiggins, 1962), or only with aggressive (J. Doris and Fierman, 1956) or nonsense humor (Spiegel, Brodkin, and Keith-Spiegel, 1969). One study even found some significant correlations between participants' funniness ratings of jokes containing anal themes (i.e., jokes about defecation and flatulence) and measures of "anal" personality traits such as obstinacy, negativism, hostility, cleanliness, and thrift (O'Neill, Greenberg, and Fisher, 1992).

As in the psychoanalytically inspired research, humor appreciation tests were also used in many of the studies investigating disparagement theories of humor (also reviewed in Chapter 2). These tests typically comprised hostile humor that was categorized by the researchers according to the identity of the proponents and targets of the jokes. Overall, these studies demonstrated that people tend to enjoy disparagement humor that makes fun of people toward whom they have some antipathy (La Fave et al., 1976; Wicker et al., 1980; Wolff et al., 1934; Zillmann and Cantor, 1972, 1976). As noted in Chapter 5, researchers have also used similar methods to study the relationship between sexist attitudes and the enjoyment of sexist humor (e.g., Henkin and Fish, 1986; Moore et al., 1987; Thomas and Esses, 2004).

In summary, a large number of studies have been conducted over the years with humor appreciation tests containing theoretically derived, content-based categories of humorous stimuli. Most of this research was conducted prior to the 1980s, although some researchers have continued to employ this approach more recently to study subjects' appreciation for particular types of humor, such as "sick" jokes (Herzog and Bush, 1994; Herzog and Karafa, 1998), sexist humor (Greenwood and Isbell, 2002; Ryan and Kanjorski, 1998), or "perspective-taking" humor (Lefcourt et al., 1997).

Although some interesting results have been obtained, this approach to classifying humorous materials is subject to several criticisms (Ruch, 1992). Researchers typically did not empirically evaluate the reliability and validity of their humor classifications, nor did they test the assumption of homogeneity of participants' responses to humorous stimuli within a given category. As Eysenck (1972) observed, individuals often do not agree about which aspects of a joke or cartoon they find salient or why they consider it to be funny or unfunny. The dimensions used by a researcher in categorizing humorous stimuli may therefore not be relevant to the way the participants themselves perceive and respond to them. In this regard, an early study by Landis and Ross (1933) found no relation between subjects' classifications of a number of jokes and the way these jokes had been classified by the experimenters, even when the subjects were provided with the categories and their definitions.

In addition, because researchers using this approach selected particular humorous stimuli to fit their theories, they were unable to determine whether their classification systems applied to all kinds of humor or merely to a subset. Finally, since many of the humor appreciation tests were used in only one or two studies by individual researchers, it is difficult to compare the results across different studies. Because of these weaknesses, this approach has not led to much accumulation of knowledge about the nature of sense of humor.

Early Factor Analytic Studies

An alternative to the theoretically derived content-based method of categorizing humor stimuli involves the use of factor analysis techniques. Rather than constructing a test based on a particular theory, this approach seeks to build a theory on the basis of empirically derived factor dimensions. Factor analysis is a statistical technique for examining correlations among a large set of variables and identifying a smaller number of dimensions (i.e., factors) that account for most of the variance. This method has been used extensively by personality researchers to search for basic personality traits, as in the FFM mentioned earlier. Over the years, some humor researchers have also applied this technique to identify basic dimensions of humor appreciation.

The general strategy in this approach is to obtain a large number of jokes, cartoons, and other humorous stimuli that are considered to be representative of the whole domain. These materials are then rated for funniness by a large number of research participants. By factor-analyzing these ratings, researchers can determine the implicit dimensions underlying people's appreciation of humor. Jokes and cartoons whose ratings are highly correlated tend to cluster together in the same factor, whereas those whose ratings are uncorrelated fall into different factors. By examining the characteristics that are shared by the humorous stimuli that load on each factor, researchers can identify the relevant dimensions that people implicitly use in their appraisals of these stimuli.

Early factor analytic studies of humor appreciation were conducted by Hans Eysenck, a well-known German-British personality researcher (reviewed by Nias, 1981). Noting that most theories of humor were developed by philosophers and based on speculation, Eysenck sought to develop a theory based on empirical evidence. To do this, he administered collections of verbal jokes, cartoons, and incongruous photographs to 16 participants (a very small sample by today's standards) who were asked to rank-order them for funniness and to indicate which ones they enjoyed (Eysenck, 1942). Factor analyses of these data revealed a small general factor, indicating individual differences in the degree to which people find any kind of humor to be funny. In addition, the analyses revealed three specific factors or dimensions of humor, which were labeled as (1) sexual versus nonsexual; (2) simple versus complex; and (3) personal versus impersonal.

Eysenck also examined the correlations between participants' ratings of humor on the three factors and their scores on a personality test. Sexual and simple jokes were found to be preferred by extraverted individuals, while complex and nonsexual jokes were preferred by introverts. These factor analytic results were generally replicated by Eysenck (1943) in another study in which he administered five sets of humorous stimuli, including jokes, cartoons, and funny limericks, to 100 adults representing a broad cross section of British society.

Based on these factor analytic findings, Eysenck (1942) proposed a theoretical model of humor comprising three components or facets: cognitive (corresponding to the complexity of the humor), conative (having to do with motivation or impulse expression), and affective (relating to emotional aspects). He further combined the conative and affective components under the term *orectic*, which has to do with the "joyful consciousness of superior adaptation" associated with humor. He noted that different traditional theories of humor focus on one or another of these humor facets. The cognitive aspects are emphasized in incongruity theories of humor, the conative in superiority/disparagement theories, and the affective in theories that stress the positive emotions associated with laughter. According to Eysenck, Freud's theory combined elements of all three components.

Eysenck also suggested that each of these components may be present in a given joke to varying degrees, and individual differences in sense of humor may be conceptualized in terms of the degree to which people enjoy humor containing these different elements. For example, he suggested that introverts are more likely to enjoy humor in which the cognitive element predominates, whereas extraverts tend to prefer humor in which the orectic aspects are paramount. Further support for this view was provided by Wilson and Patterson (1969) who found a significant correlation between participants' scores on a measure of extraversion and their funniness ratings of sexual jokes. However, as we will see, other researchers have failed to replicate this finding (Ruch, 1992). Overall, then, Eysenck was one of the first researchers who attempted to develop a general theory of sense of humor based on factor analytic studies of humor appreciation.

Raymond Cattell was another well-known pioneer of general personality research who conducted early factor analytic studies of humor appreciation. Cattell and Luborsky (1947) collected a set of 100 jokes that were considered to be representative of a broad range of humor and relatively free of cultural bias. A sample of 50 male and 50 female undergraduate students were asked to rate the funniness of each joke on two different occasions. Factor analyses revealed 13 clusters of jokes that appeared to have adequate internal consistency and test-retest reliability. Subjects' scores on each of these clusters were subsequently submitted to an additional factor analysis, resulting in five fairly orthogonal (i.e., uncorrelated) factors. Based on the themes of the jokes loading on each factor, the factors were tentatively labeled as: (1) good-natured self-assertion; (2) rebellious dominance; (3) easy going sensuality; (4) resigned derision; and (5) urbane sophistication. The authors suggested that these clusters and factors of humor appreciation might be related to the 12 to 16 general personality factors identified by Cattell (1947) in his factor analyses of personality traits.

To test these ideas, in a subsequent study Luborsky and Cattell (1947) examined the correlations between individuals' funniness scores on the 13 joke clusters and their scores on 10 personality dimensions measured by the Guilford-Martin temperament inventory. Six of these personality dimensions were found to be significantly correlated with funniness ratings of various joke clusters, allowing for further refinement of the cluster labels. These findings caused the authors to be quite optimistic about the possibility of using these humor appreciation factors as a method of assessing more general dimensions of personality. For example, one joke factor was found to be correlated with extraversion, and it was suggested that those jokes could be used as an objective measure of this trait. These ideas were subsequently incorporated into the IPAT Humor Test of Personality (Cattell and Tollefson, 1966), which was designed to assess humor preferences in each of these factors as a way of indirectly measuring more general personality traits.

Despite the effort that went into developing the IPAT humor test, it had several weaknesses and was never widely used. The reliabilities of the scales were quite low, and the stability of the factor structure was questionable. Other researchers factor-analyzed the same set of jokes and found an entirely different factor structure (Yarnold and Berkeley, 1954). Part of the problem seems to have been the use of a forced-choice response format, resulting in the overextraction of numerous weak and unstable factors and suppression of stronger and more stable factors (Ruch, 1992). In addition, very little research was conducted to evaluate the validity of the humor factor scores as measures of more general personality traits. This test has been used in only a few published studies to investigate such topics as personality traits of effective counselors (Kush, 1997), the relation between humor appreciation and perceived physical health (Carroll, 1990), and gender differences in humor appreciation (Carroll, 1989; Hickson, 1977).

Ruch's Factor-Analytic Investigations

The early factor-analytic studies of humor appreciation were limited by small sample sizes and a number of methodological weaknesses. In the early 1980s, Willibald Ruch, an Austrian psychologist who is now at the University of Zurich in Switzerland, set out to investigate the factor structure of humor appreciation in a more thorough and systematic way (for a review, see Ruch, 1992). To ensure a comprehensive representation of humor types, he began by amassing a set of 600 jokes and cartoons that were obtained from a wide range of sources. Many were taken randomly from popular magazines and joke books, while others were selected as representative of the categories discussed in the humor literature and used in previous studies.

Over a series of factor-analytic studies conducted by Ruch and his colleagues, differing but overlapping sets of jokes and cartoons from this initial pool were administered to a number of samples of male and female participants representing a broad range of ages, social class, occupations, and health status (Hehl and Ruch, 1985; McGhee, Ruch, and Hehl, 1990; Ruch, 1981, 1984, 1988; Ruch, McGhee, and Hehl, 1990). The materials were also translated into several languages, and studies were conducted with samples in Austria, Germany, England, Turkey, France, Italy, and the United States (Forabosco and Ruch, 1994; Ruch and Forabosco, 1996; Ruch and Hehl, 1998; Ruch et al., 1991).

These factor-analytic studies revealed three stable and robust factors that appear to account for most of the variance in humor appreciation and are consistently found across different humorous stimuli and in all populations studied. Interestingly, the first two factors have to do with structural aspects of humor, rather than content themes. The first of these, labeled *incongruity-resolution* humor (INC-RES), comprises jokes and cartoons in which the incongruity introduced by the punch line can be resolved by information available elsewhere in the joke. In these jokes, there is a sense of having "gotten the point" or understood the joke once it is resolved. Most of the "canned" jokes that people relate in social settings, consisting of a setup and a punch line, fit into this category. This type of humor is consistent with the two-stage incongruity-resolution models of humor discussed in Chapter 3 (e.g., Suls, 1972).

The second factor, labeled *nonsense* humor (NON), also relates to joke structure rather than content. Jokes and cartoons in this category also contain a surprising or incongruous element, but the incongruity is not fully resolved, giving the appearance of making sense without actually doing so. This type of humor might be described as bizarre, fanciful, off-the-wall, or zany. In this humor there is not a sense of "getting" the joke, but rather one of enjoying a fanciful incongruity for its own sake. Many of Gary Larsen's *Far Side* cartoons, as well as the zany humor of *Monty Python's Flying Circus* have been found to load on this factor (Ruch, 1992, 1999). Thus, contrary to the assumption made by earlier researchers that humor should be categorized according to its content or themes, Ruch's research demonstrated that people's humor preferences have more to do with structure than with content.

The third factor, labeled *sexual* humor (SEX) is composed of jokes and cartoons containing obvious sexual content themes, indicating that people tend to be fairly consistent in the degree to which they enjoy or dislike sexual humor. Most of these sexual humor materials were also found to have secondary loadings on one or the other of the first two structural factors, depending on whether the humor contained resolved or unresolved incongruity. An example of a SEX joke with a secondary INC-RES loading is the following:

> "So how was Scotland?" the father asked his daughter, who had just returned from a vacation. "Is it true they all have bagpipes?" "Oh, that's just one of those silly stereotypes," replied the daughter. "All the ones I met had quite a normal one."

The incongruity of the daughter's reply is resolved when we recognize that she misunderstood her father's question about bagpipes to be referring to the appearance of Scottish men's genitals. In contrast, a cartoon that loaded on the SEX factor with a secondary NON loading shows a hen lying on her back with her legs in the air, saying to a rooster who is facing her, "Just once . . . for a change." A hen desiring sex in the "missionary position" is incongruous, and this incongruity cannot be resolved by finding some additional information that enables one to "get the joke."

The SEX factor, which was the only one found by Ruch that had to do with content, has also consistently been found in other factor-analytic studies (e.g., Eysenck, 1942; Herzog and Larwin, 1988). Although, as we have seen, many past researchers have classified humor stimuli on a theoretical basis into various additional content categories, such as aggressive, hostile, sexist, scatological, anal, or sick humor, Ruch's investigations did not reveal any such content factors, even though he was careful to include examples of all these kinds of humor among his stimuli. Instead, humor containing these sorts of themes always loaded on one or the other of the two structural factors. Thus, apart from sexual themes, individuals do not appear to respond in any consistent way to jokes or cartoons based on the topic of the humor. Instead, the degree to which people enjoy humor seems to be primarily influenced by whether or not the incongruity is resolved, or "makes sense" in some way.

Besides factor-analyzing the humor *stimuli*, Ruch also investigated the factor structure of participants' *responses* to humor. Using a number of different positive and negative rating scales, Ruch found two response factors: (1) a positive enjoyment or *funniness* factor, and (2) an *aversiveness* or rejection factor. These were only weakly negatively correlated, indicating that individuals who find a particular joke to be very funny do not necessarily rate it as low on aversiveness. For example, an individual might view a sexist or racist joke as very funny but also very aversive. Thus, funniness or enjoyment ratings alone do not adequately assess people's responses to humor; it is also important to evaluate their negative reactions. Furthermore, research by Igor Gavanski (1986) indicated that these sorts of funniness and aversiveness ratings primarily reflect people's cognitive evaluations of humor stimuli, rather than their emotional response (i.e., the degree of mirth experienced), which is more strongly gauged by the amount of smiling and laughter displayed. This partial dissociation between cognitive and emotional responses to humor explains why many studies have found only weak correlations between funniness ratings and the degree of smiling and laughter.

Based on his factor-analytic studies, Ruch (1983) constructed the 3WD (*Witz-dimensionen*) humor test to assess individuals' ratings of funniness and aversiveness of jokes and cartoons on the three identified factors. A 50-item version (form K) and two parallel 35-item versions (forms A and B) are available. The jokes and cartoons are printed in test booklets, and respondents are instructed to rate their funniness and aversiveness on 6-point scales. The total funniness and aversiveness scores for each factor have been shown to have good internal consistencies and test-retest reliabilities. Scores on the three factors are moderately positively intercorrelated, indicating that, to some degree, individuals who enjoy (or dislike) one type of humor also tend to enjoy (or dislike) the others.

Personality Correlates of the 3WD Dimensions

Numerous studies have been conducted to examine correlations between scores on the three factors of the 3WD humor test and a variety of personality traits (reviewed in Ruch, 1992; Ruch and Hehl, 1998). The total funniness ratings across the three factors have been found to be weakly correlated with extraversion, indicating that extraverts are somewhat more likely than introverts to enjoy all kinds of jokes and cartoons. In addition, the total aversiveness scores are weakly correlated with neuroticism, indicating that people who generally experience more negative emotions such as anxiety, depression, or guilt tend to dislike all kinds of jokes and cartoons. This is particularly true for neurotic individuals who are also introverted and who are high on tender-mindedness, a construct relating to empathy, concern for others, tolerance, and democratic values. These findings are consistent with recent fMRI findings (discussed in Chapter 6) that people who are high in extraversion and those who are low in neuroticism show greater activation of the reward centers in the limbic system of the brain on exposure to humorous cartoons (Mobbs et al., 2005). Interestingly, total funniness scores on the 3WD have also been found to be negatively correlated with religious fundamentalism and orthodoxy, indicating that people who are high in these types of conservative religious orientation are less likely to enjoy all types of jokes and cartoons (Saroglou, 2003).

Much of Ruch's research has focused on personality traits having to do with conservatism, tolerance of ambiguity, and sensation seeking in relation to the two structure-related humor dimensions (NON and INC-RES). Since the appreciation of nonsense humor requires the individual to tolerate and even enjoy residual incongruity, bizarreness, and absurdity, Ruch hypothesized that this type of humor would be enjoyed by people who have a high tolerance for ambiguity, a general sensation-seeking orientation, and a preference for complex, novel, and unstructured stimuli. On the other hand, since INC-RES humor is more unambiguous and uncomplicated, and generally involves the application of stereotypes to resolve the incongruity, the enjoyment of this type of humor was predicted to be related to greater conservatism and a general need for structured, uncomplicated, stable, unambiguous, and safe forms of stimulation.

Research conducted by Ruch and others has provided a good deal of support for these predictions. Measures of conservative and authoritarian personality traits and attitudes have consistently been found to be positively correlated with funniness ratings of INC-RES humor and with aversiveness ratings of NON humor (Hehl and Ruch, 1990; Ruch, 1984; Ruch and Hehl, 1986a, 1986b). Thus, individuals who espouse more conservative views (as measured by scales of intolerance of minorities, militarism, religious fundamentalism, education to submission, traditional family ideology, capitalism, economic values, and value orthodoxy) and authoritarian attitudes (punitiveness, intolerance of ambiguity, law-and-order attitude) are more likely to enjoy humor in which the incongruity is resolved and one can "get the joke," and to dislike more bizarre or zany humor that does not seem to "make sense."

In one study, for example, Ruch and his colleagues asked participants to indicate the degree to which they believe criminals should be punished for a range of crimes such as fraud, robbery, rape, and murder (Ruch, Busse, and Hehl, 1996). As predicted, the results revealed that the more these individuals enjoyed INC-RES humor, the more severely they thought criminals should be punished for all types of crime (i.e., longer prison terms). If you are charged with a crime, you may wish to avoid a judge who enjoys these kinds of jokes! Not surprisingly, since older people generally tend to be more conservative than younger people, they also tend to enjoy INC-RES jokes more (Ruch et al., 1990).

Sensation seeking is a personality trait involving a need for varied, novel, and complex sensations and experiences, and a willingness to take risks. People who are high on sensation seeking tend to enjoy having new and stimulating experiences through art, music, travel, food, and even taking psychedelic drugs and living an unconventional lifestyle. Research with the 3WD has shown that individuals with high scores on measures of sensation seeking, as well as related constructs such as venturesomeness and hedonism, enjoy nonsense humor significantly more than incongruity-resolution humor (Hehl and Ruch, 1985, 1990; Ruch, 1988). Enjoyment of NON humor has also been found to be positively correlated with the openness to experience dimension of the FFM (Ruch and Hehl, 1998). In addition, greater enjoyment of NON humor is weakly related to higher intelligence, whereas enjoyment of INC-RES humor tends to correlate with lower intelligence (Ruch, 1992).

Other studies have examined preferences for stimulus uncertainty and complexity in relation to these structural factors of humor appreciation. In one study, participants were asked to wear prism glasses that distort the normal visual field by flipping it upside-down or left-to-right. Those with higher funniness ratings of NON humor kept the glasses on for a longer time and moved around more while wearing them, indicating a greater willingness to experiment with this novel experience (Ruch and Hehl, 1998). Enjoyment of NON humor was also shown to be significantly correlated with preference for more complex and abstract forms of art, whereas enjoyment of INC-RES humor was related to preference for simpler, more representational types of art. When research participants were instructed to arrange black and white plastic squares into an aesthetically pleasing configuration, the productions of individuals with greater appreciation of NON humor were judged to be more complex (Ruch and Hehl, 1998).

Overall, then, the two humor structures appear to partly represent the opposite poles of some personality dimensions (e.g., simplicity-complexity), while also partly relating to entirely different dimensions. In particular, INC-RES humor tends to correlate with conservative and authoritarian *attitudes* and *values*, whereas NON humor relates to variables involving *imagination* and *fantasy*. The relation between conservative attitudes and values and the enjoyment of INC-RES humor is likely due to the fact that stereotypical attitudes (e.g., about particular ethnic groups) need to be invoked in order to resolve the incongruity of most of these kinds of jokes. Individuals with more conservative attitudes may have easier access to the information required for resolving the incongruity and may also derive greater satisfaction from the resulting support that is provided to their belief systems. On the other hand, the stronger association of imagination and fantasy with enjoyment of NON humor is likely explained by the fact that this type of humor involves a greater deviation from reality and requires a willingness to accept improbable events and enter the world of fantasy.

With regard to the content factor of sexual humor, research with the 3WD indicates that enjoyment of this category of humor relates most strongly to the toughminded versus tenderminded dimension of social attitudes. Toughmindedness is characterized by independent, rational, self-sufficient, and unfanciful dispositions, whereas tendermindedness has to do with empathy, concern for others, sentimentality, tolerance, and democratic values. Regardless of the structure of the joke or cartoon, toughminded individuals tend to show greater enjoyment of sexual humor, whereas tenderminded people tend to rate such humor as being more aversive (Ruch and Hehl, 1986b). Moreover, the more highly a given joke or cartoon loads on the sexual factor, the stronger the correlation between its funniness ratings and the toughmindedness versus tendermindedness dimension, indicating that the enjoyment of sexual humor may be viewed as an indicator of toughminded attitudes (Ruch, 1992).

Some additional correlations have been found when SEX humor is divided into NON and INC-RES types on the basis of its structure. For example, enjoyment of sexual humor with the incongruity-resolution structure (INC-RES SEX) is correlated positively with both conservatism and toughmindedness, resulting also in positive correlations with variables such as authoritarianism, intolerance of ambiguity, political and economic conservatism, technical interests, and support for education toward submissiveness, and negative correlations with aesthetic and social interests (Hehl and Ruch, 1990; Ruch and Hehl, 1986b, 1987). Thus, enjoyment of sexual humor that is based on the incongruity-resolution structure (i.e., the most common kinds of sexual jokes that people frequently tell in social situations) has little to do with sex *per se*, but instead has to do with toughminded conservatism (authoritarianism). Interestingly, since authoritarian individuals tend to have exaggerated concerns about "sexual goings-on," their enjoyment of sexual humor of the incongruity-resolution type seems to have more to do with rigid sexual preoccupations than with sexual permissiveness or pleasure (Ruch, 1992).

On the other hand, enjoyment of sexual humor that is based on the nonsense structure (NON SEX), and is therefore more fanciful and bizarre, is unrelated to conservative attitudes (although still related to toughmindedness), but is positively correlated with scales of disinhibition, sensation seeking, hedonism, interest in sex, and sexual libido, permissiveness, pleasure, and experience (Hehl and Ruch, 1990; Ruch and Hehl, 1986b, 1988). Thus, it is only the appreciation of sexual humor of the nonsense structure type that is related to positive sexual attitudes and experience.

In summary, Ruch's research with the 3WD has gone a long way in clarifying the nature of individual differences in appreciation of jokes and cartoons. An important finding is that people's enjoyment of these forms of humor is determined not so much by the content but by the structure of the humor. In particular, individuals tend to respond quite differently to jokes and cartoons in which the incongruity is resolved and there is a sense of "getting the joke" versus those in which the incongruity is unresolved and which might be described as bizarre, fanciful, off-the-wall, or zany. Sexual topics are the only content domain in humor for which individuals show consistent response patterns.

This research also indicates that there is truth to the long-held view that the type of jokes a person enjoys tells us something about his or her personality. However, the particular personality traits associated with humor appreciation are not as self-evident as one might expect. It may be surprising to many that people who enjoy the sorts of jokes that are most commonly told in social contexts (i.e., incongruity-resolution jokes) tend to be individuals with conservative values and attitudes. When such jokes are of a sexual nature, their enjoyment also indicates toughminded, unsympathetic, intolerant, and authoritarian attitudes. On the other hand, the enjoyment of the more bizarre and fanciful nonsense humor (which is more likely to be encountered in cartoons, literature, and films than in canned jokes) indicates greater openness, tolerance for ambiguity, sensation seeking, intelligence, and enjoyment of novelty and complexity. When this sort of humor contains sexual themes, its enjoyment indicates more liberal (although still toughminded) attitudes and greater sexual permissiveness and enjoyment.

SELF-REPORT MEASURES OF SENSE OF HUMOR DIMENSIONS

The humor appreciation approach to conceptualizing and measuring sense of humor, discussed in the previous section, focuses on canned jokes and cartoons which, as I have pointed out in earlier chapters, comprise only a small fraction of the forms of humor that people encounter in their daily lives. Moreover, this approach is limited to people's enjoyment of these types of humor, and does not include their tendency to create humor spontaneously and to amuse other people in their everyday lives. Consequently, this approach to sense of humor, although it has produced many interesting research findings, seems to address only a limited aspect of the many ways individuals may habitually differ from one another in regard to humor.

In the mid-1970s, researchers began to develop self-report measures of sense of humor as an alternative to the humor appreciation approach, in order to investigate some of these other humor-related individual-difference dimensions. This change in methodology was associated with a shift in interest toward the everyday functions of humor, including its role in interpersonal relationships, coping with stress, and mental and physical health. These sorts of research questions required measures that assess the degree to which people create, enjoy, and engage in humor in their daily lives, and researchers with this perspective began to question whether humor appreciation measures were appropriate for these purposes (Lefcourt and Martin, 1986).

Although the humor appreciation approach provided a great deal of interesting information about the personality traits of individuals who enjoy particular types of humor (and indeed, Ruch was just beginning to conduct his more systematic research on this topic around the same time), this approach did not seem to capture some of the dimensions of sense of humor that were of interest to this new generation of researchers. The fact that an individual rates jokes and cartoons as funny does not necessarily mean that he or she engages in humor in daily life. Indeed, in a large multitrait-multimethod study of sense of humor, Elisha Babad (1974) found no relationship between individuals' scores on humor appreciation tests and either peer- or self-ratings of their tendency to appreciate, produce, or reproduce humor in their daily lives. In contrast, self-ratings were significantly correlated with peer-ratings of these dimensions of sense of humor.

Thus, it appeared that self-report measures may be a more valid approach for assessing certain aspects of sense of humor that are not tapped by humor appreciation tests. An initial concern of researchers was that self-report humor tests might be particularly susceptible to a social desirability bias. In other words, because a sense of humor is such a desirable characteristic, research participants might not be objective when rating their own sense of humor and might tend to overestimate it. Although this may well occur when people are asked to rate their overall sense of humor, subsequent research indicates that questions focusing on specific humor-related behaviors or attitudes do not seem to be strongly contaminated by social desirability (Lefcourt and Martin, 1986). Over the years, a number of different self-report scales have been developed, each designed to measure a somewhat different component or aspect of sense of humor. In the following sections, I will discuss a few of the more widely used measures (for a more complete listing, see Ruch, 1998b).

Svebak's Sense of Humor Questionnaire

Norwegian psychologist Sven Svebak (1974a, 1974b), now at the Norwegian University of Science and Technology in Trondheim, was one of the first researchers to break with the tradition of focusing on humor appreciation using funniness ratings of jokes and cartoons, and initiated the measurement of sense of humor using self-report questionnaires. In one of the earliest articles to specifically present a theory of sense of humor as a personality trait, Svebak (1974b) observed that smooth social functioning requires the construction of a shared, rational "social world." However, this shared perspective on the world is somewhat arbitrary, and can also be constraining and stifling. Sense of humor, like creativity, is "the ability to imagine . . . irrational social worlds, and to behave according to such fantasies *within* the existing (real) social frame in such a way that the latter is not brought into a state of collapse" (Svebak, 1974b, p. 99). Thus, "humor may be said to be a defense against the monotony of culture more than against bodily displeasure" (p. 100).

Svebak suggested that individual differences in sense of humor involve variations in three separate dimensions: (1) *meta-message sensitivity*, or the ability to take an irrational, mirthful perspective on situations, seeing the social world as it might be rather than as it is; (2) *personal liking* of humor and the humorous role; and (3) *emotional permissiveness*, or the tendency to laugh frequently in a wide range of situations. With regard to the components of humor that I have discussed in earlier chapters, the first of these dimensions relates primarily to the cognitive component, having to do with a nonserious outlook and an ability to shift perspective in a creative manner. The second dimension involves playful attitudes and a lack of defensiveness toward humor, and the third relates to the positive emotion of mirth and its expression through laughter.

Svebak (1974a) constructed the Sense of Humor Questionnaire (SHQ) to measure individual differences in each of the three dimensions posited in his theory, with seven items for each dimension. Examples of the items in each subscale are as follows: (1) metamessage sensitivity (M): "I can usually find something comical, witty, or humorous in most situations"; (2) liking of humor (L): "It is my impression that those who try to be funny really do it to hide their lack of self-confidence" (disagreement with this statement results in higher scores on the scale); and (3) emotional expressiveness (E): "If I find a situation very comical, I find it very hard to keep a straight face even when nobody else seems to think it's funny." Individuals completing the measure are instructed to rate the degree to which each item is descriptive of them, using a four-point Likert-type scale. Initial research revealed moderate correlations between the M and L and the M and E dimensions, and no correlation between L and E, indicating that the three dimensions were relatively independent of one another.

Subsequent research using this measure indicated acceptable psychometric properties (reliability and validity) for the M and L scales, but inadequate values for the E scale (Lefcourt and Martin, 1986). In studies employing this measure, therefore, researchers tended to use only the first two subscales. Support for the validity of these two scales has been provided by significant correlations with peer ratings of humor, as well as with other self-report humor tests (to be described below). The measure was used in research on stress-buffering effects of sense of humor, which I will discuss in Chapter 9. Svebak (1996) later published a shorter, six-item version of the SHQ (SHQ-6) which comprises three items each from the original M and L scales. These six items were found to form a single factor in a factor analysis of SHQ data from nearly 1000 participants, and reliability analysis of the scale revealed a good internal consistency. The SHQ-6 has also been used in research on humor and stress (Svebak, Götestam, and Jensen, 2004), and Svebak (1996) recommended its use in large-scale survey research in which a short measure of sense of humor is required.

The Situational Humor Response Questionnaire

Herbert Lefcourt and I developed the Situational Humor Response Questionnaire (SHRQ) at the University of Waterloo for use in our research on the stress-moderating effects of sense of humor (R. A. Martin and Lefcourt, 1984). In developing this scale, we focused particularly on the emotional-expressive component of humor, that is, smiling and laughter. Thus, we defined sense of humor as the frequency with which a person smiles, laughs, and otherwise displays amusement in a wide variety of situations. In adopting this definition, we were making the assumption that overt expressions of smiling and laughter are indicators of the emotion of mirth that is elicited by the perception, creation, and enjoyment of humor in one's daily life.

The scale comprises 18 items that present participants with brief descriptions of situations (e.g., "if you were eating in a restaurant with some friends and the waiter accidentally spilled a drink on you"). These include both pleasant and unpleasant situations, ranging from specific and structured to general and unstructured, and from relatively common to relatively unusual. For each item, respondents are asked to rate the degree to which they would be likely to laugh in such a situation, using five response options ranging from "I would not have been particularly amused" to "I would have laughed heartily." In addition to the 18 situational items, the scale contains three self-descriptive items relating to the frequency with which the participant generally laughs and smiles in a wide range of situations.

The SHRQ has been found to have acceptable internal consistency and test-retest reliability (Lefcourt and Martin, 1986). Males and females typically do not obtain different mean scores. The validity support for the SHRQ is quite extensive (see Lefcourt and Martin, 1986; R. A. Martin, 1996). For example, individuals with higher scores on the SHRQ displayed higher frequency and duration of spontaneous laughter during unstructured interviews and also recorded more frequent daily laughter in three-day diaries (R. A. Martin and Kuiper, 1999). SHRQ scores also have been found to correlate significantly with peer ratings of participants' frequency of laughter and tendency to use humor in coping with stress. In addition, scores have correlated significantly with the rated funniness of monologues created by participants in the laboratory. Individuals with higher SHRQ scores were also found to make more spontaneously funny comments in a nonhumorous creativity task. The SHRQ is uncorrelated with measures of social desirability, providing evidence of discriminant validity (Lefcourt and Martin, 1986). The measure has been used extensively in research on sense of humor in relation to mental and physical health, which will be discussed in Chapters 9 and 10.

Lambert Deckers and Willibald Ruch (1992b) found no significant correlations between the SHRQ and either the total score or the three factor scores on Ruch's 3WD measure of humor appreciation. Thus, as Lefcourt and I (1986) had hypothesized, tests of humor appreciation employing respondents' ratings of the funniness or aversiveness of jokes and cartoons represent a completely different construct from that assessed by self-report humor measures such as the SHRQ. Individuals might rate particular types of jokes and cartoons on the 3WD as being very humorous without necessarily engaging in much humor in their daily lives.

On the other hand, the SHRQ has been found to be positively correlated with extraversion (Ruch and Deckers, 1993), indicating that individuals who tend to laugh readily in a range of situations (as indicated by high scores on the SHRQ) tend also to be characterized by extraverted traits such as sociable, people-oriented, active, talkative, optimistic, fun-loving, and joyful. In addition, the SHRQ is correlated with sensation-seeking, a variable that is also associated with extraversion, indicating that individuals who tend to laugh frequently also tend to seek highly arousing thrills, adventure, and varied experiences, and are easily bored (Deckers and Ruch, 1992a). Interestingly, social drinkers with higher scores on the SHRQ have also been found to have higher rates of alcohol consumption (Lowe and Taylor, 1993). This finding may also be a function of extraversion, since other research indicates that extraverted individuals tend to drink more alcohol than do introverts (M. Cook et al., 1998).

The SHRQ has been criticized for defining sense of humor purely in terms of laughter frequency (Thorson, 1990). Indeed, as I have acknowledged, laughter can occur without humor, and there can be humor without laughter (R. A. Martin, 1996). Nonetheless, correlations between the SHRQ and various measures of personality and well-being are comparable to those found with other self-report humor measures such as the Coping Humor Scale (to be discussed next), suggesting that it assesses a more general sense of humor trait than simply the tendency to laugh. A study by Lourey and McLachlan (2003) indicates that the SHRQ relates to perceptions of humor and not merely laughter frequency. Moreover, research showing positive correlations between participants' scores on the SHRQ and their humor production ability indicates that it taps into humor creation and not just laughter responsiveness. This broader construct validity of the measure may be due to the inclusion of a number of items describing unpleasant or mildly stressful situations. Consequently, more than merely assessing the frequency of laughter *per se*, the SHRQ appears to address the tendency to maintain a humorous perspective when faced with unpleasant or potentially embarrassing events.

A potentially more serious shortcoming of this measure is that the situations described in the items are specific to university students' experiences (and even more particularly those of Canadian students), and it is therefore less suitable for other populations. Furthermore, the situations described in the items have become somewhat dated over time and may be difficult for many people to relate to today. For these reasons, the SHRQ would likely benefit from a careful revision if it is to be used in further research.

The Coping Humor Scale

The Coping Humor Scale (CHS) is another measure that Herbert Lefcourt and I developed in the context of our research on sense of humor as a stress-moderating personality trait (R. A. Martin and Lefcourt, 1983). Instead of attempting to assess a broad sense of humor construct, this test was designed to measure more narrowly the degree to which individuals report using humor in coping with stress. Thus, it focused specifically on one particular function of humor. The CHS contains seven items that are self-descriptive statements such as "I have often found that my problems have been greatly reduced when I tried to find something funny in them" and "I can usually find something to laugh or joke about even in trying situations." Research with the CHS has demonstrated marginally acceptable internal consistency and acceptable test-retest reliability (R. A. Martin, 1996).

There is also considerable support for the construct validity of this scale (summarized by Lefcourt and Martin, 1986; R. A. Martin, 1996). For example, scores on the CHS have correlated significantly with peer ratings of individuals' tendency to use humor to cope with stress and not take themselves too seriously. In addition, the CHS was significantly correlated with the rated funniness of participants' humorous monologues created while watching a stressful film, but not with the spontaneous funniness of responses in a nonstressful creativity task, indicating that it specifically relates to the production of humor in stressful situations. In another study, dental patients with higher scores on the CHS were found to engage in significantly more joking and laughter before undergoing dental surgery (Trice and Price-Greathouse, 1986).

The measure is generally uncorrelated with measures of social desirability, thereby lending discriminant validity support. With regard to other personality traits, the CHS has been found to be positively related to self-esteem, stability of self-concept, realistic cognitive appraisals, optimism, sense of coherence, and extraversion, and negatively related to dysfunctional attitudes and neuroticism (R. A. Martin, 1996). Thus, it seems to primarily assess humor in an extraverted, emotionally stable type of personality. Research using the CHS in relation to mental and physical health will be discussed in more detail in Chapters 9 and 10. The CHS does have some psychometric limitations, however, particularly a relatively weak internal consistency resulting from low item-total correlations of some items.

The Humor Styles Questionnaire

Many of the self-report humor scales were developed for research on humor in relation to mental and physical health, and nearly all of these were based on the assumption that a sense of humor is inherently beneficial to health and well-being. However, as we have seen in earlier chapters of this book, humor does not always seem to be used in psychologically beneficial ways. For example, the hostile, manipulative, and coercive uses of humor that were discussed in Chapter 5 do not seem to be very conducive to healthy interpersonal relationships. Indeed, it could be argued that humor is essentially neutral with regard to mental health: its implications for health depend on how it is used by the individual in interacting with other people.

Since most humor measures do not distinguish between positive and negative uses of humor, however, they are limited in their usefulness for studying potentially detrimental aspects.

Recently, my students and I have developed the Humor Styles Questionnaire (HSQ), a measure designed to distinguish between potentially beneficial and detrimental humor styles (R. A. Martin et al., 2003). The focus of this measure is on the functions for which people spontaneously use humor in their everyday lives, particularly in the domains of social interaction and coping with life stress. Based on a review of past theoretical and empirical literature, we hypothesized four main dimensions, two of which were considered to be relatively healthy or adaptive (affiliative and self-enhancing humor) and two relatively unhealthy and potentially detrimental (aggressive and self-defeating humor).

Affiliative humor refers to the tendency to say funny things, to tell jokes, and to engage in spontaneous witty banter, in order to amuse others, to facilitate relationships, and to reduce interpersonal tensions (e.g., "I enjoy making people laugh"). This is hypothesized to be an essentially nonhostile, tolerant use of humor that is affirming of self and others and presumably enhances interpersonal cohesiveness. *Self-enhancing humor* refers to the tendency to maintain a humorous outlook on life even when one is not with other people, to be frequently amused by the incongruities of life, to maintain a humorous perspective even in the face of stress or adversity, and to use humor in coping (e.g., "My humorous outlook on life keeps me from getting overly upset or depressed about things"). This humor style is closely related to the construct assessed by the earlier Coping Humor Scale.

On the other hand, *aggressive humor* is the tendency to use humor for the purpose of criticizing or manipulating others, as in sarcasm, teasing, ridicule, derision, or disparagement humor, as well as the use of potentially offensive (e.g., racist or sexist) forms of humor (e.g., "If someone makes a mistake, I will often tease them about it"). It also includes the compulsive expression of humor even when it is socially inappropriate. This type of humor is viewed as a means of enhancing the self at the expense of one's relationships with others.

Finally, *self-defeating humor* involves the use of excessively self-disparaging humor, attempts to amuse others by doing or saying funny things at one's own expense, and laughing along with others when being ridiculed or disparaged (e.g., "I often try to make people like or accept me more by saying something funny about my own weaknesses, blunders, or faults"). Thus, it deals with the use of humor to ingratiate oneself with others, as discussed in Chapter 5. It also involves the use of humor as a form of defensive denial, to hide one's underlying negative feelings or avoid dealing constructively with problems. This style of humor is seen as an attempt to gain the attention and approval of others at one's own expense.

It is important to note that, although the HSQ assesses the way people "use" humor in their everyday lives, no assumption was made that these uses are consciously or strategically chosen. Instead, we assumed that people tend to engage in humor quite spontaneously and are often unaware of its social or psychological functions in a given situation. Thus, the items had to be worded quite carefully to address the relevant functions indirectly, much like items on a self-report measure of defense mechanisms.

The HSQ was developed using construct-based test construction procedures over a series of studies with fairly large samples of participants ranging in age from 14 to 87 years (R. A. Martin et al., 2003). This methodology resulted in four stable factors that were corroborated by means of confirmatory factor analysis. The final measure contains four eight-item scales, each of which has demonstrated good internal consistency. The HSQ has been translated into a number of languages and administered to participants in various countries in North and South America, Europe, and Asia, and the four-factor structure has been replicated in all cultures studied to date (Chen and Martin, in press; Kazarian and Martin, 2004; in press; Saroglou and Scariot, 2002).

With regard to relationships among the scales themselves, moderate correlations are typically found between self-enhancing and affiliative humor and between aggressive and self-defeating humor, indicating that the two positive and the two negative styles of humor, while conceptually and empirically distinguishable, tend to covary. In addition, aggressive humor tends to be weakly correlated with both affiliative and self-enhancing humor, suggesting that even positive styles of humor may include some aggressive elements.

Research conducted to date has provided promising evidence for the construct validity of each scale, as well as discriminant validity among the four scales (P. Doris, 2004; Kazarian and Martin, 2004; Kuiper et al., 2004; R. A. Martin et al., 2003; Saroglou and Scariot, 2002). For example, scores on each of the scales have been found to correlate significantly with peer ratings of the corresponding dimensions. The affiliative and self-enhancing humor scales also tend to be positively correlated with other well-validated self-report humor measures such as the SHQ, SHRQ, and CHS, whereas the aggressive and self-defeating humor scales are generally unrelated to other humor measures, indicating that these two presumably detrimental styles of humor are not well-measured with other tests.

One self-report measure, the Multidimensional Sense of Humor Scale (MSHS; Thorson and Powell, 1993a) has been shown to be significantly positively correlated with all four HSQ scales, indicating that this earlier humor test does not distinguish between potentially beneficial and detrimental uses of humor, making it somewhat less useful for investigating the role of humor in mental health. Not surprisingly, scores on the self-enhancing humor scale tend to be quite strongly correlated with scores on the conceptually similar Coping Humor Scale (Kuiper et al., 2004). Since the self-enhancing humor scale has better reliability than the CHS, this newer measure seems to be a better instrument for use in research on humor as a coping mechanism.

With regard to other personality and mood variables, the two measures of "healthy" styles of humor are generally positively related to indicators of psychological health and well-being such as self-esteem, positive emotions, optimism, social support, and intimacy; and negatively related to negative moods such as depression and anxiety. In contrast, aggressive humor is positively correlated with measures of hostility and aggression and negatively correlated with relationship satisfaction. Similarly, self-defeating humor is positively related to measures of psychological distress and dysfunction, including depression, anxiety, hostility, and psychiatric symptoms, and negatively related with self-esteem, psychological well-being, social support, and relationship satisfaction. These findings support the view that the different humor styles are differentially related to aspects of psychological well-being.

The four scales have also been found to correlate differentially with measures of the FFM, which posits five major dimensions accounting for most of the variance in personality traits (R. A. Martin et al., 2003; Saroglou and Scariot, 2002). Although there were some differences in the patterns of correlations found among English-speaking Canadian and French-speaking Belgian participants, extraversion was generally found to be positively correlated with affiliative, aggressive, and (more weakly) self-enhancing humor, but unrelated to self-defeating humor. Neuroticism, on the other hand, was unrelated to affiliative humor, negatively related to self-enhancing humor, and positively related to both aggressive and self-defeating humor. In turn, affiliative and self-enhancing humor were both positively correlated with openness to experience, while aggressive and self-defeating humor were both negatively correlated with agreeableness and conscientiousness. Thus, these four styles of humor appear to be located in quite different regions of the personality space represented by the FFM, suggesting that they represent disparate ways in which people with differing personality traits express and experience humor in their everyday lives.

Some research has also begun to explore relationships between the HSQ scales and measures of culture-related personality traits such as individualism and collectivism (Kazarian and Martin, 2004; in press). In general, affiliative humor appears to be related to the cultural orientation of collectivism (which emphasizes the interdependence of individuals with respect to broader social groups), whereas aggressive humor is more related to individualism (which views individual needs as taking precedence over group needs). Further cross-cultural research is needed to determine whether the HSQ dimensions reflect different styles of humor found in people from different cultures. For example, Western cultures, which tend to be more individualistic, might be expected to have more aggressive humor styles, whereas people from more collectivistic Eastern cultures may be higher on affiliative humor.

Interestingly, although negligible differences are found between men and women on the two presumably positive styles of humor, males tend to have significantly higher scores than females on the two presumably detrimental humor styles, suggesting that men tend to use negative forms of humor more than women do (cf. Crawford and Gressley, 1991). Older participants have been found to obtain lower scores than younger people on both affiliative and aggressive humor, suggesting that people may have a decreasing tendency to engage in these more extraverted types of humor as they age. Among women, self-enhancing humor was found to be higher for older than younger individuals, suggesting an increase in this coping style of humor with greater age and life experience. Longitudinal research is needed, however, to test whether these observed age differences are due to developmental changes over the lifespan or to cohort effects.

Overall, then, the HSQ assesses dimensions of humor that are not tapped by previous tests and, in particular, it is the first self-report measure to assess social and psychological functions of humor that are less desirable and potentially detrimental to well-being. In Chapter 9, I will discuss additional research that has used this measure in the study of humor and mental health.

The State-Trait Cheerfulness Inventory

When we say that someone has a good sense of humor, we may mean that the person tends to maintain a cheerful mood and a nonserious, playful attitude much of the time, even in situations where other people might be likely to become distressed. This way of conceptualizing sense of humor, which focuses on the emotional component and the playful, nonserious character of humor, was proposed some time ago by Howard Leventhal and Martin Safer (1977). More recently, Willibald Ruch and his colleagues have adopted this perspective in their investigations of trait cheerfulness, which they view as the temperamental basis of sense of humor (for a review, see Ruch and Köhler, 1998).

In this view, individual differences in sense of humor are based on presumably innate, habitual differences in cheerfulness, seriousness, and bad mood. While each of these can be viewed as temporary states or moods, individuals are assumed to differ in traitlike ways with regard to how consistently they experience these states. *Trait cheerfulness* is an affective trait or temperament involving a prevalence of cheerful mood and mirth, a generally good-humored interaction style, a tendency to smile and laugh easily, and a composed view of adverse life circumstances. *Trait seriousness* (versus playfulness) is a habitual frame of mind or mental attitude toward the world, comprising a tendency to perceive even everyday events as important, a tendency to plan ahead and set long-range goals, a preference for activities that have a rational purpose, and a sober, straightforward communication style that avoids exaggeration and irony. In Michael Apter's (2001) terminology (discussed in Chapters 1, 3, 4, and 5), this relates to the degree to which people tend to be in the telic (serious, goal-oriented) versus the paratelic (playful, activity-oriented) mode. Individuals who would typically be viewed as having a sense of humor would be those who are low on this trait. *Trait bad mood* is an affective disposition involving a prevalence of sad, despondent, and distressed moods; a generally ill-humored interaction style (sullen, grumpy, grouchy); and a negative response to cheerfulness-evoking situations and people. Again, high-humor people would tend to be low on this dimension.

Ruch and his colleagues constructed the trait form of the State-Trait Cheerfulness Inventory (STCI-T) to assess individual differences in habitual cheerfulness, seriousness, and bad mood (Ruch, Köhler, and Van Thriel, 1996). These scales have been shown to have good internal consistencies and test-retest reliabilities. Factor analyses on data obtained in several countries have consistently confirmed the existence of the three distinct factors. Cheerfulness tends to be weakly negatively correlated with seriousness and moderately negatively correlated with bad mood, while seriousness and bad mood are weakly positively correlated. A state version of the State-

Trait-Cheerfulness Inventory (STCI-S) was also constructed to assess the presence of each of the three mood states over shorter periods of time (Ruch, Köhler, and van Thriel, 1997).

A number of studies have demonstrated good validity for the STCI-T. Scores on each of the three trait scales were significantly correlated with peer ratings of the same dimensions (Ruch, Köhler, et al., 1996) and with the corresponding mood states as measured by the STCI-S (Ruch and Köhler, 1999). Studies have also shown that individuals with high scores on the trait cheerfulness scale, as compared to those with low scores, are less likely to develop a depressed mood and serious frame of mind when they are exposed to negative mood induction procedures such as reading a melancholy story or engaging in a series of boring tasks in a depressing, windowless room with black walls and poor lighting (Ruch and Köhler, 1998, 1999).

Similarly, individuals with high trait cheerfulness scores, as compared to those with low scores, are also more likely to smile and laugh (showing the Duchenne display of genuine mirth) and to have enhanced feelings of state cheerfulness in mirth-inducing situations, such as inhalation of nitrous oxide (laughing gas), exposure to a clowning experimenter, or the sudden, unexpected appearance of a jack-in-the-box (Ruch, 1997; Ruch and Köhler, 1998). These findings provide support for the validity of trait cheerfulness as representing a habitually high threshold for negative moods and a low threshold for mirth, laughter, and positive moods in general.

To examine the validity of the trait seriousness scale of the STCI-T, participants in one study were instructed to create humorous captions for a series of cartoons. As predicted, individuals with lower scores on trait seriousness (indicating greater habitual playfulness) were found to create a greater number of humorous captions, and their captions were rated as more funny, witty, and original (Ruch and Köhler, 1998). On Ruch's 3WD measure of humor appreciation, individuals with low (as opposed to high) seriousness scores tended to prefer nonsense over incongruity-resolution humor. In addition, higher seriousness scores were related to higher aversiveness ratings for all types of humor, indicating that more serious individuals are more likely to reject all forms of humor (Ruch and Köhler, 1998). These findings provided support for (low) trait seriousness as a general attitude or frame of mind characterized by a more playful perspective and a greater receptiveness to humor.

Studies have also examined the relationships between the STCI-T scales and more general personality dimensions such as the FFM, and models of positive and negative affectivity (Ruch and Köhler, 1998). Overall, cheerfulness was associated with extraversion/energy, agreeableness/friendliness, emotional stability/low neuroticism, and positive affectivity. Thus high trait cheerfulness is a characteristic of agreeable, stable, extraverted types. Bad mood, in contrast, showed the opposite pattern of correlations, but with a stronger contribution of neuroticism and negative affectivity and a weaker loading on extraversion and positive affectivity. Thus, bad mood is characteristic of disagreeable, neurotic introverts. Finally, seriousness was consistently associated with low psychoticism/conscientiousness and introversion.

In summary, this temperament-based approach provides an interesting perspective on the meaning of sense of humor. In this view, individuals who are typically described as having a "good sense of humor" tend to be people who are habitually in a cheerful mood, who maintain a playful, nonserious attitude toward life, and who are infrequently in a bad, grouchy mood. Different styles of humor may have to do with different combinations of the three traits. For example, an acerbic, caustic sense of humor might involve low seriousness, moderate cheerfulness, and high bad mood. On the other hand, people who are easily amused at others' humor but not very witty themselves might be high on cheerfulness, low on bad mood, and relatively high on seriousness.

Since trait cheerfulness has been shown to be a predictor of robustness of positive mood in experimental studies, this construct also seems to be a potentially useful way of conceptualizing sense of humor as a trait that contributes to coping with stress and enhancing psychological health. As Ruch and Köhler (1998, p. 228) suggested, individuals who are high on trait cheerfulness may "have a better 'psychological immune system,' protecting them against the negative impact of the annoyances and mishaps they meet in everyday life and enabling them to maintain good humor under adversity." This measure would therefore likely be useful in research on physical and mental health benefits of humor, particularly in the context of humor as resilience to psychosocial stress.

SENSE OF HUMOR AS AN ABILITY

Some conceptualizations of sense of humor view it as a form of creative ability or aptitude. In this approach, the ability to perceive humorous incongruities, to create jokes, funny stories, and other humorous productions, and to make other people laugh is viewed as a skill, like the ability to draw a picture or solve a math problem. Individuals who are gifted with this creative talent are presumably the amateur comedians who keep their friends "in stitches" and are the "life of the party," while the supremely talented few may become professional comedians and comedy writers. This conception of sense of humor seems to be most appropriately measured by means of ability tests that assess maximal performance, rather than the typical behavior assessed by self-report scales. This approach has been taken by a few researchers over the years.

Alan Feingold, a researcher affiliated with Yale University, has long been a proponent of the view of sense of humor as a kind of aptitude. Feingold (1982, 1983) developed tests of humor perceptiveness and humor achievement comprising questions about joke knowledge, in which participants were required to complete famous jokes (e.g., "Take my wife, _____"; Answer: "please") and identify the names of comedians associated with particular jokes (e.g., "I get no respect" linked with Rodney Dangerfield). Respondents' scores on these tests were based on the number of questions that were answered correctly. Scores on this test were positively correlated with intelligence, and (not surprisingly) individuals with high scores were found to be avid viewers of comedy television shows.

Feingold and Mazzella (1991) expanded on this earlier work, developing additional tests to assess two proposed types of verbal humor ability or wittiness: (1)

memory for humor, which they hypothesized to be akin to crystallized intelligence; and (2) *humor cognition*, thought to be comparable to fluid intelligence. Memory for humor was assessed by tests of humor information and joke knowledge (similar to Feingold's earlier measure of humor perceptiveness), while humor cognition was measured with tests of humor reasoning and joke comprehension. Again, these were all maximal performance tests in which scores were based on the number of correct answers. Their research findings revealed significant correlations between traditional measures of verbal intelligence and the tests of humor cognition, whereas memory for humor was not strongly related to intelligence. Humor reasoning was also correlated with the Remote Associates Test, a measure of creative thinking.

In a subsequent article, Feingold and Mazzella (1993) suggested that verbal wittiness may be viewed as a multidimensional construct composed of the mental ability dimension of humor cognition, in combination with social and temperamental factors influencing humor motivation and communication. Overall, then, Feingold and Mazzella's conceptualization of humor ability appears to be a fairly narrow construct, relating particularly to individuals' familiarity with well-known jokes and popular comedians. However, the psychometric properties of their measures are not well-established, and they have not gained wide acceptance among other humor researchers.

Other humor production tests have been developed by researchers over the years to examine individual differences in the ability to create or produce humor. Most of these were designed for use in individual studies, and they have typically not been standardized. In this approach, research participants are typically presented with various stimuli, such as caption-removed cartoons or silent movies, and are instructed to make up as many funny responses as they can to go with these stimuli. The funniness of their responses is then rated by the experimenters, yielding a score for humor production ability. Some of these studies have examined the relationship between humor production ability and various other personality traits.

For example, Robert Turner (1980) examined the association between humor production ability and self-monitoring, a personality trait having to do with the degree to which individuals are sensitive to environmental cues of social appropriateness and regulate their behavior accordingly. Humor ability was assessed in two ways. In one of these, participants were asked to make up witty captions to go with a series of cartoons in which the original captions had been removed. In the second method, participants were seated at a table on which were placed a number of miscellaneous objects, such as a tennis shoe, a wristwatch, and a box of crayons. The participants were instructed to create a three-minute comedy monologue, describing these objects in a funny way, after being given only 30 seconds to collect their thoughts. In both methods, the participants' humorous productions were rated by judges for wittiness.

The results revealed that, as predicted, individuals with higher scores on a measure of self-monitoring, as compared to those with lower scores, produced responses that were rated as significantly more witty on both humor production tests. The author suggested that the tendency to attend to and respond to social cues and the reactions of others enables people who are high in self-monitoring to develop skill in creating and delivering humor successfully over the course of their lives. In contrast, those who are low in self-monitoring, because they do not attend as much to the responses of others, do not learn as readily from those responses and therefore do not develop as much skill at producing humor. Consistent with these results, other research has found a positive correlation between self-monitoring and a self-report measure of the tendency to initiate humor in social interactions (Bell, McGhee, and Duffey, 1986). Thus, self-monitoring may be an important personality trait that contributes to the development of the ability to produce humor. These findings suggest that humor creativity should be viewed as a type of social skill (see also Dewitte and Verguts, 2001, for a similar selectionist account of sense of humor development).

Other researchers have used similar humor creation tests to examine the association between humor production ability and more general forms of creativity (reviewed by O'Quin and Derks, 1997). As discussed in Chapter 4, a number of theorists have noted close connections between humor and creativity, pointing out that both involve divergent thinking, incongruity, surprise, and novelty (Ferris, 1972; Murdock and Ganim, 1993; Treadwell, 1970; Wicker, 1985; Ziv, 1980). For example, Arthur Koestler (1964) considered humor, scientific discovery, and artistic creation (all of which involve the process of bisociation) to be forms of creativity.

Researchers investigating these hypotheses have assessed participants' humor creation abilities by rating the funniness of their responses to a variety of tasks, including creating humorous captions for cartoons (Babad, 1974; Brodzinsky and Rubien, 1976; Ziv, 1980) and TAT cards (Day and Langevin, 1969), generating witty word associations (Hauck and Thomas, 1972), and making up funny presidential campaign slogans (Clabby, 1980). In general, these studies revealed positive but moderate correlations between these funniness ratings and a variety of measures of creativity, including the Remote Associates Test (in which participants must identify a concept that links two seemingly unrelated words) and tests in which participants are asked to come up with unusual uses of a common object such as a brick. A meta-analysis of this research found an average correlation of .34 between humor production ability and creativity (O'Quin and Derks, 1997). These authors concluded that, although creativity and humor production do involve similar mental processes, they are nonetheless distinct. Whereas humorous productions are typically creative, individuals can be creative without being funny.

How is humor production ability related to other dimensions of sense of humor? As noted earlier, research has generally indicated little or no relation between measures of humor production and humor appreciation (Babad, 1974; Köhler and Ruch, 1996; Koppel and Sechrest, 1970), indicating that, somewhat surprisingly, people who are able to create humor successfully do not necessarily enjoy or respond with amusement to various kinds of jokes and cartoons. On the other hand, some positive but generally weak correlations have been found between measures of humor production ability and several self-report humor scales, including the SHRQ, CHS, Metamessage Sensitivity scale of the SHQ, and (low) Seriousness scale of the STCI-T (Köhler and Ruch, 1996; Lefcourt and Martin, 1986; Ruch, Köhler, et al., 1996).

The use of ability measures of humor production is an approach that merits further investigation. In addition to self-monitoring and creativity, this method would seem to be useful for evaluating other variables besides self-monitoring and creativity (e.g., intelligence, tolerance for ambiguity, curiosity) that contribute to humor production.

SENSE OF HUMOR AS STYLES OF HUMOROUS CONDUCT

When we say that someone has a sense of humor, we are implying that we have frequently observed this person engaging in a variety of humor-related behaviors in a range of situations. For example, we may have seen the person telling jokes or humorous stories, making spontaneous witty comments, laughing at a variety of amusing events, and so on. Based on these observations, we may also characterize the person's overall humorous style in various ways, using descriptors such as *reflective, sarcastic, irreverent,* or *sardonic.* Thus, the concept of sense of humor may be viewed as a socially constructed description of a person's typical humor-related conduct. In other words, sense of humor may be seen as a set of labels that we ascribe to people based on our observations during our interactions with them. What are the basic dimensions by which people classify different styles of humor in everyday conduct, and what are the patterns of humor-related behaviors that are associated with these different dimensions? These questions have been the focus of research conducted by Kenneth Craik and his colleagues at the University of California at Berkeley (Craik, Lampert, and Nelson, 1996; Craik and Ware, 1998).

To investigate the dimensions of humor based on observable behavior, Craik and his colleagues began by developing a list of 100 descriptive statements that were intended to capture all the important facets of the domain of everyday humorous conduct (described by Craik and Ware, 1998). Examples of these descriptions include: "Uses good-natured jests to put others at ease," "Has difficulty controlling the urge to laugh in solemn situations," "Enjoys witticisms which are intellectually challenging," and "Spoils jokes by laughing before finishing them." Each of these statements was then printed on a separate card to form the Humorous Behavior Q-sort Deck (HBQD). Subsequent research with this card deck employed the standard q-sort technique, in which observers are asked to sort the cards into a series of piles indicating the degree to which each description is characteristic of a particular target person.

In one study (described by Craik and Ware, 1998), participants were asked to sort the cards to describe a hypothetical person with a high sense of humor. Correlations among the card sorts of the participants revealed high agreement in the popular conception of what it means for someone to have a sense of humor. Averaging across the card sorts of all the subjects, the researchers were able to identify the humor styles that are generally perceived to be positively and negatively associated with this concept, as well as those that are seen as irrelevant. Positively related to the concept of sense of humor were items having to do with good-natured wittiness, a cheerful disposition, and skillful humor ability. Negatively associated items were those involving aggressive, inappropriate, and maladroit attempts at humor. Enjoyment of intellectual wit and ethnic jokes, along with ingratiating uses of humor, were deemed to be irrelevant to the concept. Thus, this method proved useful for exploring the way most people typically conceptualize a sense of humor.

In another study (also described by Craik and Ware, 1998), participants were asked to sort the HBQD cards to describe the styles of humor of several famous comedians, such as David Letterman, Woody Allen, and Bill Cosby. Again, good interrater reliabilities were found. Correlations between the mean card sorts for different comedians were then computed to examine the degree to which their humor styles were perceived to be similar. For example, Arsenio Hall and Whoopi Goldberg were perceived to have fairly similar styles, whereas Woody Allen and Lucille Ball were less similar. This q-sort method could be a potentially useful technique for researchers to use in quantifying the degree of similarity in humor styles between pairs of individuals, such as married couples or friends. These similarity scores could then be correlated with other relationship variables such as marital satisfaction or the long-term stability of the friendships to examine the degree to which similarity in humor styles contributes to these aspects of relationships.

To identify the major dimensions underlying different perceived styles of humor, a large number of university students were asked to describe their own humor styles using the HBQD, and these card sorts were then subjected to factor analysis (Craik et al., 1996). This analysis revealed five bipolar factors, which were labeled as: (1) socially warm versus cold; (2) reflective versus boorish; (3) competent versus inept; (4) earthy versus repressed; and (5) benign versus mean-spirited humorous styles. It was suggested that these five factors represent the major implicit dimensions by which people characterize one another's sense of humor. In future research using this procedure, an individual's humorous style could be described (either by the individual or, more preferably, by trained observers) by means of a card sort with the HBQD, and factor scores for each of the five factors could be computed for that individual. These scores could then be used in investigating their correlations with other personality, social, and affective variables that might be of interest to the researcher.

As one example of such research, Craik and colleagues (1996) examined correlations between factor scores on the (self-administered) HBQD and scores on a measure of extraversion in a sample of university students. Greater extraversion (as compared to introversion) was found to be associated with more socially warm and also more boorish humor styles. The other three humor style factors were unrelated to extraversion-introversion. Other studies examined correlations between the HBQD factors and scores on the subscales of the California Psychological Inventory (Craik et al., 1996) and the major personality dimensions of the FFM (Craik and Ware, 1998). The results demonstrated that each of these general personality dimensions is characterized by a unique constellation of humorous styles, suggesting that people with different personality traits have different corresponding styles of humor. For example, individuals who are high on the FFM dimension of agreeableness tend to be characterized by a socially warm, competent, and benign humorous style. On the other hand, neuroticism was associated with an inept (as opposed to competent) humor style. Further research is needed to replicate these findings and explore relationships with other personality constructs. In addition, this methodology may be useful for future research investigating such questions as the role of different humorous styles in interpersonal relationships, coping with stress, and mental health generally.

In summary, the HBQD represents a method for investigating sense of humor that takes a different perspective than the approaches using humor appreciation, self-report, and humor production measures. However, research using this approach has been quite limited so far, and its potential utility for exploring other facets of sense of humor remains largely unexplored. An initial step that seems necessary for future research is to determine the stability and replicability of the identified factors. In this regard, a recent factor analytic study of the items from the HBQD did not replicate the original factor structure (Kirsh and Kuiper, 2003), although this may have been due to the use of a self-rating format using Likert scales rather the original q-sort method. Because it was originally developed for use by trained observers, the use of the HBQD in a self-report format also seems questionable. Many of the items appear to be difficult to understand by untrained raters and many refer to behaviors that are not readily accessible to self-observation (e.g., "Enhances humorous impact with a deft sense of timing;" "Delights in the implicit buffoonery of the over-pompous"). Nonetheless, this approach, when used as originally intended, appears to be a potentially interesting avenue for future investigations.

HOW MANY DIFFERENT SENSES OF HUMOR EXIST?

As we saw at the beginning of this chapter, most people seem to think of sense of humor as a unitary construct, although its meaning in popular usage tends to be quite vague and ill-defined. Over the years, personality researchers have attempted to clarify and refine the meaning of this concept, defining and measuring it in a number of different ways. In the current state of the literature, with the proliferation of measurement instruments over recent years, sense of humor seems to comprise a plethora of apparently distinct trait dimensions. There are three factors of humor appreciation measured with the 3WD, numerous constructs measured by many different self-report humor tests, five styles of humorous conduct assessed by the HBQD, and an unknown number of components of humor production ability. After starting out with a seemingly simple idea, sense of humor turns out to be exceedingly complicated!

Do we really need this many different trait concepts, however, to meaningfully describe individual differences in humor? It would seem to be desirable for personality psychologists to identify the degree to which all these different traits are intercorrelated and to determine whether individual differences in humor can be captured using a more parsimonious set of basic dimensions. To answer these questions, researchers should ideally administer all the existing measures to large samples of individuals representing a broad cross section of the population across different cultures. Factor analyses could then be conducted on these data to identify the underlying factor structure. This would be similar to the approach that was taken with personality traits in the development of the FFM (John, 1990). Additional research could then explore the relations between the identified core humor factors and broader personality dimensions such as the FFM to determine the degree to which sense of humor dimensions overlap with known personality factors or are fairly unique. Only a limited amount of research along these lines has been conducted so far, focusing primarily on self-report measures.

Using data from a sample of German adults from the general population, Willibald Ruch (1994) conducted a factor analysis of seven sense of humor scales from four different self-report measures, including the SHRQ, CHS, SHQ, and Ziv's (1981) measure of humor appreciation and creativity. Also included were the three subscales of the Telic Dominance Scale (TDS) (Murgatroyd et al., 1978), which relate to seriousmindedness, planfulness, and arousal avoidance (i.e., the inverse of a habitually playful, humorous frame of mind). This analysis yielded only two factors. All the sense of humor scales loaded highly positively on the first factor, which was tentatively labeled *cheerfulness*. This finding suggests that these different self-report tests, although they were designed to measure different components or aspects of sense of humor, actually all assess a common underlying dimension. The second factor, labeled *restraint versus expressiveness*, was found to be related only to the SHRQ, the Emotional Expressiveness scale of Svebak's SHQ, and (in the opposite direction) the subscales of the TDS.

To explore these dimensions further, Ruch examined the relations of these two humor factors, as well as each of the individual humor scales, with the three superfactors of extraversion, neuroticism, and psychoticism, which were viewed by Eysenck (1990) as being the most basic, biologically based temperament dimensions of personality. All of the sense of humor scales loaded positively on extraversion, as did the first (cheerfulness) factor found in the factor analysis. Thus, these self-report humor scales all appear to relate primarily to the general personality dimension of extraversion, which comprises traits such as sociable, lively, active, assertive, sensation-seeking, carefree, dominant, and the tendency to experience positive moods. Overall, a sense of humor seems to be a characteristic of extraverts rather than introverts. In addition, the SHRQ and Emotional Expressiveness scale of the SHQ (along with the second overall humor factor) loaded positively on the psychoticism dimension, which, among other traits, relates to low impulse control. This relationship is likely due to items on the SHRQ and SHQ-E scales that describe laughing in situations in which laughter is not typically seen to be appropriate.

Somewhat surprisingly, none of the humor scales were strongly loaded on the neuroticism dimension, with only a weak negative loading for the SHQ-M scale. Thus, individuals with high scores on these humor scales do not necessarily experience less negative emotions than do those with low humor scores. Contrary to popular opinion, people with a strong sense of humor, as measured by these self-report scales, are not necessarily very emotionally stable and well-adjusted. Overall, this study indicated that the various self-report humor scales do not assess substantially different humor dimensions, but instead form one main factor that is quite strongly related to extraversion. Ruch suggested that measures of humor appreciation and the ability to produce humor are likely not related to these temperament dimensions, although he did not test this assumption in this study.

In a later study, Gabriele Köhler and Willibald Ruch (1996) conducted a similar factor analysis of 23 humor-related self-report scales using another sample of German adults. In addition to the scales used in the previous study, this analysis also included the cheerfulness and seriousness facet subscales of the STCI-T, the Multidimensional Sense of Humor Scale (MSHS; Thorson and Powell, 1993a), and the Humor Initiation Scale (HIS; Bell et al., 1986). Once again, only two factors were found. The first factor, again labeled *cheerfulness*, had strong loadings for all the scales except for the seriousness facet subscales of the STCI-T. The second factor, labeled *seriousness*, had strong positive loadings for the STCI-T seriousness scales, and generally weak negative loadings for most of the remaining humor scales.

The authors concluded that these results provided support for Ruch's model of the temperament basis of sense of humor (discussed earlier). Most self-report humor tests appear to relate strongly to trait cheerfulness, and they also tend to capture a low seriousness or playfulness component to varying degrees. Once again, the first factor was found to be strongly related to extraversion, and in this study it was also somewhat negatively related to neuroticism. In addition, the second factor was again related to psychoticism, with greater psychoticism being associated with lower seriousness, or greater playfulness. Thus, most of the variance in self-report humor scales seems to be captured by the Eysenckian temperament dimensions of extraversion and psychoticism and, less so, by (low) neuroticism.

This study also included measures of humor appreciation (the 3WD) and a test of humor production ability (a cartoon captioning task), although unfortunately these were not included in the factor analysis. Correlational analyses revealed that, as in previous research, humor appreciation and humor production measures were unrelated to each other. In addition, self-report measures purporting to assess humor appreciation were only weakly correlated with the 3WD appreciation scores, while self-report scales designed to assess humor production were generally unrelated to the rated funniness of participants' cartoon humor productions (with the exception of the SHQ-M scale). Overall, these findings suggest that three distinct humor constructs are assessed by measures of (1) humor appreciation (the 3WD), (2) humor production, and (3) self-report scales, with the latter measures reflecting the two broad dimensions of cheerfulness and, to varying degrees, (low) seriousness. Further research is needed to replicate these findings with other populations and to include newer humor measures, such as the HSQ and the HBQD.

PERSONALITY CHARACTERISTICS OF PROFESSIONAL HUMORISTS

Do professional comedians have particular personality traits that differ from those of other people? One commonly held belief is that comedians tend to be depressive individuals who hide their dysphoria behind a mask of superficial hilarity. An old story tells of a man going to a doctor to complain of feelings of depression and despondency. The doctor encourages him to attend a performance of a famous comedian who is extremely funny and will be sure to lift his spirits. The patient replies that he is that comedian.

Two studies have investigated the personality traits of professional comedians. Taking a psychoanalytic approach, Samuel Janus (1975, 1978) studied the intelligence, educational level, family background, and personality structure of 55 male and 14 female comedians, all of whom were said to be famous and successful. Data were collected using clinical interviews, early memories, dreams, handwriting analyses, projective tests, and the Wechsler Adult Intelligence Scale (WAIS). Based on his interpretations of these data, Janus concluded that comedians tended to be superior in intelligence, angry, suspicious, and depressed. In addition, their early lives were characterized by suffering, isolation, and feelings of deprivation, and they used humor as a defense against anxiety, converting their feelings of suppressed rage from physical to verbal aggression.

Many of the comedians were also described as shy, sensitive, and empathic individuals whose comedic success was due in part to an ability to accurately perceive the fears and needs of their audiences. Overall, these findings appear to provide support for the popular view of professional comedians as generally unhappy people. However, the validity of the results is questionable, due to the use of some dubious assessment methods and the lack of a control group, making it difficult to know whether these characteristics are unique to comedians or may be shared, for example, by noncomic entertainers.

Seymour Fisher and Rhoda Fisher (1981) conducted a more well-controlled study of the personality characteristics and childhood memories of 43 professional comedians and circus clowns (whom they designated collectively as "comics"). To control for possible non-comedy–related variables involved in being a public performer, these researchers included an age-matched comparison sample of professional actors. They administered a semistructured interview, the Rorschach inkblot test, the TAT, and several standardized personality questionnaires to all participants.

The two groups did not differ on measures of depression or overall psychological health, casting doubt on the view that comedians are more psychologically disturbed than other people. However, a number of interesting statistically significant differences did emerge between the two groups. Compared to the actors, the comics' responses revealed a significantly greater preoccupation with themes of good and evil, unworthiness, self-deprecation, duty and responsibility, concealment, and smallness. In addition, the comics, as compared to the actors, described their fathers in more positive terms and their mothers in a more negative manner. These findings suggested that their comic tendencies may have originated in early family dynamics.

Most of these professional comics indicated that they had developed their comedic abilities early in childhood, and many had been "class clowns" in school. In order to investigate further the possible childhood dynamics involved in becoming a comic, Fisher and Fisher conducted another study in which they used self-report questionnaires to compare the personality characteristics and attitudes of the parents of a group of children identified as class clowns with the parents of children who did not show these comic characteristics. Compared to the mothers of noncomic children, personality testing revealed that the mothers of the comic children were significantly less kind, less sympathetic, less close and intimately involved with their children, and more selfish and controlling, and that they wanted their children to take responsibility and grow up more quickly. For their part, the fathers of the comic children were more passive than those of the noncomic children.

On the basis of the combined findings from these two studies, Fisher and Fisher theorized that professional comics develop their humor skills in childhood as a means of entertaining others, gaining approval, and asserting their goodness, in the context of a relatively uncongenial family environment characterized by limited maternal affection and warmth, a need to take on adult responsibilities at an early age, and a sense that things often are not what they appear to be on the surface. Moreover, as children they tend to take on a parentified healing role, learning to provide psychological support and reassurance to their parents by means of a humorous persona. By making their parents laugh at their funny antics, they are able to gain the attention and approval of otherwise unaffectionate and rejecting parents. Thus, humor in these individuals seems to be a means of coping with feelings of anxiety and anger associated with a generally harsh and uncongenial family environment.

Overall, then, although this research does not support the popular view that professional comedians are depressed or otherwise psychologically disturbed, it does suggest that humor in these individuals serves as a defense or coping mechanism for dealing with adversity in early life. The well-honed comedic skills required for a successful career as a comic may well be developed as a means of compensating for earlier psychological losses and difficulties. As we will see in Chapter 8, similar mechanisms may be involved in the development of a comic sense of humor in at least some ordinary individuals who do not become professional comedians.

CONCLUSION

A sense of humor is seen by most people as an important personality characteristic. It is one of the main dimensions by which people tend to characterize others, and is viewed as a very desirable trait in potential friends and romantic partners (Sprecher and Regan, 2002). But what exactly *is* sense of humor? As we have seen, this concept has taken on many positive connotations over the years, while becoming increasingly vague and ill-defined. The research reviewed in this chapter suggests that sense of humor is not a unitary construct. Instead, it can be conceptualized and measured in a number of different ways, each focusing on different aspects of humor. Furthermore, these different ways of defining it are not necessarily highly correlated with one another, and they relate in quite different ways to other personality traits.

Research with a variety of different sense of humor measures is beginning to clarify the nature and correlates of these humor-related traits, showing how they interact with other dimensions of personality and behavior. With regard to the humor appreciation approach, Ruch's work with the 3WD has contributed a great deal to our understanding of individual differences in the enjoyment of humor in the form of jokes and cartoons. Interestingly, this research demonstrates that individual differences in humor appreciation have more to do with structural aspects than with the content or topic of the jokes, contrary to the assumptions of many past researchers. These investigations have also uncovered some very interesting correlations between these structural humor appreciation dimensions and a variety of more general personality traits, showing that the types of humor that individuals enjoy reflect their levels of conservative versus liberal social attitudes, sensation seeking, toughmindedness, and so on.

Other researchers have taken an ability approach to sense of humor, defining it in terms of the ability to produce humor and amuse others. People who do well on these types of tests presumably excel in the cognitive abilities needed to generate the sorts of nonserious incongruities that are the hallmark of humor. Research using this approach indicates that individuals who are more aware of and responsive to the reactions of others to their own behavior (i.e., those who are high in self-monitoring), as well as those who are generally more creative and capable of divergent thinking, tend to be better at producing humor and making others laugh. Thus, an aptitude for humor production may be viewed as a type of social skill as well as a creative ability.

The many different self-report measures that have been created in recent years were designed to assess different components or aspects of sense of humor. A considerable amount of evidence for reliability and validity has been found for several of these measures. However, factor analytic research suggests that most of these self-report scales load on only one or two major factors. The strongest factor has to do with a cheerful temperament and an extraverted, sociable disposition, while the other involves a playful, nonserious attitude. These dimensions provide support for Ruch's temperament model of sense of humor, and also reflect the social, emotional, and cognitive components of humor that I have discussed at earlier points in this book.

Until recently, a limitation of self-report humor measures has been their unique focus on positive, desirable aspects of humor. The HSQ represents a more recent tendency among researchers to consider also more negative and socially undesirable functions of humor in social interaction. As we will see in Chapter 9, researchers have recently begun to explore the implications of these and other negative humor styles for interpersonal relationships and psychological well-being. The HBQD represents another potentially interesting method of investigating individual differences in humor styles using q-sort ratings by observers. This method appears to be particularly useful for examining popular conceptions of what a sense of humor is, as well as providing a method for quantifying similarities and differences in humor styles between individuals and examining relationships between various humor styles and other personality traits and behaviors.

One view that seems to be emerging in the research is that different personality traits are reflected in different humor dimensions. In other words, people express their particular personality traits through their humor. Thus, it may be that extraverts express humor in different ways and enjoy different types of humor than do introverts. Similarly, more agreeable people tend to have a friendly style of humor, while hostile individuals tend to use humor in more aggressive ways. Other styles of humor may be differentially associated with neuroticism versus emotional stability, as well as openness and conscientiousness.

In summary, a considerable amount of research has been conducted on various dimensions of sense of humor as a personality trait, providing a growing scientific understanding of this ubiquitous tendency of humans to play with language and ideas. In the following chapters, I will discuss research investigating how these various components of sense of humor develop during childhood, and how they relate to aspects of psychological and physical health.

CHAPTER 8

The Developmental Psychology of Humor

We have seen in previous chapters that humor is a complex phenomenon involving a range of psychological functions. These include cognitive processes relating to perception, language, concept formation, memory, problem solving, and creativity; play and emotion; social relationships and communication; and biological processes taking place in the brain and extending into other parts of the body. Although nearly everyone engages in humor to some degree, individuals differ from one another in their humor comprehension and production, the types of humor that they enjoy, and the way they use and express humor in their daily lives. In this chapter, we will see that all these psychological aspects of humor begin to emerge soon after birth and continue to develop over the course of childhood and into adulthood.

What are the typical patterns of humor development in children? How do children's developing cognitive, social, and emotional capacities interact with their ability to understand, enjoy, and produce humor? What are the contributions of genetic and social environmental factors to the development of individual differences in children's sense of humor, and how does a sense of humor influence the child's cognitive, social, and emotional functioning? How does humor change over the course of adulthood, and what are the changing social and emotional functions of humor in later life? These and other related questions have been the focus of a considerable body of research that has accumulated over the past 40 years on the developmental psychology of humor.

Developmental psychologists make use of empirical research methods to study psychological development over the life span. Employing a variety of research methods, including observational studies, experiments, surveys, and case studies, and using retrospective, cross-sectional, and longitudinal designs, they seek to understand the processes of change in cognition, language, emotion, social functioning, and so forth. Developmental psychologists take a multifaceted perspective, recognizing that psychological development involves a complex interplay of genetics, biology, parental and family influences, and other social environment factors. All these aspects of psychological development in general apply as well to the development of humor. In this chapter, I will discuss theories and research findings on the developmental psychology of humor, examining the development of smiling and laughter in infancy and early childhood, the origins of humor in children's play, the relation between humor and cognitive development, humor as emotional coping in childhood and adolescence, social aspects of humor development, individual differences in humor, and humor in later adulthood and old age.

SMILING AND LAUGHTER IN INFANCY AND EARLY CHILDHOOD

Infants typically begin to smile during their first month, initially in response to tactile stimulation (e.g., tickling, rubbing the skin) accompanied by the sound of a caregiver's voice, and a month or so later in response to visual stimuli such as moving objects and lights. In the following months, babies begin to smile when they recognize objects such as the general configuration of a face and, eventually, the faces of specific individuals such as their parents or siblings, indicating that they have developed a cognitive schema, or mental representation, of that object. Smiling appears to be most likely to occur when an optimal amount of effort (not too little or too much) is required for recognition (McGhee, 1979).

Laughter first appears in the context of infant-caregiver interaction sometime between 10 and 20 weeks of age, and it quickly becomes a frequent part of the interactions between infants and their caregivers. Researchers have observed that young infants typically produce one to four laughs in a ten-minute face-to-face play session with their mother (Fogel et al., 1997). In an early study at the University of Minnesota, Alan Sroufe and Jane Wunsch (1972) investigated the stimuli that trigger laughter during the first year of life by having mothers engage in a variety of behaviors with their infants, such as making lip-popping sounds, tickling, displaying unusual facial expressions, and playing peek-a-boo games. They found that laughter occurs with increasing frequency and in response to a greater variety of maternal behaviors over the course of the year. The types of stimuli producing laughter also change over the year. Tactile and auditory stimuli that produce relatively high rates of laughter at 7 or 8 months (e.g., kissing on the bare stomach or making the sound of a horse) are less likely to do so by 12 months. In turn, visual and social actions (e.g., walking with an exaggerated waddle, or the "I'm going to get you" game) are more likely to induce laughter at 12 months than at 8 months. The authors noted that the stimuli that become most effective in inducing laughter with increasing age are those that seem to make the greatest cognitive demands on the infant.

Overall, the actions that trigger laughter seem to be ones that are unexpected or incongruous with regard to the child's developing cognitive schemas. When the mother walks like a penguin, sucks on a baby bottle, or dangles a piece of cloth from her mouth, these actions deviate from the familiar behavior that the infant has come to expect. Based on these observations, Sroufe and Wunsch proposed an incongruity-based cognitive-arousal theory of laughter in infants. They suggested that laughter occurs in response to an unexpected or incongruous event, which is appropriate to the infant's cognitive level but does not mesh with his or her developing schemas. Such incongruous events initially attract the attention of the child, inducing efforts at information processing, and producing accompanying physiological arousal. If the infant's interpretation of the event is negative due to feelings of insecurity or perceptions of threat, he or she will cry and engage in avoidance behaviors; however, if the interpretation is positive, due to perceptions of a safe and playful environment, he or she will smile or laugh and engage in approach behaviors.

The authors noted that their data provided little support for the ambivalence view of laughter that has been proposed by some theorists, according to which laughter is associated with a concurrent mixture of both positive and negative emotions. Instead, they observed that, although an infant might first respond to an incongruous stimulus with some apprehension and hesitation, once laughter begins the affective tone seems to be purely positive and is accompanied only by approach behaviors rather than vacillation. Thus, laughter in infants appears to occur in response to the perception of an incongruous object or event in a safe, playful, and nonthreatening social context. As noted in Chapter 4, contemporary theories suggest that the perception of nonserious incongruity is also the basis of humor in adults.

Some later experiments used the "peek-a-boo" game to investigate various factors that influence the amount of smiling and laughter exhibited by infants in response to incongruous events. In this game, a familiar person hides his or her face for a few seconds and then suddenly reappears in front of the infant, saying "peek-a-boo!" while smiling and making eye contact with the infant. Infants between 6 and 12 months frequently smile and laugh upon seeing the person reappear. The disappearance and reappearance of a familiar face in a playful context seems to be particularly enjoyable to infants when they are in the process of mastering "object permanence," the recognition that objects continue to exist even when they are not visible to the child (Shultz, 1976).

One study (MacDonald and Silverman, 1978) showed that one-year-old children are more likely to smile and laugh in response to this game when it is carried out by their mother as compared to a stranger (indicating the importance of familiarity and perceptions of security) and when the mother rapidly approaches them during the game rather than moving away from them (indicating the importance of increasing arousal).

Gerrod Parrott and Henry Gleitman (1989), at Georgetown University, investigated the role of expectations in six- to eight-month-old infants' enjoyment by inserting occasional "trick trials" in a series of standard peek-a-boo trials. In these trick trials, one person would hide and a different person would reappear in his or her place, or else the same person would reappear but in a different location than in the standard trials. The results showed that the infants smiled and laughed much less frequently in response to the trick trials than the standard trials, whereas the trick trials produced more eyebrow-raising, indicating surprise or puzzlement instead of amusement.

These findings suggest that infants at this age have well-formed expectations about the identity and location of the returning person, and that conformity to these expectations contributes to their enjoyment of the game, whereas large deviations from expectations induce puzzlement rather than enjoyment. The authors suggested that when deviations from expectations are too great, the infant is unable to "resolve" the incongruity by assimilating it into an overarching schema, thereby making sense of it in some way. Thus infants, like older children and adults, are not always amused by just any sort of incongruity or deviation from their expectations, but prefer deviations that can be reinterpreted in a way that makes sense. In addition to these cognitive aspects, the trick trials, being so deviant from the infants' experience, might have induced a serious, nonplayful reaction of puzzlement in the infants, interfering with the playful state of mind that is required for humor.

The importance of social factors in laughter was demonstrated by a study that found that infants never smiled or laughed in response to an impersonal analogue of the peek-a-boo game in which a toy, instead of a person, was made to disappear and suddenly reappear, whereas they frequently smiled and laughed in response to a person playing the game (Shultz, 1976). Thus, laughter right from its inception tends to be a form of social communication. Infant laughter typically occurs during interactions with parents and other caregivers, who in turn tend to laugh in response to the infants.

More recent research by Evangeline Nwokah and her colleagues at Purdue University have investigated in greater detail the social nature of laughter as a means of communicating emotional information between infants and caregivers (Fogel et al., 1997; Nwokah and Fogel, 1993; Nwokah et al., 1999; Nwokah et al., 1994). For example, Nwokah and colleagues (1994) conducted a longitudinal study in which they observed the laughter of mothers and their infants during free play sessions over the first two years of the infants' lives, to examine the timing and temporal sequence of laughter in interpersonal interaction. They found that infant laughter increased in frequency over the first year and remained fairly stable during the second year (averaging about .3 laughs per minute by age two), whereas the rate of laughter in the mothers remained quite stable over the two years (at about .55 laughs per minute). By the second year, the rate and duration of laughter was significantly correlated between mothers and infants, meaning that the more a particular mother laughed, the more her infant laughed. Thus, laughter appears to be modeled by the mother during the first year and stabilizes in the infant by the second year.

By the time the infant is one year of age, both mother and infant can anticipate that by altering their tone of voice, facial expressions, and actions, they can induce laughter in each other. For example, by engaging in incongruous behaviors such as putting a toy on her head, the mother can encourage laughter in the infant, although the likelihood of laughter also depends on such factors as the timing, element of surprise, emotional state of both the mother and infant, and attention of the infant (Fogel et al., 1997). Thus, laughter is clearly a social process, serving an emotional communication function.

As children progress into the preschool or nursery school years, their laughter occurs increasingly in the context of playful interactions with other children in addition to caregivers. Charlene Bainum and her colleagues at the University of Tennessee observed groups of three-, four-, and five-year-old children in a nursery school to investigate laughing and smiling during structured and unstructured play (Bainum, Lounsbury, and Pollio, 1984). No differences were found between girls and boys in the overall frequency of smiling and laughter across the three age groups. The social nature of smiling and laughter was again clearly demonstrated by the fact that 95 percent of these behaviors occurred when children were interacting with others, and only 5 percent occurred when alone. Laughter increased in frequency from age three to five, whereas smiling decreased over this age span. By the age of five, children laughed an average of 7.7 times per hour during play. Smiling and laughter in three-year-olds occurred more often in response to amusing nonverbal actions (e.g., funny faces or body movements), whereas in five-year-olds they appeared more frequently in response to amusing verbal behaviors (e.g., funny comments, stories, songs, or unusual word usage).

In all three age groups, laughter occurred most frequently in response to intentional humor rather than events that were unintentionally funny. Interestingly, children were somewhat more likely to laugh at the funny things they themselves said or did, rather than the behavior of others, indicating that laughter was often used as a signal to indicate that particular behaviors were meant to be funny. Although the majority of laughter occurred in response to socially positive or at least neutral humorous behavior, there was an increase from ages three to five in the proportion of laughter occurring in response to socially negative behaviors such as teasing, shoving, or ridicule.

Compared to laughter, smiling occurred in response to a wider variety of events, especially incidental (not intentionally funny) events, although it also occurred along with laughter in the context of intentional silliness/clowning events. Thus, although some instances of smiling may be viewed as a diminished form of laughter, indicating a lower level of amusement, smiling also serves a broader range of social functions than does laughter.

What are the acoustic characteristics of young children's laughter? Nwokah and her colleagues (1993) conducted acoustical analyses of 50 samples of laughter emitted by three-year-old children while interacting with their mothers. They identified four distinct types of laughter in these children: (1) *comment laughs*, comprising a single laughter syllable or note with a fundamental frequency (pitch) close to that of normal speech, and lasting about 200 milliseconds; (2) *chuckle laughs*, consisting of either one note with two peaks or two notes, with a somewhat higher pitch and a total duration of about 500 milliseconds; (3) *rhythmical laughter*, comprising three or more notes with a similar fundamental frequency as the chuckle and more complex harmonic structure, lasting 1 to 1.5 sec; and (4) *squeal laughter*, involving a single note of about 500 milliseconds duration with a very high-pitched fundamental frequency.

The duration of individual notes or syllables within all the different kinds of laughs (with the exception of squeal laughter) was very similar to that found in adult laughter (approximately 200 to 220 milliseconds). Some minor differences in acoustic structure were observed between children's and adults' laughter, largely due to children having less control over the vocal apparatus. The authors concluded that different kinds of laughs are used to communicate different degrees of emotional intensity as well as qualitatively different emotional experiences. For example, chuckle laughter often occurs in response to an accomplishment on the part of the child, whereas rhythmical laughter tends to occur in a wide variety of high-arousal social contexts, often where both partners are laughing.

HUMOR AND PLAY

As we have seen in earlier chapters of this book, humor is closely related to play. Research on laughter in chimpanzees and other animals, discussed in Chapter 6, suggests that the evolutionary origins of laughter arise in the context of rough-and-tumble social play. Developmental psychologists studying humor have also noted that laughter and humor develop in human children in the context of play (see Figure 6), and many view humor as a particular form of mental play (Barnett, 1990, 1991; Bergen, 1998b, 2002, 2003; McGhee, 1979).

What exactly is play? Although there is little agreement among play researchers and theorists about how to define this nebulous concept, most would agree that it is an enjoyable, spontaneous activity that is carried out for its own sake with no obvious immediate biological purpose (Berlyne, 1969). Michael Apter (1982) suggested that play is best viewed as a state of mind rather than a characteristic of certain types of activities. Thus, one can engage in almost any activity in a playful way, as long as one has a nonserious, activity-oriented (rather than goal-oriented) mental set.

There are many similarities between humor and play (Bergen, 2002). Laughter and play both emerge at a similar age in infants (around four to six months), and both are facilitated by similar social contexts. Humor and play are both enjoyable, and they share similar characteristics regarding motivation, control, and reality. They both involve an "as if" attitude, they are enjoyed for their own sake without having an obvious serious purpose, and they both occur in safe settings with people who are trusted. They also both seem to involve consolidation and mastery of newly acquired skills and concepts. Moreover, children are socialized into play and humor by their caregivers in similar ways and in similar contexts. Just as parents initiate their infant children into the "play frame," teaching them to recognize the verbalizations and behaviors that signal "this is play," parents also teach their children the meaning of

FIGURE 6 Humor develops during childhood in the context of social play. © SW Productions/Getty Images/Brand X Pictures

the "humor frame" by means of facial expressions, behavioral and vocal exaggerations, and verbal labels indicating "this is funny."

Doris Bergen (1998a), a developmental psychologist at Miami University in Ohio, asked parents of children from ages one to seven to keep a record of the events that the children themselves perceived to be funny. Most of the reported examples of children's humor took place in the context of play and involved playful manipulations of language and actions. Common examples included: expressed joy in mastery and movement play (e.g., tickling games, chasing), clowning (e.g., exaggerated facial or bodily movements or voices), performing incongruous actions (e.g., rolling up a red placemat and pretending to eat it as a "Fruit Roll"), and playing with sounds and word meanings (e.g., chanting or singing nonsense words).

The close connection between humor and play is also reflected in research showing that children with a greater sense of humor tend to engage in more play in general. Lynn Barnett (1990) developed a measure for assessing children's playfulness in which sense of humor is included as one of the subscales. The sense of humor scale includes items relating to the frequency of joking, playful teasing, telling funny stories, and laughing with other children. In addition to humor, the measure, which was designed to be used by adult observers to rate children's playfulness, also includes scales for physical, social, and cognitive spontaneity and manifest joy. Research with this measure has shown that the sense of humor scale is significantly correlated with a number of other measures of general playfulness in children, lending further support to the close link between humor and play (Barnett, 1991). Similarly, a study of humor in nursery school children by Paul McGhee and Sally Lloyd (1982) showed that the strongest predictor of children's verbal and behavioral humor initiation and laughter responsiveness was the frequency with which they engaged in social play.

Although humor and play are closely related, they are not exactly the same thing. A small child dressing up in her mother's fancy dress and high-heeled shoes and putting on lipstick may be engaging in enjoyable make-believe play, but she does not necessarily find it to be humorous or "funny." However, if she puts the dress on backwards, wears the shoes on her hands, or gives herself a clown face with the lipstick, she might perceive this to be humorous and expect other people to laugh at it as well. Thus, humor involves a greater degree of incongruity, bizarreness, exaggeration, or discrepancy from the way things normally are, along with a playful attitude.

At what point in a child's development can we say that humor first diverges from other forms of play? When we see a six-month-old infant laughing in response to the peek-a-boo game, it is tempting to assume that he or she is experiencing humor; however, according to some researchers, this is not necessarily the case. Laughter in infants and young children might be used to communicate a variety of positive emotions, and not just humor. When then do children begin to laugh at things that are "funny" and not just "fun"? This has been a topic of some controversy among developmental psychologists.

According to Martha Wolfenstein (1954), an early psychoanalytically-oriented researcher of humor in children, humor does not emerge until sometime in the second year of life, when make-believe play becomes differentiated into two strands, which she called "serious" make-believe and "joking" make-believe. In both kinds of make-believe, the child pretends that something is real, but knows that it is not. In serious make-believe, the focus is on the pretense or illusion of reality, whereas in joking make-believe the emphasis is on the recognition of unreality. Thus, a child engaging in serious make-believe play may become engrossed in taking on a role, pretending to be a "mommy" or a "truck driver," and carrying out activities that closely resemble those of a real mother or truck driver. In humor, however, the child will intentionally distort reality, behaving in unusual or exaggerated ways with the intention of causing someone to laugh.

Paul McGhee (1979), a prominent early developmental humor researcher, also saw a close link between humor and make-believe play. His theory of humor development was strongly influenced by the more general theory of cognitive development formulated by the well-known Swiss psychologist Jean Piaget (1970). Similarly to Wolfenstein, McGhee argued that genuine humor does not begin until the middle of the second year of life, when children begin to develop the capacity for fantasy, pretense, or make-believe play. This corresponds to the transition from the sensorimotor stage to the preoperational stage in Piaget's theory. At this stage, children begin to represent schemas internally instead of relying on direct manipulation of objects to gain knowledge of the world (the concept of cognitive schemas was discussed in Chapter 4).

The most significant achievement at this age is the ability to use symbols and signs, including words, to represent other objects. According to Piagetian theory, when a child perceives information that does not fit with his or her existing schema about a particular object or event, he or she experiences incongruity. To make sense of this incongruous information, the child normally either reinterprets the perceived information to make it fit with the existing schema (*assimilation*, in Piaget's terms), or modifies the schema so that it can incorporate the new information (*accommodation*). In this way, the incongruity is eliminated and the child's intelligence is expanded.

According to McGhee (1979), these processes for making sense of events can occur in two ways: either through "reality assimilation," which is more serious and reality-based, or "fantasy assimilation," which is more playful and makes use of pretense and make-believe. In the latter type of assimilation, which is the essence of humor, the child responds to incongruity by playfully applying the wrong schemas to objects, treating one object as if it were another one. In this way, children can create experiences in their fantasy world that they know cannot take place in reality. Thus, in McGhee's view, humor essentially involves the perception of an incongruity along with fantasy assimilation.

For example, a child might pretend to comb her hair with a pencil, thus stretching the pencil schema to make it incorporate characteristics of a comb. The schema is not permanently altered in fantasy assimilation, as it is in reality assimilation, but is temporarily applied incorrectly. Based on developmental research by Piaget and others, McGhee argued that children are not capable of this sort of fantasy assimilation until they acquire the capacity for symbolic play at around 18 months of age. In McGhee's view, then, the six-month-old infant who laughs in response to the peek-a-boo game is not really experiencing humor, even though he or she may perceive the situation to be incongruous and obviously enjoys it.

In contrast to both Wolfenstein and McGhee, developmental psychologists Diana Pien and Mary Rothbart (1980) argued that symbolic play capacities and fantasy assimilation are not necessary for the appreciation of humor. Instead, they proposed that humor requires only the recognition of incongruity along with a playful interpretation of that incongruity, and they argued that both these abilities are present by the time infants first exhibit laughter, around the fourth month. Although infants at this age do not have internalized mental schemas, they do develop sensory and motor schemas based on their interactions with the physical world, and they are able to recognize events that are incongruous with respect to these developing schemas. In support of their view, they cited the research by Sroufe and Wunsch (1972) described earlier, which indicated that infants laugh in response to visual and social events that involve discrepancy from familiar sensorimotor schemas.

Although Pien and Rothbart agreed with McGhee (and Piaget) that make-believe play does not begin until the preoperational stage, they pointed out that by four months of age infants are capable of simple forms of playful behavior involving practice, exploratory, and manipulative play with objects; motor play; and social play (see also Garner, 1998). Following Piaget, they defined play as actions that are carried out for the pleasure of the activity alone, involving assimilation with little or no serious attempt to accommodate existing schemas to fit a stimulus. They argued that this ability to respond playfully is all that is necessary for incongruity to be perceived as humorous. To respond to incongruity in a playful way, the infant merely needs to be in a safe, nonthreatening environment. In Pien and Rothbart's view, then, a six-month-old infant laughing at the peek-a-boo game is actually experiencing humor.

The question of when humor first occurs in infants may be impossible to resolve, since it depends in part on how one defines humor. Perhaps the most we can say is that humor originates in play and gradually becomes differentiated from other forms of play as the child's cognitive abilities develop (Bergen, 2003). Most researchers today seem to avoid the question of when humor begins in children, focusing on overt behaviors like smiling and laughter and avoiding making inferences about subjective cognitive experiences such as humor. Nonetheless, most would agree that by the end of their second year, children are able to distinguish between humor and other forms of play. This also becomes more evident as children's developing language skills enable them to describe certain events as "funny" or "silly," in addition to laughing at them.

HUMOR AND COGNITIVE DEVELOPMENT

As we have seen in this and earlier chapters, most researchers and theorists view incongruity as an essential component of humor. Incongruity may be viewed as a deviation or discrepancy from one's normal expectations. As discussed in Chapter 4, these expectations are based on one's cognitive schemas, the mental representations stored in memory. Children, as well as adults, tend to laugh at objects or events that do not conform to their existing schemas. Since schemas gradually develop throughout childhood as the individual gains experience and familiarity with the world, the kinds of objects and events that are perceived to be incongruous with respect to these schemas—and therefore humorous—also change over time. Things that seem incongruous and funny at an early age become mundane and less humorous at a later stage of cognitive development, whereas the older child's more sophisticated schemas enable him or her to perceive and enjoy new kinds of incongruity and more complex forms of humor that are not comprehensible to the younger child. Thus, the development of a sense of humor in children parallels their overall cognitive development. The effects of cognitive development on humor comprehension and appreciation have been the focus of a great deal of theoretical work and empirical research since the early 1970s.

McGhee's Four-Stage Model of Humor Development

Based on a variety of research findings, Paul McGhee (1979), then at Texas Tech University, proposed four stages of humor development in children that correspond to general trends in cognitive development. As we saw earlier, McGhee argued that the appreciation of humor does not begin until the middle of the second year of life, when children progress into the preoperational stage of cognitive development and acquire the capacity for make-believe or fantasy play. The first stage of humor development, which McGhee named *incongruous actions toward objects*, therefore begins at this age. According to McGhee, children at this age are able to represent objects with internal mental schemas, and their humor consists of playfully assimilating objects into schemas to which they do not normally belong.

For example, a child might hold a leaf to her ear and begin talking to it as if it were a telephone. The child's recognition of the inappropriateness of the action is an important component of the humor: if the child simply misapplies a schema without recognizing the error, this may provoke laughter in adult observers but not in the child. Indeed, one way children often learn to behave in humorous ways is when their inadvertent cognitive errors unintentionally produce laughter in their parents and others. Once they discover that such incongruous actions can cause people to laugh, they begin to intentionally engage in such behavior to evoke laughter in others (Bariaud, 1988).

McGhee's second stage of humor development, called *incongruous labeling of objects and events*, begins early in the third year, when the child is able to begin using language in playful ways. At this stage, the humorous use of language involves mislabeling objects or events. For example, children at this age may derive a great deal of amusement from calling a dog a cat, a hand a foot, an eye a nose, and so on. The child must understand the correct meaning of the word and must be aware that he or she is applying it incorrectly for it to be perceived as humorous. Thus, the child's mastery of the correct usage of the word seems to be the critical factor in determining when it will be misapplied in a playful manner to create humor.

The third humor stage, called *conceptual incongruity*, begins around three years of age when, according to Piaget, the child begins to realize that words refer to classes of objects or events that have certain key defining characteristics. Humor in this stage involves the violation of one or more attributes of a concept rather than simply mislabeling it. For example, instead of simply finding it funny to call a cat a dog, a child at this stage might find humor in imagining or seeing a picture of a cat with more than one head that says "moo" instead of "meow."

More recently, however, Johnson and Mervis (1997) questioned the cognitive basis of the transition from stage two to stage three. They pointed out that the Piagetian idea of a transition from "preconcepts" to "true concepts" at this age has not held up well in the research on children's early conceptual development. Instead, infants' prelinguistic categories have been shown to be based on the same principles as the categories of adults. These authors suggested that the transition from stage two to stage three in McGhee's model may simply reflect a change in what children tend to talk about. Children first learn names for objects, allowing them to create stage-two humor involving mislabeling of objects. Later, they begin learning words for the attributes of objects, leading to the enjoyment of stage-three humor involving incongruous attributes.

During this time, children also develop more complex syntactic abilities, enabling them to engage in various types of language play, including repetitious rhyming of words and the creation of nonsense words (e.g., "ringo, dingo, bingo"). Children at this age also begin to enjoy simple riddles, although those they typically tell may be best described as "preriddles," since they follow the structure of riddles without involving the play on words or concepts found in the true riddles enjoyed at a later stage (Yalisove, 1978).

McGhee's fourth and final stage of humor development, called *multiple meanings*, begins around seven years of age, when children progress from the preoperational to the concrete operations stage in Piaget's theory of cognitive development (Piaget, 1970). Children in the concrete operations stage are able to manipulate schemas in their minds, imagining the effects of various actions on objects (i.e., "operations") without having to carry them out behaviorally. They are also able to understand conservation, recognizing that physical matter does not magically appear or disappear despite changes in form. In addition, they are able to carry out reversibility of thinking, or the recognition that operations can be reversed so that their effects are nullified. Children at this stage also become less egocentric, and begin to be able to recognize that other people's perspectives may be different from their own. All of these cognitive abilities contribute to their ability to appreciate more sophisticated kinds of humor that play with reality in more complex ways.

With regard to linguistic abilities, children at this stage begin to recognize the ambiguity inherent in language at various levels, including phonology, morphology, semantics, and syntax (Shultz and Pilon, 1973; Shultz and Robillard, 1980). They are therefore able to enjoy the play on words and double meanings that are an important component of many jokes and riddles (Whitt and Prentice, 1977; Yalisove, 1978). For example, children at this age would be able to understand the double meaning involved in the following riddle (McGhee, 1979, p. 77):

> "Why did the old man tiptoe past the medicine cabinet?"
> "Because he didn't want to wake up the sleeping pills."

In addition to understanding puns and other jokes based on double meanings and language play, children at this age are able to understand other kinds of abstract humor based on logical inconsistencies and requiring inferential thinking. Several studies by McGhee (1971a, 1971b) showed that preoperational children had difficulty understanding the meaning of various jokes and cartoons containing abstract incongruities, whereas those who had achieved concrete operations demonstrated better comprehension.

McGhee (1979) viewed stage four humor as the final stage in humor development, noting that this type of humor continues to be enjoyed into adolescence and adulthood. However, we might speculate that some further development takes place with the onset of Piaget's formal operations stage beginning in early adolescence (Piaget, 1970). In this stage, the individual's thinking becomes more abstract and is governed more by logical principles than by perceptions and experiences. Individuals at this age have a more flexible, critical, and abstract view of the world. They are able to mentally manipulate more than two categories of variables at the same time, to detect logical inconsistencies in a set of statements, to hypothesize logical sequences of actions, and to anticipate future consequences of actions. All of these cognitive capacities no doubt enable the individual to play with ideas and concepts at a more abstract level than is possible in the concrete operations stage (Führ, 2001).

For example, individuals at this stage might begin to enjoy existential jokes about the meaning of life, as well as jokes that play with traditional joke structures and forms. In one study in which children were asked to produce their favorite riddle (Yalisove, 1978), those in grades two to seven tended to provide riddles based on language ambiguity (e.g., "Why do birds fly south? It's too far to walk"), whereas by grade ten they were more likely to give absurdity-based riddles (e.g., "How can you fit six elephants into a Volkswagen Beetle? Three in the front and three in the back"). Overall, then, the cognitive development of humor may be viewed as the development of more sophisticated mental structures and cognitive abilities with which the individual is able to engage in the perception and creation of playful incongruities.

The Role of Incongruity and Resolution in Children's Humor

Thomas Shultz and his colleagues at McGill University in Montreal conducted a number of early studies on the relationship between cognitive development and humor appreciation (for a review, see Shultz, 1976). They based their research on the incongruity-resolution theory of humor (discussed in Chapter 3), which proposes that humor is composed of an incongruity that can be resolved in some way. This model of humor is best illustrated by jokes, in which an incongruity in the punch line is typically resolved by reinterpreting some ambiguous information in the joke setup. These researchers were particularly interested in the relative contribution of incongruity and resolution to humor appreciation in children at different stages of cognitive development.

In one study, Shultz and Horibe (1974) presented children in grades one to seven with a series of intact and modified jokes. In some of the modified jokes, the incongruity was removed, and in others the incongruity remained but the resolution was removed. For example, one of the original jokes was the following:

> Woman: Call me a cab.
> Man: You're a cab.
> The resolution-removed version of this joke was:
> Woman: Call a cab for me.
> Man: You're a cab.
> The incongruity-removed version was:
> Woman: Call me a cab.
> Man: Yes, ma'am.

The results of this study showed that, for children in grades three to seven, the original jokes were perceived to be funnier than the resolution-removed jokes, which in turn were funnier than the incongruity-removed jokes. However, for children in grade one, there was no difference in perceived funniness between the original and resolution-removed jokes, whereas both were funnier than the incongruity-removed jokes. These results were interpreted as indicating that younger children find humor in incongruity alone and do not require the incongruity to be resolved. Beginning sometime between grades one and three, and presumably continuing into adulthood, resolution of the incongruity becomes important for humor appreciation. This conclusion was further supported by the fact that, when asked to explain the meaning of the original jokes, children in grade one had great difficulty in comprehending joke resolutions, particularly in identifying the hidden meaning of the ambiguity in the joke setup.

The authors noted that the transition from enjoyment of incongruity alone to resolvable incongruity seems to occur at about the same age when children typically progress from the preoperational to the concrete operational stage of cognitive development, suggesting that the increased mental abilities of this later stage may be necessary for the child to appreciate and enjoy the resolution components of humor. Thus, this transition from incongruity-only humor to incongruity-resolution humor corresponds to the beginning of McGhee's fourth stage of humor development. The conclusions drawn from this study were further supported by similar findings in another study by Shultz (1974a) using humorous riddles instead of jokes.

A subsequent study at the University of Oregon by Diana Pien and Mary Rothbart (1976), however, cast some doubt on Shultz's conclusions. These researchers pointed out that the types of jokes used in these studies were based on linguistic ambiguities that may have been too difficult for six-year-old children to understand. The failure to appreciate resolution at this age may therefore simply have been due to comprehension difficulties with the particular stimuli used, rather than a reduced importance of resolution in humor generally. Indeed, these authors demonstrated that, when simpler jokes and cartoons were used as stimuli, four- and five-year-old children were able to understand resolution of incongruity and showed a preference for jokes containing resolution rather than incongruity alone (see also similar findings by A. J. Klein, 1985).

Pien and Rothbart reasoned that these findings were inconsistent with Shultz's view that children progress from a stage of enjoying incongruity alone to the enjoyment of incongruity plus resolution. They argued instead that incongruity with or without resolution may be perceived as humorous at all ages from infancy to adulthood. This view seems to be consistent with more recent research findings. As noted earlier, the "peek-a-boo" study by Parrott and Gleitman (1989) that included "trick" trials suggested that some degree of resolution may be important for humor even in infancy. On the other hand, Ruch's factor-analytic studies of jokes and cartoons that were discussed in Chapter 7 (e.g., Ruch and Hehl, 1998) indicate that adults also can enjoy humor containing incongruity without resolution (i.e., nonsense humor). Thus, the presence or absence of resolution does not seem to be an important factor in humor development, but instead characterizes two different kinds of humor across the lifespan.

Moreover, as Bernard Lefort (1992) pointed out, jokes, riddles, and cartoons are particular narrative forms that are communicated in a social context as a sort of game between the teller and the listener. What Shultz called *resolution* may be better viewed as a particular class of techniques used in these forms of verbal humor to simultaneously activate incongruous multiple schemas (see also Attardo, 1997). In other forms of humor, such as spontaneous witticisms, these techniques may not be as necessary for incongruous schema activation. As they gain experience with jokes, children learn to organize their comprehension activity around this narrative framework, internalizing the traditional rules of the game. Thus, developmental research based on jokes and riddles, such as the studies by Shultz and colleagues, may tell us more about children's developing understanding of the traditional joke structure than about their experience of humor more generally.

Humor and Cognitive Mastery

McGhee's model of humor development suggests that, once children have mastered particular cognitive abilities, they soon begin to create humor by playing with these abilities in incongruous ways. As McGhee (1983a, p. 115) put it, "Once a child becomes confident of the normal relationship between stimulus elements or achieves a new level of understanding through acquisition of new cognitive skills, he/she enjoys distorting that knowledge or understanding in the guise of a joke." Evidence from a number of studies of children's humor indicates that children particularly enjoy humor that plays with concepts that they have only recently mastered, rather than those with which they are very familiar (McGhee, 1974).

In an early study of humor and cognitive development, researchers at Yale University presented cartoons to children in the second, third, fourth, and fifth grades (Zigler, Levine, and Gould, 1966). The researchers noted the degree to which the children smiled and laughed in response to the cartoons, and also asked them to explain the meaning of each cartoon. Not surprisingly, the children showed an increasing comprehension of the cartoons across the four grades, with fifth-grade children exhibiting the greatest understanding of the humor. However, the pattern of smiling and laughter in response to the cartoons did not follow the same pattern. The frequency of smiling and laughing increased from the second to the fourth grades, paralleling the children's increasing comprehension, but in the fifth grade there was a steep drop to the level shown by children in the second grade. Thus, although they understood the humor better, fifth-grade children did not find it nearly as funny as did those in preceding grades. At this age, the cartoons seemed to be too simple and therefore no longer amusing.

The authors proposed a "cognitive congruency" hypothesis to explain these findings, suggesting an inverted-U relationship between cognitive difficulty and enjoyment of humor. Cartoons that make too great a cognitive demand on a child are not understood and are therefore not enjoyed, but those that make too little demand are not found to be funny, even though they may be understood. Thus, humorous stimuli are enjoyed if they are congruent with the complexity of the child's cognitive schemas. Further support for this hypothesis was found in a subsequent study by the same authors in which cartoons with different levels of difficulty were administered to children at three different grade levels (Zigler et al., 1967). Children at each grade level preferred cartoons with an intermediate level of difficulty, and this optimal difficulty level increased across the three grades.

Two experiments conducted by McGhee (1976) provided additional support for this hypothesis. In the first study, children of varying ages were first assessed for their ability to understand conservation of mass using standardized tests. Conservation of mass refers to the recognition that objects, such as a piece of modeling clay, retain the same mass even when they change shape. The children were then presented with a series of jokes that were based on a humorous violation of conservation concepts. The following is an example of such jokes:

> Mr. Jones went into a restaurant and ordered a whole pizza for dinner. When the waiter asked him if he wanted it cut into six or eight pieces, Mr. Jones said: "Oh, you'd better make it six! I could never eat eight!"

Analyses of the participants' funniness ratings of the jokes revealed a significant curvilinear effect, with the highest ratings being given by children who had just recently acquired conservation skills, and lower ratings given both by those who had not yet achieved conservation and by older children who had presumably attained these skills several years earlier. A similar inverted-U pattern of results was obtained in the second study, in which children were first tested for their understanding of the Piagetian concept of class inclusion (the ability to recognize that an object can be a member of more than one class at the same time), and were then presented with jokes that involved a violation of this principle. Again, the jokes were rated as most funny by the children who had just recently mastered the concept that was violated in the jokes.

McGhee interpreted these findings as supportive of the cognitive congruency hypothesis, suggesting that children derive the greatest pleasure from humor that presents an optimal level of challenge to their cognitive structures. Humor that is too difficult or too easy to understand is not enjoyed as much. The cognitive congruency hypothesis was also supported by several studies examining associations between children's cognitive development and their comprehension and enjoyment of humorous riddles (Park, 1977; Prentice and Fathman, 1975; Whitt and Prentice, 1977; Yalisove, 1978).

Cognitive Development of Irony and Sarcasm

Most of the early empirical research on cognitive aspects of humor development focused on children's comprehension and appreciation of "canned" forms of humor, such as jokes, cartoons, and riddles. As I have noted in earlier chapters, these types of humor are context-free and portable, and are therefore quite easy to study in the laboratory. However, they represent only a small part of the humor encountered by children (as well as adults) in everyday life (Bergen, 1998b; R. A. Martin and Kuiper, 1999). Most humor in childhood arises from spontaneous verbal and nonverbal behaviors during playful social interactions, such as wordplay, silly gestures and actions, incongruous fantasy play, teasing, irony, sarcasm, and practical jokes (Bergen, 1998a; Fabrizi and Pollio, 1987b; McGhee, 1980b). Investigation of these kinds of naturally occurring humor poses greater challenges to researchers, since they depend more on the constantly changing social context. Nonetheless, in recent years there has been some research on the development of children's comprehension of certain types of conversational humor, particularly irony and sarcasm (see Creusere, 1999, for a review). This cognitive developmental research parallels the psycholinguistic research on irony and sarcasm in adults that was discussed in Chapter 4.

As noted in Chapter 4, irony is a humorous figure of speech that is used to communicate indirectly a message that is the opposite of the literal meaning of a sentence. For example, someone who says "What a beautiful day!" when the weather is cold and stormy actually intends to communicate "What an awful day." Irony is also closely related to sarcasm, which depends for its effect on "bitter, caustic, and other ironic language that is usually directed against an individual" (Gibbs, 1986, p. 3). For example, if someone says "You're so graceful" in response to someone tripping and falling, this is an ironic statement that may also be sarcastic. On the other hand, irony can also be used in making indirect compliments as well as criticisms. For example, a high-achieving student who receives an A on a test might be told by a classmate, "You'd better work harder next time!"

To understand and appreciate irony and sarcasm, children must develop the ability to make several complex linguistic and social inferences. First, they need to recognize that the intended meaning of the ironic statement is not the surface meaning, and therefore they must learn to substitute the true meaning for the literal meaning. In addition, they need to recognize the pragmatic (i.e., social and communicative) functions of irony in speech. Two such functions have been identified by researchers. First, irony is used to tinge or mute the implied criticism or praise, making the criticism less negative and the compliment less positive than they would be using literal language. Second, irony is used to convey humor, based on the incongruity between the literal and implied meanings, and is therefore meant to be funny (Dews et al., 1995). Developmental researchers have investigated how children develop an understanding of these different aspects of irony.

A number of studies have shown that the ability to understand the intended meaning of ironic statements does not develop in children until about age six (e.g., Creusere, 2000; de Groot et al., 1995; Winner et al., 1987). This comprehension ability appears to depend on the development of a "theory of mind," or the ability to infer a speaker's beliefs or intentions. In particular, to understand that a statement is meant to be ironic, one needs to infer not only what the speaker actually intends, but also that the speaker believes that the listener understands this implied meaning as well. Failure to make these inferences will lead to a misinterpretation of the irony as either a literally true statement or a lie.

Kate Sullivan and her colleagues at the University of Massachusetts (Sullivan, Winner, and Hopfield, 1995) found that children between five and eight years of age were only able to distinguish between a lie and a humorous false statement in a story if they had already developed the theory-of-mind ability to attribute second-order ignorance (i.e., recognizing that one person in a story does not know what another person knows). Interestingly, without this ability, even the presence of different vocal intonations in lies versus jokes did not enable children to recognize that a joke was not intended as a lie. However, the more difficult theory-of-mind ability to attribute second-order false belief (i.e., recognizing that one person in a story misperceives what another person is thinking) was not needed for children to be able to distinguish between a lie and a joke, indicating that only some aspects of a theory of mind are necessary for irony comprehension (see also Winner and Leekam, 1991).

Other research has investigated the development of children's comprehension of the pragmatic functions of irony. Shelly Dews and her colleagues (1996) at Boston College conducted two studies to investigate children's understanding of the muting function and humorous nature of ironic insults. In the first study, they presented groups of five- and six-year-olds, eight- and nine-year-olds, and college students with brief clips from television cartoons containing instances of ironic criticism, literal criticism, and literal compliments. The participants were tested for their understanding of the intended meanings of the statements, and were asked to rate them for meanness and funniness.

Consistent with other research, children's ability to understanding the implied meaning of the ironic criticisms was found to emerge between five and six years of age. Interestingly, the results also showed that, as soon as they were able to understand the meaning of ironic criticism, children recognized that it was less mean or insulting than literal criticism, indicating an understanding of the muting function of irony. However, an understanding of the humorous nature of irony apparently does not develop until some time later. It was not until the eight- to nine-year-old age range that children began to perceive ironic insults as being funnier than literal ones. In turn, the college students gave even higher funniness ratings to the ironic insults, suggesting that a full appreciation of the humorous aspects of irony may not develop until adolescence or early adulthood.

The second study extended these findings by manipulating the degree to which ironic criticisms were subtle or obvious, and the degree to which they were presented in a deadpan or sarcastic tone of voice. The results showed that, at all ages, more subtle forms of indirect irony are considered more insulting than are more obvious and direct forms. However, adults find the subtler forms of irony funnier, while children find the more obvious forms funnier. Thus, the appreciation that a meaner remark can also be funnier appears to develop with age. The perceived meanness and funniness of the ironic insults were also influenced by voice intonation. At all ages, a sincere or deadpan intonation made the irony seem less insulting and funnier than did a sarcastic intonation. A sarcastic tone of voice seems to convey annoyance, whereas a deadpan or sincere intonation signals playfulness and humor.

More recently, Melanie Harris and Penny Pexman (2003), at the University of Calgary, investigated the development of children's understanding of the social functions of ironic compliments as well as criticisms. Children ages five to eight were presented with puppet shows depicting ironic and literal criticisms and compliments. The results with ironic and literal criticisms generally replicated the findings of Dews et al. (1996), indicating that children recognize the muting function of ironic criticism as soon as they begin understanding the implied meaning, but the recognition of humor in ironic criticism does not begin until some time later. Indeed, even the older children in this sample did not perceive the ironic criticism to be funny.

With regard to ironic compliments, the results revealed that only a minority of children correctly interpreted the implied meaning, and the proportion of correct responses did not increase between ages five and eight. Thus, comprehension of ironic compliments seems to develop at a later age than comprehension of ironic criticisms. One possible explanation for this finding is that children may be more likely to encounter sarcasm than ironic compliments in their daily lives. Alternatively, it may be because ironic compliments involve a double negation, which is likely more difficult to understand.

In addition, this study revealed that children rated ironic compliments as less nice than literal compliments as soon as they were able to understand them, indicating that, as with ironic criticism, the muting function of irony is recognized early on. However, across all the age groups, there were no differences in the funniness ratings of ironic and literal compliments, both of which were rated as being serious, indicating that the humorous aspects of ironic compliments are not appreciated by children in this age range. Further research with children older than eight years of age is needed to determine the age at which children begin to perceive humor in this form of irony.

In summary, by investigating the development of children's comprehension of the meaning and pragmatic functions of irony and sarcasm, researchers are beginning to extend the study of cognitive aspects of humor development beyond canned jokes, cartoons, and riddles, and into conversational forms of humor that frequently occur in everyday interactions with others. These types of humor depend more on the social context, and require an understanding of a variety of linguistic and social factors such as speaker intentions, theory of mind, vocal intonation, and so on. In addition to irony and sarcasm, further research is needed to explore the development of children's ability to understand and appreciate other forms of verbal and nonverbal interpersonal humor. As well as furthering our understanding of children's humor development, research in this area may yield interesting insights into the development of social cognition more generally.

HUMOR AS EMOTIONAL COPING

Besides the cognitive aspects of humor, a number of developmental researchers have suggested that humor serves as a method for children to cope with emotionally arousing and threatening topics. By joking and laughing about issues that normally arouse feelings of anxiety and tension, children are able to feel less threatened and gain a sense of mastery. As we have seen, Freud (1960 [1905]) suggested that jokes are a way of expressing taboo topics relating to sex and aggression in a socially acceptable manner, allowing the individual to release feelings of anxiety associated with these topics. Similarly, Levine (1977) extended the idea of humor as a form of cognitive mastery (discussed earlier) to suggest that humor and laughter are a way of asserting mastery in emotional and interpersonal, as well as cognitive, domains.

In her psychoanalytically-based case studies of humor in children, Wolfenstein (1954) noted that much of children's humor relates to potentially painful, anxiety-arousing, or guilt-inducing topics such as death, violence, destruction, punishment, illness, bodily functions, sexuality, and stupidity. By engaging in the playful fantasy of humor, the child is able to transform a threatening situation into something to be laughed at and enjoyed. Writing about play more generally, Sutton-Smith (2003) suggested that "play can be defined as behavioral parody of emotional vulnerability because it both mimics and inverts the primary emotions ironically" (p. 13). The essential function of play, he suggested, "is to make fun of the emotional vulnerabilities of anger, fear, shock, disgust, loneliness, and narcissism" (p. 13). Humor, as a form of mental play, presumably serves these functions as well.

Loeb and Wood (1986) outlined a developmental model of humor based on Erikson's eight stages of psychosocial development, suggesting that humor may be one method of dealing with conflicts arising from the successive developmental crises of trust versus mistrust, autonomy versus shame, initiative versus guilt, industry versus inferiority, and so on. Similarly, Paul McGhee (1979) noted that the topics that children are most likely to make jokes and laugh about at different ages are ones that are commonly associated with tensions, conflicts, and anxieties at each stage of development. For young children going through the trials and tribulations of toilet training, when toilet-related activities and accidents increasingly become sources of emotional tension, a great deal of laughter is generated by scatological humor relating to defecation, urination, flatulence, and so on. The mere repetition of toilet-related words ("poo-poo," "pee-pee," "fart") is enough to produce howls of laughter.

As preschoolers become aware of and concerned about physical differences between the sexes, this also becomes a topic for joking. Continuing feelings of conflict and tension about sexual activity throughout childhood and into adulthood contribute to the ongoing popularity of sexual jokes. The strong emphasis placed on intellectual achievement and rationality during the school years also produces anxieties about intellectual performance, leading to a great deal of joking about stupidity and irrational behavior. The use of humor to cope with potentially threatening topics is also seen in the popularity among children and adolescents of "sick" jokes, "dead baby" jokes, and "disgusting" or "gross-out" humor in movies and television programs depicting flatulence, projectile vomiting, and other bodily functions (Herzog and Bush, 1994; Herzog and Karafa, 1998; Oppliger and Zillmann, 1997).

Although a considerable amount of research has examined the role of humor in coping in adults (which I will discuss in Chapter 9), empirical research on children's use of humor in emotional coping is unfortunately very limited (R. A. Martin, 1989).

Danish psychologist Martin Führ (2002) administered the Coping Humor Scale (CHS) along with a questionnaire about the uses of humor in coping to 960 children between the ages of 10 and 16 years. Factor analyses revealed three factors: (1) the use of humor to cope with uncertainty and stress; (2) aggressive humor making fun of others; and (3) humor as a means of improving one's mood. Boys were found to use more aggressive forms of humor in coping, whereas girls were more likely to report using humor as a mood booster. The use of humor for coping with uncertainty and stress increased with age for both boys and girls. With increasing age, girls were more likely to report using humor as a mood booster, whereas boys' reported use of this function of humor decreased slightly. Further research is needed to examine the effectiveness of different types of humor in coping with various sources of emotional distress, as well as developmental changes in the use of humor for coping beginning earlier in childhood.

INTERPERSONAL ASPECTS OF HUMOR IN CHILDREN

As we have seen, humor and laughter are essentially social phenomena. Infants begin to laugh in the context of interactions with their caregivers, and most of the laughter of preschool children occurs when they are with other children or adults. The predominantly interpersonal nature of humor is also apparent as children progress through the elementary and high school years. Besides being a form of play, humor is an important aspect of interpersonal interaction and communication, serving a variety of social functions (Chapman, Smith, and Foot, 1980). As noted in Chapter 5, the inherent incongruity and ambiguity of humor makes it useful for communicating messages and influencing others in situations in which a more direct, serious mode of communication might be problematic for a variety of reasons.

Simons and colleagues discussed a number of possible functions of humor in children's social interactions from infancy through adolescence (Simons, McCluskey-Fawcett, and Papini, 1986). In infants, humorous interactions with parents may play a role in the development of attachment relationships, which have been shown to be very important for later social and emotional development (Ainsworth, Bell, and Stayton, 1991). Humor may be one way of coping with separation anxiety and asserting oneself during the process of gaining greater autonomy during toddlerhood. During middle childhood, it may be important for socialization, establishing and maintaining peer groups, communicating and enforcing norms, and influencing social status within groups. These functions continue into adolescence, where humor also becomes important in negotiating sexual relationships. These ideas remain largely speculative at present, however, as little research has been conducted on the social functions of humor in children or the way these functions develop through childhood and adolescence. Much of the early research on social aspects of humor focused on how the presence of other children influences a child's perceptions of humor. More recently, research on teasing has begun to address the social aspects of aggressive types of humor. These research topics are discussed in the following sections.

Social Influences on Humor Appreciation and Laughter

A considerable amount of research has shown that the amount of laughter that children display in response to humor is influenced by various aspects of the social situation. For example, the effects of modeling on children's laughter were demonstrated by an experiment that found that preschool children laughed much more frequently while listening to a humorous audiotape after they had observed another child laughing at the same tape as compared to a condition in which the other child did not laugh at the tape (G. E. Brown, Wheeler, and Cash, 1980).

In a series of experiments during the 1970s, Antony Chapman, at the University of Wales, examined the effects of social context on humorous laughter in children (for a review of this research, see Chapman, 1983). In one study (Chapman, 1973b), seven-year-old children listened to a humorous audiotape on headphones either by themselves ("alone" condition), with a nonlistening companion of the same age and sex ("audience" condition), or with another child who was also listening to the same tape ("coaction" condition). The participants in the coaction condition laughed and smiled more frequently and rated the tape as funnier than did those in the audience condition, who in turn displayed more mirth and higher funniness ratings than did those in the alone condition. These results indicate that the perception and enjoyment of humor are facilitated by the mere presence of another person, and even more so when the other person also shares the humor experience.

A subsequent study showed that the amount of laughter exhibited by children while listening to a humorous audiotape was directly related to the frequency of laughter in a companion (Chapman and Wright, 1976). Other experiments revealed that children laughed and smiled more frequently at the tape when they were sitting closer to the companion (Chapman, 1975a) and when they were sitting face-to-face with the companion rather than back-to-back (Chapman, 1976). Another experiment showed that children in small groups laugh and smile more at a humorous audiotape when their companions look at them while laughing as compared to when they look at someone else (Chapman, 1975b). These studies provide further evidence that laughter is primarily a form of social communication, and that sharing the social situation with others facilitates the enjoyment of humor.

Teasing Among Children

Children become aware of the aggressive uses of humor at an early age. As early as age three, the presence of aggressive verbal and nonverbal behavior is a potent factor in determining children's perceptions of humor (Sinnott and Ross, 1976), and aggression continues to be an important determinant of humor preferences throughout childhood (Pinderhughes and Zigler, 1985). For example, by age three, boys show a preference for humor that disparages girls rather than boys (McGhee and Lloyd, 1981). As soon as children begin to develop a strong positive sense of racial-ethnic identity between three and six years of age, they begin to enjoy humor that disparages members of other racial-ethnic groups (McGhee and Duffey, 1983). Children also learn at an early age about the coercive effects of humorous ridicule. By six years of age, children will avoid behaviors for which they have observed others being ridiculed in a humorous way (Bryant et al., 1983).

Teasing is an aggressive form of humor that occurs frequently in childhood. According to Shapiro, Baumeister, and Kessler (1991), teasing comprises three components: aggression, humor, and ambiguity (see also Keltner et al., 2001). As noted in Chapter 5, the humorous and ambiguous nature of teasing allows the source to say things that would be face-threatening and potentially unacceptable if communicated in a serious mode, since the source can always say "I was just joking" if the communication is not well received by the target. The aggressive and humorous elements of teasing may be combined in different proportions. When the aggressive component predominates, teasing is perceived as more hostile and hurtful, whereas teasing containing greater humor may be perceived as benign and enjoyed by the target as well as the source.

Jeremy Shapiro and colleagues (1991), at the Child Guidance Center in Cleveland, asked children in grades three, five, and eight to describe their experiences of teasing and being teased. The most commonly reported forms of teasing were making fun of an attribute or behavior of the target (28 percent), calling the target humorous names (25 percent), and simply laughing at the target (11 percent). The most common topics of teasing were physical appearance (especially being fat), intellectual performance (especially stupidity, but also being too smart in school), and physical performance. The most common reasons given for teasing were retaliation (i.e., teasing in response to someone else's teasing) and playing or joking around. In addition, 51 percent of the participants identified aggressive bullies as the most frequent teasers, whereas 23 percent identified popular, funny, lively children. The most frequent targets of teasing were timid, physically small "losers," unpopular children, overweight children, and children with lower intelligence. Thus, teasing seems to be carried out by socially dominant children against those with less social status who do not conform to group norms. Overall, teasing seems to be a way of asserting and maintaining status within the peer group as well as censuring behaviors in others that violate group norms.

A limited amount of research has examined developmental changes in the content and form of teasing in childhood. Given the function of teasing as a way of enforcing social norms, it is not surprising that developmental changes in teasing tend to parallel changes in the types of norms that are most relevant at different ages, such as possessiveness and aggression during the preschool years, associations with members of the opposite sex during elementary school, fashion-related and dating behavior in puberty, and behaviors related to experimentation with sex and drug use during adolescence and early adulthood (Keltner et al., 2001; Warm, 1997).

The style of teasing also changes over the course of development. In particular, teasing tends to become less blatantly aggressive, more humorous and playful, and more subtle as individuals move from late childhood into adolescence (Keltner et al., 2001; Warm, 1997). These changes may be partly related to developments in the comprehension of irony and sarcasm discussed earlier. As we saw, recognition of the humorous aspects of ironic language does not develop until late childhood and adolescence, even though the potential for using irony to convey indirect criticism is recognized by age six. Younger children are therefore less able to employ playful language cues such as the use of irony to mitigate the hostility of their teasing. As a result, younger children's teasing tends to be more overtly hostile, hurtful, and insulting. Any humor that is involved is often meant for the benefit of the witnesses at the expense of the recipient (Scambler, Harris, and Milich, 1998).

These developmental changes in the style of teasing are also reflected in children's perceptions of the functions and effects of teasing. Although children of all ages emphasize the hurtful nature of teasing, older children and adolescents begin to recognize that it can sometimes also have positive functions and outcomes, such as pointing out undesirable behaviors in a playful way and indirectly communicating acceptance and friendship (Shapiro et al., 1991; Warm, 1997).

Some researchers have investigated how children respond to teasing and have attempted to identify the types of responses that might be most effective. In the survey by Shapiro et al. (1991), the most common response to teasing reported by children was reciprocating teasing with a verbal comeback or teasing of their own (39 percent), followed by ignoring the teasing (24 percent), laughing along (12 percent), fighting (10 percent), and reporting the teasing to an authority figure (4 percent). When teachers were asked what they considered to be the most effective response to teasing, 91 percent recommended simply ignoring the teaser.

Douglas Scambler and colleagues (1998), at the University of Kentucky, conducted an experiment in which they showed children between the ages of 8 and 11 one of three versions of a videotape in which a child responded in different ways to being teased by other children: (1) ignoring; (2) an angry, hostile response; and (3) a humorous response. The participants rated the humorous response as most likely to be effective, followed by ignoring, with the hostile response being rated as least effective. Interestingly, the humorous response produced more positive evaluations of the teaser as well as the recipient of the teasing. Thus, responding with humor may be even more effective than ignoring, as it might defuse the conflict situation and potentially turn it into a prosocial interaction. The authors suggested that children who are frequent targets of teasing should be taught to practice lighthearted, humorous responses to use in such situations. Similar results were obtained in a subsequent experiment by Robin Lightner and colleagues that looked at empathic responding as well as ignoring, humorous, and hostile reactions to teasing (Lightner et al., 2000).

Further research is needed to examine actual interactions, instead of artificial scenarios, to capture the emotional elements in teasing situations and examine the effectiveness of various responses with different types of teasing among children of different ages and personality characteristics.

INDIVIDUAL DIFFERENCES IN CHILDREN'S SENSE OF HUMOR

So far in this chapter I have been discussing developmental changes in humor that are characteristic of most children. However, children do not all develop a sense of humor to the same degree; the individual differences in humor that we discussed in the previous chapter begin to emerge in early childhood. Besides studying normative trends in humor development, researchers have therefore also investigated the ways children at a given age differ from one another in the degree to which they initiate and appreciate humor. Why do some children more than others develop a tendency to laugh easily and frequently, a heightened enjoyment of humor, or an ability to tell jokes and make others laugh? To what extent do genetic and environmental factors influence the development of a sense of humor? How do parental behaviors and the family environment contribute to humor development in children? What other personality characteristics and behaviors are associated with a sense of humor in children at various ages? These are some of the sorts of questions regarding individual differences in children's humor that researchers have sought to answer.

As we saw in Chapter 7, sense of humor is not a unitary concept. Individual differences in sense of humor can be conceptualized and measured in many different ways, including differences in the frequency of laughter, ability to comprehend humor, appreciation of various kinds of humorous stimuli, tendency to initiate humor and make others laugh, and so on. These different definitions of sense of humor are reflected in the various measurement approaches taken by different researchers in studying individual differences in children's humor as well. Research findings that relate to the development of one of these components of sense of humor do not necessarily apply to others.

Genetic Factors in Sense of Humor

In recent decades, numerous twin studies have provided evidence that genetic factors play a substantial role in individual differences in temperament and personality generally (Rowe, 1997). The general strategy in this research involves comparing the correlations on a particular personality trait between pairs of monozygotic (i.e., identical) and dizygotic (i.e., fraternal) twins. A genetic contribution to the trait is indicated when higher correlations are found in identical as compared to fraternal twin pairs. Using multivariate statistical modeling procedures, the relative contribution of genetic as well as shared and nonshared environmental influences can be estimated. Shared environmental influences are those that are experienced similarly by both members of a twin pair, such as the general family environment, whereas nonshared influences have to do with experiences that differ between a pair of twins both within and outside the family. A few of these types of studies have been conducted to examine the degree to which genetic and environmental factors may contribute to the development of various aspects of the sense of humor.

David Nias and Glenn Wilson (1977), at the Institute of Psychiatry in London, used the classic twin study methodology to investigate individual differences in humor appreciation in 100 pairs of young adult identical and fraternal twins. The participants were asked to rate the funniness of 48 cartoons that had been classified as nonsense, satirical, aggressive, or sexual. The correlations between the pairs of twins for each category of humor averaged about .45, but did not differ between the fraternal and identical twins, indicating that individual differences in the appreciation of these humor categories do not appear to have a genetic basis. On the other hand, the sizable magnitude of the average correlations indicated that environmental influences shared by both members of a pair play a fairly substantial role in the development of their humor preferences. Thus, shared environmental influences, such as the effects of being raised within a particular family, appear to play a more important role than genetic factors in determining the degree to which individuals enjoy particular types of humor. A subsequent more detailed analysis of the same data led to similar conclusions (G. D. Wilson, Rust, and Kasriel, 1977).

In a more recent twin study by Lynn Cherkas and colleagues at St. Thomas Hospital in London, 127 pairs of female twins (71 monozygotic and 56 dizygotic) ages 20 to 75 were asked to rate the funniness of five *Far Side* cartoons by Gary Larson (Cherkas et al., 2000). As we saw in the last chapter, these rather bizarre, "off-the-wall" cartoons have been found in previous research to load on Ruch's (1992) nonsense factor of humor appreciation, as opposed to the incongruity-resolution factor. The results replicated the earlier findings of Nias and Wilson (1977). Whereas significant correlations were found between the pairs of twins on the funniness ratings of each of the five cartoons, these correlations did not differ between the fraternal and identical twins, indicating no genetic contribution to individual differences in the enjoyment of these cartoons. Multivariate model-fitting analyses confirmed that the data were best explained by a model that allowed for the contribution of both shared and nonshared environmental factors, but not genetic effects. Thus, this study provided further evidence that a sense of humor, when defined as the appreciation of particular types of humor, develops primarily as a result of environmental influences both within and outside the family of origin.

Besides the humor appreciation approach, another way of thinking about the sense of humor construct is to view it as a temperament-based affective trait. As we saw in Chapter 7, Willibald Ruch and his colleagues have proposed that individual differences in humor may be conceptualized in terms of temperamental differences in cheerfulness (e.g., Ruch and Köhler, 1998). Temperament refers to relatively stable characteristics of response to the environment, such as activity level, sociability, and emotionality, which are observed in infants as early as the first months of life (A. H. Buss and Plomin, 1984). To explore possible genetic and environmental factors in temperament, researchers at the University of Wisconsin (Goldsmith et al., 1999) conducted a study of 302 pairs of 3- to 16-month-old infant twins (121 identical and 181 fraternal). Several dimensions of temperament were assessed by means of maternal ratings on a standardized questionnaire, as well as laboratory observations. Factor analysis of the temperament variables revealed two main factors: (1) positive affectivity, composed of frequency of smiling and laughter, duration of orienting, and soothability; and (2) negative affectivity, composed of distress in response to limitations and novelty, and activity level. The positive affectivity factor seems to be most relevant to Ruch's concept of trait cheerfulness and sense of humor in general, whereas negative affectivity likely corresponds to neuroticism and Ruch's concept of trait bad mood.

Multivariate model-fitting analyses revealed that positive affectivity was best explained by a model that included additive genetic (40 percent), shared environmental (34 percent), and nonshared environmental effects (25 percent). Very similar results were obtained when the frequency of smiling and laughter was analyzed separately. Thus, the degree to which an infant tends to respond with smiling and laughter, as well as his or her overall positive emotionality, appears to be influenced by both genetic and environmental factors. Of particular interest here is the finding of a shared environmental component, indicating that children's positive affectivity is partly influenced by factors that are common to children within the same family, such as maternal personality or attachment security. Similar findings of shared environmental effects on positive emotionality have been found in other twin studies of infants, preschoolers, and adults (Goldsmith, Buss, and Lemery, 1997; Tellegen et al., 1988).

On the other hand, the analyses revealed that negative affectivity was best explained by a model containing only additive genetic (64 percent) and nonshared environmental effects (36 percent). Thus, negative emotionality also appears to be influenced by both genetic and environmental factors. However, the environmental influences in this case are not those that are shared by all children within the same family, but instead have to do with ways in which children in the same family may have different experiences. In summary, this study indicates that sense of humor, when viewed as an emotional temperament trait, is influenced by both genetic and environmental factors.

In addition to research on humor appreciation and emotional temperament, two studies have investigated genetic and environmental contributions to sense of humor using self-report humor measures. In an early twin study, identical and fraternal adolescent twins were asked to rate the degree to which they felt they had a good sense of humor on a 7-point scale (Loehlin and Nichols, 1976). A significantly larger correlation was found between identical as compared to fraternal twins, suggesting a genetic contribution to individual differences in self-rated humor. A very weak correlation for fraternal twins indicated that environmental influences are of the nonshared rather than the shared variety.

The second study, described by Beth Manke (1998), at the University of Houston, examined individual differences in interpersonal humor expression in adolescents. Instead of using pairs of identical and fraternal twins, however, this study made use of pairs of adolescent siblings who had been raised in the same families but were either nonadopted (therefore sharing approximately 50 percent of their genes) or adopted at birth (therefore not sharing any genes). As in the twin studies, a larger correlation between nonadopted compared to adopted sibling pairs would indicate a genetic effect. A self-report questionnaire was used to assess the degree to which each participant typically engaged in humor and laughter (e.g., telling jokes and funny stories, laughing or joking about embarrassing or upsetting events, laughing at comedy movies and television programs) in their relationships with their mother, their sibling, and their best friend.

Multivariate model-fitting analyses revealed that a significant proportion (over 25 percent) of the variance in humor use with mothers and siblings can be attributed to genetic factors. In contrast, genetic influences were negligible for use of humor in relating to best friends. The author suggested that the lack of a genetic contribution to humor in interactions with friends may have been due to the shorter duration of these relationships. Genetic influences may become more apparent in longer-term relationships in which humor patterns have become more stabilized. In addition, the analyses revealed a sizable environmental influence on humor use with mothers, siblings, and friends (accounting for over 50 percent of the variance). These effects were of the nonshared variety, suggesting that growing up in the same family does not make siblings similar in their humor expression.

Overall, then, this research suggests that a sense of humor is a product of both genetics and environment, with the relative contributions of these two types of influence varying with different components of this trait. When sense of humor is defined in terms of the appreciation of particular types of humorous material, genetic influences appear to be negligible, and most of the variance can be attributed to both shared and unshared environmental effects. The types of things people laugh at are determined primarily by their past experiences within and outside their family of origin. When a temperament-based approach is taken, defining sense of humor in terms of positive emotionality and the tendency to laugh and smile frequently, genetic factors appear to play a more significant role, although both shared and unshared environmental influences are also important. Finally, a sizable genetic contribution, as well as nonshared environment influences, is found with self-report measures assessing overall sense of humor and the tendency to engage in humorous interactions with family members. Interestingly, there seem to be differences in the degree to which genetic factors contribute to humor expression in different relationships, with humor in relating to peers showing less genetic contribution than with family members. It is important to note that these studies allow for the estimation of the overall effects of genetic and environmental influences, but they are not able to identify the specific genes or environmental factors that are responsible for individual differences in humor. Further research is needed to address these questions.

Family Environment Factors in Sense of Humor Development

These heritability studies suggest that, although genetics play a role, environmental factors are also important in the development of most dimensions of sense of humor. One influential aspect of the environment is the family. Children likely learn to express and enjoy humor in the context of their early relationships with their parents and other family members. Two competing hypotheses have been proposed concerning the way interactions with parents may influence the development of a sense of humor, referred to as the modeling/reinforcement and the stress and coping hypotheses (Manke, 1998). According to the Modeling/Reinforcement Hypothesis, parents who enjoy humor themselves and who laugh and joke a good deal serve as humorous role models and are likely to positively reinforce their children's attempts at humor initiation, leading to greater humor and laughter in the children (McGhee, Bell, and Duffey, 1986). On the other hand, the Stress and Coping Hypothesis suggests that a sense of humor may develop in children as a way of coping with distress, conflict, and anxiety in an uncongenial family environment. For these children, humor may be a way of releasing hostile feelings or gaining attention and approval from parents who are otherwise rejecting and nonnurturing (McGhee, 1980b). There is some research evidence in support of both of these hypotheses.

Paul McGhee (1980b) described a study of nursery school and elementary school children at the Fels Research Institute in Ohio, in which observational ratings were obtained for the children's frequency of laughter and behavioral and verbal attempts to initiate humor during peer interactions in free-play sessions. Because these children were part of an ongoing longitudinal study, data were also available on a number of measures of antecedent maternal behaviors that had been assessed during their infancy and earlier childhood. In support of the stress and coping hypothesis, correlational analyses with the nursery school children revealed that those who showed greater amounts of humor tended to have mothers who babied and overprotected them but showed little affection and closeness.

Among both boys and girls at the elementary school age, greater humor expression was associated with a greater tendency of mothers to leave the children alone to solve problems on their own, even when some assistance would have been appropriate. Greater humor in elementary school girls was also related to a lack of maternal protectiveness and a home environment characterized by conflict, unpleasantness, repression, and insecurity. Thus, the development of a sense of humor in children seemed to be associated with rather uncongenial parental behaviors toward the children. No relation was found between children's humor behaviors and their mothers' own tendency to engage in humor during interactions with the child, casting doubt on the Modeling/Reinforcement Hypothesis.

Further support for the Stress and Coping Hypothesis was provided by a study of male adolescents conducted at Vanderbilt University (Prasinos and Tittler, 1981). Using a peer nomination technique, the participants were divided into humor-oriented, moderately humor-oriented, and non–humor-oriented groups. Individuals in the humor-oriented group, as compared to those in the other two groups, reported significantly less cohesion and greater conflict in their families on a family environment measure and significantly greater distance from their father in a figure-placement test.

The research by Fisher and Fisher (1981) on professional comedians and comic children, described in Chapter 7, also lends support to the Stress and Coping Hypothesis. Professional comedians described their relationships with their mothers as more negative than did noncomic entertainers. Questionnaire data also revealed that the mothers of comic children, as compared with mothers of noncomic children, were significantly less kind, less sympathetic, less close and intimately involved with their children, and more selfish and controlling, and they wanted their children to take responsibility and grow up more quickly. Taken together, these studies provide some support for the view that children may develop a sense of humor as a way of coping with feelings of anger and anxiety, and as a means of gaining attention and approval from parents who are otherwise distant and unsupportive.

On the other hand, some support for the Modeling/Reinforcement Hypothesis was found in a study by Paul McGhee and colleagues (1986) at Texas Tech University. Male and female university students and a group of elderly women completed a self-report measure of humor initiation as well as a questionnaire about their parents' tendency to engage in humor when they were growing up. Among male students, humor initiation was positively correlated with father's humor, whereas female students showed a positive correlation between laughter responsiveness and mother's humor. Among the elderly women, those with higher scores on humor initiation and laughter responsiveness reported that their mothers engaged in higher levels of joking, clowning, and playful teasing when the participants were growing up. No significant correlations were found between participants' humor scores and the modeling of humor by the opposite-sex parent. These findings suggested that the greatest early modeling influences on humor development may come from the same-sex parent. However, these findings should be viewed as rather tentative, since they were based on recall data that may be subject to memory biases.

Overall, the existing research seems to lend stronger support to the Stress and Coping Hypothesis than to the Modeling/Reinforcement Hypothesis. However, more thorough investigation is required before firm conclusions may be drawn. Most of the evidence to date is based on studies with small sample sizes, and the Modeling/Reinforcement Hypothesis in particular has not been adequately investigated. Future research should examine possible effects of family environment and parental behaviors on a broader range of aspects of children's sense of humor, and the possibility of curvilinear relationships should also be examined.

In the end, there may be some validity to both the Modeling/Reinforcement and the Stress and Coping hypotheses. Some children raised in uncongenial family environments may develop a sense of humor to cope and gain acceptance, especially if they learn that their humorous behaviors are positively reinforced by attention and approval from parents who are otherwise harsh and unaffectionate. Other children, who are raised in more secure and nurturing environments, may develop a sense of humor as a consequence of parental modeling and reinforcement. As we have seen in previous chapters, humor serves a variety of different social functions, and there are likely to be several different pathways in the development of individual differences in humor.

An additional weakness of this research is that it does not control for possible genetic confounds in the observed relations. Any associations that are found between parents' behavior and their children's later sense of humor may be due to the genes that are shared by parents and children rather than to causal effects of the parental behavior on the child's sense of humor. One way to test for this possibility is to compare the associations between family environment and children's sense of humor in adoptive and nonadoptive families. If a stronger relation is found for nonadoptive than for adoptive children, this would suggest that the effect is at least partially mediated by the greater genetic similarity between parents and nonadopted children.

This approach was taken in a study reported by Beth Manke (1998) that investigated the relation between family environment variables and interpersonal humor expression in male and female adolescents who were either raised by their biological parents or were adopted at birth. In this longitudinal study (part of which was described in the previous section), the general family environment and maternal parenting practices had been assessed when the adolescents were 9 to 11 years of age by means of questionnaires completed by the mothers. The data analyses revealed only a few significant correlations between these family environment measures and measures of interpersonal humor that were completed several years later by the adolescents. The results provided weak and somewhat contradictory support for the Stress and Coping Hypothesis.

Of particular interest to the present discussion, though, was the finding that any significant associations that did emerge occurred only with the nonadopted children and not with the adopted children. This finding suggests that associations between the family environment and children's sense of humor development may be genetically mediated, rather than being a direct causal effect. In other words, certain combinations of genes (which are passed from parents to their biological children) may contribute both to particular parenting practices and to the development of a sense of humor in children, whereas these parenting practices might not directly influence sense of humor development. These conclusions are only tentative, however, since this is the only study of this kind conducted so far, the sample size was fairly small, and the parenting behaviors were assessed only during middle childhood.

Further research along these lines is clearly needed, using a variety of approaches to measure sense of humor in children, and broader, more objective assessments of parental behaviors and family environment beginning at an earlier age in the children's development. An alternative method of controlling for the confounding effects of genetics in studying effects of parenting on children's sense of humor is the "children of twins" design, which compares parent-child associations in identical versus fraternal twins and their offspring (D'Onofrio et al., 2003).

Personality and Behavioral Correlates of Children's Sense of Humor

What other personality traits, abilities, and behaviors are associated with having a sense of humor in children? Once again, the answer depends in part on how we define sense of humor. Several studies have investigated individual differences in children's tendency to initiate humor and make other children laugh in the playground and classroom. Associations between these humor initiation measures and various other interpersonal behaviors, traits, and abilities have been examined in children of different ages. In one study of four- and five-year-old nursery school children, those who were rated by their teachers as being more likely to initiate humor in interactions with peers were found to have more advanced language skills and were rated by their mothers as having a temperament characterized by greater activity and approach, rather than social withdrawal (Carson et al., 1986).

In the longitudinal study by Paul McGhee (1980b) discussed earlier, associations were examined between children's general interpersonal behavior during free play in their preschool years and their later frequency of verbal and behavioral humor initiation and laughter with peers when they were either in nursery school or elementary school. Among nursery-school-age children, those who engaged in more frequent laughter and initiation of humor had previously been observed to engage in more frequent unprovoked verbal and physical aggression and retaliation to aggression with their peers. More humorous children also tended to be those who were taller and heavier and who had exerted more effort on mastery of gross-motor skills (which are particularly involved in physical play activities seen in the playground) and less effort on intellectual activities and mastery of fine-motor skills (which are needed for writing, art, and other academic activities observed in the classroom). In addition, while unrelated to overall intelligence, greater verbal humor initiation was observed in children who had developed better language abilities at an earlier age. Overall, these findings suggest that humorous behavior with peers in nursery school children occurs particularly in aggressive, physically large, active children with better gross-motor than fine-motor skills and precocious language development.

Similar patterns were observed with the elementary school children. Among both boys and girls, those who engaged in greater amounts of verbal and nonverbal humor initiation and who were rated by observers as having a greater sense of humor tended to be those who had previously been rated as being more physically and verbally aggressive, more dominant, and exerting more effort on activities requiring gross-motor rather than fine-motor skills. High-humor children also tended to have had more precocious speech development and better language skills, and were rated by observers as being more creative at an early age (McGhee, 1980a). In addition, they were rated as seeking more help, attention, and affection from adults, and were more likely to engage in imitation during play. By elementary school, greater humor was no longer associated with weight or height, although it was still related to greater social dominance.

A study by Sandra Damico and William Purkey (1978), at the University of Florida, examined personality traits of 96 eighth-grade children in 10 different junior high schools who were identified by their classmates as being "class clowns" (i.e., students who "joke and clown around a lot" and "make others laugh"). In comparison with a randomly selected group of nonclown classmates, the class clowns (who were much more likely to be male than female) were rated by their teachers as being higher in social assertiveness, cheerfulness, and leadership, but also more unruly and attention-seeking, and less likely to complete their academic work. On a measure of self-concept, class clowns were more likely to describe themselves as leaders, vocal in expressing ideas and opinions, confident about speaking up in class, satisfied with themselves, and self-confident. However, they also rated themselves as being less well-understood by their parents and displayed more negative attitudes toward their teachers and principal.

Although humorous children may be perceived by their teachers as somewhat unruly and disruptive, other studies indicate that they tend to be very popular with their classmates. Lawrence Sherman (1988), at Miami University in Ohio, had children in three fourth-grade classes rate the sense of humor and the degree to which they liked the other children in their class. The mean liking ratings for each child were used to compute a measure of the child's social distance within the class. A strong correlation was found between the mean humor ratings and social distance scores, indicating that children who were perceived to have a better sense of humor were more well-liked by their peers. This association between perceived humor and social distance was stronger among same-sex peers than among opposite-sex classmates.

These findings were replicated in a subsequent study using classes of 9-, 12-, and 15-year-old children (Warners-Kleverlaan, Oppenheimer, and Sherman, 1996). The latter study revealed that, among 12- and 15-year-olds, the association between sense of humor and social distance became equally strong for cross-gender and within-gender ratings. Thus, as children enter adolescence and begin to take a stronger interest in members of the opposite sex, a sense of humor seems to be an important component of one's popularity with both sexes. This study also indicated that pre-adolescent children tend to define a sense of humor in terms of funny actions and joke-telling, whereas adolescents define it more in terms of witty verbal skills.

Some additional research suggests that the pattern of behavioral and personality correlates of the tendency to initiate humor with peers may change as individuals progress into adolescence. Michael Fabrizi and Howard Pollio (1987b), at the University of Tennessee, observed children in grades 3, 7, and 11 during classroom periods, and coded how frequently each child initiated humor and made other children laugh. No differences were found between boys and girls in the frequency of humor initiation. Among children in grade three, the frequency of humor initiation was unrelated to the children's general classroom behavior or their interactions with their teachers.

However, by grade seven, children who engaged in more frequent humor initiation tended to be those who were generally more disruptive in class, calling out rather than raising their hands for permission to speak, frequently leaving their seat, interacting more often with peers, and spending less time doing their school work. Not surprisingly, the more humorous children were also more likely to receive disapproval and reprimands for off-target behavior from their teachers. Although the pattern of correlations was similar in grade 11, humor in these older children seemed to be somewhat less disruptive. The authors concluded that, whereas humor initiation in grade 7 seemed to be part of a constellation of acting-out behaviors, by grade 11 it seemed to be associated with being a popular child who knows the rules of the classroom and is sought out by his or her peers.

In a subsequent study, Fabrizi and Pollio (1987a) found that children in grade seven who engaged in more frequent humor initiation in the classroom and were more frequently nominated by their peers as being "the funniest in the class" tended to have lower scores on a measure of self-esteem. By grade 11, however, there was no association between humor initiation and self-concept. These findings seem to be inconsistent with the positive self concept found in class clowns in the Damico and Purkey (1978) study, although the differences may be due to the fact that the latter study used a more extreme group of humorous children drawn from a larger population, rather than examining correlations within the classroom.

On the other hand, whereas no correlation was found between humor initiation and creativity among children in grade 7, more frequent humor initiation in grade 11 was significantly correlated with higher scores for originality, flexibility, and elaboration on a test of creative thinking as well as higher teacher ratings of creativity. These findings suggest that being funny with peers is associated with different behaviors and personality characteristics at these different ages. During early adolescence (grade seven), making one's peers laugh is associated with going against authority, acting out, being silly, and having low self-esteem. In later stages of adolescence (grade 11), making one's peers laugh is less strongly related to disruptive behavior and low self-esteem, and more strongly related to creativity and popularity with peers.

Although this correlational research does not permit us to draw conclusions about causality, these studies, taken together, provide some indication of the possible developmental trajectory of children who become particularly adept at initiating humor and amusing their peers. Temperamentally outgoing and active preschoolers who are verbally and physically aggressive learn at an early age that aggressive behavior is likely to meet with disapproval from adults as well as rejection from peers. Those children with strong verbal skills or gross-motor abilities may learn that a more acceptable way of gaining acceptance from peers and minimizing disapproval from adults is to channel these abilities into verbal and physical humor that generates laughter in others. In elementary and junior high school, the ability to make others laugh leads to increased popularity and a position of dominance and leadership among peers, but it also increasingly brings the child into conflict with the demands of the classroom, resulting in these children having a conflicted relationship with authority figures and being perceived by teachers as disruptive and unruly. By high school, humorous children continue to be socially dominant and assertive, but somewhat less disruptive, and as they hone their humor abilities they also become more creative in their thinking in general.

This description of the hypothesized course of humor development seems consistent with the existing data. However, because most of the research to date has used cross-sectional designs, we do not know for certain if the children who are most humorous in kindergarten are the same ones who make their friends laugh in high school, or whether different children take on this humorous role at different age levels. Longitudinal research is needed to examine the stability of humor initiation across childhood and adolescence.

Besides defining sense of humor in terms of humor initiation during interactions with peers, researchers have also examined individual differences in children's humor appreciation and their ability to comprehend and produce humor using jokes and cartoons. Ann Masten (1986), at the University of Minnesota, assessed the sense of humor of children in grades five to eight using measures of humor appreciation (funniness ratings of cartoons), amount of laughter and smiling in response to the cartoons, humor comprehension (ability to explain the point of the cartoons), and humor production (ability to generate witty cartoon captions). The children's social competence was also assessed by means of teacher and peer ratings on a standardized questionnaire, and their academic competence was measured using intelligence and achievement tests.

With regard to social competence, children with higher levels of humor comprehension and production were rated by their peers as higher on sociability and leadership and lower on emotional sensitivity and social isolation. They were also rated by their teachers as showing more cooperativeness, attention, and initiative. Correlations with the amount of laughter and funniness ratings of cartoons showed similar, although somewhat weaker, patterns. With regard to academic competence, correlational analyses showed that children who displayed more laughter in response to cartoons, humor comprehension, and humor production tended to have higher IQ and academic achievement scores. None of the humor measures were significantly correlated with peer or teacher ratings of aggressiveness, oppositional behavior, or disruptiveness in the classroom.

Using the same humor measures as in the Masten (1986) study, a similar pattern of findings emerged in a subsequent investigation of social and academic competence in children ages 9 to 14 (Pellegrini et al., 1987). Factor analyses of a variety of social and cognitive competence measures revealed that the amount of laughter in response to cartoons, humor appreciation, comprehension, and production measures all loaded on a "social comprehension" factor, along with measures of interpersonal understanding and means-ends problem solving. Thus, these sense of humor measures formed part of a social cognition dimension involving maturity of understanding about the social world and the ability to achieve social goals and solve interpersonal problems. This dimension was in turn positively related to teacher and peer ratings of social competence, popularity, friendliness, and leadership. It was also significantly but weakly related to academic achievement. In addition, humor comprehension and production both loaded on a factor of divergent thinking, along with measures of creativity and cognitive reflectivity and accuracy (cf. Brodzinsky, 1975; Brodzinsky, 1977).

Overall, the findings of these two studies suggest that when sense of humor is defined in terms of humor production ability and comprehension and appreciation of cartoons, it tends to be positively correlated with social competence and maturity, sociability, cooperative behaviors, academic achievement, and intellectual abilities, and unrelated to aggressiveness and disruptive classroom behavior. Of course, the direction of causality in these correlational findings is unknown. These findings are quite different from the pattern of correlations described earlier in research defining sense of humor in terms of children's tendency to make their peers laugh. In that research, humor initiation tended to be related to a history of aggressiveness, disruptive classroom behavior, inattention to school work, and a generally conflicted relationship with authority figures. Thus, correlations between sense of humor and particular personality traits, competencies, and behaviors may be quite different, depending on the way sense of humor is defined and measured.

HUMOR AND AGING

How does the sense of humor change as people progress through adulthood and into old age? Our discussion of humor development in this chapter has focused particularly on the period from infancy to adolescence. However, further developments in the production, comprehension, enjoyment, and social functions of humor likely occur throughout the lifespan, along with changes in cognitive abilities, psychosocial needs and concerns, social relationships, attitudes, coping with adverse life events, and so on. Because only a few studies have investigated humor in older adults, however, our knowledge in this area is very limited.

A major limitation of research comparing aspects of humor in older and younger adults is that this approach does not permit us to determine whether any observed differences are due to developmental changes that occur with aging, or whether they are due to cohort effects. If elderly people are found to differ from younger people in their humor abilities, styles, comprehension, or appreciation, this may be due to the fact that they grew up in a different era, with different cultural norms and expectations, different popular role models, different educational opportunities, and so on. Longitudinal research, following individuals over many years, is needed to investigate changes in humor over the course of individuals' lives. Since no studies of this kind have been conducted, we must be cautious in our interpretation of the existing cross-sectional research.

Some research suggests that declines in cognitive abilities in the elderly may be associated with reduced comprehension of humor. A study at Purdue University found that, among participants ages 50 to 80 years, greater age was associated with lower comprehension but also greater appreciation (higher funniness ratings) of jokes (Schaier and Cicirelli, 1976). In addition, those older participants who were found to have a reduced understanding of conservation of volume on standard Piagetian tasks also showed lower comprehension and appreciation of jokes involving violations of conservation, but not nonconservation jokes.

The authors concluded that these findings provide further support for the cognitive congruency hypothesis (discussed earlier). In the first part of life, increases in cognitive abilities enable children to understand and appreciate more cognitively challenging forms of humor; however, as their abilities increase still more and a joke becomes too easy, their appreciation decreases. In the later part of life, as cognitive ability begins to decline with age, comprehension of jokes also declines. This leads to an increased appreciation of the humor as the joke places more cognitive demand on the individual, up to the point where he or she no longer understands the joke, when appreciation again declines.

In a more recent study at the University of Toronto, elderly participants (mean age = 73 years), as compared to younger people (mean age = 29 years), made significantly more errors in selecting the humorous punch line on a joke completion test and also made more errors in selecting the funnier cartoon when presented with pairs of nonverbal cartoon drawings (Shammi and Stuss, 2003). In contrast, the two age groups did not differ in their performance on a nonhumorous story completion task, indicating an equal ability to understand narrative language. In the elderly participants, performance on the verbal joke test was also significantly correlated with performance on neuropsychological tests of working memory and verbal abstract ability, while the nonverbal cartoon test was significantly related to measures of working memory, speed of visual scanning, mental flexibility, and visual perceptual abilities. All of these abilities have been found in previous research to be related to frontal lobe functioning. The deficits in performance on the verbal and nonverbal humor tests in the elderly were much less severe, however, than those seen in patients with right frontal lobe brain damage. With regard to humor appreciation, the elderly participants, in comparison to the younger ones, rated humorous materials as significantly funnier. Drawing on findings from previous brain research on humor comprehension (discussed in Chapter 6), the authors of this study concluded that subtle declines in frontal lobe functioning in the elderly may lead to some impairment in cognitive processing of humor, while leaving the affective enjoyment of humor intact.

To investigate age differences in humor appreciation in adults, Willibald Ruch and colleagues (1990) examined correlations between age and humor appreciation on the 3WD humor test in a sample of more than 4000 German participants ranging in age from 14 to 66 years. Enjoyment of incongruity-resolution (INC-RES) humor increased significantly across the age span in a linear fashion, whereas enjoyment of nonsense (NON) humor decreased with age. These age differences in the enjoyment of the two categories of humor were found to be fully accounted for by a corresponding increase with age in scores on a measure of conservatism. As noted in Chapter 7, greater preferences for INC-RES over NON humor are related to more conservative social attitudes.

Thus, the more conservative attitudes of older as compared to younger adults are reflected in differences in the kind of humor that they enjoy. In particular, older people are more likely to enjoy humor in which incongruity is resolved (as in most "canned" jokes) and less likely to enjoy the more offbeat types of humor containing unresolved incongruity. Of course, as with all of this cross-sectional research, we do not know whether the older participants became increasingly conservative and had corresponding changes in their humor appreciation over the course of their lifetime, or whether they were always more conservative and always enjoyed INC-RES humor more than did the group born at a later time.

Some research has also examined age differences in younger and older adults' scores on self-report humor measures. A study using the Multidimensional Sense of Humor Scale (MSHS) with a sample of adults ages 18 to 90 found no age differences in overall humor scores (Thorson and Powell, 1996). However, older participants were somewhat more likely than younger ones to report producing and appreciating humor and using humor to cope with stress, whereas they tended to report a more negative attitude toward humorous people. My colleagues and I also examined age differences in scores on the Humor Styles Questionnaire in more than 1000 participants ranging in age from 14 to 87 years (R. A. Martin et al., 2003). Older adults were found to have significantly lower scores than younger ones on both affiliative and aggressive humor, indicating that older people are less likely to engage in friendly joking and laughing with others and are also less likely to use humor to disparage, ridicule, or manipulate others. On the other hand, older women (but not men) had higher scores than younger ones on self-enhancing humor, indicating a generally more humorous outlook on life and greater use of perspective-taking and coping humor. No age differences were found with the self-defeating humor scale.

Taken together, these findings suggest that humor may serve different functions for adults at different periods of the lifespan. In younger people, humor may be more important for expressing aggression in socially acceptable ways, establishing relationships, and testing one's social standing in the peer group, whereas humor in older people (especially women) may have more to do with coping with stress and maintaining a humorous outlook on life. These findings suggest potentially interesting avenues for future longitudinal research exploring changes in humor abilities, enjoyment, and functions over the lifespan.

CONCLUSION

Laughter begins to emerge in infants around four months of age, and occurs in response to perceptions of incongruity in a playful, safe context. Right from its inception, laughter functions as a form of social communication. The incongruous tactile stimuli, actions, sounds, and facial expressions that trigger laughter in infants gradually evolve into an internalized sense of humor, as developing schemas enable the child to manipulate mental representations of concepts and language in incongruous ways.

Much research has examined associations between humor development and the development of cognitive abilities through childhood. As cognitive capacities become more complex, children are able to perceive and enjoy more sophisticated forms of playful incongruity. Humor appreciation signals mastery of concepts, as humor that playfully violates recently acquired concepts is funnier than humor that is either cognitively too difficult or too simple. Children's ability to understand and enjoy conversational forms of humor such as irony and sarcasm also depends on their level of cognitive development.

Social and emotional aspects of humor continue to play a major role throughout childhood. Humor as a form of communication serves many social functions in children as well as adults. Joking and laughing with others about taboo topics and anxiety-arousing issues and experiences is an important way for children to manage negative emotions such as anxiety, guilt, and insecurity in the face of an often bewildering and threatening world.

Individual differences in sense of humor begin to emerge in early childhood. The relative proportion of genetic and environmental influences on sense of humor differs depending on how humor is defined and measured. With regard to familial influences on sense of humor development, research has tended to support the Stress and Coping Hypothesis, although evidence has also been found for the Modeling/Reinforcement Hypothesis. Some children may develop a strong sense of humor due to a rather dysfunctional family environment in which humor emerges as a way of coping with negative emotions and gaining attention and approval from otherwise nonnurturing parents, whereas others may develop a sense of humor as a result of growing up in a well-functioning family in which humor is valued and modeled.

Sense of humor defined as a tendency to frequently initiate humor and amuse one's peers is associated with having been physically active, dominant, and aggressive, and having precocious language abilities in the preschool years, and disruptive classroom behavior during elementary school, but also popularity among peers and creativity in high school. Sense of humor defined as the ability to comprehend and produce humor in the laboratory is associated with social competence, cooperativeness, initiative, and leadership.

In the latter part of the life span, declining cognitive abilities may be associated with reduced comprehension of humor, but no reduction in humor appreciation and enjoyment. More conservative attitudes in older as compared to younger adults are associated with greater enjoyment of incongruity-resolution and reduced enjoyment of nonsense humor. Older adults tend to use humor in less aggressive and affiliative ways, but their greater breadth of life experience may enable them to have a generally more humorous outlook on life and an increased ability to use humor in coping with life stress.

The study of humor development in childhood and across the lifespan offers many interesting research opportunities. Although many studies have examined the role of cognitive development in the comprehension and appreciation of "canned" jokes, cartoons, and riddles, only a limited amount of research has examined cognitive developmental aspects of more spontaneous forms of verbal and nonverbal humor that occur in everyday social interactions. Further research is also needed on the social functions of humor in infancy and childhood and changes in these functions through childhood and adolescence. Research on developmental aspects of the role of humor in emotional coping is also needed.

With regard to individual differences in sense of humor, our knowledge of familial and other social environmental influences on humor development is still very limited. Research on this topic needs to employ methodologies that enable researchers to control for possible genetic confounds. Finally, further research is needed on changes in various components of sense of humor in later life, as well as changes in the social and emotional functions of humor in the elderly. In all these areas, longitudinal research designs are needed to augment the findings of cross-sectional research. Thus, although the existing research has provided a great deal of interesting information about the development of humor, many questions remain to be answered.

CHAPTER 9

Humor and Mental Health

In recent decades, a sense of humor has come to be viewed not only as a very socially desirable personality trait but also as an important component of mental health. Besides boosting positive emotions and counteracting negative moods like depression and anxiety, humor is thought to be a valuable mechanism for coping with stressful life events and an important social skill for initiating, maintaining, and enhancing satisfying interpersonal relationships (Galloway and Cropley, 1999; Kuiper and Olinger, 1998; Lefcourt, 2001). A good deal of research in the psychology of humor in the past two decades has focused on the relation between humor and various aspects of mental health.

Our discussion of the implications of humor for mental health in this chapter brings us to clinical psychology, the branch of psychology having to do with the study, assessment, and treatment of psychological disorders, as well as the study and promotion of factors contributing to positive mental health and well-being (Seligman and Peterson, 2003). Clinical psychology is both a research discipline and an applied profession. In this chapter, I will focus on the research aspect, exploring empirical findings concerning the role of humor in psychological health and well-being; applied issues will be the focus in Chapter 11, where I will consider applications of humor to psychotherapy.

Mental health is often defined in negative terms as the absence of psychological disturbance or emotional distress. In this chapter, I will take a more positive approach, defining it in terms of three general capacities that seem to be essential for an individual to thrive and flourish. These are: (1) the ability to regulate negative emotions and enjoy positive emotions; (2) the ability to cope with stress and adapt to change; and (3) the ability to establish close, meaningful, and enduring relationships with others. In the following sections I will describe research investigating the potential benefits of humor for each of these three components of positive mental health.

HUMOR AND EMOTIONAL WELL-BEING

As we have seen in earlier chapters, one component of humor is the positive emotion of mirth that is elicited. When people engage in humor and laughter, they tend to feel more cheerful and energetic, and less depressed, anxious, irritable, and tense. In the short term, at least, humor seems to boost positive moods and counteract negative emotions. Thus, one way a sense of humor may be beneficial to mental health is by contributing to one's ability to regulate or manage emotions, which is an essential aspect of mental health (Gross and Muñoz, 1995).

Experimental Investigations of Humor and Emotions

The effects of humor on mood have been demonstrated in a number of laboratory experiments. In two studies, Willibald Ruch (1997) exposed participants to humor either by having them interact with a clowning experimenter or by showing them comedy videotapes. The frequency, intensity, and duration of their smiling and laughter were coded using the criteria for the Duchenne display which, as we saw in Chapter 6, indicates genuine amusement. The more the participants smiled and laughed in this way, the more their self-reported feelings of cheerfulness and mirth increased over baseline. Thus, smiling and laughter are an expression of the positive emotion of mirth that is induced by the perception of humor, and the more intense this emotion, the greater the laughter. Interestingly, there were no correlations between the participants' pre-existing (baseline) moods and the degree to which they smiled and laughed at the humorous stimuli, confirming that positive emotions were a consequence rather than a cause of humorous amusement.

Other research suggests that smiling and laughter by themselves, even without humor, can induce positive feelings of mirth. For example, when participants were asked to rate the funniness of cartoons while holding a pen in their mouth in a way that caused them to contract the facial muscles normally associated with smiling (as compared to subjects who held the pen in a way that inhibited such muscle contractions), they rated the cartoons as funnier and reported greater increases in positive mood (Strack, Martin, and Stepper, 1988). Laboratory studies have also found significant increases in positive mood in subjects following sessions of forced, nonhumorous laughter (Foley, Matheis, and Schaefer, 2002; Neuhoff and Schaefer, 2002). Thus, the act of smiling and laughing, even when done artificially, seems to induce feelings of amusement and mirth, at least temporarily.

Besides increasing positive moods, there is experimental evidence that humor can reduce negative moods. One experiment found that exposure to a four-minute humorous film led to a significant reduction in reported feelings of anxiety relative to baseline (C. C. Moran, 1996). Another study compared the mood effects of watching a 20-minute comedy videotape, running on a treadmill for 20 minutes, and watching a nonhumorous documentary video (Szabo, 2003). Compared to the aerobic exercise, the comedy video produced similar increases in positive mood and decreases in emotional distress and even greater reductions in anxiety, and both comedy and exercise showed significantly stronger mood effects than did the nonhumorous control video (these results were replicated by Szabo, Ainsworth, and Danks, 2005). Taken together, these findings suggest that humor produces positive short-term emotional changes that are at least comparable if not superior to the effects of vigorous physical exercise.

There is also some evidence that humor can counteract the effects of experimentally induced depressed moods. Using a standard laboratory mood-induction technique, Amy Danzer and her colleagues (1990) induced dysphoric moods in female undergraduate students and then randomly assigned them to either humorous audiotape (stand-up comedy), nonhumorous audiotape (an interesting but unfunny geography lecture), or no tape conditions. Participants in all three groups showed significant increases in self-reported depressed moods following the mood induction, indicating that this procedure was effective, but only those in the humor condition showed a significant posttreatment reduction in dysphoria back to baseline levels, suggesting that humor counteracted the depressed mood.

Besides influencing positive and negative moods, there is experimental evidence that humor-related mirth affects one's general outlook on life. One study found that participants who watched a comedy videotape, as compared to those who viewed a nonhumorous video, reported a significantly greater increase in feelings of hopefulness (Vilaythong, Arnau, Rosen, and Mascaro, 2003). Another experiment suggested that humor can change one's perceptions of a boring task into an interesting one (Dienstbier, 1995). After watching either a comedy or nonhumorous videotape, participants engaged in several repetitive and boring proofreading tasks. Those who had viewed the comedy video, as compared to those in the control group, reported higher levels of energy and elation and rated these tasks as being more challenging and invigorating, although they did not actually achieve better performance on the tasks. Thus, the positive emotion associated with humor seems to make people more hopeful, more energetic, and less susceptible to boredom.

The preceding experiments provided fairly consistent evidence of short-term effects of humor on positive and negative moods and feelings of well-being in the laboratory. Based on these findings, one would expect that exposing people to humorous stimuli repeatedly over a number of weeks or months should result in overall improvements in their prevailing moods and general outlook on life. However, when researchers have investigated longer-term psychological effects of repeated exposure to humorous stimuli over fairly extended time periods, the results have generally been rather disappointing.

In one study, patients with chronic schizophrenia in one ward of a psychiatric hospital were shown 70 comedy movies over a three-month period, while those in another ward were shown an equal number of nonhumorous dramatic movies (Gelkopf, Kreitler, and Sigal, 1993). After these interventions, comparisons were made between the two groups on 21 measures relating to staff-rated and self-rated moods, psychiatric symptoms, physical health symptoms, physiological variables, and cognitive functioning. Significant benefits were found on only six of these variables, most of which involved perceptions of the patients by hospital staff. In particular, the patients who had watched the comedy movies, compared to those in the other group, were rated by the staff as having significantly lower levels of verbal (but not behavioral) hostility, anxiety/depression, and tension, and the patients themselves reported greater perceived social support from the staff. The authors of the study acknowledged that these rather meager findings may have had more to do with the effects of the movies on the perceptions of the hospital staff than on the actual functioning of the patients.

Even fewer psychological benefits of humor were found in other intervention studies. James Rotton and Mark Shats (1996) randomly assigned patients recovering from orthopedic surgery to watch either four feature-length comedy movies, four dramatic but nonhumorous movies, or no movies during the two days postsurgery. The results showed no differences between the humorous and non-humorous movie conditions in levels of self-rated emotional distress and pain over the two days. However, both of the movie-watching groups reported less distress and pain than did those in the no-movie control condition, indicating a beneficial effect of watching movies of any kind, but no particular benefit of humor.

Similarly, in a study of elderly residents of a long-term care facility, no significant differences in self-reported prevailing moods were found after six weeks of watching humorous versus nonhumorous feature-length movies three days per week, although both groups showed equal improvements in mood over the course of the study (E. R. Adams and McGuire, 1986). Finally, in an experiment in which undergraduate participants were randomly assigned to six weekly $1\frac{1}{2}$-hour sessions of either laughter-induction exercises, relaxation training, or didactic health education presentations, the laughter-induction sessions were found to be no more effective than the nonhumorous health education lectures, and significantly less effective than the relaxation sessions, in reducing total mood disturbance and anxiety (White and Camarena, 1989).

In summary, although the experimental laboratory research indicates that humor and laughter have beneficial short-term mood effects, there is little evidence of longer-term psychological benefits of repeated exposure to humorous movies or participation in laughter sessions over a period of days or weeks. These findings raise questions about the benefits of humor interventions such as those provided by laughter clubs, in which members meet regularly to engage in laughter-induction exercises (Kataria, 2002).

Although the research in this area is still quite limited, the evidence to date suggests that simply laughing for an hour or two a few times a week has little lasting effect on individuals' overall well-being. This may be because the humor is not integrated into the participants' day-to-day experiences. Perhaps such interventions would have greater benefits if they were designed to increase the frequency of humor and laughter arising spontaneously during people's everyday social interactions, influencing the way they respond to ongoing life experiences, and thus contributing to more effective emotion regulation. This would presumably require training people how to take a more humorous perspective on their daily experiences and to produce humor in their interactions with others.

However, very little research has investigated the degree to which people can actually be taught to increase their tendency to engage in humor in the course of their daily lives. In the only published study of this kind, Ofra Nevo and her colleagues evaluated the effectiveness of a seven-week, 21-hour training program for increasing sense of humor in high school teachers, but found only limited evidence of success (Nevo, Aharonson, and Klingman, 1998). The program led to increased peer ratings of humor production and appreciation, as well as more positive attitudes toward humor in the participants, but it did not improve their ability to produce humor, as assessed by tests of humor creativity, or their scores on self-report humor measures. Unfortunately, the effects of the intervention on psychological well-being were not examined. In view of the efforts being made by some health care professionals to promote mental and physical health by means of various interventions designed to improve people's sense of humor (e.g., McGhee, 1999), there is clearly a need for further research to determine whether it is even possible to change the quantity or quality of people's everyday use of humor.

Correlational Studies of Trait Humor and Emotional Well-Being

If humor in general is beneficial to psychological well-being, then individuals who engage in humor more frequently in their everyday lives (i.e., those with a greater sense of humor) should tend to be generally less depressed, anxious, and pessimistic, less likely to experience burnout and to develop psychiatric disorders, and they should have greater self-esteem, optimism, and overall feelings of well-being. Numerous studies have investigated these hypotheses by examining correlations between individuals' scores on various trait measures of sense of humor and a variety of measures of emotional and psychological well-being.

Studies of university students using the Coping Humor Scale (CHS), Situational Humor Response Questionnaire (SHRQ), and Sense of Humor Questionnaire Metamessage Sensitivity (SHQ-M) and Liking of Humor (SHQ-L) scales (discussed in Chapter 7) have found moderate negative correlations between some (but not all) of these humor scales and measures of neuroticism, anxiety, and depression, and positive correlations with self-esteem (Deaner and McConatha, 1993; Kuiper and Borowicz-Sibenik, 2005; Kuiper and Martin, 1993). Which humor scales are significantly correlated with which well-being measures tends to vary across studies. Research using the Multidimensional Sense of Humor Scale (MSHS) has also found significant but generally weak negative correlations between this humor test and measures of depression, death anxiety, pessimism, and the tendency to worry about various life concerns (Kelly, 2002; Thorson and Powell, 1993b, 1994; Thorson et al., 1997).

Some studies investigating stress-moderating effects of humor (which will be described in more detail later in this chapter) have also reported significant negative correlations between various self-report humor scales and measures of depression (Anderson and Arnoult, 1989; Nezu, Nezu, and Blissett, 1988; Overholser, 1992; Porterfield, 1987; Safranek and Schill, 1982), mood disturbance (Labott and Martin, 1987; Lefcourt et al., 1995), and emotional burnout (P. S. Fry, 1995). However, some other studies found no simple correlation between sense of humor tests and anxiety (Nezu et al., 1988), mood disturbance (R. A. Martin and Lefcourt, 1983), or positive moods (Kuiper, Martin, and Dance, 1992).

To investigate the association between sense of humor and self-esteem, Nicholas Kuiper and I examined correlations between four humor scales (CHS, SHRQ, SHQ-M, and SHQ-L) and various measures of self-concept in undergraduate participants (Kuiper and Martin, 1993). All four humor tests were found to be positively correlated with a measure of self-esteem. In addition, three of them were negatively related to the discrepancy between participants' actual and ideal self-ratings on a series of 60 self-descriptive adjectives, indicating that those with higher humor scores had a greater congruence between the way they actually perceived themselves and the way they would ideally like to be. In addition, two of the humor tests were significantly related to the temporal stability of self-ratings on these adjectives over a one-month period, indicating that participants with higher humor scores had a more stable self-concept. Finally, participants with higher scores on all four humor scales were significantly less likely to endorse dysfunctional, unrealistic, and perfectionistic self-evaluative standards. Overall, this study indicated that individuals with higher scores on at least some of these humor measures tend to have a more positive, congruent, stable, and realistic self-concept.

In addition to research on university students, a study of elderly residents of assisted living facilities found that those with higher scores on the CHS tended to have higher levels of emotional health, positive mood, and zest for life (Celso, Ebener, and Burkhead, 2003). A study of well-being among noninstitutionalized elderly women and men also found that higher scores on the SHRQ and CHS were significantly associated with better morale but unrelated to overall life satisfaction (Simon, 1990). In addition, a study of the relation between humor and burnout among instructors in a school of nursing found that higher scores on the CHS were related to significantly lower levels of depersonalization and higher levels of perceived personal accomplishment, but were unrelated to emotional exhaustion (Talbot and Lumden, 2000).

Whereas the preceding research was conducted with nonclinical samples, a few studies have also investigated whether psychiatric patients have lower sense of humor scores, on average, than do people without diagnosed psychiatric disorders. One study compared a group of hospitalized adolescent psychiatric patients and a group of normal adolescents and found no differences in their average scores on the CHS or measures of humor creation ability and humor appreciation, casting some doubt on the benefits of humor for mental health (Freiheit, Overholser, and Lehnert, 1998). Similarly, a study of defensive styles in clinically depressed patients found no difference in humor scores between those who had recently attempted suicide and those who had not (Corruble et al., 2004).

One study did report that hospitalized adult psychiatric patients diagnosed with depression or schizophrenia had significantly lower scores on at least some trait humor measures as compared to scale norms derived from university students (Kuiper et al., 1998). However, it is questionable whether this was an appropriate comparison group, due to differences in age, education level, and social background. Overall, then, although the research on this question is quite limited, there is little evidence that high humor individuals are less likely to have psychiatric disorders than are those with less of a sense of humor. Some clinicians have pointed out that clinically depressed people do not necessarily display less humor than others, but their humor tends to be rather black, cynical, hostile, and excessively self-disparaging (e.g., Kantor, 1992).

Nonetheless, there is some evidence that, within groups of individuals diagnosed with clinical depression, greater emotional disturbance is associated with lower trait humor scores. In the study of hospitalized adolescent psychiatric patients, higher scores on the CHS were associated with lower levels of depression and higher self-esteem, although they were unrelated to feelings of hopelessness (Freiheit et al., 1998). The study of hospitalized adult psychiatric patients found that higher sense of humor scores tended to be associated with lower depression and higher self-esteem and positive moods among the clinically depressed patients (Kuiper et al., 1998). However, sense of humor was unrelated to symptom severity among patients diagnosed with schizophrenia. Another study of humor in hospitalized schizophrenic patients similarly found no relation between scores on the CHS and several self-report and psychiatrist-rated measures of hostility, aggression, and anger (Gelkopf and Sigal, 1995). Thus, although a greater sense of humor seems to be related to lower severity of disturbance in clinically depressed individuals, this does not seem to be the case among persons with schizophrenia.

In the correlational research described so far, the overall evidence for mental health benefits of a sense of humor is not overwhelming. Some correlations have been found between sense of humor, as measured by self-report scales, and various components of emotional well-being, but the associations often tend to be quite weak and the findings have been somewhat inconsistent across studies. Nicholas Kuiper and I (1998a) examined the results of five correlational studies to determine how sense of humor compares with another positive personality characteristic commonly thought to be important for mental health, namely optimism. These studies employed four sense of humor scales (CHS, SHRQ, SHQ-M, and SHQ-L), a test of dispositional optimism, and various measures of psychological well-being. The analyses revealed that higher scores on the sense of humor scales were only weakly associated with greater optimism. In relation to a multidimensional measure of psychological well-being, higher scores on the humor tests were associated with only one subscale assessing personal growth, but they were unrelated to self-acceptance, positive relations with others, autonomy, environmental mastery, and purpose in life. In contrast, optimism was much more strongly related to all six of these components of psychological well-being.

The humor scales were also almost entirely uncorrelated with a measure of mental health-related assumptions about the world and other people, whereas optimism was significantly related in positive ways to most of these world beliefs. Consistent with other research, the sense of humor scales did show moderate positive correlations with self-esteem, and negative correlations with anxiety, depression, fear of negative evaluations, and social avoidance and distress. However, optimism was more strongly related to all of these well-being measures. Thus, although these sense of humor measures are associated with some aspects of emotional well-being, the correlations appear to be generally weaker and less extensive than are those with other "positive personality" constructs such as optimism.

These rather weak and inconsistent associations between trait measures of sense of humor and well-being can perhaps be explained by research (discussed in Chapter 7) showing that most self-report humor tests load primarily on the general personality factor of extraversion, but only weakly, if at all, on the neuroticism factor (Köhler and Ruch, 1996; Ruch, 1994). Extraversion has to do with the general tendency to experience positive emotions, as well as traits such as sociable, lively, and active. On the other hand, neuroticism, which is unrelated to extraversion, involves emotional instability, moodiness, irritability, and the tendency to experience negative emotions, such as depression, anxiety, and hostility. Not surprisingly, most measures of psychological well-being load primarily (negatively) on the neuroticism factor (DeNeve, 1999).

The fact that the two broad personality dimensions of extraversion and neuroticism are uncorrelated with each other may explain why the sense of humor measures (relating primarily to extraversion) tend to be only weakly associated with well-being measures (relating mainly to neuroticism). Since dispositional optimism is more strongly (inversely) associated with neuroticism than are the humor measures, it also tends to correlate more strongly with well-being measures. This begs the question of whether there are some dimensions of humor that are more strongly associated with neuroticism, either negatively or positively, which are not well measured by the self-report humor tests used in the research discussed so far. This question is addressed in the next section.

Distinguishing Potentially Healthy and Unhealthy Humor Styles

People use humor in their interactions with others in many different ways and for different purposes. As noted in Chapter 5, humor serves numerous interpersonal functions, some of which may contribute to greater social cohesiveness and enhanced communication between people, whereas others may be more coercive, disparaging, or ingratiating. Although overall sense of humor may be weakly related to emotional health, as suggested by research described in the previous section, perhaps some of the ways people use humor are more strongly associated with well-being, whereas other forms of humor may even be associated with poorer psychological health.

This way of thinking about the connection between humor and mental health is consistent with the views of psychologists writing about this topic in the past. For example, when Sigmund Freud (1928) referred to humor as the "highest of the defense mechanisms" (p. 216) and described it as "something fine and elevating" (p. 217), he was not speaking about humor in the broad sense that we generally associate with it today, but instead he was giving it a narrow meaning, consistent with the terminology of the nineteenth century. As noted in Chapter 1, humor in this sense referred exclusively to a sympathetic, tolerant, and benevolent form of amusement, and was distinguished from wit, which was viewed as more sarcastic, biting, and cruel (Wickberg, 1998).

In a similar way, psychologists like Abraham Maslow (1954), Gordon Allport (1961), and Walter O'Connell (1976) suggested that especially well-adjusted individuals are characterized by a particular style of humor that is nonhostile, philosophical, and self-deprecating while remaining self-accepting. These authors viewed this healthy form of humor as relatively rare, in contrast with most of the humor occurring in everyday social interactions and in the media. Interestingly, they also suggested that healthy forms of humor are not necessarily extremely funny, being more likely to trigger a chuckle than a hearty laugh. Maslow (1954) even suggested that the particularly well-adjusted people that he characterized as "self-actualizing" would likely be perceived by the average person as "rather on the sober and serious side" (p. 223).

These ideas suggest that psychological health relates not only to the *presence* of certain kinds of adaptive humor but also to the *absence* of other more unhealthy forms of amusement. Rather than assuming that humor in general is beneficial for mental health and well-being, as most recent researchers seem to have done, it may therefore be important to return to earlier views which made a distinction between beneficial and detrimental forms of humor.

This view of humor as being potentially detrimental as well as beneficial to mental health was the rationale for our development of the Humor Styles Questionnaire (HSQ; R. A. Martin et al., 2003), which I described in Chapter 7. In developing this measure, we identified two styles of humor that have been discussed in the literature as being potentially unhealthy: one involving the use of humor to enhance the self at the expense of others, and the other involving the use of humor to gain approval and attention from others at the expense of one's own psychological needs. We hypothesized that these two humor styles may capture some of the forms of humor that psychologists like Allport and Maslow viewed as less likely to be found in people who are particularly psychologically healthy.

The first of these, *aggressive humor*, is the tendency to use humor for the purpose of criticizing or manipulating others, as in sarcasm, teasing, ridicule, derision, or disparagement humor (e.g., "If someone makes a mistake, I will often tease them about it"), as well as the use of potentially offensive (e.g., racist or sexist) forms of humor.

It also includes the compulsive expression of humor even when it is socially inappropriate (e.g., "Sometimes I think of something that is so funny that I can't stop myself from saying it, even if it is not appropriate for the situation"). Most of us know people who tend to use humor in these sorts of aggressive and domineering ways.

The other potentially unhealthy style, *self-defeating humor*, involves the use of humor to ingratiate oneself with others, attempts to amuse others by doing or saying funny things at one's own expense, excessively self-disparaging humor, and laughing along with others when being ridiculed or disparaged (e.g., "I often try to make people like or accept me more by saying something funny about my own weaknesses, blunders, or faults"). It also involves the use of humor as a form of defensive denial (Marcus, 1990), to hide one's underlying negative feelings or avoid dealing constructively with problems ("If I am having problems or feeling unhappy, I often cover it up by joking around, so that even my closest friends don't know how I really feel").

A prominent example of what we consider to be the use of self-defeating humor was Chris Farley, a popular American comedian in the early 1990s who honed his zany comedic skills as an overweight child with a desperate need to be liked by others. Despite the outstanding success that he achieved as a young adult through his hilarious and rather compulsive sense of humor, he seemed to harbor a deep self-loathing, destroying himself at an early age through alcohol, drugs, and overeating. Rather than contributing to effective coping, his humor seemed to be a way of denying the severity of his problems and deflecting the concerns of his friends. John Belushi, who met a similar end in the midst of a brilliant comedy career, seems to be another example of this self-defeating humor style. Interestingly, in our research with the HSQ, aggressive and self-defeating humor turned out to be significantly positively correlated with each other, indicating that people who use one potentially unhealthy style tend to use the other as well.

We also identified two styles of humor that we thought might be positively associated with psychological well-being, one having to do with the use of humor to promote positive interpersonal relationships and the other with the use of humor to cope with stress and regulate emotions. The first of these, *affiliative humor*, refers to the tendency to say funny things, to tell jokes, and to engage in spontaneous witty banter, in order to amuse others, to facilitate relationships, and to reduce interpersonal tensions (e.g., "I enjoy making people laugh"; "I don't have to work very hard at making other people laugh—I seem to be a naturally humorous person"). We viewed this as an essentially nonhostile, tolerant use of humor that is affirming of self and others and presumably enhances interpersonal cohesiveness. However, research with the HSQ has shown that, at least in North American samples, affiliative humor turns out to be weakly correlated with aggressive humor, suggesting that it may tap into the use of teasing, which may at times be friendly and prosocial, but also risks becoming aggressive.

The second presumably healthy humor style is *self-enhancing humor*, which refers to the tendency to be frequently amused by the incongruities of life, to maintain a humorous perspective even in the face of stress or adversity, and to use humor as an emotion-regulation mechanism (e.g., "My humorous outlook on life keeps me from getting overly upset or depressed about things"). This humor style is closely related to the construct assessed by the earlier Coping Humor Scale. Subsequent research has found that self-enhancing humor tends to be fairly strongly related to affiliative humor, a finding that emphasizes the essentially social nature of humor, but it is unrelated to aggressive and self-defeating humor, suggesting that this may be the healthiest of the four humor styles. We consider it to be the closest of the four to the traditional, narrowly defined concept of humor, which was viewed by Freud (1928) as a healthy defense mechanism or coping style.

Research examining correlations between the subscales of the HSQ and previous self-report humor scales provided support for our view that this new measure taps into distinct dimensions of humor that are not well differentiated (or not even assessed at all) by the earlier measures (R. A. Martin et al., 2003). For example, the CHS, although quite strongly related to self-enhancing (as well as affiliative) humor, has also been found to be correlated with aggressive humor, suggesting that it may not be as pure a measure of positive humor uses as the self-enhancing humor scale. Worse still, the MSHS was found to be positively correlated with all four HSQ scales, indicating that it taps into potentially unhealthy aggressive and self-defeating humor as well as potentially healthy forms of humor. This may account for the generally weak correlations with well-being measures found in research using the MSHS.

Other humor measures such as the SHRQ, SHQ, and Cheerfulness scale of the State-Trait Cheerfulness Inventory (STCI-T) were found to be positively correlated with affiliative and self-enhancing humor, but unrelated to aggressive and self-defeating humor. Thus, although there is less evidence that these earlier humor measures capture unhealthy aspects of humor, the addition of the two negative forms of humor in the HSQ might be useful for exploring these more negative aspects of humor that have not been assessed by previous scales. Interestingly, with regard to gender, whereas negligible differences have been found between men and women on the two presumably healthy styles of humor, men on average tend to have higher scores on the two potentially negative styles, suggesting that men and women do not differ in their healthy uses of humor, but men may be more likely to use humor in unhealthy ways (R. A. Martin et al., 2003).

Our initial studies with the HSQ provided general support for our view that these different humor styles are differentially related to psychological health and well-being (R. A. Martin et al., 2003). Affiliative and self-enhancing humor were found to be negatively correlated with anxiety and depression, and positively correlated with self-esteem and a measure of overall psychological well-being, the correlations with self-enhancing humor being somewhat stronger than those with affiliative humor. In contrast, higher scores on self-defeating humor were found to be associated with greater anxiety, depression, and psychiatric symptoms, and lower self-esteem and overall well-being. Aggressive and self-defeating humor styles were also both related to hostility and aggression. Thus, as expected, less use of these negative humor styles (particularly self-defeating humor) seems to be related to more healthy psychological functioning.

When the four HSQ scales were entered together into regression equations to predict the various measures of emotional well-being, sizable multiple correlations were found (averaging about .50). These correlations were considerably stronger than those typically found in earlier studies of humor and well-being, indicating that, by combining uses of humor that are negatively related to well-being with those that are positively related, we were able to account for a greater proportion of the variance in well-being variables. With regard to the broad personality dimension of neuroticism, affiliative humor was found to be unrelated, whereas self-enhancing humor was negatively related, and both aggressive and self-defeating humor were positively related to this personality factor. Thus, as expected, the different HSQ scales seem to differentiate styles of humor that are positively related, negatively related, and neutral with regard to neuroticism, suggesting that emotional stability is associated not just with the *presence* of certain styles of humor, but also with the *absence* of other styles. Humor appears to be neither inherently healthy nor unhealthy; its relation to mental health depends on how it is used in everyday life.

Several additional recent studies with the HSQ have added to these findings. Nicholas Kuiper and his colleagues (2004) found that higher scores on self-enhancing humor were associated with lower levels of depression, anxiety, and negative affect, and higher levels of self-esteem and positive affect. The pattern of correlations with affiliative humor was similar, but generally weaker. In contrast, self-defeating humor showed the exact opposite pattern of correlations: greater use of this type of humor was associated with higher levels of depression, anxiety, and negative affect, and lower levels of self-esteem. Aggressive humor, however, was unrelated to the emotional well-being measures. In another study, Vassilis Saroglou and Christel Scariot (2002) administered a French translation of the HSQ to Belgian university and high school students, and found that individuals with higher self-esteem reported greater use of affiliative humor and lower use of self-defeating humor. Self-defeating and aggressive humor were also both associated with lower levels of motivation for academic success.

Paul Frewen and his colleagues similarly found that individuals who reported higher levels of depressed moods tended to report lower use of self-enhancing and (to a lesser degree) affiliative humor, and greater use of self-defeating humor (Frewen, Brinker, Martin, and Dozois, in press). This study also looked at measures of sociotropy and autonomy, two personality dimensions that have been found to be vulnerability factors for depression. *Sociotropy* refers to the degree to which one's sense of self-worth is based excessively on one's perceived likableness to others, making one socially dependent and vulnerable to depression when experiencing interpersonal criticism or rejection. On the other hand, *autonomy* has to do with the degree to which one is invested in preserving independence and defining self-worth in terms of personal achievement, and it is associated with increased vulnerability to depression when people experience achievement-related failures. After controlling for current depression levels, sociotropy was found to be negatively related to self-enhancing humor and positively related to self-defeating humor. Autonomy, in turn, was associated with both self-defeating and aggressive humor. Thus, negative forms of humor appear to be associated with personality traits that make people vulnerable to depression. On the other hand, self-enhancing humor, being negatively related to sociotropy, may serve to protect the individual from becoming depressed during experiences of social rejection.

Previous research has shown that individuals who engage in the cognitive style of rumination (i.e., those who tend to repeatedly go over negative events and feelings in their mind) are particularly vulnerable to depression. A recent study of university students using the HSQ found that individuals with higher scores on self-enhancing and (more weakly) affiliative humor are less likely to engage in rumination (M. L. Olson et al., 2005). Moreover, this study found evidence that these two positive humor styles can buffer the effect of rumination on depression. In particular, participants with lower scores on these two humor styles showed a strong correlation between their frequency of rumination and dysphoric mood symptoms, whereas those with higher humor scores did not show any association between these two variables.

Overall, the correlational findings obtained so far suggest that self-enhancing humor is particularly related in a positive way to emotional well-being, supporting our view that this is an especially healthy humor style. For its part, affiliative humor seems to be somewhat more weakly related to emotional health, producing correlations that are more in line with those found with previous trait humor measures. In contrast, self-defeating humor is consistently negatively associated with well-being measures, indicating that this use of humor to ingratiate oneself with others at one's own expense and deny the presence of negative emotion is particularly related to unhealthy functioning. On the other hand, aggressive humor appears to be largely unrelated to overall psychological well-being. Although earlier theorists such as Freud, Maslow, and Allport seemed to view aggressive forms of humor as being particularly problematic for overall psychological health, our research findings do not provide much support for this view. As we will see later in this chapter, however, aggressive humor seems to play a particularly negative role in regard to the quality of one's close interpersonal relationships.

Before leaving this topic, it is important to note that all of these findings are correlational, and they therefore do not permit us to determine the direction of causality between sense of humor and mental health. For example, the frequent use of self-defeating humor may cause people to be more prone to depression, have lower self-esteem, and so on, but it is equally possible that people engage in this humor style as a consequence of having low levels of psychological well-being. Similarly, although the frequent use of self-enhancing humor may cause people to be less prone to emotional disturbance, it is also possible that being more psychologically healthy causes people to use humor in this way. It may also be the case that humor styles and components of psychological health have no causal connection at all, but are both consequences of a third variable, such as neuroticism. The most we can say at the present time is that emotional well-being tends to be associated with the presence of self-enhancing and affiliative uses of humor and the absence of self-defeating humor.

One way for researchers to address these questions of causality may be through the use of daily experience methods or event-sampling procedures, in which the use of different styles of humor as well as various aspects of psychological well-being are assessed repeatedly in individuals over a period of days or weeks (Reis and Gable, 2000). By examining time-lagged associations, it may be possible to determine whether more frequent use of particular styles of humor is followed or preceded by changes in well-being over hours or days, providing some indication of the direction of causality in these associations. I will have more to say about these sorts of research methods later in this chapter.

HUMOR, STRESS, AND COPING

A second general way humor may potentially be beneficial to mental (as well as physical) health has to do with its use in coping with stressful life experiences. A considerable amount of research has shown that high levels of stressful events, such as natural disasters, relationship conflicts, work pressures, and financial problems, can have adverse effects on one's mental and physical health, producing such negative outcomes as emotional disturbance, cognitive inefficiency, and behavioral impairments (A. K. Johnson and Anderson, 1990; Sanderson, 2004).

However, these sorts of negative outcomes of stress are not inevitable. Based on the theoretical framework of Richard Lazarus and his colleagues (e.g., Lazarus and Folkman, 1984), a great deal of research has shown that psychological appraisal and coping processes play an important role in determining whether or not potentially stressful life experiences result in adverse physiological and psychological outcomes. Over the years, many theorists have suggested that the ability to respond with humor in the face of stress and adversity may be an important and effective coping skill (Freud, 1928; Lefcourt, 2001; Lefcourt and Martin, 1986). Norman Dixon (1980) even suggested that humor may have evolved in humans specifically for this purpose.

Many authors have noted that humor, because it inherently involves incongruity and multiple interpretations, provides a way for individuals to shift perspective on a stressful situation, reappraising it from a new and less-threatening point of view. As a consequence of this humorous reappraisal, the situation becomes less stressful and more manageable, and the individual is less likely to experience a stress response (Dixon, 1980). Walter O'Connell (1976) described humorous people as being "skilled in rapid perceptual-cognitive switches in frames of reference" (p. 327), an ability that presumably enables them to reappraise a problem situation, distance themselves from its immediate threat, and thereby reduce the often paralyzing feelings of anxiety and helplessness. Similarly, Rollo May (1953) stated that humor has the function of "preserving the self . . . It is the healthy way of feeling a 'distance' between one's self and the problem, a way of standing off and looking at one's problem with perspective" (p. 54).

As noted in Chapter 2, superiority theory, which views humor as a form of playful aggression, can also be seen as a basis for conceptualizing humor as a coping mechanism. By poking fun at other people and situations that would normally be viewed as threatening or constricting, one is able to gain a sense of liberation and freedom from threat and thereby experience positive feelings of well-being and efficacy. As Horace Kallen (1968) wrote, "I laugh at that which has endangered or degraded or has fought to suppress, enslave, or destroy what I cherish and has failed. My laughter signalizes its failure and my own liberation" (p. 59). Other authors, taking an existential approach, have emphasized the sense of liberation, mastery, and self-respect provided by humor in the face of adversity (Knox, 1951; Mindess, 1971). Thus, as a means of asserting one's superiority through playful aggression, humor is a way of refusing to be overcome by the people and situations that threaten one's well-being. At the same time, though, with the use of aggressive forms of humor in coping there is a risk of cynicism, hostility, and impairment of social relationships.

Although coping humor may at times involve an aggressive element, some theorists have also emphasized the importance of being able to laugh at one's own faults, failures, and limitations, while maintaining a positive sense of self-esteem. Gordon Allport (1950) stated, for example, that "the neurotic who learns to laugh at himself may be on the way to self-management, perhaps to cure" (p. 280). By not taking oneself too seriously, one is able to let go of excessively perfectionistic expectations while remaining motivated to achieve realistic goals. There is an important distinction, however, between self-deprecating humor based on a fundamental sense of self-worth and excessively self-disparaging humor arising from a negative self-concept, as measured by the self-defeating humor scale of the HSQ.

Experimental Investigations of Humor as a Stress Moderator

A number of experiments have been conducted to investigate the effectiveness of a humor manipulation in mitigating the emotional or psychophysiological effects of mildly stressful laboratory stressors. Herbert Lefcourt and I (Lefcourt and Martin, 1986) instructed university students to make up either a humorous narrative, a non-humorous "intellectual" narrative, or no narrative while they were watching a silent film entitled *Subincision*, which depicts a rather gory and evidently painful circumcision ritual performed on adolescent boys in a tribe of Australian aborigines. The results revealed that, among female participants, those who created a humorous narrative (as compared to those in the other two conditions) reported less negative emotions and displayed fewer behavioral indicators of distress (e.g., averted gaze, grimacing, hand-rubbing) while watching the film, providing evidence of a stress-moderating effect of humor. The male participants, however, showed minimal distress in all three conditions, suggesting that the film was not very stressful for them.

A similar methodology was used by Michelle Newman and Arthur Stone (1996) in an experiment in which male college students were instructed to create either a humorous or a serious narrative while watching a film depicting gruesome accidents in a lumber mill. Compared to those in the serious narrative condition, the participants in the humorous condition reported less emotional distress and had lower skin conductance and heart rate and higher skin temperature for up to 15 minutes following the film, indicating a reduced stress response. Taken together, these studies provided some evidence that participants who actively create humor to reframe a potentially stressful situation have a lower stress response, as measured by self-rated moods, behaviors, and physiological reactions (see also Lehman et al., 2001).

Instead of having participants create humorous narratives during stressful situations in the laboratory, other researchers have used comedy videotapes as a humor manipulation. Arnie Cann and his colleagues showed male and female participants either a humorous stand-up comedy video, a nonhumorous nature video, or no video, after they had viewed a stressful segment of a movie depicting an airplane crash (Cann, Holt, and Calhoun, 1999). Analyses of self-rated moods following the intervention revealed that the humorous video enhanced positive emotions but did not reduce anxiety relative to the nonhumorous video.

In a subsequent experiment, Cann and his colleagues compared the effects of exposure to a humorous versus a neutral videotape either before or after participants watched a stressful film depicting scenes of death (Cann, Calhoun, and Nance, 2000). Regardless of whether the intervention preceded or followed the stressful film, the humorous video produced lower ratings of depression and anger and higher positive moods compared to the neutral video. For anxiety-related moods, however, the humorous intervention was only effective when it was presented before the stressful film rather than after it. The authors suggested that the elevated positive emotions associated with humor may serve to counteract feelings of depression and anger, whereas the effects of humor on anxiety may be more cognitively mediated: humor preceding the stressor might work as a cognitive prime, changing the way subsequent events are interpreted and thereby reducing subsequent anxiety.

In addition to the use of emotionally distressing films, researchers interested in the effects of humor on stress have employed various types of frustrating tasks, such as unsolvable anagrams and difficult mental arithmetic problems, to produce mild stress in the laboratory. One study found that exposure to humorous cartoons mitigated the performance-impairing effect of working on unsolvable anagrams (Trice, 1985). Another experiment similarly found that exposure to a humorous videotape, compared to a nonhumorous video, was effective in reducing anxiety following an unsolvable anagram task, but only among male participants (Abel and Maxwell, 2002). However, a study using a 10-minute mental arithmetic task to induce a mild state of anxiety found no differences among comedy, relaxation, and neutral videotapes on state anxiety, heart rate, or skin conductance (White and Winzelberg, 1992). Although this study failed to demonstrate a stress-moderating effect of humor, this may have been due to the minimally stressful nature of the arithmetic task.

In an experiment by Nancy Yovetich and her colleagues, stress was induced by falsely informing participants that they would receive a painful electric shock 12 minutes later (Yovetich, Dale, and Hudak, 1990). While waiting for the supposed shock, the participants listened either to a humorous audiotape, a nonhumorous tape, or no tape. Overall, the participants showed increasing levels of self-rated anxiety and heart rate across the 12-minute period, indicating increased anticipatory anxiety. However, those in the humorous tape condition showed a less steep increase in self-reported anxiety (but no difference in heart rate) as compared to those in the other two conditions, providing some evidence of a stress-buffering effect of humor.

In summary, although the results have not always replicated, these experimental laboratory studies provide some support for the hypothesized stress-buffering effects of humor. When participants actively create humor during mildly stressful experiences, or when they are exposed to comedy before or after such events, they tend to report more positive and less negative moods and show less stress-related physiological arousal as compared to participants in control groups. These studies extend the findings of the laboratory experiments described earlier, indicating that the general effects of humor on moods also occur in mildly stressful conditions.

Although these lab experiments allow researchers to identify the direction of causality between humor and stress responses, their rather artificial nature makes it difficult to generalize the findings to everyday experiences. In particular, the stressors used in these experiments are much milder and of shorter duration than real-life stressors, and the humor manipulations with solitary subjects in the laboratory are only an approximation of the way humor is typically experienced in everyday life. It is therefore important to augment these laboratory findings with more naturalistic types of research examining the use of humor in coping with real-life stressors. I will discuss this sort of research in the following sections.

Correlational Studies of Sense of Humor and Coping Styles

As we saw earlier, theorists have suggested a number of possible ways in which humor might serve to mitigate the effects of stress. For example, taking a humorous perspective on a stressful situation might enable individuals to alter their frame of reference, changing appraisals of negative threat into ones of positive challenge, and increasing feelings of mastery and control over the situation. Other potential coping-related functions of humor include enhancing social support, denying reality, venting aggressive feelings, and providing distraction. A number of studies have explored these different hypotheses by examining correlations between various sense of humor scales and measures assessing the types of cognitive appraisals and coping styles participants typically use when dealing with stress.

In one study, Nick Kuiper and colleagues (1993) examined the relationship between the Coping Humor Scale and university students' cognitive appraisals of their first midterm examination in an Introductory Psychology course. The results showed that, prior to the exam, students with higher scores on the CHS appraised it as more of a positive challenge rather than a negative threat. Following the exam, those with high CHS scores reappraised the exam as being more important and positively challenging if they had done well on it, but lowered their importance and challenge ratings if they had done poorly. They also adjusted their expectations of how well they would do on the next exam in a realistic manner, based on their performance on the previous one. In contrast, those with low CHS scores rated the exam as being more important if they did poorly rather than well on it, and failed to adjust their expectations about the next exam according to their past performance.

Higher CHS scores were also found to be associated with lower scores on a measure of dysfunctional attitudes involving unrealistic and perfectionistic expectations about achievement and social relationships. These findings provide some support for the idea that one way a sense of humor may relate to better coping with stress has to do with the types of cognitive appraisals that individuals make about potential stressors. Those with a greater tendency to use humor in coping with stress appear to appraise potentially stressful situations as more challenging rather than threatening, and to evaluate their own performance and adjust their expectations for future performance in a less perfectionistic and more realistic and self-protective manner.

The relation between sense of humor and appraisal processes was also investigated in other research by Nicholas Kuiper and his colleagues (Kuiper, McKenzie, and Belanger, 1995). In one study they had participants complete a negative life events measure for the past month, and then asked them questions about the degree to which they were able to change their perspective or point of view when attempting to cope with these stressful events. Individuals with high scores on the CHS, in comparison with low scorers, reported that they were more likely to make a conscious effort to view their problems from alternate perspectives and were better able to do so, and that these changes in perspective resulted in more positive perceptions of the events. In a second study, they examined subjects' cognitive appraisals while completing a challenging picture-drawing task. Participants with higher sense of humor scores appraised the task as being more of a positive challenge and less of a negative threat and reported putting more effort into accomplishing it, providing further evidence that individual differences in humor are related to different ways of appraising potentially stressful events.

Several studies have also examined correlations between sense of humor scales and measures of people's typical styles of coping with stress. One study (Kuiper et al., 1993) found that the CHS was positively correlated with both emotional distancing (e.g., "Don't let it get to me;" "Refuse to think too much about it") and a confrontive coping style (e.g., "Stand my ground and fight for what I want"), suggesting that the use of humor in coping involves both emotional self-protection and active confrontation of problems. A study of humor and coping in women business executives (P. S. Fry, 1995) found that the CHS and SHRQ were positively associated with both emotion-focused (i.e., regulation of one's emotional reactions) and existential (i.e., taking a detached, philosophical approach to problems) coping orientations. Specific coping strategies associated with humor included seeking practical and emotional social support, expressiveness (venting emotions), tension-reduction (e.g., use of relaxation techniques), and acceptance ("Accept each day as it comes;" "No matter how bad things are, they could always be worse").

In another study examining correlations between several self-report humor scales (CHS, SHRQ, and SHQ) and a measure of defensive coping styles, these sense of humor measures were generally found to be related to the coping styles of minimization (denial), replacement (sublimation), substitution (displacement), and reversal (reaction formation), although the pattern of correlations differed for different humor scales and for males and females (Rim, 1988). Finally, a study using the MSHS found that higher scores on this humor scale were associated with greater use of planful problem solving, positive reappraisal, distancing oneself, and emotional self-management (Abel, 2002).

Overall, these studies suggest that high-humor individuals tend to have more realistic and flexible and less threat-related cognitive appraisals of potentially stressful situations, and that they tend to deal with stress using a variety of coping strategies and defenses, particularly those involving self-protective cognitive reframing and emotional management. Once again, however, it is important to note that the correlational approach of these studies does not permit us to determine the direction of causality. It may be that humor directly contributes to these cognitive appraisal and coping styles, but it is also possible that humor is simply a by-product of these styles of coping, or that both humor and associated coping styles are independent consequences of some other traits (e.g., extraversion). Also, this trait approach to measuring humor and coping styles does not provide much insight into the actual processes involved when humor is used in coping, or the context in which this occurs.

Humor in Coping with Specific Life Stressors

There is a great deal of anecdotal evidence, as well as some empirical research, indicating that humor can be beneficial for emotional survival in dealing with extreme and uncontrollable stressful situations such as prisoner of war and concentration camps. One study evaluated the psychological health of 82 surviving crew members of the *USS Pueblo* shortly after their release from 11 months of imprisonment in North Korea in 1969 (C. V. Ford and Spaulding, 1973). Humor was one of several coping strategies that were found to be significantly associated with better psychological adjustment. Coping humor in this stressful situation took the form of joking about the characteristics of captors, giving funny nicknames to the guards and fellow prisoners, and telling jokes to one another.

More recently, Linda Henman (2001) reported a qualitative study based on interviews with more than 60 American servicemen who had been prisoners of war (POWs) in Vietnam. Despite being in captivity for over seven years and enduring isolation, starvation, torture, and beatings, these individuals showed a remarkable level of adjustment. When asked about their methods of coping, most of the participants emphasized the importance of humor in maintaining their resilience. Humor was described as a way of eliciting positive emotions, maintaining group cohesion and morale, and fighting back at the captors. By cracking jokes about the guards and about the hardships they endured, the POWs were able to gain a sense of mastery and invincibility in a situation over which they had no real control. It is worth noting that the use of humor in coping occurred primarily during interactions among the POWs, rather than while they were alone. One participant observed that "the larger the group, the more lighthearted things were. The smaller the group, the more intense things were" (p. 86). Some of the prisoners even risked torture to tell a joke through the walls to another prisoner who needed cheering up.

The importance of humor in coping with atrocities has also been emphasized by concentration camp survivors. In recounting his experiences as a prisoner in a Nazi concentration camp during World War II, Viktor Frankl (1984) described humor as "another of the soul's weapons in the fight for self-preservation" (p. 63). Recognizing the importance of humor in maintaining morale, he and his fellow prisoners agreed to tell each other amusing stories every day. One favorite form of humor involved joking about the ways their experience of imprisonment might affect them after their liberation. For example, one prisoner joked that at future dinner engagements they might forget themselves and ask the hostess to ladle the soup from the bottom of the pot to get the treasured vegetables instead of the watery broth on top. Their jokes also included a good deal of mockery of the guards, which gave them a feeling of superiority over their captors. Such uses of humor were also depicted in Roberto Benigni's 1997 movie, *Life is Beautiful*, in which a Jewish father engages in humorous antics to shield his son from the horrors of a Nazi death camp, denying reality by pretending that the Holocaust is nothing but a game in which the winner gets to ride in a tank.

Although humor appears to be an effective way of coping with the extreme and uncontrollable horror of being a prisoner of war, research on the use of humor in less severe and more controllable stressful situations has been less clear-cut. For example, studies investigating the use of humor in coping with high-stress occupations have produced mixed results. One study provided evidence for the effectiveness of humor in coping with stress among soldiers undergoing an intensive combat training course in the Israeli army (Bizi, Keinan, and Beit-Hallahmi, 1988). Humor production and appreciation were assessed using both self-report measures and peer ratings, and the quality of coping under stress was evaluated using ratings by peers and commanding officers. Greater peer-rated (but not self-rated) humor was found to be significantly related to higher peer ratings of performance under stress and higher commander ratings of initiative and responsibility. This was especially true for active humor (generating joking comments rather than merely laughing at others' humor). These findings were interpreted as providing support for the view that a sense of humor is associated with better coping during stressful military training.

In contrast, however, a recent study of health care staff working with AIDS and cancer patients suggested that the use of humor as a coping strategy may actually have *negative* rather than positive consequences (Dorz et al., 2003). The coping styles of 528 physicians and nurses in 20 hospitals in northern Italy were assessed using a measure called the Coping Orientations to Problem Experiences (COPE) (Carver, Scheier, and Weintraub, 1989), which contains a scale assessing the use of humor in coping. In addition, the participants completed measures of anxiety, depression, and emotional burnout. Surprisingly, the data analyses revealed that higher levels of humor in coping were associated with *greater* emotional exhaustion and feelings of depersonalization. Since this study was correlational, the direction of causality between humor use and burnout is unclear. Nonetheless, the results cast some doubt on the overall effectiveness of humor in coping in a high-stress health care setting.

Some qualitative research on the use of humor in stressful occupations helps to shed some light on these puzzling findings. Using a participant observer approach, Joan Sayre (2001) observed the use of humor among staff in a psychiatric unit. She found that it could be divided into two broad categories, a fairly benign "whimsical" type (incongruous witticisms, bravado, and self-denigrating humor) and a more aggressive "sarcastic" type (discounting, malicious, and gallows humor). Sarcastic humor was more common than whimsical humor among the staff, and most of the humor was directed at making fun of patient behaviors when out of earshot of the patients. Although the relative benefits of the different types of humor were not directly tested in this study, the author suggested that, whereas some of these uses of humor seemed to be beneficial in managing anxiety in a socially acceptable manner, the more aggressive forms appeared to promote negative, cynical attitudes toward patients, which might actually have impaired therapeutic effectiveness and contributed to morale problems.

A similarly mixed view of the benefits of humor emerged in a qualitative study in which emergency personnel were interviewed about their methods of coping with the stress of handling dead bodies following major disasters such as airplane crashes and explosions (McCarroll et al., 1993). Although some participants viewed humor as an important tension reducer, others expressed reservations about its appropriateness. Similar reservations were also expressed in a review of research relating to the potential benefits and risks of the use of humor for coping in emergency work (C. Moran and Massam, 1997). Overall, then, the use of humor in coping with work-related stress seems to have mixed benefits. As we have seen earlier in this chapter, probably not all forms of humor are beneficial for coping; instead, whether or not it contributes to better coping likely depends on the style or type of humor used.

Research on the use of humor in coping with life-threatening illness has also yielded somewhat equivocal findings. In one study, 59 women who had been diagnosed with breast cancer were asked to complete measures of moods and coping strategies (using the COPE) before surgery, immediately after surgery, and at 3-, 6-, and 12-month follow-ups (Carver et al., 1993). Greater use of humor in coping was found to be associated with reduced emotional distress, but this relation was significant at only two of the five assessment times (three-month and six-month follow-up).

In a larger study of coping with breast cancer, 236 patients completed the COPE as well as measures of emotional distress (Culver et al., 2004). No significant correlations were found between humor in coping and any of the measures of emotional distress, raising questions about the overall effectiveness of humor as a means of coping with breast cancer. However, a limitation of both of these studies, as well as some of the research on coping with work-related stress described earlier, was the use of the COPE humor scale. This test has been shown to be positively correlated with all four subscales of the Humor Styles Questionnaire, indicating that it does not distinguish between potentially beneficial affiliative and self-enhancing humor and potentially detrimental aggressive and self-defeating humor styles (R. A. Martin et al., 2003).

Using observational methods instead of relying on self-report humor scales, a longitudinal study of bereavement by George Bonanno and Dacher Keltner (1997) provided evidence for a beneficial effect of benign humor in coping with the death of one's spouse. Men and women who had lost their spouse six months previously were videotaped during an interview about their relationship with their deceased partner. The tapes were subsequently coded for Duchenne and non-Duchenne smiles and laughter, and measures of emotional adjustment and physical health were obtained at 14 and 25 months postloss. Analyses showed that a greater frequency of Duchenne smiling and laughter (indicating genuine amusement) during the interview was a significant predictor of fewer grief symptoms (e.g., intrusive memories of the deceased, emotional numbness, inability to part with the deceased person's possessions, depressed mood) at 14 and 25 months, even after controlling for moods at the time of the interview. Thus, the ability to experience humor early in bereavement, as demonstrated by smiling and laughter showing genuine mirth while talking about the deceased spouse, was associated with better emotional adjustment more than a year later. Further analyses of the same data by Keltner and Bonanno (1997) found that individuals who displayed more frequent Duchenne (but not non-Duchenne) laughter during the interview reported more positive and less negative moods and showed a greater dissociation between verbal reports of distress and autonomic arousal, suggesting that one of the benefits of genuine humor in coping may be that it enables the individual to dissociate from negative emotions.

In summary, although many authors have proposed that humor may be a beneficial way of coping with occupational stress, bereavement, illness, and other major stressors (e.g., Sumners, 1988; van Wormer and Boes, 1997), empirical evidence for such benefits is limited and somewhat mixed. Once again, the inconsistent findings may be due to a failure on the part of researchers to distinguish among different uses of humor, some of which may be effective for coping in some types of situations but less so in others, while other uses of humor may actually be detrimental in coping with certain stressors. For example, highly aggressive or macabre gallows humor may be almost essential to survival in the nearly hopeless situation of a prison camp, but may contribute to feelings of cynicism, alienation, and burnout in a stressful work environment where other more constructive forms of coping are available. In addition, mildly self-deprecating and whimsical uses of humor might enhance group morale and cohesiveness in a work setting, but frequent teasing and practical jokes might impair morale. Because of the multifaceted functions of humor and their widely varied social and emotional effects, it seems to be overly simplistic to view humor in general as a purely beneficial method of coping. Further research is clearly needed to investigate in more detail the potential benefits and pitfalls of different styles of humor in coping with particular stressors.

Sense of Humor as a Stress Moderator

The idea that humor is beneficial for coping with stress suggests that people with a greater sense of humor should be less likely to suffer the adverse emotional and physiological consequences of stressful life events. Although high-humor individuals may be just as likely as their low-humor counterparts to experience stressors such as financial losses, occupational pressures, unemployment, death of a loved one, and relationship breakups, their more frequent use of humor might enable them to appraise these stressors as less threatening, garner more social support, and generally cope more effectively, resulting in less likelihood of becoming emotionally distressed and physically ill as a consequence of the stressors.

A popular way of testing this hypothesis is the stress-moderator paradigm (Cohen and Edwards, 1989), in which researchers use questionnaires and other testing procedures to assess three types of variables: (1) some aspect of sense of humor measured as a personality trait; (2) the frequency of major stressful life events or minor daily hassles experienced over a specified period of time in the recent past, such as the preceding six months; and (3) current levels of particular adaptational outcomes, such as prevailing levels of depression or anxiety or the number of different illness symptoms experienced recently. By using hierarchical multiple regression analyses with a stressor x sense of humor interaction term, researchers can determine whether the strength of the association between the frequency of stressors and adaptational outcomes varies as a function of level of sense of humor. The stress-buffering hypothesis is supported when the correlation between stressors and negative outcomes is found to become weaker as sense of humor increases across participants, and when high levels of stressors are associated with less disturbance among high-humor as compared to low-humor individuals (Figure 7). A number of studies using this paradigm have been conducted over the past two decades, using a variety of different sense of humor tests, stressor measures, and outcome variables.

Herbert Lefcourt and I reported three studies that employed different methods of assessing sense of humor and found fairly consistent evidence of a stress-moderating effect of humor (R. A. Martin and Lefcourt, 1983). In each of these studies, we used a life events checklist to assess the number of major life stressors that our undergraduate participants had experienced during the preceding year, and a test of overall mood disturbance (depression, anxiety, tension, anger, fatigue) as our outcome measure. Each study employed different methods of assessing sense of humor. In the first study, using self-report trait humor measures, we found a significant stress-buffering effect with the SHRQ, CHS, and SHQ-L, indicating that individuals with higher scores on these measures were less likely to report disturbed moods after experiencing high levels of stressful experiences.

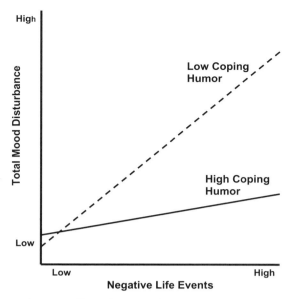

FIGURE 7   Stress-moderating effect of sense of humor. As the number of stressful life events increases, individuals with higher scores on the Coping Humor Scale show a less steep increase in mood disturbance as compared to those with lower scores on this humor measure (from Martin & Lefcourt, 1983).

In the second study, we assessed sense of humor using a behavioral measure of humor production ability. Participants were asked to make up a humorous narrative in the laboratory, describing a number of objects in a funny way, and these monologues were subsequently rated for overall funniness. Once again, the results revealed a significant stress-moderating effect: individuals who were better able to make up a funny monologue on demand in this rather difficult task showed less likelihood of becoming emotionally distressed following high levels of life stress.

The third study employed a similar humor-production approach, this time involving an even more stressful laboratory situation. The participants were instructed to create a humorous narrative while watching the *Subincision* film, and when the rated funniness of their narratives was used as the measure of humor in regression analyses, the results once again revealed a significant stress-buffering effect of humor production ability. We speculated that those individuals who were able to create funnier narratives in these mildly stressful conditions in the laboratory might also be the ones who tend to engage in humor more frequently during times of stress in their everyday lives, enabling them to cope more effectively and therefore become less emotionally distressed.

These encouraging initial findings were subsequently followed up in a number of similar studies by various researchers, some of which replicated our stress-moderator findings while others did not. One study using both cross-sectional (within one time period) and prospective analyses (assessing stressors and sense of humor at one time point to predict prevailing moods two months later), found a significant stress-moderating effect of the CHS and SHRQ in the prediction of depression but not anxiety (Nezu et al., 1988).

A study of coping among women business executives also found significant stress-buffering effects of the CHS and SHRQ using a measure of minor daily hassles as the stressor measure and tests of self-esteem and emotional burnout as the outcome measures (P. S. Fry, 1995). Another study found a significant stress-moderating effect of the MSHS in the prediction of illness symptoms and anxiety, although the anxiety finding was only significant for male participants (Abel, 1998). In addition, my student James Dobbin and I found stress-buffering effects of three self-report humor scales on the negative relationship between daily hassles and levels of salivary immunoglobulin-A, a measure of immunity, indicating that high-humor individuals, compared to those with less of a sense of humor, were less likely to have reduced immunity after experiencing high numbers of stressful hassles (R. A. Martin and Dobbin, 1988).

Taking a somewhat different approach, Nicholas Kuiper, Kathy Dance, and I (1992) used the stress-moderator paradigm to examine interactions between sense of humor measures and both positive and negative life events in predicting positive rather than negative moods. Consistent with the stress-buffering hypothesis, we found significant interactions between the frequency of stressful negative life events and the CHS, SHRQ, and SHQ-M in predicting positive affect. Among individuals with low scores on these humor scales, more frequent negative events were associated with lower levels of positive moods, whereas those with high humor scores tended to maintain high levels of positive moods regardless of the number of negative events they had experienced. Analyses using the frequency of recent positive life events (e.g., enjoyable experiences, successful achievements) in the place of negative stressors also revealed significant interactions with the two subscales of the SHQ in predicting positive affect, indicating that the frequency of positive events was more strongly related to increased positive moods for high-humor as compared to low-humor individuals. These results suggested that, besides helping one to maintain one's positive moods during times of stress, a sense of humor seems to enhance the enjoyment of positive events.

In a later study, Kuiper and I (1998b) employed a daily diary approach to investigate the stress-buffering hypothesis. In this study, adult men and women from the community were asked to keep a three-day record of each time they laughed, as well as completing measures of the number of stressful events they experienced over the course of each day and their levels of positive and negative moods each evening. Interestingly, correlational analyses revealed that people who laughed more frequently over the three days did not necessarily experience more positive or less negative moods overall. Instead, the relationship between laughter and moods depended on their levels of daily stress. In particular, a significant stress-moderating effect revealed that greater numbers of stressful life events were associated with more negative moods, but only among individuals with a low frequency of laughter. In contrast, individuals with a higher frequency of daily laughter had relatively low levels of negative moods regardless of their stress levels. Similar effects were found with positive moods, but only among men.

A recent study examined the potential role of humor in coping with the effects of mathematics performance anxiety in women (T. E. Ford et al., 2004). Female college students were administered a mathematics test in either high- or low-threat conditions. In the high-threat condition, they were told that this test assesses mathematical aptitude and has been found to be more difficult for women than men; in the low-threat condition, they were told that it assesses the process of general problem solving and that men and women tend to perform equally well on it. In support of the stress-buffering hypothesis, the results revealed a significant interaction between scores on the CHS and threat condition in predicting performance on the test and self-reported anxiety. Whereas all participants performed well on the test and had low anxiety scores in the low-threat condition, greater coping humor was related to better test performance and lower anxiety in the high-threat condition. These results suggested that the use of humor in coping with stress may reduce the effects of stereotype threat on women's mathematics-related anxiety and performance.

Although the foregoing research was generally quite supportive of the hypothesis that a sense of humor may buffer the adverse psychological effects of stress, some other investigations have failed to replicate these findings. One early study found no evidence of a stress-buffering effect of humor on depression or anxiety (Safranek and Schill, 1982). However, sense of humor was assessed in this study by means of a humor appreciation test in which participants were asked to rate the funniness of several categories of jokes. The null results may have been due to the fact that the enjoyment of various types of jokes likely has little to do with the degree to which individuals actually use humor in coping with life stress (Lefcourt and Martin, 1986).

A more serious challenge to the stress-buffering hypothesis came from a study by Albert Porterfield (1987) with more than 200 participants that did not find any evidence of stress-moderating effects of humor using the CHS and SHRQ as humor measures, the same test of major life stressors that Lefcourt and I had used in our original studies, and measures of depression and physical illness symptoms as the outcome variables. Another study with more than 700 participants also failed to find a stress-moderating effect of the CHS in predicting physical illness symptoms (Korotkov and Hannah, 1994). Similarly, a study of 334 undergraduates did not find a significant stress-moderating effect of coping humor on mood disturbance (Labott and Martin, 1987).

Even more confusing results were found in a study by Craig Anderson and Lynn Arnoult (1989). In this study, undergraduates completed the CHS, a measure of major life stressors, and tests of negative affect, depression, insomnia, physical illness symptoms, and an overall health rating. No evidence of a stress-moderating effect of coping humor was found on negative affect, depression, or illness symptoms. On the other hand, the interaction between CHS and stressors was significant in the prediction of overall wellness and insomnia. However, closer examination of the interaction revealed that the results for wellness were in the wrong direction: high-humor individuals showed a *stronger* association between stressful events and poor health than did low-humor individuals. Only the results for insomnia were in the predicted direction.

A study by James Overholser (1992) also produced some results contradicting the stress-buffering hypothesis. Undergraduate participants completed three different types of humor measures: the CHS, humor appreciation (participants' funniness ratings of a set of cartoons), and humor production ability (rated funniness of cartoon captions created by participants). The outcome measures were tests of depression, loneliness, and self-esteem. Regression analyses using the CHS revealed a significant interaction with major life stressors only in the prediction of depression, among females but not males. However, the correlation tables reveal that this effect was in the wrong direction: females with high CHS scores showed a stronger association between stress and depression than did those with low scores on this humor test. A few significant interactions were also found between stressors and humor production ability in predicting loneliness (for both males and females) and self-esteem (for females only). However, since the direction of these effects was not reported, it is unknown whether they also were in the wrong direction.

In summary, the stress-moderator research using the multiple regression approach has yielded some rather inconsistent evidence for stress-buffering effects of a sense of humor. Nine studies found at least some significant stress-moderating effects, three obtained no significant results, and two produced results in the wrong direction. There does not seem to be any clear pattern to the particular humor scales, stressor measures, or outcome variables that did and did not produce significant findings. Although there are enough positive findings in this research to warrant some optimism about the stress-buffering potential of a sense of humor, it is difficult to discern from this research which particular uses of humor are beneficial for coping with which sorts of stressors to produce which types of outcomes.

Process Approaches to Investigating Humor in Coping

The inconsistent patterns of findings from the stress-moderator studies described in the previous section may be due in part to several inherent weaknesses of this research methodology (Somerfield and McCrae, 2000). These include reliance on trait measures of humor, retrospective assessment of stressors occurring over a period of time, and use of a between-person, cross-sectional design. Since the variables are typically assessed at only one point in time, this stress-moderator paradigm provides only a static "snapshot" of what is an inherently dynamic coping process. Furthermore, a high score on a trait measure of sense of humor does not necessarily mean that an individual actually used humor to cope with the particular stressors that are measured by the life events checklists. Consequently, this approach does not allow researchers to examine directly how particular types of humor are used on a day-to-day basis to cope with specific ongoing stressors.

Howard Tennen and colleagues have advocated the use of a more "real-time" approach to stress and coping research, assessing proximal stressors, coping efforts, and adaptational outcome variables repeatedly in individuals as they occur over a period of days or weeks (Tennen et al., 2000). By capturing these variables closer to their actual occurrence, researchers can minimize recall error while studying coping processes within individuals over time. Such data can be analyzed using multilevel analysis procedures such as Hierarchical Linear Modeling (HLM; Bryk and Raudenbush, 1992), which combine the advantages of both an idiographic and a nomothetic approach. This approach to analyzing stress-moderating effects of humor is conceptually similar to the multiple regression method described in the previous section, but the focus is on changes within individuals over time rather than differences between individuals at one time. In other words, the methodology enables researchers to examine whether individuals show evidence of higher or lower levels of well-being on days when they engage in particular styles of humor to cope with particular types of stressors, relative to other days when they experience similar stressors but do not use those humor styles.

So far, this process-oriented approach has been used in only one study examining potential stress-buffering effects of humor, which was conducted by my former graduate student, Patricia Doris (2004), as part of her PhD research. Twice a week for three weeks, university students participating in this study were asked to log onto an Internet website at the end of the day and complete a brief questionnaire, recording their stressful experiences, negative moods, and uses of humor during that day. The humor questions were modified items from the Humor Styles Questionnaire, asking participants how frequently they had engaged in affiliative, self-enhancing, aggressive, and self-defeating styles of humor that day. Thus, humor was assessed in terms of the frequency with which individuals engaged in various humor behaviors on a particular day, rather than their typical or habitual humor tendencies, as in trait measurement approaches. Stressful events and moods were also assessed for the same day, rather than being measured retrospectively over weeks or months. HLM analyses were used to examine the interactions between day-to-day stressors and humor use in relation to daily negative moods both within and between participants concurrently.

The results revealed significant stress-moderating effects for self-enhancing, aggressive, and self-defeating humor, but not affiliative humor. In each case, a higher number of stressful events was associated with more negative moods on days when participants did not engage in these types of humor, whereas stressful events did not result in such negative moods on days in which participants engaged more frequently in these three humor styles. Although these findings will need to be replicated before we can place much confidence in them, they provide preliminary evidence for the stress-buffering effects of three of the four HSQ humor styles.

The results with self-enhancing humor were exactly as expected, suggesting that the use of this healthy style of humor to cope with stress is an effective way of regulating one's moods when experiencing daily stressors. The finding of similar results with both aggressive and self-defeating humor may at first seem surprising, but they also make some sense. As suggested earlier, although aggressive uses of humor may be potentially injurious to relationships in the long run, aggressively making fun of people and situations that are perceived as threatening to one's well-being may be a way of reducing immediate feelings of threat and associated negative moods. Similarly with self-defeating humor, on days when one is experiencing a great deal of stress, the use of humor to ingratiate oneself with others and deny one's feelings may be a way of boosting one's spirits and mitigating the negative emotional effects of stress, at least in the short run. Moreover, the temporary alleviation of negative emotion may act as a reinforcer for the use of these aggressive and self-defeating types of humor, even though the longer-term effects may be detrimental to well-being, explaining why these potentially maladaptive uses of humor tend to be maintained in some individuals as habitual coping styles. Thus, although aggressive and self-defeating humor styles may mitigate the emotional effects of stress in the short term, they may be more maladaptive in the longer run.

Interestingly, the use of affiliative humor did not appear to moderate the effects of daily stress on negative moods. Instead, this type of humor showed a direct mood effect, with greater uses of daily affiliative humor being associated with less negative and more positive moods regardless of stress levels. It is worth noting that in this study, Doris also used the traditional cross-sectional multiple regression paradigm to examine stress-moderating effects of humor, using several trait measures of humor including the HSQ, CHS, and SHRQ, major life events assessed retrospectively over six months, and prevailing moods. The failure to find any significant stress-moderating effects in these analyses further underscores the weaknesses of the cross-sectional trait approach.

The process-oriented repeated measures approach, using multilevel analysis procedures such as HLM, appears to be a promising methodology for further research on the role of humor in coping with stress. Future research could also examine the relative benefits of particular styles of humor in coping with different types of stressors. For example, stressors could be categorized on the basis of whether they involve conflicts with close friends or acquaintances, problems at work, failures to achieve an academic or work goal, and so on, as well as the participant's degree of perceived control over the events. Different styles of humor may be more or less effective with different types of stressors.

Researchers might also wish to consider other potentially relevant styles of humor besides those assessed by the HSQ. Other adaptational outcomes should also be examined, including specific mood states, psychophysiological arousal levels, illness symptoms, and so forth. In addition, different sampling procedures could be used over different time periods. For example, the availability of small handheld computers now makes it possible to collect ongoing data relating to stressors, humor use, moods, and even physiological arousal in "real time" over the course of the day. These methods may enable researchers to examine the process of humor use in coping in a more fine-grained manner.

INTERPERSONAL ASPECTS OF HUMOR IN MENTAL HEALTH

As we have seen throughout this book, humor typically occurs in the context of social interaction. Until recently, however, as in other areas of the psychology of humor, much of the research on humor and mental health has tended to ignore its inherently social nature. Viewing humor as a form of interpersonal interaction allows us to think about how it may contribute to social relationships, which in turn may have an impact on the individual's psychological health.

There is a great deal of research indicating that social relationships have a profound influence on one's level of happiness and general psychological well-being (for a review, see Berscheid and Reis, 1998). Summarizing the research in this area, Harry Reis (2001) stated that "there is widespread evidence that socially involved persons are happier, healthier, and live longer than socially isolated persons do" (p. 58). For example, married people, on average, tend to have better mental and physical health than do unmarried people. Research has also shown that people with better social skills, enabling them to form close and satisfying relationships, are less likely to experience depression, anxiety disorders, and other forms of psychological disturbance (Segrin, 2000). Meaningful relationships with others are also important for the provision of social support, which can protect the individual from the adverse effects of stress (Berscheid and Reis, 1998). On the other side of the coin, there is an abundance of research showing that loneliness is related to unhappiness and a range of mental and physical problems (Berscheid and Reis, 1998).

The importance of social connectedness for well-being likely has a biological basis. Evolutionary psychologists view social relationships as one of the most important factors responsible for the survival of the human species (D. M. Buss and Kenrick, 1998). The evolutionary significance of close relationships is also emphasized by attachment theory (Bowlby, 1982), which suggests that the ability to form secure interpersonal attachments originates in the relationship between infants and their caregivers, and continues to play an important role in one's close relationships and in the ability to regulate emotions throughout one's life.

In view of the social functions of humor discussed previously in this book, it seems reasonable to propose that humor may play a role in the initiation and maintenance of satisfying and enduring social relationships, such as those with close friends, marriage partners, and colleagues at work (Shiota et al., 2004). These relationships, in turn, can contribute in positive ways to the individual's level of mental health. Besides enhancing partners' enjoyment of the relationship through playful interactions, socially skilled uses of humor may aid in confronting and resolving difficulties and facilitate the resolution of conflicts that inevitably occur in all relationships.

In addition, the humor that is shared by relationship partners during times of life stress may be an important way they help each other to cope. Thus, humorous interactions between partners can be a way of regulating emotion, augmenting positive enjoyment and reducing feelings of distress originating either within or outside the relationship itself. On the other hand, maladaptive uses of humor, such as aggressive teasing or self-defeating humor, may have detrimental effects on relationships. In particular, individuals who use humor in these unhealthy ways may have difficulty initiating and maintaining close relationships, leading to adverse consequences for well-being.

Humor as a Facilitator of Healthy Relationships

Some correlational studies have examined associations between trait measures of humor and several variables relevant to personal relationships. For example, self-report humor scales have been found to be positively correlated with measures of intimacy (Hampes, 1992, 1994), empathy (Hampes, 2001), social assertiveness (Bell et al., 1986), and interpersonal trust (Hampes, 1999). As noted in Chapter 5, studies of dating and married couples have shown that individuals who perceive their partner to have a good sense of humor tend to be more satisfied with their relationship, as compared to those who view their partner as less humorous (Rust and Goldstein, 1989; Ziv and Gadish, 1989). Moreover, people who are happily married often attribute their marital satisfaction, at least in part, to the humor they share with their spouse (Lauer et al., 1990; Ziv, 1988a). Researchers observing styles of interaction between married spouses during discussions of problems in their marriage have found that spouses who are more satisfied with their marriage, as compared to those who are unhappily married, show higher levels of humor and laughter and more reciprocated laughter during these problem discussions (Carstensen et al., 1995; Gottman, 1994).

However, there is also some evidence that humor may play a negative as well as a positive role in close relationships, particularly in men. Herbert Lefcourt and I found that, among women, scores on the CHS were positively correlated with marital satisfaction and positive engagement in a problem discussion between spouses, whereas for men higher CHS scores were associated with lower marital satisfaction and greater destructiveness (negative affect and verbal negativity) during the discussion (Lefcourt and Martin, 1986). A study of newly married couples (described in Chapter 5) found that greater humor expression by husbands during a problem discussion, when accompanied by higher levels of major stressful events in the couple's life, predicted a greater likelihood that couples would be separated or divorced 18 months later (Cohan and Bradbury, 1997). The authors suggested that husbands' use of humor during times of stress may be a way for them to temporarily deflect problems and avoid the anxiety associated with talking about them, but without actively confronting and resolving them. Hence, humor expressed by the husband in the context of major life stress might be associated with less distress in the short term but not with longer-term marital stability.

The possibility of negative as well as positive effects of humor in relationships is consistent with our discussion throughout this chapter. It is only quite recently, however, that researchers have begun to address these issues in the context of relationships, attempting to identify negative as well as positive forms of humor. In a qualitative study of dating relationships, for example, Amy Bippus (2000b) drew a distinction between humor that serves a bonding function and more negative types, such as cruel, inappropriate, and overbearing humor that may be injurious to the relationship. In addition, the recently developed Relational Humor Inventory, which was designed for studying humor in close relationships, contains separate scales for assessing positive, negative, and instrumental uses of humor by each partner (de Koning and Weiss, 2002). Preliminary data indicate that these different scales are differentially associated with marriage partners' levels of relationship satisfaction.

A few recent studies have also made use of the HSQ to examine associations between these potentially healthy and unhealthy humor styles and variables having to do with close relationships. For example, in our initial studies with the HSQ (R. A. Martin et al., 2003), we found that individuals with higher scores on affiliative humor and lower scores on self-defeating humor tended to report higher levels of intimacy in their close relationships. In addition, self-enhancing humor was positively related to the degree to which participants felt satisfied with the social support provided by their friends, whereas self-defeating humor was negatively correlated with this variable.

One of my graduate students, Gwen Dutrizac, and I found that higher affiliative and self-enhancing humor scores were associated with lower levels of loneliness and interpersonal anxiety, whereas higher self-defeating humor was related to higher levels of these negative feelings (R. A. Martin and Dutrizac, 2004). Some studies have also examined associations between the HSQ scales and measures relevant to attachment. In a study of Lebanese university students, Shahe Kazarian and I found that participants with higher scores on the self-defeating humor scale were significantly more likely to report anxious attachment in their relationships with close friends (Kazarian and Martin, 2004). On the other hand, those with higher affiliative humor scores were significantly less likely to report avoidant attachment styles.

Similarly, in their study of Belgian high school and university students, Saroglou and Scariot (2002) reported a correlation between self-defeating humor and insecure attachment in participants' relationships both with their friends and with their mothers. Self-defeating humor was also associated with more fearful-avoidant and anxious-ambivalent models of the self. Overall, these findings indicate that affiliative and self-enhancing humor are associated with a variety of positive relationship indicators, whereas self-defeating humor is particularly related to more negative experiences of relationships in general.

Other studies have examined associations between humor styles on the HSQ and participants' satisfaction with specific relationships. As part of her doctoral dissertation, Patricia Doris (2004) asked university students who were in a dating relationship to rate their own and their partners' humor styles using the HSQ, as well as their satisfaction with the relationship. Self-ratings and partner ratings of affiliative and self-enhancing humor were found to be associated with greater relationship satisfaction. On the other hand, greater use of aggressive humor in oneself or one's partner was associated with greater dissatisfaction with the dating relationship.

Similarly, in a study of humor in the initiation and maintenance of same-sex friendships among university students, another one of my students, Jennie Ward (2004), found that individuals who engaged in more affiliative and less aggressive humor were rated by their friends as being more enjoyable to interact with, and as fulfilling more positive friendship functions, such as companionship, intimacy, emotional security, and affection. These studies suggest that the use of affiliative and (to a somewhat lesser extent) self-enhancing humor may be beneficial for relationship satisfaction, whereas aggressive humor in either partner seems to be particularly associated with relationship dissatisfaction.

These differential correlations between HSQ scales and satisfaction in close relationships suggest that healthy humor styles may be viewed as a type of social competence, whereas unhealthy humor styles may be related to social skills deficits. To test this hypothesis, Jeremy Yip and I examined the HSQ, as well as the trait form of the STCI, in relation to subscales of the Interpersonal Competence Questionnaire (ICQ) (Buhrmester et al., 1988), a measure of the degree to which participants perceive themselves to have various social skills needed to initiate and maintain satisfying relationships (Yip and Martin, in press). The results showed that higher scores on affiliative and self-enhancing humor and trait cheerfulness were associated with greater reported abilities in both initiating relationships (e.g., "Finding and suggesting things to do with new people whom you find interesting and attractive") and personal disclosure (e.g., "Confiding in a new friend and letting her or him see your softer, more sensitive side").

In contrast, greater use of aggressive humor was related to lower reported abilities both in providing emotional support (e.g., "Helping a close companion cope with family or roommate problems") and conflict management (e.g., "When angry at a companion, being able to accept that he or she has a valid point of view even if you don't agree with that view"), whereas trait cheerfulness was positively associated with both of these abilities. Finally, greater use of self-defeating humor was associated with lower ability to engage in negative assertion (e.g., "Telling a companion you don't like a certain way she or he has been treating you").

Similar patterns of correlations between the HSQ and the ICQ were also reported by Nicholas Kuiper and his colleagues (2004). Overall, these findings provide support for the idea that the positive forms of humor may be viewed as a type of social skill, whereas aggressive and self-defeating humor may be considered to be social skills deficits. These correlational findings need to be followed up with further research exploring in more detail the appropriate and inappropriate ways humor is actually used in each of these social skill domains.

The studies discussed so far have examined correlations between humor scales and overall ratings of relationship satisfaction. This approach to measuring satisfaction requires participants to make generalizations about a large number of interactions with another person that have taken place over an extended period of time, and to summarize this complex process in a single rating. To obtain more process-oriented and proximal assessments of the quality of social interactions, two recent studies have employed daily diary methods, obtaining repeated assessments of participants' positive and negative experiences with daily social interactions as they occurred over a period of several weeks.

John Nezlek and Peter Derks (2001) had participants keep a daily record every day for two weeks, recording all of their social interactions lasting more than 10 minutes, and rating each one for enjoyment, level of intimacy, and feelings of self-confidence. Using HLM to analyze the data, the researchers found that participants with higher scores on the Coping Humor Scale rated their daily social interactions as being more satisfying and they also reported feeling greater self-confidence during these interactions. However, coping humor was unrelated to the total number of people interacted with each day or to the perceived intimacy of interactions. The authors suggested that people who use humor to cope may be more enjoyable to be with, providing others with more positive forms of support through their humor, resulting in greater enjoyment and efficacy in interactions.

In the other study of this kind, Gwen Dutrizac and I conducted a similar daily diary study of social interactions using the HSQ as our measure of humor (R. A. Martin and Dutrizac, 2004). We had undergraduate participants keep a diary of daily social interactions two days a week for three weeks. We focused only on interactions with "close others," such as close friends, romantic partners, parents, and siblings. At the end of each day, the participants indicated how many close others they interacted with that day, the number of positive and negative verbal interactions and activities they had with these people, and the frequency of both giving and receiving empathic responses in these interactions.

HLM analyses revealed that higher affiliative humor on the HSQ was associated with more frequent daily positive activities with close others (doing enjoyable things together), while self-enhancing humor was correlated with more frequent positive verbal interactions (engaging in enjoyable conversations). On the other hand, both aggressive humor and self-defeating humor were related to more frequent negative verbal communications and activities (e.g., arguments and criticism). In addition, self-enhancing humor was associated with more giving and receiving of empathic responses, whereas aggressive humor was related to less giving and receiving of empathy. Like Nezlek and Derks (2001), we found no correlation between HSQ scales and the overall frequency of interactions with others, suggesting that humor is related to the quality but not the quantity of social interactions. Taken together, these two studies provide further evidence that greater use of adaptive humor styles and less use of aggressive and self-defeating humor styles are related to more satisfying day-to-day interactions with others.

Another approach to investigating the role of different humor styles in relationships is to observe directly individuals' humor while they are interacting with relationship partners. We have recently developed a reliable observational coding system for rating the degree to which individuals engage in each of the four styles of humor identified by the HSQ during social interactions. This method was used in a recent study to rate the degree to which each member of pairs of heterosexual dating couples used affiliative and aggressive humor during a 10-minute discussion of a problem in their relationship (Martin, Campbell, and Ward, 2006). The results indicated that, although both styles of humor were positively correlated with observer ratings of funniness (demonstrating that both are indeed humorous), they had very different relationship outcomes. The more an individual was observed to use affiliative humor during the discussion, the more his or her partner reported increased feelings of closeness, less emotional distress, greater perception that the problem had been resolved, and greater overall satisfaction with the relationship. In contrast, the more individuals were observed to use aggressive humor, the less their partners felt the problem had been resolved and the less satisfied they were with the relationship overall. Thus, this study was able to show a direct link between these positive and negative styles of humor and relationship partners' subsequent feelings and perceptions, demonstrating that humor can have both positive and negative effects on close relationships, depending on whether it is used in affiliative or aggressive ways.

In summary, the research on social relationships using the HSQ, although as yet quite limited, has provided general support for the view that these positive and negative styles of humor are differentially correlated with a number of variables having to do with individuals' experiences of close relationships, which in turn are important for mental health. Higher levels of both affiliative and self-enhancing humor tend to be associated with greater skill in initiating relationships and self-disclosure of personal information, more positive interactions with close others, more satisfying relationships with friends and dating partners, and lower levels of loneliness and interpersonal anxiety. Affiliative humor is also related to lower levels of avoidant attachment and greater intimacy in relationships, while self-enhancing humor is associated with greater perceived social support and giving and receiving of empathy.

In contrast, greater use of aggressive humor is related to more frequent negative interactions with others, less giving and receiving of empathy, reduced ability to manage conflict and provide empathy in social relationships, and lower satisfaction with dating relationships and friendships, both for oneself and one's partner. Thus, although aggressive humor is less strongly related to overall emotional well-being variables (as we saw previously), it seems to be particularly associated with social skills deficits and maladaptive social interaction styles and therefore more unsatisfactory relationships.

Finally, greater use of self-defeating humor tends to be associated with a reduced ability to assert oneself in relationships, more negative interactions with close others, higher levels of loneliness, interpersonal anxiety, and anxious and insecure attachment, and lower perceptions of intimacy and social support. Overall, then, the neuroticism-related characteristics of self-defeating humor that were seen with general well-being variables seem to carry over into one's feelings about social relationships as well, although, unlike aggressive humor, this negative style of humor does not seem to be related to negative feelings and dissatisfaction in one's relationship partners.

It is important to note, however, that many of these studies were correlational, using trait measures of humor, and were therefore unable to determine the direction of causality between humor and relationship satisfaction. Additional research using observational methods is needed to determine whether different styles of humor have causal effects on relationship outcomes. Also, further research using event-sampling procedures might be useful for studying humor use in everyday social events as they occur in natural contexts (for a discussion of this methodology, see Reis, 2001).

Interpersonal Aspects of Coping Humor

While humor appears to play a role in facilitating healthy personal relationships, it is also important to note that social relationships likely play a significant role in the use of humor in coping with life stress, which I discussed earlier. As we have seen throughout this book, humor typically occurs in the context of social interactions, and this is also likely true of the use of humor in coping. As seen in the study of POWs in Vietnam (Henman, 2001), individuals usually do not begin laughing or cracking jokes about their problems when they are all by themselves. Instead, coping humor typically takes the form of joking comments and other types of playful communication among individuals during or shortly after the occurrence of stressful events.

For example, by cracking jokes with one another during the course of a particularly stressful work situation, coworkers may be able to alter their appraisals of the situation and thereby minimize the amount of negative emotion that might otherwise be elicited. Alternatively, while sitting together in a coffee shop at the end of a stressful day, they might begin jesting and laughing about some of the day's events, enabling them to relieve tension and manage residual emotions. Similarly, coping humor can arise when one person is describing his or her experiences of a recent or ongoing stressful situation to a close friend or romantic partner. Humor may be introduced into the discussion either by the individual who experienced the stressor or by the listener who is providing emotional support. In either case, the humor may provide the stressed individual an alternative way of looking at the stressor, alleviating feelings of distress and enhancing positive emotions. Thus, as sociologist Linda Francis (1994) pointed out, humor may be used to manage other people's emotions as well as one's own.

To date, only a few studies have examined these interpersonal aspects of humor as a coping mechanism. In one recent study, Sharon Manne and her colleagues (2004) observed 10-minute interactions between women who were undergoing treatment for breast cancer and their spouses. These dyads were instructed to discuss a cancer-related issue identified by the patient as being a problem and about which she wanted support from her partner. Each turn of speech during the discussion was coded for various types of social interaction, including benign, nonsarcastic humor. Sequential analyses showed that when husbands responded with humor to the cancer patients' self-disclosures, the patients subsequently tended to report significantly lower levels of distress about their cancer. These findings suggest that a husband's sensitive use of humor in response to his wife sharing her worries and concerns about breast cancer may lessen the threat of the cancer, helping her to gain perspective and reduce feelings of distress.

Research by John Gottman and his colleagues (1998), which was discussed in Chapter 5, also shows how humor may be a way of regulating emotions in one's marriage partner. This study found that, when married couples were engaged in discussions about problems in their marriage, the use of nonsarcastic humor by wives was predictive of greater marital stability over the following six years, but only when the wives' humor led to a reduction in their husbands' heart rate during the conversation. This finding suggests that humor may be beneficial during times of marital stress when it is used as a way of emotionally calming one's spouse and thereby enabling him to remain engaged in problem-solving efforts.

Amy Bippus (2000a) also investigated the outcomes experienced by individuals when their friends use humor in attempting to comfort them during times of stress. In this study, university students were asked to complete a questionnaire about a recent time when they confided to a friend about an emotionally upsetting experience or problem and the friend responded with humor. The results indicated that the effectiveness of the friend's humorous response (i.e., the degree to which it resulted in increased positive moods and feelings of empowerment, and decreased rumination about the problem) depended on the quality (i.e., funniness and appropriate timing) of the humor, its relevance to the problem, and the degree to which it seemed to be given purposefully. In addition, humor responses appeared to be most effective when they were given in the context of a relationship in which humor is a typical part of the interactions between the partners, where both partners normally use humor in coping with stress (as shown by high scores on the CHS), and when the humor was presented in a way that conveyed feelings of concern and a lack of negative criticism or disparagement, and provided an alternate perspective on the problem.

In summary, a limited amount of research has examined the interpersonal context in which humor is used to cope with stress, and the processes of social interaction that are involved. This is a potentially very fruitful topic for future investigation. For example, future research could investigate the effects of humor when it is introduced by the person who is experiencing stress as compared to when it is introduced by the person providing social support, as well as the relative benefits of different styles and topics of humor with different types of stressors.

CONCLUSION

As we have seen in previous chapters of this book, humor is a complex process involving cognitive, emotional, and interpersonal aspects. All of these facets of humor have implications for mental health and emotional well-being. When people joke with one another about their problems or about a potentially threatening life situation, they are able to change their perceptions of the situation, their emotional state, and the nature of their relationships with each other. However, the research reviewed in this chapter suggests that the link between humor and psychological health is more complex than it might first seem.

Experimental laboratory research has provided a considerable amount of support for the view of humor as an emotion-regulation mechanism. At least in the short term, humor produces an increase in positive feelings of exhilaration and well-being, along with perceptions of mastery and control, and a reduction in negative feelings such as anxiety, depression, and anger. There is also research evidence that humor can mitigate the negative emotions, physiological arousal, and behavioral impairments that often occur as a result of stressful life experiences.

While humor may be a useful mechanism for regulating emotions and coping with stress in the short term, however, correlational research using trait measures of sense of humor suggests that the longer-term implications for mental health may depend on the way people use humor in their daily lives. Individuals who use humor to cope in ways that are sensitive to their own and other people's broader psychological needs are likely to experience enhanced feelings of self-esteem and emotional well-being and more satisfying relationships with others in the longer term. On the other hand, if humor is used to temporarily boost one's positive emotions and mitigate stress at the expense of others by means of sarcasm, teasing, or other types of aggressive humor, it may lead in the longer term to interpersonal difficulties and conflicts, and generalized feelings of alienation from others. Similarly, if humor is used at one's own psychological expense by ingratiating oneself with others, excessively disparaging oneself, or avoiding dealing constructively with the underlying causes of one's problems, it may produce temporary feelings of well-being, but at the cost of less healthy functioning in the longer term.

Overall, then, it would appear that humor is inherently neither psychologically healthy nor unhealthy. Just because someone is very funny and able to make others laugh does not necessarily mean that he or she is particularly well-adjusted psychologically. As suggested by earlier psychologists such as Maslow (1954) and Allport (1961), the role of humor in mental health seems to have as much to do with the kinds of humor an individual does *not* display as the kinds of humor he or she *does* express.

Another way of putting this is that a healthy sense of humor is an important component of overall mental health. People who are psychologically well-adjusted, with satisfying personal relationships, tend to use humor in ways that enhance their own well-being and closeness to others. For example, they may engage in friendly joking to communicate an optimistic outlook on a stressful situation, to encourage others during times of distress, or to express underlying feelings of acceptance and affection in the midst of an argument. However, less well-adjusted individuals who are aggressive and hostile, or those with low self-esteem and a vulnerability to negative emotionality, tend to use humor to communicate their aggression and cynicism, to manipulate, demean, or control others, to ingratiate themselves, or to hide their true feelings from others. Indeed, since no one is completely psychologically healthy or completely unhealthy, most people likely use humor to some degree in all of these ways at different times and in different contexts.

Throughout this chapter, I have noted several limitations of the existing research as well as promising questions and methodologies for future research. A major limitation of much of the research in this area is the use of correlational methodologies, which do not allow researchers to determine the direction of causality between humor and well-being. It is unclear from the existing research whether more healthy forms of humor contribute to greater psychological health or whether different styles of humor are merely a consequence of healthy and unhealthy psychological functioning. Other methodological limitations include the use of cross-sectional designs, self-report trait measures of sense of humor, retrospective assessments of stressors, and general, traitlike evaluations of well-being and relationship satisfaction. All of these preclude the possibility of studying the ongoing processes involved in the use of humor in coping with stress and negotiating interpersonal interactions. These approaches also tend to ignore the interpersonal nature and functions of humor.

Rather than merely seeking to find simple correlations between sense of humor scales and various aspects of mental health, or interactions between sense of humor and life stress measures in predicting overall well-being, future research should attempt to determine which types of humor in which social contexts are beneficial and detrimental for which aspects of mental health. Some humor styles, such as aggressive humor, may be beneficial for some aspects of mental health (e.g., short-term regulation of one's own emotions) but deleterious for others (e.g., long-term maintenance of close relationships). They may also be more beneficial for coping with some types of stressors (e.g., being a prisoner of war) than others (e.g., dealing with difficult patients in a psychiatric ward).

To address these kinds of questions, I have suggested that future research could make use of daily experience methods or event-sampling procedures, in which the actual use of different styles of humor during the course of the day is evaluated in "real time" over a period of days or weeks (Reis and Gable, 2000). This approach could be used to study humor as a coping mechanism by including repeated assessments of stressful events and ongoing indicators of emotional and physical well-being. The role of humor in social relationships could also be examined by including measures of various aspects of daily social interactions. Another potentially useful approach for further research is the use of observational methods to study the processes of humor in interpersonal interactions. For example, the social functions of humor, as well as its effect on coping with stress, could be examined during conversations between dyads (friends, married partners, or even strangers) while they are discussing a stressful situation that has recently been experienced by one or both of them.

Finally, there has been little research examining the question of whether individuals can improve their sense of humor and learn to use it in more healthy and less unhealthy ways. To address this question, intervention studies are needed, making use of role-playing procedures, creativity exercises, and other techniques over multiple sessions to train individuals in effective humor skills. Outcome measures could be used to examine the effectiveness of such humor-training sessions, relative to other non-humorous interventions, in improving humor usage and enhancing aspects of psychological well-being. This type of research is necessary before we can begin to advocate the use of humor and laughter to promote mental health.

CHAPTER 10

Humor and Physical Health

The idea that humor and laughter are good for one's health has become very popular in recent years, among the general public as well as many health care practitioners. This is actually not a new idea; the health benefits of laughter have been touted for centuries. The medicinal value of mirth and cheerfulness, as well as the health-impairing effects of negative emotions, were affirmed thousands of years ago in a biblical proverb which states that "a merry heart does good like a medicine, but a broken spirit dries the bones" (Proverbs 17:22).

Since the time of Aristotle, a number of physicians and philosophers have suggested that laughter has important health benefits, such as improving blood circulation, aiding digestion, restoring energy, counteracting depression, and enhancing the functioning of various organs of the body (for reviews, see Goldstein, 1982; Moody, 1978). This idea has become increasingly popular in recent years, as modern medical discoveries like endorphins, cytokines, natural killer cells, and immunoglobulins have been added to the list of bodily substances that are thought to be beneficially affected by humor and laughter.

Within psychology, research on the potential benefits of humor on physical health falls within the domain of health psychology, which is concerned with the way behavior, cognitions, and emotions can influence health, wellness, and illness. Health psychologists conduct research on such topics as the physiological effects of psychosocial stress; the influence of cognitive appraisals, coping, social support, and other psychological factors on stress; the effects of emotions on immunity; psychological aspects of pain and disease; the promotion and maintenance of health; and the relationship between patients and health care providers.

Rejecting the traditional biomedical model of health and illness as overly simplistic, health psychologists espouse a biopsychosocial model, which views health as determined by psychological, social, and cultural factors, in addition to biological causes (Engel, 1977). Clinical health psychology is a professional specialty area within clinical psychology that seeks to apply the research findings of health psychology and related disciplines to the development of treatment interventions for helping people to cope effectively with stress, modify their behavior in more health-enhancing ways, manage pain, cope with chronic illness, and so forth.

Over the past two decades, about 50 published articles have reported empirical investigations that bear on the relationship between humor and physical health. In addition to psychologists, these studies have been conducted by researchers from medicine, nursing, and other fields. In this chapter, I will begin by discussing recent developments in the popularization of claims for health benefits of humor and laughter. I will then explore several theoretical mechanisms by which humor and laughter could potentially influence health. In the remainder of the chapter, I will provide an overview of research on the effects of humor on various aspects of health, including immunity, pain tolerance, blood pressure, illness symptoms, and longevity, examining the current state of the evidence and discussing some of the questions that remain to be answered (for a more detailed review of this research, see R. A. Martin, 2001).

POPULAR BELIEFS ABOUT HUMOR AND HEALTH

The current popularity of ideas about medicinal benefits of humor and laughter can be traced in large part to the publication by Norman Cousins of an article in the *New England Journal of Medicine* entitled "Anatomy of an illness" (Cousins, 1976), which was later expanded into a best-selling book by the same name (Cousins, 1979). Cousins, a well-known American magazine editor, recounted in these writings how he had been diagnosed in the early 1960s with a very painful, chronic, and debilitating rheumatoid disease called *ankylosing spondylitis*, and was told by his doctor that he had only a 1-in-500 chance of recovering fully. Aware that medical science had little to offer in the way of cure except medication to ease the pain of the disease, Cousins searched through the medical literature and learned about recent research suggesting health-impairing effects of stress-related negative emotions, as well as potential benefits of vitamin C. With the cooperation of his physician, he decided to check himself out of the hospital and undergo a self-prescribed treatment plan involving frequent daily laughter, along with massive doses of vitamin C. To induce positive feelings which, he hoped, would counteract any adverse effects of negative emotions, he laughed as often as possible by watching old episodes of the television program *Candid Camera*, Marx Brothers movies, and other comedy films, and reading joke books. The story of his eventual recovery from the disease is now well-known.

During the course of this treatment, Cousins observed that 10 minutes of hearty laughter had a reliable analgesic effect, providing two hours of pain-free sleep. In addition, he reported that episodes of laughter reliably resulted in reductions in the sedimentation rate, the rate at which red blood cells descend in a test tube, which is a measure of inflammation. These observations led to the hypothesis that laughter reduces pain, perhaps by stimulating the production of endorphins, the morphinelike substances produced by the brain, as well as the suggestion that laughter enhances immune system functioning.

Although the story of Norman Cousins is widely cited as evidence for the health benefits of laughter, it is important to note that such anecdotal cases do not provide scientific evidence, but need to be followed up with controlled experiments. It is unknown whether his recovery was due to the laughter, the Vitamin C, particular personality traits such as the will to live, or to some totally unrelated factor, or whether the disease may even have been misdiagnosed in the first place. Indeed, in a later article, Cousins (1985) himself downplayed the role of laughter in his recovery, emphasizing the importance of positive emotions in general as a context for the application of traditional medical treatments.

The case of Norman Cousins appeared at a time when many North Americans were becoming dissatisfied with traditional Western medicine, and alternative approaches to medicine were growing in popularity. The idea that laughter could have curative properties fit well with this zeitgeist. Over the years since then, numerous popular magazine articles have reported claims of scientific research purportedly showing evidence of beneficial effects of humor and laughter on various aspects of health, further bolstering these beliefs in the public mind. As one example, an article in a recent issue of *Reader's Digest* (Rackl, 2003) claimed that scientists have demonstrated that humor and laughter can alleviate allergy symptoms, increase pain tolerance, strengthen the immune system, reduce the risk of stroke and heart disease, and even help diabetics control their blood sugar levels.

Stimulated by these ideas, a burgeoning "humor and health movement" has developed, made up of nurses, physicians, social workers, psychotherapists, educators, clowns, and comedians, who enthusiastically promote the therapeutic benefits of humor through conferences, seminars, workshops, books, videotapes, and Internet websites. As noted in Chapter 1, the Association for Applied and Therapeutic Humor (AATH) is a professional society of individuals whose members are interested in the application of humor and laughter in medicine, social work, psychotherapy, education, and so on (available at www.aath.org).

In addition, the "laughter club movement," which was started in India in 1995 by a physician named Madan Kataria, has witnessed remarkable growth in the past decade, forming chapters throughout the world. Believing that even nonhumorous laughter is beneficial for physical, mental, interpersonal, and spiritual health, adherents of this movement meet regularly to engage in group laughter as a form of yogic exercise. According to Kataria (2002), the mission of the movement is nothing less than to bring about "world peace through laughter!" The humor and health movement also received a boost in 1998 with the release of the movie *Patch Adams*, starring Robin Williams, which depicted the true story of an unconventional physician who augmented his medical interventions by making his patients laugh in response to his comic interactions with them (described also in P. Adams and Mylander, 1998). Laughter rooms, comedy carts, and "therapeutic clowns" have now become familiar sights in many hospitals.

The remarkable range of bodily functions that are said to be helped by laughter and humor, according to contemporary claims, reminds one of the advertised benefits of patent medicines a century ago. Laughter is said to provide exercise for the muscles and heart, produce muscle relaxation, improve blood circulation, reduce the production of stress-related hormones such as catecholamines and cortisol, enhance a wide range of immune system variables, reduce pain by stimulating the production of endorphins, reduce blood pressure, enhance respiration, regulate blood sugar levels, and remove carbon dioxide and water vapor from the lungs (W. F. Fry, 1994; McGhee, 1999). As such, laughter has been said to provide some degree of protection against cancer, heart attacks, stroke, asthma, diabetes, pneumonia, bronchitis, hypertension, migraine headaches, arthritis pain, ulcers, and all sorts of infectious diseases ranging from the common cold to AIDS (W. F. Fry, 1994; McGhee, 1999). With such a range of effects, it would seem that laughter threatens to put the major pharmaceutical companies out of business!

Many of the claimed health benefits of laughter are unproven and appear quite fanciful. For example, although it is often claimed that laughter provides the same health benefits as jogging and other forms of physical exercise, there is no published research evaluating this claim. It seems likely that one would need to laugh for quite a long time in order to consume a significant number of calories; people are likely better off taking up a more vigorous form of exercise if they wish to lose weight or enhance their cardiovascular fitness.

Other claims are essentially unfalsifiable and therefore of little scientific merit. An example is the suggestion that laughter reduces the risk of bronchial infections and pneumonia by expelling moist residual air from the lungs, resulting in a reduction of excess moisture that would otherwise encourage pulmonary bacterial growth (W. F. Fry, 1994). The difficulty with this claim (apart from the fact that there is no empirical evidence that laughter actually reduces moisture levels in the lungs) is that one could make an equally convincing argument for health-enhancing benefits of laughter regardless of the direction of its physiological effects. If it turned out that laughter somehow increased, rather than decreased, the pulmonary moisture level, one could come up with an equally plausible-sounding argument that it is beneficial because it keeps the lungs from drying out and shriveling up. Thus, regardless of what effect laughter may have on a particular system of the body, a "just-so story" can be concocted to explain why this effect is beneficial. It is interesting to note that one curmudgeonly nineteenth-century author used similar kinds of arguments in the opposite way to support his contention that laughter is actually *harmful* to physical health (Vasey, 1877)!

Part of the attraction of humor and laughter as a form of alternative medicine is that it is inherently enjoyable and, unlike many other health-promoting activities, it does not require giving up pleasurable habits like smoking and overeating. The fact that it is free, in contrast to the high costs of many traditional and nontraditional treatments, makes it even more attractive. Given the popularity of these views, one runs the risk of being labeled as a killjoy if one questions whether humor and laughter actually produce the medical benefits that are claimed. However, a scientific approach requires that we examine the evidence.

As we saw in the previous chapter, there is good reason to believe that laughter can improve one's mood and that a healthy sense of humor can be beneficial for coping with stress and enriching one's relationships with others, enhancing one's quality of life. What is the evidence, however, that humor and laughter can also have a beneficial impact on aspects of physical health, such as strengthening the immune system, reducing pain, or prolonging the duration of one's life? As we will see, the existing evidence is rather weaker and more inconsistent than the media reports would lead us to believe.

HOW MIGHT HUMOR AFFECT HEALTH?

The idea of health benefits of humor is more complex than it might first appear. For one thing, physical health is not a unitary concept. There are many different aspects and components of health, and they are not all correlated. Factors that are beneficial for some aspects of health might even be harmful for others. In addition, as previous chapters of this book have shown, humor is a complex phenomenon, involving cognitive, emotional, behavioral, physiological, and social aspects. Different components of humor could conceivably affect different aspects of health in a variety of ways (R. A. Martin, 2001).

If humor is beneficial for health, then presumably people with a greater sense of humor enjoy better physical health and live longer lives. But what aspects or components of "sense of humor" are likely to be health-enhancing? As noted in Chapter 7, there are numerous ways of conceptualizing this personality trait. Different dimensions of sense of humor might be related to health in different ways, and some may be more relevant to health than others. Indeed, some aspects or styles of humor (e.g., aggressive or self-defeating humor) might actually be detrimental to health in some ways.

Thus, it is important to consider the possible mechanisms by which humor could influence health. Systematic research is needed to investigate each of these potential mechanisms and to determine which components and aspects of humor are important and which are not. Only when we have gained such knowledge can we begin to design effective therapeutic interventions based on these findings. In general, five potential mechanisms may be considered, each involving different aspects of humor (and hence different ways of conceptualizing what it means to have a "healthy" sense of humor), and each suggesting different implications for health care interventions.

First, health benefits might result from some of the physiological effects of *laughter* itself, as suggested by many people over the years. As we saw in Chapter 6, laughter is a facial and vocal expression of the emotion of mirth that involves respiratory, muscular, and vocal activity. As mentioned earlier, psychiatrist William Fry (1994) suggested that the muscular activity occurring in many parts of the body during vigorous laughter may be viewed as a form of aerobic exercise, burning calories and providing many of the well-known health benefits of physical exertion. He also suggested that laughter enhances pulmonary function, enabling the lungs to expel stale residual air containing built-up carbon dioxide and water vapor, thereby potentially reducing the risk of bronchial bacterial infections.

These ideas are quite speculative, but if they are correct, then it would be necessary for people to actually laugh in order to gain such benefits; simply being amused or feeling cheerful without laughing would not be enough. Indeed, laughter might even be expected to provide these effects without humor (e.g., feigned or forced laughter), as advocated by leaders of the laughter club movement (Kataria, 2002). The object of one's laughter would also seem to be unimportant: hostile laughter directed at other people should be just as effective as more friendly forms. From this perspective, the person with a "healthy" sense of humor is the one who laughs uproariously as often as possible, and therapeutic humor interventions should be aimed simply at encouraging people to engage in frequent and intense laughter.

A second potential mechanism whereby humor could conceivably influence health is through the physiological effects of the *positive emotion* (*i.e., mirth*) that accompanies humor and is expressed by laughter. As noted in Chapter 6, this pleasurable emotion is mediated by activity in the limbic system and other parts of the brain and, like other emotions, produces changes in the autonomic nervous system and endocrine system that extend throughout the body. Some of these physiological effects of mirth might have beneficial health effects. For example, the increased heart rate resulting from sympathetic arousal might provide a sort of cardiac workout (W. F. Fry, 1994).

We also saw in chapter 6 that there is evidence from animal studies suggesting the production of endorphins and other opiates during play, which might also occur with humor-related mirth, resulting in a greater tolerance for pain (Panksepp, 1998). Researchers are just beginning to explore the various neuropeptides that are released by the brain during states of positive as well as negative emotions (Panksepp, 1993), and some of these mirth-related biochemicals might conceivably have beneficial effects on various components of the immune system as well as other bodily functions (W. F. Fry, 1994).

It should be noted that, although popular writings on humor and health often attribute these sorts of physiological changes to vigorous laughter, they are more properly viewed as effects of the emotion that is communicated by laughter, as noted in Chapter 6. Thus, actually laughing out loud may not be necessary to achieve these effects: humor-induced feelings of mirth may be all that is needed. Nonhumorous exercises for inducing laughter, such as those used in laughter clubs, might not be very effective unless they also elicit the positive emotion of mirth along with the laughter.

In addition, it is worth noting that these potential benefits might not be specific to mirth, but might also result from other positive emotions that are not specifically humor-related, such as joy, happiness, and love, which might share many of the same brain circuits (Panksepp and Burgdorf, 2003). Thus, positive emotions, regardless of how they are generated, may have analgesic (Bruehl, Carlson, and McCubbin, 1993) or immunoenhancing effects (Stone et al., 1987) or may have an "undoing" effect on the potentially harmful cardiovascular consequences of negative emotions (Fredrickson and Levenson, 1998). If these hypotheses are correct, then they give humor and laughter a less unique role in health enhancement, as they are only one means of increasing positive emotions. In this view, a "healthy" sense of humor would involve a generally cheerful temperament characterized by happiness, joy, optimism, and a playful approach to life (Ruch and Carrell, 1998), and therapeutic interventions should aim at increasing people's positive emotions by a variety of means in addition to humor. The promotion of laughter would be less important than seeking to enhance positive emotions.

Third, humor might benefit health through *cognitive* mechanisms, by moderating the adverse effects of psychosocial stress on health. A large body of research has demonstrated that stressful life experiences can have adverse effects on various aspects of health, such as suppression of the immune system (Uchino, Kiecolt-Glaser, and Glaser, 2000) and increased risk of heart disease (Esler, 1998), through the chronic production of various stress-related hormones such as catecholamines and cortisol. As noted in Chapter 9, humor may be an effective way of coping with stress, reducing its adverse effects on physical health as well as moods. A humorous outlook on life and the ability to see the funny side of one's problems may enable individuals to cope more effectively with stress by allowing them to gain perspective and distance themselves from stressful situations, enhancing their feelings of mastery and well-being in the face of adversity (R. A. Martin et al., 1993; R. A. Martin and Lefcourt, 1983). As a consequence, these individuals may experience fewer of the adverse effects of stress on their physical health.

In this hypothesized stress-moderator mechanism, the cognitive-perceptual aspects of humor would be more important than laughter, and the ability to maintain a humorous outlook during times of stress and adversity would be particularly important; humor during nonstressful times would be less relevant to health. This view also introduces the possibility that certain types of humor (e.g., perspective-taking humor) may be more adaptive and health-enhancing than others (e.g., excessively self-disparaging humor). If this view is correct, therapeutic humor interventions should be viewed as a component of stress management training, focusing on teaching individuals ways of using humor to cope with stress in their daily lives.

Fourth, humor might indirectly benefit health through an *interpersonal* mechanism by increasing one's level of social support. As noted in Chapter 9, individuals who are able to use humor effectively to reduce interpersonal conflicts and tensions and to enhance positive feelings in others may consequently enjoy more numerous and satisfying social relationships. As a result, they may enjoy the well-established stress-buffering and health-enhancing effects of close relationships (House, Landis, and Umberson, 1988; Kiecolt-Glaser and Newton, 2001). This hypothesized mechanism focuses on interpersonal aspects of humor and the social competence with which individuals express humor in their relationships, rather than the frequency with which they engage in laughter. The target and nature of the humor becomes even more important in this model. Here, a "healthy" sense of humor would involve the use of humor to enhance relationships with others in an affiliative and nonhostile manner. Therapeutic humor interventions would be seen as an adjunct to social skills training, teaching individuals to develop a socially facilitative sense of humor, along with other skills for developing, maintaining, and enhancing intimate relationships.

Finally, a fifth (*behavioral*) mechanism by which humor might hypothetically have a beneficial effect on health is by promoting a healthy lifestyle. For example, one could speculate that people with a better sense of humor, because of their presumably higher self-esteem and more optimistic outlook on life, are more likely to engage in healthy behaviors such as obtaining regular physical exercise, eating healthy foods, maintaining an appropriate body weight, and refraining from smoking and excess alcohol consumption. However, research evidence bearing on this hypothesis, although rather limited, actually suggests that, if anything, the effects are the opposite: high-humor individuals seem to be more likely to engage in unhealthy lifestyles.

For example, in a longitudinal study of humor and physical health among Finnish police officers, Paavo Kerkkänen, Nicholas Kuiper, and I (2004) found that higher scores on some sense of humor scales (but not others) were associated with greater obesity, increased smoking, and factors associated with greater risk of cardiovascular disease. Similarly, the Terman life-cycle study, which followed a large sample of highly gifted individuals over many decades (to be discussed in more detail later in this chapter), found that those who were rated as being more cheerful as children (i.e., having a higher sense of humor and greater optimism) were more likely to smoke and consume alcohol as adults (L. R. Martin et al., 2002).

These apparent associations between humor and unhealthy lifestyle behaviors may be due in part to the more extraverted personality traits of high-humor individuals (Ruch, 1994). Past research has shown that extraverted individuals, in comparison with introverts, are more likely to drink alcohol (M. Cook et al., 1998), to smoke (Patton, Barnes, and Murray, 1993), and to be obese (Haellstroem and Noppa, 1981). Although such findings of an association between sense of humor and unhealthy lifestyle behaviors need to be studied in more detail before we make too much of them, they do suggest that humor may actually have some deleterious as well as potentially beneficial health consequences.

In summary, there are several different theoretical models of the mechanisms by which humor might potentially influence health. Each model suggests different approaches to the application of humor in health care and health promotion. In order to ensure that treatments are likely to be effective, systematic research should be conducted to test each of these models before developing such interventions.

HUMOR AND IMMUNITY

The immune system is an exceedingly complex and dynamic network of many types of white blood cells (lymphocytes) and biochemical molecules distributed throughout all parts of the body, whose function is to discriminate between "self" and "nonself" antigens and protect the body from foreign invaders (Sanders, Iciek, and Kasprowicz, 2000; Uchino et al., 2000). Given the large number of components and the dynamic nature of the immune system, there is no single way of measuring overall immunocompetence. In recent years, research in the field of psychoneuroimmunology has demonstrated that there are intimate connections between the immune system and the brain, which communicate with one another by means of a variety of molecules such as neurotransmitters, hormones, neuropeptides, and cytokines. Psychological factors can therefore influence immunity, just as immunological factors can affect psychological functioning.

There is now considerable evidence that different emotional states have an influence on immunity through these brain-immune system communication channels (for a review, see Booth and Pennebaker, 2000). In particular, some research indicates that negative emotions, such as anger, depression, and fear, can adversely affect various components of immunity, and that these effects can result in poorer health. However, the effects vary for different aspects of immunity, with some immunity components also showing improvement in response to negative moods. The effects also seem to depend in part on the psychosocial context. It is therefore incorrect to assume that there is a one-to-one correspondence between specific emotions and specific immune system changes (Booth and Pennebaker, 2000).

Overall, potential effects of positive emotions on immunity are less well-documented than the effects of negative emotions, although this may be due to less attention having been given to positive emotions by researchers. Nonetheless, several studies have investigated hypothesized effects on immunity of the positive emotion associated with humor.

Experimental Investigations

To study effects of humor on immunity, researchers have conducted experiments in which they obtained blood or saliva samples before and after participants watched humorous videotapes in the laboratory, and then conducted assays on these samples to determine the levels of various components of immunity, such as the secretion rates of various immunoglobulins and the ability of different types of lymphocytes to detect and combat antigens. A significant prevideotape to postvideotape change in these immunological variables suggests possible effects of humor on immunity.

Of course, these experiments also require appropriate control conditions, in which participants also watch nonhumorous (but equally interesting) videotapes, to ensure that any observed effects are due to humor and not some other factor, such as simply watching an interesting and enjoyable videotape, or the increases and decreases in biological variables (diurnal cycles) that occur naturally over the course of the day.

To determine whether any observed effects are specific to humor, or are also found with other positive or negative emotions, it is also desirable to include control conditions in which other emotions are elicited.

In addition, to explore possible mechanisms of any observed humor-related changes in immunity, researchers should examine the correlations between these immunological changes and such variables as the frequency of laughter and ratings of funniness, enjoyment, and moods obtained from the participants in the comedy condition. The relative strengths of these correlations can provide an indication of whether the effects are due to laughter in particular, or to the positive emotions associated with humor, or to other factors. For example, if changes in immunity are found to be significantly related to the duration or intensity of laughter, even after controlling for mood changes, this would suggest that laughter influences immunity even beyond the effects of mirth. Unfortunately, most of the research to date has not included the control conditions and observational measures needed to explore these sorts of questions.

The majority of the immunity-related experiments that have been conducted so far have examined only secretory immunoglobulin A (S-IgA), a component of the immune system found in saliva that is involved in the body's defense against upper respiratory infections. A number of investigations outside of the humor field have shown phasic (short-term) increases in levels of S-IgA in saliva while subjects are performing emotionally stressful, exciting, or challenging tasks in the laboratory (Harrison et al., 2000), whereas more tonic (longer-lasting) decreases in S-IgA levels have been found during times of life stress, such as when students are writing major examinations (Deinzer et al., 2000).

In the first published study of humor and immunity, Kathleen Dillon and her colleagues had nine college students individually watch a 30-minute comedy videotape (Richard Pryor performing stand-up comedy) and an emotionally neutral control videotape in counterbalanced order (Dillon, Minchoff, and Baker, 1985). The data analyses revealed a significant increase in the levels of S-IgA in saliva while the participants watched the comedy film, whereas no change in S-IgA was observed during the control film. Thus, humor appeared to produce at least a short-term improvement in this component of immunity.

These findings inspired Herbert Lefcourt and his colleagues to conduct a series of three experiments with larger sample sizes examining effects of exposure to comedy on S-IgA (Lefcourt, Davidson-Katz, and Kueneman, 1990). In each study, participants either listened to a comedy audiotape or watched a comedy videotape in small groups. All three studies showed significant increases in S-IgA following exposure to comedy relative to a baseline measure, providing further support for the findings of Dillon and her colleagues (1985). However, these studies had some methodological weaknesses that made the results somewhat inconclusive. Many of the baseline assessments of S-IgA were taken on different days, at different times of day, and in different locations than the postcomedy measures. In addition, these studies did not have adequate control groups. It is therefore difficult to know whether the observed effects were specifically due to humor or whether they may have resulted from some other uncontrolled variables.

Better controls were used by David McClelland and Adam Cheriff (1997) in a series of three studies in which participants were shown either a comedy or a documentary control videotape. No consistent prevideotape to postvideotape increases in S-IgA were observed in the documentary videotape control conditions, whereas, in the comedy conditions, more subjects showed an increase than a decrease in S-IgA. Similar findings of humor-related increases in S-IgA have been obtained in three other experiments (Labott et al., 1990; Lambert and Lambert, 1995; Perera et al., 1998). However, two additional well-controlled experiments failed to replicate these findings (Harrison et al., 2000; Njus, Nitschke, and Bryant, 1996), casting some doubt on their reliability.

Besides the research on S-IgA, a few other laboratory experiments have examined effects of exposure to comedy videotapes on a variety of immunological variables assayed in blood samples. One of these, conducted by Lee Berk and his colleagues (1989), received a great deal of attention in the media and has frequently been cited in the humor and health literature. The participants in this study were 10 male medical personnel, five of whom were assigned as a single group to watch a 60-minute comedy video, whereas the other five sat quietly in a room together for an hour. Blood samples were collected via intravenous catheters in the forearm at several intervals before, during, and after the stimulus conditions, and assays were conducted for 19 immunity and endocrine-related variables. Among the participants in the comedy video group, the results showed significant increases from baseline in six immunity-related variables (T cell helper/suppressor ratio, blastogenesis, IgG, IgM, natural killer cell activity, and complement C3), suggesting immunoenhancing effects of humor. However, since comparisons were not reported for the control condition, we can only assume that similar changes did not also occur in those participants who did not watch the humorous video.

Although some promising results were obtained in this study, there are a number of methodological limitations that weaken our ability to draw firm conclusions. These include a small sample size, an inadequate control condition, and a very large number of statistical analyses, increasing the risk that the observed effects could simply have been due to chance. In addition, most of the immunity-related results of this study were never published in a peer-reviewed journal article, but were only reported in conference papers, leaving many details of the methodology and analyses unknown and therefore difficult to evaluate. Since the researchers did not measure the amount of laughter or moods of the participants, they were unable to examine the degree to which these factors mediated the effects. Overall, although this study showed some intriguing findings, it does not provide the sort of conclusive scientific evidence of immunoenhancing effects of laughter that have often been claimed for it.

Some additional experiments have also reported humor-related changes in various components of immunity measured in blood samples (L. S. Berk et al., 2001; Itami, Nobori, and Texhima, 1994; Kamei, Kumano, and Masumura, 1997; Mittwoch-Jaffe et al., 1995; Yoshino, Fujimori, and Kohda, 1996). However, these studies also tended to have only small numbers of participants and inadequate controls. In addition, the results were rather inconsistent across the studies, with some showing immuno-enhancing effects, others showing immunosuppressive effects, and still others showing no significant effects with particular components of immunity. For example, whereas Berk and colleagues (2001) reported increases in T-cell helper-suppressor ratio and Natural Killer (NK) cell activity with exposure to comedy, Kamei and associates (1997) did not replicate the T-cell ratio finding and found a *decrease* in NK cell activity. Overall, then, although the existing experimental laboratory research suggests that exposure to comedy may have some short-term effects on some components of immunity, more systematic and well-controlled research is needed before any firm conclusions can be drawn concerning the exact nature of these effects.

There appears to be a particular interest in the potential health benefits of humor among researchers in Japan, as witnessed by some of the studies mentioned above, as well as several other more recent investigations that were conducted in that country. Hajime Kimata recently reported research suggesting that humor can reduce allergic reactions in individuals with allergies. In one study, after watching a humorous movie, individuals with dermatitis showed less severe allergic reactions in response to skin prick tests involving allergens such as house dust mites and cat dander, as compared to the more severe reactions that occurred after they watched a nonhumorous documentary film (Kimata, 2001).

In another study comprising two separate experiments, patients with allergy-related bronchial asthma showed reduced asthmatic reactions to allergens after they had watched a comedy videotape, whereas no such effect was found with a nonhumorous control film (Kimata, 2004b). This same researcher also found that watching a comedy film, but not a nonhumorous control film, resulted in a reduction in certain allergy-related immunoglobulins in the tears of patients with allergic conjunctivitis, an inflammatory eye condition (Kimata, 2004a). Taken together, these experiments suggest that, rather than enhancing immunity, humor may suppress the excessive immune responses that occur in certain allergic reactions by reducing the secretion of immunoglobulins such as IgE and IgG.

In another Japanese study, after watching a comedy videotape, healthy participants were found to have a significant increase in free radical scavenging capacity (FRSC), as indicated by increased levels (relative to baseline) of certain molecules in their saliva that are involved in the elimination of free radicals from the mouth (Atsumi et al., 2004). Free radicals are molecules that have been implicated in inflammation, aging, and the development of some types of cancer. Although this study was limited by the fact that it did not include a nonhumorous control condition, the amount of increase in FRSC was found to be significantly correlated with participants' ratings of their enjoyment of the videotape, suggesting a possible mediating role of mirth.

An additional Japanese study, although unrelated to immunity, is worth mentioning here. In this investigation, individuals with type 2 diabetes were found to have significantly lower blood glucose levels after eating a meal on a day when they had previously attended a comedy show, as compared to a day when they had attended a nonhumorous, monotonous lecture (Hayashi et al., 2003). The authors theorized that neuroendocrine effects of mirthful emotion may have suppressed the elevation of glucose, suggesting that engaging in humor might be beneficial to people with diabetes to help control their glucose levels. These recent Japanese investigations suggest a number of intriguing possibilities of beneficial immunological and endocrine effects of humor-related positive emotion and laughter. However, the evidence is still far from conclusive. Further research is needed to replicate and explore the mechanisms of these effects in greater detail, using larger samples and more rigorous methodologies, before we can be confident of their reliability and clinical utility.

Correlational Studies

A limitation of the sorts of experiments described in the previous section is that they are not able to determine whether there are any long-term health benefits of humor and laughter on immunity. Even though there may be statistically significant short-term changes in immunity-related variables with exposure to comedy in the laboratory, it is important to determine whether such changes have any longer-term clinical significance. If humor has clinically meaningful beneficial effects on the immune system, then it should be possible to demonstrate that individuals who engage in laughter and humor more frequently (i.e., those with a greater sense of humor) have generally greater immunocompetence and are less likely to suffer from infectious illnesses over time. In other words, there should be a positive correlation between sense of humor and immunity-related variables and a negative correlation between sense of humor and rates of infectious illnesses. Although research on this question is limited, the results to date have generally been disappointing.

With regard to infectious illnesses, McClelland and Cheriff (1997) found no correlation between several self-report measures of sense of humor and the frequency or severity of colds experienced by participants, either retrospectively or prospectively over a period of three months. Several studies have also examined correlations between levels of S-IgA measured in saliva and participants' sense of humor as assessed by self-report scales. Although two early studies with very small sample sizes reported sizable positive correlations between scores on the Coping Humor Scale (CHS) and S-IgA (Dillon et al., 1985; Dillon and Totten, 1989), some later studies with larger sample sizes failed to replicate these findings (Labott et al., 1990; Lefcourt et al., 1990; R. A. Martin and Dobbin, 1988).

It should be noted, however, that immunity levels are likely to fluctuate considerably over time, so that levels obtained in a single assay may be too unreliable to expect significant correlations with a trait measure of humor. Future research should aggregate immune measures across a number of assays over a period of time and examine correlations with trait humor test scores. An even better method would be to take a longitudinal approach, examining possible associations between day-to-day fluctuations in participants' experiences of humor, laughter, and cheerfulness, and corresponding fluctuations in their levels of various immunity variables over a number of days or weeks. A link between humor and immunity would be supported if increases and decreases in immunity from day to day are systematically related to the experience of more or less humor on those days.

Finally, James Dobbin and I conducted a study to determine whether sense of humor as a personality trait might moderate the effects of life stress on immunity (R. A. Martin and Dobbin, 1988). Numerous past studies have shown that stress can have an adverse effect on various components of the immune system (Uchino et al., 2000). As we saw in Chapter 9, there is some evidence that people with a greater sense of humor are better able to cope with stress, and they might therefore also be less likely to experience the adverse effects of stress on immunity. In our study, using undergraduate students as participants, we administered a measure of daily stress and assayed S-IgA levels in saliva samples on two different occasions $1\frac{1}{2}$ months apart. Sense of humor was assessed using several self-report scales, including the SHRQ, CHS, and SHQ.

The results revealed that daily stress scores at Time 1 were negatively related to S-IgA levels at Time 2, indicating an immunosuppressive effect of stress. More importantly, significant stress-moderating effects were found on this relationship with three of the four sense of humor measures. In each case, participants with low humor scores showed strong negative correlations between stress and immunoglobulins, whereas this association was much weaker or even nonexistent among those with high humor scores. Although these findings are in need of replication, they suggest that the stress-moderating effects of humor that have been found in other studies with mood measures may also extend to effects of stress on immunity.

Overall, despite the claims that are often made in the popular media and "humor and health" literature, the existing evidence for beneficial effects of humor on immunity is still rather weak and inconclusive. Although a number of laboratory experiments have found significant changes in some components of immunity while participants were watching humorous videotapes, these findings have not always been replicated, with some results even going in opposite directions in different studies. The correlational studies have generally failed to find significant associations between sense of humor and immunity, raising questions about the long-term clinical significance of the short-term effects that have been found in the laboratory.

It should also be noted that none of the laboratory studies assessed the frequency of Duchenne laughter and smiling or the funniness of the comedy videotapes. Future research should include such measures to examine whether they are correlated with the strength of any observed changes in immunity, thereby providing further evidence that the effects are due to mirth. The studies also have tended to be very small, with numerous methodological weaknesses. Part of the difficulty here seems to be that, unfortunately, very little funding is available for conducting these sorts of experiments, which tend to be quite costly. Research on possible effects of humor on immunity does not seem to have a high priority for the government granting agencies and pharmaceutical companies that fund most of the health-related research. Consequently, researchers in this area have had to make do with small-scale studies, cutting corners on the types of control groups and other design features that are needed in order to draw firm conclusions.

HUMOR AND PAIN

As noted earlier in the chapter, the case of Norman Cousins suggested that laughter may have a pain-reducing effect, perhaps due to the hypothesized release of endorphins in the brain when people are experiencing mirthful emotion. Since then, several experiments have been conducted to determine whether humor can be shown to increase pain tolerance under controlled laboratory conditions. These investigations have employed research designs similar to those used in the immunity research, testing participants' pain threshold or tolerance before and after exposing them to comedy videotapes and comparing the findings with those obtained in nonhumorous control conditions.

Pain threshold and tolerance are measured using procedures that were developed in traditional experimental studies of pain, in which participants are exposed to painful (but not harmful) stimuli. The most popular of these is the cold pressor procedure, in which participants are asked to immerse their arm in a tub of ice cold water for up to a few minutes. Pain threshold is defined as the amount of time elapsed before the participant reports the stimulus to be painful, while pain tolerance is the duration of time before the individual cannot tolerate the stimulus any longer and wishes to terminate it (i.e., remove his or her arm from the ice water).

These experiments have generally been more carefully controlled and methodologically rigorous than the immunity research (likely because they are less expensive to conduct). Most of the studies have had several control groups, controlling for such factors as distraction, relaxation, and negative emotion. For example, Rosemary Cogan and her colleagues conducted an experiment in which college students were randomly assigned to either humor (an audiotape of Lily Tomlin performing stand-up comedy), relaxation (a progressive muscle relaxation tape), dull narrative (a lecture on ethics), or no-treatment control conditions (Cogan, Cogan, Waltz, and McCue, 1987). The results showed no difference between the laughter and relaxation groups on pain threshold measures obtained following the manipulation; however, thresholds for both of these groups were significantly higher than those for the dull narrative and no-treatment conditions. Thus, exposure to humor and relaxation both produced increases in the amount of noxious stimulus that participants were able to experience before they began to perceive it as painful, suggesting that humor, like relaxation, may have an analgesic effect.

In a second study, these same authors sought to rule out other possible alternative explanations for these findings by assigning students to either comedy (an audiotape of Bill Cosby performing stand-up comedy), interesting narrative (an absorbing Edgar Allen Poe story), dull narrative (an ethics lecture), active distraction (performing a multiplication task), or no-treatment conditions. The results revealed that participants' pain thresholds following these conditions were significantly higher in the comedy condition than in all the other groups. These results indicate that the humor-related increase in pain tolerance was not simply due to distraction or absorption, suggesting a possible physiological mechanism. Similar results have been obtained in other well-controlled experiments (J. Weaver and Zillmann, 1994; Weisenberg, Tepper, and Schwarzwald, 1995; Zillmann, Rockwell, Schweitzer, and Sundar, 1993), providing fairly consistent evidence that exposure to comedy results in increased pain threshold and tolerance.

There is also some evidence that the analgesic effects of humor observed in the laboratory may extend to clinical interventions, but perhaps only with moderate rather than severe levels of pain. In a field study, James Rotton and Mark Shats (1996) assigned hospitalized orthopedic surgery patients to one of three conditions: (1) a humorous movie group, who watched four feature-length comedy movies during the two days post-surgery; (2) a nonhumorous movie group, who watched four dramatic movies; or (3) a no-movie control group. The results showed lower levels of minor analgesic (e.g., aspirin) usage during the two days post-surgery in participants watching the humorous movies as compared to those in the other two groups. However, these effects did not extend to the use of major analgesics such as Demerol and Percodan. Furthermore, these findings were only obtained among patients in the humorous movie condition who were permitted to choose which movies they would watch; those who were not given any choice over the comedy movies they were to watch actually showed significantly *higher* levels of analgesic usage compared to the control groups. Thus, watching humorous films that are not consistent with one's own humor preferences may be aversive rather than beneficial.

Although these studies suggest that exposure to humor can reduce pain, it is interesting to note that similar effects are also found with negative emotions. Experiments that have included negative emotion control conditions, in addition to comedy conditions, have demonstrated similar increases in pain threshold and tolerance with exposure to videotapes inducing emotions like disgust, horror, or sadness. For example, Matisyohyu Weisenberg and colleagues (1995) found equal increases in pain tolerance in a group of participants exposed to a comedy film and a group exposed to a disgusting horror film, both of which showed greater pain tolerance than those in neutral-film and no-film control conditions. Similar results were found in other studies comparing the effects of humor to tragedy (Zillmann et al., 1993) and sadness (J. Weaver and Zillmann, 1994). These findings suggest that the observed analgesic effects may occur with both positive and negative emotional arousal, rather than being specific to mirth.

Although these humor-related increases in pain tolerance and threshold appear to be quite robust, the exact mechanisms involved are still not clear. The effects appear to take some time to build up, since they have only been found in studies that tested pain tolerance after the comedy film ended and not while participants were still watching the film (Nevo, Keinan, and Teshimovsky-Arditi, 1993). Furthermore, Weisenberg and colleagues found that the increased pain threshold and tolerance continued for 30 minutes after exposure to a humorous videotape, even after participants' self-rated moods had returned to baseline (Weisenberg, Raz, and Hener, 1998). The authors interpreted these findings as indicating that humor-related mirth induces physiological changes that affect the sensory components of pain, rather than simply altering the cognitive-affective-motivational components of pain, and that these physiological changes take some time to develop and continue even after initial mood changes have dissipated.

A study by Diana Mahony and her colleagues suggests that humor-related increases in pain tolerance may be mediated by expectancies (Mahony, Burroughs, and Hieatt, 2001). In this study, before being shown a humorous videotape, the participants were told either that humor is known to increase pain tolerance (positive expectancy condition), or that humor has been shown to *decrease* pain tolerance (negative expectancy condition), or they were told nothing about the effects of humor on pain (no expectancy condition). The positive expectancy and no expectancy groups both showed significantly greater increases in pain thresholds following exposure to the comedy videotape, as compared to the negative expectancy group. These results suggest that the analgesic effects of humor may be a sort of placebo effect. However, this does not negate the possibility that they are mediated by physiological processes, since placebo analgesic effects have been shown in other studies to be mediated by physiological mechanisms including endorphin production in the brain (Benedetti, 2002).

Until recently, none of the humor and pain studies had examined correlations between the frequency of participants' laughter during the comedy film and changes in their pain tolerance, and it was therefore unclear whether the effects are due to laughter in particular, to the positive emotion of mirth, or to some other factor such as the cognitions involved in humor. A recent experiment by Karen Zweyer and her colleagues was designed to address this question. In this study, participants watched a comedy film (*Mr. Bean at the Dentist*) that contained sound effects but no dialogue, and they were instructed to either (1) enjoy the film but inhibit all smiling and laughter, (2) smile and laugh as much as possible during the film, or (3) produce a humorous narrative while watching the film (Zweyer, Velker, and Ruch, 2004). Using the cold pressor procedure, pain tolerance was measured before, immediately after, and 20 minutes after the film. The researchers also videotaped the participants during the procedure, and subsequently coded their facial expressions for genuine (Duchenne) and forced (non-Duchenne) smiling and laughter, using the Facial Action Coding System (which was described in Chapter 6).

Overall, the three conditions yielded similar significant increases in pain threshold and tolerance relative to baseline, which were evident immediately after the film and continued 20 minutes later. These results indicate that neither laughter nor humor production are necessary, beyond feelings of amusement, for the pain reduction effect to occur. Moreover, the observed increases in pain tolerance were found to be positively associated with genuine enjoyment smiles (Duchenne display), but not with the frequency or intensity of laughter. In fact, voluntary efforts to exhibit or amplify laughter-related positive emotions were actually *negatively* associated with pain tolerance. Although these findings should be replicated before we can draw firm conclusions, they cast doubt on the hypothesis (derived from the case of Norman Cousins) that hearty laughter is necessary for the increase in pain tolerance to occur. Instead, the results suggest that the mechanisms have more to do with the amusement-related positive emotion of mirth. Laughter does not seem to be necessary and, in fact, forcing oneself to laugh seemed to have a contrary effect (a finding that may be problematic for the laughter club movement).

In summary, there is quite consistent empirical support for Norman Cousins' observation that laughter reduces pain, although the evidence suggests that the effect is not due to laughter *per se*, but rather to the positive emotion of mirth that accompanies humor and that is typically expressed by laughter. The research also indicates that these analgesic effects occur with negative as well as positive emotions. We still do not know, however, whether the humor-related increases in pain tolerance are mediated by endorphins. Indeed, the popular view that humorous mirth is associated with endorphin production in the brain has not yet been substantiated by research. In fact, experiments that have assessed levels of beta-endorphin in blood samples have not found any changes in this variable when participants were exposed to comedy films (L. S. Berk et al., 1989; Itami et al., 1994). However, blood tests may not be sensitive to changes in opiate levels occurring in the brain. One potential method for investigating the endorphin mediation hypothesis would be to determine whether humor-associated increases in pain tolerance disappear when participants are first given the opiate antagonist Naloxone. If Naloxone, which blocks endorphin receptors in the brain, cancels out the pain-reducing effect of humor, this would indicate that the effect is mediated by endorphins. This is an interesting question that should be pursued in future research.

HUMOR, BLOOD PRESSURE, AND HEART DISEASE

Although some authors have speculated that frequent hearty laughter may lead to a reduction in blood pressure (e.g., McGhee, 1999), experimental studies indicate that laughter is actually associated with short-term increases in blood pressure and heart rate, but no longer-term effects. Sabina White and Phame Camarena (1989) conducted a six-week intervention study to examine the effects of laughter on systolic blood pressure (SBP), diastolic blood pressure (DBP), and heart rate (HR). They randomly assigned participants to a laughter treatment group, a relaxation group, or a health-education control group, each of which met for 6 weekly sessions of $1\frac{1}{2}$ hours. The results showed no significant presession to postsession changes in DBP, SBP, or HR in the laughter or health-education groups, whereas the relaxation group showed significantly lower postsession HR and SBP in comparison with both of the other groups. Thus, this study did not support the hypothesis that sustained laughter results in lower levels of heart rate and blood pressure over time.

In a study of the relation between trait sense of humor and blood pressure, Herbert Lefcourt and his colleagues examined correlations between participants' scores on the Situational Humor Response Questionnaire (SHRQ) and the Coping

Humor Scale (CHS) and their SBP and DBP levels during a series of stressful laboratory tasks (Lefcourt, Davidson, Prkachin, and Mills, 1997). No significant correlations were found between the sense of humor scales and DBP, but an interesting sex difference was revealed in the pattern of correlations with SBP. Women with higher scores on the sense of humor measures, as compared to women with lower scores, were found to have generally lower levels of SBP, supporting the idea that a sense of humor is negatively related to blood pressure. However, the opposite relation was found for men: those with higher humor scores had *higher* overall levels of SBP as compared to their low-humor male counterparts. The authors suggested that these findings may be due to differences in the way men and women express humor, with women perhaps engaging in more tolerant, self-accepting, and adaptive forms of humor, potentially leading to more beneficial physiological effects (Crawford and Gressley, 1991). In contrast, greater humor in men may reflect greater competitiveness and aggressiveness, resulting in more elevated blood pressure. These findings hint at the possibility that different styles or types of humor may have quite different health consequences.

Adam Clark and his colleagues conducted a study at the University of Maryland Medical Center to determine whether there is a correlation between coronary heart disease (CHD) and sense of humor (A. Clark, Seidler, and Miller, 2001). They administered the SHRQ (which, as noted in Chapter 7, assesses the degree to which individuals frequently laugh and smile in a wide variety of situations) to 300 consecutive patients diagnosed with CHD, as well as biological family members of these patients. The results showed that, on average, the CHD patients had significantly lower SHRQ scores than did their healthy relatives, suggesting that a lower sense of humor may be a risk factor for heart disease. Scores on this sense of humor measure were unrelated to other risk factors such as diabetes, hypertension, or cigarette smoking. However, individuals with higher SHRQ scores had significantly lower scores on a measure of hostility, which has previously been shown to be related to a greater risk of heart disease (Williams et al., 1980). Although these findings suggest that a sense of humor may provide some protection against heart disease, a serious weakness of the study is that the humor test was administered after patients had already developed the disease. The causal effect may therefore be opposite to what is proposed: people who have recently had a heart attack may be less inclined to respond to situations with humor and laughter, resulting in lower SHRQ scores. Further research is therefore needed using prospective designs to determine whether nonsymptomatic people with lower humor scores are more likely to develop heart disease at a later time.

HUMOR AND ILLNESS SYMPTOMS

If humor and laughter confer beneficial effects on immunity and other aspects of health, individuals who laugh more frequently and have a better sense of humor should be generally less likely to become ill. To test this hypothesis, several researchers have examined simple correlations between trait measures of sense of humor, such as the

SHRQ and CHS, and overall health, as measured by self-report physical symptom checklists. Some of these studies have found the predicted negative correlations between these variables, indicating that individuals with a greater sense of humor tend to report fewer medical problems and illness symptoms (Boyle and Joss-Reid, 2004; Carroll and Shmidt, 1992; Dillon and Totten, 1989; P. S. Fry, 1995; Ruch and Köhler, 1999). Other studies, however, have failed to replicate these findings (Anderson and Arnoult, 1989; Labott and Martin, 1990; Porterfield, 1987).

Additionally, two studies found a significant stress-moderating effect of sense of humor on self-reported illness symptomatology, indicating that individuals with higher sense of humor scores were less likely to report becoming ill following high levels of stressful life events (Abel, 1998; P. S. Fry, 1995). However, these findings were not replicated in other studies with larger sample sizes (Korotkov and Hannah, 1994; Porterfield, 1987). One study even found an interaction between humor and stress that was opposite to predictions, with high-humor individuals showing a greater tendency to report illness following negative life events (Anderson and Arnoult, 1989). Thus, there is no consistent evidence that people with a greater sense of humor are less likely to become ill.

It is important to note that self-report measures of illness symptoms are often confounded with negative emotionality or neuroticism, making them somewhat unreliable measures of objective health status (D. Watson and Pennebaker, 1989). People who generally experience more negative moods, as compared to less neurotic individuals, tend to perceive themselves as being less healthy, even though they may not differ in objective health status. Because sense of humor tests tend to be somewhat negatively related to neuroticism, observed correlations between sense of humor and self-reported illness symptoms may be due to this shared neuroticism component rather than any objective health benefits of humor. It is therefore important for researchers to partial out the effects of neuroticism in such research. This was done in only one study, and in that study the correlation between sense of humor and physical illness symptoms disappeared after controlling for neuroticism (Korotkov and Hannah, 1994).

A recent study by Sven Svebak and colleagues represented a unique opportunity to include a measure of sense of humor in a large population health study that involved the entire adult population of a county in Norway (Svebak, Martin, and Holmen, 2004). Besides completing a three-item humor measure derived from Svebak's (1996) Sense of Humor Questionnaire (SHQ-6), over 65,000 participants completed a survey about their illness symptoms in a variety of domains (e.g., nausea, diarrhea, pounding heart, dyspnea, musculoskeletal pain) and their overall health satisfaction, and were also assessed for blood pressure, height, and weight (allowing for computation of body mass index, a measure of obesity). As such, this is the largest correlational study of sense of humor and health ever conducted. However, the results provided very little evidence for a direct association between sense of humor and health. After controlling for age, no meaningful correlations were found between sense of humor and either illness symptoms or objective health indicators, although the study did find a weak relation between sense of humor and satisfaction with health.

These results suggest that, although high-humor individuals do not seem to have objectively better health, they are somewhat more subjectively satisfied with their health.

In view of the very large sample size of this survey, the broad age range of participants, and the unselected nature of the sample, these data provide quite convincing evidence that people with a greater sense of humor (at least as defined by high scores on such self-report tests as the SHQ) are no more healthy overall than are their low-humor counterparts. If a sense of humor does confer any health benefits, it would appear that either they are too subtle to be captured by such a cross-sectional design, or the type of humor involved is not adequately captured by the SHQ. For example, this study did not include a measure of life stress, so the authors were unable to examine the possibility of a stress-moderating effect of sense of humor on health. In addition, the possibility remains that effects of humor on health might emerge over time in a longitudinal design.

A study by Nicholas Kuiper and Sorrel Nicholl (2004) also bears on the relation between sense of humor and satisfaction with health. These authors suggested that it may be important to distinguish between actual and perceived physical health, and proposed that a sense of humor may contribute to more positive perceptions of physical health than may actually be warranted. Using a sample of undergraduate students, they found that individuals with higher scores on sense of humor measures reported more positive health-related perceptions, such as less fear of serious disease or death, less negative bodily preoccupation, and less concern about pain. These results are consistent with the finding of Svebak et al. (2004) that higher sense of humor is related to greater subjective satisfaction with health but not with more objective indicators of health status. These findings may help to explain the popularity of the idea that humor is beneficial for one's health. People with a greater sense of humor may perceive themselves to be healthier, showing less concern and preoccupation with symptoms of illness, even though they are not objectively healthier. Thus, although the direction of causality is unclear in correlational research such as this, it may be that humor contributes to one's quality of life without making one physically healthier.

HUMOR AND LONGEVITY

If humor has beneficial effects on physical health, then it should be possible to demonstrate that, on average, people who more frequently engage in humor and laughter tend to live longer than their less humorous counterparts. Indeed, this would seem to be the most important test of the humor-health hypothesis. Although one could still argue that frequently engaging in humor and laughter can at least improve the quality if not the duration of life, it is difficult to see how claims for actual physical health benefits of humor can be sustained if it does not prolong life. Unfortunately, the research evidence in this regard, although limited, is not very encouraging.

James Rotton (1992), in a series of four separate studies, found no differences in the life duration of comedians and comedy writers, as compared with that of serious entertainers and authors. Interestingly, though, he found that both professional humorists and serious entertainers died at a significantly *younger* age than did people who were famous for other reasons, perhaps due to the stresses or unhealthy lifestyles of people in the entertainment industry. Thus, the ability to create humor and to make other people laugh (as epitomized in individuals who make a living by their comedic abilities) does not appear to confer any health benefits resulting in greater longevity.

Another study suggests that having a sense of humor may actually cause people to die at an *earlier* age than they would otherwise. Howard Friedman and his colleagues conducted analyses of data from 1178 male and female participants from the well-known Terman Life-Cycle Study, a longitudinal investigation that followed a cohort of intellectually gifted individuals for many decades beginning when they were children in the 1920s (Friedman, Tucker, Tomlinson-Keasey, Schwartz, et al., 1993). A composite measure of cheerfulness was derived from parent and teacher ratings of sense of humor and optimism that had been obtained on these individuals at the age of 12. Surprisingly, survival analyses revealed that those individuals who were rated as having higher cheerfulness at age 12 had significantly *higher* mortality rates throughout the ensuing decades. Thus, on average, more cheerful individuals were more likely to die at a younger age as compared to their less cheerful counterparts. The higher mortality rates were found in both men and women, and applied to all causes of death.

The authors suggested that these surprising results may be due to more cheerful individuals being less concerned about health risks and taking less care of themselves, as compared to more serious people. Ironically, the greater health satisfaction and lowered concern about health problems found in high-humor individuals (Kuiper and Nicholl, 2004; Svebak, Martin et al., 2004) may lead to a more blasé attitude toward health risks and consequently higher mortality rates.

Proponents of the health benefits of humor have sought to dismiss the findings of this study in a number of ways, suggesting, for example, that the definition of sense of humor was inappropriate, or that the results were due to the optimism component of the composite cheerfulness measure rather than the sense of humor component, or that cheerfulness in this study reflected a lack of emotional adjustment. However, these arguments do not appear to stand up under closer scrutiny. The question that was used for rating sense of humor in this study had at its positive pole the following description: "Extraordinarily keen sense of humor. Witty. Appreciates jokes. Sees the funny side of everything," and at its negative pole the following: "Extremely lacking in sense of humor. Serious and prosy. Never sees the funny side." It seems difficult to argue that this description is very different from the way most people today (including advocates of the "humor and health" movement) would describe a sense of humor.

Moreover, a follow-up analysis of these data found that the higher mortality rates remained even when the sense of humor rating was used by itself, and not just in combination with optimism (L. R. Martin et al., 2002). These analyses also found that individuals who were rated higher on cheerfulness as children were no more likely to be neurotic or to have emotional problems later in life and, indeed, they were better adjusted and more carefree in adulthood, as well as being more extraverted. On the other hand, the analyses showed that children who were rated as more cheerful in childhood went on to smoke more cigarettes, consume more alcohol, and engage in more risky hobbies as adults, although these unhealthy lifestyle behaviors did not completely account statistically for their higher mortality rates. Overall, then, rather than supporting the hypothesis that a sense of humor increases longevity, the existing evidence, though limited, suggests that a sense of humor may actually be an illness risk factor.

CONCLUSION

Of all the health benefits claimed for humor and laughter, the most consistent research support has been found for the hypothesized analgesic effects. After watching humorous films in the laboratory, individuals tend to be able to tolerate increased levels of pain, and there is some limited clinical evidence that humor can reduce post-surgical pain. The research suggests that the observed pain-reducing effects are likely due to amusement-related positive emotion, rather than to laughter *per se*, although similar effects are also found with negative emotions. The popular idea that these effects are mediated by the production of endorphins or other opiates in the brain has not yet been investigated, although this appears to be a plausible explanation. More extensive research is needed to explore these mechanisms and to determine whether these effects are strong enough to be useful for applications of humor in the treatment of pain resulting from clinical conditions.

With regard to possible effects of humor and laughter on immunity, the research to date is not as consistent or conclusive. Some short-term effects of exposure to comedy on some components of immunity have been observed in the laboratory, and recent findings of reduced allergic reactions are intriguing. However, these studies tend to be quite small, with many methodological limitations, and some of the findings have been inconsistent across studies. More systematic and rigorous research is needed to replicate these findings and explore possible mechanisms before firm conclusions can be drawn. Research in the general field of psychoneuroimmunology indicates that emotional states can influence immunity through the many communication channels linking the brain and the immune system. There is therefore reason to expect interactions between the emotion of mirth and immunity as well. However, these complex interactions are still not well understood, and there does not appear to be a simple one-to-one relation between specific emotions and particular changes in immunity (Booth and Pennebaker, 2000).

Although the research offers some interesting suggestions of possible effects of humor on immunity, there is little evidence that people who have a better sense of humor and laugh more frequently have better immunity, enjoy better health overall, or live longer lives. There is even some research suggesting that more humorous and cheerful people may actually die at an earlier age than their more serious counter-parts. This may be due to high-humor individuals having less concern about health issues, a more risky lifestyle, or a reduced tendency to take health problems seriously and seek appropriate medical treatment when needed.

Nonetheless, even though more humorous and cheerful people may not live longer, they may enjoy a better quality of life and greater overall life satisfaction. It also remains possible that different types of humor may affect different aspects of health in different ways. Although a cheerful sense of humor might contribute to earlier mortality by causing people to take less care of themselves overall, it remains possible that mirth could produce biochemical changes having some health benefits, or that the use of certain styles of humor could facilitate coping with stress or enhance intimate relationships, indirectly producing some positive health effects.

Those who advocate humor and laughter as a pathway to better health seem to have moved too quickly to promote their views on the basis of rather flimsy research evidence. Besides the need for more basic research in this area, the effectiveness of humor-based interventions needs to be carefully evaluated before they are widely implemented. For some proponents, this health fad may be seen as an opportunity for making money through promotional books and workshops, but many others appear to be motivated by genuine concern about helping others. In either case, a strong commitment to belief in health benefits of humor and laughter can make it difficult for advocates to evaluate the research objectively.

One could perhaps argue in defense of proponents of the "humor and health" movement that, although humor may not produce all the health benefits that have been claimed, at least it is not likely to be harmful and it can enhance people's enjoy-ment if not the duration of their lives. There is certainly some merit to this line of argument. There is undoubtedly nothing wrong with encouraging people to enjoy humor and to laugh more often, especially if they are suffering from a serious illness that would otherwise reduce their enjoyment of life. However, there is a risk that unfounded claims of health benefits of humor and laughter may raise false hopes in sick individuals.

There is also a danger that an emphasis on the health benefits of humor and laughter could lead to an unjustified perception that people have more control over their health than they actually do, fostering a subtle tendency to blame people for their illnesses. Consequently, those who become ill may begin to feel guilty because they supposedly did not laugh enough. In addition, exaggerated claims about unfounded health benefits of humor and laughter can contribute to perceptions that this is nothing more than a fringe movement and a passing fad, which could dissuade researchers and funding agencies from conducting and funding well-designed large-scale experiments in this field, thereby delaying progress in identifying those health effects that may be genuine.

Theories about possible health benefits of humor need to be based on plausible biological mechanisms. From an evolutionary perspective, it seems unlikely that the primary function of humor and laughter is to improve people's physical health. As noted in Chapter 6, comparative research suggests that the positive emotion associated with humor is related to social play, and that laughter is an expressive behavior communicating playful emotions and intentions to others. In Chapter 5, I also discussed in some detail the many social functions of humor and laughter. Thus, the origins of humor and laughter seem to have more to do with social interaction and the social nature of human existence than with physical health. Nonetheless, it remains possible that these emotions and behaviors may have some physiological and psychological concomitants that could indirectly affect aspects of health.

The interactions between emotions and immunity that have been found by researchers likely have to do with the fact that both are involved in constructing and maintaining relationships between the individual and his or her environment (Booth and Pennebaker, 2000). Emotional feelings of distress and well-being are signals concerning the state of the organism, providing useful information for the immune system, which is also concerned with individual integrity and well-being. Hence, feelings of cheerfulness and a playful, humorous perspective may be in part a signal that one's physiological resources are adequate for dealing with threats to well-being, as well as perhaps contributing to the mobilization of those resources (Leventhal and Patrick-Miller, 2000). Thus, there are some theoretical grounds for proposing possible effects of humor on some health-related variables, even though these effects may not be the primary function of humor from an evolutionary perspective.

Despite the limitations of the existing research evidence, more systematic investigation in this area appears to be warranted by the suggestive research findings, as well as the theoretical plausibility of some sort of humor-health connections. As discussed earlier, future experimental research should include appropriate control conditions to rule out alternative explanations for findings, as well as examining the role of laughter and mirth in mediating any observed effects. Animal research may also be helpful in clarifying neural and biochemical mechanisms involved in physiological effects of play-related emotions (Panksepp and Burgdorf, 2003).

Future research should also examine the different theoretical models linking humor and health that I discussed earlier in this chapter. Most of the existing research has focused on hypothesized direct effects of laughter and mirthful emotion on physiological variables such as immunity. Little research has been conducted on possible indirect effects, such as potential health benefits of enhanced interpersonal relationships and more effective coping with stress resulting from a healthy sense of humor. Here, as suggested in the Chapter 11, it would seem to be important to distinguish between different types or styles of humor, some of which may be beneficial to health while others may even have adverse effects. In the end, it may be that, as with psychological health, the absence of certain deleterious types of humor (e.g., hostile humor) may be as important (or perhaps even more important) for physical health as the presence of other more benign forms of humor.

CHAPTER 11

Applications of Humor in Psychotherapy, Education, and the Workplace

Over the past two decades, there has been a growing interest in potential applications of humor in a variety of professional domains. In Chapter 10, I discussed possible benefits of humor and laughter for physical health, as well as the use of various humor-based interventions by health care providers. In this chapter, I will explore potential benefits (and also possible risks) of humor applied to the fields of psychotherapy and counseling, education, and the workplace.

A number of individuals working in each of these areas have enthusiastically promoted the use of humor-related techniques and interventions in their respective disciplines, and numerous articles in professional and trade journals, books, and Internet websites have appeared on this topic. Among its membership, the Association for Applied and Therapeutic Humor (AATH) includes psychotherapists, marriage and family counselors, teachers, and consultants to business and industry, along with physicians, nurses, and other health care practitioners, all of whom are interested in the way humor and laughter may be applied to their respective fields.

Most of the claims that have been made about potential benefits of humor in these different areas are based on anecdotal evidence and personal experiences, although humor advocates also frequently cite various research findings to bolster their arguments. Although the empirical research in each of these areas is quite limited, in the following sections I will explore the relevant findings, attempting to weigh the evidence for various claims, as well as pointing out those questions that still require further study.

The topics of this chapter bring us to the applied areas of psychology, particularly clinical and counseling, educational, and industrial-organizational (I/O) psychology. Each of these branches of psychology represents a combination of professional practice and science. As practitioners, psychologists working in these fields seek to apply relevant findings and principles derived from the more basic research areas of the discipline to solve real-world problems relating to individual emotional and behavioral disturbance, teaching and education, and the world of business and industry, respectively. As scientists, they conduct empirical research to examine the effectiveness of their interventions and to answer important theoretical and practical questions relating to their fields.

As a consequence of this scientific orientation, applied psychologists tend to be rather skeptical about unsubstantiated claims regarding novel treatment interventions, teaching methods, or business practices, emphasizing instead the importance of applying empirical methods to investigate the validity of these sorts of practices. Thus, while maintaining an open mind about possible benefits of humor-related applications in these areas, a psychological perspective requires that we carefully sift through the evidence and avoid being carried away by unfounded enthusiasm.

HUMOR IN PSYCHOTHERAPY AND COUNSELING

Based on the idea that humor has important benefits for mental health (as discussed in Chapter 9), therapists from a variety of different theoretical perspectives are showing a growing interest in the potential role of humor in psychotherapy and counseling. A number of journal articles and books have been written on this topic in recent years (Buckman, 1994; Franzini, 2000, 2001; W. F. Fry and Salameh, 1987, 1993; Gelkopf and Kreitler, 1996; Haig, 1988; Kuhlman, 1984; Lemma, 1999; Rutherford, 1994; Saper, 1987; Strean, 1994). Humor-based interventions have been advocated in the treatment of a wide variety of psychological problems ranging from depression (Richman, 2003), stress-related disorders (Prerost, 1988), obsessive-compulsive disorders (Surkis, 1993), and phobias (Ventis, Higbee, and Murdock, 2001), to antisocial personality disorder (Martens, 2004), schizophrenia (Witztum, Briskin, and Lerner, 1999), and mental retardation (Davidson and Brown, 1989).

Humor has been recommended as a useful tool in individual therapy and counseling (Rutherford, 1994), group therapy (Bloch, 1987; Bloch, Browning, and McGrath, 1983), family and marital counseling (Odell, 1996), and in the treatment of children and adolescents (Bernet, 1993) and the elderly (Prerost, 1993; Richman, 1995). The therapeutic benefits of humor have been lauded by therapists from many different theoretical schools, including Adlerian (Rutherford, 1994), behavioral (Franzini, 2000; Ventis et al., 2001), cognitive (Gelkopf and Kreitler, 1996), psychoanalytic (Bergmann, 1999; Korb, 1988), rational-emotive (Borcherdt, 2002), and strategic family therapy (Madanes, 1987).

Clinical psychologist Louis Franzini (2001) defined therapeutic humor as "the intentional and spontaneous use of humor techniques by therapists and other health care professionals, which can lead to improvements in the self-understanding and behavior of clients or patients" (p. 171). He suggested that therapeutic humor can take almost any form, including formal jokes or riddles (although these would be relatively rare), spontaneous puns or spoonerisms, behavioral or verbal parapraxes (i.e., unintentional humorous "Freudian slips"), humorous comments pointing out absurdities or illogical reasoning, exaggerations to the extreme, humorous self-deprecations on the part of the therapist, illustrations of universal human frailties, and comical observations of current social events. In order for humor to be beneficial in therapy, according to Franzini, the point of the humor should be clearly relevant to a current therapeutic issue, such as an inner conflict or a personal characteristic of the client. The immediate consequence of such therapeutic uses of humor is typically a positive emotional experience shared by the therapist and the client, ranging in intensity from quiet empathic amusement to loud laughter.

There are three general ways of thinking about potential applications of humor to therapy. First, some authors have advocated a sort of "*humor as therapy*" approach, attempting to develop a whole system of therapy that is based largely on humor. Second, humor could be the basis of *specific therapeutic techniques* that clinicians might have in their repertoire (along with a number of other, non-humor–based interventions) and which they could apply to the treatment of particular types of client problems. Third, humor may be viewed as a *communication skill* that, like other therapist characteristics such as empathy and genuineness, contributes to a therapist's overall effectiveness regardless of his or her theoretical orientation.

In the following sections, I will explore each of these approaches in turn, examining research evidence where it exists, followed by a discussion of potential risks in the use of humor in psychotherapy and counseling. Although my focus here is on psychotherapy and counseling, much of this discussion is also relevant to the use of humor in other helping and health care professions such as social work, medicine, nursing, physiotherapy, occupational therapy, and so on (cf. du Pre, 1998; Leber and Vanoli, 2001).

Humor-Based Therapies

A large number of different "schools" of psychotherapy were developed and promoted by various clinicians during the 1960s and 1970s. A few of these approaches emphasized the importance of fostering a healthy sense of humor as one of the main goals of therapy. According to these approaches, a humorous perspective on life is not only an important indicator of psychological health, but also a means to maintain and strengthen healthy functioning. Some of these approaches employed specific humor-based techniques to induce change in clients, while others emphasized the role of the therapist in modeling a humorous outlook and encouraging any humor that emerges naturally as the client gains a more realistic outlook and a greater ability to cope with life.

One well-known approach to therapy that makes extensive use of humor is Rational-Emotive Therapy (RET), which was developed by Albert Ellis (e.g., Ellis and Grieger, 1986). According to this approach, people develop psychological disturbance as a consequence of having irrational beliefs, dysfunctional attitudes, and unrealistic absolute standards. The aim of therapy is therefore to challenge and dispute clients' false beliefs and to replace them with more realistic and adaptive assumptions and attitudes. One way of doing this is for the therapist to use humorous exaggeration and even sarcasm to point out the absurdity of clients' irrational belief systems. Ellis (1977) wrote that "human disturbance largely consists of exaggerating the significance or the seriousness of things, and the ripping up of such exaggerations by humorous counter-exaggeration may well prove one of the main methods of therapeutic attack" (p. 4).

Besides being a way of disputing the irrational assumptions of clients, Ellis suggested that humor is beneficial in therapy because it brings enjoyment and mirth, makes life seem more worthwhile, and provides alternative ways of dealing with problems. Although Ellis's use of humor appears to be quite aggressive, he emphasized that it must be done in a way that communicates acceptance of clients and encourages them to accept themselves despite their errors and human fallibilities. Nonetheless, many clinicians are uncomfortable with such a confrontational style of humor in therapy. Most would agree that, due to its potential for harm, such humor must be employed very cautiously and skillfully, if at all.

Another therapeutic approach that employs humor to actively confront and challenge clients is Provocative Therapy, which was developed by Frank Farrelly and his colleagues (Farrelly and Brandsma, 1974; Farrelly and Lynch, 1987). Originally devised for the treatment of chronic schizophrenia, this approach was subsequently promoted as being beneficial for many types of psychological problems. Based on the assumption that clients can change their self-defeating behavior patterns and overcome psychological disturbance if they take responsibility for their own behavior, the goal of this therapy is to provoke an emotional response in clients that results in changes in their perceptions and actions. This is done by using humor to attack their beliefs, feelings, and behaviors through exaggeration and sarcasm, causing them to fight back against the therapist and eventually gain a detached, humorous perspective on their dysfunctional behavior patterns.

Although this therapeutic approach, like RET, appears to be very aggressive and even hostile, Farrelly and Lynch (1987) emphasized that the client must experience the therapist as "warmly caring and fundamentally supportive" (p. 90). Similarly, Farrelly and Brandsma (1974) stressed that "if the client is not laughing during at least part of the therapeutic encounter, the therapist is not doing provocative therapy and what he is doing may at times turn out to be destructive" (p. 95). Like Ellis's approach, provocative therapy appears to have a potential for harm if used by an unskilled therapist.

A less confrontational therapeutic system giving an important place to humor is Walter O'Connell's (1981; 1987) Natural High Therapy, a humanistic approach that borrows heavily from the ideas of Carl Jung and Alfred Adler. According to this approach, psychological symptoms are manifestations of displaced creative energies and personality constrictions resulting from frustrating life experiences. The goal of therapy is to increase self-actualization, helping the client to move from the constrictions of being controlled by the environment and inner compulsions to a healthy sense of autonomy based on self-esteem and satisfying relationships with others. A healthy sense of humor is seen as a defining characteristic of self-actualization.

Using a didactic-experiential format and combining individual and group treatment modalities, Natural High Therapy employs a variety of techniques to promote self-actualization, including psychodrama, role playing, guided imagery, and meditation. Humor, which O'Connell (1981, p. 561) viewed as "the royal road toward self-actualization," is an intrinsic part of all of these methods. However, for O'Connell, humor was more an end than a means. Rather than forcing it onto clients, the therapist's role is one of modeling a humorous outlook and encouraging any humor that emerges spontaneously in the client.

Other clinicians who have promoted humor as an essential component of psychotherapy include Harvey Mindess (1971, 1976), Martin Grotjahn (1966, 1971), and Waleed Salameh (1987). Unfortunately, like many of the schools of therapy that arose in past decades, little research has been conducted to evaluate the effectiveness of most of these humor-based therapy systems or to compare them with other types of treatment.

Humor as a Specific Therapeutic Technique

Rather than creating a whole system of therapy with humor as a central ingredient, some clinicians have developed specific humor-based intervention techniques for treating particular clients with particular problems. For example, Larry Ventis, a clinical psychologist at the College of William and Mary, developed an application of humor in systematic desensitization for the treatment of phobias and other fear-related conditions. Systematic desensitization is a behavioral intervention in which clients vividly imagine themselves experiencing a series of progressively more threatening fear-evoking situations while engaging in muscle relaxation exercises. The repeated pairing of a relaxation response with exposure to a feared stimulus gradually diminishes the feelings of anxiety evoked by the stimulus, enabling the individual to overcome the phobic aversion.

In an early case study, Ventis (1973) described the successful use of humorous imagery instead of muscle relaxation during a session of systematic desensitization in the treatment of a young woman who suffered from social anxiety. In another case study published around the same time, Ronald Smith (1973) reported that the use of humor in nine sessions of systematic desensitization was highly effective in reducing strong, maladaptive anger responses in a 22-year-old woman, after previous attempts at treatment using standard muscle relaxation procedures had failed.

More recently, Ventis and his colleagues (2001) conducted a more carefully controlled clinical study to investigate the use of humor in systematic desensitization in the treatment of spider phobias. Forty undergraduate students with spider phobias were randomly assigned to either four individual weekly treatment sessions using traditional systematic desensitization with muscle relaxation, four sessions of desensitization using humor, or a no-treatment control condition. In the humor treatment condition, participants were given humor creation exercises and weekly homework assignments in which they were encouraged to generate humorous statements and images relating to spiders. In each therapy session, they were also taken through a hierarchy of mental imagery scenarios in which humorous images were paired with anxiety-evoking situations having to do with exposure to spiders.

The results revealed that participants in both the humor desensitization group and the standard muscle relaxation group showed significant and equally large reductions in their fear of spiders on self-report and behavioral outcome measures, whereas those in the no-treatment group did not show any significant improvement. Further analyses revealed that the reduction of spider phobia in the two treatment groups was mediated by increased feelings of self-efficacy. The authors suggested that the experience of humor-related positive emotion may have altered the cognitive appraisals of participants in the humor treatment group, providing them with an increased sense of self-efficacy and a greater willingness to approach and interact with spiders. Overall, this study provided evidence that a humor-based intervention may be just as effective as (but not necessarily more effective than) standard muscle relaxation in systematic desensitization for the treatment of phobias.

Another well-known therapeutic technique that has often been viewed as being based on humor is "paradoxical intention," which was developed by Viktor Frankl (1960) and has been used for treating various problems including obsessive-compulsive symptoms, anxiety, depression, and agoraphobia. In this technique, clients are encouraged to try to increase the frequency and exaggerate the severity of their symptoms. It is assumed that these paradoxical efforts put the clients into a sort of "double bind" that can only be resolved by recognizing the absurdity of their symptoms, enabling them to develop the ability to laugh at their neurotic behavior patterns and gain a feeling of detachment from them. It might therefore seem reasonable to expect that clients with a greater sense of humor would derive more benefit from this type of treatment.

However, contrary to this hypothesis, a study by Geraldine Newton and Thomas Dowd (1990) found that the use of paradoxical interventions in the treatment of students with test anxiety was much more effective with clients having low (rather than high) scores on measures of sense of humor. The authors suggested that the high-humor participants may have treated the paradoxical intervention as merely a joke that was not to be taken seriously, and were therefore unable to experience the therapeutic "double bind" that is required for the intervention to be effective. In contrast, low-humor participants may have taken the intervention more seriously and attempted to cooperate with the therapist, resulting in the paradoxical effectiveness of the treatment. These findings suggest that, although paradoxical interventions may work by stimulating a humorous perspective toward one's neurotic symptoms, they need to be initially taken seriously to be effective. Individuals who normally approach life with a humorous outlook may be less likely to benefit from them.

Eliezer Witztum and his colleagues (1999) described the use of paradoxical interventions and other humor-based techniques to treat delusions and hallucinations in 12 patients with chronic schizophrenia who had been hospitalized for at least eight years. After three months of more serious "persuasion therapy" failed to produce any therapeutic improvement in the patients, the therapists began using a humorous approach in individual and group therapy sessions. This involved making joking comments in a sympathetic and lighthearted manner to satirize and trivialize the patients' delusions and hallucinations, highlighting the irony and absurdity of these symptoms through playful exaggeration, and thereby encouraging the patients not to take them overly seriously. At the end of three months of this humor treatment, evaluations of the patients' mental state using a psychiatric rating scale revealed significant improvements in functioning in most of the patients, and these gains were found to be maintained in a three-month follow-up assessment. Although further research is needed, this small study provided promising evidence of the potential benefits of humor-based techniques in treating chronic psychotic symptoms.

Humor as a Therapist Skill

A third approach to the role of humor in therapy is to view it as a type of social skill or interpersonal competence that contributes to therapists' overall effectiveness, regardless of their theoretical orientation or the specific techniques they employ (e.g., Franzini, 2001; Saper, 1987). In other words, it may be important for psychotherapists to have a "good sense of humor." As we have seen throughout this book, humor may be viewed as a form of interpersonal communication that can serve a wide variety of social functions, ranging from prosocial to aggressive. Psychotherapy is an interpersonal process, in which the relationship between the therapist and the client is arguably the main vehicle for therapeutic change (Teyber, 1988). As in most types of interpersonal relationships, humor and laughter occur quite frequently in the interactions between therapists and their clients.

One recent study of individual psychotherapy sessions found that laughter in either the client or therapist occurred on average every three minutes, with clients laughing more than twice as often as therapists (Marci et al., 2004). The ability to use humor effectively with clients may be viewed as a therapeutic skill that clinicians need to practice and refine, just as they need to develop a number of other communication skills such as empathic understanding, active listening, nonverbal communication, and so forth. In this view, then, humor is something that occurs spontaneously and naturally in the normal interactions between therapist and client, which may be used with varying degrees of skill and may be more or less beneficial to the client, rather than being a specific technique that is intentionally employed by the therapist. Humor in itself is not inherently therapeutic; to be effective, it must be used in a therapeutic manner.

A good deal of therapy outcome research indicates that the most effective therapists are those who convey an attitude of empathy, caring, and genuineness toward their clients (Bachelor and Horvath, 1999). Humor is therefore most likely to be therapeutic if it is used in a genuine manner, communicating empathic understanding and concern for the client. On the other hand, humor may be nontherapeutic, and even harmful, if it leaves clients feeling misunderstood, if it conveys a sense of dismissing or denigrating their feelings and perceptions, or if it is used by therapists to mask their own feelings of discomfort with the issues raised by their clients.

Rather than engaging in humor unthinkingly simply because it is enjoyable, therapists need to be cognizant of the functions being served by their own use of humor and that of their clients at each stage of therapy, and evaluate its likely therapeutic effects. In view of the important role of humor in social interaction generally, and the potential benefits and risks of humor in psychotherapy, Franzini (2001) has argued that the topic of humor should be a formal component of the curriculum in the training of all psychotherapists and counselors.

Although specific techniques vary across different approaches, most types of therapy share several common goals. These include: (1) establishing positive rapport with the client; (2) gaining an accurate understanding of the client's thoughts, feelings, and behavior patterns; (3) helping clients to gain insight into their difficulties, recognize unrealistic aspects of their thinking, and develop alternative perspectives and new ways of thinking; (4) reducing levels of emotional distress and increasing feelings of well-being; and (5) modifying dysfunctional behavior patterns. A number of authors have suggested that, when used in a sensitive and empathic manner, humor might be useful to further each of these therapeutic goals (Gelkopf and Kreitler, 1996; Kuhlman, 1984; Pierce, 1994; Saper, 1987).

With regard to *establishing rapport*, it has been suggested that humor may be used to put the client at ease and reduce tension, to make the therapist seem more human, to increase the attractiveness of the therapist to the client, and to create a transitional "play space" in which the therapist and client can engage in rewarding interchange and shared reality (Gelkopf and Kreitler, 1996). Laughing together may promote feelings of intimacy and friendliness and facilitate the client's trust in the therapist. A well-timed humorous comment on the part of the therapist can often be a way of conveying empathic understanding by succinctly encapsulating ironic aspects of a client's experience, evoking a chuckle of recognition from the client. By using mildly self-deprecating humor or taking a humorous perspective on a potentially embarrassing or threatening situation that arises in the course of therapy, the therapist can also serve as a role model for the appropriate use of humor. For example, if a client criticizes or complains to the therapist, a humorous rather than a defensive response from the therapist can communicate that he or she remains hopeful and is not overwhelmed by the client's criticism and problems (H. A. Olson, 1994).

Humor may also be a vehicle for helping the therapist to *gain an accurate understanding of the client* by paying close attention to the client's humor productions. Research indicates that clients in psychotherapy are much more likely to initiate humor than are therapists, and that both clients and therapists are more likely to laugh in response to humorous comments made by the client than to therapist-initiated humor (Marci et al., 2004). This client-generated humor may be a rich source of information about the client's perceptions, attitudes, assumptions, and feelings. Clients' humor may be used diagnostically as an indicator of their mental status and level of functioning, as well as a way of assessing progress in therapy and the effectiveness of particular interventions. For example, the presence or absence of humor may indicate the degree to which a client is feeling some control over his or her problems or is feeling overwhelmed. Clients' humor may also signal areas of conflict when the client laughs spontaneously at things that do not at first appear to be amusing, or may indicate issues of aggression or depression. Therapists should also be alert to the possibility of countertransference feelings when they find themselves using humor excessively or avoiding it altogether with particular clients (Gelkopf and Kreitler, 1996).

Since humor inherently involves the simultaneous perception of incongruous or seemingly incompatible ideas or perspectives (i.e., bisociation), it also often occurs in therapy in the context of helping the client to *gain insight and alternative perspectives*. As clients begin to overcome rigid defenses, become more aware of unconscious assumptions and attitudes, and gain new perspectives on their life situation, they often experience an "aha" experience that strikes them as humorous and produces spontaneous laughter. When therapists join into this laughter, they celebrate these new insights with their clients and further reinforce their new perspectives. In addition, therapists can also often nudge clients toward these types of insights by gently using humor to highlight the irrationality or absurdity of their assumptions and attitudes. Such humor on the part of the therapist may also help clients to gain a sense of proportion, recognizing that their problems are not as large as they seem. Appropriate uses of humor by the therapist can also help clients to take a more tolerant view of life, accepting their own imperfections as well as the limitations and uncertainties of the world around them (Ellis, 1977).

Humor may also be helpful in therapy as a means of *reducing emotional distress*. As noted in Chapter 9, a considerable amount of research indicates that humor functions as an emotion regulation mechanism, reducing negative emotions such as depression, anxiety, and hostility, and increasing positive moods. By modeling and encouraging a humorous outlook, therapists can help clients to regulate their emotions.

Laughter may also play a role in helping clients to *modify dysfunctional behavior patterns*. Shared laughter can be a form of positive reinforcement following desirable behavior change, such as when a therapist and client laugh together following the client's successful enactment of a new way of dealing assertively with a problematic interpersonal situation. In helping clients to develop assertiveness and to find more adaptive ways of coping with interpersonal problems, therapists can also teach them methods of using humor as an effective social skill. In sum, humor seems to be an important therapist communication skill which, when used judiciously, can help to work toward the goals of therapy.

Research on Humor in the Therapeutic Process

Empirical investigations of the effects of humor as a therapist communication skill are unfortunately quite limited, and the overall findings have not been very promising. One approach to this type of research has been to ask participants to rate their perceptions of simulated therapy sessions containing humorous and nonhumorous interventions. In one study, adults who were currently in outpatient psychotherapy were presented with a series of audio recordings of therapy sessions in which the therapists either did or did not use humor in their responses to their clients (Rosenheim and Golan, 1986). The participants were asked to rate how helpful and understanding each therapist appeared to be and the degree to which they themselves would be willing to be treated by the therapist. Contrary to predictions, the results revealed that the nonhumorous interventions, as compared to the humorous ones, were rated as being significantly more effective and were more strongly preferred by the therapy clients.

Similar findings were reported in another study using the same methodology in which the participants were schizophrenic patients in the early stages of remission from an acute psychotic episode (Rosenheim, Tecucianu, and Dimitrovsky, 1989). Once again, the results revealed a consistent preference for the nonhumorous over the humorous interventions among all patients, regardless of age, gender, education, and diagnosis (paranoid versus nonparanoid). In particular, patients rated the nonhumorous interactions as being more helpful, more likely to strengthen the therapeutic relationship, and displaying more empathy and understanding. These findings suggest that humorous interventions run the risk of not being well received by clients, and underscore the need for care in their use.

In another study, university students were asked to rate one of three videotapes of simulated counseling sessions containing no humor, facilitative (empathic and supportive) humor, or nonfacilitative (mildly derisive or distracting) humor initiated by the counselor (J. A. Foster and Reid, 1983). The results indicated that the counselor was rated as more approachable and better able to create a positive relationship in both the facilitative humor and no-humor conditions as compared to the nonfacilitative humor condition, but no differences were found between the facilitative humor and no-humor conditions. Moreover, no differences were found across all three groups in ratings of the counselor's ability to help the client achieve greater self-understanding. Overall, this study suggested that nonfacilitative humor might have an adverse effect on some aspects of treatment, but facilitative humor does not seem to show any greater therapeutic benefits compared to no humor at all.

Other studies have analyzed tape recordings of actual therapy sessions to examine the effects of humorous therapist interventions on the ongoing therapy process. Clinical psychologist Barbara Killinger (1987) studied tape recordings of 85 therapy sessions involving different clients and therapists in two different university counseling centers. Interestingly, no differences were found in the overall frequency of humor initiated by novice versus more experienced therapists or during early versus later therapy sessions. The effectiveness of the humorous interventions was examined by comparing therapist-client interactions in which the therapist made a humorous comment with randomly selected control interactions in which the therapist made a nonhumorous comment. Trained judges rated the degree to which these therapist statements facilitated subsequent client exploration and understanding and led to a more positive attitude of the client toward the therapist. Overall, the results revealed that the humorous therapist statements did not seem to produce any greater benefits than did the nonhumorous control statements. On the contrary, those humorous comments that elicited laughter in clients were actually judged to produce significantly *less* client exploration and understanding as compared to nonhumorous statements.

Further analyses of the types of humor used by therapists in this study revealed that about 20 percent of the humor instances could be categorized as aggressive (superiority or ridicule). Although clients typically responded somewhat negatively to this type of humor, therapists were generally able to mitigate any lasting negative consequences through the immediate use of a "recovery statement," which softened the humor in some way. Nonetheless, this typically led to a shift away from the current topic of discussion and an interruption of client self-exploration. In sum, this study further highlighted potential risks of the use of humor by therapists and the need for caution.

A similar method was used by Patrick Peterson and Howard Pollio (1982) to study therapeutic effects of client-initiated humor in group rather than individual therapy. Analyzing video recordings of five sessions of a single therapy group, they found that over 75 percent of the humor generated by group members was negatively targeted toward another group member or someone outside the group, while only seven percent involved positive remarks of any sort. Analyses of the immediate effects of laughter on the therapeutic climate of the group revealed that laughter in response to humor directed at another group member led to a significant reduction in therapeutic effectiveness, whereas laughter at humor targeting generalized others outside the group led to an increase in effectiveness. Qualitative analyses indicated that most of the humor targeting other group members appeared to be a means of diverting group discussion away from the current topic of conversation, whereas humor targeting generalized others seemed to be a method of offering support and promoting group feeling.

Jacob Megdell (1984) examined the effects of therapist-initiated humor on clients' feelings of attraction or liking for the therapist during individual counseling sessions taking place at two alcoholism treatment centers. After the sessions, videotapes of the sessions were reviewed by the counselor and the client separately, and continuous ratings were made of each individual's perceptions of therapist-initiated humor. The clients also made continuous ratings of their feelings toward the therapist during the session. The results revealed that client liking of the therapists tended to increase significantly following segments that were perceived as being humorous by both the therapist and the client, but not following humor that was perceived as funny by only one of them. These findings suggest a potential benefit of humor, but only when it is enjoyed by both the client and the therapist together.

Some other studies that may be relevant to psychotherapy have examined the effects of humor in physician-patient interactions. In one of these, researchers analyzed audiotapes of interactions between primary care physicians and their patients during routine office visits, in order to identify interpersonal behavior patterns that might differentiate between physicians who had had two or more malpractice insur-ance claims against them and those who had none (Levinson et al., 1997). Besides using more facilitation comments (e.g., informing patients about what to expect, solic-iting their opinions, checking on their understanding), physicians with no malprac-tice claims were found to laugh more frequently and to use more humor in their interactions with their patients.

In another study, various types of humor initiated by physicians and patients were examined in audiotapes of physician-patient visits that were given either very high or very low satisfaction ratings by the patients following the sessions (Sala, Krupat, and Roter, 2002). The results revealed that high-satisfaction as compared to low-satisfaction visits were characterized by significantly more frequent physician use of positive types of humor (e.g., playful, light humor expressing caring, support, and warmth, and relieving tension), but did not differ in physician use of negative types of humor (e.g., humor putting down self, patient, or others), which in any case occurred extremely rarely. With regard to patient-initiated humor, during high-satisfaction visits the patients were significantly more likely to engage in lighthearted, tension-relieving humor and less likely to engage in humor that disparaged them-selves or the physician. The patients were also much more likely to laugh at the physi-cians' humorous comments during high-satisfaction as compared to low-satisfaction visits. Since this study did not involve an experimental manipulation, it is impossible to determine whether positive humorous interactions between physicians and patients were a cause or merely a concomitant of patients' feelings of satisfaction.

In summary, research on the effects of humor on the therapeutic process has been quite limited, with mixed results. Some studies have suggested that humorous inter-ventions may be less helpful than nonhumorous ones, others have shown no differ-ence in effectiveness, and still others have indicated some therapeutic benefits of humor. These contradictory findings may be due to the fact that different types or uses of humor can have quite different effects in therapy. Although some researchers made an effort to distinguish between positive and negative types of humor, these past studies may not have succeeded in identifying the crucial differences between therapeutic and nontherapeutic forms of humor. More carefully refined research is needed to investigate in more detail the potential benefits and risks of different types of humor in therapy. In view of the ubiquity of humor and laughter in therapy, and the many seemingly plausible hypotheses concerning its potential benefits (as well as its potential risks), this is clearly a research topic that merits further attention.

Risks of Humor in Therapy

Although humor may potentially be beneficial for therapy, many clinicians have also pointed out that it has some inherent risks. As we have seen in previous chap-ters, humor may be used for many different purposes in everyday social interactions, including such negative uses as disparagement and ridicule, enforcing conformity to social norms, and avoiding dealing with problems. Even though most therapists are careful to avoid using humor in these ways, there is a risk that their humor may be misunderstood by clients and misperceived as coercive or aggressive. Since humor is inherently ambiguous, there is always a possibility of misunderstanding. Therapists therefore need to be alert to the way their humorous comments are perceived by clients and how they affect their feelings and perceptions.

In a frequently cited article, Lawrence Kubie (1970), a psychoanalytically oriented therapist, expressed particularly strong reservations about the use of humor in psychotherapy, pointing out a number of potential risks. He noted that therapists' use of humor may convey to clients that they do not take their problems very seriously. If therapists have to explain that something they said was only intended as a joke, this is an indication that the humor was likely used inappropriately and insensitively, since the client's failure to recognize it as humor indicates a lack of therapist attunement to the client's feelings and needs. Kubie also argued that humor is sometimes used inappropriately by therapists as a defense against their own anxieties or as a way of narcissistically showing off their own wittiness. When used by clients, humor may also be an unhealthy defense mechanism, a way of avoiding dealing with problems, or a means of devaluing their own strengths and characteristics in a self-mocking way (i.e., self-defeating humor). In addition, clients may have a maladaptive aggressive humor style. By engaging in humorous interactions with these sorts of clients, the therapist may inadvertently reinforce an unhealthy style of humor.

Another risk of humor, according to Kubie, is that when the therapist treats certain topics in a humorous manner, the client may take this to mean that these topics are taboo and are not to be discussed seriously. In addition, clients may feel a need to laugh along with a therapist to show that they have a "good sense of humor," even when this superficial joviality covers underlying feelings of distress or resentment. The use of humor by the therapist may thus make it difficult for the client to express negative feelings or disagreement. Kubie (1970) concluded his article by stating, "Humor has its place in life. Let us keep it there by acknowledging that one place where it has a very limited role, if any, is in psychotherapy" (p. 866).

Although few clinicians writing on this topic have taken such an extreme view as Kubie, most seem to agree that there is some validity to his arguments. Just as they need to monitor carefully the impact of all their communications in therapy, clinicians need to be especially alert to the effects of their humor on their clients. However, this does not mean that therapy should always be serious and devoid of humor. Taking a more moderate approach, Thomas Kuhlman (1984) suggested a number of potential benefits of humor, but also pointed out that when a client is struggling emotionally with an issue, humor can be inappropriate if it diverts the client's attention away from the problem rather than facilitating the ongoing processing of information. Similarly, Robert Pierce (1994) suggested that, although it can often be beneficial, humor is inappropriate in therapy (1) when it is used to belittle, laugh at, or mimic the client; (2) when it is used defensively to divert attention away from an emotionally charged problem onto safer topics; and (3) when it is irrelevant to the therapeutic purpose, gratifying the therapist's own need for amusement and wasting valuable therapy time and energy.

Waleed Salameh (1987) developed a five-point rating scale for evaluating the appropriateness of therapists' use of humor in therapy sessions. Level 1 refers to *destructive uses of humor*, such as sarcastic and vindictive humor that elicits feelings of hurt and distrust in clients. Level 2 is *harmful humor*, which includes humor that is irrelevant or not attuned to clients' needs. This would include uses of humor where the therapist subsequently has to retract it or make amends by reassuring the client that it was not intended seriously. Level 3 refers to *minimally helpful humor*, which promotes a positive therapist-client interaction, but remains mostly a response to the client's own humor rather than being initiated by the therapist. Level 4 is described as *very helpful humor* that is initiated by the therapist and is attuned to the client's needs, facilitating self-exploration and self-understanding. Finally, Level 5 refers to *outstandingly helpful humor* that conveys a deep understanding of the client, is spontaneous and well-timed, and accelerates the process of client growth and change. Although the reliability and validity of this rating scale still need to be evaluated, it might be a useful tool for researchers wishing to investigate therapeutic humor, as well as for supervisors to evaluate the use of humor by therapists in training.

Therapists need to be especially careful in using humor with clients who have particular humor-related difficulties. Willibald Ruch and Rene Proyer (in press) have coined the term "gelatophobia" to refer to a psychological disorder characterized by a morbid fear of being laughed at and not taken seriously. They created a reliable self-report scale to assess this trait, which is thought to develop from repeated experiences of being the object of ridicule and mockery early in life. Investigations using this measure have demonstrated that clinically identified gelatophobic individuals could be reliably distinguished from patients with other types of social anxiety and depressive disorders as well as nonclinical control subjects.

The study found that people with gelatophobia are fearful of exposing themselves to others lest they be laughed at, tend to be socially avoidant and anxious, and have high levels of neuroticism and introversion and low self-esteem. They have great difficulty enjoying any kinds of humor in their social interactions, since they are always suspicious that others are laughing at their expense. Clearly, the use of humor in therapy with such individuals is fraught with difficulties, and needs to be approached with great sensitivity to avoid retraumatizing the client. Indeed, one of the goals of therapy in such cases might be to help clients gradually to overcome their aversion to humor by means of techniques that have been developed for treating other types of phobias.

A very different type of humor-related difficulty is seen in clients who use humor excessively as a way of trivializing their problems and avoiding dealing with difficulties. Psychiatrist Ned Marcus (1990) described certain types of therapy clients who engage in a pathological form of humor during therapy, treating their psychological problems and the therapeutic process itself as "all one big joke." Such uses of humor may be accompanied by other avoidant behaviors, such as frequently arriving late for sessions, failing to complete homework assignments, and generally devaluing the therapeutic process. In treating these clients, the therapist needs to be careful not to join into the humor and thereby reinforce the avoidant behavior. Marcus advocated the use of cognitive therapy techniques to help these clients become aware of the dysfunctional automatic thoughts underlying their humor (e.g., unaccountability, incongruity, inconsequentiality), and to encourage them to gain a more realistic perspective. The goal here is not to eliminate the client's sense of humor, but to make it more integrated with reality and therefore healthier.

Conclusion

There appears to be a growing interest among many psychotherapists and counselors in the potential role of humor in treatment. Clinicians who have written on this topic have ranged from those who enthusiastically advocate humor as a highly beneficial component of therapy, to those who express a more cautious and balanced approach, to those who perceive the risks of humor in therapy as far outweighing any potential benefits. The existence of such strongly opposing views suggests that the truth likely lies somewhere in the middle. As we have seen throughout this book, humor may be viewed as a form of interpersonal communication that can be used in therapy, just as in other social relationships, for a variety of purposes, both prosocial and aggressive.

Not surprisingly, humor occurs quite frequently in psychotherapy, just as it does in all sorts of interpersonal interactions. Like any type of communication, it can be used effectively or ineffectively in therapy. On one hand, it can be used empathically and in a caring and genuine manner to foster the therapeutic relationship and to encourage client self-exploration, insight, and change. On the other hand, it can be used inappropriately, either in an extreme way by denigrating the client to further the therapist's own needs at the client's expense, or in a more mild way by distracting from and interfering with the therapeutic process. Thus, the ability to use humor effectively and appropriately seems to be best viewed as a type of social competence (Yip and Martin, in press) that novice therapists naturally possess to varying degrees. The ability to use humor therapeutically is a skill that needs to be developed and honed by therapists in training, just as they need to learn a variety of other clinical skills.

Most of the existing literature on humor in therapy is based on case examples and clinical impressions. In recent years, there is growing recognition of the importance of evidence-based approaches to therapy, and the need for clinicians to employ treatment interventions that have demonstrated effectiveness. Unfortunately, apart from a few therapy outcome and process studies, there is currently little empirical research examining the effectiveness of humor-based interventions or the types of humor that may be appropriate or inappropriate for therapy. Further research is clearly needed to investigate which uses of humor may be beneficial or detrimental in treating which sorts of problems with which types of clients.

HUMOR IN EDUCATION

Although education was traditionally seen as a rather serious and solemn undertaking, pedagogical trends in recent decades have shifted toward the promotion of a more relaxed learning environment and an emphasis on "making learning fun." The current prevailing philosophy of education argues that students are much more likely to be motivated to learn and to retain information if they are happy and amused than if they are feeling anxious and threatened (Oppliger, 2003). Consistent with this trend, many educators in recent years have recommended that teachers introduce humor into the classroom by sprinkling funny anecdotes, examples, and illustrations throughout their lessons, displaying comical images and sayings on the classroom walls, and encouraging frequent humor production in their students.

A number of popular books and articles in education journals written by teachers and educational experts have touted humor as a very useful and effective teaching tool with a wide range of benefits (e.g., Cornett, 1986; Struthers, 2003; Tamblyn, 2003). One author described humor as one of the teacher's "most powerful instructional resources" and claimed that it can be used for such diverse purposes as correcting reading difficulties, controlling behavioral problems, building vocabulary, teaching foreign languages, and integrating students who are socially isolated (Cornett, 1986, p. 8).

In general, it has been suggested that humor in the classroom helps to reduce tension, stress, anxiety, and boredom; enhances student-teacher relationships; makes the classroom less threatening for students; makes learning enjoyable, creating positive attitudes toward learning; stimulates interest in and attention to educational messages; increases comprehension, cognitive retention, and performance; and promotes creativity and divergent thinking (R. A. Berk and Nanda, 1998; A. P. Davies and Apter, 1980; Ziegler, Boardman, and Thomas, 1985). The use of humor has been seen as an especially useful tool in teaching students about sensitive, anxiety-arousing topics such as death and suicide (H. A. Johnson, 1990), and in teaching courses that are typically associated with negative attitudes and anxiety, such as undergraduate statistics (R. A. Berk and Nanda, 1998). Based on the presumed cognitive, emotional, social, and physiological benefits of humor, some educators have even suggested that one of the goals of education should be to facilitate the development of a good sense of humor in students (Bernstein, 1986; Masselos, 2003).

Most of these enthusiastic endorsements of humor are based on anecdotal evidence and teachers' reports of their own experiences in the classroom. Empirical research evaluating the claimed educational benefits of humor is unfortunately quite limited, much of it is over two decades old, little replication has taken place, and the findings have been rather mixed (Teslow, 1995). Nonetheless, there is some research on humor in education addressing the following questions: (1) How often and in what ways do teachers typically use humor in the classroom? (2) Does humor improve the classroom environment and make learning more enjoyable for students? (3) Does humor in teaching improve students' ability to learn and retain information? (4) Does the inclusion of humor in tests and exams help to reduce test anxiety and improve student performance on the tests? and (5) Does humor in textbooks help to make them more understandable and improve students' ability to learn the material? In the following sections I will review research findings addressing each of these questions, followed by some general caveats concerning the use of humor in education (for more detailed reviews of research in this area, see Bryant and Zillmann, 1989; Oppliger, 2003; Teslow, 1995).

Descriptive Studies of Teachers' Use of Humor in the Classroom

Evidence from several studies indicates that many teachers tend to use humor quite frequently in classroom settings. For example, an analysis of tape recordings of typical lectures by university professors found an average of a little over three instances of humor per 50-minute class (Bryant et al., 1980). Similar rates of humor have also been found among high school and elementary school teachers (Bryant and Zillmann, 1989; Gorham and Christophel, 1990; Neuliep, 1991). There is some evidence that male teachers tend to use humor in the classroom more frequently than do female teachers, although this sex difference appears to have diminished over the past 20 years (Bryant et al., 1980; Gorham and Christophel, 1990; Neuliep, 1991; Van Giffen, 1990).

What kinds of humor do teachers use? Although most educational experts recommend that teachers avoid the use of teasing and ridicule, there is evidence that aggressive forms of humor are actually fairly common in the classroom. In a study by Joan Gorham and Diane Christophel (1990), college students were asked to write brief descriptions of all humorous comments made by instructors during classes. Analyses of these humor descriptions indicated that over half of all instances of humor by the college instructors could be categorized as "tendentious" or aggressive, in that they involved poking fun at a person, a group of people, or an institution. As many as 20 percent of all humorous comments by instructors made fun of an individual student in the classroom or the class as a whole, while other tendentious humor targeted the topic or subject of the course, the instructor's academic department, the university, the state, or famous people at the national or international level. About 12 percent of the humor was targeted at the instructors themselves, in what might be described as self-deprecating or perhaps self-defeating humor. Less than half of the college instructors' humor did not have an obvious target. These nontendentious forms of humor included either personal or general anecdotes and stories that were either related or unrelated to the subject of the lecture, "canned" jokes, and physical or vocal comedy ("schtick"). In all, only about 30 percent of the humor was related to the lecture topic.

In another study, James Neuliep (1991) conducted a large-scale survey of high school teachers about their use of humor. The respondents were asked to describe in some detail the most recent situation in which they had used humor in the classroom. Responses to this question were used by the researcher to develop a taxonomy of teachers' humor, which contained the following categories: (1) teacher-directed humor (e.g., self-deprecation, describing an embarrassing personal experience); (2) student-targeted humor (e.g., joking insult, teasing a student about a mistake); (3) untargeted humor (e.g., pointing out incongruities, joke-telling, punning, tongue-in-cheek or facetious interactions, humorous exaggeration); (4) external source humor (e.g., relating a humorous historical incident, showing a cartoon that is related or unrelated to the subject, humorous demonstrations of natural phenomena); and (5) nonverbal humor (e.g., making a funny face, humorous vocal style, physical bodily humor). Although teachers seemed to be generally aware of the potential risks of using overly aggressive forms of humor directed at students, humor involving teasing, insults, and joking about students' mistakes still accounted for more than 10 percent of their overall humor.

In summary, teachers appear to use humor in a wide variety of ways, including some that appear rather aggressive, such as teasing and playful put-downs of students. While much of their humor appears to be used to illustrate a pedagogical point, to make a lesson more vivid and memorable, or simply to add some levity and playful fun to the learning environment, teachers also appear to use humor for the same sorts of purposes for which humor is used in other interpersonal contexts. As noted in Chapter 5, humor serves a variety of social communication functions (e.g., social probing, enforcing social norms and control, status and hierarchy maintenance, etc.), and teachers use humor in their interactions with students for many of these purposes, just as they do in their interactions with other people.

Teachers' Use of Humor and the Classroom Environment

Does humor improve the classroom environment and make learning more enjoyable? Research on this question has provided a fair amount of evidence that the judicious use of humor by teachers in the classroom increases students' enjoyment of learning, their perceptions of how much they learn, and how positively they feel about the course and the instructor (e.g., Wanzer and Frymier, 1999). Indeed, teachers with a good sense of humor tend to be especially popular with their students (see Figure 8). Student surveys have found that a sense of humor is typically rated as one of the most desirable characteristics of an effective teacher (Check, 1986; Fortson and Brown, 1998; Powell and Andresen, 1985).

Other research has shown that teachers who are observed to use more humor in the classroom are rated more positively by their students. One study employing tape recordings of classroom lectures to evaluate the frequency of humor used by college instructors found that teachers who told more funny stories and jokes in the classroom received more positive overall evaluations from their students, and were rated as being more effective and appealing and having a better delivery, but were not necessarily seen as being more competent or intelligent (Bryant et al., 1980).

Other research indicates, however, that some types of humor used by the teacher may have a negative rather than a positive impact on student evaluations. For example, Gorham and Christophel (1990) found that, whereas a greater proportion of humorous anecdotes and stories in college instructors' humor was positively associated with students' perceptions of how much they learned in the course and their positive attitudes toward the instructor and the course, a greater proportion of tendentious or aggressive humor was associated with less positive evaluations by students.

Some early research suggested that these effects of humor use on student appraisals occurred primarily for male instructors, whereas for female teachers humor

FIGURE 8 Teachers' use of humor in the classroom contributes to greater immediacy. © David Buffington/Getty Images/PhotoDisc

did not appear to have much of an effect one way or the other (Bryant et al., 1980). However, more recent research suggests that this gender difference may have disappeared, perhaps due to changes in sex role expectations in the general culture. Gorham and Christophel (1990) found significant correlations between instructors' humor use and positive student evaluations for female as well as male teachers, although the effects were still somewhat stronger for males. In contrast, Katherine Van Giffen (1990) found that college students' ratings of the degree to which an instructor used humor were *more* strongly predictive of teacher evaluations for female than for male instructors.

The value of humor in the classroom may be particularly related to its role in promoting a sense of immediacy. Immediacy is an educational concept referring to the degree to which the teacher makes a close personal connection with students, as opposed to remaining distant and aloof (Andersen, 1979). It has been found to be enhanced by such teacher behaviors as using personal examples from one's own life, encouraging students to enter into discussions in class, addressing students by name, praising students' work, and looking and smiling at the class while speaking. Past research has indicated that greater levels of immediacy are associated with more positive student attitudes toward the class and instructor, greater enjoyment and motivation, and greater perceived learning (Andersen, 1979; Gorham, 1988; D. H. Kelley and Gorham, 1988). Humor may be another method for instructors to reduce the psychological distance between themselves and their students, and thereby increase the level of immediacy.

In the study by Gorham and Christophel (1990) mentioned earlier, college students were asked to observe and record instances of humor by professors during lectures, as well as completing a measure of the degree to which these instructors engaged in a variety of verbal and nonverbal immediacy behaviors. The results revealed significant positive correlations between the frequency of positive types of humor observed in the lectures and the instructors' overall verbal and nonverbal immediacy. More specifically, teachers with higher overall immediacy told proportionately more humorous anecdotes and stories and exhibited more physical/vocal comedy; however, they also used less tendentious (aggressive) and self-deprecating (likely self-defeating) humor. Interestingly, no differences were found in the degree to which the humor used by teachers with high versus low immediacy was related to the lecture topic or course content.

Melissa Wanzer and Ann Frymier (1999) also found that college students' ratings of the degree to which particular professors engaged in humor were positively associated with measures of the instructors' immediacy and responsiveness to students. In addition, analyses revealed that the significant associations found between instructors' humor and students' course evaluations and perceptions of learning were largely (but not entirely) accounted for by immediacy. Thus, humor seems to be one component of a broader set of teacher behaviors that contribute to a sense of immediacy in the classroom, which in turn results in more positive teacher and course evaluations and greater perceived learning in the students.

Teachers' Use of Humor and Students' Learning

Educators advocating the use of humor in teaching have claimed that humor not only promotes a positive, enjoyable atmosphere in the classroom but also helps students to learn and retain information better, leading to higher levels of academic performance. Several mechanisms have been proposed to explain why lecture material that is accompanied by humor might be learned and remembered better than information that is presented in a more serious manner (Oppliger, 2003; Teslow, 1995). First, the positive emotion accompanying humor (i.e., mirth) may become associated with the overall learning experience, giving students a more positive attitude toward education in general and increasing their motivation to learn, resulting in higher academic achievement. Second, the novelty and emotionally arousing properties of humor may help to attract and sustain students' attention onto the lesson, thus facilitating acquisition of information. Third, the incongruous mental associations that are an inherent characteristic of humor may facilitate the process of cognitive elaboration, helping in the storage and retention of information in long-term memory. Finally, humorous memory cues associated with previously learned information may facilitate the retrieval of this information from long-term memory at a later date when students are answering questions on a test or examination.

Early studies investigating children's attention to humorous educational television programs have provided some evidence of the hypothesized attention-drawing effects of humor, at least in young children. For example, one study found that, when given a choice of educational television programs to watch, first- and second-grade children were more likely to select those containing humor, especially if the humor was fast-paced (Wakshlag, Day, and Zillmann, 1981). Similar findings were obtained by Dolf Zillmann and his colleagues (1980), who concluded that "the educator who deals with an audience whose attentiveness is below the level necessary for effective communication should indeed benefit from employing humor early on and in frequent short bursts" (p. 178).

Beyond the attention-grabbing effects of humor, a number of studies over the years have investigated the question of whether information that is taught in a humorous way is learned and remembered better than information that is presented in a more serious manner. The results of early educational research on this topic were quite disappointing. Charles Gruner (1976) reviewed nine such studies and concluded that all except one failed to show any influence of humor on learning. Outside of the educational context, early research on the effects of humor on memory for speeches also generally found no differences in learning between humorous and serious speeches (Gruner, 1967).

A few later educational studies showed more promising results, although the findings across studies continued to be mixed. For example, Ann Davies and Michael Apter (1980) randomly assigned children between the ages of 8 and 11 to view either humorous or nonhumorous versions of several 20-minute audio-visual educational programs on topics such as language, science, history, and geography. The humorous versions of the programs were identical to the nonhumorous versions except for the random insertion of a number of funny cartoons. In support of the hypothesis that humor enhances learning, testing revealed that the children in the humorous condition recalled a significantly greater amount of information from these presentations than did those in the nonhumorous condition, both immediately after the presentations and at one-month follow-up, although this difference in memory retention was no longer apparent nine months later.

The strongest evidence for beneficial effects of humor on learning in an educational context comes from two naturalistic experiments conducted by Avner Ziv (1988b). Criticizing earlier laboratory studies for their methodological flaws, artificiality, lack of ecological validity, and short duration, Ziv examined the effects of humorous lectures on student performance in an actual course over a whole semester. In the first experiment, students in an introductory statistics course were randomly assigned to receive the same 14-week course from the same instructor in either a humorous or a nonhumorous condition. In the humorous condition, the instructor, who had received training on the effective use of humor in education, inserted three or four funny anecdotes, jokes, or cartoons into each lecture to illustrate key concepts. Thus, humor was used as a sort of mnemonic device, or memory aid, to help students remember important points. The nonhumorous condition contained the same course material without the humorous illustrations. At the end of the semester, analyses of the students' grades on the final exam revealed that those in the humor condition obtained significantly higher average grades, with a difference of nearly 10 percentage points being found between the two groups.

These remarkable findings were replicated by Ziv in a second experiment using two classes of female students taking an introductory psychology course in a teachers' college. Once again, students in the humorous condition achieved an average grade that was about 10 percentage points higher than that obtained by those in the nonhumorous condition, using the same multiple-choice final exam. In his discussion of these results, Ziv argued that the stronger findings of these two experiments, compared with the generally disappointing earlier educational research on this topic, may have been due to the fact that the humor was directly relevant to the course material, it was limited to only a few instances per lecture hour, and the teachers were trained in its effective use.

Ziv's conclusions appear to be generally supported by several more recent carefully-controlled laboratory studies on the effects of humor on memory (Derks, Gardner et al., 1998; Schmidt, 1994, 2002; Schmidt and Williams, 2001). As noted in the review of this research in Chapter 4, these experiments provide quite consistent evidence that humorous information is recalled better than nonhumorous information when both are presented in the same context. If only humorous material is presented, however, there is no apparent benefit for memory. Moreover, it is important to note that the enhanced recall of humorous material occurs at the expense of memory for any nonhumorous material that is presented at the same time. In other words, the inclusion of humorous illustrations in a lecture may enhance students' memory for the humorous material, but it might also diminish their memory for other information in the same lecture that is not accompanied by humor.

These findings suggest that, if teachers wish to use humor to facilitate students' learning of course material, they should ensure that the humor is closely tied to the course content. In addition, the constant use of humor throughout a lesson will have little effect on retention. Instead, humor should be used somewhat sparingly to illustrate important concepts and not peripheral material.

Effects of Humor in Tests and Exams

Do students perform better on examinations containing some humorous questions as compared to exams with no humor? Some authors have suggested that the inclusion of humorous questions in examinations may help to reduce test anxiety and consequently lead to improved performance. A number of studies have investigated this hypothesis by examining test scores when students are randomly assigned to receive either humorous or nonhumorous versions of the same multiple-choice tests (e.g., Deffenbacher, Deitz, and Hazaleus, 1981; McMorris, Urbach, and Connor, 1985; Townsend and Mahoney, 1981; Townsend, Mahoney, and Allen, 1983). In this research, humorous versions of the tests are typically created by modifying several of the questions so that they contain either a funny "stem" or an amusing response option. Several of these studies looked at tests in university psychology classes, while others used English grammar or mathematics tests with elementary school children ranging from third to eighth grade.

The results of this research have generally been quite disappointing. A review of 11 studies of this type concluded that there is no convincing evidence that humorous tests lead to better overall performance than do nonhumorous tests (McMorris, Boothroyd, and Pietrangelo, 1997). In fact, the only clearly significant main effect indicated *poorer* performance among students receiving the humorous version of a test. Most of these studies also examined potential moderating effects of trait anxiety, hypothesizing that humorous tests may be most effective in increasing the performance of highly anxious students but less effective for students who were low on anxiety. However, these results were decidedly mixed. Only one study showed a significant interaction in the predicted direction, with a humorous version of an exam boosting the performance of highly anxious students but not those low on anxiety (R. E. Smith et al., 1971). In contrast, a few studies found the opposite pattern, with high-anxious students scoring better on the nonhumorous test and low-anxious students scoring better on the humorous one (e.g., Townsend and Mahoney, 1981). Yet other studies found no significant interaction at all between anxiety level and humor intervention in the prediction of test scores (e.g., Deffenbacher et al., 1981).

One important variable may be whether or not the students actually find the humorous items to be funny. Some students may not understand the humor, may not think it is particularly amusing, or may even find these items to be annoying, perhaps interfering with performance. Only one study asked students in the humorous exam condition to rate the funniness of the items. This study produced a significant interaction, with students who rated the test as funny having significantly higher scores on the test than did those who did not find it funny (McMorris et al., 1997). Although this finding needs to be replicated, it suggests that teachers wishing to use humorous exam items should be careful to ensure that the humor is understandable and enjoyable to the students.

Although there is little evidence that humorous test items improve students' actual performance on a test, findings from these studies do suggest that students generally respond favorably to tests that include some humorous items. When asked about their reactions to the humorous versions of the tests, the vast majority of students perceived them to be enjoyable and helpful rather than detrimental to their performance. In their review of this literature, McMorris and colleagues (1997) concluded that, although there is no evidence that humor in tests either helps or hinders students' performance, the judicious use of humor may be beneficial in making exams more enjoyable to the students. They noted, though, that it is important to ensure that the humor is positive, constructive, and appropriate for the students.

Effects of Humor in Textbooks

Many high school and college textbooks contain funny cartoons and other humorous materials to illustrate the information in the text. Does the inclusion of this sort of humor actually help students to learn the material better? In one study designed to investigate this question, students were randomly assigned to read different versions of a draft chapter of a college textbook containing either no humor, moderate amounts of humor, or extensive humor in the form of cartoons illustrating points in the text (Bryant et al., 1981). No differences were found across the three humor conditions on a subsequent test of recall of information from the chapter, suggesting that the presence of humorous cartoons had no effect on learning. However, the humor did apparently have some influence on the participants' enjoyment and perceptions of the chapters. In particular, humorous as compared to nonhumorous versions were rated as more enjoyable, but they were also rated as less persuasive and showing less author credibility. On the other hand, the amount of humor did not affect students' ratings of interest, likelihood of reading more of the book, or likelihood of taking a course with this book as the text.

In another study, college students were asked to rate a randomly assigned chapter from an introductory psychology textbook on a number of dimensions such as level of interest, enjoyableness, persuasiveness, and so on (D. M. Klein, Bryant, and Zillmann, 1982). The chapters were then analyzed by the researchers for the amount of humor they contained. Correlational analyses revealed that textbooks containing more humor tended to be rated by the students as more enjoyable, but the amount of humor was unrelated to ratings of interest, persuasiveness, capacity for learning, or desire to read more on the topic. Although research on this topic is quite limited, the overall findings suggest that humor in textbooks may be useful for boosting student appeal (and perhaps increasing the likelihood of adoption by course instructors), but it does not seem to improve students' ability to learn the information or their perceptions of the credibility of the book.

Caveats in the Use of Humor in Education

Most educators who advocate the use of humor in teaching are careful to note that aggressive forms of humor such as sarcasm, ridicule, and put-down humor have no place in the classroom. Nonetheless, as Jennings Bryant and Dolf Zillmann (1989) pointed out, research indicates that many teachers actually use hostile forms of humor with their students, including ridicule, sarcasm, and teasing. These types of humor may be perceived by some teachers as a potent method of correcting undesirable behavior in their students such as tardiness, inattention, failure to complete assignments, disruptive behavior, and so on. By teasing or ridiculing a student, teachers may feel that they can correct individual students as well as setting an example for the rest of the class. Indeed, research evidence suggests that these techniques may be quite effective as behavioral deterrents, since observing another person being ridiculed can have a powerful inhibiting effect on children's behavior by the time they reach six years of age (Bryant et al., 1983).

However, there is also abundant evidence that ridicule and other forms of aggressive humor can have a detrimental effect on the overall emotional climate of a classroom. For example, in a study discussed in Chapter 5, college students who observed another person being ridiculed became more inhibited, more conforming and fearful of failure, and less willing to take risks (Janes and Olson, 2000). The research by Gorham and Christophel (1990) discussed earlier also indicates that teachers who use more aggressive forms of humor in the classroom are evaluated more negatively by their students. Clearly, the use of humor to poke fun at students for their ineptness, slowness to learn, ignorance, or inappropriate behavior can be damaging, creating an atmosphere of tension and anxiety, and stifling creativity.

Another potential risk of humor in education, particularly with younger children, is that it might be misunderstood and lead to confusion (Bryant and Zillmann, 1989). Humor often involves exaggeration, understatement, distortion, and even contradiction (e.g., in irony). These types of humor might inadvertently cause students to fail to understand the intended meaning and to learn inaccurate information. Because of the novelty of the images that such distorting humor can convey, such inaccuracies may also be particularly easy to remember and especially resistant to memory decay.

These potential risks of humor with primary school children are supported by two studies finding that educational television programs containing humorous exaggeration or irony led to distortions in children's memory for the information being taught (J. Weaver, Zillmann, and Bryant, 1988; Zillmann et al., 1984). These memory-distorting effects of humor were found in children from kindergarten to grade four. Interestingly, even when the researchers added statements that identified and corrected the factual distortions introduced by the humor, this was not enough to overcome the distorting effects of humor on children's recall. The authors of these studies concluded that the vividness of the humorous images was recalled and not the verbal corrections. Thus, teachers of young children who use humor need to be careful to ensure that their humorous statements are not misunderstood.

Conclusion

As with humor in psychotherapy and, indeed, in all types of social interactions, the role of humor in education turns out to be more complex than it might first appear. Consistent with our conclusions about humor in psychotherapy, humor seems to be best viewed as a form of interpersonal communication that can be used for a variety of purposes in teaching. Humor may be used by teachers in potentially beneficial ways to illustrate pedagogical points, to make lessons more vivid and memorable, and to make the learning environment generally more enjoyable and interesting for students. On the other hand, it may be used in more negative ways that are coercive or demeaning to students, and it can distract students' attention away from more important points or distort their understanding of the information. As Bryant and Zillmann (1989) observed, success in teaching with humor "depends on employing the right type of humor, under the proper conditions, at the right time, and with properly motivated and receptive students" (p. 74).

Although empirical research on the effects of humor in education has been quite limited and the findings have been somewhat inconsistent, the existing research does suggest that appropriate uses of humor by teachers in the classroom are associated with more positive teacher evaluations, greater enjoyment of the course, and greater perceived learning by the students. However, the use of aggressive types of humor is associated with more negative student evaluations. The judicious use of humor seems to be particularly beneficial in increasing the level of immediacy in the classroom, reducing the psychological distance between teachers and students.

In addition, although the research results have been rather mixed, there is evidence from some naturalistic classroom studies, as well as some recent well-controlled laboratory experiments on humor and memory, indicating that information that is presented in a humorous manner is remembered better than information presented in a serious way when both occur in the same context. However, the enhanced learning of humorous material occurs at the expense of poorer learning for nonhumorous information. Teachers who wish to employ humor in their lessons to help students remember the material should therefore be careful to use humor sparingly and to associate it with key concepts rather than irrelevant information.

Finally, there is little evidence that the inclusion of humorous questions on tests reduces test anxiety and improves test performance or that funny cartoons and illustrations in textbooks enhance students' ability to learn the information in the text, although these uses of humor do appear to make the tests and textbooks more enjoyable to the students.

HUMOR IN THE WORKPLACE

Work is typically viewed as "serious business" and it seems to be the very antithesis of play. In recent years, however, there has been considerable interest in the potential benefits of increasing the amount of humor that occurs in the workplace. A number of people have suggested that a more playful work environment in which humor is encouraged might produce a happier, healthier, less stressed, and more productive work force, engendering better social interactions among workers and managers, and fostering more creative thinking and problem solving (e.g., Morreall, 1991). Although research evidence for a link between worker happiness and productivity is controversial (Iaffaldano and Muchinsky, 1985; Judge, Thoresen, Bono, and Patton, 2001), the assumption seems to be that the improved rapport, teamwork, and creativity resulting from humorous interactions will not only make for a more enjoyable work environment but will also translate into greater productivity and a better bottom line for the company. Articles extolling the benefits of humor in the workplace have appeared in numerous business magazines and trade journals (e.g., W. J. Duncan and Feisal, 1989), and popular books have been written on the topic (e.g., Kushner, 1990).

In the past two decades these ideas have also given rise to a new breed of business consultants who specialize in the promotion of humor at work (Gibson, 1994). Besides producing newsletters, websites, books, and audiotapes proclaiming the advantages of workplace humor, these "humor consultants" are frequently hired by organizations to conduct entertaining workshops and seminars in which they teach employees how to become more playful and humorous at work. While cautioning against the use of inappropriate and offensive types of humor, they advocate that workers engage in such playful activities as telling funny stories during breaks, making a collection of jokes and cartoons to look at during times of stress, and posting amusing baby pictures of fellow employees on a bulletin board.

Most of these presentations take the form of motivational sessions that involve humorous hands-on activities designed to loosen up the audience and overcome their seriousness and inhibitions, such as having them juggle scarves or balloons, wear red clown noses, balance pennies on their foreheads, or tell each other amusing personal anecdotes. As Gibson (1994) noted, these efforts to promote humor at work are appealing to management as well as employees, since they give both groups a greater feeling of control. At the level of the individual, humor is seen as a tool for gaining control over stress levels and relationships with fellow employees, while it gives organizations a sense of control over their employees, increasing their motivation, productivity, and efficiency.

Gibson pointed out that the view of humor taken by these humor consultants is a "rational/utilitarian" one. In other words, they see humor as a planned activity that can be controlled and used as a tool for success, rather than a spontaneous social behavior comprising emotional and unconscious elements that are often difficult to control and manage. In addition, the type of humor that they advocate is one that does not question the corporate status quo and is aimed at putting up with the system rather than challenging or trying to alter it. Unfortunately, there does not appear to be any empirical research on the effectiveness of these sorts of humor interventions in business, although their continued popularity suggests that they meet with a receptive audience among both workers and management.

Indeed, very little psychological research of any kind has been conducted on the general topic of humor in the workplace. This is a potentially fruitful domain for industrial-organizational psychologists to explore. Nonetheless, several largely descriptive qualitative studies of humor in the work environment have been conducted by sociologists and anthropologists. Many of these have been ethnographic studies in which the researchers acted as participant observers in various work settings, carefully observing the occurrence and effects of humor. These sorts of qualitative studies have investigated humor among staff members in a psychiatric hospital (Coser, 1960), a child care center (J. C. Meyer, 1997), and a hotel kitchen (R. B. Brown and Keegan, 1999); factory workers (Collinson, 1988; Ullian, 1976); members of a petroleum exploration party (Traylor, 1973); and managers in a large multinational computer company (Hatch and Ehrlich, 1993), a metropolitan zoo (D. M. Martin, 2004), and various private companies (Grugulis, 2002).

In the following sections, I will briefly review some of the findings of these investigations as they pertain to the social functions of humor in the workplace, humor and the corporate culture, the use of humor in negotiations and mediation, and the role of humor in leadership (see also W. J. Duncan, Smeltzer, and Leap, 1990).

Social Functions of Humor in the Workplace

As I have already noted, humor serves a number of important social functions in interpersonal communication. Besides being a form of play that enables individuals to release tension and increase enjoyment, humor is a mode of communication that is frequently used to convey certain types of information that would be more difficult to express using a more serious mode (Mulkay, 1988). In particular, humor is often used to communicate a socially risky message in an ambiguous context in a way that allows both the speaker and the audience to "save face" if the message is not well received.

Since the work situation is often characterized by ambiguity and uncertainty, it is not surprising that humor is quite frequently used for these purposes at work. For example, a worker who disagrees with a decision made by a supervisor can make a joking comment about it in order to "test the water," rather than openly opposing the superior. In this way, the worker can easily retract the criticism by saying it was "only a joke" if the supervisor takes offense. These sorts of humorous comments can often be quite funny and may generate a considerable amount of mirthful laughter, but they also have a more serious underlying communication function. Humor of this sort is a ubiquitous form of social communication that occurs frequently in interactions between people in the work environment just as in other social settings.

Although humor consultants frequently make the claim that most workplaces are much too serious, research indicates that humor and laughter actually occur quite frequently at work. Janet Holmes and Meredith Marra (2002a) analyzed tape recordings of a large number of team meetings of both blue-collar and white-collar workers in various government departments, nonprofit organizations, and private companies, and found that humorous comments and laughter among team members occurred an average of once every two to five minutes. Humor and laughter occurred most frequently in the meetings of factory workers and office workers in private companies, and somewhat less often (although still quite frequently) in government offices and nonprofit organizations. Although the frequency of humor and laughter in these work settings was considerably less (about one-eighth as often) than that observed in groups of close friends during casual interactions in the home (J. Holmes and Marra, 2002b), these findings indicate that humor is much more common in the workplace than is often assumed.

Some of the qualitative studies of humor at work have focused on potentially beneficial effects of humor for relieving stress, enhancing enjoyment, and facilitating cohesiveness among workers. For example, in a participant observation study of humor in a small family-owned business, Karen Vinton (1989) concluded that humor, in the form of telling humorous anecdotes, friendly teasing, and witty banter, served a variety of largely beneficial social functions. In particular, humor was used as a means of socializing new employees into the organizational culture, creating a more pleasant work environment, lessening status differentials between people and thereby making it easier for them to work cooperatively, and as a relatively nonconfrontational way of prodding people to get their work done.

In a study of humor occurring in task-oriented managerial meetings, Carmine Consalvo (1989) observed that humor and laughter occurred most frequently during transition points, such as when group members moved from a problem-identification phase to a problem-solving phase in their discussions. She concluded that humor at these times signaled a willingness to work together to solve the problem and conveyed an open, accepting, and mutually supportive attitude among group members.

On the other hand, much of the research on humor in the workplace also reveals the paradoxical nature of humor, showing that although it can be used to increase cohesiveness and facilitate working relationships, it can also be used in subversive ways to express disagreement and create divisions among people. In a content analysis of the humor observed in tape recordings of a number of mixed-gender team meetings in two large business organizations, Holmes and Marra (2002b) distinguished between humor that serves to strengthen existing solidarity and power relationships ("reinforcing humor") and humor that challenges existing power relationships ("subversive humor"). Reinforcing humor consisted of amusing anecdotes and joking comments that served to emphasize and maintain friendly and collegial relationships among participants.

These researchers found, however, that almost 40 percent of the humor in these organizational meetings could be characterized as subversive. Interestingly, the frequency of these more negative uses of humor in the workplace was about 10 times that observed in groups of friends in casual nonwork settings, likely because of the greater tensions and power differentials present in the workplace. Nearly half of this subversive humor targeted specific individuals who were present in the team meetings, often for the purpose of undermining their power or status. Another sizable proportion of subversive humor was aimed at the group as a whole or the larger organization, challenging or criticizing particular values, attitudes, or goals. Finally, a small proportion was directed at the societal level, questioning the ideology of the business community or broader institutional or societal values.

The subversive humor that was observed in this study took a variety of forms. The most frequent of these was the use of *quips*, defined as short witty or ironic comments about the ongoing action or topic under discussion, which occurred much more frequently in the work setting than in casual friendship groups. Other common forms of subversive humor included jocular abuse (a witty insult or put-down remark aimed at someone present), and role-play, in which one person parodied another person's style of speaking.

Based on these qualitative analyses, the authors suggested that subversive humor in business meetings is a socially acceptable mechanism for subordinates to challenge or criticize superiors, disagree with others, or question group decisions. For managers and team leaders, it is an acceptable method of commenting on nonconformist or uncooperative behavior and generally controlling participants in an interaction. Thus, these uses of humor serve a purpose of furthering the goals of individual participants in team discussions, although they do not necessarily contribute to the overall cohesiveness of the team.

In a review of sociological studies of humor in the workplace, Tom Dwyer (1991) similarly concluded that humor occurs very frequently in most organizations and that it often reflects the tensions and power dynamics within the organization. According to Dwyer, humor can be used either to conserve and reinforce the status quo or to undermine the authority of particular individuals and change the equilibrium of power. For example, observational studies have shown that workers often use humor to joke about the inadequacies of managers, to complain about poor working conditions, and to protest against seemingly arbitrary rules. For their part, managers use humor to mask the authoritarian nature of a message or to create divisions among subordinates so as to weaken their collective power.

Dwyer also noted that joking is often used as a way of enforcing norms and expectations, as well as a tool for constructing and defending group identity. The joking and playful banter that frequently goes on among workers helps to define the different social groupings, reinforces the ranking of group members within and between groups, and clarifies the status of groups in relation to each other. According to Dwyer, the relative power and goals of individuals in the work setting determine who tells jokes, who is the target of the jokes, and who laughs at them. Thus, an analysis of the humor and laughter that occurs in an organization could be a useful tool for exploring the power structures, tensions, and dynamics within the organization.

These varied social functions of humor are well illustrated in an observational study by David Collinson (1988) examining the humor of male shop-floor workers in the parts division of a lorry (truck) factory in England. Collinson observed that these workers engaged in nearly constant joking, humorous banter, witty repartee, and horseplay in their interactions with one another. While much of this humor could be viewed on one level as a way of finding fun and releasing tension in the monotony of tightly controlled, repetitive work tasks, on another level it could be seen as serving several important social functions. One of these functions was putting up resistance to the social organization of the company. For example, humor often involved making fun of managers and white-collar staff, emphasizing the workers' self-differentiation from, and antagonism toward, these groups.

Although the managers often tried to use humor to engage the workers and obscure the conflict and power differential inherent in their relationships, the workers tended to resist these overtures, excluding the managers from their joking relationships. In addition to expressing antagonism and resistance toward management, humor on the shop floor served to enforce conformity among the workers themselves. A good deal of humor, in the form of highly aggressive teasing, sarcastic put-downs, and practical jokes, seemed to be a way of communicating and enforcing group norms and expectations, particularly concerning behaviors associated with working-class masculinity. Anyone who deviated from these social norms would be subjected to constant teasing and practical jokes, providing a powerful incentive to conform.

In summary, this brief review of the existing observational research suggests that, although humor may be a way of releasing tension, having fun, and improving morale at work, it also often serves more "serious" social functions. Humor can be a way of increasing cohesiveness, facilitating communication, and reducing interpersonal tensions, but it can also be a method of communicating disagreement, enforcing norms, excluding individuals, and emphasizing divisions between groups.

In view of the complexity, subversiveness, uncontrollability, and paradoxical qualities of humor revealed by these analyses, it seems rather simplistic and naïve to suggest, as do some humor consultants, that simply increasing the level of humor and fun in an organization will result in many desirable changes and improved productivity. Since humor is already ubiquitous in the workplace, serving many different functions and reflecting the social structures and power dynamics of the organization, the task for managers seems to be not so much to increase the level of fun and laughter, but to understand the meaning of the humor that already exists and to attempt to channel it in productive directions. This is likely easier said than done, however, and more carefully controlled empirical research on this topic is clearly needed before we can confidently provide useful guidance to business organizations about how best to promote positive humor in the workplace.

Humor as a Reflection of Organizational Culture

The concept of corporate or organizational culture refers to the sense of shared values, norms, and behavior patterns that bind members of an organization together and give it a distinctive identity (Deal and Kennedy, 1982). Organizational researchers view corporate culture as an important factor in determining the degree to which an organization is able to remain productive and competitive. Some research indicates that part of what makes for a successful organizational culture is a sense of camaraderie among employees and feeling good about what they do. Some authors have suggested that the sharing of humor among members of an organization is an important aspect of a successful corporate culture (e.g., Clouse and Spurgeon, 1995).

In their study of humor in work team meetings described earlier, Holmes and Marra (2002a) examined the way in which the frequency, type, and style of humor that arises in a particular workplace reflects the broader culture of the organization. For example, they found that blue-collar employees in a fairly cohesive and mutually dependent factory work team tended to produce high-frequency humor in the form of brief single quips using a competitive humor style (i.e., each trying to outdo the other in wittiness), but in a socially supportive manner (i.e., using humor to agree with, add to, elaborate, or strengthen the argument of a previous speaker). On the other hand, during meetings of white-collar staff in a private commercial organization, there was also a good deal of humor, but it took the form of more extended, somewhat competitive humor sequences, and tended to be much more contestive than supportive (i.e., using humor to challenge, disagree with, or undermine the authority of previous speakers), reflecting the individualistic and competitive culture of this private business.

Yet another pattern of humor was observed during staff meetings in government departments and nonprofit organizations, where humor took the form of extended sequences, a collaborative humor style (i.e., building on and extending one another's humorous comments rather than trying to outdo one another with humor), and a more supportive than contestive use of humor, reflecting a generally collegial, focused, and cooperative style of interactions in these organizations as a whole. Thus, the overall culture, goals, and emphases of a given organization seem to be reflected in the ways individuals in the organization use humor in their interpersonal communication. As suggested earlier, analysis of the humor occurring in an organization might be a useful method of evaluating its overall corporate culture. This is another topic that may yield interesting findings in future research.

Humor in Negotiation and Mediation

Some authors have suggested that humor may be an important tool for facilitating negotiations and mediation, particularly during times of conflict and tension between parties. John Forester (2004) emphasized that the use of humor in mediation is not simply a matter of telling jokes, but involves the expression of spontaneous humor in the flow of conversation to alter perspectives, change disabling expectations, reframe relationships, and provide multiple points of view on topics. The use of humor to "test the water" and to communicate potentially risky or threatening messages in a face-saving way, as discussed earlier, seems to be particularly relevant in this context, where interpersonal tensions and conflicting points of view are an inevitable part of the process.

These communication functions of humor were illustrated in a qualitative study of humor observed in a video recording of sales negotiations between a salesman from a parts supply company and a potential buyer who was a proprietor of a photographic equipment shop (Mulkay, Clark, and Pinch, 1993). This study suggested that humor is used to deal with difficulties arising in these types of interactions in a way that avoids confrontation and enables both parties to save face while still furthering their own goals. For example, the prospective buyer used a great deal of humor as a way of refusing to buy the salesman's products, requesting concessions, halting a persistent sales pitch, suggesting that the prices were too high, and hinting that the goods were of inferior quality. For his part, the salesman made use of humor to try to overcome the buyer's resistance, to make fun of his various excuses for not buying the products, and to forestall further criticism. Thus, humor seems to be a commonly used method for dealing with problems and tensions that are inherent in these types of business transactions, enabling individuals to express their views without appearing overly confrontational.

Viveka Adelsward and Britt-Marie Oberg (1998) also conducted qualitative research on the role of humor in business negotiations by analyzing all utterances that were followed by laughter in tape recordings of a number of business meetings and telephone conversations between buyers and sellers. As in the study by Consalvo (1989) mentioned earlier, they found that during negotiation sessions, humor frequently occurred around topic transitions, such as when a group was moving from initial introductions to the discussion of a problem, or from the presentation of a problem to a negotiation phase. They suggested that this use of humor served as a way of structuring the ongoing process by signaling a desire of some participants to move on to a different topic without appearing to be too abrupt or controlling. In addition, humor often appeared to be used to smooth tensions between participants and to find common ground.

The researchers noted that the occurrence of laughter during negotiations was often a sign that the participants were dealing with particularly difficult or sensitive topics, such as haggling over a price. They also found that whether or not others laughed at a humorous comment made by a speaker depended on the relative status or power advantage of the speaker. In particular, joint laughter was much more likely to occur when the speaker had higher status (e.g., the team leader) or had some other advantage (e.g., being the buyer rather than the seller). In contrast, when a humorous comment was made by a speaker with lower status or one who was at some sort of disadvantage, he or she was often the only one who laughed. This research suggests that the ability to use humor effectively may be an important social skill for individuals involved in sensitive negotiations.

Humor in Leadership

It has often been suggested that a good sense of humor is an important characteristic for effective leadership, along with other abilities such as intelligence, creativity, persuasiveness, good speaking ability, and social skills. Research on leadership behavior indicates that effective leadership requires skills in the general areas of (1) giving and seeking information, (2) making decisions, (3) influencing people, and (4) building relationships (Yukl and Lepsinger, 1990). These broad skill areas have been further divided into a variety of component behaviors, many of which have to do with interpersonal relations and communication, such as the ability to communicate and get along well with subordinates, peers, and superiors, to manage conflict, motivate others, and enhance group cohesion and cooperation. As an important communication skill, humor can be seen as potentially useful to leaders and managers in many of these areas. For example, the use of humor could be beneficial for teaching and clarifying work tasks, helping to motivate and change behavior, promoting creativity, coping with stress, and generally making the interactions between the manager and subordinates more positive and less tense (Decker and Rotondo, 2001).

A few survey studies have examined the correlation between sense of humor and perceived leadership qualities by asking workers to rate their supervisors on these dimensions. In a survey of 290 workers, Wayne Decker (1987) found that those who rated their supervisors as being high in sense of humor also reported greater job satisfaction and rated these supervisors as having generally more positive leadership characteristics as compared to participants who rated their supervisors as low in sense of humor.

Similarly, in two survey studies in which military cadets were asked about the personality traits of particularly good and bad leaders that they had worked with, Robert Priest and Jordan Swain (2002) found that good leaders were rated as having a significantly more warm, competent, and benign humorous style, whereas bad leaders were rated as having a more cold, inept, and mean-spirited humorous style. On the other hand, the two types of leaders did not differ in the degree to which they were perceived to display boorish (versus reflective) or earthy (versus repressed) styles of humor.

Wayne Decker and Denise Rotondo (2001) conducted a study to determine whether the importance of a sense of humor for effective leadership differs for male versus female leaders. These researchers asked a large number of men and women employed in a variety of organizations and geographic areas to evaluate their managers' use of positive and negative humor, task behaviors, relationship behaviors, and overall leadership effectiveness. Positive humor referred to the managers' use of humor to communicate, enjoyment of jokes, and use of nonoffensive humor, whereas negative humor was their use of sexual and insulting humor.

Regression analyses showed that greater perceived use of positive humor by managers was associated with more successful task and relationship behaviors and greater overall effectiveness, whereas greater use of negative humor was related to lower ratings on these measures of managerial competence. With regard to sex differences, although male managers were rated as using both more positive and more negative humor than female managers, the associations between humor and leadership competence measures were found to be stronger for women than for men. Thus, the use of benign humor by female as compared to male managers was more strongly positively associated with workers' perceptions of their leadership skills, and by the same token the use of sexual or offensive humor was more negatively related to perceived leadership in women than in men.

Overall, these studies provide evidence that supervisors who are perceived by their subordinates to have a positive sense of humor also tend to be viewed as being effective leaders, although leaders who use humor inappropriately tend to receive more negative evaluations of their leadership skills. Of course, the correlational and rather subjective nature of this research makes it difficult to determine the direction of causality. A greater sense of humor may cause a leader to be more effective, but these findings may also simply be due to a "halo effect," whereby greater overall liking of a supervisor may cause subordinates to perceive him or her as having a better sense of humor as well as better leadership skills. Future research should employ more objective assessments of humor and leadership instead of relying solely on employee ratings. Further research is also needed to investigate the ways in which effective leaders actually express humor and how this humor might contribute to their leadership competence.

Conclusion

Humor consultants and others who advocate the promotion of humor in the workplace often claim that increased levels of humor at work will result in a variety of benefits, including greater teamwork and cooperation, improved social interactions among workers and managers, better worker morale and health, reduced stress, and greater creativity, problem solving, and productivity. Although most of the studies of humor in the workplace are qualitative and descriptive, the existing research suggests that these sorts of enthusiastic claims are somewhat simplistic. Although the workplace is often viewed as excessively serious and devoid of humor, the research indicates that humor and laughter actually occur quite frequently in most organizations.

In addition, this research suggests that humor in the workplace serves a variety of functions, including ones that could be detrimental to worker morale and a productive work environment, as well as ones that contribute to teamwork and cooperation. Besides being a form of play that is useful for relieving tension and making work more enjoyable, humor serves important functions as a mode of communication that is useful for expressing potentially risky messages in the ambiguous context of work. As such, humor can be used to convey many different types of messages and to achieve many different goals. It may be used to lessen or to reinforce status differences, to express agreement or disagreement, to facilitate cooperation or resistance, to include others in a group or to exclude them, to strengthen solidarity and relationships, or to undermine power and status.

Thus, simply increasing the level of humor at work is not likely to have purely positive consequences. Although most humor consultants would agree that certain types of humor are inappropriate and detrimental in the workplace, it is not a simple matter to distinguish between detrimental and facilitative forms of humor, or to promote one type of humor and not the other. For example, it is often difficult to know where friendly teasing and playful banter end and where ridicule and unwanted joking begin.

As in psychotherapy and education, there are potential risks as well as benefits associated with humor in the workplace. One particularly negative type of humor that has received considerable attention in recent decades is the use of derogatory humor as a form of harassment. Duncan, Smeltzer, and Leap (1990) noted that work-related sexual and racial harassment and discrimination cases are often precipitated by jokes, teasing, and pranks of a sexual or racial nature. In a survey of 13,000 federal employees, the most prevalent form of sexual harassment was unwanted sexual teasing and joking. Humor that involves horseplay and practical jokes can also create a stressful work environment, cause disruptions or safety hazards, or result in property damage.

As in other areas, humor in the context of work seems to be best viewed as a type of social skill or interpersonal competence (Yip and Martin, in press) that can be used for negative as well as positive purposes. Thus, the task of managers and business consultants is not simply to increase the levels of humor among employees, but to attempt to understand the ways in which the humor that already exists reflects the power dynamics and general culture within the organization. Improving the quality of humor in the workplace may require efforts to change the overall organizational culture and power structures rather than simply having workers attend a workshop where they learn to tell funny stories and engage in silly activities.

GENERAL DISCUSSION

A number of practitioners in the fields of psychotherapy and counseling, education, and business consulting have touted the supposed benefits of humor and laughter in each of these domains, claiming that greater uses of humor might improve the effectiveness of therapy and counseling, increase student enjoyment and learning in education, and enhance health, morale, and productivity in the workplace. Most of these claims are based on anecdotes and the personal experiences of practitioners. Although empirical work in these areas is quite limited, our review of the relevant

research literature suggests a gap between many of the enthusiastic claims of practitioners and the evidence of science.

Interestingly, although in some respects these advocates of humor applications
may be seen as going too far in their claims about the potential benefits of humor, in
other respects it can also be argued that they do not go far enough in recognizing the
prevalence and importance of humor in all types of social interaction. Although humor
promoters often claim that that there is not enough humor in psychotherapy, education, and the workplace, studies indicate that humor and laughter actually occur quite
frequently in all of these domains. Since humor is a ubiquitous aspect of nearly all
interpersonal relationships, we should not be surprised to discover that it is frequently
encountered in the interactions between therapists and clients, between teachers and
students, and among individuals working in the same organizations.

Although practitioners who actively promote humor in these fields tend to view
it as generally positive and beneficial to mental and physical health, educational
achievement, and cooperative relationships at work, research indicates that humor can
be used for a wide range of purposes and to achieve many different goals, some of
which may be detrimental to the broader goals of therapists, educators, and business
organizations. In each of these fields, humor advocates tend to take a "rational/utili-
tarian" approach to humor (Gibson, 1994), seeing it as something that can be manipulated, planned, and controlled in a rational way. However, a more complex view of
humor has emerged in the research that we have explored throughout this book, portraying it as a phenomenon that often occurs spontaneously and has unconscious
(as well as conscious) emotional and cognitive determinants that are not so easily
managed or controlled. Indeed, humor that is consciously created by therapists, teachers, or managers with the goal of having a particular effect on others is likely to come
across as stilted, forced, and artificial.

A more realistic view of humor seems to be that it is an inevitable and important
aspect of human social interaction in all areas of our lives, including therapy, education, and the workplace. As such, it can serve many different social functions, depending on the goals, status, motives, and needs of the individual. Rather than simply trying
to increase the level of humor in each of the fields that we have discussed, we need
to try to gain a more thorough understanding of the ways humor is already being used
and the many functions served by different types of humor in these contexts. In this
way, we can begin to identify appropriate and beneficial types of humor that further
the goals of therapists, educators, and business leaders, as well as inappropriate and
detrimental forms of humor.

One research question that also requires further attention is the degree to which
it is even possible to modify people's sense of humor. Many of the applications of
humor that we have discussed involve helping people to increase the amount of humor
that they engage in or to change their predominant styles of humor (cf. McGhee,
1999). However, it is still not clear whether this is even possible. As noted in Chapter
9, the only published study addressing this question was one conducted by Ofra Nevo
and her colleagues (1998). In this study, 101 female high school teachers were
randomly assigned to either an active-production humor training program (which

provided training in a variety of humor creation techniques), a passive-appreciation humor program (focusing on ways to increase opportunities for enjoying humor in one's daily life), a nonhumorous activity control group, or a waiting list control group. All but the waiting list group met for seven weekly three-hour sessions.

At the end of the program, testing revealed that the two humor training groups were only partially successful in improving participants' sense of humor. On the positive side, the participants in the humor groups, compared to those in the control groups, reported significantly more positive attitude towards humor and were rated by their peers as having higher levels of humor production and appreciation. On the negative side, however, they did not show any improvements on objective measures of their ability to actually produce humor, and there were no changes in their scores on self-report humor scales. There is clearly a need for further research to determine the degree to which it is possible to increase the quantity or improve the quality of people's habitual uses of humor and, if so, what training methods may be most effective. This sort of program evaluation research should be carried out by practitioners before they attempt to promote the widespread implementation of unproven humor interventions.

The general topic of humor applications presents many interesting questions and potentially fertile topics for future research in the applied areas of clinical/counseling, educational, and industrial-organizational psychology. In each of these fields, further research is needed to investigate the role and functions of humor, the ways people use it to achieve their personal goals, and the types of humor that are potentially beneficial as well as detrimental to broader professional goals.

Although practitioners who advocate humor applications in health care, psychotherapy, education, and business have drawn attention to potentially interesting research questions, there is also a risk that their excessive claims and simplistic, pop-psychology writings may drive away some basic and applied researchers in psychology, who may perceive these ideas as trivial and unimportant or may not wish to be seen as promoting overly simplistic and unscientific agendas. However, this would be unfortunate.

As I have tried to show throughout this book, humor is a ubiquitous aspect of human behavior that touches on every area of psychology. It is an interesting phenomenon in its own right that merits further investigation to understand more fully how it works and what functions it serves in human cognition, emotion, and social behavior. Basic research of this kind may lead to interesting new insights about potential applications in various domains. Whether the focus is on basic processes or practical applications, the psychology of humor continues to be a fascinating topic of research that promises many more interesting and useful discoveries.

REFERENCES

Abel, M. H. (1998). Interaction of humor and gender in moderating relationships between stress and outcomes. *Journal of Psychology, 132*(3), 267–276.

Abel, M. H. (2002). Humor, stress, and coping strategies. *Humor: International Journal of Humor Research, 15*(4), 365–381.

Abel, M. H., & Maxwell, D. (2002). Humor and affective consequences of a stressful task. *Journal of Social & Clinical Psychology, 21*(2), 165–190.

Abelson, R. P. (1981). Psychological status of the script concept. *American Psychologist, 36*, 715–729.

Adams, E. R., & McGuire, F. A. (1986). Is laughter the best medicine? A study of the effects of humor on perceived pain and affect. *Activities, Adaptation & Aging, 8*(3–4), 157–175.

Adams, P., & Mylander, M. (1998). *Gesundheit!: Bringing good health to you, the medical system, and society through physician service, complementary therapies, humor, and joy.* Rochester, VT: Healing Arts Press.

Adelsward, V., & Oberg, B.-M. (1998). The function of laughter and joking in negotiation activities. *Humor: International Journal of Humor Research, 11*(4), 411–429.

Ainsworth, M. D. S., Bell, S. M., & Stayton, D. J. (1991). Infant-mother attachment and social development: 'Socialisation' as a product of reciprocal responsiveness to signals. In M. Woodhead, R. Carr & P. Light (Eds.), *Becoming a person* (pp. 30–55). London: Routledge.

Alexander, R. D. (1986). Ostracism and indirect reciprocity: The reproductive significance of humor. *Ethology & Sociobiology, 7*(3–4), 253–270.

Allport, G. W. (1950). *The individual and his religion.* New York: Macmillan.

Allport, G. W. (1961). *Pattern and growth in personality.* New York: Holt, Reinhart & Winston.

American Psychiatric Association. (1994). *Diagnostic and statistical manual of mental disorders* (4th ed.). Washington, DC: American Psychiatric Association.

Andersen, J. F. (1979). Teacher immediacy as a predictor of teaching effectiveness. In D. Nimmo (Ed.), *Communication Yearbook 3* (pp. 543–559). New Brunswick, NJ: Transaction Books.

Anderson, C. A., & Arnoult, L. H. (1989). An examination of perceived control, humor, irrational beliefs, and positive stress as moderators of the relation between negative stress and health. *Basic & Applied Social Psychology, 10*(2), 101–117.

Andrews, R. (1993). *The Columbia dictionary of quotations*. New York: Columbia University Press.

Apte, M. L. (1985). *Humor and laughter: An anthropological approach*. Ithaca, NY: Cornell University Press.

Apter, M. J. (1982). *The experience of motivation: The theory of psychological reversals*. London: Academic Press.

Apter, M. J. (1991). A structural-phenomenology of play. In J. H. Kerr & M. J. Apter (Eds.), *Adult play: A reversal theory approach* (pp. 13–29). Amsterdam: Swets & Zeitlinger.

Apter, M. J. (1992). *The dangerous edge: The psychology of excitement*. New York: Free Press.

Apter, M. J. (Ed.). (2001). *Motivational styles in everyday life: A guide to reversal theory*. Washington, DC: American Psychological Association.

Apter, M. J., & Smith, K. C. P. (1977). Humour and the theory of psychological reversals. In A. J. Chapman & H. C. Foot (Eds.), *It's a funny thing, humour* (pp. 95–100). Oxford: Pergamon Press.

Arriaga, X. B. (2002). Joking violence among highly committed individuals. *Journal of Interpersonal Violence, 17*(6), 591–610.

Arroyo, S., Lesser, R. P., Gordon, B., Uematsu, S., Hart, J., Schwerdt, P., et al. (1993). Mirth, laughter and gelastic seizures. *Brain, 116*, 757–780.

Askenasy, J. J. (1987). The functions and dysfunctions of laughter. *Journal of General Psychology, 114*(4), 317–334.

Aspinwall, L. G., & Staudinger, U. M. (2003). *A psychology of human strengths: Fundamental questions and future directions for a positive psychology*. Washington, DC: American Psychological Association.

Atsumi, T., Fujisawa, S., Nakabayashi, Y., Kawarai, T., Yasui, T., & Tonosaki, K. (2004). Pleasant feeling from watching a comical video enhances free radical-scavenging capacity in human whole saliva. *Journal of Psychosomatic Research, 56*(3), 377–379.

Attardo, S. (1994). *Linguistic theories of humor*. Hawthorne, NY: Mouton de Gruyter.

Attardo, S. (1997). The semantic foundations of cognitive theories of humor. *Humor: International Journal of Humor Research, 10*(4), 395–420.

Attardo, S. (1998). The analysis of humorous narratives. *Humor: International Journal of Humor Research, 11*(3), 231–260.

Attardo, S., Hempelmann, C. F., & Di Maio, S. (2002). Script oppositions and logical mechanisms: Modeling incongruities and their resolutions. *Humor: International Journal of Humor Research, 15*(1), 3–46.

Attardo, S., & Raskin, V. (1991). Script theory revis(it)ed: Joke similarity and joke representation model. *Humor: International Journal of Humor Research, 4*(3–4), 293–347.

Averill, J. R. (1969). Autonomic response patterns during sadness and mirth. *Psychophysiology, 5*, 399–414.

Azim, E., Mobbs, D., Jo, B., Menon, V., & Reiss, A. L. (2005). Sex differences in brain activation elicited by humor. *Proceedings of the National Academy of Sciences, 102*(45), 16496–16501.

Babad, E. Y. (1974). A multi-method approach to the assessment of humor: A critical look at humor tests. *Journal of Personality, 42*(4), 618–631.

Bachelor, A., & Horvath, A. (1999). The therapeutic relationship. In M. A. Hubble, B. L. Duncan & S. D. Miller (Eds.), *The heart and soul of change: What works in therapy* (pp. 133–178). Washington, DC: American Psychological Association.

Bachorowski, J.-A., & Owren, M. J. (2001). Not all laughs are alike: Voiced but not unvoiced laughter readily elicits positive affect. *Psychological Science, 12*(3), 252–257.

Bachorowski, J.-A., & Owren, M. J. (2003). Sounds of emotion: Production and perception of affect-related vocal acoustics. *Annals of the New York Academy of Sciences, 1000.*

Bachorowski, J.-A., Smoski, M. J., & Owen, M. J. (2001). The acoustic features of human laughter. *Journal of the Acoustical Society of America, 110*(3, Pt 1), 1581–1597.

Bainum, C. K., Lounsbury, K. R., & Pollio, H. R. (1984). The development of laughing and smiling in nursery school children. *Child Development, 55*(5), 1946–1957.

Bariaud, F. (1988). Age differences in children's humor. *Journal of Children in Contemporary Society, 20*(1–2), 15–45.

Barnett, L. A. (1990). Playfulness: Definition, design, and measurement. *Play & Culture, 3*(4), 319–336.

Barnett, L. A. (1991). The playful child: Measurement of a disposition to play. *Play & Culture, 4*(1), 51–74.

Baron, R. A. (1978a). Aggression-inhibiting influence of sexual humor. *Journal of Personality & Social Psychology, 36*(2), 189–197.

Baron, R. A. (1978b). The influence of hostile and nonhostile humor upon physical aggression. *Personality & Social Psychology Bulletin, 4*(1), 77–80.

Baron, R. A., & Ball, R. L. (1974). The aggression-inhibiting influence of nonhostile humor. *Journal of Experimental Social Psychology, 10*(1), 23–33.

Bartlett, F. C. (1932). *Remembering.* Cambridge: Cambridge University Press.

Bateson, P. (2005). The role of play in the evolution of great apes and humans. In A. D. Pellegrini & P. K. Smith (Eds.), *The nature of play: Great apes and humans* (pp. 13–24). New York: Guilford Press.

Belanger, H. G., Kirkpatrick, L. A., & Derks, P. (1998). The effects of humor on verbal and imaginal problem solving. *Humor: International Journal of Humor Research, 11*(1), 21–31.

Bell, N. J., McGhee, P. E., & Duffey, N. S. (1986). Interpersonal competence, social assertiveness and the development of humour. *British Journal of Developmental Psychology, 4*(1), 51–55.

Benedetti, F. (2002). How the doctor's words affect the patient's brain. *Evaluation & the Health Professions, 25*(4), 369–386.

Bergen, D. (1998a). Development of the sense of humor. In W. Ruch (Ed.), *The sense of humor: Explorations of a personality characteristic* (pp. 329–358). Berlin, Germany: Walter de Gruyter.

Bergen, D. (1998b). Play as a context for humor development. In D. P. Fromberg & D. Bergen (Eds.), *Play from birth to twelve and beyond: Contexts, perspectives, and meanings* (pp. 324–337). New York: Garland.

Bergen, D. (2002). Finding the humor in children's play. In J. L. Roopnarine (Ed.), *Conceptual, social-cognitive, and contextual issues in the fields of play* (pp. 209–220). Westport, CT: Ablex Publishing.

Bergen, D. (2003). Humor, play, and child development. In A. J. Klein (Ed.), *Humor in children's lives: A guidebook for practitioners* (pp. 17–32). Westport, CT: Praeger.

Berger, A. A. (1995). *Blind men and elephants: Perspectives on humor.* New Brunswick, NJ: Transaction Publishers.

Bergmann, M. S. (1999). The psychoanalysis of humor and humor in psychoanalysis. In J. W. Barron (Ed.), *Humor and psyche: Psychoanalytic perspectives* (pp. 11–30). Hillsdale, NJ: The Analytic Press.

Bergson, H. (1911). *Laughter: An essay on the meaning of the comic.* Oxford: Macmillan.

Berk, L. S., Felten, D. L., Tan, S. A., Bittman, B. B., & Westengard, J. (2001). Modulation of neuroimmune parameters during the eustress of humor-associated mirthful laughter. *Alternative Therapies, 7*(2), 62–76.

Berk, L. S., Tan, S. A., Fry, W. F., Napier, B. J., Lee, J. W., Hubbard, R. W., et al. (1989). Neuroendocrine and stress hormone changes during mirthful laughter. *American Journal of the Medical Sciences, 298*, 390–396.

Berk, R. A., & Nanda, J. P. (1998). Effects of jocular instructional methods on attitudes, anxiety, and achievement in statistics courses. *Humor: International Journal of Humor Research, 11*(4), 383–409.

Berkowitz, L. (1970). Aggressive humor as a stimulus to aggressive responses. *Journal of Personality & Social Psychology, 16*(4), 710–717.

Berlyne, D. E. (1960). *Conflict, arousal, and curiosity.* New York, NY: McGraw-Hill.

Berlyne, D. E. (1969). Laughter, humor, and play. In G. Lindzey & E. Aronson (Eds.), *The handbook of social psychology* (2nd ed., Vol. 3, pp. 795–852). Reading, MA: Addison-Wesley.

Berlyne, D. E. (1972). Humor and its kin. In J. H. Goldstein & P. E. McGhee (Eds.), *The psychology of humor: Theoretical perspectives and empirical issues* (pp. 43–60). New York: Academic Press.

Bernet, W. (1993). Humor in evaluating and treating children and adolescents. *Journal of Psychotherapy Practice & Research, 2*(4), 307–317.

Berns, G. S. (2004). Something funny happened to reward. *Trends in Cognitive Sciences, 8*(5), 193–194.

Bernstein, D. K. (1986). The development of humor: Implications for assessment and intervention. *Topics in Language Disorders, 6*(4), 65–71.

Berscheid, E., & Reis, H. T. (1998). Attraction and close relationships. In D. T. Gilbert, S. T. Fiske & G. Lindzey (Eds.), *The handbook of social psychology* (4th ed., Vol. 2, pp. 193–281). Boston: McGraw-Hill.

Besemer, S. P., & Treffinger, D. J. (1981). Analysis of creative products: Review and synthesis. *Journal of Creative Behavior, 15*, 158–178.

Bihrle, A. M., Brownell, H. H., & Gardner, H. (1988). Humor and the right hemisphere: A narrative perspective. In H. A. Whitaker (Ed.), *Contemporary reviews in neuropsychology* (pp. 109–126). New York: Springer-Verlag.

Bihrle, A. M., Brownell, H. H., & Powelson, J. A. (1986). Comprehension of humorous and nonhumorous materials by left and right brain-damaged patients. *Brain & Cognition, 5*(4), 399–411.

Bill, B., & Naus, P. (1992). The role of humor in the interpretation of sexist incidents. *Sex Roles, 27*(11–12), 645–664.

Binsted, K., Pain, H., & Ritchie, G. (1997). Children's evaluation of computer-generated punning riddles. *Pragmatics and Cognition, 5*(2), 309–358.

Binsted, K., & Ritchie, G. (1997). Computational rules for generating punning riddles. *Humor: International Journal of Humor Research, 10*(1), 25–76.

Binsted, K., & Ritchie, G. (2001). Towards a model of story puns. *Humor: International Journal of Humor Research, 14*(3), 275–292.

Bippus, A. M. (2000a). Humor usage in comforting episodes: Factors predicting outcomes. *Western Journal of Communication, 64*(4), 359–384.

Bippus, A. M. (2000b). Making sense of humor in young romantic relationships: Understanding partners' perceptions. *Humor: International Journal of Humor Research, 13*(4), 395–417.

Bizi, S., Keinan, G., & Beit-Hallahmi, B. (1988). Humor and coping with stress: A test under real-life conditions. *Personality & Individual Differences, 9*(6), 951–956.

Blakemore, S. J., Wolpert, D. M., & Frith, C. D. (1998). Central cancellation of self-produced tickle sensation. *Nature Neuroscience, 1*(7), 635–640.

Bloch, S. (1987). Humor in group therapy. In W. F. Fry & W. A. Salameh (Eds.), *Handbook of humor and psychotherapy: Advances in the clinical use of humor* (pp. 171–194). Sarasota, FL: Professional Resource Exchange.

Bloch, S., Browning, S., & McGrath, G. (1983). Humour in group psychotherapy. *British Journal of Medical Psychology, 56*(1), 89–97.

Bonanno, G. A., & Keltner, D. (1997). Facial expressions of emotion and the course of conjugal bereavement. *Journal of Abnormal Psychology, 106*(1), 126–137.

Booth, R. J., & Pennebaker, J. W. (2000). Emotions and immunity. In M. Lewis & J. M. Haviland-Jones (Eds.), *Handbook of emotions* (2nd ed., pp. 558–570). New York: Guilford.

Borcherdt, B. (2002). Humor and its contributions to mental health. *Journal of Rational-Emotive & Cognitive Behavior Therapy, 20*(3–4), 247–257.

Bowlby, J. (1982). *Attachment* (2nd ed.). New York: Basic Books.

Boyle, G. J., & Joss-Reid, J. M. (2004). Relationship of humour to health: A psychometric investigation. *British Journal of Health Psychology, 9*(1), 51–66.

Breckler, S. J., Olson, J. M., & Wiggins, E. C. (2006). *Social psychology alive*. Belmont, CA: Thompson-Wadsworth.

Bressler, E. R., & Balshine, S. (2006). The influence of humor on desirability. *Evolution and Human Behavior, 27*(1), 29–39.

Bressler, E. R., Martin, R. A., & Balshine, S. (2006). Production and appreciation of humor as sexually selected traits. *Evolution and Human Behavior, 27*(2), 121–130.

Brodzinsky, D. M. (1975). The role of conceptual tempo and stimulus characteristics in children's humor development. *Developmental Psychology, 11*(6), 843–850.

Brodzinsky, D. M. (1977). Children's comprehension and appreciation of verbal jokes in relation to conceptual tempo. *Child Development, 48*(3), 960–967.

Brodzinsky, D. M., Barnet, K., & Aiello, J. R. (1981). Sex of subject and gender identity as factors in humor appreciation. *Sex Roles, 12*, 195–219.

Brodzinsky, D. M., & Rubien, J. (1976). Humor production as a function of sex of subject, creativity, and cartoon content. *Journal of Consulting & Clinical Psychology, 44*(4), 597–600.

Brown, G. E., Brown, D., & Ramos, J. (1981). Effects of a laughing versus a nonlaughing model on humor responses in college students. *Psychological Reports, 48*(1), 35–40.

Brown, G. E., Wheeler, K. J., & Cash, M. (1980). The effects of a laughing versus a nonlaughing model on humor responses in preschool children. *Journal of Experimental Child Psychology, 29*(2), 334–339.

Brown, P., & Levinson, S. C. (1987). *Politeness: Some universals in language usage*. New York: Cambridge University Press.

Brown, R. B., & Keegan, D. (1999). Humor in the hotel kitchen. *Humor: International Journal of Humor Research, 12*(1), 47–70.

Brown, S. L., & Schwartz, G. E. (1980). Relationships between facial electromyography and subjective experience during affective imagery. *Biological Psychology, 11*, 49–62.

Brownell, H. H., & Gardner, H. (1988). Neuropsychological insights into humour. In J. Durant & J. Miller (Eds.), *Laughing matters: A serious look at humour* (pp. 17–34). Essex, England: Longman Scientific and Technical.

Brownell, H. H., Michel, D., Powelson, J., & Gardner, H. (1983). Surprise but not coherence: Sensitivity to verbal humor in right-hemisphere patients. *Brain & Language, 18*(1), 20–27.

Brownell, H. H., & Stringfellow, A. (2000). Cognitive perspectives on humor comprehension after brain injury. In L. T. Connor & L. K. Obler (Eds.), *Neurobehavior of language and cognition: Studies of normal aging and brain damage* (pp. 241–258). Boston: Kluwer Academic.

Bruehl, S., Carlson, C. R., & McCubbin, J. A. (1993). Two brief interventions for acute pain. *Pain, 54*(1), 29–36.

Bryant, J. (1977). Degree of hostility in squelches as a factor in humour appreciation. In A. J. Chapman & H. C. Foot (Eds.), *It's a funny thing, humour* (pp. 321–327). Oxford: Pergamon Press.

Bryant, J., Brown, D., Parks, S. L., & Zillmann, D. (1983). Children's imitation of a ridiculed model. *Human Communication Research, 10*(2), 243–255.

Bryant, J., Brown, D., Silberberg, A. R., & Elliott, S. M. (1981). Effects of humorous illustrations in college textbooks. *Human Communication Research, 8*(1), 43–57.

Bryant, J., Comisky, P. W., Crane, J. S., & Zillmann, D. (1980). Relationship between college teachers' use of humor in the classroom and students' evaluations of their teachers. *Journal of Educational Psychology, 72*(4), 511–519.

Bryant, J., & Zillmann, D. (1989). Using humor to promote learning in the classroom. In P. E. McGhee (Ed.), *Humor and children's development: A guide to practical applications* (pp. 49–78). New York: Haworth Press.

Bryk, A. S., & Raudenbush, S. W. (1992). *Hierarchical linear models: Applications and data analysis methods.* Thousand Oaks, CA: Sage Publications.

Buckman, E. S. (Ed.). (1994). *The handbook of humor: Clinical applications in psychotherapy.* Melbourne, FL: Robert E. Krieger.

Buhrmester, D., Furman, W., Wittenberg, M. T., & Reis, H. T. (1988). Five domains of interpersonal competence in peer relationships. *Journal of Personality & Social Psychology, 55*(6), 991–1008.

Burling, R. (1993). Primate calls, human language, and nonverbal communication. *Current Anthropology, 34*(1), 25–53.

Buss, A. H., & Plomin, R. (1984). *Temperament: Early developing personality traits.* Hillsdale, NJ: Lawrence Erlbaum Associates.

Buss, D. M. (1989). Sex differences in human mate preferences: Evolutionary hypotheses tested in 37 cultures. *Behavioral and Brain Sciences, 12*(1–49).

Buss, D. M., & Kenrick, D. T. (1998). Evolutionary social psychology. In D. T. Gilbert, S. T. Fiske & G. Lindzey (Eds.), *The handbook of social psychology* (4th ed., Vol. 2, pp. 982–1026). Boston: McGraw-Hill.

Butovskaya, M. L., & Kozintsev, A. G. (1996). A neglected form of quasi-aggression in apes: Possible relevance for the origins of humor. *Current Anthropology, 37*(4), 716–717.

Byrne, D. (1956). The relationship between humor and the expression of hostility. *Journal of Abnormal & Social Psychology, 53,* 84–89.

Byrne, D. (1961). Some inconsistencies in the effect of motivation arousal on humor preferences. *Journal of Abnormal & Social Psychology, 62,* 158–160.

Cacioppo, J. T., Berntson, G. G., Larsen, J. T., Poehlmann, K. M., & Ito, T. A. (2000). The psychophysiology of emotion. In M. Lewis & J. M. Haviland-Jones (Eds.), *Handbook of emotions* (2nd ed., pp. 173–191). New York: Guilford.

Cann, A., & Calhoun, L. G. (2001). Perceived personality associations with differences in sense of humor: Stereotypes of hypothetical others with high or low senses of humor. *Humor: International Journal of Humor Research, 14*(2), 117–130.

Cann, A., Calhoun, L. G., & Banks, J. S. (1997). On the role of humor appreciation in interpersonal attraction: It's no joking matter. *Humor: International Journal of Humor Research*, *10*(1), 77–89.

Cann, A., Calhoun, L. G., & Nance, J. T. (2000). Exposure to humor before and after an unpleasant stimulus: Humor as a preventative or a cure. *Humor: International Journal of Humor Research*, *13*(2), 177–191.

Cann, A., Holt, K., & Calhoun, L. G. (1999). The roles of humor and sense of humor in responses to stressors. *Humor: International Journal of Humor Research*, *12*(2), 177–193.

Cantor, J. R. (1976). What is funny to whom? The role of gender. *Journal of Communication*, *26*(3), 164–172.

Cantor, J. R., Bryant, J., & Zillmann, D. (1974). Enhancement of humor appreciation by transferred excitation. *Journal of Personality & Social Psychology*, *30*(6), 812–821.

Caron, J. E. (2002). From ethology to aesthetics: Evolution as a theoretical paradigm for research on laughter, humor, and other comic phenomena. *Humor: International Journal of Humor Research*, *15*(3), 245–281.

Carroll, J. L. (1989). Changes in humor appreciation of college students in the last twenty-five years. *Psychological Reports*, *65*(3, Pt 1), 863–866.

Carroll, J. L. (1990). The relationship between humor appreciation and perceived physical health. *Psychology: A Journal of Human Behavior*, *27*(2), 34–37.

Carroll, J. L., & Shmidt, J. L. (1992). Correlation between humorous coping style and health. *Psychological Reports*, *70*(2), 402.

Carson, D. K., Skarpness, L. R., Schultz, N. W., & McGhee, P. E. (1986). Temperament and communicative competence as predictors of young children's humor. *Merrill-Palmer Quarterly*, *32*(4), 415–426.

Carstensen, L. L., Gottman, J. M., & Levenson, R. W. (1995). Emotional behavior in long-term marriage. *Psychology and Aging*, *10*(1), 140–149.

Carver, C. S., Pozo, C., Harris, S. D., Noriega, V., Scheier, M. F., Robinson, D. S., et al. (1993). How coping mediates the effect of optimism on distress: A study of women with early stage breast cancer. *Journal of Personality & Social Psychology*, *65*(2), 375–390.

Carver, C. S., Scheier, M. F., & Weintraub, J. K. (1989). Assessing coping strategies: A theoretically based approach. *Journal of Personality & Social Psychology*, *56*(2), 267–283.

Casadonte, D. (2003). A note on the neuro-mathematics of laughter. *Humor: International Journal of Humor Research*, *16*(2), 133–156.

Cashion, J. L., Cody, M. J., & Erickson, K. V. (1986). "You'll love this one . . .": An exploration into joke-prefacing devices. *Journal of Language & Social Psychology*, *5*(4), 303–312.

Cattell, R. B. (1947). Confirmation and clarification of primary personality factors. *Psychometrica*, *12*, 197–220.

Cattell, R. B., & Luborsky, L. B. (1947). Personality factors in response to humor. *Journal of Abnormal & Social Psychology*, *42*, 402–421.

Cattell, R. B., & Tollefson, D. L. (1966). *The IPAT humor test of personality*. Champaign, IL: Institute for Personality and Ability Testing.

Celso, B. G., Ebener, D. J., & Burkhead, E. J. (2003). Humor coping, health status, and life satisfaction among older adults residing in assisted living facilities. *Aging & Mental Health*, *7*(6), 438–445.

Chafe, W. (1987). Humor as a disabling mechanism. *American Behavioral Scientist*, *30*(1), 16–25.

Chapman, A. J. (1973a). An electromyographic study of apprehension about evaluation. *Psychological Reports*, *33*, 811–814.

Chapman, A. J. (1973b). Social facilitation of laughter in children. *Journal of Experimental Social Psychology*, *9*(6), 528–541.

Chapman, A. J. (1975a). Eye contact, physical proximity and laughter: A re-examination of the equilibrium model of social intimacy. *Social Behavior & Personality*, *3*(2), 143–155.

Chapman, A. J. (1975b). Humorous laughter in children. *Journal of Personality & Social Psychology*, *31*(1), 42–49.

Chapman, A. J. (1976). Social aspects of humorous laughter. In A. J. Chapman & H. C. Foot (Eds.), *Humour and laughter: Theory, research, and applications* (pp. 155–185). London: John Wiley & Sons.

Chapman, A. J. (1983). Humor and laughter in social interaction and some implications for humor research. In P. E. McGhee & J. H. Goldstein (Eds.), *Handbook of humor research, Vol. 1: Basic issues* (pp. 135–157). New York: Springer-Verlag.

Chapman, A. J., & Foot, H. C. (1976). *Humour and laughter: Theory, research and applications*. Oxford, England: John Wiley & Sons.

Chapman, A. J., & Gadfield, N. J. (1976). Is sexual humor sexist? *Journal of Communication*, *26*(3), 141–153.

Chapman, A. J., Smith, J. R., & Foot, H. C. (1980). Humour, laughter, and social interaction. In P. E. McGhee & A. J. Chapman (Eds.), *Children's humour* (pp. 141–179). Chichester: John Wiley & Sons.

Chapman, A. J., & Wright, D. S. (1976). Social enhancement of laughter: An experimental analysis of some companion variables. *Journal of Experimental Child Psychology*, *21*(2), 201–218.

Chattopadhyay, A., & Basu, K. (1990). Humor in advertising: The moderating role of prior brand evaluation. *Journal of Marketing Research*, *27*(4), 466–476.

Check, J. F. (1986). Positive traits of the effective teacher–negative traits of the ineffective one. *Education*, *106*(3), 326–334.

Chen, G., & Martin, R. A. (in press). Humor styles, coping humor, and mental health among Chinese university students. *Humor: International Journal of Humor Research*.

Cherkas, L., Hochberg, F., MacGregor, A. J., Snieder, H., & Spector, T. D. (2000). Happy families: A twin study of humour. *Twin Research*, *3*, 17–22.

Chomsky, N. (1957). *Syntactic structures*. The Hague: Mouton.

Chomsky, N. (1971). Deep structure, surface structure, and semantic interpretation. In D. D. Steinberg & L. A. Jakobovits (Eds.), *Semantics: An interdisciplinary reader in philosophy, linguistics, and psychology* (pp. 183–216). Cambridge: Cambridge University Press.

Christie, I. C., & Friedman, B. H. (2004). Autonomic specificity of discrete emotion and dimensions of affective space: A multivariate approach. *International Journal of Psychophysiology*, *51*, 143–153.

Clabby, J. F. (1980). The wit: A personality analysis. *Journal of Personality Assessment*, *44*(3), 307–310.

Clark, A., Seidler, A., & Miller, M. (2001). Inverse association between sense of humor and coronary heart disease. *International Journal of Cardiology*, *80*, 87–88.

Clark, H. H., & Gerrig, R. J. (1984). On the pretense theory of irony. *Journal of Experimental Psychology: General*, *113*, 121–126.

Clouse, R. W., & Spurgeon, K. L. (1995). Corporate analysis of humor. *Psychology: A Journal of Human Behavior*, *32*(3–4), 1–24.

Cogan, R., Cogan, D., Waltz, W., & McCue, M. (1987). Effects of laughter and relaxation on discomfort thresholds. *Journal of Behavioral Medicine*, *10*(2), 139–144.

Cohan, C. L., & Bradbury, T. N. (1997). Negative life events, marital interaction, and the longitudinal course of newlywed marriage. *Journal of Personality & Social Psychology, 73*(1), 114–128.

Cohen, S., & Edwards, J. R. (1989). Personality characteristics as moderators of the relationship between stress and disorder. In R. W. J. Neufeld (Ed.), *Advances in the investigation of psychological stress* (pp. 235–283). New York: Wiley.

Collinson, D. L. (1988). "Engineering humour": Masculinity, joking and conflict in shop-floor relations. *Organization Studies, 9*(2), 181–199.

Colston, H. L., Giora, R., & Katz, A. (2000). *Joke comprehension: Salience and context effects.* Paper presented at the 7th International Pragmatics Conference, Budapest.

Consalvo, C. M. (1989). Humor in management: No laughing matter. *Humor: International Journal of Humor Research, 2*(3), 285–297.

Conway, M., & Dube, L. (2002). Humor in persuasion on threatening topics: Effectiveness is a function of audience sex role orientation. *Personality & Social Psychology Bulletin, 28*(7), 863–873.

Cook, K. S., & Rice, E. (2003). Social exchange theory. In J. Delamater (Ed.), *Handbook of social psychology* (pp. 53–76). New York: Plenum.

Cook, M., Young, A., Taylor, D., & Bedford, A. P. (1998). Personality correlates of alcohol consumption. *Personality & Individual Differences, 24*, 641–647.

Cornett, C. E. (1986). *Learning through laughter: Humor in the classroom.* Bloomington, IN: Phi Delta Kappa Educational Foundation.

Corruble, E., Bronnec, M., Falissard, B., & Hardy, P. (2004). Defense styles in depressed suicide attempters. *Psychiatry & Clinical Neurosciences, 58*(3), 285–288.

Coser, R. L. (1960). Laughter among colleagues: A study of the functions of humor among the staff of a mental hospital. *Psychiatry, 23*, 81–95.

Coulson, A. S. (2001). Cognitive synergy. In M. J. Apter (Ed.), *Motivational styles in everyday life: A guide to reversal theory* (pp. 229–248). Washington, DC: American Psychological Association.

Coulson, S., & Kutas, M. (2001). Getting it: Human event-related brain response to jokes in good and poor comprehenders. *Neuroscience Letters, 316*, 71–74.

Cousins, N. (1976). Anatomy of an illness (as perceived by the patient). *New England Journal of Medicine, 295*, 1458–1463.

Cousins, N. (1979). *Anatomy of an illness as perceived by the patient: Reflections on healing and regeneration.* New York: W. W. Norton.

Cousins, N. (1985). Therapeutic value of laughter. *Integrative Psychiatry, 3*(2), 112.

Craik, K. H., Lampert, M. D., & Nelson, A. J. (1996). Sense of humor and styles of everyday humorous conduct. *Humor: International Journal of Humor Research, 9*(3–4), 273–302.

Craik, K. H., & Ware, A. P. (1998). Humor and personality in everyday life. In W. Ruch (Ed.), *The sense of humor: Explorations of a personality characteristic* (pp. 63–94). Berlin, Germany: Walter de Gruyter.

Crawford, M. (1989). Humor in conversational context: Beyond biases in the study of gender and humor. In R. K. Unger (Ed.), *Representations: Social constructions of gender* (pp. 155–166). Amityville, NY: Baywood Publishing.

Crawford, M. (1992). Just kidding: Gender and conversational humor. In R. Barreca (Ed.), *New perspectives on women and comedy* (pp. 23–37). Philadelphia, PA: Gordon and Breach.

Crawford, M. (2003). Gender and humor in social context. *Journal of Pragmatics, 35*(9), 1413–1430.

Crawford, M., & Gressley, D. (1991). Creativity, caring, and context: Women's and men's accounts of humor preferences and practices. *Psychology of Women Quarterly, 15*(2), 217–231.

Creusere, M. A. (1999). Theories of adults' understanding and use of irony and sarcasm: Applications to and evidence from research with children. *Developmental Review, 19*(2), 213–262.

Creusere, M. A. (2000). A developmental test of theoretical perspectives on the understanding of verbal irony: Children's recognition of allusion and pragmatic insincerity. *Metaphor & Symbol, 15*(1–2), 29–45.

Culver, J. L., Arena, P. L., Wimberly, S. R., Antoni, M. H., & Carver, C. S. (2004). Coping among African-American, Hispanic, and non-Hispanic White women recently treated for early stage breast cancer. *Psychology & Health, 19*(2), 157–166.

Cunningham, W. A., & Derks, P. (2005). Humor appreciation and latency of comprehension. *Humor: International Journal of Humor Research, 18*(4), 389–403.

Damasio, A. R. (1994). *Descartes' error: Emotion, reasoning, and the human brain*. New York: G. P. Putnam.

Damico, S. B., & Purkey, W. W. (1978). Class clowns: A study of middle school students. *American Educational Research Journal, 15*(3), 391–398.

Daniel, H. J., O'Brien, K. F., McCabe, R. B., & Quinter, V. E. (1985). Values in mate selection: A 1984 campus survey. *College Student Journal, 19*(1), 44–50.

Danzer, A., Dale, J. A., & Klions, H. L. (1990). Effect of exposure to humorous stimuli on induced depression. *Psychological Reports, 66*(3, Pt 1), 1027–1036.

Darwin, C. (1872). *The expression of the emotions in man and animals*. London: Murray.

Davidson, I. F. W. K., & Brown, W. I. (1989). Using humour in counselling mentally retarded clients: A preliminary study. *International Journal for the Advancement of Counselling, 12*, 93–104.

Davies, A. P., & Apter, M. J. (1980). Humour and its effect on learning in children. In P. E. McGhee & A. J. Chapman (Eds.), *Children's humour* (pp. 237–253). Chichester: John Wiley & Sons.

Davies, C. (1990a). *Ethnic humor around the world: A comparative analysis*. Bloomington, IN: Indiana University Press.

Davies, C. (1990b). An explanation of Jewish jokes about Jewish women. *Humor: International Journal of Humor Research, 3*, 363–378.

Davis, G. A., & Subkoviak, M. J. (1975). Multidimensional analysis of a personality-based test of creative potential. *Journal of Educational Measurement, 12*(1), 37–43.

Davis, J. M., & Farina, A. (1970). Humor appreciation as social communication. *Journal of Personality & Social Psychology, 15*(2), 175–178.

Day, H. I., & Langevin, R. (1969). Curiosity and intelligence: Two necessary conditions for a high level of creativity. *Journal of Special Education, 3*, 263–268.

de Groot, A., Kaplan, J., Rosenblatt, E., Dews, S., & Winner, E. (1995). Understanding versus discriminating nonliteral utterances: Evidence for a dissociation. *Metaphor & Symbol, 10*(4), 255–273.

de Koning, E., & Weiss, R. L. (2002). The Relational Humor Inventory: Functions of humor in close relationships. *American Journal of Family Therapy, 30*(1), 1–18.

Deal, T. E. D., & Kennedy, A. A. (1982). *Corporate cultures: The rites and rituals of corporate life*. Reading, MA: Addison-Wesley.

Deaner, S. L., & McConatha, J. T. (1993). The relationship of humor to depression and personality. *Psychological Reports, 72*(3, Pt 1), 755–763.

Decker, W. H. (1987). Managerial humor and subordinate satisfaction. *Social Behavior & Personality, 15*(2), 225–232.

Decker, W. H., & Rotondo, D. M. (2001). Relationships among gender, type of humor, and perceived leader effectiveness. *Journal of Managerial Issues, 13*(4), 450–465.

Deckers, L. (1993). On the validity of a weight-judging paradigm for the study of humor. *Humor: International Journal of Humor Research, 6*(1), 43–56.

Deckers, L. (1998). Influence of mood on humor. In W. Ruch (Ed.), *The sense of humor: Explorations of a personality characteristic* (pp. 309–328). Berlin, Germany: Walter de Gruyter.

Deckers, L., & Buttram, R. T. (1990). Humor as a response to incongruities within or between schemata. *Humor: International Journal of Humor Research, 3*(1), 53–64.

Deckers, L., & Carr, D. E. (1986). Cartoons varying in low-level pain ratings, not aggression ratings, correlate positively with funniness ratings. *Motivation & Emotion, 10*(3), 207–216.

Deckers, L., & Edington, J. (1979). *Facial expressions of mirth as a log-log function of the degree of incongruity in a psychophysical task.* Paper presented at the Midwestern Psychological Association Convention, Chicago.

Deckers, L., Edington, J., & VanCleave, G. (1981). Mirth as a function of incongruities in judged and unjudged dimensions of psychophysical tasks. *Journal of General Psychology, 105*(Pt 2), 225–233.

Deckers, L., & Hricik, D. (1984). Orienting and humor responses: A synthesis. *Motivation & Emotion, 8*(3), 183–204.

Deckers, L., Jenkins, S., & Gladfelter, E. (1977). Incongruity versus tension relief: Hypotheses of humor. *Motivation & Emotion, 1*, 261–272.

Deckers, L., & Kizer, P. (1974). A note on weight discrepancy and humor. *Journal of Psychology, 86*(2), 309–312.

Deckers, L., & Kizer, P. (1975). Humor and the incongruity hypothesis. *Journal of Psychology, 90*(2), 215–218.

Deckers, L., Pell, C., & Lundahl, B. (1990). *Smile amplitude or duration as an indicator of humor?* Paper presented at the Midwestern Psychological Association Convention, Chicago.

Deckers, L., & Ruch, W. (1992a). Sensation seeking and the Situational Humour Response Questionnaire (SHRQ): Its relationship in American and German samples. *Personality & Individual Differences, 13*(9), 1051–1054.

Deckers, L., & Ruch, W. (1992b). The Situational Humour Response Questionnaire (SHRQ) as a test of "sense of humour": A validity study in the field of humour appreciation. *Personality & Individual Differences, 13*(10), 1149–1152.

Deckers, L., & Salais, D. (1983). Humor as a negatively accelerated function of the degree of incongruity. *Motivation & Emotion, 7*(4), 357–363.

Deffenbacher, J. L., Deitz, S. R., & Hazaleus, S. L. (1981). Effects of humor and test anxiety on performance, worry, and emotionality in naturally occurring exams. *Cognitive Therapy & Research, 5*(2), 225–228.

Deinzer, R., Kleineidam, C., Stiller-Winkler, R., Idel, H., & Bachg, D. (2000). Prolonged reduction of salivary immunoglobulin A (sIgA) after major academic exam. *International Journal of Psychophysiology, 37*(3), 219–232.

DeNeve, K. M. (1999). Happy as an extraverted clam? The role of personality for subjective well-being. *Current Directions in Psychological Science, 8*(5), 141–144.

Derks, P. (1987). Humor production: An examination of three models of creativity. *Journal of Creative Behavior, 21*, 325–326.

Derks, P., & Arora, S. (1993). Sex and salience in the appreciation of cartoon humor. *Humor: International Journal of Humor Research, 6*(1), 57–69.

Derks, P., & Berkowitz, J. (1989). Some determinants of attitudes toward a joker. *Humor: International Journal of Humor Research, 2*(4), 385–396.

Derks, P., Gardner, J. B., & Agarwal, R. (1998). Recall of innocent and tendentious humorous material. *Humor: International Journal of Humor Research, 11*(1), 5–19.

Derks, P., Gillikin, L. S., Bartolome-Rull, D. S., & Bogart, E. H. (1997). Laughter and electroencephalographic activity. *Humor: International Journal of Humor Research, 10*(3), 285–300.

Derks, P., & Hervas, D. (1988). Creativity in humor production: Quantity and quality in divergent thinking. *Bulletin of the Psychonomic Society, 26*(1), 37–39.

Derks, P., Kalland, S., & Etgen, M. (1995). The effect of joke type and audience response on the reaction to a joker: Replication and extension. *Humor: International Journal of Humor Research, 8*(4), 327–337.

Derks, P., Staley, R. E., & Haselton, M. G. (1998). "Sense" of humor: Perception, intelligence, or expertise? In W. Ruch (Ed.), *The sense of humor: Explorations of a personality characteristic* (pp. 143–158). Berlin, Germany: Walter de Gruyter & Co, 1998, x, 498.

Dewitte, S., & Verguts, T. (2001). Being funny: A selectionist account of humor production. *Humor: International Journal of Humor Research, 14*(1), 37–53.

Dews, S., Kaplan, J., & Winner, E. (1995). Why not say it directly? The social functions of irony. *Discourse Processes, 19*(3), 347–367.

Dews, S., Winner, E., Kaplan, J., Rosenblatt, E., Hunt, M., Lim, K., et al. (1996). Children's understanding of the meaning and functions of verbal irony. *Child Development, 67*(6), 3071–3085.

Dienstbier, R. A. (1995). The impact of humor on energy, tension, task choices, and attributions: Exploring hypotheses from toughness theory. *Motivation & Emotion, 19*(4), 255–267.

Dillon, K. M., Minchoff, B., & Baker, K. H. (1985). Positive emotional states and enhancement of the immune system. *International Journal of Psychiatry in Medicine, 15*(1), 13–18.

Dillon, K. M., & Totten, M. C. (1989). Psychological factors, immunocompetence, and health of breast-feeding mothers and their infants. *Journal of Genetic Psychology, 150*(2), 155–162.

Dixon, N. F. (1980). Humor: A cognitive alternative to stress? In I. G. Sarason & C. D. Spielberger (Eds.), *Stress and anxiety* (Vol. 7, pp. 281–289). Washington, DC: Hemisphere.

D'Onofrio, B. M., Turkheimer, E. N., Eaves, L. J., Corey, L. A., Berg, K., Solaas, M. H., et al. (2003). The role of the Children of Twins design in elucidating causal relations between parent characteristics and child outcomes. *Journal of Child Psychology & Psychiatry, 44*(8), 1130–1144.

Donoghue, E. E., McCarrey, M. W., & Clement, R. (1983). Humour appreciation as a function of canned laughter, a mirthful companion, and field dependence: Facilitation and inhibitory effects. *Canadian Journal of Behavioural Science, 15*(2), 150–162.

Doris, J., & Fierman, E. (1956). Humor and anxiety. *Journal of Abnormal & Social Psychology, 53*, 59–62.

Doris, P. (2004). *The humor styles questionnaire: Investigating the role of humor in psychological well-being.* Unpublished doctoral dissertation, University of Western Ontario, London, Ontario.

Dorz, S., Novara, C., Sica, C., & Sanavio, E. (2003). Predicting burnout among HIV/AIDS and oncology health care workers. *Psychology & Health, 18*(5), 677–684.

du Pre, A. (1998). *Humor and the healing arts: A multimethod analysis of humor use in health care.* Mahwah, NJ: Lawrence Erlbaum Associates.

Duchowny, M. S. (1983). Pathological disorders of laughter. In P. E. McGhee & J. H. Goldstein (Eds.), *Handbook of humor research, Vol. 2: Applied studies* (pp. 89–108). New York: Springer-Verlag.

Dunbar, R. I. M. (1996). *Grooming, gossip and the evolution of language.* London: Faber and Faber.

Duncan, C. P., & Nelson, J. E. (1985). Effects of humor in a radio advertising experiment. *Journal of Advertising, 14*(2), 33–40.

Duncan, C. P., Nelson, J. E., & Frontzak, N. L. (1984). The effect of humor on advertising comprehension. In T. C. Kinnear (Ed.), *Advances in consumer research* (pp. 432–437). Chicago: Association for Consumer Research.

Duncan, W. J., & Feisal, J. P. (1989). No laughing matter: Patterns of humor in the workplace. *Organizational Dynamics, 17*(4), 18–30.

Duncan, W. J., Smeltzer, L. R., & Leap, T. L. (1990). Humor and work: Applications of joking behavior to management. *Journal of Management, 16*(2), 255–278.

Dworkin, E. S., & Efran, J. S. (1967). The angered: Their susceptibility to varieties of humor. *Journal of Personality & Social Psychology, 6*(2), 233–236.

Dwyer, T. (1991). Humor, power, and change in organizations. *Human Relations, 44*(1), 1–19.

Eagly, A. H., Ashmore, R. D., Makhijani, M. G., & Longo, L. C. (1991). What is beautiful is good, but . . . : A meta-analytic review of research on the physical attractiveness stereotype. *Psychological Bulletin, 110*, 109–128.

Eastman, M. (1936). *Enjoyment of laughter.* New York: Simon and Schuster.

Ekman, P., Davidson, R. J., & Friesen, W. V. (1990). The Duchenne smile: Emotional expression and brain physiology: II. *Journal of Personality & Social Psychology, 58*(2), 342–353.

Ekman, P., & Friesen, W. V. (1978). *Facial action coding system.* Palo Alto, CA: Consulting Psychologists Press.

Ellis, A. (1977). Fun as psychotherapy. *Rational Living, 12*(1), 2–6.

Ellis, A., & Grieger, R. (1986). *Handbook of rational-emotive therapy.* New York: Springer.

Engel, G. L. (1977). The need for a new medical model: A challenge for biomedicine. *Science, 196*(4286), 129–136.

Epstein, S., & Smith, R. (1956). Repression and insight as related to reaction to cartoons. *Journal of Consulting Psychology, 20*, 391–395.

Ervin-Tripp, S. M. (1993). Conversational discourse. In J. B. Gleason & N. B. Ratner (Eds.), *Psycholinguistics* (pp. 237–270). Fort Worth, TX: Harcourt Brace Jovanovich.

Esler, M. D. (1998). Mental stress, panic disorder and the heart. *Stress Medicine, 14*(4), 237–243.

Eysenck, H. J. (1942). The appreciation of humour: an experimental and theoretical study. *British Journal of Psychology, 32*, 295–309.

Eysenck, H. J. (1943). An experimental analysis of five tests of "appreciation of humor." *Educational & Psychological Measurement, 3*, 191–214.

Eysenck, H. J. (1972). Foreword. In J. H. Goldstein & P. E. McGhee (Eds.), *The psychology of humor: Theoretical perspectives and empirical issues* (pp. xii-xvii). New York: Academic Press.

Eysenck, H. J. (1990). Biological dimensions of personality. In L. A. Pervin (Ed.), *Handbook of personality: Theory and research* (pp. 244–276). New York: Guilford.

Fabrizi, M. S., & Pollio, H. R. (1987a). Are funny teenagers creative? *Psychological Reports, 61*(3), 751–761.

Fabrizi, M. S., & Pollio, H. R. (1987b). A naturalistic study of humorous activity in a third, seventh, and eleventh grade classroom. *Merrill-Palmer Quarterly, 33*(1), 107–128.

Fagen, R. (1981). *Animal play behavior.* New York: Oxford University Press.

Farrelly, F., & Brandsma, J. (1974). *Provocative therapy.* Cupertino, CA: Meta Publications.

Farrelly, F., & Lynch, M. (1987). Humor in provocative therapy. In W. F. Fry & W. A. Salameh (Eds.), *Handbook of humor and psychotherapy: Advances in the clinical use of humor* (pp. 81–106). Sarasota, FL: Professional Resource Exchange.

Feingold, A. (1981). Testing equity as an explanation for romantic couples "mismatched" on physical attractiveness. *Psychological Reports, 49*(1), 247–250.

Feingold, A. (1982). Measuring humor: A pilot study. *Perceptual & Motor Skills, 54*(3, Pt 1), 986.

Feingold, A. (1983). Measuring humor ability: Revision and construct validation of the Humor Perceptiveness Test. *Perceptual & Motor Skills, 56*(1), 159–166.

Feingold, A. (1992). Gender differences in mate selection preferences: A test of the parental investment model. *Psychological Bulletin, 112*(1), 125–139.

Feingold, A., & Mazzella, R. (1991). Psychometric intelligence and verbal humor ability. *Personality & Individual Differences, 12*(5), 427–435.

Feingold, A., & Mazzella, R. (1993). Preliminary validation of a multidimensional model of wittiness. *Journal of Personality, 61*(3), 439–456.

Felmlee, D. H. (1995). Fatal attractions: Affection and disaffection in intimate relationships. *Journal of Social & Personal Relationships, 12*(2), 295–311.

Ferris, D. R. (1972). Humor and creativity: Research and theory. *Journal of Creative Behavior, 6*, 75–79.

Fine, G. A. (1977). Humour in situ: The role of humour in small group culture. In A. J. Chapman & H. C. Foot (Eds.), *It's a funny thing, humour* (pp. 315–318). Oxford: Pergamon Press.

Fisher, S., & Fisher, R. L. (1981). *Pretend the world is funny and forever: A psychological analysis of comedians, clowns, and actors.* Hillsdale, NJ: Erlbaum.

Flugel, J. C. (1954). Humor and laughter. In G. Lindzey (Ed.), *Handbook of social psychology.* Cambridge, MA: Addison-Wesley.

Fogel, A., Dickson, K. L., Hsu, H.-C., Messinger, D., Nelson-Goens, G. C., & Nwokah, E. E. (1997). Communication of smiling and laughter in mother-infant play: Research on emotion from a dynamic systems perspective. In K. C. Barrett (Ed.), *The communication of emotion: Current research from diverse perspectives* (pp. 5–24). San Francisco, CA: Jossey-Bass.

Foley, E., Matheis, R., & Schaefer, C. (2002). Effect of forced laughter on mood. *Psychological Reports, 90*(1), 184.

Forabosco, G. (1992). Cognitive aspects of the humor process: The concept of incongruity. *Humor: International Journal of Humor Research, 5*(1–2), 45–68.

Forabosco, G. (1994). "Seriality" and appreciation of jokes. *Humor: International Journal of Humor Research, 7*(4), 351–375.

Forabosco, G. (1998). The ill side of humor: Pathological conditions and sense of humor. In W. Ruch (Ed.), *The sense of humor: Explorations of a personality characteristic* (pp. 271–292). Berlin, Germany: Walter de Gruyter.

Forabosco, G., & Ruch, W. (1994). Sensation seeking, social attitudes and humor appreciation in Italy. *Personality & Individual Differences, 16*(4), 515–528.

Ford, C. V., & Spaulding, R. C. (1973). The Pueblo incident: A comparison of factors related to coping with extreme stress. *Archives of General Psychiatry, 29*(3), 340–343.

Ford, T. E. (2000). Effects of sexist humor on tolerance of sexist events. *Personality & Social Psychology Bulletin, 26*(9), 1094–1107.

Ford, T. E., & Ferguson, M. A. (2004). Social consequences of disparagement humor: A prejudiced norm theory. *Personality & Social Psychology Review, 8*(1), 79–94.

Ford, T. E., Ferguson, M. A., Brooks, J. L., & Hagadone, K. M. (2004). Coping sense of humor reduces effects of stereotype threat on women's math performance. *Personality & Social Psychology Bulletin*, *30*(5), 643–653.

Ford, T. E., Wentzel, E. R., & Lorion, J. (2001). Effects of exposure to sexist humor on perceptions of normative tolerance of sexism. *European Journal of Social Psychology*, *31*(6), 677–691.

Forester, J. (2004). Responding to critical moments with humor, recognition, and hope. *Negotiation Journal*, *20*(2), 221–237.

Fortson, S. B., & Brown, W. E. (1998). Best and worst university instructors: The opinions of graduate students. *College Student Journal*, *32*(4), 572–576.

Foster, J. A., & Reid, J. (1983). Humor and its relationship to students' assessments of the counsellor. *Canadian Counsellor*, *17*(3), 124–129.

Foster, P. S., Webster, D. G., & Williamson, J. (2002). The psychophysiological differentiation of actual, imagined, and recollected mirth. *Imagination, Cognition & Personality*, *22*(2), 163–180.

Fraley, B., & Aron, A. (2004). The effect of a shared humorous experience on closeness in initial encounters. *Personal Relationships*, *11*(1), 61–78.

Francis, L. E. (1994). Laughter, the best mediation: Humor as emotion management in interaction. *Symbolic Interaction*, *17*(2), 147–163.

Frank, M. G., & Ekman, P. (1993). Not all smiles are created equal: The differences between enjoyment and nonenjoyment smiles. *Humor: International Journal of Humor Research*, *6*(1), 9–26.

Frankl, V. E. (1960). Paradoxical intention: A logotherapeutic technique. *American Journal of Psychotherapy*, *14*, 520–535.

Frankl, V. E. (1984). *Man's search for meaning*. New York: Washington Square Press.

Franzini, L. R. (2000). Humor in behavior therapy. *Behavior Therapist*, *23*(2), 25–29, 41.

Franzini, L. R. (2001). Humor in therapy: The case for training therapists in its uses and risks. *Journal of General Psychology*, *128*(2), 170–193.

Fredrickson, B. L. (1998). What good are positive emotions? *Review of General Psychology*, *2*(3), 300–319.

Fredrickson, B. L. (2001). The role of positive emotions in positive psychology: The broaden-and-build theory of positive emotions. *American Psychologist*, *56*(3), 218–226.

Fredrickson, B. L., & Branigan, C. (2005). Positive emotions broaden the scope of attention and thought-action repertoires. *Cognition & Emotion*, *19*(3), 313–332.

Fredrickson, B. L., & Levenson, R. W. (1998). Positive emotions speed recovery from the cardiovascular sequelae of negative emotions. *Cognition & Emotion*, *12*(2), 191–220.

Fredrickson, B. L., Mancuso, R. A., Branigan, C., & Tugade, M. M. (2000). The undoing effect of positive emotions. *Motivation and Emotion*, *24*(4), 237–258.

Freiheit, S. R., Overholser, J. C., & Lehnert, K. L. (1998). The association between humor and depression in adolescent psychiatric inpatients and high school students. *Journal of Adolescent Research*, *13*(1), 32–48.

Freud, S. (1928). Humour. *International Journal of Psychoanalysis*, *9*, 1–6.

Freud, S. (1935). *A general introduction to psycho-analysis*. New York: Liveright Publishing.

Freud, S. (1960 [1905]). *Jokes and their relation to the unconscious*. New York: Norton.

Frewen, P. A., Brinker, J., Martin, R. A., & Dozois, D. J. A. (in press). Humor styles and personality-vulnerability to depression. *Humor: International Journal of Humor Research*.

Fridlund, A. J., & Loftis, J. M. (1990). Relations between tickling and humorous laughter: Preliminary support for the Darwin-Hecker hypothesis. *Biological Psychology, 30*(2), 141–150.

Fried, I., Wilson, C. L., MacDonald, K. A., & Behnke, E. J. (1998). Electric current stimulates laughter. *Nature, 391*(66–68), 650.

Friedman, H. S., Tucker, J. S., Tomlinson-Keasey, C., Schwartz, J. E., et al. (1993). Does childhood personality predict longevity? *Journal of Personality & Social Psychology, 65*(1), 176–185.

Fry, D. P. (2005). Rough-and-tumble social play in humans. In A. D. Pellegrini & P. K. Smith (Eds.), *The nature of play: Great apes and humans* (pp. 54–85). New York: Guilford Press.

Fry, P. S. (1995). Perfectionism, humor, and optimism as moderators of health outcomes and determinants of coping styles of women executives. *Genetic, Social, & General Psychology Monographs, 121*(2), 211–245.

Fry, W. F. (1963). *Sweet madness: A study of humor*. Palo Alto, CA: Pacific Books.

Fry, W. F. (1994). The biology of humor. *Humor: International Journal of Humor Research, 7*(2), 111–126.

Fry, W. F., & Rader, C. (1977). The respiratory components of mirthful laughter. *Journal of Biological Psychology, 19*(2), 39–50.

Fry, W. F., & Salameh, W. A. (Eds.). (1987). *Handbook of humor and psychotherapy: Advances in the clinical use of humor*. Sarasota, FL: Professional Resource Exchange.

Fry, W. F., & Salameh, W. A. (Eds.). (1993). *Advances in humor and psychotherapy*. Sarasota, FL: Professional Resource Press.

Führ, M. (2001). Some aspects of form and function of humor in adolescence. *Humor: International Journal of Humor Research, 14*(1), 25–36.

Führ, M. (2002). Coping humor in early adolescence. *Humor: International Journal of Humor Research, 15*(3), 283–304.

Fuller, R. G., & Sheehy-Skeffington, A. (1974). Effects of group laughter on responses to humorous material: A replication and extension. *Psychological Reports, 35*(1, Pt 2), 531–534.

Gallivan, J. (1992). Group differences in appreciation of feminist humor. *Humor: International Journal of Humor Research, 5*(4), 369–374.

Galloway, G., & Cropley, A. (1999). Benefits of humor for mental health: Empirical findings and directions for further research. *Humor: International Journal of Humor Research, 12*(3), 301–314.

Gamble, J. (2001). Humor in apes. *Humor: International Journal of Humor Research, 14*(2), 163–179.

Garner, B. P. (1998). Play development from birth to age four. In D. P. Fromberg & D. Bergen (Eds.), *Play from birth to twelve and beyond: Contexts, perspectives, and meanings* (pp. 137–145). New York: Garland.

Gavanski, I. (1986). Differential sensitivity of humor ratings and mirth responses to cognitive and affective components of the humor response. *Journal of Personality & Social Psychology, 51*(1), 209–214.

Gelb, B. D., & Zinkhan, G. M. (1986). Humor and advertising effectiveness after repeated exposures to a radio commerical. *Journal of Advertising, 15*(2), 15–20.

Gelkopf, M., & Kreitler, S. (1996). Is humor only fun, an alternative cure or magic: The cognitive therapeutic potential of humor. *Journal of Cognitive Psychotherapy, 10*(4), 235–254.

Gelkopf, M., Kreitler, S., & Sigal, M. (1993). Laughter in a psychiatric ward: Somatic, emotional, social, and clinical influences on schizophrenic patients. *Journal of Nervous & Mental Disease, 181*(5), 283–289.

Gelkopf, M., & Sigal, M. (1995). It is not enough to have them laugh: Hostility, anger, and humor-coping in schizophrenic patients. *Humor: International Journal of Humor Research*, *8*(3), 273–284.

Gerber, W. S., & Routh, D. K. (1975). Humor response as related to violation of expectancies and to stimulus intensity in a weight-judgment task. *Perceptual & Motor Skills*, *41*(2), 673–674.

Gervais, M., & Wilson, D. S. (2005). The evolution and functions of laughter and humor: A synthetic approach. *Quarterly Review of Biology*, *80*(4), 395–430.

Gibbs, R. W. (1986). On the psycholinguistics of sarcasm. *Journal of Experimental Psychology: General*, *115*, 3–15.

Gibbs, R. W. (1994). *The poetics of mind*. Cambridge: Cambridge University Press.

Gibson, D. E. (1994). Humor consulting: Laughs for power and profit in organizations. *Humor: International Journal of Humor Research*, *7*(4), 403–428.

Gilbert, D. T., Fiske, S. T., & Lindzey, G. (1998). *The handbook of social psychology* (4th ed.). Boston: McGraw-Hill.

Gillikin, L. S., & Derks, P. L. (1991). Humor appreciation and mood in stroke patients. *Cognitive Rehabilitation*, *9*(5), 30–35.

Giora, R. (1985). A text-based analysis of non-narrative texts. *Theoretical Linguistics*, *12*, 115–135.

Giora, R. (1991). On the cognitive aspects of the joke. *Journal of Pragmatics*, *16*, 465–485.

Giora, R. (1995). On irony and negation. *Discourse Processes*, *19*, 239–264.

Giora, R., & Fein, O. (1999). Irony comprehension: The graded salience hypothesis. *Humor: International Journal of Humor Research*, *12*(4), 425–436.

Giora, R., Fein, O., & Schwartz, T. (1998). Irony: Graded salience and indirect negation. *Metaphor and Symbol*, *13*, 83–101.

Godkewitsch, M. (1974). Correlates of humor: Verbal and nonverbal aesthetic reactions as functions of semantic distance within adjective-noun pairs. In D. E. Berlyne (Ed.), *Studies in the new experimental aesthetics: Steps towards an objective psychology of aesthetic appreciation* (pp. 279–304). Washington, DC: Hemisphere.

Godkewitsch, M. (1976). Physiological and verbal indices of arousal in rated humour. In A. J. Chapman & H. C. Foot (Eds.), *Humor and laughter: Theory, research, and applications* (pp. 117–138). London: John Wiley & Sons.

Goel, V., & Dolan, R. J. (2001). The functional anatomy of humor: Segregating cognitive and affective components. *Nature Neuroscience*, *4*(3), 237–238.

Goffman, E. (1967). *Interaction ritual: Essays on face-to-face behavior*. Garden City, NY: Anchor Books.

Goldsmith, H. H., Buss, K. A., & Lemery, K. S. (1997). Toddler and childhood temperament: Expanded content, stronger genetic evidence, new evidence for the importance of environment. *Developmental Psychology*, *33*(6), 891–905.

Goldsmith, H. H., Lemery, K. S., Buss, K. A., & Campos, J. J. (1999). Genetic analyses of focal aspects of infant temperament. *Developmental Psychology*, *35*(4), 972–985.

Goldstein, J. H. (1982). A laugh a day: Can mirth keep disease at bay? *The Sciences*, *22*(6), 21–25.

Goldstein, J. H., Harman, J., McGhee, P. E., & Karasik, R. (1975). Test of an information-processing model of humor: Physiological response changes during problem- and riddle-solving. *Journal of General Psychology*, *92*(1), 59–68.

Goldstein, J. H., & McGhee, P. E. (Eds.). (1972). *The psychology of humor: Theoretical perspectives and empirical issues*. Oxford, England: Academic Press.

Goldstein, J. H., Suls, J. M., & Anthony, S. (1972). Enjoyment of specific types of humor content: Motivation or salience? In J. H. Goldstein & P. E. McGhee (Eds.), *The psychology of humor: Theoretical perspectives and empirical issues* (pp. 159–171). New York: Academic Press.

Gollob, H. F., & Levine, J. (1967). Distraction as a factor in the enjoyment of aggressive humor. *Journal of Personality & Social Psychology, 5*(3), 368–372.

Goodenough, F. L. (1932). Expression of the emotions in a blind-deaf child. *Journal of Abnormal & Social Psychology, 27*, 328–333.

Goodwin, R. (1990). Sex differences among partner preferences: Are the sexes really very similar? *Sex Roles, 23*(9–10), 501–513.

Goodwin, R., & Tang, D. (1991). Preferences for friends and close relationships partners: A cross-cultural comparison. *Journal of Social Psychology, 131*(4), 579–581.

Gorham, J. (1988). The relationship between verbal teacher immediacy behaviors and student learning. *Communication Education, 37*(1), 40–53.

Gorham, J., & Christophel, D. M. (1990). The relationship of teachers' use of humor in the classroom to immediacy and student learning. *Communication Education, 39*(1), 46–62.

Gottman, J. M. (1993). The roles of conflict engagement, escalation, and avoidance in marital interaction: A longitudinal view of five types of couples. *Journal of Consulting & Clinical Psychology, 61*(1), 6–15.

Gottman, J. M. (1994). *What predicts divorce?: The relationship between marital processes and marital outcomes*. Hillsdale, NJ: Lawrence Erlbaum Associates.

Gottman, J. M., Coan, J., Carrere, S., & Swanson, C. (1998). Predicting marital happiness and stability from newlywed interactions. *Journal of Marriage and the Family, 60*, 5–22.

Gottman, J. M., & Levenson, R. W. (1999). Rebound from marital conflict and divorce prediction. *Family Process, 38*, 287–292.

Gould, S. J. (2002). *The structure of evolutionary theory*. Cambridge, MA: Harvard University Press.

Graeven, D. B., & Morris, S. J. (1975). College humor in 1930 and 1972: An investigation using the humor diary. *Sociology & Social Research, 59*(4), 406–410.

Graham, E. E., Papa, M. J., & Brooks, G. P. (1992). Functions of humor in conversation: Conceptualization and measurement. *Western Journal of Communication, 56*(2), 161–183.

Grammer, K. (1990). Strangers meet: Laughter and nonverbal signs of interest in opposite-sex encounters. *Journal of Nonverbal Behavior, 14*(4), 209–236.

Gray, J. A. (1994). Three fundamental emotion systems. In P. Ekman & R. J. Davidson (Eds.), *The nature of emotion: Fundamental questions* (pp. 243–247). New York: Oxford University Press.

Greenwood, D., & Isbell, L. M. (2002). Ambivalent sexism and the dumb blonde: Men's and women's reactions to sexist jokes. *Psychology of Women Quarterly, 26*, 341–350.

Gregory, J. C. (1924). *The nature of laughter*. Oxford, England: Harcourt, Brace.

Greig, J. Y. T. (1923). *The psychology of laughter and comedy*. New York: Dodd, Mead.

Groch, A. S. (1974). Generality of response to humor and wit in cartoons, jokes, stories, and photographs. *Psychological Reports, 35*, 835–838.

Gross, J. J., & Muñoz, R. F. (1995). Emotion regulation and mental health. *Clinical Psychology: Science & Practice, 2*(2), 151–164.

Grotjahn, M. (1966). *Beyond laughter: Humor and the subconscious*. New York, NY: McGraw-Hill.

Grotjahn, M. (1971). Laughter in group psychotherapy. *International Journal of Group Psychotherapy, 21*(2), 234–238.

Grugulis, I. (2002). Nothing serious? Candidates' use of humour in management training. *Human Relations, 55*(4), 387–406.

Gruner, C. R. (1967). Effect of humor on speaker ethos and audience information gain. *Journal of Communication, 17*(3), 228–233.

Gruner, C. R. (1976). Wit and humour in mass communication. In A. J. Chapman & H. C. Foot (Eds.), *Humor and laughter: Theory, research, and applications* (pp. 287–311). London: John Wiley & Sons.

Gruner, C. R. (1978). *Understanding laughter: The workings of wit and humor.* Chicago: Nelson-Hall.

Gruner, C. R. (1997). *The game of humor: A comprehensive theory of why we laugh.* New Brunswick, NJ: Transaction Publishers.

Grziwok, R., & Scodel, A. (1956). Some psychological correlates of humor preferences. *Journal of Consulting Psychology, 20*, 42.

Haellstroem, T., & Noppa, H. (1981). Obesity in women in relation to mental illness, social factors and personality traits. *Journal of Psychosomatic Research, 25*, 75–82.

Haig, R. A. (1988). *The anatomy of humor: Biopsychosocial and therapeutic perspectives.* Springfield, IL, England: Charles C Thomas, Publisher.

Hall, G. S., & Allin, A. (1897). The psychology of tickling, laughing, and the comic. *American Journal of Psychology, 9*(1), 1–44.

Hammes, J. A., & Wiggins, S. L. (1962). Manifest anxiety and appreciation of humor involving emotional content. *Perceptual & Motor Skills, 14*, 291–294.

Hampes, W. P. (1992). Relation between intimacy and humor. *Psychological Reports, 71*(1), 127–130.

Hampes, W. P. (1994). Relation between intimacy and the Multidimensional Sense of Humor Scale. *Psychological Reports, 74*(3, Pt 2), 1360–1362.

Hampes, W. P. (1999). The relationship between humor and trust. *Humor: International Journal of Humor Research, 12*(3), 253–259.

Hampes, W. P. (2001). Relation between humor and empathic concern. *Psychological Reports, 88*(1), 241–244.

Happé, F., Brownell, H., & Winner, E. (1999). Acquired "theory of mind" impairments following stroke. *Cognition, 70*(3), 211–240.

Harris, C. R. (1999). The mystery of ticklish laughter. *American Scientist, 87*(4), 344–351.

Harris, C. R., & Alvarado, N. (2005). Facial expressions, smile types, and self-report during humour, tickle, and pain. *Cognition & Emotion, 19*(5), 655–669.

Harris, C. R., & Christenfeld, N. (1997). Humour, tickle, and the Darwin-Hecker Hypothesis. *Cognition & Emotion, 11*(1), 103–110.

Harris, C. R., & Christenfeld, N. (1999). Can a machine tickle? *Psychonomic Bulletin & Review, 6*(3), 504–510.

Harrison, L. K., Carroll, D., Burns, V. E., Corkill, A. R., Harrison, C. M., Ring, C., et al. (2000). Cardiovascular and secretory immunoglobin A reactions to humorous, exciting, and didactic film presentations. *Biological Psychology, 52*(2), 113–126.

Hatch, M. J., & Ehrlich, S. B. (1993). Spontaneous humour as an indicator of paradox and ambiguity in organizations. *Organization Studies, 14*(4), 505–526.

Hauck, W. E., & Thomas, J. W. (1972). The relationship of humor to intelligence, creativity, and intentional and incidental learning. *Journal of Experimental Education, 40*(4), 52–55.

Hay, J. (2000). Functions of humor in the conversations of men and women. *Journal of Pragmatics, 32*(6), 709–742.

Hayashi, K., Hayashi, T., Iwanaga, S., Kawai, K., Ishii, H., Shoji, S. I., et al. (2003). Laughter lowered the increase in postpriandal blood glucose. *Diabetes Care, 26*(5), 1651–1652.

Hebb, D. O. (1955). Drives and the C.N.S. (Conceptual Nervous System). *Psychological Review, 62*, 243–254.

Hehl, F.-J., & Ruch, W. (1985). The location of sense of humor within comprehensive personality spaces: An exploratory study. *Personality & Individual Differences, 6*(6), 703–715.

Hehl, F.-J., & Ruch, W. (1990). Conservatism as a predictor of responses to humour: III. The prediction of appreciation of incongruity resolution based humour by content saturated attitude scales in five samples. *Personality & Individual Differences, 11*(5), 439–445.

Hemmasi, M., Graf, L. A., & Russ, G. S. (1994). Gender-related jokes in the workplace: Sexual humor or sexual harassment? *Journal of Applied Social Psychology, 24*(12), 1114–1128.

Henkin, B., & Fish, J. M. (1986). Gender and personality differences in the appreciation of cartoon humor. *Journal of Psychology, 120*(2), 157–175.

Henman, L. D. (2001). Humor as a coping mechanism: Lessons from POWs. *Humor: International Journal of Humor Research, 14*(1), 83–94.

Herzog, T. R., & Bush, B. A. (1994). The prediction of preference for sick humor. *Humor: International Journal of Humor Research, 7*(4), 323–340.

Herzog, T. R., & Karafa, J. A. (1998). Preferences for sick versus nonsick humor. *Humor: International Journal of Humor Research, 11*(3), 291–312.

Herzog, T. R., & Larwin, D. A. (1988). The appreciation of humor in captioned cartoons. *Journal of Psychology, 122*(6), 597–607.

Hickson, J. (1977). Differential responses of male and female counselor trainees to humor stimuli. *Southern Journal of Educational Research, 11*(1), 1–8.

Hillson, T. R., & Martin, R. A. (1994). What's so funny about that?: The domains-interaction approach as a model of incongruity and resolution in humor. *Motivation & Emotion, 18*(1), 1–29.

Hobden, K. L., & Olson, J. M. (1994). From jest to antipathy: Disparagement humor as a source of dissonance-motivated attitude change. *Basic & Applied Social Psychology, 15*(3), 239–249.

Holland, N. N. (1982). *Laughing: A psychology of humor.* Ithaca, NY: Cornell University Press.

Holmes, D. S. (1969). Sensing humor: Latency and amplitude of response related to MMPI profiles. *Journal of Consulting & Clinical Psychology, 33*(3), 296–301.

Holmes, J., & Marra, M. (2002a). Having a laugh at work: How humour contributes to workplace culture. *Journal of Pragmatics, 34*(12), 1683–1710.

Holmes, J., & Marra, M. (2002b). Over the edge? Subversive humor between colleagues and friends. *Humor: International Journal of Humor Research, 15*(1), 65–87.

House, J. S., Landis, K. R., & Umberson, D. (1988). Social relationships and health. *Science, 241*(4865), 540–545.

Hubert, W., & de Jong-Meyer, R. (1990). Psychophysiological response patterns to positive and negative film stimuli. *Biological Psychology, 31*, 73–93.

Hubert, W., & de Jong-Meyer, R. (1991). Autonomic, neuroendocrine, and subjective responses to emotion-inducing film stimuli. *International Journal of Psychophysiology, 11*, 131–140.

Hubert, W., Moeller, M., & de Jong-Meyer, R. (1993). Film-induced amusement changes in saliva cortisol levels. *Psychoneuroendocrinology, 18*(4), 265–272.

Iaffaldano, M. T., & Muchinsky, P. M. (1985). Job satisfaction and job performance: A meta-analysis. *Psychological Bulletin, 97*(2), 251–273.

Isen, A. M. (1993). Positive affect and decision making. In M. Lewis & J. M. Haviland (Eds.), *Handbook of emotions* (pp. 261–277). New York: Guilford.

Isen, A. M. (2003). Positive affect as a source of human strength. In L. G. Aspinwall & U. M. Staudinger (Eds.), *A psychology of human strengths: Fundamental questions and future directions for a positive psychology* (pp. 179–195). Washington, DC: American Psychological Association.

Isen, A. M., & Daubman, K. A. (1984). The influence of affect on categorization. *Journal of Personality and Social Psychology, 47,* 1206–1217.

Isen, A. M., Daubman, K. A., & Nowicki, G. P. (1987). Positive affect facilitates creative problem solving. *Journal of Personality and Social Psychology, 52,* 1122–1131.

Isen, A. M., Johnson, M. M. S., Mertz, E., & Robinson, G. F. (1985). The influence of positive affect on the unusualness of word associations. *Journal of Personality and Social Psychology, 48,* 1413–1426.

Itami, J., Nobori, M., & Texhima, H. (1994). Laughter and immunity. *Japanese Journal of Psychosomatic Medicine, 34,* 565–571.

Iwase, M., Ouchi, Y., Okada, H., Yokoyama, C., Nobezawa, S., Yoshikawa, E., et al. (2002). Neural substrates of human facial expression of pleasant emotion induced by comic films: A PET study. *NeuroImage, 17,* 758–768.

Janes, L. M., & Olson, J. M. (2000). Jeer pressures: The behavioral effects of observing ridicule of others. *Personality & Social Psychology Bulletin, 26*(4), 474–485.

Janus, S. S. (1975). The great comedians: Personality and other factors. *American Journal of Psychoanalysis, 35*(2), 169–174.

Janus, S. S., Bess, B. E., & Janus, B. R. (1978). The great comediennes: Personality and other factors. *American Journal of Psychoanalysis, 38*(4), 367–372.

John, O. P. (1990). The "Big Five" factor taxonomy: Dimensions of personality in the natural language and in questionnaires. In L. A. Pervin (Ed.), *Handbook of personality: Theory and research* (pp. 66–100). New York: Guilford.

Johnson, A. K., & Anderson, E. A. (1990). Stress and arousal. In J. T. Cacioppo & L. G. Tassinary (Eds.), *Principles of psychophysiology: Physical, social, and inferential elements* (pp. 216–252). Cambridge, England: Cambridge University Press.

Johnson, H. A. (1990). Humor as an innovative method for teaching sensitive topics. *Educational Gerontology, 16*(6), 547–559.

Johnson, K. E., & Mervis, C. B. (1997). First steps in the emergence of verbal humor: A case study. *Infant Behavior & Development, 20*(2), 187–196.

Jones, E. E. (1990). *Interpersonal perception.* New York: W. H. Freeman.

Jones, J. A. (2005). The masking effects of humor on audience perception of message organization. *Humor: International Journal of Humor Research, 18*(4), 405–417.

Jones, J. M., & Harris, P. E. (1971). Psychophysiological correlates of cartoon humor appreciation. *Proceedings of the Annual Convention of the American Psychological Association, 6,* 381–382.

Judge, T. A., Thoresen, C. J., Bono, J. E., & Patton, G. K. (2001). The job satisfaction–job performance relationship: A qualitative and quantitative review. *Psychological Bulletin, 127*(3), 376–407.

Kallen, H. M. (1968). *Liberty, laughter and tears: Reflection on the relations of comedy and tragedy to human freedom.* DeKalb, IL: Northern Illinois University Press.

Kamei, T., Kumano, H., & Masumura, S. (1997). Changes of immunoregulatory cells associated with psychological stress and humor. *Perceptual & Motor Skills, 84*(3, Pt 2), 1296–1298.

Kane, T. R., Suls, J., & Tedeschi, J. T. (1977). Humour as a tool of social interaction. In A. J. Chapman & H. C. Foot (Eds.), *It's a funny thing, humour* (pp. 13–16). Oxford: Pergamon Press.

Kantor, M. (1992). *The human dimension of depression: A practical guide to diagnosis, understanding, and treatment.* New York: Praeger.

Kaplan, R. M., & Pascoe, G. C. (1977). Humorous lectures and humorous examples: Some effects upon comprehension and retention. *Journal of Educational Psychology, 69*(1), 61–65.

Kataria, M. (2002). *Laugh for no reason* (2nd ed.). Mumbai, India: Madhuri International.

Katz, A. N., Blasko, D. G., & Kazmerski, V. A. (2004). Saying what you don't mean: Social influences on sarcastic language processing. *Current Directions in Psychological Science, 13*(5), 186–189.

Katz, B. F. (1993). A neural resolution of the incongruity-resolution and incongruity theories of humour. *Connection Science, 5*(1), 59–75.

Kazarian, S. S., & Martin, R. A. (2004). Humor styles, personality, and well-being among Lebanese university students. *European Journal of Personality, 18*(3), 209–219.

Kazarian, S. S., & Martin, R. A. (in press). Humor styles, culture-related personality, well-being, and family adjustment among Armenians in Lebanon. *Humor: International Journal of Humor Research.*

Keith-Spiegel, P. (1972). Early conceptions of humor: Varieties and issues. In J. H. Goldstein & P. E. McGhee (Eds.), *The psychology of humor: Theoretical perspectives and empirical issues* (pp. 3–39). New York: Academic Press.

Kelley, D. H., & Gorham, J. (1988). Effects of immediacy on recall of information. *Communication Education, 37*(3), 198–207.

Kelley, H. H. (1972). Attribution theory in social interaction. In E. E. Jones, D. E. Kanouse & H. H. Kelley (Eds.), *Attribution: Perceiving the causes of behavior* (pp. 1–26). Morristown, NJ: General Learning Press.

Kellogg, R. T. (1995). *Cognitive psychology.* Thousand Oaks, CA: Sage Publications.

Kelly, W. E. (2002). An investigation of worry and sense of humor. *Journal of Psychology, 136*(6), 657–666.

Keltner, D., & Bonanno, G. A. (1997). A study of laughter and dissociation: Distinct correlates of laughter and smiling during bereavement. *Journal of Personality & Social Psychology, 73*(4), 687–702.

Keltner, D., Capps, L., Kring, A. M., Young, R. C., & Heerey, E. A. (2001). Just teasing: A conceptual analysis and empirical review. *Psychological Bulletin, 127*(2), 229–248.

Keltner, D., Young, R. C., Heerey, E. A., Oemig, C., & Monarch, N. D. (1998). Teasing in hierarchical and intimate relations. *Journal of Personality and Social Psychology, 75*(5), 1231–1247.

Kennedy, S., Glaser, R., & Kiecolt-Glaser, J. (1990). Psychoneuroimmunology. In J. T. Cacioppo & L. G. Tassinary (Eds.), *Principles of psychophysiology: Physical, social, and inferential elements* (pp. 177–190). Cambridge, England: Cambridge University Press.

Kenny, D. T. (1955). The contingency of humor appreciation on the stimulus-confirmation of joke-ending expectations. *Journal of Abnormal & Social Psychology, 51*, 644–648.

Kenrick, D. T., Sadalla, E. K., Groth, G., & Trost, M. R. (1990). Evolution, traits, and the stages of the parental investment model. *Journal of Personality, 58*, 97–117.

Kerkkänen, P., Kuiper, N. A., & Martin, R. A. (2004). Sense of humor, physical health, and well-being at work: A three-year longitudinal study of Finnish police officers. *Humor: International Journal of Humor Research, 17*(1–2), 21–35.

Kiecolt-Glaser, J. K., & Newton, T. L. (2001). Marriage and health: His and hers. *Psychological Bulletin, 127*(4), 472–503.

Killinger, B. (1987). Humor in psychotherapy: A shift to a new perspective. In W. F. Fry & W. A. Salameh (Eds.), *Handbook of humor and psychotherapy: Advances in the clinical use of humor* (pp. 21–40). Sarasota, FL: Professional Resource Exchange.

Kimata, H. (2001). Effect of humor on allergen-induced wheal reactions. *JAMA: Journal of the American Medical Association, 285*(6), 737.

Kimata, H. (2004a). Differential effects of laughter on allergen-specific immunoglobulin and neurotrophin levels in tears. *Perceptual & Motor Skills, 98*(3, Pt 1), 901–908.

Kimata, H. (2004b). Effect of viewing a humorous vs. nonhumorous film on bronchial responsiveness in patients with bronchial asthma. *Physiology & Behavior, 81*(4), 681–684.

Kintsch, W., & Bates, E. (1977). Recognition memory for statements from a classroom lecture. *Journal of Experimental Psychology: Human Learning and Memory, 3*, 150–159.

Kipper, S., & Todt, D. (2001). Variation of sound parameters affects the evaluation of human laughter. *Behaviour, 138*(9), 1161–1178.

Kipper, S., & Todt, D. (2003a). Dynamic-acoustic variation causes differences in evaluations of laughter. *Perceptual & Motor Skills, 96*(3), 799–809.

Kipper, S., & Todt, D. (2003b). The Role of Rhythm and Pitch in the Evaluation of Human Laughter. *Journal of Nonverbal Behavior, 27*(4), 255–272.

Kirsh, G. A., & Kuiper, N. A. (2003). Positive and negative aspects of sense of humor: Associations with the constructs of individualism and relatedness. *Humor: International Journal of Humor Research, 16*(1), 33–62.

Klein, A. J. (1985). Humor comprehension and humor appreciation of cognitively oriented humor: A study of kindergarten children. *Child Study Journal, 15*(4), 223–235.

Klein, D. M., Bryant, J., & Zillmann, D. (1982). Relationship between humor in introductory textbooks and students' evaluations of the texts' appeal and effectiveness. *Psychological Reports, 50*(1), 235–241.

Kline, P. (1977). The psychoanalytic theory of humour and laughter. In A. J. Chapman & H. C. Foot (Eds.), *It's a funny thing, humour* (pp. 7–12). Oxford: Pergamon Press.

Knox, I. (1951). Towards a philosophy of humor. *Journal of Philosophy, 48*, 541–548.

Koestler, A. (1964). *The act of creation.* London: Hutchinson.

Köhler, G., & Ruch, W. (1996). Sources of variance in current sense of humor inventories: How much substance, how much method variance? *Humor: International Journal of Humor Research, 9*(3/4), 363–397.

Koppel, M. A., & Sechrest, L. (1970). A multitrait-multimethod matrix analysis of sense of humor. *Educational & Psychological Measurement, 30*(1), 77–85.

Korb, L. J. (1988). Humor: A tool for the psychoanalyst. *Issues in Ego Psychology, 11*(2), 45–54.

Korotkov, D., & Hannah, T. E. (1994). Extraversion and emotionality as proposed superordinate stress moderators: A prospective analysis. *Personality & Individual Differences, 16*(5), 787–792.

Kowalski, R. M., Howerton, E., & McKenzie, M. (2001). Permitted disrespect: Teasing in interpersonal interactions. In R. M. Kowalski (Ed.), *Behaving badly: Aversive behaviors in interpersonal relationships* (pp. 177–202). Washington, DC: American Psychological Association.

Kubie, L. S. (1970). The destructive potential of humor in psychotherapy. *American Journal of Psychiatry, 127*(7), 861–866.

Kuhlman, T. L. (1984). *Humor and psychotherapy.* Homewood, IL: Dow Jones–Irwin Dorsey Professional Books.

Kuhlman, T. L. (1985). A study of salience and motivational theories of humor. *Journal of Personality & Social Psychology, 49*(1), 281–286.

Kuiper, N. A., & Borowicz-Sibenik, M. (2005). A good sense of humor doesn't always help: Agency and communion as moderators of psychological well-being. *Personality & Individual Differences, 38*(2), 365–377.

Kuiper, N. A., Grimshaw, M., Leite, C., & Kirsh, G. A. (2004). Humor is not always the best medicine: Specific components of sense of humor and psychological well-being. *Humor: International Journal of Humor Research, 17*(1–2), 135–168.

Kuiper, N. A., & Martin, R. A. (1993). Humor and self-concept. *Humor: International Journal of Humor Research, 6*(3), 251–270.

Kuiper, N. A., & Martin, R. A. (1998a). Is sense of humor a positive personality characteristic? In W. Ruch (Ed.), *The sense of humor: Explorations of a personality characteristic* (pp. 159–178). Berlin, Germany: Walter de Gruyter.

Kuiper, N. A., & Martin, R. A. (1998b). Laughter and stress in daily life: Relation to positive and negative affect. *Motivation & Emotion, 22*(2), 133–153.

Kuiper, N. A., Martin, R. A., & Dance, K. A. (1992). Sense of humour and enhanced quality of life. *Personality & Individual Differences, 13*(12), 1273–1283.

Kuiper, N. A., Martin, R. A., & Olinger, L. J. (1993). Coping humour, stress, and cognitive appraisals. *Canadian Journal of Behavioural Science, 25*(1), 81–96.

Kuiper, N. A., Martin, R. A., Olinger, L. J., Kazarian, S. S., & Jette, J. L. (1998). Sense of humor, self-concept, and psychological well-being in psychiatric inpatients. *Humor: International Journal of Humor Research, 11*(4), 357–381.

Kuiper, N. A., McKenzie, S. D., & Belanger, K. A. (1995). Cognitive appraisals and individual differences in sense of humor: Motivational and affective implications. *Personality & Individual Differences, 19*(3), 359–372.

Kuiper, N. A., & Nicholl, S. (2004). Thoughts of feeling better? Sense of humor and physical health. *Humor: International Journal of Humor Research, 17*(1–2), 37–66.

Kuiper, N. A., & Olinger, L. J. (1998). Humor and mental health. In H. S. Friedman (Ed.), *Encyclopedia of mental health* (Vol. 2, pp. 445–457). San Diego, CA: Academic Press.

Kush, J. C. (1997). Relationship between humor appreciation and counselor self-perceptions. *Counseling & Values, 42*(1), 22–29.

Kushner, M. (1990). The light touch: How to use humor for business success. In. New York: Simon & Schuster.

La Fave, L. (1972). Humor judgments as a function of reference groups and identification classes. In J. H. Goldstein & P. E. McGhee (Eds.), *The psychology of humor: Theoretical perspectives and empirical issues* (pp. 195–210). New York: Academic Press.

La Fave, L., Haddad, J., & Maesen, W. A. (1976). Superiority, enhanced self-esteem, and perceived incongruity humour theory. In A. J. Chapman & H. C. Foot (Eds.), *Humor and laughter: Theory, research, and applications* (pp. 63–91). London: John Wiley & Sons.

La Fave, L., Haddad, J., & Marshall, N. (1974). Humor judgments as a function of identification classes. *Sociology & Social Research, 58*(2), 184–194.

La Gaipa, J. J. (1977). The effects of humour on the flow of social conversation. In A. J. Chapman & H. C. Foot (Eds.), *It's a funny thing, humour* (pp. 421–427). Oxford: Pergamon Press.

Labott, S. M., Ahleman, S., Wolever, M. E., & Martin, R. B. (1990). The physiological and psychological effects of the expression and inhibition of emotion. *Behavioral Medicine, 16*(4), 182–189.

Labott, S. M., & Martin, R. B. (1987). The stress-moderating effects of weeping and humor. *Journal of Human Stress, 13*(4), 159–164.

Labott, S. M., & Martin, R. B. (1990). Emotional coping, age, and physical disorder. *Behavioral Medicine, 16*(2), 53–61.

Lamb, C. W. (1968). Personality correlates of humor enjoyment following motivational arousal. *Journal of Personality & Social Psychology, 9*(3), 237–241.

Lambert, R. B., & Lambert, N. K. (1995). The effects of humor on secretory Immunoglobulin A levels in school-aged children. *Pediatric Nursing, 21*, 16–19.

Lampert, M. D., & Ervin-Tripp, S. M. (1998). Exploring paradigms: The study of gender and sense of humor near the end of the 20th century. In W. Ruch (Ed.), *The sense of humor: Explorations of a personality characteristic* (pp. 231–270). Berlin, Germany: Walter de Gruyter.

Landis, C., & Ross, J. W. H. (1933). Humor and its relation to other personality traits. *Journal of Social Psychology, 4*, 156–175.

Landy, D., & Mettee, D. (1969). Evaluation of an aggressor as a function of exposure to cartoon humor. *Journal of Personality & Social Psychology, 12*(1), 66–71.

Langevin, R., & Day, H. I. (1972). Physiological correlates of humor. In J. H. Goldstein & P. E. McGhee (Eds.), *The psychology of humor: Theoretical perspectives and empirical issues* (pp. 129–142). New York: Academic Press.

Lauer, R. H., Lauer, J. C., & Kerr, S. T. (1990). The long-term marriage: Perceptions of stability and satisfaction. *International Journal of Aging & Human Development, 31*(3), 189–195.

Lazarus, R. S. (1991). Cognition and motivation in emotion. *American Psychologist, 46*(4), 352–367.

Lazarus, R. S., & Folkman, S. (1984). *Stress, appraisal, and coping.* New York: Springer.

Leacock, S. B. (1935). *Humor: Its theory and technique.* New York: Dodd, Mead.

Leak, G. K. (1974). Effects of hostility arousal and aggressive humor on catharsis and humor preference. *Journal of Personality & Social Psychology, 30*(6), 736–740.

Leber, D. A., & Vanoli, E. G. (2001). Therapeutic use of humor: Occupational therapy clinicians' perceptions and practices. *American Journal of Occupational Therapy, 55*(2), 221–226.

LeDoux, J. E. (1994). Emotion-specific physiological activity: Don't forget about CNS physiology. In P. Ekman & R. J. Davidson (Eds.), *The nature of emotion: Fundamental questions* (pp. 248–251). New York: Oxford University Press.

Lefcourt, H. M. (2001). *Humor: The psychology of living buoyantly.* New York: Kluwer Academic.

Lefcourt, H. M., Davidson, K., Prkachin, K. M., & Mills, D. E. (1997). Humor as a stress moderator in the prediction of blood pressure obtained during five stressful tasks. *Journal of Research in Personality, 31*(4), 523–542.

Lefcourt, H. M., Davidson, K., Shepherd, R., & Phillips, M. (1997). Who likes "Far Side" humor? *Humor: International Journal of Humor Research, 10*(4), 439–452.

Lefcourt, H. M., Davidson, K., Shepherd, R., Phillips, M., Prkachin, K. M., & Mills, D. E. (1995). Perspective-taking humor: Accounting for stress moderation. *Journal of Social & Clinical Psychology, 14*(4), 373–391.

Lefcourt, H. M., Davidson-Katz, K., & Kueneman, K. (1990). Humor and immune-system functioning. *Humor: International Journal of Humor Research, 3*(3), 305–321.

Lefcourt, H. M., & Martin, R. A. (1986). *Humor and life stress: Antidote to adversity.* New York: Springer-Verlag.

Lefort, B. (1992). Structure of verbal jokes and comprehension in young children. *Humor: International Journal of Humor Research, 5*(1–2), 149–163.

Lehman, K. M., Burke, K. L., Martin, R., Sultan, J., & Czech, D. R. (2001). A reformulation of the moderating effects of productive humor. *Humor: International Journal of Humor Research, 14*(2), 131–161.

Lemma, A. (1999). *Humour on the couch: Exploring humour in psychotherapy and everyday life.* London, England: Whurr Publishers, Ltd.

Levenson, R. W. (1994). Human emotions: A functional view. In P. Ekman & R. J. Davidson (Eds.), *The nature of emotion: Fundamental questions* (pp. 123–126). New York: Oxford University Press.

Leventhal, H., & Patrick-Miller, L. (2000). Emotions and physical illness: Causes and indicators of vulnerability. In M. Lewis & J. M. Haviland-Jones (Eds.), *Handbook of emotions* (2nd ed., pp. 523–537). New York: Guilford.

Leventhal, H., & Safer, M. A. (1977). Individual differences, personality, and humour appreciation: Introduction to symposium. In A. J. Chapman & H. C. Foot (Eds.), *It's a funny thing, humour* (pp. 335–349). Oxford: Pergamon Press.

Levi, L. (1965). The urinary output of adrenalin and noradrenalin during pleasant and unpleasant emotional states: A preliminary report. *Psychosomatic Medicine, 27,* 80–85.

Levine, J. (1977). Humour as a form of therapy: Introduction to symposium. In A. J. Chapman & H. C. Foot (Eds.), *It's a funny thing, humour* (pp. 127–137). Oxford: Pergamon Press.

Levine, J., & Abelson, R. P. (1959). Humor as a disturbing stimulus. *Journal of General Psychology, 60,* 191–200.

Levine, J., & Redlich, F. C. (1955). Failure to understand humor. *Psychoanalytic Quarterly, 24,* 560–572.

Levinson, W., Roter, D. L., Mullooly, J. P., Dull, V. T., et al. (1997). Physician-patient communication: The relationship with malpractice claims among primary care physicians and surgeons. *JAMA: Journal of the American Medical Association, 277*(7), 553–559.

Lewis, P. (1997). Debate: Humor and political correctness. *Humor: International Journal of Humor Research, 10*(4), 453–513.

Lewis, P. (2006). *Cracking up: American humor in a time of conflict.* Chicago, IL: University of Chicago Press.

Lightner, R. M., Bollmer, J. M., Harris, M. J., Milich, R., & Scambler, D. J. (2000). What do you say to teasers? Parent and child evaluations of responses to teasing. *Journal of Applied Developmental Psychology, 21*(4), 403–427.

Lippman, L. G., & Dunn, M. L. (2000). Contextual connections within puns: Effects on perceived humor and memory. *Journal of General Psychology, 127*(2), 185–197.

Lloyd, E. L. (1938). The respiratory mechanism in laughter. *Journal of General Psychology, 19,* 179–189.

Loeb, M., & Wood, V. (1986). Epilogue: A nascent idea for an Eriksonian model of humor. In L. Nahemow, K. A. McCluskey-Fawcett & P. E. McGhee (Eds.), *Humor and aging* (pp. 279–284). Orlando, FL: Academic Press.

Loehlin, J. C., & Nichols, R. C. (1976). *Heredity, environment, and personality.* Austin, TX: University of Texas Press.

Long, D. L., & Graesser, A. C. (1988). Wit and humor in discourse processing. *Discourse Processes, 11*(1), 35–60.

Losco, J., & Epstein, S. (1975). Humor preference as a subtle measure of attitudes toward the same and the opposite sex. *Journal of Personality, 43*(2), 321–334.

Lourey, E., & McLachlan, A. (2003). Elements of sensation seeking and their relationship with two aspects of humour appreciation-perceived funniness and overt expression. *Personality & Individual Differences, 35*(2), 277–287.

Love, A. M., & Deckers, L. H. (1989). Humor appreciation as a function of sexual, aggressive, and sexist content. *Sex Roles, 20*(11–12), 649–654.

Lowe, G., Britton, R., Carpenter, E., Castle, H., Clayton, C., Hulme, C., et al. (1997). Social drinking and laughter. *Psychological Reports, 81*(2), 684.

Lowe, G., & Taylor, S. B. (1993). Relationship between laughter and weekly alcohol consumption. *Psychological Reports, 72*(3, Pt 2), 1210.

Luborsky, L. B., & Cattell, R. B. (1947). The validation of personality factors in humor. *Journal of Personality, 15*, 283–291.

Ludovici, A. M. (1933). *The secret of laughter.* New York: Viking Press.

Lundy, D. E., Tan, J., & Cunningham, M. R. (1998). Heterosexual romantic preferences: The importance of humor and physical attractiveness for different types of relationships. *Personal Relationships, 5*(3), 311–325.

Lyons, V., & Fitzgerald, M. (2004). Humor in autism and Asperger syndrome. *Journal of Autism & Developmental Disorders, 34*(5), 521–531.

Lyttle, J. (2001). The effectiveness of humor in persuasion: The case of business ethics training. *Journal of General Psychology, 128*(2), 206–216.

Lyubomirsky, S., King, L., & Diener, E. (2005). The benefits of frequent positive affect: Does happiness lead to success? *Psychological Bulletin, 131*(6), 803–855.

MacDonald, N. E., & Silverman, I. W. (1978). Smiling and laughter in infants as a function of level of arousal and cognitive evaluation. *Developmental Psychology, 14*(3), 235–241.

Mackie, D. M., & Worth, L. T. (1989). Processing deficits and the mediation of positive affect in persuasion. *Journal of Personality and Social Psychology, 57*(1), 27–40.

MacLean, P. D. (1987). The midline frontolimbic cortex and the evolution of crying and laughter. In E. Perecman (Ed.), *The frontal lobes revisited* (pp. 121–140). New York, NY: IRBN Press.

Madanes, C. (1987). Humor in strategic family therapy. In W. F. Fry & W. A. Salameh (Eds.), *Handbook of humor and psychotherapy: Advances in the clinical use of humor* (pp. 241–264). Sarasota, FL: Professional Resource Exchange.

Madden, T. J., & Weinberger, M. G. (1982). The effects of humor on attention in magazine advertising. *Journal of Advertising, 11*(3), 8–14.

Magnavita, J. J. (2002). *Theories of personality: Contemporary approaches to the science of personality.* New York: Wiley.

Mahony, D. L., Burroughs, W. J., & Hieatt, A. C. (2001). The effects of laughter on discomfort thresholds: Does expectation become reality? *Journal of General Psychology, 128*(2), 217–226.

Maio, G. R., Olson, J. M., & Bush, J. E. (1997). Telling jokes that disparage social groups: Effects on the joke teller's stereotypes. *Journal of Applied Social Psychology, 27*(22), 1986–2000.

Mandler, J. M. (1979). Categorical and schematic organization in memory. In C. R. Puff (Ed.), *Memory organization and structure* (pp. 259–299). New York: Academic Press.

Manke, B. (1998). Genetic and environmental contributions to children's interpersonal humor. In W. Ruch (Ed.), *The sense of humor: Explorations of a personality characteristic* (pp. 361–384). Berlin, Germany: Walter de Gruyter.

Manne, S., Sherman, M., Ross, S., Ostroff, J., Heyman, R. E., & Fox, K. (2004). Couples' support-related communication, psychological distress, and relationship satisfaction among women with early stage breast cancer. *Journal of Consulting & Clinical Psychology, 72*(4), 660–670.

Mannell, R. C., & McMahon, L. (1982). Humor as play: Its relationship to psychological well-being during the course of a day. *Leisure Sciences, 5*(2), 143–155.

Marci, C. D., Moran, E. K., & Orr, S. P. (2004). Physiologic evidence for the interpersonal role of laughter during psychotherapy. *Journal of Nervous & Mental Disease, 192*(10), 689–695.

Marcus, N. N. (1990). Treating those who fail to take themselves seriously: Pathological aspects of humor. *American Journal of Psychotherapy, 44*(3), 423–432.

Markiewicz, D. (1974). Effects of humor on persuasion. *Sociometry, 37*(3), 407–422.

Martens, W. H. J. (2004). Therapeutic use of humor in antisocial personalities. *Journal of Contemporary Psychotherapy, 34*(4), 351–361.

Martin, D. M. (2004). Humor in middle management: Women negotiating the paradoxes of organizational life. *Journal of Applied Communication Research, 32*(2), 147–170.

Martin, G. N., & Gray, C. D. (1996). The effects of audience laughter on men's and women's responses to humor. *Journal of Social Psychology, 136*(2), 221–231.

Martin, L. R., Friedman, H. S., Tucker, J. S., Tomlinson-Keasey, C., Criqui, M. H., & Schwartz, J. E. (2002). A life course perspective on childhood cheerfulness and its relation to mortality risk. *Personality & Social Psychology Bulletin, 28*(9), 1155–1165.

Martin, R. A. (1984). *Telic dominance, humor, stress, and moods.* Paper presented at the International Symposium on Reversal Theory, Gregynog, Wales.

Martin, R. A. (1989). Humor and the mastery of living: Using humor to cope with the daily stresses of growing up. In P. E. McGhee (Ed.), *Humor and children's development: A guide to practical applications* (pp. 135–154). New York: Haworth Press.

Martin, R. A. (1996). The Situational Humor Response Questionnaire (SHRQ) and Coping Humor Scale (CHS): A decade of research findings. *Humor: International Journal of Humor Research, 9*(3–4), 251–272.

Martin, R. A. (1998). Approaches to the sense of humor: A historical review. In W. Ruch (Ed.), *The sense of humor: Explorations of a personality characteristic* (pp. 15–60). Berlin, Germany: Walter de Gruyter.

Martin, R. A. (2000). Humor and laughter. In A. E. Kazdin (Ed.), *Encyclopedia of psychology* (Vol. 4, pp. 202–204). Washington, DC: American Psychological Association.

Martin, R. A. (2001). Humor, laughter, and physical health: Methodological issues and research findings. *Psychological Bulletin, 127*(4), 504–519.

Martin, R. A. (2002). Is laughter the best medicine? Humor, laughter, and physical health. *Current Directions in Psychological Science, 11*(6), 216–220.

Martin, R. A. (2003). Sense of humor. In S. J. Lopez & C. R. Snyder (Eds.), *Positive psychological assessment: A handbook of models and measures* (pp. 313–326). Washington, DC: American Psychological Association.

Martin, R. A., Campbell, L., & Ward, J. R. (2006). Observed humor styles, relationship quality, and problem resolution in a conflict discussion between dating couples. Paper presented at the annual conference of the International Society for Humor Studies, Copenhagen, Denmark.

Martin, R. A., & Dobbin, J. P. (1988). Sense of humor, hassles, and immunoglobulin A: Evidence for a stress-moderating effect of humor. *International Journal of Psychiatry in Medicine, 18*(2), 93–105.

Martin, R. A., & Dutrizac, G. (2004). *Humor styles, social skills, and quality of interactions with close others: A prospective daily diary study.* Paper presented at the Annual Conference of the International Society for Humor Studies, Dijon, France.

Martin, R. A., & Kuiper, N. A. (1999). Daily occurrence of laughter: Relationships with age, gender, and Type A personality. *Humor: International Journal of Humor Research, 12*(4), 355–384.

Martin, R. A., Kuiper, N. A., Olinger, L. J., & Dance, K. A. (1993). Humor, coping with stress, self-concept, and psychological well-being. *Humor: International Journal of Humor Research*, *6*(1), 89–104.

Martin, R. A., Kuiper, N. A., Olinger, L. J., & Dobbin, J. P. (1987). Is stress always bad? Telic versus paratelic dominance as a stress moderating variable. *Journal of Personality and Social Psychology*, *53*, 970–982.

Martin, R. A., & Lefcourt, H. M. (1983). Sense of humor as a moderator of the relation between stressors and moods. *Journal of Personality & Social Psychology*, *45*(6), 1313–1324.

Martin, R. A., & Lefcourt, H. M. (1984). Situational Humor Response Questionnaire: Quantitative measure of sense of humor. *Journal of Personality & Social Psychology*, *47*(1), 145–155.

Martin, R. A., Puhlik-Doris, P., Larsen, G., Gray, J., & Weir, K. (2003). Individual differences in uses of humor and their relation to psychological well-being: Development of the Humor Styles Questionnaire. *Journal of Research in Personality*, *37*(1), 48–75.

Martineau, W. H. (1972). A model of the social functions of humor. In J. H. Goldstein & P. E. McGhee (Eds.), *The psychology of humor: Theoretical perspectives and empirical issues* (pp. 101–125). New York: Academic Press.

Maslow, A. H. (1954). *Motivation and personality*. New York: Harper.

Masselos, G. (2003). "When I play funny it makes me laugh": Implications for early childhood educators in developing humor through play. In D. E. Lytle (Ed.), *Play and educational theory and practice* (pp. 213–226). Westport, CT: Praeger Publishers/Greenwood Publishing.

Masten, A. S. (1986). Humor and competence in school-aged children. *Child Development*, *57*(2), 461–473.

May, R. (1953). *Man's search for himself*. New York: Random House.

Mayne, T. J. (2001). Emotions and health. In T. J. Mayne & G. A. Bonanno (Eds.), *Emotions: Current issues and future directions* (pp. 361–397). New York: Guilford.

McCarroll, J. E., Ursano, R. J., Wright, K. M., & Fullerton, C. S. (1993). Handling bodies after violent death: Strategies for coping. *American Journal of Orthopsychiatry*, *63*(2), 209–214.

McCauley, C., Woods, K., Coolidge, C., & Kulick, W. (1983). More aggressive cartoons are funnier. *Journal of Personality & Social Psychology*, *44*(4), 817–823.

McClelland, D. C., & Cheriff, A. D. (1997). The immunoenhancing effects of humor on secretory IgA and resistance to respiratory infections. *Psychology & Health*, *12*(3), 329–344.

McComas, H. C. (1923). The origin of laughter. *Psychological Review*, *30*, 45–56.

McCrae, R. R., & John, O. P. (1992). An introduction to the five-factor model and its applications. *Journal of Personality*, *60*(2), 175–215.

McDougall, W. (1903). The theory of laughter. *Nature*, *67*, 318–319.

McDougall, W. (1922). Why do we laugh? *Scribners*, *71*, 359–363.

McGhee, P. E. (1971a). Cognitive development and children's comprehension of humor. *Child Development*, *42*(1), 123–138.

McGhee, P. E. (1971b). The role of operational thinking in children's comprehension and appreciation of humor. *Child Development*, *42*(3), 733–744.

McGhee, P. E. (1972). On the cognitive origins of incongruity humor: Fantasy assimilation versus reality assimilation. In J. H. Goldstein & P. E. McGhee (Eds.), *The psychology of humor: Theoretical perspectives and empirical issues* (pp. 61–80). New York: Academic Press.

McGhee, P. E. (1974). Cognitive mastery and children's humor. *Psychological Bulletin*, *81*(10), 721–730.

McGhee, P. E. (1976). Children's appreciation of humor: A test of the cognitive congruency principle. *Child Development, 47*(2), 420–426.

McGhee, P. E. (1980a). Development of the creative aspects of humour. In P. E. McGhee & A. J. Chapman (Eds.), *Children's humour* (pp. 119–139). Chichester: John Wiley & Sons.

McGhee, P. E. (1980b). Development of the sense of humour in childhood: A longitudinal study. In P. E. McGhee & A. J. Chapman (Eds.), *Children's humour* (pp. 213–236). Chichester: John Wiley & Sons.

McGhee, P. E. (1983a). Humor development: Toward a life span approach. In P. E. McGhee & J. H. Goldstein (Eds.), *Handbook of humor research, Vol. 1: Basic issues* (Vol. 1, pp. 109–134). New York: Springer-Verlag.

McGhee, P. E. (1983b). The role of arousal and hemispheric lateralization in humor. In P. E. McGhee & J. H. Goldstein (Eds.), *Handbook of humor research, Vol. 1: Basic issues* (pp. 13–37). New York: Springer-Verlag.

McGhee, P. E. (1999). *Health, healing and the amuse system: Humor as survival training* (3rd ed.). Dubuque, Iowa: Kendall/Hunt.

McGhee, P. E. (Ed.). (1979). *Humor: Its origin and development*. San Francisco, CA: W. H. Freeman.

McGhee, P. E., Bell, N. J., & Duffey, N. S. (1986). Generational differences in humor and correlates of humor development. In L. Nahemow, K. A. McCluskey-Fawcett & P. E. McGhee (Eds.), *Humor and aging* (pp. 253–263). Orlando, FL: Academic Press.

McGhee, P. E., & Duffey, N. S. (1983). Children's appreciation of humor victimizing different racial-ethnic groups: Racial-ethnic differences. *Journal of Cross-Cultural Psychology, 14*(1), 29–40.

McGhee, P. E., & Goldstein, J. H. (Eds.). (1983). *Handbook of humor research* (Vols. 1 and 2). New York: Springer-Verlag.

McGhee, P. E., & Lloyd, S. A. (1981). A developmental test of the disposition theory of humor. *Child Development, 52*(3), 925–931.

McGhee, P. E., & Lloyd, S. A. (1982). Behavioral characteristics associated with the development of humor in young children. *Journal of Genetic Psychology, 141*(2), 253–259.

McGhee, P. E., Ruch, W., & Hehl, F.-J. (1990). A personality-based model of humor development during adulthood. *Humor: International Journal of Humor Research, 3*(2), 119–146.

McMorris, R. F., Boothroyd, R. A., & Pietrangelo, D. J. (1997). Humor in educational testing: A review and discussion. *Applied Measurement in Education, 10*(3), 269–297.

McMorris, R. F., Urbach, S. L., & Connor, M. C. (1985). Effects of incorporating humor in test items. *Journal of Educational Measurement, 22*(2), 147–155.

Mednick, S. A. (1962). The associative basis of the creative process. *Psychological Review, 69,* 220–232.

Megdell, J. I. (1984). Relationship between counselor-initiated humor and client's self-perceived attraction in the counseling interview. *Psychotherapy: Theory, Research, Practice, Training, 21*(4), 517–523.

Mendez, M. F., Nakawatase, T. V., & Brown, C. V. (1999). Involuntary laughter and inappropriate hilarity. *Journal of Neuropsychiatry & Clinical Neurosciences, 11*(2), 253–258.

Mettee, D. R., Hrelec, E. S., & Wilkens, P. C. (1971). Humor as an interpersonal asset and liability. *Journal of Social Psychology, 85*(1), 51–64.

Meyer, J. C. (1997). Humor in member narratives: Uniting and dividing at work. *Western Journal of Communication, 61*(2), 188–208.

Meyer, M., Zysset, S., von Cramon, D. Y., & Alter, K. (2005). Distinct fMRI responses to laughter, speech, and sounds along the human peri-sylvian cortex. *Cognitive Brain Research, 24*(2), 291–306.

Middleton, R. (1959). Negro and white reactions to racial humor. *Sociometry, 22,* 175–183.

Miller, G. F. (1997). Protean primates: The evolution of adaptive unpredictability in competition and courtship. In A. Whiten & R. W. Byrne (Eds.), *Machiavellian intelligence II: Extensions and evaluations* (pp. 312–340). New York, NY: Cambridge University Press.

Miller, G. F. (2000). *The mating mind: How sexual choice shaped the evolution of human nature.* New York: Doubleday.

Mindess, H. (1971). *Laughter and liberation.* Los Angeles: Nash Publishing.

Mindess, H. (1976). The use and abuse of humour in psychotherapy. In A. J. Chapman & H. C. Foot (Eds.), *Humor and laughter: Theory, research, and applications* (pp. 331–341). London: John Wiley & Sons.

Minsky, M. (1977). Frame-system theory. In P. N. Johnson-Laird & P. C. Wason (Eds.), *Thinking: Readings in cognitive science* (pp. 355–376). Cambridge: Cambridge University Press.

Mio, J. S., & Graesser, A. C. (1991). Humor, language, and metaphor. *Metaphor & Symbolic Activity, 6*(2), 87–102.

Mittwoch-Jaffe, T., Shalit, F., Srendi, B., & Yehuda, S. (1995). Modification of cytokine secretion following mild emotional stimuli. *NeuroReport, 6,* 789–792.

Mobbs, D., Greicius, M. D., Abdel-Azim, E., Menon, V., & Reiss, A. L. (2003). Humor modulates the mesolimbic reward centers. *Neuron, 40,* 1041–1048.

Mobbs, D., Hagan, C. C., Azim, E., Menon, V., & Reiss, A. L. (2005). Personality predicts activity in reward and emotional regions associated with humor. *Proceedings of the National Academy of Sciences, 102*(45), 16502–16506.

Moody, R. A. (1978). *Laugh after laugh: The healing power of humor.* Jacksonville, FL: Headwaters Press.

Moore, T. E., Griffiths, K., & Payne, B. (1987). Gender, attitudes towards women, and the appreciation of sexist humor. *Sex Roles, 16*(9–10), 521–531.

Moran, C., & Massam, M. (1997). An evaluation of humour in emergency work. *Australasian Journal of Disaster and Trauma Studies, 1*(3).

Moran, C. C. (1996). Short-term mood change, perceived funniness, and the effect of humor stimuli. *Behavioral Medicine, 22*(1), 32–38.

Morreall, J. (1991). Humor and work. *Humor: International Journal of Humor Research, 4*(3–4), 359–373.

Morreall, J. (Ed.). (1987). *The philosophy of laughter and humor.* Albany, NY: State University of New York Press.

Morse, S., & Gergen, K. (1970). Social comparison, self-consistency, and the concept of self. *Journal of Personality and Social Psychology, 16,* 148–156.

Mowrer, D. E. (1994). A case study of perceptual and acoustic features of an infant's first laugh utterances. *Humor: International Journal of Humor Research, 7*(2), 139–155.

Mowrer, D. E., LaPointe, L. L., & Case, J. (1987). Analysis of five acoustic correlates of laughter. *Journal of Nonverbal Behavior, 11*(3), 191–199.

Mueller, C. W., & Donnerstein, E. (1983). Film-induced arousal and aggressive behavior. *Journal of Social Psychology, 119*(1), 61–67.

Mulkay, M. (1988). *On humor: Its nature and its place in modern society.* New York: Basil Blackwell.

Mulkay, M., Clark, C., & Pinch, T. (1993). Laughter and the profit motive: The use of humor in a photographic shop. *Humor: International Journal of Humor Research, 6*(2), 163–193.

Murdock, M. C., & Ganim, R. M. (1993). Creativity and humor: Integration and incongruity. *Journal of Creative Behavior, 27*(1), 57–70.

Murgatroyd, S., Rushton, C., Apter, M., & Ray, C. (1978). The development of the Telic Dominance Scale. *Journal of Personality Assessment, 42*(5), 519–528.

Murstein, B. I., & Brust, R. G. (1985). Humor and interpersonal attraction. *Journal of Personality Assessment, 49*(6), 637–640.

Nerhardt, G. (1970). Humor and inclination to laugh: Emotional reactions to stimuli of different divergence from a range of expectancy. *Scandinavian Journal of Psychology, 11*(3), 185–195.

Nerhardt, G. (1976). Incongruity and funniness: Towards a new descriptive model. In A. J. Chapman & H. C. Foot (Eds.), *Humor and laughter: Theory, research, and applications* (pp. 55–62). London: John Wiley & Sons.

Nerhardt, G. (1977). Operationalization of incongruity in humour research: A critique and suggestions. In A. J. Chapman & H. C. Foot (Eds.), *It's a funny thing, humour* (pp. 47–51). Oxford: Pergamon Press.

Neuhoff, C. C., & Schaefer, C. (2002). Effects of laughing, smiling, and howling on mood. *Psychological Reports, 91*(3, Pt 2), 1079–1080.

Neuliep, J. W. (1991). An examination of the content of high school teachers' humor in the classroom and the development of an inductively derived taxonomy of classroom humor. *Communication Education, 40*(4), 343–355.

Nevo, O., Aharonson, H., & Klingman, A. (1998). The development and evaluation of a systematic program for improving sense of humor. In W. Ruch (Ed.), *The sense of humor: Explorations of a personality characteristic* (pp. 385–404). Berlin, Germany: Walter de Gruyter.

Nevo, O., Keinan, G., & Teshimovsky-Arditi, M. (1993). Humor and pain tolerance. *Humor: International Journal of Humor Research, 6*(1), 71–88.

Nevo, O., & Nevo, B. (1983). What do you do when asked to answer humorously? *Journal of Personality & Social Psychology, 44*(1), 188–194.

Newman, M. G., & Stone, A. A. (1996). Does humor moderate the effects of experimentally-induced stress? *Annals of Behavioral Medicine, 18*(2), 101–109.

Newton, G. R., & Dowd, E. T. (1990). Effect of client sense of humor and paradoxical interventions on test anxiety. *Journal of Counseling & Development, 68*(6), 668–672.

Nezlek, J. B., & Derks, P. (2001). Use of humor as a coping mechanism, psychological adjustment, and social interaction. *Humor: International Journal of Humor Research, 14*(4), 395–413.

Nezu, A. M., Nezu, C. M., & Blissett, S. E. (1988). Sense of humor as a moderator of the relation between stressful events and psychological distress: A prospective analysis. *Journal of Personality & Social Psychology, 54*(3), 520–525.

Nias, D. K. (1981). Humour and personality. In R. Lynn (Ed.), *Dimensions of personality: Papers in honour of H. J. Eysenck* (pp. 287–313). Oxford: Pergamon Press.

Nias, D. K., & Wilson, G. D. (1977). A genetic analysis of humour preferences. In A. J. Chapman & H. C. Foot (Eds.), *It's a funny thing, humour* (pp. 371–373). Oxford: Pergamon Press.

Niethammer, T. (1983). Does man possess a laughter center? Laughing gas used in a new approach. *New Ideas in Psychology, 1*(1), 67–69.

Nilsen, A. P., & Nilsen, D. L. F. (2000). *Encyclopedia of 20th-century American humor*. Phoenix, AZ: Oryx Press.

Njus, D. M., Nitschke, W., & Bryant, F. B. (1996). Positive affect, negative affect, and the moderating effect of writing on sIgA antibody levels. *Psychology & Health, 12*(1), 135–148.

Norrick, N. R. (1984). Stock conversational witticisms. *Journal of Pragmatics, 8*, 195–209.

Norrick, N. R. (1986). A frame-theoretical analysis of verbal humor. *Semiotica, 60,* 225–245.

Norrick, N. R. (1993). *Conversational joking: Humor in everyday talk.* Bloomington, IN: Indiana University Press.

Norrick, N. R. (2003). Issues in conversational joking. *Journal of Pragmatics, 35*(9), 1333–1359.

Nwokah, E. E., Davies, P., Islam, A., Hsu, H.-C., & Fogel, A. (1993). Vocal affect in three-year-olds: A quantitative acoustic analysis of child laughter. *Journal of the Acoustical Society of America, 94*(6), 3076–3090.

Nwokah, E. E., & Fogel, A. (1993). Laughter in mother-infant emotional communication. *Humor: International Journal of Humor Research, 6*(2), 137–161.

Nwokah, E. E., Hsu, H.-C., Davies, P., & Fogel, A. (1999). The integration of laughter and speech in vocal communication: A dynamic systems perspective. *Journal of Speech, Language, & Hearing Research, 42*(4), 880–894.

Nwokah, E. E., Hsu, H.-C., Dobrowolska, O., & Fogel, A. (1994). The development of laughter in mother-infant communication: Timing parameters and temporal sequences. *Infant Behavior & Development, 17*(1), 23–35.

Obrdlik, A. (1942). Gallows humor: A sociological phenomenon. *American Journal of Sociology, 47,* 709–716.

O'Connell, W. E. (1960). The adaptive functions of wit and humor. *Journal of Abnormal & Social Psychology, 61,* 263–270.

O'Connell, W. E. (1969). The social aspects of wit and humor. *Journal of Social Psychology, 79*(2), 183–187.

O'Connell, W. E. (1976). Freudian humour: The eupsychia of everyday life. In A. J. Chapman & H. C. Foot (Eds.), *Humor and laughter: Theory, research, and applications* (pp. 313–329). London: John Wiley & Sons.

O'Connell, W. E. (1981). Natural high therapy. In R. J. Corsini (Ed.), *Handbook of innovative psychotherapies* (pp. 554–568). New York: John Wiley & Sons.

O'Connell, W. E. (1987). Natural high theory and practice: The humorist's game of games. In W. F. Fry & W. A. Salameh (Eds.), *Handbook of humor and psychotherapy: Advances in the clinical use of humor* (pp. 55–79). Sarasota, FL: Professional Resource Exchange.

Odell, M. (1996). The silliness factor: Breaking up repetitive and unproductive conflict patterns with couples and families. *Journal of Family Psychotherapy, 7*(3), 69–75.

Olson, H. A. (1994). The use of humor in psychotherapy. In H. S. Strean (Ed.), *The use of humor in psychotherapy* (pp. 195–198). Northvale, NJ: Jason Aronson.

Olson, J. M., Maio, G. R., & Hobden, K. L. (1999). The (null) effects of exposure to disparagement humor on stereotypes and attitudes. *Humor: International Journal of Humor Research, 12*(2), 195–219.

Olson, M. L., Hugelshofer, D. S., Kwon, P., & Reff, R. C. (2005). Rumination and dysphoria: The buffering role of adaptive forms of humor. *Personality and Individual Differences, 39*(8), 1419–1428.

Omwake, L. (1939). Factors influencing the sense of humor. *Journal of Social Psychology, 10,* 95–104.

O'Neill, R. M., Greenberg, R. P., & Fisher, S. (1992). Humor and anality. *Humor: International Journal of Humor Research, 5*(3), 283–291.

Oppliger, P. A. (2003). Humor and learning. In J. Bryant, D. Roskos-Ewoldsen & J. R. Cantor (Eds.), *Communication and emotion: Essays in honor of Dolf Zillmann* (pp. 255–273). Mahwah, NJ: Lawrence Erlbaum Associates.

Oppliger, P. A., & Zillmann, D. (1997). Disgust in humor: Its appeal to adolescents. *Humor: International Journal of Humor Research, 10*(4), 421–437.

O'Quin, K., & Aronoff, J. (1981). Humor as a technique of social influence. *Social Psychology Quarterly, 44*(4), 349–357.

O'Quin, K., & Derks, P. (1997). Humor and creativity: A review of the empirical literature. In M. A. Runco (Ed.), *The creativity handbook* (Vol. 1, pp. 227–256). Cresskill, NJ: Hampton Press.

Oring, E. (1994). Humor and the suppression of sentiment. *Humor: International Journal of Humor Research, 7*(1), 7–26.

Osgood, C. E., Suci, G. J., & Tannenbaum, P. H. (1957). *The measurement of meaning.* Urbana, IL: University of Illinois Press.

Overeem, S., Lammers, G. J., & Van Dijk, J. G. (1999). Weak with laughter. *Lancet, 354*, 838.

Overeem, S., Taal, W., Gezici, E. Ö., Lammers, G. J., & Van Dijk, J. G. (2004). Is motor inhibition during laughter due to emotional or respiratory influences? *Psychophysiology, 41*(2), 254–258.

Overholser, J. C. (1992). Sense of humor when coping with life stress. *Personality & Individual Differences, 13*(7), 799–804.

Owren, M. J., & Bachorowski, J.-A. (2001). The evolution of emotional experience: A "selfish-gene" account of smiling and laughter in early hominids and humans. In T. J. Mayne & G. A. Bonanno (Eds.), *Emotions: Currrent issues and future directions* (pp. 152–191). New York, NY: Guilford.

Owren, M. J., & Bachorowski, J.-A. (2003). Reconsidering the evolution of nonlinguistic communication: The case of laughter. *Journal of Nonverbal Behavior, 27*(3), 183–200.

Palmer, C. T. (1993). Anger, aggression, and humor in Newfoundland floor hockey: An evolutionary analysis. *Aggressive Behavior, 19*(3), 167–173.

Panksepp, J. (1993). Neurochemical control of moods and emotions: Amino acids to neuropeptides. In M. Lewis & J. M. Haviland (Eds.), *Handbook of emotions* (pp. 87–107). New York: Guilford.

Panksepp, J. (1994). The clearest physiological distinctions between emotions will be found among the circuits of the brain. In P. Ekman & R. J. Davidson (Eds.), *The nature of emotion: Fundamental questions* (pp. 258–260). New York: Oxford University Press.

Panksepp, J. (1998). *Affective neuroscience: The foundations of human and animal emotions.* New York: Oxford University Press.

Panksepp, J. (2000). The riddle of laughter: Neural and psychoevolutionary underpinnings of joy. *Current Directions in Psychological Science, 9*(6), 183–186.

Panksepp, J., & Burgdorf, J. (2000). 50-kHz chirping (laughter?) in response to conditioned and unconditioned tickle-induced reward in rats: Effects of social housing and genetic variables. *Behavioural Brain Research, 115*(1), 25–38.

Panksepp, J., & Burgdorf, J. (2003). "Laughing" rats and the evolutionary antecedents of human joy? *Physiology & Behavior, 79*(3), 533–547.

Park, R. (1977). A study of children's riddles using Piaget-derived definitions. *Journal of Genetic Psychology, 130*(1), 57–67.

Parrott, W. G., & Gleitman, H. (1989). Infants' expectations in play: The joy of peek-a-boo. *Cognition & Emotion, 3*(4), 291–311.

Parvizi, J., Anderson, S. W., Martin, C. O., Damasio, H., & Damasio, A. R. (2001). Pathological laughter and crying: A link to the cerebellum. *Brain, 124*(9), 1708–1719.

Paskind, H. A. (1932). Effect of laughter on muscle tone. *Archives of Neurology & Psychiatry*, 623–628.

Patton, D., Barnes, G. E., & Murray, R. P. (1993). Personality charactistics of smokers and ex-smokers. *Personality & Individual Differences, 15*, 653–664.

Paulos, J. A. (1980). *Mathematics and humor*. Chicago, IL: University of Chicago Press.

Pellegrini, D. S., Masten, A. S., Garmezy, N., & Ferrarese, M. J. (1987). Correlates of social and academic competence in middle childhood. *Journal of Child Psychology & Psychiatry & Allied Disciplines, 28*(5), 699–714.

Perera, S., Sabin, E., Nelson, P., & Lowe, D. (1998). Increases in salivary lysozyme and IgA concentrations and secretory rates independent of salivary flow rates following viewing of a humorous videotape. *International Journal of Behavioral Medicine, 5*(2), 118–128.

Peterson, J. P., & Pollio, H. R. (1982). Therapeutic effectiveness of differentially targeted humorous remarks in group psychotherapy. *Group, 6*(4), 39–50.

Petty, R. E., & Cacioppo, J. T. (1986). *Communication and persuasion*. New York: Springer-Verlag.

Pexman, P. M., & Harris, M. (2003). Children's perceptions of the social functions of verbal irony. *Discourse Processes, 36*(3), 147–165.

Pexman, P. M., & Zvaigzne, M. T. (2004). Does irony go better with friends? *Metaphor & Symbol, 19*(2), 143–163.

Piaget, J. (1970). Piaget's theory. In P. H. Mussen (Ed.), *Carmichael's manual of child psychology* (3rd ed., Vol. 1, pp. 703–732). New York: Wiley.

Pien, D., & Rothbart, M. K. (1976). Incongruity and resolution in children's humor: A reexamination. *Child Development, 47*(4), 966–971.

Pien, D., & Rothbart, M. K. (1977). Measuring effects of incongruity and resolution in children's humor. In A. J. Chapman & H. C. Foot (Eds.), *It's a funny thing, humour* (pp. 211–213). Oxford: Pergamon Press.

Pien, D., & Rothbart, M. K. (1980). Incongruity humour, play, and self-regulation of arousal in young children. In P. E. McGhee & A. J. Chapman (Eds.), *Children's humour* (pp. 1–26). Chichester: John Wiley & Sons.

Pierce, R. A. (1994). Use and abuse of laughter in psychotherapy. In H. S. Strean (Ed.), *The use of humor in psychotherapy* (pp. 105–111). Northvale, NJ: Jason Aronson.

Pinderhughes, E. E., & Zigler, E. (1985). Cognitive and motivational determinants of children's humor responses. *Journal of Research in Personality, 19*(2), 185–196.

Plutchik, R. (1991). Emotions and evolution. In K. T. Strongman (Ed.), *International review of studies in emotion* (pp. 37–58). Chichester: John Wiley & Sons`.

Poeck, K. (1985). Pathological laughter and crying. In P. J. Vinken, G. W. Bruyn & H. L. Klawans (Eds.), *Handbook of clinical neurology* (Vol. 45, pp. 219–225). Amsterdam: Elsevier Science Publishers.

Pollio, H. R., & Mers, R. W. (1974). Predictability and the appreciation of comedy. *Bulletin of the Psychonomic Society, 4*(4-A), 229–232.

Pollio, H. R., Mers, R. W., & Lucchesi, W. (1972). Humor, laughter, and smiling: Some preliminary observations of funny behaviors. In J. H. Goldstein & P. E. McGhee (Eds.), *The psychology of humor: Theoretical perspectives and empirical issues* (pp. 211–239). New York: Academic Press.

Porterfield, A. L. (1987). Does sense of humor moderate the impact of life stress on psychological and physical well-being? *Journal of Research in Personality, 21*(3), 306–317.

Porterfield, A. L., Mayer, F. S., Dougherty, K. G., Kredich, K. E., Kronberg, M. M., Marsee, K. M., et al. (1988). Private self-consciousness, canned laughter, and responses to humorous stimuli. *Journal of Research in Personality, 22*(4), 409–423.

Powell, J. P., & Andresen, L. W. (1985). Humour and teaching in higher education. *Studies in Higher Education, 10*(1), 79–90.

Prasinos, S., & Tittler, B. I. (1981). The family relationships of humor-oriented adolescents. *Journal of Personality, 49*(3), 295–305.

Prentice, N. M., & Fathman, R. E. (1975). Joking riddles: A developmental index of children's humor. *Developmental Psychology, 11*(2), 210–216.

Prerost, F. J. (1977). Environmental conditions affecting the humour response: Developmental trends. In A. J. Chapman & H. C. Foot (Eds.), *It's a funny thing, humour* (pp. 439–441). Oxford: Pergamon Press.

Prerost, F. J. (1983). Changing patterns in the response to humorous sexual stimuli: Sex roles and expression of sexuality. *Social Behavior & Personality, 11*(1), 23–28.

Prerost, F. J. (1984). Reactions to humorous sexual stimuli as a function of sexual activeness and satisfaction. *Psychology: A Journal of Human Behavior, 21*(1), 23–27.

Prerost, F. J. (1988). Use of humor and guided imagery in therapy to alleviate stress. *Journal of Mental Health Counseling, 10*(1), 16–22.

Prerost, F. J. (1993). A strategy to enhance humor production among elderly persons: Assisting in the management of stress. *Activities, Adaptation & Aging, 17*(4), 17–24.

Prerost, F. J., & Brewer, R. E. (1977). Humor content preferences and the relief of experimentally aroused aggression. *Journal of Social Psychology, 103*(2), 225–231.

Prerost, F. J., & Ruma, C. (1987). Exposure to humorous stimuli as an adjunct to muscle relaxation training. *Psychology: A Journal of Human Behavior, 24*(4), 70–74.

Preuschoft, S., & van Hooff, J. A. (1997). The social function of "smile" and "laughter": Variations across primate species and societies. In U. C. Segerstrale & P. Molnar (Eds.), *Nonverbal communication: Where nature meets culture* (pp. 171–190). Hillsdale, NJ, England: Lawrence Erlbaum Associates.

Priest, R. F., & Swain, J. E. (2002). Humor and its implications for leadership effectiveness. *Humor: International Journal of Humor Research, 15*(2), 169–189.

Priest, R. F., & Thein, M. T. (2003). Humor appreciation in marriage: Spousal similarity, assortative mating, and disaffection. *Humor: International Journal of Humor Research, 16*(1), 63–78.

Provine, R. R. (1992). Contagious laughter: Laughter is a sufficient stimulus for laughs and smiles. *Bulletin of the Psychonomic Society, 30*(1), 1–4.

Provine, R. R. (1993). Laughter punctuates speech: Linguistic, social and gender contexts of laughter. *Ethology, 95*(4), 291–298.

Provine, R. R. (1996). Laughter. *American Scientist, 84*, 38–45.

Provine, R. R. (2000). *Laughter: A scientific investigation.* New York: Penguin.

Provine, R. R. (2004). Laughing, tickling, and the evolution of speech and self. *Current Directions in Psychological Science, 13*(6), 215–218.

Provine, R. R., & Fischer, K. R. (1989). Laughing, smiling, and talking: Relation to sleeping and social context in humans. *Ethology, 83*(4), 295–305.

Provine, R. R., & Yong, Y. L. (1991). Laughter: A stereotyped human vocalization. *Ethology, 89*(2), 115–124.

Rackl, L. (2003). But seriously folks: Humor can keep you healthy. *Reader's Digest* (September), 62–71.

Radcliffe-Brown, A. R. (1952). *Structure and function in primitive society: Essays and addresses.* New York: Free Press.

Ramachandran, V. S. (1998). The neurology and evolution of humor, laughter, and smiling: The false alarm theory. *Medical Hypotheses, 51*, 351–354.

Rapp, A. (1951). *The origins of wit and humor.* Oxford, England: Dutton.

Raskin, V. (1985). *Semantic mechanisms of humor.* Dordrecht: D. Reidel.

Redlich, F. C., Levine, J., & Sohler, T. P. (1951). A Mirth Response Test: preliminary report on a psychodiagnostic technique utilizing dynamics of humor. *American Journal of Orthopsychiatry, 21*, 717–734.

Reis, H. T. (2001). Relationship experiences and emotional well-being. In C. D. Ryff & B. H. Singer (Eds.), *Emotion, social relationships, and health* (pp. 57–86). New York: Oxford University Press.

Reis, H. T., & Gable, S. L. (2000). Event-sampling and other methods for studying everyday experience. In H. T. Reis & C. M. Judd (Eds.), *Handbook of research methods in social and personality psychology* (pp. 190–222). New York: Cambridge University Press.

Richman, J. (1995). The lifesaving function of humor with the depressed and suicidal elderly. *Gerontologist, 35*(2), 271–273.

Richman, J. (2003). Therapeutic humor with the depressed and suicidal elderly. In C. E. Schaefer (Ed.), *Play therapy with adults* (pp. 166–192). New York, NY: John Wiley & Sons.

Rim, Y. (1988). Sense of humour and coping styles. *Personality & Individual Differences, 9*(3), 559–564.

Ritchie, G. (1999). *Developing the incongruity-resolution theory.* Paper presented at the AISB Symposium on Creative Language: Stories and Humour, Edinburgh.

Ritchie, G. (2001). Current directions in computational humour. *Artificial Intelligence Review, 16*(2), 119–135.

Ritchie, G. (2004). *The linguistic analysis of jokes.* London: Routledge.

Ritchie, G. (in press). Reinterpretation and viewpoints. *Humor: International Journal of Humor Research.*

Rizzolatti, G., & Craighero, L. (2004). The mirror-neuron system. *Annual Review of Neuroscience, 27*, 169–192.

Robinson, D. T., & Smith-Lovin, L. (2001). Getting a laugh: Gender, status, and humor in task discussions. *Social Forces, 80*(1), 123–158.

Roeckelein, J. E. (2002). *The psychology of humor: A reference guide and annotated bibliography.* Westport, CT: Greenwood Press.

Rosenheim, E., & Golan, G. (1986). Patients' reactions to humorous interventions in psychotherapy. *American Journal of Psychotherapy, 40*(1), 110–124.

Rosenheim, E., Tecucianu, F., & Dimitrovsky, L. (1989). Schizophrenics' appreciation of humorous therapeutic interventions. *Humor: International Journal of Humor Research, 2*(2), 141–152.

Rosenwald, G. C. (1964). The relation of drive discharge to the enjoyment of humor. *Journal of Personality, 32*(4), 682–698.

Rothbart, M. K. (1976). Incongruity, problem-solving and laughter. In A. J. Chapman & H. C. Foot (Eds.), *Humor and laughter: Theory, research, and applications* (pp. 37–54). London: John Wiley & Sons.

Rotton, J. (1992). Trait humor and longevity: Do comics have the last laugh? *Health Psychology, 11*(4), 262–266.

Rotton, J., & Shats, M. (1996). Effects of state humor, expectancies, and choice on postsurgical mood and self-medication: A field experiment. *Journal of Applied Social Psychology, 26*(20), 1775–1794.

Rowe, D. C. (1997). Genetics, temperament, and personality. In R. Hogan, J. Johnson & S. Briggs (Eds.), *Handbook of personality psychology* (pp. 367–386). San Diego: Academic Press.

Ruch, W. (1981). Humor and personality: A three-modal analysis. *Zeitschrift für Differentielle und Diagnostische Psychologie, 2*, 253–273.

Ruch, W. (1983). *Humor-Test 3 WD (Forms A, B, and K)*.Unpublished manuscript, University of Dusseldorf, Germany.

Ruch, W. (1984). Conservatism and the appreciation of humor. *Zeitschrift fur Differentielle und Diagnostische Psychologie*, 5, 221–245.

Ruch, W. (1988). Sensation seeking and the enjoyment of structure and content of humour: Stability of findings across four samples. *Personality & Individual Differences*, 9(5), 861–871.

Ruch, W. (1992). Assessment of appreciation of humor: Studies with the 3 WD Humor Test. In C. D. Spielberger & J. N. Butcher (Eds.), *Advances in personality assessment* (Vol. 9, pp. 27–75). Hillsdale, NJ: Lawrence Erlbaum Associates.

Ruch, W. (1993). Exhilaration and humor. In M. Lewis & J. M. Haviland (Eds.), *Handbook of emotions* (pp. 605–616). New York, NY: Guilford.

Ruch, W. (1994). Temperament, Eysenck's PEN system, and humor-related traits. *Humor: International Journal of Humor Research*, 7(3), 209–244.

Ruch, W. (1997). State and trait cheerfulness and the induction of exhilaration: A FACS study. *European Psychologist*, 2(4), 328–341.

Ruch, W. (1998a). Sense of humor: A new look at an old concept. In W. Ruch (Ed.), *The sense of humor: Explorations of a personality characteristic* (pp. 3–14). Berlin, Germany: Mouton de Gruyter.

Ruch, W. (1998b). *The sense of humor: Explorations of a personality characteristic*. Berlin, Germany: Mouton de Gruyter.

Ruch, W. (1999). The sense of nonsense lies in the nonsense of sense. Comment on Paolillo's (1998) "Gary Larsen's Far Side: Nonsense? Nonsense!" *Humor: International Journal of Humor Research*, 12(1), 71–93.

Ruch, W., Attardo, S., & Raskin, V. (1993). Toward an empirical verification of the General Theory of Verbal Humor. *Humor: International Journal of Humor Research*, 6(2), 123–136.

Ruch, W., Busse, P., & Hehl, F.-J. (1996). Relationship between humor and proposed punishment for crimes: Beware of humorous people. *Personality & Individual Differences*, 20(1), 1–11.

Ruch, W., & Carrell, A. (1998). Trait cheerfulness and the sense of humour. *Personality & Individual Differences*, 24(4), 551–558.

Ruch, W., & Deckers, L. (1993). Do extraverts "like to laugh"? An analysis of the Situational Humor Response Questionnaire (SHRQ). *European Journal of Personality*, 7(4), 211–220.

Ruch, W., & Ekman, P. (2001). The expressive pattern of laughter. In A. Kaszniak (Ed.), *Emotion, qualia and consciousness* (pp. 426–443). Tokyo: World Scientific.

Ruch, W., & Forabosco, G. (1996). A cross-cultural study of humor appreciation: Italy and Germany. *Humor: International Journal of Humor Research*, 9(1), 1–18.

Ruch, W., & Hehl, F.-J. (1986a). Conservatism as a predictor of responses to humour: I. A comparison of four scales. *Personality & Individual Differences*, 7(1), 1–14.

Ruch, W., & Hehl, F.-J. (1986b). Conservatism as a predictor of responses to humour: II. The location of sense of humour in a comprehensive attitude space. *Personality & Individual Differences*, 7(6), 861–874.

Ruch, W., & Hehl, F.-J. (1987). Personal values as facilitating and inhibiting factors in the appreciation of humor content. *Journal of Social Behavior & Personality*, 2(4), 453–472.

Ruch, W., & Hehl, F.-J. (1988). Attitudes to sex, sexual behaviour and enjoyment of humour. *Personality & Individual Differences*, 9(6), 983–994.

Ruch, W., & Hehl, F.-J. (1998). A two-mode model of humor appreciation: Its relation to aesthetic appreciation and simplicity-complexity of personality. In W. Ruch (Ed.), *The sense of humor: Explorations of a personality characteristic* (pp. 109–142). Berlin, Germany: Walter de Gruyter.

Ruch, W., Köhler, G., & Van Thriel, C. (1996). Assessing the "humorous temperament": Construction of the facet and standard trait forms of the State-Trait-Cherrfulness-Inventory-STCI. *Humor: International Journal of Humor Research, 9*(3–4), 303–339.

Ruch, W., Köhler, G., & van Thriel, C. (1997). To be in good or bad humor: Construction of the state form of the State-Trait-Cheerfulness-Inventory-STCI. *Personality & Individual Differences, 22*(4), 477–491.

Ruch, W., & Köhler, G. (1998). A temperament approach to humor. In W. Ruch (Ed.), *The sense of humor: Explorations of a personality characteristic* (pp. 203–228). Berlin, Germany: Walter de Gruyter.

Ruch, W., & Köhler, G. (1999). The measurement of state and trait cheerfulness. In I. Mervielde, I. J. Deary, F. De Fruyt & F. Ostendorf (Eds.), *Personality psychology in Europe* (pp. 67–83). Tilburg, Netherlands: Tilburg University Press.

Ruch, W., McGhee, P. E., & Hehl, F.-J. (1990). Age differences in the enjoyment of incongruity-resolution and nonsense humor during adulthood. *Psychology & Aging, 5*(3), 348–355.

Ruch, W., Ott, C., Accoce, J., & Bariaud, F. (1991). Cross-national comparison of humor categories: France and Germany. *Humor: International Journal of Humor Research, 4*(3–4), 391–414.

Ruch, W., & Proyer, R. T. (in press). Gelatophobia: A distinct and useful new concept? *Humor: International Journal of Humor Research.*

Rumelhart, D. E., & Ortony, A. (1977). The representation of meaning in memory. In R. C. Anderson, R. J. Spiro & W. E. Montague (Eds.), *Schooling and the acquisition of knowledge* (pp. 99–135). Hillsdale, NJ: Erlbaum.

Russell, J. A., Bachorowski, J.-A., & Fernandez-Dols, J. M. (2003). Facial and vocal expressions of emotion. *Annual Review of Psychology, 54,* 329–349.

Rust, J., & Goldstein, J. (1989). Humor in marital adjustment. *Humor: International Journal of Humor Research, 2*(3), 217–223.

Rutherford, K. (1994). Humor in psychotherapy. *Individual Psychology, 50*(2), 207–222.

Ryan, K. M., & Kanjorski, J. (1998). The enjoyment of sexist humor, rape attitudes, and relationship aggression in college students. *Sex Roles, 38*(9–10), 743–756.

Safranek, R., & Schill, T. (1982). Coping with stress: Does humor help. *Psychological Reports, 51*(1), 222.

Sala, F., Krupat, E., & Roter, D. (2002). Satisfaction and the use of humor by physicians and patients. *Psychology & Health, 17*(3), 269–280.

Salameh, W. A. (1987). Humor in integrative short-term psychotherapy (ISTP). In W. F. Fry & W. A. Salameh (Eds.), *Handbook of humor and psychotherapy: Advances in the clinical use of humor* (pp. 195–240). Sarasota, FL: Professional Resource Exchange.

Sander, K., & Scheich, H. (2001). Auditory perception of laughing and crying activates human amygdala regardless of attentional state. *Cognitive Brain Research, 12*(2), 181–198.

Sanders, V. M., Iciek, L., & Kasprowicz, D. J. (2000). Psychosocial factors and humoral immunity. In J. T. Cacioppo, L. G. Tassinary & G. G. Berntson (Eds.), *Handbook of psychophysiology* (2nd ed., pp. 425–455). Cambridge, England: Cambridge University Press.

Sanderson, C. A. (2004). *Health psychology.* Hoboken, NJ: Wiley.

Sanville, J. B. (1999). Humor and play. In J. W. Barron (Ed.), *Humor and psyche: Psychoanalytic perspectives* (pp. 31–55). Hillsdale, NJ: Analytic Press.

Saper, B. (1987). Humor in psychotherapy: Is it good or bad for the client? *Professional Psychology: Research & Practice, 18*(4), 360–367.

Saper, B. (1995). Joking in the context of political correctness. *Humor: International Journal of Humor Research, 8*(1), 65–76.

Saroglou, V. (2003). Humor appreciation as function of religious dimensions. *Archiv fur Religionpsychologie, 24,* 144–153.

Saroglou, V., & Scariot, C. (2002). Humor Styles Questionnaire: Personality and educational correlates in Belgian high school and college students. *European Journal of Personality, 16*(1), 43–54.

Sayre, J. (2001). The use of aberrant medical humor by psychiatric unit staff. *Issues in Mental Health Nursing, 22*(7), 669–689.

Scambler, D. J., Harris, M. J., & Milich, R. (1998). Sticks and stones: Evaluations of responses to childhood teasing. *Social Development, 7*(2), 234–249.

Schachter, S., & Wheeler, L. (1962). Epinephrine, chlorpromazine, and amusement. *Journal of Abnormal & Social Psychology, 65*(2), 121–128.

Schaier, A. H., & Cicirelli, V. G. (1976). Age differences in humor comprehension and appreciation in old age. *Journal of Gerontology, 31*(5), 577–582.

Schank, R. C., & Abelson, R. (1977). *Scripts, plans, goals, and understanding.* New York: Wiley.

Schmidt, S. R. (1994). Effects of humor on sentence memory. *Journal of Experimental Psychology: Learning, Memory, & Cognition, 20*(4), 953–967.

Schmidt, S. R. (2002). The humour effect: Differential processing and privileged retrieval. *Memory, 10*(2), 127–138.

Schmidt, S. R., & Williams, A. R. (2001). Memory for humorous cartoons. *Memory & Cognition, 29*(2), 305–311.

Schultz, W. (2002). Getting formal with dopamine and reward. *Neuron, 36*(2), 241–263.

Segrin, C. (2000). Social skills deficits associated with depression. *Clinical Psychology Review, 20*(3), 379–403.

Seligman, M. E. P., & Csikszentmihalyi, M. (2000). Positive psychology: An introduction. *American Psychologist, 55*(1), 5–14.

Seligman, M. E. P., & Peterson, C. (2003). Positive clinical psychology. In L. G. Aspinwall & U. M. Staudinger (Eds.), *A psychology of human strengths: Fundamental questions and future directions for a positive psychology* (pp. 305–317). Washington, DC: American Psychological Assocation.

Shammi, P., & Stuss, D. T. (1999). Humour appreciation: A role of the right frontal lobe. *Brain, 122*(4), 657–666.

Shammi, P., & Stuss, D. T. (2003). The effects of normal aging on humor appreciation. *Journal of the International Neuropsychological Society, 9*(6), 855–863.

Shapiro, J. P., Baumeister, R. F., & Kessler, J. W. (1991). A three-component model of children's teasing: Aggression, humor, and ambiguity. *Journal of Social & Clinical Psychology, 10*(4), 459–472.

Sharkey, N. E., & Mitchell, D. C. (1985). Word recognition in a functional context: The use of scripts in reading. *Journal of Memory and Language, 24,* 253–270.

Sher, P. K., & Brown, S. B. (1976). Gelastic epilepsy: Onset in neonatal period. *American Journal of Diseases of Childhood, 130,* 1126–1131.

Sherman, L. W. (1988). Humor and social distance in elementary school children. *Humor: International Journal of Humor Research, 1*(4), 389–404.

Shiota, M. N., Campos, B., Keltner, D., & Hertenstein, M. J. (2004). Positive emotion and the regulation of interpersonal relationships. In P. Philippot & R. S. Feldman (Eds.), *The regulation of emotion* (pp. 127–155). Mahwah, NJ: Lawrence Erlbaum Associates.

Shultz, T. R. (1972). The role of incongruity and resolution in children's appreciation of cartoon humor. *Journal of Experimental Child Psychology, 13*(3), 456–477.

Shultz, T. R. (1974a). Development of the appreciation of riddles. *Child Development, 45*(1), 100–105.

Shultz, T. R. (1974b). Order of cognitive processing in humour appreciation. *Canadian Journal of Psychology, 28*(4), 409–420.

Shultz, T. R. (1976). A cognitive-developmental analysis of humour. In A. J. Chapman & H. C. Foot (Eds.), *Humor and laughter: Theory, research, and applications* (pp. 11–36). London: John Wiley & Sons.

Shultz, T. R., & Horibe, F. (1974). Development of the appreciation of verbal jokes. *Developmental Psychobiology, 10*, 13–20.

Shultz, T. R., & Pilon, R. (1973). Development of the ability to detect linguistic ambiguity. *Child Development, 44*(4), 728–733.

Shultz, T. R., & Robillard, J. (1980). The development of linguistic humour in children: Incongruity through rule violation. In P. E. McGhee & A. J. Chapman (Eds.), *Children's humour* (pp. 59–90). Chichester: John Wiley & Sons.

Shultz, T. R., & Scott, M. B. (1974). The creation of verbal humour. *Canadian Journal of Psychology, 28*(4), 421–425.

Shurcliff, A. (1968). Judged humor, arousal, and the relief theory. *Journal of Personality & Social Psychology, 8*(4), 360–363.

Simon, J. M. (1990). Humor and its relationship to perceived health, life satisfaction, and morale in older adults. *Issues in Mental Health Nursing, 11*(1), 17–31.

Simons, C. J. R., McCluskey-Fawcett, K. A., & Papini, D. R. (1986). Theoretical and functional perspectives on the development of humor during infancy, childhood, and adolescence. In L. Nahemow, K. A. McCluskey-Fawcett & P. E. McGhee (Eds.), *Humor and aging* (pp. 53–80). Orlando, FL: Academic Press.

Simpson, J. A., & Weiner, E. S. C. (1989). *The Oxford English dictionary* (2nd ed., Vol. 7). Oxford: Clarendon Press.

Singer, D. L. (1968). Aggression arousal, hostile humor, catharsis. *Journal of Personality and Social Psychology Monograph Supplement, 8*(1), 1–14.

Singer, D. L., Gollob, H. F., & Levine, J. (1967). Mobilization of Inhibitions and the enjoyment of aggressive humor. *Journal of Personality, 35*(4), 562–569.

Sinnott, J. D., & Ross, B. M. (1976). Comparison of aggression and incongruity as factors in children's judgments of humor. *Journal of Genetic Psychology, 128*(2), 241–249.

Smith, J. E., Waldorf, V. A., & Trembath, D. L. (1990). "Single white male looking for thin, very attractive . . ." *Sex Roles, 23*(11/12), 675–685.

Smith, P. K. (1982). Does play matter? Functional and evolutionary aspects of animal and human play. *Behavioral & Brain Sciences, 5*(1), 139–184.

Smith, R. E. (1973). The use of humor in the counterconditioning of anger responses: A case study. *Behavior Therapy, 4*(4), 576–580.

Smith, R. E., Ascough, J. C., Ettinger, R. F., & Nelson, D. A. (1971). Humor, anxiety, and task performance. *Journal of Personality & Social Psychology, 19*(2), 243–246.

Smoski, M. J., & Bachorowski, J.-A. (2003). Antiphonal laughter between friends and strangers. *Cognition & Emotion, 17*(2), 327–340.

Snider, J. G., & Osgood, C. E. (1969). *Semantic differential technique: A sourcebook*. Chicago: Aldine.

Somerfield, M. R., & McCrae, R. R. (2000). Stress and coping research: Methodological challenges, theoretical advances, and clinical applications. *American Psychologist, 55*(6), 620–625.

Spencer, G. (1989). An analysis of JAP-baiting humor on the college campus. *Humor: International Journal of Humor Research, 2*(4), 329–348.

Spencer, H. (1860). The physiology of laughter. *Macmillan's Magazine, 1*, 395–402.

Sperber, D. (1984). Verbal irony: Pretense or echoic mention. *Journal of Experimental Psychology: General, 113*, 130–136.

Spiegel, D., Brodkin, S. G., & Keith-Spiegel, P. (1969). Unacceptable impulses, anxiety and the appreciation of cartoons. *Journal of Projective Techniques and Personality Assessment, 33*, 154–159.

Spradley, J. P., & Mann, B. J. (1975). *The cocktail waitress: Woman's work in a man's world*. New York: Wiley.

Sprecher, S., & Regan, P. C. (2002). Liking some things (in some people) more than others: Partner preferences in romantic relationships and friendships. *Journal of Social & Personal Relationships, 19*(4), 463–481.

Sroufe, L. A., & Wunsch, J. P. (1972). The development of laughter in the first year of life. *Child Development, 43*(4), 1326–1344.

Stearns, F. R. (1972). *Laughing: Physiology, pathophysiology, psychology, pathopsychology, and development*. Oxford, England: Charles C Thomas.

Stewart, M., & Heredia, R. (2002). Comprehending spoken metaphoric reference: A real-time analysis. *Journal of Experimental Psychology, 49*, 34–44.

Stillion, J. M., & White, H. (1987). Feminist humor: Who appreciates it and why? *Psychology of Women Quarterly, 11*(2), 219–232.

Stone, A. A., Cox, D. S., Valdimarsdottir, H., Jandorf, L., & Neale, J. M. (1987). Evidence that secretory IgA antibody is associated with daily mood. *Journal of Personality & Social Psychology, 52*(5), 988–993.

Strack, F., Martin, L. L., & Stepper, S. (1988). Inhibiting and facilitating conditions of the human smile: A nonobtrusive test of the facial feedback hypothesis. *Journal of Personality & Social Psychology, 54*(5), 768–777.

Strean, H. S. (1994). *The use of humor in psychotherapy*. Northvale, NJ: Jason Aronson.

Strickland, J. F. (1959). The effect of motivational arousal on humor preferences. *Journal of Abnormal & Social Psychology, 59*, 278–281.

Strother, G. B., Barnett, M. M., & Apostolakos, P. C. (1954). The use of cartoons as a projective device. *Journal of Clinical Psychology, 10*, 38–42.

Struthers, A. (2003). No laughing! Playing with humor in the classroom. In A. J. Klein (Ed.), *Humor in children's lives: A guidebook for practitioners* (pp. 85–94). Westport, CT: Praeger.

Sullivan, K., Winner, E., & Hopfield, N. (1995). How children tell a lie from a joke: The role of second-order mental state attributions. *British Journal of Developmental Psychology, 13*(2), 191–204.

Suls, J. M. (1972). A two-stage model for the appreciation of jokes and cartoons: An information-processing analysis. In J. H. Goldstein & P. E. McGhee (Eds.), *The psychology of humor: Theoretical perspectives and empirical issues* (pp. 81–100). New York: Academic Press.

Suls, J. M. (1977). Cognitive and disparagement theories of humour: A theoretical and empirical synthesis. In A. J. Chapman & H. C. Foot (Eds.), *It's a funny thing, humour* (pp. 41–45). Oxford: Pergamon Press.

Suls, J. M. (1983). Cognitive processes in humor appreciation. In P. E. McGhee & J. H. Goldstein (Eds.), *Handbook of humor research, Vol. 1: Basic issues* (pp. 39–57). New York: Springer-Verlag.

Sumners, A. D. (1988). Humor: Coping in recovery from addiction. *Issues in Mental Health Nursing, 9*, 169–179.

Surkis, A. A. (1993). Humor in relation to obsessive-compulsive processes. In W. F. Fry & W. A. Salameh (Eds.), *Advances in humor and psychotherapy* (pp. 121–141). Sarasota, FL: Professional Resource Press.

Sutton-Smith, B. (2003). Play as a parody of emotional vulnerability. In D. E. Lytle (Ed.), *Play and educational theory and practice* (pp. 3–17). Westport, CT: Praeger.

Svebak, S. (1974a). Revised questionnaire on the sense of humor. *Scandinavian Journal of Psychology, 15*, 328–331.

Svebak, S. (1974b). A theory of sense of humor. *Scandinavian Journal of Psychology, 15*(2), 99–107.

Svebak, S. (1975). Respiratory patterns as predictors of laughter. *Psychophysiology, 12*(1), 62–65.

Svebak, S. (1977). Some characteristics of resting respiration as predictors of laughter. In A. J. Chapman & H. C. Foot (Eds.), *It's a funny thing, humour* (pp. 101–104). Oxford: Pergamon Press.

Svebak, S. (1982). The effect of mirthfulness upon amount of discordant right-left occipital EEG alpha. *Motivation & Emotion, 6*(2), 133–147.

Svebak, S. (1996). The development of the Sense of Humor Questionnaire: From SHQ to SHQ-6. *Humor: International Journal of Humor Research, 9*(3–4), 341–361.

Svebak, S., & Apter, M. J. (1987). Laughter: An empirical test of some reversal theory hypotheses. *Scandinavian Journal of Psychology, 28*(3), 189–198.

Svebak, S., Götestam, K. G., & Jensen, E. N. (2004). The significance of sense of humor, life regard, and stressors for bodily complaints among high school students. *Humor: International Journal of Humor Research, 17*(1–2), 67–83.

Svebak, S., & Martin, R. A. (1997). Humor as a form of coping. In S. Svebak & M. J. Apter (Eds.), *Stress and health: A reversal theory perspective* (pp. 173–184). Washington, DC: Taylor & Francis.

Svebak, S., Martin, R. A., & Holmen, J. (2004). The prevalence of sense of humor in a large, unselected county population in Norway: Relations with age, sex, and some health indicators. *Humor: International Journal of Humor Research, 17*(1–2), 121–134.

Szabo, A. (2003). The acute effects of humor and exercise on mood and anxiety. *Journal of Leisure Research, 35*(2), 152–162.

Szabo, A., Ainsworth, S. E., & Danks, P. K. (2005). Experimental comparison of the psychological benefits of aerobic exercise, humor, and music. *Humor: International Journal of Humor Research, 18*(3), 235–246.

Talbot, L. A., & Lumden, D. B. (2000). On the association between humor and burnout. *Humor: International Journal of Humor Research, 13*(4), 419–428.

Tamblyn, D. (2003). *Laugh and learn: 95 ways to use humor for more effective teaching and training.* New York: Amcom.

Tannen, D. (1986). *That's not what I meant.* New York: William Morrow.

Tannen, D. (1990). *You just don't understand.* New York: Ballantine.

Tellegen, A., Lykken, D. T., Bouchard, T. J., Wilcox, K. J., et al. (1988). Personality similarity in twins reared apart and together. *Journal of Personality & Social Psychology, 54*(6), 1031–1039.

Tennen, H., Affleck, G., Armeli, S., & Carney, M. A. (2000). A daily process approach to coping: Linking theory, research, and practice. *American Psychologist, 55*(6), 626–636.

Terrion, J. L., & Ashforth, B. E. (2002). From "I" to "we": The role of putdown humor and identity in the development of a temporary group. *Human Relations, 55*(1), 55–88.

Terry, R. L., & Ertel, S. L. (1974). Exploration of individual differences in preferences for humor. *Psychological Reports, 34*(3, Pt 2), 1031–1037.

Teslow, J. L. (1995). Humor me: A call for research. *Educational Technology Research & Development, 43*(3), 6–28.

Teyber, E. (1988). *Interpersonal process in psychotherapy: A guide for clinical training*. Chicago: Dorsey Press.

Thomas, C. A., & Esses, V. M. (2004). Individual differences in reactions to sexist humor. *Group Processes & Intergroup Relations, 7*(1), 89–100.

Thorson, J. A. (1990). Is propensity to laugh equivalent to sense of humor? *Psychological Reports, 66*(3, Pt 1), 737–738.

Thorson, J. A., & Powell, F. C. (1993a). Development and validation of a multidimensional sense of humor scale. *Journal of Clinical Psychology, 49*(1), 13–23.

Thorson, J. A., & Powell, F. C. (1993b). Relationships of death anxiety and sense of humor. *Psychological Reports, 72*(3, Pt 2), 1364–1366.

Thorson, J. A., & Powell, F. C. (1994). Depression and sense of humor. *Psychological Reports, 75*(3, Pt.2), 1473–1474.

Thorson, J. A., & Powell, F. C. (1996). Women, aging, and sense of humor. *Humor: International Journal of Humor Research, 9*(2), 169–186.

Thorson, J. A., Powell, F. C., Sarmany-Schuller, I., & Hampes, W. P. (1997). Psychological health and sense of humor. *Journal of Clinical Psychology, 53*(6), 605–619.

Torrance, E. P. (1966). *Torrance tests of creative thinking*. Princeton, NJ: Personnel Press.

Townsend, M. A., & Mahoney, P. (1981). Humor and anxiety: Effects on class test performance. *Psychology in the Schools, 18*(2), 228–234.

Townsend, M. A., Mahoney, P., & Allen, L. G. (1983). Student perceptions of verbal and cartoon humor in the test situation. *Educational Research Quarterly, 7*(4), 17–23.

Trappl, R., Petta, P., & Payr, S. (Eds.). (2002). *Emotions in humans and artifacts*. Cambridge, MA: MIT Press.

Traylor, G. (1973). Joking in a bush camp. *Human Relations, 26*(4), 479–486.

Treadwell, Y. (1970). Humor and creativity. *Psychological Reports, 26*(1), 55–58.

Trice, A. D. (1985). Alleviation of helpless responding by a humorous experience. *Psychological Reports, 57*(2), 474.

Trice, A. D., & Price-Greathouse, J. (1986). Joking under the drill: A validity study of the Coping Humor Scale. *Journal of Social Behavior & Personality, 1*(2), 265–266.

Trick, L., & Katz, A. (1986). The domain interaction approach to metaphor processing: Relating individual differences and metaphor characteristics. *Metaphor and Symbolic Activity, 1*, 203–244.

Turnbull, C. M. (1972). *The mountain people*. New York: Touchstone.

Turner, R. G. (1980). Self-monitoring and humor production. *Journal of Personality, 48*(2), 163–172.

Uchino, B. N., Kiecolt-Glaser, J., & Glaser, R. (2000). Psychological modulation of cellular immunity. In J. T. Cacioppo, L. G. Tassinary & G. G. Berntson (Eds.), *Handbook of psychophysiology* (2nd ed., pp. 397–424). Cambridge, England: Cambridge University Press.

Ullian, J. A. (1976). Joking at work. *Journal of Communication, 26*(3), 129–133.

Ullmann, L. P., & Lim, D. T. (1962). Case history material as a source of the identification of patterns of response to emotional stimuli in a study of humor. *Journal of Consulting Psychology, 26*(3), 221–225.

Vaid, J. (1999). The evolution of humor: Do those who laugh last? In D. H. Rosen & M. C. Luebbert (Eds.), *Evolution of the psyche* (pp. 123–138). Westport, CT: Praeger Publishers/Greenwood Publishing.

Vaid, J. (2002). Humor and laughter. In V. S. Ramachandran (Ed.), *Encyclopedia of the human brain* (Vol. 2, pp. 505–516). San Diego, CA: Academic Press.

Vaid, J., Hull, R., Heredia, R., Gerkens, D., & Martinez, F. (2003). Getting a joke: The time course of meaning activation in verbal humor. *Journal of Pragmatics, 35*(9), 1431–1449.

Vaillant, G. E. (2000). Adaptive mental mechanisms: Their role in a positive psychology. *American Psychologist, 55*(1), 89–98.

Van Giffen, K. (1990). Influence of professor gender and perceived use of humor on course evaluations. *Humor: International Journal of Humor Research, 3*(1), 65–73.

van Hooff, J. A. (1972). A comparative approach to the phylogeny of laughter and smiling. In R. A. Hinde (Ed.), *Non-verbal communication*. Oxford, England: Cambridge U. Press.

van Hooff, J. A., & Preuschoft, S. (2003). Laughter and smiling: The intertwining of nature and culture. In F. B. M. de Waal & P. L. Tyack (Eds.), *Animal social complexity: Intelligence, culture, and individualized societies* (pp. 260–287). Cambridge, MA: Harvard University Press.

van Wormer, K., & Boes, M. (1997). Humor in the emergency room: A social work perspective. *Health & Social Work, 22*(2), 87–92.

Vasey, G. (1877). *The philosophy of laughter and smiling* (2nd ed.). London: J. Burns.

Ventis, W. L. (1973). Case history: The use of laughter as an alternative response in systematic desensitization. *Behavior Therapy, 4*(1), 120–122.

Ventis, W. L., Higbee, G., & Murdock, S. A. (2001). Using humor in systematic desensitization to reduce fear. *Journal of General Psychology, 128*(2), 241–253.

Vettin, J., & Todt, D. (2004). Laughter in conversation: Features of occurrence and acoustic structure. *Journal of Nonverbal Behavior, 28*(2), 93–115.

Vilaythong, A. P., Arnau, R. C., Rosen, D. H., & Mascaro, N. (2003). Humor and hope: Can humor increase hope? *Humor: International Journal of Humor Research, 16*(1), 79–89.

Vinton, K. L. (1989). Humor in the workplace: It is more than telling jokes. *Small Group Behavior, 20*(2), 151–166.

Wakshlag, J. J., Day, K. D., & Zillmann, D. (1981). Selective exposure to educational television programs as a function of differently paced humorous inserts. *Journal of Educational Psychology, 73*(1), 27–32.

Walle, A. H. (1976). Getting picked up without being put down: Jokes and the bar rush. *Journal of the Folklore Institute, 13*, 201–217.

Wanzer, M. B., & Frymier, A. B. (1999). The relationship between student perceptions of instructor humor and student's reports of learning. *Communication Education, 48*(1), 48–62.

Wapner, W., Hamby, S., & Gardner, H. (1981). The role of the right hemisphere in the apprehension of complex linguistic materials. *Brain & Language, 14*(1), 15–33.

Ward, J. R. (2004). *Humor and its association with friendship quality.* Unpublished Masters thesis, University of Western Ontario, London, Ontario.

Warm, T. R. (1997). The role of teasing in development and vice versa. *Journal of Developmental & Behavioral Pediatrics, 18*(2), 97–101.

Warners-Kleverlaan, N., Oppenheimer, L., & Sherman, L. (1996). To be or not to be humorous: Does it make a difference? *Humor: International Journal of Humor Research, 9*(2), 117–141.

Watson, D., & Pennebaker, J. W. (1989). Health complaints, stress, and distress: Exploring the central role of negative affectivity. *Psychological Review, 96*, 234–254.

Watson, K. K., Matthews, B. J., & Allman, J. M. (in press). Brain activation during sight gags and language-dependent humor. *Cerebral Cortex*.

Weaver, J., & Zillmann, D. (1994). Effect of humor and tragedy on discomfort tolerance. *Perceptual & Motor Skills, 78*(2), 632–634.

Weaver, J., Zillmann, D., & Bryant, J. (1988). Effects of humorous distortions on children's learning from educational television: Further evidence. *Communication Education, 37*(3), 181–187.

Weaver, J. B., Masland, J. L., Kharazmi, S., & Zillmann, D. (1985). Effect of alcoholic intoxication on the appreciation of different types of humor. *Journal of Personality & Social Psychology, 49*(3), 781–787.

Wegener, D. T., Petty, R. E., & Smith, S. M. (1995). Positive mood can increase or decrease message scrutiny: The hedonic contingency view of mood and message processing. *Journal of Personality and Social Psychology, 69*(1), 5–15.

Weinberger, M. G., & Gulas, C. S. (1992). The impact of humor in advertising: A review. *Journal of Advertising, 21*(4), 35–59.

Weisenberg, M., Raz, T., & Hener, T. (1998). The influence of film-induced mood on pain perception. *Pain, 76*(3), 365–375.

Weisenberg, M., Tepper, I., & Schwarzwald, J. (1995). Humor as a cognitive technique for increasing pain tolerance. *Pain, 63*(2), 207–212.

Weisfeld, G. E. (1993). The adaptive value of humor and laughter. *Ethology & Sociobiology, 14*(2), 141–169.

White, S., & Camarena, P. (1989). Laughter as a stress reducer in small groups. *Humor: International Journal of Humor Research, 2*(1), 73–79.

White, S., & Winzelberg, A. (1992). Laughter and stress. *Humor: International Journal of Humor Research, 5*(4), 343–355.

Whitney, I., & Smith, P. K. (1993). A survey of the nature and extent of bullying in junior/middle and secondary schools. *Educational Research, 35*(1), 3–25.

Whitt, J. K., & Prentice, N. M. (1977). Cognitive processes in the development of children's enjoyment and comprehension of joking riddles. *Developmental Psychology, 13*(2), 129–136.

Wickberg, D. (1998). *The senses of humor: Self and laughter in modern America.* Ithaca, NY: Cornell University Press.

Wicker, F. W. (1985). A rhetorical look at humor as creativity. *Journal of Creative Behavior, 19*(3), 175–184.

Wicker, F. W., Barron, W. L., & Willis, A. C. (1980). Disparagement humor: Dispositions and resolutions. *Journal of Personality & Social Psychology, 39*(4), 701–709.

Wicker, F. W., Thorelli, I. M., Barron, W. L., & Ponder, M. R. (1981). Relationships among affective and cognitive factors in humor. *Journal of Research in Personality, 15*(3), 359–370.

Wild, B., Rodden, F. A., Grodd, W., & Ruch, W. (2003). Neural correlates of laughter and humour. *Brain, 126*(10), 2121–2138.

Williams, R. B., Haney, T. L., Lee, K. L., Kong, Y. H., Blumenthal, J. A., & Whalen, R. E. (1980). Type A behavior, hostility, and coronary atherosclerosis. *Psychosomatic Medicine, 42*(6), 539–549.

Wilson, D. W., & Molleston, J. L. (1981). Effects of sex and type of humor on humor appreciation. *Journal of Personality Assessment, 45*(1), 90–96.

Wilson, G. D., & Patterson, J. R. (1969). Conservatism as a predictor of humor preferences. *Journal of Consulting & Clinical Psychology, 33*(3), 271–274.

Wilson, G. D., Rust, J., & Kasriel, J. (1977). Genetic and family origins of humor preferences: A twin study. *Psychological Reports, 41*(2), 659–660.

Wilson, W. (1975). Sex differences in response to obscenities and bawdy humor. *Psychological Reports, 37*(3, Pt 2), 1074.

Winner, E., & Leekam, S. (1991). Distinguishing irony from deception: Understanding the speaker's second-order intention. *British Journal of Developmental Psychology, 9*(2), 257–270.

Winner, E., Windmueller, G., Rosenblatt, E., Bosco, L., Best, E., & Gardner, H. (1987). Making sense of literal and nonliteral falsehood. *Metaphor & Symbolic Activity, 2*(1), 13–32.

Witztum, E., Briskin, S., & Lerner, V. (1999). The use of humor with chronic schizophrenic patients. *Journal of Contemporary Psychotherapy, 29*(3), 223–234.

Wolfenstein, M. (1954). *Children's humor: A psychological analysis*. Glencoe, IL: The Free Press.

Wolff, H. A., Smith, C. E., & Murray, H. A. (1934). The psychology of humor. *Journal of Abnormal & Social Psychology, 28*, 341–365.

Wyer, R. S. (2004). *Social comprehension and judgment: The role of situation models, narratives, and implicit theories*. Mahwah, NJ: Lawrence Erlbaum Associates.

Wyer, R. S., & Collins, J. E. (1992). A theory of humor elicitation. *Psychological Review, 99*(4), 663–688.

Yalisove, D. (1978). The effect of riddle structure on children's comprehension of riddles. *Developmental Psychology, 14*(2), 173–180.

Yarnold, J. K., & Berkeley, M. H. (1954). An analysis of the Cattell-Luborsky Humor Test into homogeneous scales. *Journal of Abnormal & Social Psychology, 49*, 543–546.

Yip, J. A., & Martin, R. A. (in press). Sense of humor, emotional intelligence, and social competence. *Journal of Research in Personality*.

Yoshino, S., Fujimori, J., & Kohda, M. (1996). Effects of mirthful laughter on neuroendocrine and immune systems in patients with rheumatoid arthritis [letter]. *Journal of Rheumatology, 23*, 793–794.

Yovetich, N. A., Dale, J. A., & Hudak, M. A. (1990). Benefits of humor in reduction of threat-induced anxiety. *Psychological Reports, 66*(1), 51–58.

Yukl, G., & Lepsinger, R. (1990). Preliminary report on validation of the Management Practices Survey. In K. E. Clark & M. B. Clark (Eds.), *Measures of leadership* (pp. 223–237). West Orange, NJ.: Leadership Library of America.

Zajdman, A. (1995). Humorous face-threatening acts: Humor as strategy. *Journal of Pragmatics, 23*(3), 325–339.

Zeilig, G., Drubach, D. A., Katz-Zeilig, M., & Karatinos, J. (1996). Pathological laughter and crying in patients with closed traumatic brain injury. *Brain Injury, 10*(8), 591–597.

Ziegler, V., Boardman, G., & Thomas, M. D. (1985). Humor, leadership, and school climate. *Clearing House, 58*, 346–348.

Zigler, E., Levine, J., & Gould, L. (1966). Cognitive processes in the development of children's appreciation of humor. *Child Development, 37*(3), 507–518.

Zigler, E., Levine, J., & Gould, L. (1967). Cognitive challenge as a factor in children's humor appreciation. *Journal of Personality & Social Psychology, 6*(3), 332–336.

Zillmann, D., & Bryant, J. (1974). Retaliatory equity as a factor in humor appreciation. *Journal of Experimental Social Psychology, 10*(5), 480–488.

Zillmann, D., & Bryant, J. (1980). Misattribution theory of tendentious humor. *Journal of Experimental Social Psychology, 16*(2), 146–160.

Zillmann, D., Bryant, J., & Cantor, J. R. (1974). Brutality of assault in political cartoons affecting humor appreciation. *Journal of Research in Personality, 7*(4), 334–345.

Zillmann, D., & Cantor, J. R. (1972). Directionality of transitory dominance as a communication variable affecting humor appreciation. *Journal of Personality & Social Psychology, 24*(2), 191–198.

Zillmann, D., & Cantor, J. R. (1976). A disposition theory of humour and mirth. In A. J. Chapman & H. C. Foot (Eds.), *Humor and laughter: Theory, research, and applications* (pp. 93–115). London: John Wiley & Sons.

Zillmann, D., et al. (1980). Acquisition of information from educational television programs as a function of differently paced humorous inserts. *Journal of Educational Psychology, 72*(2), 170–180.

Zillmann, D., Masland, J. L., Weaver, J. B., Lacey, L. A., Jacobs, N. E., Dow, J. H., et al. (1984). Effects of humorous distortions on children's learning from educational television. *Journal of Educational Psychology, 76*(5), 802–812.

Zillmann, D., Rockwell, S., Schweitzer, K., & Sundar, S. S. (1993). Does humor facilitate coping with physical discomfort? *Motivation & Emotion, 17*(1), 1–21.

Ziv, A. (1976). Facilitating effects of humor on creativity. *Journal of Educational Psychology, 68*(3), 318–322.

Ziv, A. (1980). Humor and creativity. *Creative Child & Adult Quarterly, 5*(3), 159–170.

Ziv, A. (1981). The self concept of adolescent humorists. *Journal of Adolescence, 4*(2), 187–197.

Ziv, A. (1984). *Personality and sense of humor*. New York: Springer.

Ziv, A. (1988a). Humor's role in married life. *Humor: International Journal of Humor Research, 1*(3), 223–229.

Ziv, A. (1988b). Teaching and learning with humor: Experiment and replication. *Journal of Experimental Education, 57*(1), 5–15.

Ziv, A., & Gadish, O. (1989). Humor and marital satisfaction. *Journal of Social Psychology, 129*(6), 759–768.

Ziv, A., & Gadish, O. (1990). The disinhibiting effects of humor: Aggressive and affective responses. *Humor: International Journal of Humor Research, 3*(3), 247–257.

Zwerling, I. (1955). The favorite joke in diagnostic and therapeutic interviewing. *Psychoanalytic Quarterly, 24*, 104–114.

Zweyer, K., Velker, B., & Ruch, W. (2004). Do cheerfulness, exhilaration, and humor production moderate pain tolerance? A FACS study. *Humor: International Journal of Humor Research, 17*(1–2), 85–119.

SUBJECT INDEX

AUTHOR INDEX